DR. GEORGE SHEEHAN
— ON —
GETTING FIT
&
FEELING GREAT

DR. GEORGE SHEEHAN

ON

GETTING FIT

&

FEELING GREAT

THREE VOLUMES IN ONE

**How to Feel Great 24 Hours a Day
Running and Being
This Running Life**

George A. Sheehan, M.D.

WINGS BOOKS   NEW YORK
AVENEL, NEW JERSEY

This omnibus was originally published in separate volumes under the titles:

How to Feel Great 24 Hours a Day, copyright © 1983 by George A. Sheehan, M.D.
Running and Being, copyright © 1978 by George A. Sheehan, M.D.
This Running Life, copyright © 1980 by George A. Sheehan, M.D.
(The chart entitled "Basic Temperamental Traits," which appears in Chapter 1, is reprinted from *Psychology Today* Magazine. Copyright 1970 Ziff-Davis Publishing Company. Used by permission.)

This 1992 edition is published by Wings Books, distributed by Outlet Book Company, Inc., a Random House Company, 40 Engelhard Avenue, Avenel, New Jersey 07001, by arrangement with Simon and Schuster.

Printed and bound in the United States of America

Library of Congress Cataloging-in-Publication Data

Sheehan, George.
    Dr. George Sheehan on getting fit and feeling great / George A. Sheehan.
      p.   cm.
    "Three volumes in one."
    Originally published in 3 v. : New York : Simon & Schuster, 1978–1983.
    Contents: How to feel great 24 hours a day — Running and being — This running life.
    ISBN 0-517-08462-7
    1. Running. 2. Running—Psychological aspects. 3. Sheehan, George. 4. Track and field athletes—United States—Biography. 5. Physical fitness. 6. Physical fitness—Philosophy. I. Title. II. Title: On fitness and running.
    GV1061.S5 1992
    796.42—dc20   92-15351
                                                CIP

8 7 6 5 4 3 2 1

CONTENTS

BOOK

How to Feel Great
24 Hours a Day

DRAWINGS BY MONICA SHEEHAN

To those who will weigh and consider
what is contained herein—
and will test against their own truth

CONTENTS

INTRODUCTION

THE MORNING AFTER . . . There's always a morning after, when he wakes up to find he's not a celebrity but a sixty-three-year-old man badly in need of his first dose of caffeine. It's a new day, a new week, and he has to go out and prove himself all over again. He says he welcomes that challenge, but his face says otherwise.

George Sheehan looks tired from a hard weekend on the road. He spoke at a sports medicine conference on Saturday, raced 10 kilometers on Sunday, then spoke again after the race.

"I'm in a fog," he says. "They gave me a standing ovation after that last talk. Those don't come very often—at least not for me. But I can't remember what I said to deserve it."

Like a runner who has just had a great race, Sheehan's feelings are mixed. He's proud of that performance but wonders, What do I do to top this? Elation blends with depression right after the cheering stops.

The man with one of the best-known faces in running walks unnoticed through a crowded airport. He wears his all-purpose uniform of nondesigner jeans, running shoes, turtleneck shirt, sweater and sleeve-less down-filled jacket—all in varying shades of blue. He dresses this way, give or take a layer, whether he's practicing medicine, giving a talk, or writing a column or book.

Sheehan speaks as casually as he dresses. The tone of his talks and writings is informal and relaxed. Runners are attracted to him the way news viewers were attracted to Walter Cronkite: not because his infor-mation is that much different from other commentators' but because of how it is delivered. Sheehan, like Cronkite, calms and reassures his audiences. They feel as comfortable with him as they would with a kindly uncle.

But poke through Sheehan's public manner and you find a man who works very hard at making it all look easy. He speaks nearly a hundred times a year but still gets so nervous before going on stage that he can hardly remember his own name. He writes a column each week for his local newspaper in New Jersey (all his magazine and book work begins there), revising as many as four times—"then once more for spontaneity."

This pace leaves him tired early on a Monday morning. The doctor opens a Tab, sits down to start work on this, his sixth book, and the fatigue quickly slips from his face. George Sheehan is at his best when working. He thrives when he's stretching and testing himself, whatever his medium is at the moment.

He says, "That's the reason why at sixty-three I'm not sitting watching the ocean, which I could do—I've paid my dues. Lots of people my age are sitting in Florida now, but I feel I've never achieved what I could. I haven't run as fast as I can, I haven't spoken as well as I can, and I haven't written as well as I can. If you take less than that view, you're finished."

—Joe Henderson
Senior Editor, *Running* Magazine

PROLOGUE

Why Fitness?

EXPERTS DISAGREE ABOUT FITNESS. For every physician who claims it confers longevity and decreases the risk of a heart attack, you can find one who states that no such relationship exists.

This debate seems unending. Acceptable scientific research on the effects of fitness on disease will take years to complete. At present, neither side can prove itself right and the other wrong. It is this impasse that has led fitness proponents to adopt the slogan "Fitness has to do with the quality of life, not the quantity."

Fitness does indeed give us those qualities necessary for leading the good life. We acquire zest and vitality to face the day and its tasks with confidence and enthusiasm. We also produce creative energy, which enables us to be free and spontaneous in problem solving. Fitness opens up the circuits in the amazing storage-and-retrieval system that is our brain. And it gives us another form of energy, the willpower that comes with discipline and the ascetic life.

So the effect of fitness on the quality of life is unquestionable. The fit person develops those qualities that are fundamental to a proper existence. If instructions on how to live were issued to human beings, those qualities would be seen to be most important. Few thinkers presume to tell us *how* to act and respond. But they are unanimous in stating that we *must* act and respond countless times during the waking day.

Fitness gives us the qualities to make responses and to perform acts in accordance with our highest nature.

The case for the quality of life seems unshaken. Fitness makes a person a good animal—an animal at home in the environment, no longer alien to it but filled with a new appreciation of the body and its contribution to the life of the mind and the life of the spirit.

What should also be evident is that the quantity of life is also increased. I do not speak of future quantity, of longevity. I doubt whether we can affect that, except in a negative way. We are born with a longevity quotient similar to our intelligence quotient. We cannot increase that inborn time allotted to us. We can, of course, decrease it—by smoking and drinking and jumping out of windows.

Fitness does not add to life in the future but adds to life *today*. There it has a measurable effect on the quantity of our lives. When we are fit, we can by definition do more work. The day does not end at noon or at five. The day becomes filled with physical, mental and emotional activity. Because I am fit, I am able to do what must be done when I must do it.

Because I am fit, the end of my work is the beginning of my day. Fitness allows for the full use of the body from sunup until bedtime. People who say they cannot find the time to become fit should realize that a fitness program actually produces *more* time.

Running gives me a body that performs better at everything that I must do during the day. Because of my fitness, I can now accept the Olympic ideal—farther, faster, higher—as part of my day. Because I am fit, I am now an athlete.

Accept that, and you can see the absurdity of saying that fitness has nothing to do with quantity of life. The athlete is consumed with the idea of quantity. Everything he does is concerned with time and distance and measurable factors in performance. And so it is with any life-style play activity; the quantity of life increases. The day is filled with activity.

When you are fit, you fill your day. When unfit, you kill it.

PART

1

The Human Machine

1

On Learning

"

**If you recognize these rules
it might not be because they go back
to the Greeks and the Romans
but because they go back to
the Mets and the Knicks and the Rangers.**

"

UNLIKE MOTORCARS and almost every other mechanical device in this technological age, people do not come in new and improved models. Infants born this year will differ little from those born in the fifth century B.C. The rules for the sound body in which to house the sound mind are still the same. In health and fitness there is indeed nothing new under the sun.

Our science is, of course, much more complex. We have discovered more and more of the sophisticated mechanisms that make the body work. Yet all that we know can be reduced to one rule: "Use the benefits or lose them," and one admonition: "Use the benefits correctly."

The general rule has to be applied to a particular body. Each one of us must know what is best for us. By the time we are twenty-one the individualities of our particular bodies should be apparent to us. We should be ready to live our own personal version of the good physical life, following Breslow's seven rules, based on the research of this famous husband-wife team of public health experts at UCLA.

EAT A GOOD BREAKFAST: Culture, experience and tradition have made breakfast our principal meal. Wherever hard work is done, a big breakfast becomes the rule. When I travel the country I see the evidence of that still on the menus. In Arizona, the cowboy's breakfast; in Anaheim, the trucker's breakfast; in Minnesota, the farmer's breakfast.

DON'T EAT BETWEEN MEALS: This rule becomes easy to follow after a good breakfast. Otherwise we continue to follow the 90-minute feeding cycle of infancy. For the adult animal such behavior is inappropriate. We are responding to messages that are not there.

15

THE HUMAN MACHINE

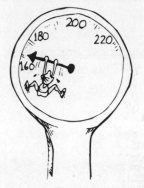

MAINTAIN YOUR WEIGHT: This must, however, be lean body weight. We should not gain in fat, and/or lose muscle. We should weigh what we did in our youth. If we do, we find that the rate of aging is so slow as to go almost unnoticed. Our weight and percentage of body fat are good indicators of how seriously we take our obligation to be fit.

DON'T SMOKE: Tobacco is simply an obvious example of any number of substances hazardous to our health. We should avoid all pollutants to whatever extent is possible. Arthur Morgan, the famous educator and

16

founder of Antioch College, once said he treated his body like a Stradivarius.

DRINK MODERATELY: Unlike tobacco or other harmful agents, alcohol in small amounts seems to add to life rather than diminish it. High-mileage runners never smoke, but some have as many as three or four drinks a day. The evidence is mounting that two drinks a day may help an individual to live longer than one who drinks more or less. The reasons for this are not clear.

GET A GOOD NIGHT'S SLEEP: Sleep needs are clearly particular to each individual. It is essential to discover one's own sleep requirements. Incorporation of naps, now generally discredited, may bring us additional benefits.

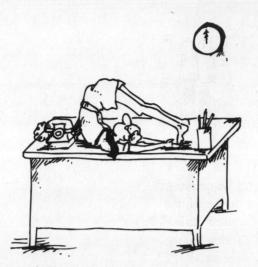

EXERCISE REGULARLY: The fitness formula is a matter of mode, intensity, frequency and duration. We must use large muscle groups as we do in walking, cycling, swimming, jogging, cross-country skiing, rowing or any other similar activities. This exercise should be done at a comfortable pace (that middle ground between hard and easy) for 30 minutes, four times a week.

If you recognize these rules it might not be because they go back to the Greeks and the Romans but because they go back to the Mets and the Knicks and the Rangers.

If an individual decides to exercise, or go into training, or become an athlete, just how should he go about it? In other words, what is the fitness formula? What factors go into the equation that provides us with energy and the ability to do work?

Most experts in exercise agree on the specifics. Few take exception to fundamentals of exercise physiology as they are now understood. You can be confident that attention to the following four factors will make you fit.

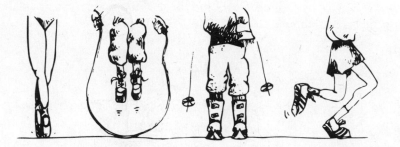

MODE OF EXERCISE: Large muscle mass must be involved in the exercise. The majority of the benefits of exercise occur in the muscles; therefore, the more muscle used during the exercise, the better. Walking, jogging, swimming and cycling are the staple methods. As are, of course, aerobic dancing, cross-country skiing, rowing, backpacking, rope skipping and other activities that might come to mind.

You are looking for stamina, so conventional weight lifting and body building are not recommended. Muscle men do very poorly when they get on a treadmill and go on to exhaustion. Only by turning lifting into an endurance activity, by using very light weights and innumerable repetitions, will you achieve fitness through weight lifting.

DURATION: The average workout should be at least 30 minutes, with a cumulative total of at least two hours a week. This activity should be continuous, as it is in running and swimming. Otherwise, as in tennis and other racket sports, it is best to have a friend hold a stopwatch on you to see how much of the time you are actually in motion.

This "30 minutes" eliminates any attention to miles or laps. There is no need to count anything except minutes. The training effect has to do with time and—the next variable we must consider:

INTENSITY: Most exercisers want to know how fast they should go. At what speed should the activity be performed. The answer is simple. Listen to your body. Go at the effort that the body says is comfortable—somewhere between fairly light and somewhat hard. This factor is based on the Swedish physiologist G. A. Borg's theory of Perceived Exertion, the idea that the body knows what it is doing.

"Most individuals," writes Dr. William Morgan, the sports psychologist, "are capable of rating the perceptual cost of physical work in an accurate, precise and consistent manner." Apparently about 90 percent of us can rate exertion better than any test procedure, because this perception involves processes that are not as yet accessible to our technology.

So when you exercise use Perceived Exertion. Dial your body to comfortable. Put it on automatic pilot, and then forget what you are doing. If this is all too new to you, you could also start by using the "Talk Test": the ability to converse comfortably with a companion and exercise at the same time. This will keep you in the correct aerobic range until you relearn the ability to read your own body.

FREQUENCY: The usual recommendation is to exercise every other day. This gives the body a chance to recoup. Glycogen replacement in the muscles will usually take 48 hours. Other neuroendocrine stresses probably take this long to adapt as well. Rest, as Olympic runner Noel Carroll has pointed out, is when the training effect takes place in the body. This is the time when the body adapts to the applied stress.

I prefer going 45 minutes or so instead of 30. My mind seems to open up more with the longer runs. When I stop at 30 minutes I feel I am missing something. So I usually do 45 minutes or an hour, two or three times a week. A friend of mine (a walker) once told me of similar feelings. "The first 30 minutes is for my body," she said. "The second 30 minutes is for my soul."

Running is a low-budget sport. Except for shoes everything you need is already in the house. Once you have bought a good pair of shoes the only other expense should be entry fees. The total outlay for the year should average little more than pennies a day.

It will, but only if you learn to deal with your injuries. Running is an inexpensive pursuit on paper, but not on the roads. Once mileage builds up, most runners develop injuries. And most injuries develop doctor's bills. Costs begin to mount. In the course of treating shin splints or runner's knee a person can run the gamut of health care specialists and incur bills that exceed the monthly rent.

I follow two rules in treating my running injuries. First, I treat myself. I do this even though I could see my colleagues without charge. I have discovered that I know more than they do. Not because I am a physician but because I am an experienced runner and now know things I was not taught in medical school. Given some surgical felt and a pair of scissors, I can shape any number of devices to put in my shoes and help my troubles.

I have also discovered a number of materials and appliances that have been useful in treating my various injuries and overuse syndromes. A little diligent searching in drug stores, running shops and surgical supply houses has uncovered most of the equipment I have used over the years. A partial listing would include the following:

ARCH SUPPORTS: These range from Dr. Scholl's Flexos available in drug stores to the heavier and more expensive ones displayed in shoe stores and surgical supply places. Dr. Scholl's 610's, Spenco and other serviceable ones are generally available.

ORTHOTICS: These differ from arch supports in providing correct placement at all points of the foot strike. They are especially needed when pronation is severe. Mine are made for me by a sports podiatrist. There are however cheaper over-the-counter ones available.

SHOCK ABSORBERS: The first and still the favorite is the Spenco innersole. A new entrant untried by me is sorbothane, a much heavier material.

HEEL LIFTS: I avoid compressible sponge rubber. Mostly I use surgical felt, which tends to bottom out but usually not before it has done its job. For permanent heel lifts inside the shoes, the best are leather, available in shoe repair shops.

AIR STIRRUPS: These new and quite marvelous devices allow a person to run with a sprain or even a stress fracture. They cast the leg, preventing lateral movement but allowing both plantar and dorsiflexion.

KNEE STRAP: Another new and effective device. A simple band that goes just below the kneecap and reduces symptoms in most knee problems. It acts on the same principle as the tennis elbow strap. It reduces the movement of the patellar tendon.

ZONAS TAPE: Made by Johnson and Johnson and not sold in drug stores. It must be obtained at surgical supply houses. It tears easily, molds to the skin and is superb for the treatment and prevention of blisters.

TINCTURE OF BENZOIN: This is sticky stuff that can be sprayed on the skin before you apply the tape.

HEEL COUNTER SUPPORTS: These are plastic bands that can be cemented around the heel of the shoe to give better protection against pronation.

They can convert a shoe from being the cause of the injury into becoming the cure.

HOT AND COLD PACKS: To be used on injured area before (hot) and after (cold) running. Just as good, and perhaps better, is the ice-massage Popsicle you can make yourself with a paper cup and a tongue depressor placed in the freezer.

SAND WEIGHTS: These are a luxury but do make strengthening exercises for the shin and quads more convenient and a lot easier. Much less awkward than the paint can, the usual home trainer.

SACROGARD: A small sacroiliac belt for about $10 which maintains the pelvis in proper position. No replacement for a girdle of muscles but will do part of the job until you do the rest.

SURGICAL FELT: With this and a pair of scissors you can become your own podiatrist. You can make almost anything needed to support the foot. These can then be taped to the foot or a Spenco innersole.

The self-treating runner may use all this equipment and fail to make the one change necessary for relief. A change in shoes. I have found that when these measures fail it is usually the shoes that have caused the problem. The heels are worn down, or the heel no longer controls the foot. Getting a shoe with excellent rear foot control can be decisive.

My second rule? If these efforts fail, see the best. I go to someone who has learned how to treat injured runners through treating thousands of injured runners. The books on this have yet to be written. It is worth the travel and the expense to see the expert.

It pays, as they say, in the long run.

2

On Planning

"
How many of us put things off,
living for a future when we will have more time?
How many of us live on the allotted 24 hours a day?
How many are waiting for a new day with more time?
"

IN 1910, ARNOLD BENNETT wrote a book on "the daily miracle," our supply of time. We wake in the morning, and our day is magically filled with 24 hours. No one can take it from you, and no one receives more or less than you receive. Genius is not rewarded with even an extra hour. Time cannot be bought. And no matter how much you waste it, the next day's supply will not be withheld from you. It is impossible to go into debt for time. Tomorrow is always there.

Out of the 24-hour day we have to spin a complex web of health, pleasure, contentment, respect and the evolution of our immortal souls. So our happiness depends upon how we use our time.

Yet how many of us put things off, living for a future when we will have more time? How many of us live on the allotted 24 hours a day? How many are waiting for a new day with more time?

"We shall never have any more time," Bennett writes. *"We have and we always had all the time there is."*

Let us review rapidly how we spend our day.

"Most of us," said Robert Louis Stevenson, "lead lives that two hours' reflection would lead us to disown."

At the least, we are haunted by a suppressed dissatisfaction with our daily life. That is the way it is with me. I am one of that band of innumerable souls who are haunted by the feeling that the years are slipping by—and we have not yet been able to get our lives in working order.

Like so many, I find the day gone and nothing to show for it. Night falls, and I have not added a thing. I go to bed, and nothing has changed in my inner or outer world. I rise, earn the bread and kill time. For that indeed is what I do, as surely as if I took a knife to an animal and let its lifeblood seep out.

Time passes hourly, daily, weekly, monthly, annually, with little or nothing to show for it. The questions hang in the air: "What have you done with your youth? What are you doing with your age?" Things do indeed go slip-sliding along. There is no end to the broken promises, most of them made to ourselves. Starting over is easy: I've done it thousands of times.

Bennett proposes that in one way or another we find 90 minutes a day for our own exclusive use. With this one and a half hours, he promises to help us approach each day with zest. We will rise then, as Marcus

25

Aurelius said, to the work of a human being, rid of the nagging knowledge that we are doing less than our best.

Amiel, the Swiss philosopher, wrote in his journal that "the morning air breathes a new and laughing energy into the veins and marrow. Every dawn is a new contract with existence." The dawn, Amiel said, is a time for projects, for resolution, for the birth of action.

Early to bed, early to rise, is good advice whether you arrive home tired out or not. It is, for one thing, the classic physiology. It is the first choice of our body, the natural way to live. Were we to follow our body rhythms, those circadian cycles, it would be the normal way to spend our allotted, unchanging 24 hours. The gradual buildup in our physiological function and then the gradual decline, the flooding and ebbing of the tides in our body, are matched by our physical and mental activity. The closer we get to following the rhythm of the earth, the closer we get to our own internal rhythms.

Early rising puts us in harmony with those rhythms. It is truly a great beginning. Early rising followed by an early morning workout is an even better one.

There are those of us who are always about to live. We are waiting until things change, until there is more time, until we are less tired, until we get a promotion, until we settle down—until, until, until. It always seems as if there is some major event that must occur in our lives before we begin living.

Bennett rejects that excuse. He asks for minor adjustments, advises that we start modestly. He gives us simple, monosyllabic advice: Rise an hour earlier, bring your mind to heel, avoid the harsh word. Everything that he suggests requires little more than the will to do it.

The psychologist Abraham Maslow, in describing fully functioning people, said much the same thing: "People who are self-actualizers go about it in these little ways: They listen to their own voice; they are honest, and they work hard."

They find out who they are, said Maslow, not only in terms of their mission in life but in other ways: ". . . in terms of the way their feet hurt when they wear such and such a pair of shoes, and whether or not they like eggplant, or stay up all night if they drink too much beer."

That is what the real self means, declared Maslow. These people find their own biological nature, their congenital nature, which is difficult to change or is irreversible.

We must become expert in ourselves; we must listen to our body, learn its strengths and weaknesses, yet all the while refusing to accept less than what we can do. There are great limits, and we do not know where they are until we get there.

The little ways we reach these great limits begin with knowing our bodies. This perception that things are right or wrong is much more sensitive than people give it credit for. Hans Selye, the expert on stress, once said that the thing that mystified him most was how people know they are sick. What moves a person to come to a doctor's office and announce that something is wrong—often when the most sophisticated medical testing is unable to find anything amiss. Science cannot make a diagnosis; yet the body knows that its homeostasis has been upset.

What we must do is perceive the static-free messages from inner space which tell us there is intelligent life there and it is attempting to communicate with us. For information to come through loud and clear, we must purify the body, must conform in every way to its proper workings. Research is always going on in the hope of helping us in this. But more often than not, the research simply proves what we already know. When we listen to our body, we need no textbook. When we are doing what our body tells us is best, we can be assured we are physiologically correct. There is not a single test that tells us as much as the body and what it perceives to be happening.

Maslow's self-actualizers discovered their own individual ways of fulfilling their potential. As Seurat's tiny dots eventually made a masterpiece, so the self-actualizers' minute attention to daily details made their lives works of art. They became specialists in the only subject that warrants being a specialist: the study of the self, the one science that makes you a successful practitioner in life.

This is not to say that success is assured, Bennett continually warns us. Always proceed with little steps, he advised. Never forget you are dealing with human nature. Always remember we want the easy way out. We want something for nothing. We blame others when things go wrong. We deny that we have control over our mind and body. We have become civilized animals and have lost the will to survive and the capability of doing so.

I once wondered why Maslow, when he places self-actualization as the highest need, put survival as the basic one. Now it is evident that we must learn to survive—becoming that wild, instinctive animal again, seeing plainly how destructive our life style is.

We must live on the alert. Then we can get on with the business of becoming perfect.

3

On Changing

“

**Once you find something that is playful
and addictive and filled with satisfaction,
your daily budget takes care of itself.
New priorities are set.
A new perspective,
a new sense of proportion,
takes over.**

”

WHEN I WAS PRACTICING MEDICINE and running every day, writing weekly sports columns and racing almost every Sunday, people would ask me how I did it. The 24 hours did not seem long enough to allow for all those activities. How was I able to budget my time so effectively?

It was difficult at first. I found that running could not be simply added to my day. I would not get up early in the morning and do it, and running before bedtime was too much after my long day. Something had to go to afford running and writing full play.

And because both running and writing are play—play of the body and play of the mind—I was able to take my 24 hours and find a place for them. *Once you find something that is playful and addictive and filled with satisfaction, your daily budget takes care of itself.* New priorities are set. A new perspective, a new sense of proportion, takes over. Once I became a runner and then a writer, my expenditures of time were made only when they were compatible with those roles.

Over a period of time, I eliminated a number of activities from my usual day. Most of this surgery was painless. Lunch, I discovered, was unnecessary. Eating a big breakfast left me with no need for midday food. All I missed was the idle chatter at the doctors' table at the hospital, and that noonday chatter became more inconsequential in its absence. Thoreau once said that we should not lunch with people unless we have a new idea to impart. On that basis, my luncheons could be reduced to monthly events.

Movies are no problem. Most are not worth seeing. A year's output in film is reduced to a handful that can stir me to tears or laughter or action. The others are no more than killers of time.

My rules for books are equally simple. I read the classics and prefer authors who are dead or older than I. If you are of another mind, pick up a best-seller list from 10 years ago, and you will get an idea how little of what is current will live on. A classic is a book that appeals from one generation to another. When people urge me to read a new book, I go home and read an old one. There are few good reasons to read novels. Robert Frost said he read no novels because he was too busy living his own life.

The passive role imposed by both the movies and novels puts me off. Like Frost, I want to be part of the action. I do not want to be a spectator. The trade-off for watching and reading is the stimulation of new ideas and the good quotes. For good quotes, books by the great thinkers are the best. Newspapers that contain the truth expressed by the common man come next. Movies are bad, TV the worst.

How many hours can you watch TV without hearing a remark clever and witty and insightful enough to repeat, much less treasure? How many months can you watch a late-night show and not learn one new thing that will change or illuminate your life?

My rules for budgeting my 24 hours are simple. No lunch, no novels, little TV, a rare movie, few magazines, a quick pass through the newspaper. Thus I reduce those hours in which I am a consumer and a spectator and increase the time when I am living my own life.

Do not underestimate the difficulty of turning over a new leaf. Be aware that even minor changes in our daily routine are resisted by forces as powerful as any commitment we can make.

We believe that change is a matter of willpower. Once we become determined enough, once a truly firm decision has been made, the new life will take place.

It doesn't work that way. It is true that we have to recognize the need for a change, true also that we must make the pledge to do it, true always that such a commitment follows observation and judgment. But *no matter how long and proper the preparation, no matter how strong and enduring the motivation, we cannot add a new activity to our life without taking something else out.*

Should I decide that I want to become fit and I am currently using up my allotted hours a day, then I must take something out of that day to make room for my new thing—in this case fitness.

Why not add it to the end of the day or the beginning? Because removing time from sleep ultimately fails. It does happen, particularly in the beginning of an athletic program, that less sleep is required because of less fatigue. But as activity increases, so does the need for sleep.

Nor is it easy to decide what is to be thrown away. We have to decide between good things, not good and bad. We have a surfeit of riches. Each has value, each is worth doing. But decide we must. Either we choose the status quo and our feeling of missing out, or we break the pattern and change course.

Whatever success you will have will begin with giving up something

31

presently in your life for the new activity. Just how difficult this can be is seen from an analogy with government.

When Jerry Brown was running for governor of California, he campaigned on reduced government spending and elimination of unnecessary jobs. When he became governor, he suddenly discovered how difficult this was to do. Every job, regardless of its importance, had its constituency—people and groups ready to battle anyone who would change the status quo. Eventually Brown saw that the only way to decrease or eliminate a government job was to have a new one created in the private sector.

So too with human potential. You have to learn that everything you do every day has a deep-seated reason. It gratifies a need and offers psychological support. Therefore, begin where the rewards of the new activity can clearly outweigh what is being sacrificed.

"A prig," says the *American Heritage Dictionary*, is "a person regarded as overprecise, affectedly arrogant, smug, or narrow-minded." Many fitness addicts become prigs. They pass through that obnoxious stage, attempting to proselytize those mired in physical sin. Prigs become arrogant about their resting pulse, boastful about their weight loss, and insufferable about their weekly mileage or laps of the pool. If their attitude is not holier-than-thou, it most certainly is better-than-you. Their reaction to their nonexercising brethren ranges from contempt to condescension.

In one's failures in other areas—creative, mental and spiritual—the eternal battle with self and a sense of humor should be the best antidotes to this attitude. It will be found that in taking care of oneself one has quite all to do.

Putting arrogance and self-satisfaction aside, there is still the danger of allowing a fitness schedule to run you. It must be respected, not worshipped. Such a daily program is not a religion. Born-again athletes come late to this realization. The sport, first a passion, becomes a duty. The mental exercise, the other part of the schedule, becomes sacrosanct. Nothing is allowed to interfere. No deviation is permitted.

Simply following a schedule risks the danger of looking ahead to your next programmed activity. This is part of the "hurry sickness" and a form of living in the future. One becomes product-centered instead of concentrating on the process.

The beginning athlete, thinker, hero, saint, has to skirt many dangers —almost all of them a matter of attitude. It is entirely within my power —without moving from my desk, without indeed moving a muscle—to cast out priggishness. It may return in a few minutes, but at least I understand how this can be done and what effort it entails.

So too with letting my daily program become an obsession. It may come to rule my life, to make me its slave rather than master. A successful rebellion against this conformity can be made in a rocking chair. Tyranny can be conquered in the mind.

The drive to live in the future may be strong but no stronger than that available concentration of attention we call willpower. Living in the present is our primary aim. Once we make that our focus, we can avoid the trap of thinking ahead—of living in a delusion.

But all these dangers presuppose an initially successful program. They are the dangers of success while the chief danger is the risk of failure at the commencement of a program. Your chance to change your life may well go aglimmering before your plans ever really get underway.

You will never have a chance to be a born-again prig if you don't first become an athlete. Nor will you gain in your mental and creative and spiritual life if the initial phases of such training are a failure.

The rule, then, is to begin modestly. Do not talk about what you are going to do; simply begin. Being born again can mean crawling before you walk and walking before you run.

What exactly is my goal physically? What should I aim for in physical fitness? Like almost everything else in life, it depends on what I am called to be. How will I best express myself through my body? I am looking, in a real sense, for my physical profession—just as I am my creative and mental and spiritual profession. We cannot all be professional athletes—but to a degree each one of us is an athlete; each is capable of becoming fit.

I express myself with and through my body. I am called to be the body I become. My profession is how my body plays, what becomes my body's sport. So my physical education is no less important than any other part of my education. And the physical manifestation of myself deserves, indeed *requires,* equal time with my other functions.

I will be fit because I must. I will find my sport because without it I

33

will be incomplete. If I am fortunate I will find an area where movement of body joins movement of the mind and movement of the spirit—and discover that activity in which the subsequent repose coincides with heightened states of being, and affirmation of myself and all creation.

4

On Sleeping

"

The human animal was built for early rising.
The human condition is best worked out
when we get up with the dawn.

"

IN RECENT YEARS I have become an early riser. I have had to. My home is now a large Victorian house on the ocean in Ocean Grove, New Jersey. I sleep in a room on the third floor. It faces the beach and opens out onto a porch with a white railing and a vista of ocean and sky.

The sun rises in that room. All I can see when I am awakened by that enormous light is the new day coming up in the east.

There is no sleeping from then on. The sun and light and sky will not permit it. Their brightness fills my mind as it fills my senses. Not only the flesh but the spirit as well is awakened in those moments that herald another miracle to be.

The sun is a clarion that sends out a message heard in every cell of my body. And it has the same effect on others in our town. Before too long, I see walkers and runners and cyclists out on the boardwalk. In the few minutes it takes for me to don my bathing suit and plunge into the ocean, people have their dogs on the leash and are out for their morning stroll.

Given the proper circumstances, we tend to follow the cycle of the day, of light and dark, as naturally and unconsciously as do the animals. We respond in our efforts and energies as the animals we are. My life in Ocean Grove has proven that.

It is an older community, a town of senior citizens—which may be a factor. With age comes wisdom and a need of economy. Time is getting short; it must be used well. Energy is not as plentiful; it must be used efficiently. Conformity to the rules of nature becomes imperative when you get a bit older.

Some wags call this town "Ocean Grave." No life there, they say. True, we have no bars, no discos, very little noise. The cars give way to pedestrians. But then we are a walking town; we old folks keep moving. Our boardwalk is alive. From dawn to sundown, there is always a parade —singly or in groups, on foot and on bicycles—of people keeping their minds and bodies in motion.

The day that begins early also ends early. On week nights, there are band concerts and sing-alongs. They end a little after nine o'clock, and by 10 P.M. there is very little stirring. Lights start going out all over town.

When we moved to Ocean Grove, our friends thought I had gone mad. My children took off and got their own apartments. What was the sense of living in an anachronism, a town still living as people did almost 100 years ago? This little hamlet, a square mile wide with all the gingerbread Victorians and the American flags, was a museum piece—not a place to make a life.

But Ocean Grove is more than a historic site. It represents a normal functioning in nature, much the same way the wetlands and the pine barrens do. It and its ways must be preserved. The customs and practices in the Grove are part of our ecology. Rising with the sun, the early morning walk or run or cycle, the pace that allows for meditation—all are necessities to the practice of living. Simple, plain food served three times a day is another part of the daily schedule. I rarely see a smoker. What drinking is done is in moderation.

Dull you might say. I find it otherwise. The days are full. And in the early evening, porches are filled with people in lively conversation. My neighbors, whatever their age, are independent and energetic. They are filled with enthusiasm. They give this little seaside town a feeling of movement I never felt anywhere else. I lived before in a suburb where I was frequently the only person on the roads. Visitors frequently stopped me on my run to get directions, because there were no other signs of life in the town.

But more than anything else, living in Ocean Grove has returned my body-mind to its natural schedule. I am responding to those tides that have ebbed and flowed since my birth. My body is now in unison with those cycles that follow the turning of the earth.

The human machine, the body-mind complex, operates on a program set by the most sophisticated computer ever devised. This human machine is a marvelous integration of innumerable changes occurring progressively during 24 hours. We need not and mostly do not conform to its schedule. But when we do, we are conforming exactly to our nature.

The human animal was built for early rising. The human condition is best worked out when we get up with the dawn.

One of the joys of aging is sleep. As I grow older my sleep has become a delight. I no longer approach my bed with the reluctance of youth and even middle age. I cannot wait to stretch out my limbs, put my body at rest, and enjoy the workings of my mind.

What I have come to treasure is not so much the sleep but the getting to sleep. As they grow older, many people complain about difficulty in falling asleep, only to be then awakened sometime during the night. They now have periods of wakefulness for various reasons. Trips to the bathroom for one. Nagging back for another. I find such interruptions no annoyance at all. They afford me another opportunity to repeat the thinking process that occurred before I went to sleep.

For me this time before sleep has become very special. Next to running, it is my best time for thinking. I have this essay I am writing. I have the information. I have already written pages of words and sentences and paragraphs. I have one problem. I do not know the first word, the first sentence, the first paragraph. I do not yet know the theme, and how to introduce it.

So I lie there letting this consciousness stream past me. I lie there searching for the few sentences that will contain the fullness of the essay when it is completed. Usually, of course, sleep intervenes. I sink down still hunting for that elusive opening. Oblivion comes with my task not yet accomplished.

Then age intervenes. I am awakened, for whatever reason, and once more I can search for the opening that contains everything that will follow. And again I go off to sleep still in this pursuit.

Who would complain about such good fortune? Too much time is spent in sleep anyway. We need, to be sure, the refreshment and energy it supplies. We require sleep to store memories and fill our subconscious. We must have sleep to replenish the zest and enthusiasm that have dwindled away during the previous day.

But must we use up so many hours to accomplish this replenishment? Sleep, it seems, demands much for what it gives. One third of my life spent with unconsciousness. One third of my time on earth in a coma. The only true benefit being that twilight zone before it finally takes over my existence.

If I must sleep eight hours, then these interruptions and repetitions, this twilight zone, are its recompense. These are the times for words and phrases and the absolutely right sentences. These are the times for Eliot's "Raids on the inarticulate." Words always fail but less so in those free-flowing periods between the light of day and the dark of sleep.

So there is nothing that gives me more pleasure than a bad night's sleep. Those hours I spent in bed now have something to show for them in the morning. I may sacrifice some benefits during those waking periods. I may lose out on some of the biochemical and metabolic effects of the various stages of sleep. What I gain is more than worth the loss. I have plundered my memory and subconscious and come back with material I did not know was there.

The absolute quiet for sleep is an effective setting for the creative impulse. It offers a peace and solitude rarely present during the rest of the day. "I have often said," wrote Pascal, "that all the troubles of man come from him not knowing how to sit still." I could extend that to being still before sleep.

When I was younger I either fought sleep or sought it. I never accepted. Age has brought with it that relaxed concentration that makes the best of whatever the circumstances.

Like everything else in life sleep is a very complex maneuver that works best if you don't try hard to do it. As I grow older it becomes easier. As tomorrow becomes less important and the now becomes the focus of my life, sleep and its comings and goings contain the meaning of my day.

Nature's way is the right way. So it is with our circadian rhythms. These self-sustained biological clocks tell us unerringly what is best for the human animal.

When I get up with the dawn, eat the right food, exercise at the proper time, and retire soon after dark, I am conforming to these built-in oscillators that control my internal functions. The light/dark, eat/not eat, exercise/rest rhythms synchronize my physiological watches.

The daily cycles will occur in any event, of course. In isolations from environmental fluctuations in light, temperature and humidity, the clocks maintain their spontaneous periodicities. I cooperate with these cycles and lock them into my daily activities to get the most out of my physical and mental capabilities.

I know, however, that my body-mind complex can adapt to alterations in this schedule. Should I get up late in the morning and go to bed late at night, I would in time believe that I am the same person I was before. But it would be settling for less than my best. I would have silenced the protest of the animal within. I would be compromising with life and working against my body.

The major ethical advance of this century, according to Thomas Merton, has been the development of the ecological conscience. Ecology derives from the Greek word for "house." Ecology is a study of the interrelationships within our environment, both internal and external.

Basically, it is the matter of keeping our house in order. We have littered and polluted and dirtied our house over the past century; now we are trying to put it in order. The same ecological conscience applies to the house that is our body.

In raising our awareness toward what technology is doing to our environment, we ignore what technology is doing to our inner environment. The indifference and arrogance we have expressed toward our natural resources, we are still expressing by abusing our personal resources—psychological and spiritual.

Former California Governor Jerry Brown speaks of the stewardship we have been given for the earth. We have the same responsibility to care for our bodies and minds—and not merely because that is the ethical and moral thing to do, but because it is the intelligent and rewarding thing to do.

Hans Selye, the world expert on stress, when asked for a philosophy of life, said we should practice a selfish altruism. What we do for the common good should be done for ourselves as well. The more we conform to the workings of the universe and nature, the better we succeed personally and socially.

Circadian rhythms are a fascinating subject. They demonstrate once again the truth of the dictum of Pythagoras that we can learn about the cosmos from inside ourselves. But these tides within the body are too important to be used simply for the delight of the mind. They must be lived. They must be acted out so that each of us gets the most out of the bodies we inhabit.

The study of our body clocks cannot be an esoteric specialty for a group of scientists. It is a vital concern for all of us. It has to do with health and homeostasis, with performance and productivity. Yet we do not look, we do not listen, we do not heed. We ignore the information the clocks give us. We are indeed blind and deaf tenants of our bodies.

The Olympic skier Suzy Chaffee once asked me, "It's 10 P.M. Do you know where your body is?" I didn't. I had never inspected my body to see where it was or where it should be. Only recently, with the sun bursting into my room morning after morning, have I discovered where my body is from minute to minute during the day—and better yet, I have enjoyed it.

40

5

On Dieting

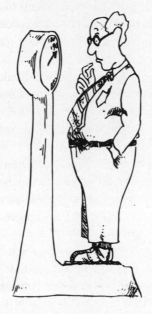

"

**Millions upon millions
of fitness-conscious Americans
are now involved in training and competition.
All of them are concerned about
the relationship of diet and performance.
They are looking for something
that will make a difference. . . .**

"

THERE IS ALWAYS A NEED for orthodoxy. Whether it be true or false, we look for an accepted dogma, and when we find it, it becomes a fixed point of reference. There must be something unchanging if we are going to occupy ourselves with change. Even the wildest of radicals are aware of this necessity for a bedrock of conservatism. If we are to rebel we want something substantial to rebel against. If we are to start a revolution we require something permanent and unalterable to counterbalance that revolt. If we would have order at the end, we must have order at the beginning.

Which is to say that the rebels and reformers and revolutionaries in the field of nutrition should be delighted that the American Dietetic Association has issued an opinion paper on "Nutrition and Fitness." This professional society numbers 28,000 dieticians among its members; its voice is that of practitioners who daily advise or prepare meals for millions of people. Orthodoxy has finally spoken. Here is a syllabus of dietary truths as these hardliners see them. Deviate from them at your own peril. Which is to say, do your own experimenting, but don't expect us to believe what happens. Not unless you document in it the basic orthodox conservative way every Establishment demands.

Those of us who have been interested spectators of the battles going on over diet and nutrition should find the ADA guidelines of value. We read claims and counterclaims on diet almost daily in the papers and magazines. International experts take opposite positions on almost every issue. Controversy is the appetizer, entree and dessert of every meeting where diet is the topic. The press naturally is having a field day with dispatches from the front lines of these wars about vitamins and trace minerals and cholesterol and any number of things we eat and don't eat.

At such times there is a need to ask, "Where are we?" A need to stop and answer the question, "What exactly do we know?" The ADA has attempted to do just that.

Their statement is divided into two parts. Part I is directed toward the general public. Part II contains recommendations for athletes involved in training or competition.

I find no surprises in the section aimed at the general public. The statement takes a conservative approach that is right down the middle of the fairway. Nothing new here. Just common sense and the wisdom of the human race. It could have been written by Hippocrates. The question it raises is whether or not there will ever be any progress in dietetics. Will nutrition ever add in some new and special way to the good life?

The ADA supports the following recommendations:

1. A nutritionally adequate diet and exercise are major contributing factors to physical fitness and health.

The ADA feels that there is substantial evidence that such a diet should avoid excess intake of calories, fat, cholesterol, sugar, salt and highly refined foods lacking in fiber.

2. Weight loss and weight maintenance should be achieved by a combination of dietary modifications, change in eating behavior, and regular aerobic exercise.

The key is balancing energy intake with energy output. As we get older our energy output diminishes so we have to reduce our energy intake. Exercise allows us to increase our energy output and thereby control or reduce our weight.

3. Skin-fold measurements should be used to determine level of body fatness.

Acceptable levels of body fat range from 7 to 15 percent for men, to 12 to 25 percent for women. However, with well-trained runners body fat is seldom higher than 6 percent in males and 12 percent in females.

The skin-fold method is the most practical test although not the most precise. Even with that deficiency, it is fortunate that skin-fold testing is not routine in the doctor's office. If we had a quick, reliable way to do mass screening for percentage of body fat, America, with all its over-eaters, would be in a panic.

4. The generally healthy individual who regularly consumes a diet that supplies the Recommended Dietary Allowances receives all the necessary nutrients for a physical conditioning program.

Here is the point where most opponents of the balanced diet separate from the herd. The precise individual needs for nutrients is the area where most of the fight occurs. Still, it is nice to have that big, shiny target to fire at.

5. Intensity, duration, frequency of exercise should be determined according to the age, physical condition and health status of the individual.

I find this recommendation by dieticians another example of experts making pronouncements outside their competence. Such matters are the province of the exercise physiologist, not the nutritionist. Still it is common practice these days to see professionals style themselves as authorities in another specialty.

This does not mean that what professional nutritionists say is not true. We have to establish their competence for ourselves.

6. The habits of a nutritionally balanced diet and physical fitness should be established during childhood and maintained throughout life.

Everyone agrees to this. The question is how correct food habits, even if universally known and accepted, can be taught. Enriching foods has been the most successful way of getting needed necessary nutrients into the everyday diet. The next best, I suspect, is to get people interested in their own performance as a consequence of eating the right food.

The second part of the American Dietetic Association's statement on "Nutrition and Fitness" is directed toward athletes. It comes at an appropriate time. Millions upon millions of fitness-conscious Americans are now involved in training and competition. All of them are concerned about the relationship of diet and performance. They are looking for something that will make a difference, some diet, vitamin, mineral, amino acid or other nutrient that will take them into longer training and better "personal bests." They, especially, are asking the questions "What do we really know?" "How much can I believe about helping my performance?"

The *Journal of the American Medical Association* takes note of these questions in a review of nutrition in the past decade. "It became obvious during the 70s," states the J.A.M.A., "that people in general expect too much of nutrition." While orthodox scientific organizations were striving for "scientific" truths, reports this review, a large segment of the population was supporting the counterculture of nutrition and holistic medicine.

The ADA statement takes the claims of this counterculture into consideration. It admits to some breakthroughs in the nutrition of the athlete but denies others or, at least, denies the fact that they have been proven scientifically. When the ink had dried, the far right in nutrition, those advocating caffeine, baked goods and beer, had won two out of three. The advocates of natural foods, bee pollen, megavitamins and such were still in the antechamber awaiting approval. No substantive evidence, said the association.

The ADA recommendations for athletes in training and competition are as follows:

1. The athlete should meet increased caloric needs by increasing "calorie plus nutrient" foods. The RDA's of thiamine and some other vitamins are increased by increased caloric intake. So an athlete using 6,000 calories a day requires more vitamins. Increase in bread-cereal and the fruit-vegetable group should be emphasized. Enriched bread and enriched cereals should keep anyone out of dietary trouble.

2. The athlete should maintain a hydrated state by consuming fluid before, during and after exercise. Runners can lose as much as 2–4 quarts of sweat (5–9 pounds) an hour. A 3 percent weight loss can impair performance. Symptoms gradually increase with further losses, and a 10 percent drop in weight can lead to heat stroke. Weighing before and after training will give you guidelines. One quart equals 2.2 pounds.

My habit is to drink enough liquid during the two hours before a race so that I have to urinate once or twice. This convinces me I am hydrated. Then I take 20 ounces just before the race starts and 10 ounces every 20 minutes thereafter. Thirst is an inaccurate indicator of water need. A full bladder is the only proof that you have taken enough.

3. The athlete should meet needs for additional electrolytes from foods ordinarily consumed. In other words, salt and potassium requirements can be met simply by diet. There is no need for anything but water and sugar during a race. The ADA recommends foods rich in potassium before an athletic event. As far as salt is concerned, we usually take too much anyway, but a little extra *after* the race may be helpful for leg cramps.

4. The athlete should use electrolyte supplements only on the advice of a physician. This is a corollary of the above. Supplementary electrolytes are not really needed. The recommendation to see a physician is virtually useless since most physicians have no idea of what goes on in a long-distance race or, indeed, of most exercise physiology. However, when sweat losses are going to be great, say four quarts or more, it is probably best to take a half-strength "ade." According to the ADA guidelines, all "ades" except Body Punch contain too much salt, too much sugar, and an incorrect amount of potassium.

5. A high carbohydrate intake prior to competition can be beneficial to some athletes competing in endurance events. This carbohydrate "unloading and reloading" should not be used indiscriminately. It is of no

45

advantage in short-term, high-intensity competition. The ADA frowns on such an intake for adolescents and thinks the full depletion-repletion, unloading-reloading cycle should not be attempted more than two or three times a year. I would agree except that I partially load two to three times a week. After every long race and 10-mile training run I eat Italian-style to put that sugar back in my muscles.

6. There is no definite performance value in products such as wheat germ, wheat germ oil, vitamin E, ascorbic acid, lecithin, honey, gelatin, phosphates, sunflower seeds, bee pollen, kelp or brewer's yeast. Many athletes, of course, think otherwise. Nevertheless, there is no conclusive scientific evidence that any of these substances can help them do better.

7. Beer, wine or more potent alcoholic beverages should not be used as a source of calories, as a muscle relaxant or as an ergogenic (performance) aid. The ADA lists the bad effects of alcohol—among them, that alcohol acts as a diuretic causing water loss and may lessen the capability of the heart to do work—and considers the evidence that there is a better way to get hydrated and increase sugar store. I have taken beer on occasion before and during a race, but now I find I prefer defizzed, diluted soft drinks.

8. The pre-event meal should be a light one, taken three to four hours prior to competition. The best meal is one that the athlete tolerates well and one he is convinced will help him do well. Some protein, minimal amounts of fat and liberal complex carbohydrates are recommended. This statement yields some ground to the mystical. It tells us that psychology still plays a part in the effect of diet.

The ADA has spoken. This is the known nutritional world. These may be its eventual limits, but I doubt it. Before us lie great discoveries in this field. We are about to find new and creative ways in which diet will help us to cope with stress, increase physical and mental performance, and allow us to explore fully our human potential.

We were 30 minutes into Orlando's Tangerine Bowl Half-Marathon, with no water station in sight, when I saw a woman standing on the curb. She was holding a six-pack of beer and a sign that read, "Pit stop for Murphys."

I ran up to her, said, "I'm Murphy," and took one of the beers. Then I rejoined the race, drinking as I ran.

In a pinch, and sometimes by preference, when I need fluid or energy,

I will take a beer from a spectator. I know of a few other runners who do this.

The Murphys in Orlando apparently like their beer. So does Dr. Thomas Bassler, the former editor of the American Medical Joggers publication. Bassler usually runs 25 miles on Sunday, taking a beer every few miles. He calls it "Jogging a six-pack." I once ran the Reno marathon with Dr. Jack Scaff, the cardiologist who fathered the distance-running boom in Hawaii. He had arranged for caches of beer along the Reno course.

Still, it would be fair to say I am virtually alone in my willingness to take beer before and during a race. I have gained a certain notoriety by appearing at the start of a marathon with two cans of beer in my hands. If I accept a beer along the way, the other runners instantly know who I am.

I take it as a personal affront, therefore, that the American College of Sports Medicine has issued a position paper on "The Use of Alcohol in Sports." Since I am the rare runner drinking alcohol among the thousands at marathons, the ACSM statement must be for my benefit.

Or could it be that the College wants to stop the revolution before it starts? The strength of a movement derives not from the numbers of its supporters but from the appeal of the cause it espouses. Alcohol has a lot of appeal.

The ACSM gives its position straight and with no chaser: Alcohol won't do you any good, and in the long run it is going to do you harm.

"Some athletes," says Dr. Melvin Williams, who wrote the final draft, "drink alcohol before or during a sports performance because they think it is an efficient form of energy or that it will aid performance. But we know these assumptions are wrong."

There undoubtedly are more efficient sources of energy than alcohol, other replacement drinks that have better physiological effects than beer. I sometimes start a distance race with two cans of Coke and often choose it along the route. The scientists also have been reluctant to confirm the value of sugar taken during long races, but runners know better.

The one advantage of alcohol over sweet drinks is that it requires no digestion and imposes no absorption problems. Some people even worry that it works too well—acting as a diuretic, which further depletes the runner of water. Yet the experiments show otherwise, and the ACSM statement does not even mention this in its negative evidence.

The ACSM tells us that alcohol can affect our physiological tests adversely. Its authors present the following judgments, and I present my reactions.

1. "The acute ingestion of alcohol can exert a deleterious effect on a wide variety of psychomotor skills." (My experience is that beer during racing has no effect on my running style. It's such a simple psychomotor skill that it escapes deterioration.)

2. "Acute ingestion of alcohol will not substantially influence metabolic or physiological functions essential to performance." (The scientists want to warn me that beer will not improve my time. I never thought it would. I drink beer not for a personal best but for personal survival, not to get better but to get to the finish line.)

3. "Acute alcohol ingestion will not improve and may decrease strength, power, speed and cardiovascular endurance." (There is, however, no definitive evidence that alcohol diminishes performance. My perception is that when I get down too far, the beer brings me up. If I am dehydrated and hypoglycemic, how can beer make me worse?)

4. "Alcohol is the most abused drug in the United States, and a major contributing factor to accidents and their consequences." (The authors of this report now show their real concern: excessive drinking after the athletic event, drinking not for performance but for pleasure. I believe they are overreacting here as well.)

I would point out that most runners are normally two-drinks-a-day individuals. The race is unlikely to change that. A little alcohol goes a long way when you have not eaten in four hours and have just run up to 26.2 miles. I get a nice buzz on after a race with two cans of beer, and I have no urge to drink more.

Beer during the race may not be an altogether satisfactory drink, but it is the ideal fluid replacement. We should never forget that sport also includes that wonderful period following the contest—a time that is filled, as Johann Huizinga observes, "with mirth and relaxation." Try that with an "ade" drink.

It's time to confront the real caffeine problem. My addiction is caffeine. I cannot begin my day without a cup of coffee, preferably light with Sweet 'n Low. Every 90 minutes from then on I have a diet cola or coffee until I reach day's end and take my two beers and go to bed. The few times I tried to break this habit were halfhearted and unsuccessful. I have never been convinced that coffee was bad for me. It has been an ever-ready antidote for those physical and mental troughs that occur during the day.

Now comes some unsettling news out of Minneapolis. Dr. Arthur Leon and his colleagues at the University of Minnesota School of Public Health have uncovered evidence that caffeine may lessen endurance performance.

Their subjects were 175 apparently healthy middle-aged men. These men first completed a questionnaire on habitual physical activity, smoking, beverage consumption and sleep habits. Then they were given a variety of tests including EKGs, cholesterol, grip strength, and a body mass ponderal index (relation of height to weight). Finally, these characteristics were correlated to the duration of treadmill exercise, the end point being when they developed symptoms of exhaustion and were unable to continue further.

This is the sort of research that interests me. If I am going to change my life it should be for the right reason. We are constantly being harangued by the media about changing our lifestyles. Hardly a day goes by when I don't read or hear that something I eat or drink or breathe or touch is likely to do me in. But these admonitions have to do with longevity, which is no longer of concern to me. My goal is Dr. Leon's goal-performance. If I achieve maximal performance it seems reasonable I will get the maximum out of my life span as well.

Most of the information from this study is not surprising. Treadmill times were higher with habitual heavy leisure activity, especially when it involved sweating and shortness of breath. Such activity was, in fact, the most potent independent variable in predicting exercise duration on the treadmill.

The study group also found a positive correlation of ability with slow resting pulse and low body mass index (weight/height squared). These are indicators I have in common with most serious runners. Running is a leisure-time activity associated with sweat and shortness of breath that leads to a low body mass and a slow resting pulse.

More reassuring information followed. Endurance capacity was apparently not influenced by a number of factors we are constantly warned about. Blood pressure, serum cholesterol, alcohol consumption (12 drinks a week), irregular heartbeat and sleep habits had no predictable consequences.

In these matters we can apparently listen to our body. Within reason we can do what our body wants to do. Eat what we like. Sleep as we please. Take our two drinks a day. All will go well. And those ominous findings we hear about during our annual physical: the blood pressure and the irregular heartbeat and the cholesterol are, it appears, not ominous at all.

What were the factors associated with low treadmill times? What were the life-style practices that most interfered with endurance? First and foremost: cigarette smoking. This predicted poor performance to the same extent that the leisure-time activity predicted the opposite. Then came the same other negative variables: a high resting pulse and a high body mass.

At this point I had a perfect grade. I was doing everything right. Then came the cruncher. Next to cigarette smoking, the most important single predictor of poor achievement on the treadmill was caffeine consumption. An average of 42 caffeine drinks a week had almost the same adverse effect as smoking.

My first reaction was disbelief. Previous reports on caffeine had never contained any threat to my 10-kilometer time. Investigators had written about coffee and a possible association with tumors of the pancreas (now discredited), but they had never even hinted that it might slow me down. Could the old-timers have been wrong who recommended coffee before a race and gave out tea and honey on the course? Was cola something that made me feel good while I was running bad?

My next response was a rush of hope. At sixty-three I am no longer getting better. I can no longer break the six-minute-a-mile barrier in my 5,000- and 10,000-meter runs. If caffeine is good for me, I am the best I will ever be. Suppose, however, it is not me but the caffeine that is holding me back? Rid myself of that habit, and I could have a season of running to rival the good old days. A few caffeineless weeks might make me a winner in this perpetual struggle with the digital clock.

Make mine Sanka, light, with Sweet 'n Low.

There are those who think the consequence of dietary affluence is disease. When food becomes plentiful, they say, so does heart disease and hypertension and diabetes. If the effect of diet on a nation's health is still a matter for debate, there are still some results from a country's nutrition that we can agree upon. This much is certain. A surplus in food has two effects, one good and one bad.

The bad effect is obesity. Depending on what criterion you use, the figures for obesity in any advanced country can be alarming. Studies in Canada, for instance, reported that more than 60 percent of all Canadians should be considered obese.

Such figures, however, frequently do not allow for the bone and muscle components of an individual. Weights are given, it is true, for big frames, medium frames and small frames. These personal estimations of skeletal size are quite rough and in great part subjective. What is needed is a quick and relatively accurate way to estimate percentage of body fat.

My percentage of body fat is around 9. I am 5 feet 10 inches and weigh 136 pounds. There are others who are 5′10″, weigh as much as 150 pounds and have less body fat than I have. Wrestlers and 150-pound football players are clear demonstrations of this. They are virtually all bone and muscle.

Runners who are thin-boned and lightly muscled like me have a relatively simple formula for an ideal weight: simply double your height in inches and the result is your ideal weight in pounds. I am 70 inches and, therefore, should weigh 140 or less. And, of course, less is always more for the runner. Now every pound I lose results in a drop of 0.8 percent in body fat. Should I lose 10 pounds, therefore, I would be in the neighborhood of 2 percent body fat and ready for a world's record.

For others who are not sure of their bone structure, the ideal weight can be a difficult figure to arrive at. People frequently ask me what they should weigh. I have even been asked this on radio talk shows where the listeners could phone in but where I couldn't see them. I recall once when a caller, a man, said, "I weigh 220 pounds and I'm 6 feet tall. What should I weigh?" My answer was in the form of a question. "What did you weigh when you were married?" There was a long silence. Then the man said, "One hundred and forty-five pounds." There was his ideal weight, and there was no way he could get out of it. "Well," I said, "you haven't been putting on muscle since you've been married."

If the what-did-you-weigh-when-you-were-married question doesn't give the game away, there is another one that may. "What did you weigh when you got out of basic?" In this era, however, people tend not to get

51

married or experience basic training, so I ask what they weighed when they were twenty years old. Statistics show that the average twenty-year-old male is about 10 percent body fat, a quite acceptable figure for anyone.

The bad effect of food in quantity is obesity. The beneficial effect is on growth and particularly stature. As the amount and quality of our country's food supply has increased so has the average height of the populace. Records have been kept on the height of students entering Harvard. They have shown a decade by decade increase over the years. The influence of diet, especially dietary protein and enriched foods, on our average height has been quite evident.

The most dramatic example of the impact of diet on stature has been in postwar Japan. Before the war most adult Japanese men and women were of small stature. This is still true of Japanese persons over forty years of age. It is no longer true, however, for Japanese teenagers and young adults. Their average size now is virtually the same as of our own teenagers and young adults.

We knew, of course, that height is in great part hereditary. I know of one basketball coach who always asks his young recruits how tall their parents are. What we did not realize is that the full effect of this genetic factor depends to a great extent on the amount of protein and fat and calories you have as an infant and child and adolescent.

In Japan there has been a profound change in the national diet over the past few decades. Between 1950 and 1975 the average consumption of milk increased 15 times. This means a 1,500 percent increase in milk intake. At the same time there was a 7.5 times (750 percent) increase in consumption of meat and eggs, and a 600 percent increase in fat. Simultaneously, the per capita consumption of rice and potato decreased significantly. And in one generation of affluence they caught up to us in height.

What affluence principally buys is more protein. After that comes the refined carbohydrates, and we adapt to them by enriching them as we have bread and cereal. What we don't adapt to are those carbohydrate calories that lead to obesity.

What parents, physicians, coaches and trainers might learn from these observations is, first, the necessity of protein in quantity for the growing child. The much richer and abundant diet in advanced countries does lead to maximum stature and physical potential. Once that has occurred, then attention can be paid to the bad effects of such diets —specifically, obesity.

The Canadian study showed very little difference in the food intake in those who were considered obese and those that were not. What divided the fat from the lean was activity. Those who were lean were expending calories in movement, either at work or in leisure-time fitness programs.

It was not what we ate when we were twenty that kept us at 10 percent body fat; it was what we were doing with our bodies.

Now you know, what keeps your diet honest is honest sweat.

The rules for diet, like the rules for everything else in life, should be kept simple and tailored to the individual. In this respect, we have no better instruction than that inscribed in the ancient Greek shrine at Delphi. The rule: "Nothing in excess." The application: "Know thyself."

Perhaps the greatest excess in the field of diet is the number of books on the subject. Every bookstore is swollen with books offering the last word on diet. Diet books are perennial bestsellers. There is hardly a list of the most sought-after books that does not include one that claims to be the final answer on how to feed your body.

Nevertheless, the truly important aspects of food intake can be summarized on a page or two in our notebooks. Our dietary aims are simple: to maintain optimum weight, to provide energy, and to avoid deficiencies. The rules, too, should be equally simple. Godfrey Fowlere, an Oxford University physician, has summarized them well:

1. The main task is to avoid obesity. This is more the province of exercise. We are not overweight, we are overfat. Only exercise will give us muscle to replace that fat. When you exercise consistently your preoccupation with diet will disappear.

2. Average sugar intake should be halved. Cut down on candy, soft drinks, sugar in tea or coffee.

3. Fat should be reduced to about 30 percent of the diet. Cut down on butter, margarine, cream, fat on meats and fried foods.

4. Increase intake of fiber. Use whole-grain cereals or, in a pinch, Metamucil.

5. Alcohol intake should be kept to two "units" a day (two pints of beer or glasses of wine).

As you can see, dieting need not be complicated. An obsession with calories is not necessary. These basic rules come down to what is now called "the prudent diet." It has a reduced sugar and fat content with some increase in fiber. Salts and alcohol are also reduced but not to limits that would interfere with normal bodily appetites.

In fact, such a diet is a response to normal bodily appetites. It will satisfy the healthy body, which is to say the exercising body. Our eating should be a matter of doing what comes naturally. This occurs only when everything else we do is natural to the body: satisfying the need for motion and activity, enjoying a daily constitutional whether it be a walk or a run.

"Nothing in excess" liberates you from the nonsense of constantly weighing oneself and checking calorie charts; you can throw away those charts of the calorie contents of foods—and the bathroom scale along with them. A school child could follow the nothing-in-excess rule without any additional instructions.

You must, of course, still obey the other Grecian counsel. You should know thyself, know what foods agree or disagree with you. My pre-race drink might cause you to throw up. So be it; choose your own. My allergies are not your allergies. Be aware of this and deal with it. The whites of two eggs contain all the essential amino acids we need for the day, but if they give you headaches or an itch or simply make you feel bad, you must find another way to get those food values. It might be that additives cause problems, but more likely it is some good nutritious food, such as milk or wheat, to which we are allergic. Once you listen to your body, once you can read it like a book, you can forever get rid of those diet books constantly being advertised.

6

On Eating

"

I look for two special requirements from my diet:
first, I must carry the least weight possible;
second, I must have the most energy available.
The first must be accomplished without losing strength,
the second without gaining weight.

"

EINSTEIN WAS ONCE ASKED if he carried a notebook in which to write down new ideas. He replied that he didn't get many new ideas. And it appears that no one else does, either. There is, as they say, nothing new under the sun. So when faced with a problem, it is best not to wait for inspiration. Chances are, the solution lies not in a new idea but in taking a new look at an old one.

Covert Bailey, author of the book *Fit or Fat*, has done just that with the problem of obesity. He has taken a new look at an old idea— exercise—and has found a solution.

"The ultimate cure for obesity," he states, "is exercise."

Obesity is conquered as we increase our muscle mass and increase the muscle enzymes that burn up the fats and carbohydrates we eat. The way to do this—the *only* way we can do it, Bailey maintains—is to exercise regularly.

Bailey is not strictly concerned with weight. His emphasis is on fitness. His theories are based on Webster's definition of obesity: "excessive bodily fat." People are not overweight; they are overfat. The higher the fat figure, the less lean body mass there is. You can weigh 250 pounds and be virtually all muscle and bone, or weigh 100 pounds and be overfat.

In recent years, efforts have been made to control weight without consideration of percentage of body fat. The significance of this figure in the development of obesity and the rationale of its treatment have gone unnoticed. We have, however, begun to observe that most fat people actually eat less than skinny people. The endurance athlete, a lean and active creature, is often an insatiable eater yet gains no weight.

Our common sense, then, tells us that exercise keeps us slim. The idea that exercise melts fat is part of our inherited wisdom. Still, scientists and nutritionists have never quite believed it. The whole idea seems to go against Newton's law of the conservation of energy.

If it takes 10 miles of running to use up the 1,000 calories in a cheeseburger, milkshake and french fries at McDonald's, the scientists have reasoned, then exercise must be an impractical method of losing weight. The scientific way to lose body fat must be to reduce energy intake, not to increase energy output.

Some people are having second thoughts about this traditional view. Dr. Eric Newsholmes of Oxford, an internationally known physiologist, has proposed that the exercised body develops what he calls "futile cycles." It acquires the ability to dissipate calories in the absence of body movement, possibly through the production of heat. When an athlete rests, the wheels are still spinning, still using up energy in these futile cycles. Such cycling, says Newsholmes, may persist for two or three days after exercise—perhaps even longer.

These cycles may contribute to other beneficial effects of exercise, as noted by Swedish medical investigator Per Bjorntrop. Exercise, he says, has a positive effect on obese people even when they are on unrestricted diets. Such people, Bjorntrop reports, undergo "a metabolic rehabilitation." He has documented decreases in hyperinsulemia (excess insulin in the blood), hypertension and high blood fats in obese people who exercise.

What apparently happens is that exercise of the aerobic type causes a hypermetabolic state. When we run or cycle or row or cross-country ski on a daily basis, all our functions are reset at a higher level. We now use the same amount of energy at rest that other people do when they are moving. We are no longer spectators gaining fat; we have become athletes losing it.

Diet alone will not do the job. Dieting reduces muscle as well as fat. It produces haggard people who do not look good or feel good. Covert Bailey is quick to point this out; he will have no truck with dieting. Men of average size, he claims, should ingest no less than 1,500 calories daily; women of average size, no less than 1,200. When an exercise program becomes intense, of course, this intake has to be increased.

Nor is Bailey impressed with pounds lost. When a person tells him that he or she has lost 12 pounds or more on a diet, he asks, "Twelve pounds of what?"

Some of it is fat, of course. But some of it is water, which means nothing. And some of it is muscle, which means the dieter has actually lost ground rather than gained it. This means that gaining weight will be even easier once the diet is stopped.

So what should be monitored if you are overfat and embark on an exercise program? First, do not keep checking your weight. You may even gain weight (two to three pounds) in the beginning because of increased muscle mass. Bailey advises people to throw out the bathroom scales. Stop shooting for an ideal weight, he says. Shoot for health instead. Become aerobically fit, and the fat will take care of itself.

The resting pulse, especially on awakening in the morning, is a good indicator of progressive improvement in fitness. The change in body fat can be checked by body measurements, particularly at the chest, hip and thigh. These are better signs of your improving fitness than is your weight.

Fitness tests, such as the Cooper 12-minute test (which measures maximum distance covered by walking and/or jogging for 12 minutes), will tell you that good things are happening to your muscles and muscle enzymes. When these muscles are tuned up, says Bailey, you have more stamina, more energy, more drive—all because of better utilization of food and less conversion of food into fat.

We may someday discover more complete explanations of these effects of exercise on obesity, but they will not change Bailey's basic premise. The choice is fitness or fatness, to exercise or not to exercise.

This is not a new idea. It is much like an old spiritual concept of which Chesterton said, "It has not been tried and found wanting. It has been found difficult and left untried."

In 1967, Scandinavian investigators reported that endurance performance depends upon the amount of sugar stored in the muscle. When this muscle glycogen is increased by heavy intakes of carbohydrates, physical-work capacity can improve as much as 100 percent. When preceded by exhaustive preliminary exercise, subsequent high-carbohydrate intake can increase the time at a given workload as much as 300 percent.

This research led to the popularity of the "carbohydrate-loading" diet before races. Now we're learning that runners crave loads of carbohydrates *all the time.* Such a diet is aimed not at disease but at performance. It is designed not for longevity but for longer training; not a lower death rate but lower racing times. It is a diet that is part scientific, part anecdotal and part experimental. My diet has evolved by this process. I read the literature to see what the scientists are saying. Next I find out what other runners do. Then I conduct my own experiments.

I look for two special requirements from my diet: first, I must carry the least weight possible; second, I must have the most energy available. The first must be accomplished without losing strength, the second without gaining weight.

In champion male distance runners body fat is rarely more than 6 percent of the body weight. In champion female runners the figure is usually 12 percent or less. In a study of elite runners in Dallas a few years back, the men were found to average 4.7 percent. That is my goal, and diet must help me reach it. I need enough fat and protein to allow for wear and tear on the body, to maintain body functions and to keep my appetite down. Yet I need enough carbohydrates to replace the 100 calories a mile of glycogen used up in my runs.

What I have come up with is a diet that is balanced in overall fat, protein and carbohydrate intake but not balanced in the way I take them.

Breakfast is almost all fat and protein. They are slowly absorbed and converted into sugar. This is bad when replacing glycogen but good when avoiding low blood sugar. Steak or bacon and eggs give me a slowly rising blood sugar. I am free from any 10 A.M. letdown or the fattening desire to go from one Danish-and-coffee break to another. I may not even have an appetite for lunch.

I run my 10 miles at midday, and following that may have some yogurt and a diet cola. I eat nothing more until supper. That is the meal where the replacement of glycogen must begin; otherwise I will not be ready for my training run the next day. Fat and protein alone can take as long as three or four days to restore muscle glycogen.

Supper, therefore, always includes potatoes or rice or spaghetti, along with fruit and vegetables and bread. Desserts, especially when I am not overweight, become important.

Then before bed comes the "night lunch." I make fair game of anything that can be eaten without being cooked: ice cream, cereal with bananas, pretzels, saltines, a beer or two.

My eating day is then over—unless I am awakened to go to the bathroom. Then I make a side trip for some milk and crackers.

If you run, your diet should maintain your proper weight, give you energy for your training run and help you race your best. It should also be a diet you enjoy. It might even include Twinkies.

Nathan Pritikin is a master magician. He has our eyes glued on his diet. He draws our attention to the dangers of eggs, points out the evils of red meat, diagrams the difficulties our bodies have with sugar, dramatizes the hazards of salt, and inveighs against alcohol and caffeine. He throws a spotlight on the terrible things food can do to you. And all the while he has something up his sleeve—exercise.

Pritikin has always espoused exercise. His plan is called the Pritikin Program for diet and exercise. But both he and his critics have focused on his diet in evaluating the efficiency of his program. And while medical observers debate the merits of his diet and dispute the claims made for it, lean, enthusiastic disciples are emerging from Pritikin centers in increasing numbers. While scientists are saying it cannot happen, it does.

The question is not whether the Pritikin Program works, it is why? The people who come for his help are in most instances symptomatic and on drugs. They have received the maximum benefits of orthodox medical treatment and yet are still living lives that are diminished and restricted.

It is a matter of record that spectacular changes do occur with the Pritikin regimen. In many instances Pritikin patients have no further need for drugs. Almost 80 percent of the hypertensives are controlled without medication. An even higher percentage of adult-onset diabetics no longer require insulin or oral hypoglycemic agents. Heart patients with vascular diseases frequently dispense with all the therapy that has been prescribed for them.

It is also a matter of record that most of this success has been attributed to the diet. Pritikin and his colleagues certainly emphasize it. Our basic problem in America, as they see it, is our standard diet, which contains 40 percent fat and 30 percent simple sugars. One journalist has summarized their attitude: "We have met the enemy, and he is fat."

It would be more accurate, and Pritikin's success proves it, to say that our enemy is fat—not fat in our diet, however important, but fat in our bodies. The problem in America is not food but inertia. And overcoming inertia is what the Pritikin program does well and certainly better than any other medical program in this country. The key to the miracle performed at Pritikin centers is exercise and more exercise.

Physicians who view the Pritikin diet as spartan and austere are usually unaware that the exercise program is even more demanding. In some instances patients are encouraged to walk two miles after each meal along with daily periods of supervised exercise. In his book *Live Longer Now*, Pritikin recommends "roving" (walk/jog) up to 10 miles a day. In the present Pritikin Hospital Plan there is a three-hour exercise program in the morning after breakfast and another three-hour period after dinner at night. His guests are doing more in one day than most fitness programs advise for a week.

This level of exercise has two effects. One, on fitness, the other, on fatness. The fitness equation is 30 minutes at a comfortable pace four times a week. Pritikin's patients have accomplished that Monday morning. Adherence to his schedule results in a superior level of fitness—not mere capacity to do work, but the capacity to do demanding work.

Exercise has metabolic consequences as well as physical endurance. The internal milieu is put to rights. The human machine functions like the Rolls-Royce it is meant to be. Blood pressure, circulation, blood chemistries, the use of sugar and fat and protein are all restored to normal. The limitations of disease are no longer experienced.

Exercise also reduces body fat and, even more important, replaces it with muscle. No diet can do that. Diet alone may reduce fat, but it reduces muscle as well. Dieters lose weight but lose energy along with it. Then, when the weight is regained the percentage of body fat is higher than it was before the dieting began. Even the best diet is secondary to exercise in restoring fitness.

There are good things about the Pritikin Diet: the complex carbohydrates, the high fiber, even the lowering of fat content, although reducing fat by 10 percent would try the faith and zeal of a Trappist monk. A total level of 30 percent would make for a more palatable diet and take care of weight and metabolism as well.

Nathan Pritikin is a pioneer in the nonpharmacological approach to disease. It is unfortunate that the acceptance of his program has been based on his theories on diet rather than on his insistence on high doses of exercise. The reason people come out of his centers looking like athletes is that they have become athletes. They feel better, look better and live better.

When I read the contradictory advice about diets, I am reminded of Goethe's statement about religion. "All religions," he says, "are true in what they affirm but wrong in what they deny."

There is, you see, no one way to salvation. The dietary experts would have you believe otherwise, of course. Each proposes his way to nutritional redemption, adopting the same attitude as the True Believers in religion. So we see the Pritikin Diet and Atkins Diet and Stillman Diet, each extolling completely different types of foodstuffs.

On the one hand, we have the disciples of Pritikin advocating complex carbohydrates. Then there are the partisans for Dr. Atkins and his high-fat regimen; they form a sect whose rituals include everything the Pritikin congregation sees as sacrilege. Still others follow the creed of Dr. Stillman and accept meat and protein as the approved food. And here and there are various schismatic groups that believe in anything from high fiber to the drinking man's diet. Fads in diets emerge occasionally much like religious cults and are accepted with equal fervor.

In such an atmosphere, I prefer to remain neutral. I am a dietary agnostic. I am not ready to join in any of the holy wars being fought by the followers of the new religions on food intake. I have a continuing doubt about the existence of a perfect diet. I am unwilling, on the available evidence, to commit myself to any single doctrine on nutrition.

I think it best in these matters to be a freethinker. It is best to suspend belief and to admit there are things we do not yet know. There are in the field of nutrition large elements that are traditional and cultural and religious. Anthropologists have shown us that. Several recent books have demonstrated how many of our dietary practices stem from restrictions and regulations set up for us by religious laws.

The way I see it, every one of these diets has something good about it. There is a case for complex carbohydrates. There is also a substantial argument in favor of high-protein intake, even for a high-fat diet. All over the world, we see people flourishing even though they espouse completely different types of diets.

There are the Tarahumara Indians, who rarely see meat or fish and subsist primarily on grain and vegetables. Then we have the Eskimos, who eat virtually no carbohydrates. The Irish have perhaps the highest protein intake in the entire world yet show no ill effects.

So let Pritikin affirm his complex carbohydrates. Let Atkins preach in favor of fat. Let the Stillman faction give sermons on protein. But let them not deny each other. There is room here to pick and choose, room to see the good in each and then use it when appropriate.

I prefer an attitude of skepticism toward this subject. There is more we do not know about nutrition than what we do know. The known facts are a lot fewer than one would suspect. An official in the U.S. Department of Agriculture has stated that we know a good deal more about feeding animals than we do about feeding humans. He said it will take another 20 to 30 years to fill the gaps in our knowledge.

Such statements should appeal for tolerance in a field where bigotry abounds. Yet this inability to hold a reasonable conversation on diet does not absolve us from the need to act. Diet has assumed a new importance. We no longer are interested in mere survival; we are concerned with living life at our full potential. *Our diet is part of our search for the good and better life. We are attempting to live at our physical, mental and spiritual peak. What we eat may well have a decisive function in that attempt.*

We cannot expect everything to be proven before we act. Nevertheless, adherence to a fundamentalist approach that excludes all other possibilities does not seem justified. We must make our own decisions—using the best information, certainly, but ultimately using the final arbiter—our bodies.

I find my body in total agreement with all these zealots in one area. In diet as with everything else, less is more. Too many calories is the capital sin. So before a diet is even decided upon, it is agreed that calories must be restricted and lean body weight must be attained.

Whether overweight predisposes to illness or decreases longevity is still conjectural. But it does sap energy. It lowers initiative. In general, it dims the full light of the day and dulls our sensitivity to all that is exciting and wonderful around us.

Under special circumstances, any one of the popular diets may be effective. There will be times when carbohydrates are necessary, or protein or fat or fiber—or even alcohol. There is *never* a time for over-eating. Whatever the diet, whatever the belief, obesity must be avoided.

Here again we see the influence of religion. Fasting or lessening food intake has always been part of the life of the mystic and the saint. There is a saying concerning food that puts it all in perspective: "The stuffed prophet sees no visions."

Nor shall we.

7

On Relaxing

"

**Exercise has the effect of defusing
anger and rage, fear and anxiety.
Like music, it soothes the savage in us
that lies so close to the surface.
It is the ultimate tranquilizer.**

"

"Whenever i have a problem that upsets me every time I think about it," a runner said to me, "I take it out on the roads. Then I am able to come to grips with it without my emotions getting in the way."

I told him I had made the same discovery. In almost two decades of running, I have never been mad at anyone during my daily run. My hour of solitude on the road has never been marred by what William James called the "coarser emotions."

Exercise has the effect of defusing anger and rage, fear and anxiety. Like music, it soothes the savage in us that lies so close to the surface. It is the ultimate tranquilizer. Why is this so? What is it about exercise that blocks these destructive feelings? How does it take us out of a world that is an adversary situation and replace it with one that is one-for-all-and-all-for-one, a world filled with sanity and good humor?

The best explanation, it seems to me, lies in the James-Lange theory of emotions. This is one of psychology's most unlikely hypotheses and one usually given little credence. Yet as with most ideas espoused by James, time gives us more and more evidence that he was right.

According to James, I do not first get angry and then exhibit that anger in my body. The actual process is the reverse. My *body* gets angry, and then I become angry. My body perceives the object or idea that causes anger, reacts with the usual physiological phenomena—rapid pulse, flushing of the face, etc.—and only then do I feel the emotion of anger.

When I first read this explanation, I found it incredible. The truth, as I saw it, was obvious: I saw or remembered or dreamed up an object or idea that frightened me or angered me, causing me to feel guilty or to know hate—and then my body reacted to that feeling. The James-Lange theory was, in a word, absurd.

Now I think otherwise. James seems to be correct. If my body does not react to the object or idea, I now realize that I don't feel these emotions. It is not until the physiological effects occur that the emotion becomes apparent. If the usual signs and symptoms of rage are blocked, then I will not feel rage in my mind.

Such blocking can occur in two ways: first, by flooding the various systems of the body with activity so that there is no reserve to produce the reaction identified with the emotion; second, by substituting some positive emotion in its place. (Act happy, look happy, speak happily,

65

said James, and you will be happy. Act like an enthusiast, and you will become an enthusiast.)

When I run, both of these events take place. Running completely occupies my body. It fills every cell. I am all movement, effort, sweat. I become the running as the dancer becomes the dance. The entire functioning of my body is focused on this one action. There is no room for the coarser emotions. Only the higher and more subtle feelings are now able to enter my consciousness.

And indeed they do. Now I can imagine myself a hero and have my body feel heroic; think of myself as a success and find failure unimaginable; know that part of me is good and whole and true, and feel faith flooding through me. My body takes me through the friendly vistas of my river road to even friendlier vistas of my soul. My mind can now think what it likes. It runs ahead of me, investigating things along the way. It is no longer impeded or affected by the negative emotions my body usually creates.

My body usually creates the typical physiological patterns that I know as anger or fear, guilt or rage. And for me, running is the best way to prevent these particular patterns from developing. When I run, I am absolved from those feelings that destroy rather than create, that lead to darkness rather than light. I am cleansed of the passions that arise when I see the world as Them or Us, or rail against Fate, or attempt to change things over which I have no control.

Is running necessary for this? Of course not. The Stoics knew this centuries ago. There is no better guide to tranquility than Marcus Aurelius, no better antidote to anxiety than reading Epictetus. But for those of us made of lesser stuff, the pragmatist James has shown an easier way.

We have discovered an alternative path to peace and serenity. We are coping with life—and quite well, thank you—on the move.

The most dangerous thing a man possesses is a logical mind. A logical mind is practical and pragmatic. It knows the price of everything and the value of nothing. It reacts appropriately to danger and inappropriately to love. It accepts work but not play, understands science but not religion. The logical mind ends where a sense of humor starts.

Almost equally dangerous are our appetites and emotions. Unchecked appetites change us from free men to slaves. The negative emotions of hate and envy and despair can kill the good life as surely as a bullet.

What we need is something to synthesize these forces—something to bring harmony to these opposites, create unity out of this diversity, fuse the body, mind and spirit into the unique person each of us is.

Surprisingly, philosophers have suggested that this is best accomplished in sports. "Man at his utmost," "self-completion (through excellence)" and "self-actualization through self-extension" are a few of the descriptions they give of the effect of sports on the athlete.

The surfer is not merely seeking the perfect wave, the skier the perfect slope, the runner the perfect race. Each is seeking his own perfection, seeking to purge the negative emotions, seeking to quell the animal appetites, seeking to keep the brain at work on things the brain should do, but most of all seeking a total acceptance of himself and his universe, a loving of himself and his fellows and his Creator. For the athlete, sport is not a religion; it is a religious act that brings together work and play, love and religion.

I would be less certain of this if I had not read William Gibson's *A Season in Heaven,* an account of his experience studying Transcendental Meditation in Spain under Maharishi Mahesh Yogi. Gibson went because TM had transformed his son who had been drowning in "eddies of self-hatred" into a smiling, loving person.

Scientists tell us that TM is a physiological method of obtaining relaxation and a hypometabolic state. Dr. Herbert Benson of Harvard University has reported a lowering of blood pressure, a decrease in oxygen intake, and a slowing of the pulse while deep in TM. Many other advantageous metabolic changes are also known to occur. ("I had a letting-go inside," writes Gibson, "which was the first waking rest I'd had from myself in 50 years.")

The key to this is the mantra. This is a simple Vedic sound without meaning (Benson claims any word may do). What it does is throw the reasoning brain off the scent while you descend into the absolute— moving away from the stresses that surround you, the disharmony, the diversity, the opposites, all the evidence you have of your mortality. The mantra allows you to get out of that bind into unity.

This unity is the promise of TM: a body free from stress and a mind open to boundless energy, intelligence, creativity, skill in action and better behavior toward others. This result comes gradually. Recruits to this method initially feel an increase in energy, both mental and physical. They make complete turnabouts as to drugs and alcohol and tobacco. There is even some talk about celibacy. Only later comes the religion that sees God as It.

For Gibson, the religion that opened up to him was his own. A nonbelieving Catholic since the age of fourteen, he returned home as a daily Mass-goer. He was able, he said, to convince his logical mind to leave his nonrational religion alone. He had found in TM a solution to his own conflicts, and also an antidote to the counsel of our best minds—"despair, impotence and self-loathing."

I have also gone the TM route—brought the flowers and the fruit and the $75 required to attend a series of four lectures. I agree with much of what Gibson writes, and I am interested in his spiritual odyssey. But I'm inclined to think, at least for me, that running offers more.

What sport does additionally is to bring the body and mind on this trip into what Maharishi calls "cosmic consciousness," the level where we deal in absolutes only, and because running does that, it takes me totally body-mind-soul into this new experience. I am man fully functioning, and there is no one on God's earth I would trade places with at that moment.

One of the more effective ways of relieving stress is the relaxation response. This is an altered state of consciousness in which the mind and the body are deeply relaxed. At the same time, your awareness of the world and its worries diminishes and you are temporarily at peace. The methods used to attain this state are primarily those of Transcendental Meditation and the technique described by Dr. Benson in his book *The Relaxation Response*.

From personal experience, I can tell you they work. The TM and Benson procedures are simple and, except for the mantra, identical. It is suggested you sit in a comfortable chair, relax your muscles, close your eyes, breathe deeply and slowly with your belly and then repeat your mantra or the word "one." This is done in tempo with your heart beat (if as slow as mine) or with your breathing. Distracting thoughts are not fought; they succumb to the recitation of the word.

To many, these measures seem quite superficial. They depart from the traditional psychological approach of changing physiological responses by unmasking the psychological factors and feelings that produce them. Stress, say these experts, must first be understood, then dealt with.

Relaxation responses, of course, do the opposite. They treat the effect, not the cause; the result, not the reason. What they seek is oblivion, a mind cleansed of thought, muscles relaxed to jelly. This type of meditation is not active or passive; it is negative. It is the way of detachment, of elimination, of emptiness.

What happens, then, is a reaction that prescinds from the cause of our hurry and worry, that cares not why or how we become tense or anxious. There is no need for psychoanalysis or psychotherapy, no need for insight and acceptance, no need to ask the Great Questions or to debate the answers, no need to study our unconscious or subconscious or even our conscious. Just follow the simple instructions and drift away.

These procedures return me to my resting state. When I use them I am in effect hunkering down, turning my tail to the wind and riding out the storm. These techniques give me a respite, a timeout, a period when I can get my breath, regain my composure, remember my game plan.

That last, I suppose, is most important. One basketball coach told me that about timeouts. "There is not much you can do," he said, "except remind them of what they do best."

When I come back from a relaxation timeout, I am reminded of what I do best. I have lost, for the most part, the tension, the feeling of straining, of being in over my head. I have regained, if only temporarily, the rhythm of my game.

That rhythm is different for each one of us. It is, however, always similar in principle. I am, as you are, like a reciprocating motor. Deep in my chest, I feel the pulsation of my heart, alternately filling and emptying. And this same systole and diastole occur in all my other activities.

There is work and play, effort and rest, times when I store energy and other times when I discharge it. The good life is a product of this balance, this alternation that enables me to accept and make the most out of the inevitable tensions and stresses I meet.

It is interesting that stress expert Hans Selye sees no need for these relaxation techniques. We would be better occupied, he states, in taking a different attitude toward the events in our life. Attitude determines whether we perceive an experience as pleasant or unpleasant. It is in adopting the right attitude, he says, that we can convert a negative stress into a positive one.

His criticism is true to an extent. The effect of a period of relaxation is brief. When I come back, nothing has been radically changed—any more than it would be if I had taken a nap. I might have been given time to remember my game plan, but I haven't discovered anything new about myself or the game.

So Selye is right. There may be a place for sitting still and making my mind a blank. But what I need more is some positive method of relaxation—one that is associated with play and movement, with creation and contemplation. So for me the supreme relaxation technique is, again, running.

Selye himself swims or bikes in the morning, then swims and lifts weights at night. These are periods of time where he is, it seems to me, employing his own relaxation techniques, which are quite similar to mine.

What we should remember is that, in dealing with stress, good intentions are not enough. In the final analysis, we need the tools, we need the skill, we need the techniques. *We have come to a time when a person who cannot play is illiterate, a person who cannot relax is a barbarian, and a person who cannot meditate has not yet learned to live.*

8

On Adapting

66

**Stress makes us fit, ready of mind,
people of virtue and courage.
Stress is what makes us complete.
Through it we advance, grow,
stay alive—but not without danger.
Stress is a struggle that can also destroy.**

99

STRESS IS THE STUFF that shapes me, the force that forces me to do my best, the stimulus that makes me the person I am.

But as society changes, so does stress. We are faced now with less and less physical stress, more and more mental and psychological stress. That is our way of doing things. Man is a technician. He expends effort to decrease effort. He strives to remove the need to work and thereby concentrates on living well. The mission of technology consists in releasing man for the task of being himself.

The result is increasing security and leisure, protection from the elements, a decrease in physical work. A great deal of physical stress has been eliminated from our day-to-day living—particularly the stresses that led to the strength of the body, the maintenance of vigor and the development of endurance.

Physical stress is no longer obligatory. Technology has liberated us from these boons to our physiology. Now we have indoor plumbing and central heating, air conditioning and hot showers. We have transportation that virtually removes the need to walk. Time and space have been conquered. We have all sorts of labor-saving devices. We have even reached the ultimate; we have put men in orbit and removed the final stress—gravity.

Physical stress therefore must be sought. It must be self-administered. We have come to a point in our physical existence much like the spiritual crisis described by Pelagius: "If we wish not to go backwards, we must run." Unless we become athletes, we can never become the self that is our project on this earth.

For each of us, this athlete inside is different, and the stress needed to become an athlete is necessarily different. Mine is the stress needed to become a long-distance runner. I administer it in measured doses of time and frequency and intensity. I run this far, this fast, this often. And then I rest at a certain plateau of performance, readying myself for another assault on the summit.

The principle for everyone is the same: the application of stress, which is the alarm period; then the period of adaptation, of mastery, followed by rest and recuperation. There is thus a general formula for fitness, and yet there is no absolute formula for fitness. The body alone knows, and every body is different.

Training is not a cookbook system. Guidelines work only up to a

72

point. I must listen to my body, know my body's wisdom, learn to reach what is going on inside.

Technique is another matter. There I must go with the best, learn how to minimize stress. So I run with the least effort. I shorten and shorten my stride until it is as if I am riding a bicycle in low gear.

So too I must learn the best methods of rest and recuperation—sleep and naps, of course, but also relaxation techniques and biofeedback. All help to restore and revitalize. All set me up for another day, another try at my peak.

There are always missteps, to be sure. That climb is never uninterrupted. Sometimes the stress is too much, the rest period too short. I break down with a cold or am possessed with exhaustion. Then nothing pleases me. The run is a bore, the race a disaster.

But this only shows that I am responsible, not only for defeat but for victory as well. I can no longer blame chance or fate or technology for the bad things that happen, but I can take credit if things go well.

Stress has been defined as any condition or situation that imposes on a person demands for adjustment. It is therefore a fact of life—omnipresent, inevitable. Stress is a constant presence in our day. Whether it be physical or mental or emotional, it is unavoidable. And should we take to our beds and pull the covers over our heads, we simply substitute other stresses: the stress of inactivity on the body, the stress of guilt on the psyche, the stress of isolation on the mind.

Stress therefore must be accepted, must be seen for the good it does, and then managed so the bad consequences are minimized. It must be welcomed, because with it we would be less than our best. In accepting stress, we know the truth of Nietzsche's words, "What does not destroy me makes me strong."

Stress makes us fit, ready of mind, people of virtue and courage. Stress is what makes us complete. Through it we advance, grow, stay alive—but not without danger. Stress is a struggle that can also destroy. It can weaken me physically, make me ill, cause a nervous breakdown, force me to lose my faith in myself and in creation.

But there is no alternative. Were I not to engage in this continuous encounter, I would give up the possibility of being stretched to my limit. I would give up all chance I have of realizing, as Theodore Rozak put it, my original splendor—the potential I had at birth.

The business of life, then, is stress. By using instinct and intelligence, discipline and humor, a sense of play, a feeling of self-esteem, I must first identify stress and then learn how to handle it.

The principles of stress and its effects are quite simple. There is the first stage of shock or alarm in which the whole force of physical and mental and psychological resources is brought to bear on the situation. Then, in the second stage, there is the gradual return to equilibrium, the restoration of the internal milieu. The whole organism, the person I am, then comes to a balance a notch higher than when the stress was imposed. At times, of course, the opposite happens. The stress is too great, the time allowed for recuperation is too short, and exhaustion or breakdown occurs.

Stress comes in large, small or medium sizes. It can be physical, emotional, mental or spiritual, or combinations of any or all of these. The crisis that confronts us may be running a marathon or passing an examination, a domestic quarrel or a deadline on an assignment, as major as the acceptance of death or as minor as a faulty carburetor.

Each of us perceives and reacts differently to these stresses. This is as it should be. I am a unique individual. My body and mind and soul were made for me and no other. My reaction is in my own style, as personal as my fingerprints. To find it, I must be an experiment-of-one. No facts should be sacred, no other's experience accepted. My task is to know myself, to learn whether I am primarily made for flight or fight, to understand what stresses I handle best.

Let it be said, however, that there are no bad stresses, just as there are no bad experiences. Everything is part of the great experiment, part of the learning process. Stress is a necessity for the good life—that is the first great lesson to learn. The second and no less important is that all of us have our own special way of dealing with it.

I am my own consultant; my own subject. I do not look for advice; nor should you. I subscribe to Emerson's thought on this matter.

"Cannot we let people be themselves and enjoy life in their way?" he asked. "You are trying to make that man another you. One's enough."

One is indeed enough. *I am satisfied to make my own lonely struggle. So in my running and my day-to-day living, I seek stress—but my own stress, the stress that my body welcomes, that my mind enjoys and that makes my soul happy.*

* * *

Suppose I accept the belief that physical fitness is essential to the good life, that training and conditioning are necessary to my day-to-day living. And suppose I do train, become a good animal, an athlete, a runner, a swimmer, a cyclist. What then?

What I mean is, where does all of this fit into the scheme of things? Will this physical health translate into mental health? Will this physical fitness contribute to psychological fitness? Will this ability to deal with physical stress do something to help me in my struggle with psychological stress?

I know from my athletic friends that it can. One friend credits running for his coping with the death of his wife. Others have become recovered alcoholics. Still others have survived long periods of anxiety and depression. And there are legions of men and women who have experienced other affirmative psychological effects from their sports.

There is also a reinforcing reverse evidence. Athletes who are injured and have to give up their sport frequently go through a period of depression that is relieved only by the resumption of activity. Until they can move freely again, they are unable to withstand even the most minor misfortune. Indeed, daily living becomes too much for them.

Why all this should be so is a mystery to me. The problem of the body-soul relationship has stumped minds infinitely more capable than mine. There is general agreement that a relationship, either direct or in parallel, exists—and that it would be best to consider the body and the soul as different functions of the same thing. Whatever happens to one effects the other.

"We often hear," said the late Paul Dudley White, "of the effect of the mind on the body. We should not forget the effect of the body on the mind."

I can attest to that effect, especially the immediate one. When I have had it up to here, when my levels of frustration have reached a critical point, when I know I will assault—at least verbally—the next person I meet, when I am in a situation where the usual advice is to count to 10, I run to 10—miles, that is.

I take off and run until that heat dissipates, and when I get back, I have usually forgotten what upset me. I am pleasantly fatigued. I have what the psychiatrists call a global feeling of well-being.

This response is a complicated interaction of physiological and psychological effects, each relating to the other. There are two ways, you

75

see, to handle stress. One is modifying the physiological response to that stress. The other is improving psychological health.

We determine our own stress. What is stressful to me might be of no consequence to someone else. Our reactions are equally individual. We are equipped with instincts that impel us to fight or take flight—or in some instances to negotiate.

My impulse, which is to flee, would have been in more primitive times, a lifesaving impulse in a life-threatening situation. Now my situation can hardly be called life-and-death. Aggravating, perhaps; frustrating, maybe; depressing, certainly—but not something associated with bodily harm. Yet the body is being mobilized to bend steel, lift cars or leap a wall at a single bound.

Before my run, the body is preparing me for a lifesaving maneuver that has to be performed maximally. To do so, it secretes hormones and, among other things, raises the pulse and blood pressure and blood sugar. It does this through a variety of marvelous physiological actions. But it also puts me in a state that has no legitimate outlet.

I give it that outlet by running. I use these energies in a healthy, happy way. Through my running, I am able to work off this excessive, inappropriate reaction. I am able to dampen those primitive responses of my autonomic nervous system. I regain control of my body in much the same way that a cowboy subdues a bucking bronco: I ride it until it tires out.

9

On Craving

"
If you are going to take something enjoyable
out of your life, you must put something
of comparable enjoyment into it.
We may think there is willpower involved,
but more likely the change is due to wantpower.
Wanting the new addiction more than the old one.
Wanting the new me in preference
to the old person I am now.
"

WHY SHOULD WE NONSMOKERS care about the smoker's problem? Why should we be concerned about what happens to these people who are dependent on nicotine? The answer is self-interest. We do wish our neighbor well, but we wish ourselves well even more. We are all dependent on something. We are addicted in some way. If not to cigarettes then to something else. What works for cigarettes and nicotine may well work for whatever we are trying to get rid of in our lives.

So whether our addiction is food or sex or TV; whether we have a burning need for just one more drink or an extra hour of sleep in the morning; whether we cannot control a controlled substance or legitimize an illegitimate relationship, the principle is the same. What helps people rid themselves of their addiction can help us handle ours.

Freud saw the answer in a substitute or surrogate activity. We need to replace these satisfying pursuits with something just as satisfying. If you are going to take something enjoyable out of your life you must put something of comparable enjoyment into it. We may think there is willpower involved, but more likely the change is due to wantpower. Wanting the new addiction more than the old one. Wanting the new me in preference to the old person I am now.

One such substitute is running. Peter Wood in his studies at Stanford discovered that runners who put in 40 miles a week on the roads did not smoke. Many of them had been two- or three-pack-a-day smokers prior to taking up running. In almost all instances they began running and then gradually gave up the cigarettes. Another study at the University of Alabama reported that only 3 percent of the joggers and runners interviewed were still smoking. In addition, the cigarette consumption was usually limited to 15 cigarettes a day.

Most of the runners I meet are ex-addicts. The addiction might have been drugs or alcohol or simply a sedentary way of life. Running turned their lives around. In every lecture I give to runners I know there is a story for each person in the audience. Each one has taken charge of their novel in the making. Each one has a tale to tell about what they were like before they began running and how they have changed for the better—physically, mentally and spiritually.

Nevertheless, an even more basic question remains unanswered: How does one become motivated to seek this substitute whether it is running or some other new life style?

George Valiant, a Harvard psychiatrist who has been studying the natural history of alcoholism, thinks he has found that answer. Alcoholics, he says, become ex-alcoholics and social drinkers through various substitutes and surrogates, but they seek that help only when they realize they have lost control of their lives.

"The key to recovery," says Valiant, "seems to be that they were no longer consciously in control of their drinking and that their use of alcohol was no longer under voluntary control." This self-discovery is a highly personal process. Unless this raising of consciousness occurs, no therapy will work. No substitute will be effective. No surrogate will take over. The addiction will continue to dominate one's life.

It is not enough, however, to stop smoking or drinking. That is an oversimplified goal. Release from bondage, however painful, says Valiant, rarely brings instant relief. Depression and divorce are common in the early stages of abstinence. The real goal is not the abstinence but a new and satisfactory existence.

In the accomplishment of this goal, there are, according to Valiant, four factors: behavior modifications, substitute dependencies, religious involvement and new relationships.

"Whoever understands human nature," wrote Sigmund Freud, "knows that hardly anything is harder for a man to give up than a pleasure he has once experienced." Freud might well have been referring to his own smoking. He was a smoker and continued to be one through thirty-three operations for cancer of the jaw and oral cavity. Apparently the father of modern psychiatry was unable to mobilize the therapeutic forces that would break the chains that bound him to this habit.

In this he has a lot in common with the common folk who smoke. There are millions of smokers who would like to be ex-smokers. Innumerable people feeding coins into cigarette machines wish they could kick the habit. Any number of our friends and neighbors wish the day would dawn when they would not have the urge to light up just one more cigarette. Most of them have gone the route of Mark Twain, who said that giving up smoking was easy. He had done it thousands of times.

I recall an interview with the actor Dennis Hopper. He had admitted frankly as he sat there smoking a cigarette that he also smoked pot. When asked whether or not he was afraid of getting addicted to marijuana, he said absolutely not. Holding up his cigarette, he said, "It's these things that I can't get rid of."

What is the basis of the pleasure that comes from cigarettes and the subsequent habituation? What it comes down to is a dependence on nicotine. Smokers have a physical dependence on nicotine. Eventually it is not only the positive effects that keep a person smoking but the negative ones as well. What happens when smoking is stopped is too awful to contemplate. And the desire to smoke remains unchanged.

The infinite variety of methods used to break this dependence and their almost universal failure show how firmly entrenched is this need. It defeats almost every attempt to cure it. The World Health Organization defines such dependence as having physiological adaptive effects. These include (1) tolerance, (2) increased capacity to metabolize and excrete the substance, (3) withdrawal symptoms.

The withdrawal symptoms are particularly distressing, and part of that is the craving that comes about through the adaptive mechanisms in the brain and nervous system. Most of these reactions are subjective and apparent only to the victim. Depression, irritability, anxiety, restlessness and difficulty in concentrating are some of these symptoms. Others are objective and demonstrable like sweating and changes in sleep electroencephalograms, and impaired ability to perform under stressful conditions.

Both subjective and objective effects can be rapidly reversed by infusing nicotine intravenously. The same result can also be achieved simply by smoking a cigarette. It is the nicotine in the cigarette that creates dependence and relieves the symptoms of withdrawal.

Some things we know about nicotine are helpful in understanding the smoker's problem. It is a drug whose primary action is stimulation of the brain and nervous system. It also can be, in later stages, a depressant. It is even a depressant in some areas and a stimulant in others. Nicotine is rapidly absorbed. Peak levels can be obtained within minutes of lighting up a cigarette. It is also rapidly metabolized by the liver. Nicotine has a half life of 30 minutes, bringing about the cigarette-every-half-hour syndrome that most smokers have.

Usually those who persist in the habit have one or more of six reasons for doing so. These have been outlined by Dr. Daniel Horn, the former director of the National Clearing House for Smoking and Health. Those reasons are 1) stimulation 2) handling 3) pleasurable relaxation 4) crutch 5) craving 6) habit. Horn has devised a self-assessment test consisting of 18 questions which he claims can pinpoint the specific needs that are being satisfied through smoking.

Horn also listed the six most powerful motives for stopping smoking: health, expense, social influence, example, esthetics and mastery. In my own medical practice I have seen all these motives fail. Threats about health rarely work. Expense in such matters is never decisive. Segregation into a smoking section is more likely to make a smoker smoke more furiously than desist. Esthetics doesn't work even for artists. This leaves mastery, which can be a most powerful weapon. When a person finally asks, "Who is in charge here, me or the butts?" changes may occur. And if they do, these changes are quite likely to become permanent.

Nevertheless, the best guide in this therapy is still the man who couldn't give up smoking himself, Sigmund Freud. "Actually we never give anything up," he said. "We exchange one thing for another. What appears to be a renunciation is really the formation of a substitute or a surrogate."

10

On Assessing

"

**. . . . pulse can tell nonathletes just how bad
things are—and how good things can be.
Individuals with a pulse in the 90s
are cheating themselves of an active life.
Those in the 70s are settling
for less than they can get.
If you are in the low 60s
you could be living those dreams of glory.**

"

MANY PEOPLE ARE UNEASY beginning a fitness program. They see fitness as a high-technology industry. Articles, brochures and advertisements bombard us with the need of specialists and their special equipment. Fitness centers abound with physiologists who use sophisticated devices to test and monitor their clients. Fitness appears to be safe and sure only when we have access to the evaluations and counseling provided by such centers. The ordinary out-of-shape individual, especially those of advanced age (the ads suggest thirty-five!), is made to feel he should not undertake a fitness program without a guide.

I am reminded of those books of my youth in which the hero must face incredible odds to survive—stories about a soft, pleasure-loving dilettante marooned on a desert island, or lost in an impenetrable forest or escaping over uninhabitable land with nothing but the clothes on his back and the contents of his pockets. The outcome is always the same. The hero rapidly learns the capabilities of his body and mind. He is soon transformed into the creature he was meant to be, the few objects in his pocket becoming the only equipment he needs to survive.

A fitness program is much the same. A soft, pleasure-loving dilettante can gain confidence, survive and prosper, with no more equipment than a few common household objects. All you need as a beginner are a mirror, a scale, a tape measure and a watch.

Begin with the mirror. Undress and stand nude in front of it. Your reflection tells all. If you look fat, you are fat. You also know where that fat is. If it is on the face and the belly, it will come off readily. If it is on the hips and thighs, it will be the last to go.

Now get on the scale. It will register fat you cannot see. Match your present weight against the weight you were when you were last active and athletic. This was most likely when you graduated from college or got married. At that point, you were probably 12 percent body fat if a male, 18 percent if a female. Everything you have gained since then is fat. A very simple calculation comparing the two weights will give you a rough estimate of your current percentage of body fat.

The scale soon assumes less importance. As you become fit, muscle will replace fat. You may even gain weight, although it generally remains constant and shows no change for some months. What will change are your measurements.

Next take the tape measure and establish those measurements. Check the circumference of your calves, thighs, hips, waist and chest. As you progress, these figures will tell you about fat loss and muscle replacement. Women will often go down as much as two dress sizes while the weight remains the same.

Finally, we come to the watch. You will use this to establish your present level of fitness. This test requires one additional object. A place where you can measure how far you can go in 12 minutes. The best setting for this is usually a quarter-mile track, usually available to you at your local high school.

Warm up with a walk or a very easy jog for 10 minutes. This will raise a sweat and get you into your "second wind." Wait about five minutes, then start. Walk or walk-jog or jog at a constant speed for 12 minutes. Now stop and measure how far you have gone.

Kenneth Cooper's aerobic tables will tell you how you rate on the fitness ladder. After 8 to 12 weeks, you can repeat the test to see how much you have improved.

Predicted Maximal Oxygen Consumption on the Basis of 12-Minute Performance

Distance (miles)	Laps (1/4 mile)	Max. Ox. Con. (ml/kg/min)
1.0	4	25
1.25	5	33
1.5	6	42.6
1.75	7	51.6
2.0	8	60.2

Levels of Fitness Based on 12-Minute Performance and Maximal Oxygen Consumption

Distance (miles)	Max. Ox. Con.	Fitness level
Less than 1	Less than 25	Very poor
1–1.25	25–33	Poor
1.25–1.5	33–42	Fair
1.5–1.75	42–51	Good
1.75 or more	51 or more	Excellent

As the program progresses, your pulse rate becomes all important. It may not be quite as fixed as the North Star, but it is the best navigational guide in traveling this uncharted land. Occasional trips to the mirror, scale and tape measure will also reassure you that you are on the right track. They will help you survive your fitness program in fine style.

My resting pulse is 48. No big deal, you might say. My resting pulse is simply part of my physical makeup. Distinctive to me but no more important than the length of my nose. My resting pulse may be slow, but that does not necessarily mean I am a superior runner. My resting pulse is, to an extent, a conversation piece. Something to drop into the discussion at the hospital lunch table or at a postrace party. It is something I possess like a condominium in Florida or a loft in Soho. Something I display much as a friend of mine wears a belt with a BMW buckle.

But this morning my pulse rate was even lower, 42 beats a minute. Six beats below normal. This is a rare treat. No matter that I don't know the physiology responsible for it; a pulse rate this low must mean great things. Just ahead are outstanding races, personal bests and feats beyond the dreams of glory.

Nonsense? Perhaps, but rightly or wrongly, runners equate their pulse rates with performance. A slow pulse rate is a runner's proudest possession. It has to do with being a runner since birth. First we are born with this capability of lowering our pulse. And then we take on the task of doing the necessary training to bring it down as far as possible. A slow pulse means that you are special. Special by birth, and special by your dedication to your sport.

My slow pulse rate does not mean I am better than another runner. It does mean that I am the best I can be. The pulse rate is, therefore, as important as runners think it is. Important physically, psychologically and spiritually. It is a numerical description of who you are, an indication of how seriously you take becoming that person.

It is an experiment anyone can perform. I once attended Grand Rounds at a midwest hospital where the medical resident presented a case study of a beginning athlete. He displayed charts showing a fall in the pulse over a period of three months, from a resting pulse of over 70 to a new level of 52.

At the end of the meeting he disclosed that he was the subject of the case. He had been assigned to conduct a meeting on the significance of the pulse rate in a fitness program and had selected himself to be the guinea pig.

This drop in the pulse rate is the almost universal result of any fitness program. Few individuals who undertake a training schedule fail to have some drop in heart rate, and sometimes the decrease can be extreme. A Finnish study of thirty-five male endurance runners using 24-hour monitoring revealed that their lowest nocturnal heart rates averaged 37 beats per minute. There has been a report in the German literature of nine runners who had resting pulses below 30, and I have had some correspondence with a Canadian marathoner whose basal pulse is 26. In such company a runner with a mediocre 48 would best remain silent.

This slow-down is usually ascribed to increased vagal influence on the heart action. The vagus nerve is part of the two-pronged autonomic nervous system that controls the heart rate. The sympathetic system speeds it up and the vagus slows it down. The relative balance between these two systems determines the rate. Training, in ways we are not sure, reduces sympathetic tone and/or increases vagal stimulation.

Slowing of the heart rate, or bradycardia, is only one of the effects that training has on the heart rate. The same Finnish study revealed other abnormalities. One third of the athletes experienced pauses in the heart rate exceeding two seconds in length, making the immediate heart rate less than 30 per minute. Another interesting finding was the presence of first-degree heart block, a slowing of the impulse time between auricle and ventricle, in 37 percent of the athletes. More than one-fifth of them had a second-degree heart block, the Wenckebach type, with varying electrical delays resulting in intermittent dropped beats. A standard second-degree block was found in an additional 8 percent. Twenty percent had a peculiarity known as junctional rhythm, in which the beat was originating elsewhere than in the usual sinus source.

Fortunately, for most runners, these oddities mostly occur only after prolonged rest. Israeli investigators discovered this when a soccer player inadvertently was left on the examination table 45 minutes waiting for an electrocardiogram. When taken, it revealed a typical Wenckebach pattern. Subsequently, studies on other athletes using a long resting period show a significant number of abnormalities.

Such findings are the result of heavy training and represent a superior state of fitness. They should not alarm the physicians, but they do. I was once asked to examine a marine captain who had been denied clearance for the Marine Corps Marathon because of a Wenckebach heart block. When I questioned him about his training he said he ran twice a day. Six miles at lunchtime with two marine friends. Eight miles at night by himself. Then I asked him about the intensity of these workouts. His evening run, he said, was leisurely. "What about your lunch-hour runs?" I asked him. "I might be able to manage a 'yes' or a 'no,' " he answered. This man was racing six miles everyday, and then adding an hour of running at night. His EKG reflected this high degree of training. His Wenckebach was not pathological, it was physiological.

The pulse rate of importance is the one when you awake in the morning. Presumably that is your resting state and represents your basal metabolic rate. You are still in torpor, doing little more than idling your engine.

As soon as you get into operation your metabolism rises. Shave, shower and dress and it will have already escalated. Now comes breakfast and coffee and it increases some more. Then the movement and effort to get to work requires a higher metabolic rate. The stress there will take it even higher.

As your metabolism increases, whatever the reason, your pulse rises also. Your pulse, therefore, presents the same problem faced in doing basal metabolism tests. Preferably they are done in bed with the individual not fully awake. Simulating this situation in a person coming to a clinical laboratory is understandably difficult. The best that can be done is to have him lie down in a quiet room, make his mind a blank, and relax.

It goes without saying that once you are told to relax you tense up.

Once your body knows it is going to have its pulse taken, it worries about the outcome. Adrenaline pours into your system; the pulse goes up rather than down. You must create a diversion if you are to catch your prey unaware.

How does one become indifferent to the whole pulse-taking procedure? My method is to hyperventilate. If I have forgotten to take my pulse before I get up out of bed, I take deep, slow breaths until I feel relaxed and a little light-headed. When I count my pulse, it is as if someone else were doing it. My attention is turned inward to the slow lub-dub of the heartbeat. All apprehension has vanished. Then I maintain this state until the minute is up and I get the answer.

You can achieve the same effect by using Benson's Relaxation Technique or some form of TM. They have been proven to produce a hypometabolic state. And that is precisely what you must be in to find out your lowest possible pulse.

It is far better, of course, to get this result before the day has begun, and to plan your life accordingly. If you are a nonathlete, this pulse rate can be a good motivator. It is not a precise statement of your level of fitness, but it does tell you roughly just where you are. It is also an indication of where you could be. Whatever your pulse, there are good reasons for doing something about it.

Should your resting pulse be in the 55–60 range, you are an out-of-shape athlete with great endurance potential. You are missing out on some particularly satisfying sports experience. A sedentary individual with a resting pulse in the 50s may well have remarkable talent for endurance events.

If your pulse is 75, you fall into the average group. This means that you are likely to be operating at a rate considerably lower than your capacity. Exercise will increase your maximum oxygen uptake as much as 25 percent and your physical work capacity as much as 300 percent.

A pulse over 90 is bad news. An Israeli study of 600 people using an equation including age, height, weight and resting-heart rate reported that those with rates in the 55–60 range had a 25 percent higher oxygen capacity than the group whose rate was 91–95.

You must interpret these numbers with caution, however. Occasionally the high pulse is due to hypermetabolism as, for instance, in a hyperthyroid state. There are also people who are hyperreactors. They can never have their pulse taken (or their blood pressure, for that matter) that it doesn't go up instantly.

Nevertheless, this baseline pulse can tell nonathletes just how bad things are—and how good things can be. Individuals with a pulse in the 90s are cheating themselves of an active life. Those in the 70s are settling for less than they can get. If you are in the low 60s you could be living those dreams of glory.

11

On Exercising

"

Great legs are a great asset.
Somewhere resident in the muscles
is the ability to withstand fatigue,
to handle stress and to get
the most out of your physical life.
So don't run for your heart
or lungs or liver or kidneys.
Run for your muscles.

"

THE WOMAN on the Denver TV program was looking at a picture of me on the cover of my new book.

"You've got great legs," she said. "I'm envious. All you runners have great legs."

It's true; we do. I know I have great legs. At every race I see proof that this woman is right. Ordinary runners have extraordinary legs.

Running, whatever else it does, is apparently good for the legs. There is controversy about other parts of the body. Does running help the heart? Is it beneficial to the lungs? These questions are debated continually, not only in the press but in medical journals as well.

The benefits of running go far beyond the appearance of the legs. I do not mention the size, configuration and definition of my legs from sheer vanity—although I do not deny that this element is present. No, I bring my legs and the legs of other runners to your attention for a specific reason—to aid you in understanding exercise physiology. These legs should give you an insight into the effect running has on the body.

You might suspect from the emphasis on cardiopulmonary fitness today that training involves mostly the heart and lungs. Guess again. No matter what you have been told, running primarily trains and conditions the muscles; the other organs merely assist in realizing this functional potential. Almost all the improvement in performance occurs because of circulatory changes in the muscles and changes in the muscle cells, the engines that transform chemical energy into mechanical energy.

We had no idea of the magnitude of such changes until the late 1960s, when muscle biopsy techniques came into general use. We then discovered an increase in the number of capillaries supplying blood to the muscles, an expanded ability of muscles to extract oxygen from the blood, and more metabolism-controlling enzymes in the muscle cells of active people. All of these improve physical work capacity. My leg muscles and yours can, with minimal change in the heart, do as much as 300 percent more work—which is why people with greatly damaged hearts can train up to the marathon level.

Cardiac rehabilitation, therefore, is mainly *muscle* rehabilitation. Heart patients conquer fatigue by developing great legs.

Physiologist Gordon Cumming points out, "The peripheral circulation regulation and the improvement in the metabolic processes in the muscle can account for the improvement in endurance performance in the absence of an increase in heart-stroke volume."

91

Dr. John Holloszy, a pioneer in this work, agrees with Cumming. "It seems unlikely," he states, "that cardiac adaptations play a role in protection against skeletal fatigue."

I have been a physician for 40 years and a runner for 18, yet this was news to me. I now realize that I never quite understood what was going on. I studied running and performance all those years and never got the hang of it.

If runners have great legs, and they obviously do, it means that fitness programs have to do with leg muscles rather than the heart muscle. The emphasis in training, therefore, ought to be on "perceived exertion"—what the body feels. Forget about heart rates and focus on training your legs.

You can see, too, that *whatever ails you, a potentially trainable pair of legs is all you need to embark upon a fitness program.* Should you have bad lungs or a bad heart, diabetes or hypertension, obesity or colitis, arthritis or depression, you can still develop great legs—and also your full functional potential.

Medical sages seem to know this. Before physicians became caught up in the technology of disease, they realized the importance of muscle tone. When the late cardiologist Paul Dudley White was called upon to assess a patient's capacity to withstand surgery, it was his custom to examine the legs. If they were firm and well muscled, he would give his approval.

Great legs are a great asset. Somewhere resident in the muscles is the ability to withstand fatigue, to handle stress and to get the most out of your physical life. So don't run for your heart or lungs or liver or kidneys. Run for your muscles. It makes more sense.

When you train three things happen to your muscles and two of them are bad. The prime movers, the power muscles, become short and inflexible. The antagonist muscles that modulate the action become relatively weak. This strength/flexibility imbalance causes or is a major contributor to injuries in our various sports.

When a person is involved in a sport that demands thousands of repetitions of a particular movement these imbalances are bound to occur. Training of the legs, for instance, results in development of the muscles of the back of the leg, the thigh and the low back. At the same time muscles of the shins, front thighs, the abdomen and the buttocks become relatively weak.

These postural weaknesses put abnormal stress on the foot, leg, knee, thigh and low back. A variety of overuse syndromes can then occur. This is especially true if there is some associated structural weakness.

The short, powerful calf muscle combines with weak shin muscle in contributing to such injuries as shinsplints, Achilles tendinitis, plantar fasciitis and calf cramps.

The muscle imbalance from the knee up causes malposition of the pelvis and a host of problems involving the low back, sciatic nerves and hip joints.

Prevention is best accomplished by regular remedial exercises. The three muscles on the back side of the body must be stretched. The three opposing muscle groups on the front of the body must be strengthened.

The stretching is easily described and appears quite simple but must be done with great care. At no time should there be pain or discomfort, the limiting point should be simply a feeling of tension.

The first exercise is performed standing an arm's length away from the wall with feet flat on the floor. Lean forward until your chest is against the wall, feet still flat and the body forming a straight line from heel to chest. Hold for 10 seconds. Then return to upright. Repeat 10 times.

The second stretch consists of standing on one leg, knee locked, and placing the other straight leg (knee locked) on a step, stool or table depending on your level of flexibility. Attempt to touch your head to your knee—you may achieve only an approximation. Again do not go beyond feeling of tension. Hold for 10 seconds then return to upright. Repeat 10 times.

The final stretch is the backover. Lie on your back on the ground, legs out straight, knees locked. Bring legs over your head toward the floor behind it. Touch floor if possible, but under no circumstances go beyond the feeling of tension. Hold for 10 seconds then return to resting state. Repeat 10 times.

The strengthening exercises involve the opposing muscles. The first two use weights of five pounds to ten pounds (or a paint can with water). Sit on the edge of a table and place the weight over the foot. Now flex the foot upward, keeping the leg immobile. Hold for 10 seconds. Relax. Repeat 10 times.

Next, still sitting on the table and using the same weights on the foot, straighten the leg and lock the knee. Hold for 10 seconds. Relax. Repeat 10 times.

The final exercise is the bent-leg situp. Lie on your back with your knees bent and your feet flat on the floor. Now tighten your buttocks and bring your head and upper chest to a 45-degree angle off the floor. Hold for 10 seconds. Relax. Repeat 10 times. Have someone hold your feet or lock them under a chair, if necessary.

Done on a daily basis, these small groups of exercises will provide considerable protection against the injuries that beset athletes. When injury does occur, they should be used in conjunction with other forms of therapy.

At those times in the past when I viewed the body as a machine rather than a function of the unified self, I pictured the heart as the engine. The heart is all noise and movement, with an independent existence. It idles even when I am at rest, and when I exert myself it dominates my senses. I can feel and hear it; I can even see it on the EKG monitor during my stress test.

But the heart, for all its evident activity, is not my engine. The muscle is. It is the individual muscle cell, joined with thousands of others, that makes my body go. The individual muscle cell is the engine that changes chemical energy into physical energy. It extracts oxygen from the blood and uses it, stores up sugar and then burns it, takes in fats and triglycerides and converts them into power. The muscle cell uses protein to manufacture the mitochondria that take up the oxygen, and it produces the enzymes that control most of the miraculous metabolic events that occur in our bodies.

By comparison, the heart does little. It is true that the heart muscle, the myocardium, enlarges with activity; true also that the cardiac output is increased. The efficiency of the heart improves. The heart becomes capable of more work. But none of the other metabolic marvels takes place. The myocardium shows no change in mitochondria, no increase in enzymes. The heart, you see, is not the engine; it is no more than a fuel pump.

The heart brings the necessary fuel to the muscle cell—the oxygen from the lungs, the food processed by the gastrointestinal tract. The muscle does the rest. More than 90 percent of our calories are burned by muscle.

When I exercise, the heart is affected only secondarily. The primary effect is on the muscle mass that is being used. It is the muscle that uses up the calories and reduces my weight. It is the muscle that removes the cholesterol and triglycerides and gives me a good lipid profile. It is the muscle that would reduce the need for insulin were I a diabetic. It is the efficiency of the muscle that allows the cardiac patient to do more work. It is the improved function of this engine that conquers fatigue.

That is why I am the best getting better when I run. Effort breeds effort. Mileage makes for more mileage. The engine does more with less. I have gotten so I can almost feel it all happening: the capillaries multiplying, the mitochondria enlarging, the enzymes increasing. I am propelled by this fantastic engine whose operation is one of the wonders of the world.

I can see why I thought it was the heart that did all those things. The term "aerobic exercise," for one thing. It is scientifically correct; the muscle performs best with an adequate supply of oxygen. But the word "aerobic" made me think of heart and lungs. It emphasizes the organs that supply the oxygen, not the muscle that uses it.

So too with the stated goal of "cardiopulmonary fitness." It is evident now that the primary aim of an exercise program is *muscular* fitness. One becomes an athlete because of the athletic things that are happening in the muscle.

Another major distraction has been the use of maximal oxygen uptake as the best measure of fitness. Not only does the name suggest that the heart and lungs are the organs at issue, but the test result actually changes very little with major improvements in fitness. Maximal oxygen uptake operates within limits preset by heredity. We can ordinarily improve it by only about 20 percent.

The indicator of physical fitness is physical work capacity. This is the ability to do submaximal work to exhaustion. My physical work capacity is entirely a matter of how good my engine muscle is. While my maximal oxygen capacity can only increase 20 percent on my running program, my physical work capacity can increase by as much as *300 percent.*

Knowing what is happening when I run has had a liberating effect on me. There is no need to use target heart rates. If the muscle is being trained, not the heart, why monitor my pulse? I listen to my body and react accordingly. When I train, I ask my muscle for a pace that I can hold indefinitely. I dial my body to "comfortable"—not too easy, not too hard—then hold it there, knowing that pace will accomplish all the physiological and biochemical events needed for fitness.

This ability of my body to know what it is doing is called "perceived exertion." It is the most liberating discovery an individual can make. I no longer need charts or graphs; all I need is my river road and some free time. Further, there has been scientific confirmation of my own experience.

"Perception of effort," states sports psychologist William Morgan, "is directly related to exertional cost in 90 percent of all the subjects tested. It is a perfect linear function."

Now I understand why my running is getting better. My muscles are functioning better and better. Athletes the world over have known that it is the legs that go first, not the heart, as the medical profession seems to believe. Athletes equate performance and fitness with the legs. That's the way it is on the run.

I had come to Dallas to champion the cause of physical exercise for patients with lung disease. I was at the respiratory therapists' annual meeting to deliver the usual message: "Treat the whole patient." Specialists tend to forget this. They forget that disease is only part of the problem, and that they must treat the patient's illness and predicament as well.

Disease is a biological process. Illness is the impact that disease has on a patient's life. The predicament is the psychosocial situation in which the patient lives. There are instances where the disease may not be improved in any way, yet treating the illness and the patient's life situation can give almost miraculous results.

Specialists—and these respiratory therapists were specialists—know too much about disease and too little about health; too much about the limitations of the body and too little about its potential; too much about what goes on in their primary interest (in this case the lungs) and too little about what goes on in the rest of the body.

Just before my talk in Dallas I had taken a tour of the convention floor. One booth after another displayed machines and devices designed for new and better ways to diagnose and treat pulmonary disease. One instrument could take ordinary air in your house and change it into 95 percent oxygen. When I took a deep breath, another converted it into a computer printout with a half-dozen tests and graphs of my exhalation.

Now I was on the podium asking the therapists to turn their backs for a moment on all this shiny equipment. I wanted them to discard their specialist mentalities about the human body. For my allotted minutes, I wanted to be talking to generalists who saw that everything was connected to something else.

The lungs, I told them, do not exist in a vacuum. In real life they are connected to the heart, and the heart to the circulatory system, and the circulatory system to the muscles. Anatomy does not begin and end with the bronchopulmonary tree.

This holistic approach to the patient is extremely important in lung disease. Without it, the therapist may not understand the use of exercise in treatment. Exercise, you should know, has a bad name among the pulmonary specialists, because it does not improve pulmonary function. Study upon study has shown that.

"Breathing exercises and similar gymnastics performed under controlled conditions," reported one investigator, "have no substantial effect on ventilatory capacity and blood-gas tensions in groups of patients with obstructive pulmonary disease." This investigator went on to suggest that any improvement that occurs is psychological and due to the enthusiasm of the physician.

I looked out on the therapists and went immediately to the attack. I conceded that pulmonary-function tests don't change. Forget about these tests, I told them. Learn exercise physiology. Learn that the adaptation to exercise occurs mainly at the level of the heart, the circulatory system and the muscles. The lungs deliver the oxygen, it's true, but the heart and muscles can learn to use it more efficiently.

The factors that influence our aerobic capacity are mostly circulatory and muscular, regardless of lung capacity. Indeed, even when the heart cannot improve, the changes at the muscular level can result in major improvements in aerobic capacity. Bengt Saltin, the Danish exercise physiologist, has made this point repeatedly.

"Increases in maximal aerobic power that accompany physical conditioning," he writes, "are predominantly due to increased muscle blood flow and muscle capillary density."

Get rid of your old ideas about the lungs, I told the therapists. They are not all-important. The lungs, I said, are no more than the gas tank. They take in the gas, which is oxygen. When you have a patient with lung disease, that gas tank is smaller. That makes things difficult but not impossible. The logical thing to do is to increase the efficiency of the car and engine so that you can get farther on that gas.

That is what exercise does. First it streamlines the body by lessening the percentage of body fat. Then it delivers more oxygen through an increase in blood volume and an increase in capillaries in the muscle tissue. The heart pump is improved, so all of this takes place more easily. And when this oxygen is sent to the muscle, more of it is taken up. Studies have shown that the difference between the oxygen going in to muscle and the oxygen in the veins coming out of the muscle is increased.

These are things none of the technology in the convention hall could do. What was needed was a solid understanding of exercise physiology. Then these specialists could treat patients with an air of confidence in an atmosphere filled with optimism. Enthusiasm always helps, but it also helps if you understand what you are doing. It is not enough to determine to treat the whole patient. You must first learn how that whole patient works.

12

On Energizing

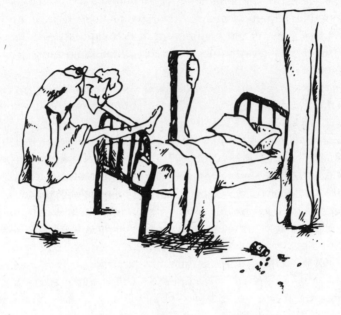

"
There is a healthy way to be ill.
Improving physical work capacity will also
improve the capacity to deal with any disease.
Whatever the disease, a patient can always
use increased energy and vitality.
Well-trained muscles can compensate
for handicaps in other systems.
"

"HAVE YOU NOTICED," asked the man at the Boston airport, "that there is one place where there are never fitness programs?"

This man was an expert on fitness, a runner who had turned his avocation into a livelihood. He had run the marathon the previous day and was now returning to California, where he headed a firm that set up fitness programs for corporations.

I also am an expert on fitness. At times, it seems that all my time is occupied by fitness. I am continually in contact with people who are engaged in some way with fitness activities. But I had no ready reply to his question.

When I asked where this place with no fitness programs was, he answered, "The hospitals."

I knew he was right. Except for an occasional cardiac rehabilitation unit, most hospitals do not have fitness programs for either their personnel or their patients. Aerobic exercise is rarely used in a hospital setting. Seldom is a patient encouraged to make the effort to become fit.

Shortly after that conversation, I learned this truth firsthand. I injured a calf muscle and was unable to run, so I went to a hospital physiotherapy department to work out on the exercise bicycle while the muscle healed.

I had not been there in some time. For the last two years, my medical chores have been limited to reading EKGs and giving stress tests. I no longer manage the day-to-day care of patients, so I have no occasion to visit most of the hospital.

The physiotherapy department was twice as big as I remembered it and filled with a variety of new electrical machines. In almost every booth, there was a patient being treated passively on a table. In the midst of this impressive professional activity was the one exercise bike, an ancient cast-iron monster called the "Everlast."

I mounted the bike and pedaled furiously for about 30 minutes. When I finished, a therapist came over to me.

"Doc," he said, "you are the first one to use that bike in two years."

The one training machine in the department, the mainstay of any fitness program for the diseased or handicapped, had not been used in all that time.

"The last one to use it," he said, "was Felix."

I remembered Felix. He had been my patient. His chronic lung ailment made him short of breath at rest, and he could hardly make it from the bed to the bathroom. Felix was in and out of the hospital like a yo-yo. When I sent for his old records, I was told they might have to be brought in with a cart. Felix was a constant problem for himself and his doctors.

One day, it occurred to me that training might help him. Before I began running, I was out of breath after running 100 yards. My improvement in endurance was not due to my lungs. My vital capacity, always high-normal, had never changed—but my fitness had. Perhaps Felix could improve without changing his lung function.

"Felix," I told him, "you are going to PT tomorrow and pedal that exercise bike until you're exhausted. And you'll do that every day until you go home."

He did, and the change was remarkable. He still wheezed at rest, but his walking improved tremendously. Felix left feeling better than he had in years.

He came back to the hospital, of course. When he got home, he just sat around. You cannot put fitness in the bank; you have to earn it every day. So Felix returned for treatment—but at longer intervals than before, and he stayed for shorter times. During each subsequent admission, he rode the bike daily.

Now nobody rides the bike. No patient in this 600-bed hospital is training for endurance. No one is working for maximal physical function, no physician is employing physiology in the treatment of disease, no physician is treating the whole patient.

Nor am I to be excused. When I left my practice, I forgot about Felix and the bike. It had been a one-time thing, and he had been the only patient I'd ever sent to the bike. It did not occur to me then that there was a major role for fitness in the hospital.

When you hear that the only exercise bike in a busy hospital physiotherapy department has not been used in two years, you begin to wonder. Why is it that hospitals do not have fitness programs? Why don't physicians urge patients to use exercise as well as medicine? Why do health-care professionals appear unconvinced of the value of physical training in the treatment of diseases?

For quite good reasons: Physicians, however little they know about exercise physiology, know a great deal about disease. They treat it daily and they study it constantly. They are suspicious of any therapies that arise outside their orthodoxy. Their tendency is to regard people outside their ranks as pushy promoters of their own interests. They demand solid scientific proof for claims of benefits for any new treatment—including exercise.

That scientific proof is not forthcoming. Physicians therefore have a tendency to see fitness as a media event with little substance. Their noncompliance indicates a basic distrust of the fitness premise, and their reading confirms that suspicion. "There is no definitive evidence," states Dr. Victor Froehlicker, a prominent heart researcher, "that exercise is effective in the primary or secondary or tertiary prevention of coronary heart disease."

Even the proselytizers for fitness acknowledge this observation. Should you listen to the leaders of the fitness movement you would find the talks are larded with qualifying words and phrases. Preceding each claim is a "may" or a "might" or a "should." The effects of exercise on disease remain speculative, and medicine is not a speculative sport.

Physicians know enough about the inexorable progression of disease to doubt that there are any lasting effects from exercise. They know pathology. They do not believe that disease can be altered simply by body movement. Theirs is a profession of skeptics and cynics. They deal in pain and suffering and death. The optimistic promises of the proponents of running and other exercise turn them off rather than on.

This suspicion even includes cardiac rehabilitation, the one program that seems to have caught on in hospitals. Even in cardiac rehab, the doctors are dragging their feet. Most patients are self-referred. They have taken it upon themselves to enter these programs, frequently against the advice of their physicians or at best with their reluctant consent.

But here, too, the doctors are on fairly solid ground. A recent review of all the available work on exercise and heart disease came to the same conclusion. According to Dr. Ezra Amsterdam, in an article in *American Heart Journal,* an exercise program will have no effect on the diseased heart. All the changes occur in the periphery, in the capillaries and the muscles.

"Numerous studies," wrote Amsterdam, "have failed to identify a direct cardiac mechanism in association with improved functional capacity following exercise training in coronary patients." That improvement occurs without cardiac improvement.

Exercise can induce the trained state regardless of disease. Every patient can be made fit. And that fitness will result in increased physical work capacity, increased oxygen intake, and reduced stress on the heart. Again it is understandable that physicians have been unaware of this. In the average American medical school only four hours in the four-year curriculum are spent on the effect of exercise on the body.

So there it is. Exercise programs have gained no foothold in hospitals for two reasons: The doctors know too much about disease and too little about exercise physiology. They rightly say there is no evidence that disease is in any way influenced by exercise. But they know so little physiology that they are unaware how exercise will profit every patient regardless of the disease.

There is a healthy way to be ill. Improving physical work capacity will also improve the capacity to deal with any disease. Whatever the disease, a patient can always use increased energy and vitality. Well-trained muscles can compensate for handicaps in other systems.

Physicians have yet to elevate their consciousness about these capabilities in their patients—and about their own opportunities to develop them. Hospital patients follow orders. They can be sent to physiotherapy, told to pedal to exhaustion, made to become fit. Physicians frustrated by their patients' not following negative injunctions such as "Stop smoking," "Stop drinking," "Stop overeating" can induce them to do something positive for their health.

Doctors have been told from their first year in medical school to treat the whole patient. They just have never been taught how. Once physicians learn the basics of exercise physiology, they will be able to offer total care—and then fitness programs will become routine in our hospitals.

What has exercise to offer? Not prevention of heart disease. Dr. Froehlicker has told us that there is no evidence that exercise is effective in the primary, secondary or tertiary prevention of coronary heart disease. Nor does exercise offer improvement for an existing disease. Dr. Amsterdam, in reviewing the available research, could not find proof that there were any direct cardiac effects of training in coronary patients.

What exercise has to offer is the attainment of maximal work capacity. Exercise will bring any individual to a trained state. Many medical reports speak of the "subjective" benefits associated with regular exercise, as if they were all in the person's mind. They are not. These results are quite objective and scientific. They can be easily tested on a bicycle or treadmill.

The limitations of disease on physical work capacity are much less than we suspect. The capabilities of handicapped people, whatever the handicap, are truly amazing. Wherever the possibilities of fitness are explored, a life is changed. There is the birth of a new capability, a new spirit, a new future.

Exercise physiology is the health science that will bring that capability, that spirit and that future to medicine. We need an exercise physiologist as part of the health care team. There should be one in every hospital, one available for consultation for every patient on the way to recovery and a new life.

One of the best-known cardiac rehabilitation units in the country is now accepting patients with diabetes. I have been notified by the University of Wisconsin at La Crosse that its rehabilitation unit is ready to treat physician-referred diabetics.

We are making progress. Cardiac rehabilitation is too valuable to be limited to cardiacs. Soon it will be available to all patients regardless of their disease. And not merely because exercise is good for the disease (which is still a question), but because it is good for the patient.

Exercise may be good for diabetes; it is even better for diabetics. Exercise may be good for hypertension; it is even better for hypertensives. Exercise may be good for asthma; it is even better for asthmatics. And so it goes. *Exercise may be good for a variety of diseases; it is even better for patients that have them.*

We are becoming aware of the immediate benefit of exercise on a number of diseases. We remain uncertain, however, as to whether the final prognoses of these diseases is changed in any way by exercise— whether, in fact, it will prolong a patient's life. What we do know is that exercise can prolong a patient's day. It can fill it with movement and stamina and endurance.

Exercise makes you fit—no more, no less. Fitness is the ability to do work—no more, no less. Fitness does not prevent disease; it does not cure disease. Fitness enables the body to function at a higher level. It makes people athletes, regardless of their ailment.

Once you realize that fitness is the ability to do work, a very confusing subject is clarified. Fitness becomes much easier to understand, as do the conflicts and arguments about it. If fitness is the ability to do work, there are many things fitness is not. Chiefly it has nothing to do with disease.

What fitness does is enable the diseased body to do more work—to push back the barriers of fatigue, exhaustion, shortness of breath, pain, or whatever it is that limits work. When a person with a disease becomes fit, work becomes possible, not because the disease is changed in any way, but because the working capacity of the body has been improved.

Physicians have been slow to understand this. Even the cardiologists who use exercise do it for the wrong reasons. Their target is the disease, not the patient. Other specialists have not even gotten that far. They do not see the life-giving and liberating effects of exercise. They focus on the pathology of the body.

These physicians argue that exercise will not help disease. They say there is no conclusive proof that training the body will cure or prevent most illnesses. A friend of mine who has written a text on preventive medicine once made that point quite clearly.

"George," he said, "if you show me that exercise prevents disease, I will add a chapter on it in my book." I never have, and he never will.

Exercise does not prevent anything. It adds to life, liberty and the pursuit of happiness. It is the way to achieve maximum function. Therefore, it is separate from disease. What it changes is the patient's life. Yet the very people whose lives are most affected by poor conditioning are being ignored. The people who need fitness most are being deprived of it.

"Deprived" may be too harsh a word, but I think not. These patients are locked into a diminished existence when they are unfit. Yet we doctors permit this to happen routinely. We restrict lives instead of expanding them. We narrow horizons instead of widening them. We reduce expectations instead of raising them.

We doctors are too concerned with disease and death. I share in that feeling of guilt we all have when we cannot prevent patients from dying. But I believe we should experience even more guilt because we prevent patients from *living*. We fear malpractice because our patients will die, which is in any case inevitable. We are actually guilty of malpractice when our patients are not taught to live.

Nevertheless, that is the current state of medicine. Even where there are cardiac rehabilitation programs, many of the patients are self-referred. Doctors see no need for such sweaty exuberances. Nor is the situation helped by the claims of the physicians who conduct such facilities. They should cease arguing that exercise helps cure a disease. They should take to high ground and tell us what exercise does for people: the decrease of fatigue, the increase in energy, the measurable improvement in physical work capacity, the enhancement of self-image.

All fitness needs in its support are the facts. What can be proven is enough. Athletes seek the ability to perform well. Cardiacs and hypertensives and diabetics and asthmatics and all those who have chronic diseases seek the same thing. Exercise will give it to them.

13

On Doctoring

"

**The doctor traditionally has been a teacher.
Being a coach and a motivator is not a new role.
It is simply one that has fallen into disuse.
Taking on that responsibility does, however,
entail becoming an athlete oneself.
If doctors want to open a new world of physical activity,
it must be their world also.**

"

WHEN DEALING WITH ACUTE ILLNESS, many physicians are superb. Our medical technology, the science of medical care, has outstripped the imagination. We read almost daily of new triumphs in the diagnosis and treatment of life-threatening disease. Every sizable hospital has physicians and technicians and machines capable of accomplishing miracles at a moment's notice.

Where doctors fail is in the treatment of chronic disease. The impressive victories won over acute illnesses are not duplicated in dealing with protracted and lifelong sickness. Such situations come down to getting the most out of what the patient has. This is hard work for both the physician and the patient, and neither seems up to it. The marvelous new technology in the laboratory and the mind-boggling devices in radiology are of little use. The new drugs are irrelevant. The information dispensed in medical journals and at conventions is of no help. This is a bare knuckles fight with an unforgiving opponent.

This therapeutic impasse has led to a search for alternative types of medical care, and the development of what is now called holistic medicine. The concept of holistic medicine is on the side of the angels. It is also on the side of the philosophers and the exercise physiologists. Its principles are simple, direct and on the mark.

The word "holistic," which is derived from the Greek word *holos,* or whole, was introduced by Jan Smuts, former prime minister of South Africa, in 1926. He took the position that things in this world tended to aggregate and form wholes. But holism is actually an ancient idea. We have heard it echoed down the centuries. Man is a whole, a unity or body-mind-spirit. And the whole is greater than the sum of the parts.

Holism is the basis of the concept of synergy. Things work better than seems possible when each part profits from what happens. Ruth Benedict pointed out this principle in primitive societies. Buckminster Fuller extended it to all sorts of physical and human equations. When the union occurs, two plus two equals five. An unpredictably beneficial result follows.

Predictably, holistic medicine has been accepted by those who believe that two plus two can equal five. Those individuals who are trying to get the most out of themselves. Those more interested in performance than disease. Holistic medicine speaks to those who believe in themselves and have faith in the universe, those who know that they are born to be a success and there is a way to do it—the athletes.

With more and more people wanting to be athletes, the influence of holistic medicine is widening. Now people with chronic disease want to test their limits and act like healthy human beings. Many are turning to the rules and regulations set up by holistic practitioners.

"The major therapeutic emphasis of the holistic physician," says Dr. C. Norman Shealy, president of the American Holistic Medical Association, "is on teaching proper life style, nutrition, adequate physical exercise and self-regulation techniques."

This sounds suspiciously like Hippocrates. And reading holistic tracts will reinforce that feeling. Attending a holistic medicine convention will give you a sense that there is little progress being made in medicine. The lectures are on procedures and techniques that go back over the ages. The talks could easily have been given a century ago. It is as if nothing has happened since.

And to some extent this is quite true. We are still dealing with the same body, the same human nature, the same chronic day-to-day problems of body-mind-spirit. We are still occupied with getting the most out of ourselves and our lives. The difference is that now we have the time and the money and the ego to do it.

When ordinary medicine fails to help, people will look to some alternative. Holistic medicine is certainly an attractive one. It rests on a solid base of philosophy and physiology. It takes notice of human nature. Holistic medicine subscribes to the reality principle. You are responsible for your own destiny. You control your fate. You are the only obstacle to your perfection.

Holistic medicine is a wonderful idea—on paper. It has the highest of goals, the purest of motives. It is the party of reform with the support of tradition.

The principles of holistic medicine read like an emancipation proclamation for the patient. Its emphasis is on prevention and self-help. The patient is a participant in whatever takes place. The holistic approach recognizes that illness is caused and maintained by an interaction of biological, psychological and social forces. On paper, holistic medicine is perfect.

In actuality, holistic medicine is like a giant flea market. Anyone can set up a table and vend his or her wares. The offerings range from pure science to far-out fantasies about the body-mind-spirit integration. And each is given equal standing. Dietary pronouncements with no proof whatsoever have the same status as the confirmed truths of exercise physiology. Therapies revealed to some mystic on a mountain receive the same attention as that given to those backed by painstaking scientific research.

In holistic medicine, conjectures become truths, hypotheses become facts, theories become axioms. Simply saying something makes it true. If said enough times, it becomes holy scripture.

These are not reformers; these are revolutionaries—each with a different cause, each with a different loyalty, each with a different path to salvation. The holistic medicine movement has generated, it is true, new ways for promoting health and treating disease. It has also regenerated the bizarre human-potential movements of past decades. Ideas and practices that began with Esalen are back.

This does not sit well with orthodox physicians. The practice of medicine, no matter what else it is, must be based on scientific grounds. Doctors may use therapies that work even though they don't know why they are effective. But even in such instances, they demand proof that the treatment does what it claims to do. Such evidence is absent in many of the prescriptions of holistic practitioners. For this reason, the medical establishment has a healthy distrust of what goes on under the banner of holism.

"For some people," writes psychologist Roger Zimmerman, "holistic medicine conjures up visions of orange-colored Zen robes, herbal teas, mantras, radical vegetarian diets, and last, but not least, the entire state of California."

Zimmerman's point: Support the concept, but stay away from the words "holistic medicine."

Dr. A. J. Lipowski, a prominent psychiatrist, takes the same view. In an article tracing the holistic-medical foundations of American psychiatry, Lipowski comments on this current movement: "Holistic medicine emerged as a catchword for an anti-scientific and anti-medical approach to health and disease. This perverted use of the term must not be confused with its traditional meaning."

The people who support the new holism have captured the best words. Their brochures are a delight to the eye and the mind and the spirit. They speak of human function, of biomedical synergistics, of the inner and outer environment, of frontiers of the mind and the body, of nutrition for performance. Everything, they say, is connected with everything else. Nothing is too trivial for their attention. What is done every moment of the day impacts on the health and fitness of the individual.

These are indeed areas that orthodox medical practitioners generally ignore—or, at best, give only passing attention. These are concerns that should be part of the traditional practice of medicine but unfortunately are not.

The supporters of holism have concentrated on the traditional concerns of treating the whole person but have ignored the equally traditional standards of science in this treatment. Our present medical establishment, on the other hand, has allowed the scientific approach to dominate medicine.

"The weight of evidence suggests," says J. Ralph Audi of the University of California Medical School in San Francisco, "that the health status of the population is not largely dependent on the quantity and quality of medical care, but the ecology (life style in its broadest sense) is the primary determinant."

This means that we the people are in control of our health. Our task is to take "holistic medicine"—a perfect idea, on paper—and make it a reality.

I frequently receive letters from runners in college who are preparing for medical school or one of the health-care specialties. They are interested, they tell me, in practicing some form of sports medicine. Some are worried that the medicine practiced today is too interested in disease and not enough in health. Their participation in running has changed their attitude toward the traditional view on what is normal. They want to treat the whole patient—and they prefer that the patient be an athlete.

In the past, when people asked me about practicing sports medicine, I said, "There are just not enough athletes to make a practice out of treating them."

There is no actual specialty of sports medicine. Only the orthopedic surgeons see enough athletes to make their care and treatment a paying proposition. Only in extraordinary situations can a physician survive seeing only athletes as patients.

Dr. Gabe Mirkin, a prominent writer on sports medicine, agrees. "I keep my allergy and dermatology practice," says Mirkin, "because sports medicine doesn't pay."

Only recently did it occur to me that it is possible for any doctor to practice sports medicine. It is, in fact, possible for any health-care specialist—nurse, nutritionist, physiotherapist or physiologist—to survive solely on sports medicine.

The solution: Turn the problem around. If there are not enough athletes who are patients, why not make every patient an athlete? Without changing the outward appearance of the practice, every physician could then become a sports physician.

Impossible, you might say. The tired housewife an athlete? The little old lady in tennis shoes? The cardiac, the asthmatic, the manic depressive, the alcoholic, the hypochondriac?

Why not? Think of how interesting those office hours would become. Treating the never-ending cycle of backache, constipation, headache and hypertension could become a delight. This approach could turn that dreary succession of patients into athletes a coach could be proud of.

The doctor traditionally has been a teacher. Being a coach and a motivator is not a new role. It is simply one that has fallen into disuse. Taking on that responsibility does, however, entail becoming an athlete oneself. If doctors want to open a new world of physical activity, it must be their world also.

They will need some new tools: a knowledge of exercise physiology, a grasp of the essentials of muscle function, some insight into the mysteries of rest and relaxation, a thorough knowledge of nutrition, continuing study of the effects of exercise on disease, and, finally, an awareness that there are exercise-induced diseases as well.

The runners who write to me have a head start. They know you don't have to be a motor genius to be an athlete; all you need is the desire. They know that normal is not average; it is the best you can be. And aging, they are beginning to realize, is more often than not a matter of rusting out. Deterioration sets in the day you stop moving.

There is still room in medicine for the new technology, the advances in medical science. When patients become athletes, they require the best of everything—the science as well as the art, holistic medicine in its widest meaning.

Practice sports medicine? The doctor should be practicing it every moment of every day.

14

On Working

"

**What health is to the individual,
morale is to the corporation.**

"

THE IBM MAN and I were sitting in the lobby of a Miami Beach hotel having the "jogger's breakfast" while waiting for the IBM award convention to start. I was there to lecture on the rewards of fitness. My job: to tell the 700 award winners of the values that come with an exercise program. My function: to motivate the best to get better.

My companion was in the IBM uniform, the suit and shirt and tie. He was wearing the corporate equivalent of the pin stripes of the New York Yankees. He was on a winning team and he knew it. His interest was not in fitness, however; it was in morale.

Once morale improves, he said, so does everything else. The rest is science and technology, never a problem at IBM. Morale is the key to the successful unit, the successful division, the successful corporation.

He was the head of a new facility in the Midwest and had gone through some problems with morale. His people were all transplants. They had come not only from other geographic areas but from other departments of the company as well. Many had been in work clothes and were now in the traditional shirt and tie.

It had been a big change, and people don't take well to change. Morale had suffered. Now, however, it was on the upswing. The plant was in a small town, a good community. People were getting involved in activities within the company and in their neighborhoods. Testing had shown marked improvement in morale. The IBM man looked pleased. His morale was quite high.

It struck me then that I had come to talk about fitness without knowing what corporations really needed. I had come with an answer without knowing the question. I had focused on my specialty and saw it as the solution to everyone's difficulty. Whatever ailed American corporations could be put to rights by fitness programs. When I preached fitness I always implied that these programs would develop enthusiastic, energetic, creative employees, and I assumed that the outcome would be enthusiastic, energetic, creative corporations. I had never considered the importance of morale.

I got up then and put in a call to my newspaper in New Jersey. I asked one of the editors to read me Webster's definition of morale. When she did, I knew the question management was asking. "Why is it that the best workers in the world, using the best technology in the world, are performing so poorly?" And I also knew the answer: "Lack of morale."

Morale, Webster tells us, is a confident, resolute, willing, courageous, self-sacrificing attitude toward a function or task demanded of an individual by a group. It is based on pride of achievement, faith in the leadership and its ultimate success, a sense of fruitful participation, and devotion and loyalty to other members.

"Morale" is one of those wonderful words the French have given us. I could almost hear the "Marseillaise" rising to a crescendo behind the voice on the phone. Morale is the quality we need for major incitements, for great deeds, and for difficult goals that require a long-term commitment.

Individual morale, according to Webster, is a state of psychological well-being and buoyancy based on such factors as mental and physical health, a sense of purpose and usefulness, and confidence in the future.

From this description, I could see that morale was of tremendous importance. Both for the individual and for the group. You could make a conscript army fit, but you would not have morale. Morale is cooperative determination, the desire to work in a common cause. Achieving good morale is the most difficult task of any leader.

Coaches know this all too well. George Allen, who transformed his over-the-hill Redskins into the best fourth-quarter team in football, said the hardest of his seven rules to put into effect was "work together." The others—work hard; improve every day; have a positive attitude; do not complain; know that no one can beat you but yourself; and, ask yourself how badly do you want it—were in comparison all easy to attain.

I remembered a statement by the coach of the Vancouver Canucks, a hockey team that had come from nowhere to get into the Stanley Cup finals. "When I took over," he said, "we had good players but a bad team. The players were totally motivated as individuals but not as a team. There was jealousy and envy. Players bragging about their success, laughing at other players." Then he brought in several young players and with them a new spirit and a winning team.

Fitness, I realized, is only part of the formula. The secret ingredient is morale. That is what motivates the best to get better. You have to be fit, but you also have to love what you do and the people you do it with.

The IBM man had left for the meeting. I followed him, eager to tell those 700 award winners what I had just learned.

What health is to the individual, morale is to the corporation. Health, as defined by the World Health Organization, is not merely the absence

115

of disease or infirmity. "It is a state of complete physical, mental and social well-being."

Health is the vital principle that enables us to meet and overcome the challenges of the day. For this, medicine and surgery are not enough. Preventive measures are only part of the picture. We must enlist all our functions, bring together body, mind and spirit to attain true health. This global approach is holistic medicine. It is medicine that sees the entire life style of the individual as important.

The same concept is now taking place in industry. Morale is no less than corporate health. It is the vital principle within a company that enables it to meet and overcome the challenges of the business day. For this, science and technology are not enough. The hard factors of production, capital investment, research and development are only part of the picture. It is necessary to enlist the soft factors—motivation, job satisfaction and collaboration—to attain true morale. This global approach could be called holistic management. It sees the entire life style of the corporation as important.

The Japanese have become masters at this. They have the hard factors in productivity. Their mastery, however, is due to the soft factors, those concerned with the human problems in productivity. The basic quality that is needed here is trust. Then there is subtlety, an acknowledgment that each individual must be accepted as a unique complex of experiences, attitudes and prejudices. Finally, there is an intimacy, a feeling of union with the others in the plant.

The Japanese do have a culture that contains and reinforces all these qualities. We live in a quite different social setting. While the Japanese have order dictated by a regard for their tradition and ancestors, we have order prescribed by law.

The two social orders are worlds apart in their effect on morale. Morale is cooperative determination, and Japanese culture reinforces and enriches it. Law creates the opposite effect. Law creates the determination not to cooperate, not to unite, but to disagree.

The law does not heal wounds, it causes them. It does not create relationships, it destroys them. The law is a poor substitute for the peace that comes from identifying with others. We live in a country, work at plants and reside in homes where life is becoming an adversary situation. It is not I and Thou; it is I *or* Thou.

Our need is for management and labor to develop our own versions of trust and subtlety and intimacy. Technical skill and skill with people rarely go hand in hand. We need supervisors and administrators who have the right instinct for people, who are experts in those things that cannot be taught and know just what to do and say when facing another human being.

Primarily, they must care and make that caring felt. The workers must know that the corporation cares. That is the role of holistic management: great involvement with every employee in the organization. How this will be developed will differ in almost every instance, but the desire and commitment alone can be decisive.

I once had as a patient an elderly Russian lady whose apartment was a profusion of beautiful plants and flowers. On the floor above her lived a woman whose plants just would not grow. She looked for advice from my patient, who told her she must love her plants for them to flourish.

"I tell my plants, 'I love you,' " my patient said to me, "and they know I do. She tells hers, 'I love you, I love you,' but they don't grow. They know she doesn't really love them."

Love has nothing to do with logic. Caring has nothing to do with technology. Yet without love and caring there will be no health in the individual or morale in the corporation.

15

On Aging

"

**Most people live nowhere near their limits.
They settle for an accelerated aging,
an early and precipitous fall.
They give aging a bad name.
Too many people entering their forties
are performing at physiological levels
more appropriate to somebody sixty years old.**

"

WHEN I TOOK UP RUNNING at the age of forty-five I joined a high school cross-country team. I had to. There were no older runners in my area and extremely few competitive events. So I kept my gear in my car and would consult the local paper for the time and place of the high school meets.

My teammates quickly accepted me. At the races it was a different story. The opposing teams and their coaches would find it quite odd that someone my age would be running and actually competing. In the races, I invariably had to pass a runner twice. The first time he would be startled and immediately spurt ahead. The second time I would put him away.

These young runners had not yet had their consciousness raised to the marvelous capability of the human body. Nor, indeed, had anyone else. In those days older runners were eccentrics, especially in cross-country season, when they might appear in longjohns on the roads. No one, including these aging runners, had any idea how little attrition occurs to the human machine with aging.

Those young athletes I ran with had a sense of urgency about their performances which I did not have. They would talk to me about two more years or one more year of eligibility. They saw their participation limited to the scholastic career; meanwhile my body was telling me to take the long view. This running, it said, can go on forever. It was that body wisdom that dispelled my preconceptions about aging. Just as women later took to running despite centuries of pronouncements to the contrary. And when they did I took the role of my high school doubters. Now it was me that a woman had to pass twice. And just as the younger runners finally grasped the truth, so did I. Women of all ages not only can run, they run well. Some of them run exceptionally well.

Now races are filled with runners over forty years of age of both sexes. The average times turned in by these older athletes are remarkable. They demonstrate just how gradual is the loss of running ability as age progresses. The study on master runners conducted by Washington University School of Medicine in St. Louis, in which I am a subject, has shown the decline to be only about 5 percent a decade.

What does this all mean? It depends upon your age. If you are a high school runner, you can see that your athletic career need never end. Indeed it must not. In physiology you get what you pay for. The effects of aging are minor as long as you keep your training and weight constant. You can be an athlete at any age, but you have to work at it.

Those who are older and have deserted exercise and play and sport must get back to it. This is the time to spend your unspent youth. There is no physiological reason to accept the rocking chair and the slippers. The minimal changes due to age would not be apparent in the course of the normal active day.

Fortunately this training need take little time. The fitness requirement is half an hour of movement at a comfortable pace four times a week. The master runners do more than that, of course, and their movement is running. But even for them the outlay is little more than four hours a week devoted to this training.

Such activity is needed to satisfy the animal in us. It is what is necessary to make you and me good animals. And that forms the base from which we can operate. Given a sound and healthy and fit body, we can pursue perfection in various ways. Once we have acquired the energy to make the day easy and the crisis conquerable, age will become the youth we were promised when we were young.

When I began running I became my own coach. I had to. At that time, no one was interested in the training of a middle-aged runner. No one was writing about the conditioning of older athletes.

It was left to me to decide on goals and a training schedule. I had to determine the correct frequency and intensity and duration of my workouts. I was an experiment of one. And lacking both instruction and experience, I was forced to learn through my mistakes.

There is a saying in medical school that if you treat yourself, you have a fool for a patient. The same thing applies to coaching. Someone has to keep his head while you are losing yours. Someone must resist the pressure of pride and ambition, of wishful thinking and dreams of glory. Someone must stand back and see things as they are. Someone must make the difficult decisions. It takes a sound mind to train a sound body. And when ego is involved, sanity is likely to go out the window.

I was no different from many others. I immediately fell into the pit. I committed all the cardinal sins of coaching.

My first and most serious transgression was to set unreasonable goals. I was influenced in this by my early success. There is always that initial quantum jump in running ability. The ease with which I progressed from

120

a brisk walk to an easy two miles persuaded me that such improvement would follow an upward line to infinity.

Once I was running well, I expected to run better and better: break five minutes in the mile; go under three hours in the marathon; catch up to those youngsters twenty-five years my junior. I looked for too much, too soon.

Unreasonable goals mean unreasonable training. I had hardly broken in my shoes when I was caught in the mileage trap. I was soon putting in more weekly distance than I had done on a championship cross-country team in college. When not doing distance on the road, I did interval work on the track and then ranged anywhere within a two-hour drive of my home looking for weekly road races.

The inevitable occurred again and again: recurrent staleness, exhaustion, sickness. I finally realized that the more I did, the worse I became. I discovered that Selye was right. The body can be trained to greater performance through application of stress. But the amount of stress and the time allowed for recovery are critical to the success of this process.

Being self-coached, I developed injuries. Again, these come as part of high goals and heavy training schedules. Long mileage, hills and speed-work breed injuries. I went through shin splints and Achilles tendinitis, runner's knee and the heel-spur syndrome. Worse, I tended to ignore them. Like many another runner, I ran hurt. I would not let an injury or an illness make me miss a race for which I had trained for months.

This attitude is almost universal. The glamor events in road running always have their share of runners who would be better off as spectators. They compete despite an illness or an injury or total exhaustion. I had a telephone call from just such a runner in South Africa two days before the 56-mile Comrade's Marathon. He had gone through a week-long fever of such severity that the doctors had seen fit to do a spinal tap to rule out encephalitis. "Would it be all right," he asked, "to run the Comrade's?" He had been in training for this race for six months and could not bear to miss it.

When he finished his question, I asked one in return. "Do you have a family?" Only someone alone in this world, whose survival mattered only to himself, would run the Comrade's in that condition.

It is quite difficult when you are your own coach to take the long view, to understand that running is a lifetime activity. Short-term triumphs matter very little. There will always be another race, another marathon, another Comrade's, even another Boston. It is possible to miss the race next Sunday and survive.

I eventually lowered my goals. I know now that athletes are much like racing cars and racing boats. We have a built-in range of performance. There is, it is true, a continuing slow improvement over the years. But year in and year out, I see the same bodies around me as I near the end of a race.

Eventually I also modified my training, just as I had modified my goals. I took one day off a week, then two. Now I do as little as 30 miles a week and find I can still race well, even continue to improve. I limit my intervals to those few weeks before the three or four races a year that I want to run especially well. The times when I run well don't spur me to train more. Nor does a bad performance get me out early the next day to put in extra miles.

However, if I made mistakes, there were compensations. In time, I came to see the other values in running. Being my own coach taught me to be independent, to trust my own experience, to learn from my own mistakes. Being a coach made me an expert on myself.

The mistakes I made in coaching were no worse than the mistakes I had made in living: unreasonable goals, misguided efforts, the short-term view, the failure to recognize what is important. I see that now. Running not only made me a coach; it made me a philosopher.

When a friend of mine, a former Olympic skier, passed the landmark age of thirty, she took herself off chronological time. Now, if asked how old she is, she answers, "My biological age is nineteen."

It is the biological or, better, the *physiological* age that matters. Despite the passage of years, the body can stay young functionally. If a person continues to train for maximum performance, a smooth trajectory can be plotted: a rising curve from adolescence to a peak at about the age of twenty-eight and then a slow decline to the biblical age and beyond.

Most people live nowhere near their limits. They settle for an accelerated aging, an early and precipitous fall. They give aging a bad name. Too many people entering their forties are performing at physiological levels more appropriate to somebody sixty years old.

It is time to elevate our consciousness of normal aging. Normal is the best you can be at any age. The normal forty-year-old is capable of athletic performances within 95 percent of the healthy twenty-five-year-old. The age group record for the marathon is within 95 percent of the world record.

And this relationship holds as the years go on. The group running records at age fifty are 85 percent of the world's records. Those at sixty are 75 percent. And one should realize that millions are attempting to set world records. A relative handful are competing at the age group levels.

These record holders are, I will grant, motor geniuses. Nevertheless, the same principle holds for us lesser folk. Whatever our personal world record might have been at the age of twenty-five, we can now approach it in our forties and fifties and sixties and even seventies to the same extent that these superathletes do. We can come within 5 or 15 or 25 percent of our peak performance.

I know this to be true from my own experience. I was a 4:20 miler in college. A secondary runner who filled in on the two-mile relay; no great shakes. Yet when I train down fine I can equal the statistics I have just presented to you. I have over the years shown the gradual reduction in performance that would be anticipated. At fifty I ran a 4:47 mile. At sixty, the equivalent of a 5:10.

I am now part of a study designed to document these changes through laboratory tests. Dr. John Holloszy and his associates at the Washington University School of Medicine in St. Louis have recruited a group of 16 master runners, averaging fifty-nine years of age, and matched us with 16 young athletes having much the same ability we had in our college days. I am, for instance, teamed up with a twenty-two-year-old, a 4.22 miler.

Each group has gone through a battery of tests. Maximum oxygen uptakes, percentage body-fat determinations, and echocardiograms were done to establish our current levels of fitness. When my results were compared to those of my younger alter ego, the investigators discovered that I had deteriorated about 5 percent a decade from my peak. And this proved to be the average lowering of function for each of the master runners.

This study has been an eye opener to the physiologists. The generally accepted figure for physiological aging is about 9 percent a decade. Some reports show even greater losses. Years ago, Sidney Robinson, an outstanding worker in the field of exercise physiology, studied the effects of age on a number of nationally ranked runners. At the average age of forty-eight they had lost up to forty-two percent of the capability that had brought them to prominence.

Robinson published his findings under the title "The Physiological Aging of Champion Runners." In retrospect, we can see the source of his error. These figures were not attributable to the normal physiological effects of aging. They were the abnormal effects. These world-class runners were heavy smokers. Their natural talent had succumbed to sedentary living. They were not aging. They were rusting out. Some were rotting out.

Only when training and weight and health states are constant can the actual effects of aging be charted. The research done at St. Louis puts normal physiological aging at just about 5 percent per decade. It confirms what my running had already told me. You can use your own body to make sure that your physiological and chronological age coincide.

I am simply a normal sixty-three-year-old getting the physiological limit out of my body. My biological age is sixty-three. My friend, the ex-Olympian, has a biological age of thirty, not nineteen. She has the capabilities of her thirty-year-old body trained to its peak.

Being an Olympian may make a difference. Not in ability, which is, in any case, relative, but in attitude. When you are thinking: higher, faster, farther, you seldom worry whether some things may be out of your reach.

When people suggest you act your age, you do . . . and go for it.

"No wise man," I said, quoting Jonathan Swift, "ever wished to be younger." The 300 or so runners in my audience nodded their wise heads in agreement. It was one of those speeches I frequently give to runners the night before a race. What was different was these runners. They were, all of them, men and women over forty years of age. The race the next day was a 5-kilometer event limited to this age group: Master runners.

I stood there looking out at those bright young faces. These were people who had found what age had to offer and found it good, who had discovered that age always contains what has gone before. The sixties, said one sage, contain the twenties and the forties. Proust put it more poetically: "Man is a creature without any fixed age who has the faculty of becoming in a few seconds many years younger." We can each of us at any moment relive anything that happened to us during our life span.

124

We Masters, I told them, have acquired a repertoire of qualities and capabilities the young cannot match. Age is constantly conferring new privileges, new abilities, new insights. We have grown in wisdom and experience. We are now superior to the individuals we were in our youth. And yet we have sacrificed very little. Only in a physical sense are we inferior to those people we were in our twenties. And even there, as tomorrow would show, few in that age group can equal our deeds. Most runners in the room tonight were in better physical condition than at any previous time in their lives.

My sixties did indeed include my twenties. Tomorrow I would be twenty again. In running that race I would relive races I had run in college. I would feel the same excitement, the same surge of adrenalin, the same challenges, the same pain, the same exhaustion, the same terrible shortness of breath, the same heaviness in the legs. The same exquisite satisfaction and relief in finally crossing the line.

My sixties also include my thirties. I remember what it was like not to be a runner, not to be an athlete. I remember those dormant days doing the work of the hive, waiting, although I did not know it, for the fullness that would come with the return to play and sport. Feeling all the while the death of ambition and the dissatisfaction with success.

Those listening to me knew my talk before I gave it. They had lived it just as I had. They knew the advantage they had over the young. We could be young, but they could not be old. They cannot know what we now know, cannot have the certainty we have acquired through the years of uncertainty.

What we lose with age, said Emerson, we can afford to lose. In our passage through the years we have focused on what is important. We have discarded the second rate. We have learned that trivia is indeed trivia. We have dispensed with tricks. We have not aged as much as we have moved from one age to another. The French speak of a third age. There is the age of the student. The age of the worker. And this third age of those ready to enjoy the fruits of study and work. The Masters.

We are indeed Masters, I told them. We are professors. We are professionals. We have come into maturity. And we have matured doing what appears to be childish things. Nevertheless, our ability to live with questions and without solutions began when we took to the roads. Our belief in ourselves and in living our own lives developed through our running. It was running that released the treasures in our subconscious and gave us the creativity to put these treasures in substantial form.

Keep running, I told the forties and fifties and sixties looking up at me, the best is indeed yet to come.

Perhaps being over sixty years of age makes me more sensitive, but no matter how people praise old age I notice a touch of condescension. They give me the feeling of someone watching another human being in difficulty and marveling at how well he is handling it. Age is never considered a gift. It is one of those natural disasters that must be met, and, if possible, with equanimity. No one seems to understand that age is the ultimate peak experience. It is the time of life for which all else is preparation.

The failure to appreciate the superiority of old age is due in part to the identification of age with death. Yet as we can see from the daily obituary columns, death comes at any time. Only a few are prepared for it. The artist, the athlete, the saint and the aged. They share a common experience. They know that after the absolutely superb effort, after a personal best, after the peak experience, comes physical and creative and spiritual exhaustion. There is a morning-after when all is ashes. It is not worth the effort to get out of bed. The hero of the day before has become an ant.

These deaths to the self and our ambitions, these periods of mourning for our hopes and our desires, come along regularly. No age is free of them. Only the elders have come to expect and welcome them. In such days are the seeds of new beginnings. They are invariably followed by new insights, new ideas, new concepts, new achievements. The progress of man is cyclical, and the peaks of that progress, not death, occupy the aging.

The major exponents of this attitude toward aging are the "young-old" described by psychiatrist Bernice Naughton. "The young-old," she writes, "are a rapidly growing group of retirees and their spouses who are physically and mentally vigorous and whose major characteristic is a new leisure time. They are people seeking interesting ways to use their time, both for self-fulfillment and for contributing to their communities."

The young-old constitutes a new aristocracy, a new leisure class pursuing truth. Their leisure is in the Greek tradition: time given over to education, to making one's life a work of art. It is an evocation, a heightening of the qualities that one implicitly possesses.

We aging see the environment as one that rewards boldness and risk taking. We bring to bear in any situation the gifts and the emotions, the strengths and the enthusiasm, of any of the ages we have gone through. We can now play any role. We have played them all before.

This is not to imply that we know it all. But it is to say we have lost nothing and we have gained freedoms we never anticipated. Further, we are no longer faceless youths barely distinguishable one from the other. Each of us is an original. Our bodies and minds and spirits are the unique expression of a personality in the final stages of evolution.

I said I could play any role. What is necessary is the script. When I was young I used other playwrights. I accepted the play and the role assigned to me. Now it is different. This is my play. This is my script. This is no role; this is me. The years in rehearsal, the decades in preparation, all the hard work, all those mistakes, are now paying off.

Now you know our secret. No young-old wants to be young again. We just want to feel young.

16

On Choosing

"

Your body reveals you within and without.
It tells the perceptive observer
your philosophy, your view of the universe.

"

WHEN I TALK to college students, I preach heresy. I use heresy in the sense of the original Greek, which means choice. I preach their abiding, permanent and absolute need for choice.

Some of that never-ending responsibility they already recognize. Other preachers have spoken of the obligation to choose from the alternatives of good and evil, industry and sloth. The sermons of our youth were filled with the should's and ought's of law and duty and culture.

That is not choice but acceptance. It is not adding to our life. It limits it. Our obedience to the rule, our acceptance of the regulation maintains our traditions, our institutions, our society. It furthers identity. It reduces individuality.

The heresy I present to them begins with the body. In our present academy the body is ignored. Physical education, basic to the education of aristocrats whether they lived in Athens in the fifth century B.C. or Florence during the Renaissance or Boston at the turn of the century, is no longer important.

When George Leonard, writer on human potential, visits college campuses he usually asks to meet with the physical educators. His faculty hosts are amazed. What in the world is to be gained by that? They regard attention to the body and play and sports as diversions from the real task of the university.

I ask these students to reexamine that idea and choose the body. Not to the exclusion of the mind and soul but in conjunction with them. To see themselves as evolving wholes. Body and mind expressing the personality that is the self.

The aristocrats in Greece embraced that unity. "Arete," the root of the word "aristocrat," means to fulfill one's function, to become whatever you are. We are wholes. Body, mind and soul.

The body cannot be ignored. The body is me, I am my body. The portrait painter Alice Neale tells us how much can be seen in a face. "I paint the inside as well as the outside. I paint the person's philosophy." Your body reveals you within and without. It tells the perceptive observer your philosophy, your view of the universe.

My body can expand my life or diminish it. To live totally I must be an athlete. I must follow the laws that govern the body. When I opt for the body, I accept the obligation of training it.

Higher education, I suggest, should consist of training both mind and body, one quite as rigorously as the other. William James, one of the great American thinkers, firmly believed in this. "I hope that the ideal of the well-trained and vigorous body," said James, "will be maintained neck and neck with that of the well-trained and vigorous mind as two co-equal halves in the higher education for men and women."

The psychological and philosophical reasons for a well-trained body were deeply important to James. Yet the physiological reasons are, at least initially, greater.

"The body," as Plato said, "is the source of all energy and initiative." The trained body gives us the maximum available energy, provides us with the most powerful initiative. Why place ourselves at a disadvantage? Are we going to get the most out of the person we are—or aren't we?

In his talk on "The Energies of Man" James speaks of our defection. In perhaps the most telling phrase in all his work he said, "We lead lives inferior to ourselves." Not, I tell the students, inferior to the leading scholar or the leading activist or the leading artist or even the leading athletes in this institution. Not to the number-one person in any of those fields—but to the self each one of us can and should be.

Abraham Maslow once suggested that we study the "good choosers." Those "gold medalists" who make work a pleasure, duty a delight, and turn selfishness into altruism. That is the definition, it seems to me, of a good and healthy narcissism. Choose well, I urge the heretics-to-be in front of me. Choose yourself, but choose your body first. Become an athlete, the person James called "a secular saint."

In 1898, William James stated that our physical breakdowns were due to the turbulence of our inner environment. In 1961, Dr. Meyer Friedman agreed with him. He reported a correlation between type-A behavior and coronary artery heart disease. Type-A people, Friedman said, are engaged in a chronic incessant endeavor to accomplish more and more in less and less time. This "hurry sickness" was usually associated with a free-floating hostility ready to vent itself at the slightest provocation.

This behavior apparently has widespread multiple adverse metabolic effects. These are generally known as coronary risk factors, and most of us are familiar with them. Elevation of cholesterol, triglycerides and adrenalin substances are perhaps the best known. The probability is that even more will be detected in the future.

The medical reaction has been to attack the branches, not the roots. Steps are taken in hopes of lowering cholesterol. Efforts are made to reduce hypertension. Type-A people are encouraged to stop smoking. As each leak occurs in the dike, there is a concerted move to plug it up.

Such measures appear to Friedman to be absurd. "Attempts are being made to prevent initial or recurrent coronary heart disease by ignoring its chief cause," he writes. Physicians, he says, are concentrating solely on secondary biophysical and biomechanical abnormalities or the noxious habit patterns possibly generated by this same overlooked cause. The solution is to modify type-A behavior and thus reduce the coronary risk.

James was in full agreement with this position. In his Gospel of Relaxation he spoke again and again of changing our inner climate. He spoke out for training the body and championed a physical training equal to that of the mind. His cure for hurry sickness was to become physically fit.

Stating what should be done is not the same as doing it. Lowering cholesterol is child's play to modifying behavior. James was preaching to the converted, graduating class of the Boston School of Gymnastics. Friedman says his best results are with people who have already suffered a heart attack. Nobody wants to be saved until salvation appears lost.

Until a person has a heart attack the very idea of having one appears inconceivable. Indeed, the first reaction the heart-attack victim has is disbelief. "This cannot possibly be a heart attack," one says to oneself. All manner of ills are considered. I know of physicians who explained away their pain and went back to chopping wood, or ate a sumptuous meal, or claimed it was all due to bursitis.

The difficulty of the problem should not dissuade us from the conclusion reached by both James and Friedman. If you wish to reduce all risk you must change behavior. It's our attitude that raises the cholesterol. Our emotions that elevate the blood pressure. Our inner storms that lead us to cigarettes.

For Friedman this change is a matter of spending time with the patient, convincing the potential victim that this life style is self-defeating. James would have us find this out for ourselves. Use the body, train it, perfect it, and you will find your behavior changing with that perfection.

Many teachers would agree with James, the teacher. They know that nothing worth learning can be taught. They realize that anything that changes behavior must be self-experienced. Do not argue. Do not debate. Simply motivate. Induce them to experience their bodies, become fit, learn how to play, engage in sport. Your work will be done.

Friedman would redeem his patients through convincing them of the error of their ways. Most type-A people, he discovered, are proud of their hurry sickness and attribute their success to this dedication to work. Friedman would show them otherwise. Type-A behavior does not bring success and it breeds emotional and spiritual disease.

His tack is to convince type-A people of two things: that their success, whatever it is, is due to their other attributes—creativity, organization, professional skill. The hurry sickness has nothing to do with it. And, secondly, that this incessant single-focused pursuit has limited their growth in other areas. They are emotionally and creatively deprived. Friedman states it more plainly. They have, he says, a spiritual illness.

Reading James, I get the same impression. Here is human potential going down the drain. And neither of these men will have it. But being on the side of the angels is not enough. Good intentions are not enough. How can a life be changed?

Not by words. At least that is my belief. Or if by words, they are the perfect words to express what you have already experienced. In this Friedman may succeed. He may, by his words, recall to the person what it was like in the past. He will bring up the conversion-creating experience.

James suggests we create the experience and the desired conversion will follow. Exercise the body, train the muscles, and in due time we will find a mental health to go along with the physical one.

James telescopes this process. He suggests it is as simple as Friedman admits it is difficult. It is not all that simple. It occurs in stages. Each of them must be lived through and then the next step is taken. But millions of people have tried it and have been successful. Everyday I meet people who have gone back to their bodies and found the self they were meant to be.

Choice always leads to more choice. The heretics who opt for training the body discover that other doors must be opened. The first leads to play. Training, they find, is enough for the body. It does give energy and vitality. There is a new presence. One becomes a good animal. Training becomes a means to this end.

The choice now comes in the expression of this evolving personality. The traditional view of normality is the ability to love and to work. From Freud and his theories to George Valiant's studies of Harvard graduates, the ability to love and to work remains the chief criterion in measuring adaptation to various life situations. The graduates with stable marriages and job satisfaction had the best mental health.

There is, however, a third choice, again complementary to the other two, which is play. Play provides the third dimension—creativity. In the playful use of our bodies, we give release to the treasures in our subconscious, the experiences stored there since birth. "Genius," said James, "is simply a different way of looking at things." It is a genius we all possess and can make available in play.

In all too many instances we fear we have no inherent creativity. Yet this is not true. "If most of us tend to keep on going [through] the same familiar motions, this is not because we are short on creativity, but because we stifle it." So wrote the late Lawrence Kubie. In commenting on this observation, Bill Moyers suggests: "Discover the impediment, exorcise it, and creativity will flow."

The impediments are many, but a playful, well-trained body removes most of them. There is a special case to be made for motion. "Never trust a thought you came upon sitting down," said Nietzsche. "The muscles must be in celebration with the mind." Thoreau made a similar statement: "It seems when my legs begin walking, my mind begins working . . . any writing I do sitting down is wooden." The play of the body, as surely as purposeless walking is play, leads to the play of the mind we call creativity.

The education that stifles play stifles creativity. Play therefore becomes what Peter Berger calls a heretical imperative. We may refuse to train our bodies or subsequently use them in play, but we should be aware of the choice and all its implications. There should be informed consent.

Most consent is uninformed. Why else this endless flow from lecture to lecture, followed by long hours of study—and only a trickle to the gymnasium and the playing fields. The Greeks knew better. An hour a day at the gymnasium or palestra was the rule. Some of the Roman intellectuals like Seneca had their own trainers.

Nietzsche, who believed in motion, also believed in play. "All great ideas are conceived in play." Man's most important activity, said Hoffer. The primary energy of man, said Ortega, was sportive or playful.

Moyers, in studying creativity, describes the attributes leading to this quality. Creative people, he discovered, tolerate ambiguity, are willing to take risks, have a strong sense of self, a need to prove their worth and, finally, discipline.

A quick perusal of these attributes should make it clear that they are common also to those individuals who have trained their bodies and discovered their play. They are the basic characteristics of the "good choosers" described by Maslow.

Ultimately, however, training and play will be insufficient. Creativity is not simply concerned with novelty. What comes from seeing the old as new must be a transforming development, an evolution or unfolding of the self. For that to happen we must make another choice: risk.

Risk is a moral equivalent to war. James and others, notably Ernest Becker, have seen clearly our need to be heroes. We require, therefore, an arena for heroism, a theater where we can act out our drama as the person we want to be.

That arena is sport. Athletics are the moral equivalent of war, our games the theater for heroism. George Santayana, that urbane Harvard philosopher and most unlikely supporter of such ideas, spoke strongly to this view in his "Philosophy on the Bleachers."

"It is not the mere need of healthy exercise that brings the players," said Santayana. "Athletics have a higher function than gymnastics and deeper basis than utility." Santayana saw the intimate relation between games and war, but he observed that "the games arose from the comparative freedom from war, and the consequent liberation of martial energy from the stimulus of necessity, and the expression of it in beautiful and spectacular forms."

The martial virtues are what we need when we place ourselves at risk. To do what will be beautiful and spectacular we must be "Spartan, active, courageous, capable of serious enthusiasm and ready to endure discipline."

In Cambridge in 1894, Santayana saw sports as the student's salvation. "Our athletic life," he stated, "is the most conspicuous and promising rebellion against this industrial tyranny"—the conformity in the

United States. Now, almost a century later, it is the most promising rebellion against academic tyranny.

If we are to be heroes, and heroes we must be, sports offer us the preeminent arena in which to achieve this status. As we have so often been told, it is not in winning or losing we become heroes but in the way we play the game. The risk is always there. But the risk is not in losing to an opponent: it is in losing to your lesser self.

Oddly, this rarely happens. Just as in war there are cowards but little cowardice, so in sports there are quitters who refuse to quit. In sports the heroic becomes the commonplace.

Once we have experienced the heroic we are never the same, that experience enters our subconscious, becomes part of our memory both verbal and nonverbal (or mystical). The heroic experience becomes both source and reason for our creativity.

It is the hero who tolerates ambiguity, who is willing to take risks. The hero has a strong sense of self, a need to prove his worth and discipline. It is the hero who has all the attributes of the creative person.

PART

2

The Athletic Experience

17

On Meaning

“

**We need all three activities.
Exercise is a science.
Play is an art. Sport is both.
Exercise is mechanical. Play is free-flowing.
Sport is exercise with rules
and a reckoning at the finish.
Sport is exercise with consequences.**

”

WHEN I LECTURE on fitness I admit up front that running is boring. I know that a majority of the people in the audience hold that opinion. Many have come to that conclusion simply by observing joggers on the road. Others have actually tried running and found it to be drudgery. I am usually facing a group of people who either failed in fitness programs or never got started.

The major obstacle to a successful fitness program is boredom, the feeling of wanting to be doing something else. When you are bored you are acutely aware there are much more interesting or satisfying things to do. Places, people and activities bore you because at this very minute you want to be elsewhere. An elsewhere with pleasure and excitement and absorption. An elsewhere without feelings of inadequacy and embarrassment and discomfort. An elsewhere where you feel at home.

My object is to suggest to the people in the audience how they can be made to feel at home in a fitness program. That program, if it is to succeed, must be interesting and satisfying. It should be filled with pleasure and excitement and absorption. It must be a place where a person is rarely if ever bored.

Can all this be accomplished while doing something boring? Possibly. You might, for instance, try thinking of something interesting while you are doing something boring. If the running movement can be made automatic, the mind then can wander through meadows of thought, completely engrossed in its own activities. This is called dissociation, and most runners do it. When you see them trotting down the road, their minds are usually miles and possibly centuries away.

I find swimming boring because I am unable to dissociate while I swim. The instant I let my mind go off on its own, I sink. I have to attend constantly to the movement of my arms and legs or I flounder in the water. When I run, however, I am able to put my body on automatic pilot and let my mind loose to search for interesting ideas.

If this fails you can try another ploy. Make what is boring interesting. Take an interesting companion on the run. Good talk can halve the distance. You will come to the end of the run feeling as if you had just begun. If you are a gossip you should run with a gossip. If people form a large part of your world, your fitness world must include them as well.

Another way to make something boring interesting is to make it competitive. In running, for instance, you can add the race. An entry blank can introduce you to a new and intensely absorbing world. The jogging during the week then has a new spur, a new motive—performance against your peers.

There are races and there is The Race—the marathon. Many runners who would have been dropouts have stayed in the sport because of this 26.2 mile challenge . . . the Everest of distance running. The marathon raises running out of the ordinary and commonplace and puts it in the Olympic category. Running becomes an epic event, a place for heroes.

In many instances these measures fail; people still do not want to run. Covert Bailey, the author of *Fit or Fat* and a great proponent of running, tells of a friend's coming up to him and saying, "Covert, there is no getting away from it, running is boring."

"No, John," said Covert, "you're boring. You are so boring you can't spend a half hour alone with yourself."

Nevertheless, the truth is that there are no boring people. Those we consider bores are simply interested in subjects that are of no interest to us. In a fitness program this means searching for something interesting to do. If running cannot be made interesting, then perhaps cycling or swimming or cross country skiing can be. There are people who were repeated dropouts in a variety of activities until they discovered karate or weight lifting or aerobic dancing. Or racquet ball.

When pushed into a corner, I ask the audience to remember what they enjoyed doing as children. That form of play or something similar to it will still be satisfying to the body. If you then add the socialization or competition that you need, fitness will come without any further concern on your part. And you will seldom be bored in the process.

At birth we are all generalists. As children we are curious about everything. We insist on exploring and exploiting all our abilities. We run and play, we sing and dance, we write and draw without thought as to whether or not we are good at it. Our games change with the seasons. Our lives are lived in a classroom that is the world. This allows for an infinite variety of physical expression.

As time passes we become specialists. We constrict our interests, narrow our participation. We limit the expression of the self. This happens in our mental life. It happens in our creative life. It happens in our physical life. We find one occupation, one avocation, one sport. Everything else that is human becomes foreign to us.

This is the major indictment of distance runners. Not that we are narcissistic, but that we are so obsessed with running we devote no time to the rest of our body. We do not develop its varied strengths and skills. We never learn the other ways the body can speak and experience, can teach and be taught.

We are not alone. Most present-day athletes are specialists. They concentrate on their sport as we do on running. They, too, congregate together, speaking in their own tongue, demanding allegiance. They also are sects who see others as heathens or heretics or backsliders lost forever to the truth.

Runners do not understand why everyone is not a runner. Cyclists feel the same way about cycling. Golfers about golf. Tennis players about tennis. Each sport has its passionate advocates who have found the Grail and see no reason why they should try anything else.

Were we the children we were meant to be, we would enjoy all sports. Were we the generalists that we once were, we would delight in all the things the body loves to do. We would play the games that have withstood the test of time and progress.

I am now incapable of sports in which I was once proficient. Up until now I did not care. Running was enough. Now I am not so sure. In putting on the New Man, must I not also develop all the things the body can do? And should I not rejoin all those friends I dismissed on my way to becoming a distance runner? Is not the glory of God man who is really functioning—not merely running?

The prominence given the decathlon is one answer to these questions. The winner of the decathlon is the hero of each Olympiad. He is the athlete we remember. Yet the decathlete is a person who is fairly good at everything and rarely exceptional at anything. The decathlete is mediocrity lived and at its highest standard. The decathlete is the generalist raised to the highest level. The decathlete is the best common man.

We common men will find no better inspiration. We are better at some sports than others, but we are not really hotshots at anything. Instead of concentrating on one area of mediocrity we should vary our sports and enlarge our physical experience. We will come to know our bodies in new and satisfying mediocre ways.

The number of athletes, young and old, participating in multiple sports is growing. That is as it should be. Athletes, not poets, are the antenna of the race. The body teaches more clearly than any other agent. In childhood that meant total sports activity. Adults unfortunately take longer to learn. We have to go through being specialists before we become the generalists and decathletes we once were.

The sports psychologists had invited me to Ottawa to present an address at their international meeting. For the first time in their history, a section was being devoted to the personal meaning of sports through life. The rest of the meeting, as always, would focus on ways to enhance athletic development.

Sports psychologists can presently be classified into two distinct groups: those doing scientific studies and experimental work in sports, and those who deliver the clinical service before, during and after competition. Both groups concentrate on athletes and their problems. Both operate in a framework which deals exclusively with the athlete's performance.

My thesis was that the psychologists had taken a parochial view of their specialty. They did not recognize the full scope of their discipline, either in the range of people it should treat or in the type of activities it should cover. Two things could remedy this:

One was to consider every person a potential athlete. Thus the influence of the psychologist would extend to everyone who could have his consciousness raised to his athletic and human potential.

The other was for psychologists to extend their sports practice to include both exercise and play. These three distinct but interrelated activities would have to be understood and then integrated if sports psychology were to have a beneficial effect on the present fitness craze.

We know all the physiology we need to know to become fit. We know next to nothing, however, about the *psychology* of fitness. When we regiment people, it is easy to get them fit. What we can't do is induce them to do it on their own. We haven't devised the psychological supports needed to make fitness programs successful.

Our difficulty is not in performance but in motivation, not in world records or personal bests, but in the desire and the discipline to stay with the training required to lead the athletic life. We need expert psychological help to increase participation and then prevent dropping out.

I am not a scientist, I told these scientists. I am a specimen. I am an example of what happens when a person finds his sport and persists in it. The last twenty years have been a learning, growing period of my life. It has been marked by an awareness of what is possible for me. I have discovered new levels of performance and new feelings about myself and my body. And I have been able to express this experience in new and creative ways.

I have done this by rediscovering the athlete I was in my youth. But this time I learned from my body. I listened to what was going on inside me. I saw the effect that my running was having, not only on my body-brain complex, but also on the self that this body and brain expressed.

I learned something I always knew but did not remember: the difference between exercise and play and sports. Each is a separate and distinct entity, each with its own function, each essential and fundamental to our nature. Each fulfills in some way our need to demonstrate who we are. Each makes us feel better about ourselves and the life we lead.

For too long people have tended to use the words interchangeably.

"Does anyone here," I asked the psychologists, "know how to play this game? Does anyone here understand the difference between exercise, play and sport?"

Do you, my reader?

Of the three athletic activities—exercise, play and sport—exercise is the easiest to define. Exercise is work. In the words of Mark Twain, it is anything a body does not want to do. Exercise is dull and boring and an extremely slow way to pass the time. Exercise is counting repetitions and watching the clock. Exercise is waiting until it ends.

We all understand exercise. It is the phys. ed. we were given in school. It is the fitness programs offered us today. Exercise is pure physiology with nothing to make it palatable. Exercising consistently, therefore, requires some of the martial virtues: discipline, a sense of obligation, a realization that the results will make boredom and fatigue and suffering worthwhile. Exercise has purpose, but it has no meaning.

Play and sports are the opposite. They have meaning but no purpose. From there on, however, they differ. And that difference, unfortunately, is not generally recognized. We often use the words "play" and "sport" synonymously. There is no verb for "sport." So we use the word "play" in attempting to describe sport. We say we *play* tennis. Or we say we *play* football. But we're not playing at all. When there are rules, when there is a score, when something is at risk, it is not play. It is sport.

144

Not to see this difference is to put yourself in one of two opposite and equally defeating situations. One is to concentrate on sports so much that play becomes nonexistent. The other is to focus on play and remove sport from your life. In either instance, you will be deprived of something essential to your development and fulfillment as a human being.

We need all three activities. Exercise is a science. Play is an art. Sport is both. Exercise is mechanical. Play is free-flowing. Sport is exercise with rules and a reckoning at the finish. Sport is exercise with consequences.

The physiologist concerned with perfecting the body and assuring maximal health need not go beyond exercise. But the fact is that few people will exercise for any length of time without the additional motive of play or sport. Most need the values introduced by play and sport to make all the training worthwhile. Then what was previously a duty becomes a privilege.

This progression can easily be seen in the runner. Running begins with fitness, 30 minutes at a comfortable pace four times a week. This makes one a jogger who exercises for no other reason than the physical benefits that come with this two hours a week. The realities of weight loss and increased energy, and the promises of longevity and freedom from heart attacks, are what motivates this beginner.

Then the jogger becomes a runner. The minutes on the run become time for meditation and creativity. City streets or rural roads become havens from the press of life and the events that promote the "hurry sickness." The daily run is no longer work, it is play.

The runner now is interested in bigger things than a low cholesterol count or normal blood pressure. The inner and outer worlds have become the focus. Running has become a search for meaning, the runs fascinating meanderings in the interstices of the mind. The sights and sounds and touches of an entire life, the subconscious ready to harvest, make every run a treasure and a delight.

But finally, even that is not enough. This search for meaning needs more. It needs a challenge, a test, an experience of the self in extremity. It needs, as William James said, a theater for heroism, a moral equivalent of war. And so the runner runs from play to sport. The runner becomes a racer.

* * *

145

The distinction between play and sport may appear trivial. It is all-important. We need both. Neither alone can satisfy our inborn need for the other. There are, to be sure, certain common characteristics. Nevertheless, play and sport are different. What I ask from my body in sport becomes the source of what I create in play. Play is truly emotion recollected in tranquility. It is the art and poetry, the painting and writing—indeed any creative act—that follow from the moments when we have put ourselves at risk.

The race is sport. The race is run in a bounded area, another world operating under its own rules. And most important, the race has a closure. There are results. I am given my time and place. So the race is a perfect way to live out the trials and tests and challenges we must meet to feel good about ourselves.

There are some who would turn sport into play. Take the net down in tennis. Do not keep score in basketball. Forget about times in races. But this approach won't work. It would be disastrous to remove competition and consequences from our lives. We need them to mold us and shape us and teach us who we are and what we can become.

Sport makes us fully functioning adults. Through pushing to our limits, we grow in self-esteem and self-respect. Through doing what we do best, we attain maturity.

Play, on the other hand, returns us to childhood. It allows complete freedom. Play is unstructured and without rules. It liberates us from necessity. It asks no product, no particular performance. It refuses to be serious. Play opens up our inner world and allows our subconscious to percolate through to understanding.

For me, the race is the epitome of sport. It is a contest, a struggle, an agony. Running on the other hand is play. The emotions I feel on the run are quite different from those in the race. Alone I am at peace. I feel confident. There is a loss of the sense of time and place.

The race is systole, where I am active. The run is diastole, where I am passive. The race is complete, the run is open-ended. The race has consequences, the run has none. The differences multiply, and none is trivial.

There is sport and there is play, the race and run, the experience and the esthetic expression of the experience. We have need of both. Racers deprived of play will sooner or later desert their sport. Runners who never compete will move on to other interests, and they and their coaches will wonder why it happened.

It takes both sport and play to make our lives complete.

The race is a true experience. Only the conditions are artificial. My entire self is engaged in a genuine struggle against time and distance and those around me. All my strengths, physical and emotional and moral, are called upon to decide the issue.

The race is, as Santayana said: "A great and continuing endeavor, a representation of all the primitive virtues and fundamental gifts of man."

Because it involves these primitive virtues and these fundamental gifts, the race is an uplifting event. It tells me previously unrecognized truths about myself. It fills my subconscious with the experience of the "good me." It makes me a hero and floods my innermost life with proof of that fact.

Our highest need is to be a hero. We need heroic experiences to saturate our subconscious, to fill up our psychic reservoir. It is imperative that this "deep well of cerebration," as William James called it, contain good news rather than bad—that what later comes to the surface is positive rather than negative.

But to be a hero, we must find what best allows us to do something heroic. We must find that arena, find that event. In this duel with life, we are allowed to choose our own weapons. We have the right to fight from high ground.

James wrote of this situation in a letter to his wife: "I often thought that the best way to define personal character would be to seek out the particular mental or moral attitude in which, when it came upon him, he felt himself most deeply and intensely active and alive. At such moments, there is a voice inside which speaks and says, 'This is the real me.'"

That is the voice I hear at the race. The race is, for one thing, absolutely true. Everything is seen and felt exactly as it is. The pain is real. The suffering is real. I am challenged. I respond to that challenge. And when I come to the finish line, I am completely spent yet completely happy. I have forgotten momentarily all the bad things about myself.

But the race is more than the moment. The subconscious is being purged and rinsed and cleansed. It is being emptied of all the mean and embarrassing things I have accumulated during my life. My bedrock concept of myself and the world is being refurbished. I am replacing all the depressing memories, all the dirt and debris, with something that is bright and clean and positive. I am hearing the good news.

This is most necessary because the subconscious is the source of all our creativity. Creativity in the arts or in thought or in life situations depends upon a subconscious that contains what is good and true and joyful. It must be kept free of everything that is not.

Hemingway once wrote that he never read criticism of his works because they made his subconscious murky and muddy. And, he said, he had to be kept clean if he was to write.

We don't have to read critics to make our subconscious murky and muddy. All we have to do is go to work, or go to school, or go to church, or even perhaps go home. There are critics all around us. Rarely do we hear anything that would make us feel good about ourselves. Our subconscious is constantly being crammed with evidence of our shortcomings and failures.

The race reverses that. It tells me I am a success. It makes me feel good about myself. And later in the week, this experience percolates out of my subconscious when I am at play—on my training runs, where I am in control, feeling virtuous at an eight-minute-per-mile pace. Then I write my column, or plan my day, or think in new directions—all because of this new "me" that has come into being.

Our problems are solved creatively, or even left unsolved creatively, only by a profound and thorough alteration of our inner life.

The race is my transforming experience. It causes a profound and thorough alteration of my inner life. The training run is the play in which this experience finds its esthetic expression. The experience of the race germinating in my conscious mind comes to fruition in play.

Then the freedom of the body and mind takes the event and its meaning, and produces art—the outer form in which life finds expression and support. Whether this is a poem or a statue, a letter or a garden, a recipe or a relationship, makes little difference. Whatever the expression, it will be a new representation of you when you are deeply and intensely active and alive.

Now you can say, "This is me," and be proud to say it.

18

On Motivating

"

The common aim of athletes
is consistent top-level performance
—not longevity, not disease prevention,
not health or wellness.
Their goal is to play their game well.
Whatever helps them do this
is worthwhile. . . .

"

I DON'T BELIEVE in will power. I believe in *want* power. If you want a thing badly enough you'll do whatever is necessary to obtain it. So it is with exercise. You may just want to run, period, or walk, or swim. Your sport may be an end in itself. Or you may train as a means to something else you want badly. Either way, you develop the want power to make exercise a part of your life.

"I hate running, but I like what it does," says golfer Jack Nicklaus. "If I want to keep up with the younger players, I have to take better care of myself. That's where running comes in."

Nicklaus runs three miles five nights a week at about 8 minutes a mile.

"I just want to get it done without dying," he says. "Oh it's horrible . . . but I feel much better for doing it."

Nicklaus has given running a priority in his life, because it has become necessary for his number one priority—golf. What is at stake is his profession, the way he is in this world. He identifies himself with the way he performs on the links.

When the relationship between exercise and everyday performance is immediate and direct, there is no need for other motivation—no necessity to make exercise interesting, enjoyable and an end in itself. A person is quite willing to find room for it in his daily schedule.

Athletes, especially professional athletes, are willing to make that adjustment. Most of them become aware that their talent will not last without training. If you are an athlete, your body demands athletic care. Diet and exercise, sleep and relaxation, are elements of extreme importance.

Professional basketball players stress the importance of sufficient rest, proper diet and ability to relax. Getting enough sleep is critical.

"In an 82-game season, players' off-court habits can be the difference between winning 15 games or losing them," says Elgin Baylor of the Washington Bullets.

The legendary Bill Russell agrees: "I knew how to relax, and that's probably the most important thing. I was an excellent sleeper."

Phil Jackson, former Knicks star, sees the need for more exercise as well. "I used to run and swim for conditioning," he says. "I'd walk and walk rather than hang around the hotel. I napped about 40 minutes a day for six days a week. Because of these things, there was a marked increase in the productivity of my game. Instead of being erratic, I became consistent."

The common aim of athletes is consistent top-level performance—not longevity, not disease prevention, not health or wellness. Their goal is to play their game well. Whatever helps them do this is worthwhile, however dull and mindless and boring it might be.

Running is a bore to most golfers, yet many have accepted it. "On the PGA tour years ago," says Nicklaus, "no one ran. Now lots of fellows out there run, maybe 50 or 60."

Arnold Palmer is one of them. Observers thought Palmer was on the way to being the stereotyped middle-aged man with a paunch, puffy face, and a penchant for beer and easy chairs. Palmer noticed it, too. "I was getting a little heavy," he says. "My golf wasn't going good. I was getting tired and lethargic about my game. And I'd lost interest in finding out what was wrong and working on it."

Then Palmer turned his life around: "I started running and now run three miles every morning. As a result, I have lost 20 pounds. My disposition has improved. I've got my old stamina back and the patience to iron out the problems of my game."

A fitness program should offer what a person wants and offer it right now. Promises work with some but disillusion others. Professional athletes look for performance. For them, life expectancy is what they expect out of today's game or tomorrow's match. Athletes seek their full potential every working day, not in some future retirement. Athletes want to be living, achieving legends.

Someone asked Jack Nicklaus if he was a reluctant runner.

"Reluctant perhaps," he answered, "but a believer nevertheless. I feel good, I look better, and that's the key to everything."

When the gains are immediate and measurable, these athletes will do almost anything to get them. So will we all.

When people tell me running is boring, I know what they mean. I find swimming boring. When I have to swim because I've been injured and can't run, I can do it for what seems like a half hour and find that only five minutes have passed. Swimming is as interminable for me as running is for some people.

I am made for running, not swimming. I have low body fat, which is good for a runner, but bad for a swimmer. I lack the buoyancy and insulation that good swimmers need. I tend to sink instead of float, and I have to expend a considerable amount of energy to keep moving. Although my running form is economical, my swimming stroke is awkward and inefficient. I am always shipping water and am never quite sure what to do with my head. How anyone can enjoy swimming is beyond me.

A physical education professor recently wrote to me about his problem with dropouts in his fitness program. "Why do people who seem to be convinced of the value of cardiovascular health stop exercising?" he asked. His own answer was that psychosocial factors are the prime determinants of behavior.

I am not sure what he means by that, but if he means boredom, I agree. The real question was asked a long time ago: "Why do children who love to play hate physical education?" If we knew the answer to that, we would know why adults drop out of fitness programs. My answer is: because the programs are boring.

Still, the educator is on the right track. Fitness programs do succeed when they satisfy psychological and social needs, like Maslow's needs of belonging, esteem and self-actualization. There is little place for reason or logic. Sport, which is play intensified, is the key. It unlocks the enthusiasm and discipline necessary to satisfy these needs.

One of the most successful fitness programs was one developed by Bruno Balke at the University of Wisconsin. When I called and asked him what his method was, he told me I would have to come and observe it. There is no way, he said, that he could systematically outline his program for me.

What he did was treat each person individually. In effect, he had as many fitness programs as there were people attending. He tried to discover an activity that each person enjoyed, and he used exercise leaders who liked people. He turned his classroom into a playground.

Conversation can be the difference between a fitness program that succeeds and one that fails. I have a friend who has a high-pressure job and has been running 2 to 3 miles a day for years. He was originally a physical education teacher and runs for a number of reasons, including fitness and relaxation, but he has never really enjoyed running. He does enjoy, however, the way running makes him feel.

Some months ago another runner moved into his neighborhood. This man is the same build as my friend. He also has the same temperament:

gregarious and outgoing. They began to run together, talking all the while. The runs soon extended to 6 and 7 miles a day. Time and distance passed unnoticed. Now they have been joined by a third runner who matches them in style, interests and pace. The trio logs mile after mile, chattering like magpies.

One physical educator began a successful jogging program for dentists using the same device. He discovered that dentists rarely get to speak to other dentists, so his plan allows for a maximum of talk. "We take a long time in the locker room getting dressed," he told me. "Then we jog out to one dentist's house and have danish and coffee. Then we jog back and take a long time getting showered and dressed."

I once spoke at a highly successful fitness clinic in the Midwest run by an outstanding exercise physiologist. Afterward, when his secretary was driving me back to the airport, she confessed that she didn't participate. There was nothing in it she liked to do, she said. I asked her what she did like. "Oh, I love to dance," she told me. "I'm always the last to leave at a dance." Yet this widely imitated clinic did not have a dance program.

"Don't serve time," said bank robber Willie Sutton. "Make time serve you." Fitness programs shouldn't be cruel or unusual punishment. The time spent getting fit should be as interesting and happy as other parts of the day.

One look at the program and I knew the President's Council on Physical Fitness and Sports was taking this meeting seriously. This one-day symposium on "Health and Fitness: The Corporate View" featured all the big guns the council could muster. They had brought in experts from all over the country. The hotel register read like a *Who's Who* in health, fitness and preventive medicine.

I was there in a nonscientific capacity. Such events tend to get too serious and even a little tedious. The participants need a little diversion. I was one diversion. George Allen, the ex-football coach, was another. The Marine Corps Band was a third. Allen was to speak at the luncheon. The band and I drew the dinner.

Allen's talk followed a morning of lectures on fitness and life expectancy, fitness and disease prevention medicine, fitness and coronary risk factors, fitness and absenteeism. The afternoon promised more of the same. The same weapons, the same ammunition, the same claims of success.

All the while I knew something was missing. This fusillade of graphs and charts and statistics, I was sure, had no more moved the audience than it had moved me. I was reminded of Napoleon's comment about the cavalry charge: "It's magnificent, but it's not war."

What we were being told had everything but relevance. There was nothing that would cause the people in board rooms to conscript their troops and ready them for battle.

I thought then of Nietzsche's statement. "Once you know 'Why,' " he said, "you will accept any 'How.' " We had yet to hear a compelling "Why," yet to be told something that would spur these executives into joining this campaign for fitness.

Then George Allen gave his speech. It was untitled, but it became immediately evident it was about winning. Allen is himself a winning coach and a winning speaker. Short declarative sentences with plenty of bite: that's the Allen style. Ideas that illuminate you and the task before you. Fifteen minutes of Allen and you can't wait for the game to start. You can't wait for adversity to begin.

He told of his experience with the Washington Redskins. "We took that over-the-hill gang," he said, "and out-conditioned every team in the league." The Redskins, old as they were, became the best fourth-quarter team in football. And they did it by following Allen's rules for becoming a winner.

None of these rules is new. They go back to the Book of Genesis. And they are as American as apple pie and mother. Allen is pure Emerson. He expresses the philosophy of people in process, reaching for perfection. So he told us nothing new, forcefully. Oh, so forcefully, he told us what we had forgotten. Again and again he came back to those pioneer virtues. Work hard. Stick together. Have the right attitude. Be positive. Improve every day. And always ask the question, "How badly do I want it?" The other teams don't beat you, said Allen. You beat yourself.

What it came down to, said Allen, was winning. For the athlete winning was the goal, the applause, a new birth, the fruit of the harvest. Winning was the best getting better. And it began and ended with conditioning. There was no substitute for physical fitness.

The band opened the dinner that night. I was to close it. The Marines contributed some stirring songs, reaching a climax with "America, the

Beautiful," and closing with hymns of the various services. Now I had to put the day in focus. I was to say something that would move these executives to action, somehow induce them to take the idea of fitness and make it a reality.

During my introduction I suddenly realized what I had to say. I put my prepared talk aside, and told them the truth. And the truth was that the best thing they had heard all day was George Allen and the Marine Corps band. They had appealed to something higher and of infinitely more value than the medical rewards offered by the experts.

Corporations are engaged in competition as fierce as any encountered in the National Football League. And there is a continual corporate Olympics vying with corporations in other countries as well. Fitness can make a company a winner. Fitness is no longer a luxury; it is a necessity.

They had heard the Gospel according to George Allen. I would merely give the exegesis. "Do you," I asked them, "have the best fourth-quarter corporation in your industry? Are you coaching, training, prodding your corporate team to do its best? Have you out-conditioned the rest of your league?

"Forget longevity, heart attacks, disease prevention, absenteeism," I told them. "They have nothing to do with fitness. Besides, what is longevity to you? Of what benefit is it to the corporation if someone lives to be eighty? And there must be dozens of employees you wish would have a mild heart attack so you could replace them. And what about absenteeism? Figures show that 90 percent of absenteeism is due to 10 percent of the work force. Pick your employees like a football coach. 'Give me men,' said Lombardi, 'not players. Players are a dime a dozen.'

"Corporations are a dime a dozen, too. Think of building a winning corporation," I urged them, "filled with people capable of increased work and more production. Employees and the company then take on the same personality. They become a single entity. Winning employees make for a winning corporation. If you would have a company with energy and enthusiasm and imagination, your employees must have the same qualities."

This was important not only to the employees and to corporations, it was important to the country. America will win this corporate international war, this conflict of energy, creativity and productivity, only if each individual employee can make that identical contribution of energy, creativity and productivity.

It ended there. The symposium was over. The band was packing up the instruments. The executives were filing out. Had they decided to take action? It did not matter. In time they would have to. Even now people are doing it on their own, seeing fitness as an obligation, a personal responsibility.

I sat there still high on Allen's words and the Marine Band's music. I was, I realized, very bullish on Americans. We are in a contest where class will tell. At that moment, I was sure we had it.

19

On Psyching

❝

Motivation,
whether it be in poetry or prizefighting,
must come from deep within.
We cannot expect to find it
in a life that is completely rational.
What we need is passion.
Passion alone enables us
to face up to and even revel in stress.

❞

IN AN ADDRESS to the American Philosophical Society, William James took as his theme "The Energies of Man." He had been musing for many years, he told his colleagues, on the phenomenon of the second wind. He had observed that there was even a third wind and a fourth wind. He saw, he said, evidence of reserves of energy that we rarely called upon.

"The plain fact remains," he said, "that men the world over possess amounts of resources that only exceptional individuals push to their extremes of use." Compared to what we ought to be, he told his fellow philosophers, we are only half-awake. We have powers of various sorts we habitually fail to use.

James's purpose that night more than 75 years ago was to consider two questions: First, to what extent do we have energies? Second, what are the keys to unlocking them?

These questions are characteristic of James. He was himself a restless, driven person. He was obsessed with the problem of the energies of man—the thoroughly American problem of how to get the most out of yourself.

America is an affluent society, and now that we have the time and money to be anything we can be, the answers to the questions propounded by James seem more important.

To what extent, then, do we have energies? The almost awesome energies posited by James in the common man are rapidly becoming visible as more and more ordinary human beings turn to distance running. Millions of people are running. Hundreds of thousands enter weekly races where the most popular distance is a previously incredible 10 kilometers. Thousands upon thousands complete the marathon and runs longer than 26 miles, 385 yards.

This is not merely a movement of men at their physiological peak. These millions include people of all ages, and between 20 and 30 percent of them are women. There seems to be no limit to the endurance of young and middle-aged and elderly men and women.

What has happened is that people have become athletes and, in so doing, have discovered previously unsuspected energies that James said were there on demand.

What are the keys to unlocking these energies? James saw that as our primary question, the problem of motivation. What is it that impels this move to be all that is possible?

"To what," James mused, "do these men owe their escape?"

158

The answer, he thought, was excitement, ideas and efforts. We must discover in the social realm something that demands incredible efforts, depth beyond depth of exertions both in degree and duration. We need something heroic that will cut across all class and economic divisions. We need incitements and passions and enthusiasms. We need to give our word of honor. Any or all of these might do.

Sport does all that. Sport motivates the athlete. It is something that demands supreme effort. It is something heroic that speaks to all, something with built-in incitements and passions and enthusiasms.

I saw the questions asked by James answered clearly on a visit I made to West Point. I was taken on a tour of the gymnasium, where I saw hundreds of cadets engaged in all sorts of sports. "There are more calories expended a day in this gym," said my escort, "than in most moderate-sized cities." Later in the captain's office I saw a motto on the wall that told the story. "Every student, an athlete. For every athlete, a challenge." Once we find our sport, we become athletes. "Those secular saints," James called them. Just as he called saints "the athletes of God." Sport provides the challenge, the impetus, the motivation. It becomes the purifying discipline.

In closing his address, James suggested that human beings be studied with reference to the different ways in which their energy reserve may be released.

Present-day philosophers and investigators of human potential might begin by stopping the next runner they see on the road. People who are tapping their deeper resources are no longer the exception. There are millions who are experiencing an escape to their high selves. Most of them are athletes. Many of them are runners.

When Peter Morgan was coaching track at Princeton, I asked him about the progress of a freshman runner I knew. "He's running well," Morgan replied, "but I'm afraid we may lose him. He's a thinker.

"When a runner gets back to the dorm, someone usually asks him, 'Why are you knocking yourself out? Why go through that torture?' If the runner is a thinker, he begins to think about that and frequently fails to come up with a good answer. Then he quits."

The young runner did quit. He had learned all about stress and how to handle it, how to condition his body, and how to minimize the bad effects. He had learned how to relax and how to recuperate. He'd been taught how much his body could take and how to recognize danger signs. The coach had taught him all that. What he did not learn, and could not be taught, was the "Why?" That had to come from himself.

We all have an inner voice asking: "Why am I trying so hard? Why am I knocking myself out?" Man is a maximizer, pursuing ease or hardship, pleasure or pain with equal intensity. We can direct all our energies into making life easy, or we can undergo the worst sufferings to achieve an ideal. We are willing to take on hand-to-hand struggle or minute-by-minute, day-by-day conflict with ourselves only if we know why we are doing it. The German philosopher Friedrich Nietzsche, as we have observed, told us that if we have a why to live, we will also find a how.

Philosopher William James addressed this topic in his speech, "What Makes a Life Significant." The answer, he said, was the marriage of an unhabitual ideal with some fidelity, courage and endurance. When that miracle occurs, we not only accept stress, we welcome it.

The poet John Berryman said much the same thing. "What happens to my poetic work in the future," he said, "will not depend upon my sitting calmly on my ass, but by my being knocked in the face and thrown flat and given all sorts of illnesses short of senile dementia." Poet Marianne Moore, speaking of former heavyweight boxing champion Floyd Patterson, said his motivation was a matter of "powerful feeling and the talent to use it."

Such motivation, whether it be in poetry or prizefighting, must come from deep within. We cannot expect to find it in a life that is completely rational. What we need is passion. Passion alone enables us to face up to and even revel in stress. What is necessary is a cause, an experience, a value, even some suffering that will enflame us, not just for a moment, but continuously.

That is another difficulty. Anyone can get fired up for a while, because most of us have ideals. We all wish, but we don't always have the desire or the ambition required to make our wishes happen. We don't really want to change the world; we'd rather go down to the corner and have a beer.

The need still exists, however, for a continuing ideal, a persistent value for which we will live, love and fight during every waking hour— some meaning for which we would be willing to die. That is the paradox.

But how do we find such motivation? How do we begin this search for meaning? One way is to face up to psychiatrist Viktor Frankl's question to the despairing patient: "Why not, then, commit suicide?"

Why don't we? Because faced with that choice we begin to see what we want. We realize that our life has meaning, that we can leave a mark, and the world will be aware that we were here.

One way to do this, as the poet Robert Frost suggested, is to achieve form. It matters little, he said, what form it is. A basket, a letter, a garden, a room, an idea, a picture, a poem would do. This is the artist's view. Inspiration followed by perspiration. Passion followed by precision.

Whatever we do must be preceded by our will to achieve; the will to search for these things and then be committed to accomplishing them.

The thinker, as Coach Morgan said, is always in danger. We athletes who tend to be thinkers, rather than doers or talkers, know that. But once we see the light, there is nothing we won't do to reach it.

If there is a race I should avoid, it is the Trevira Twosome. It comes only six days after the Boston Marathon, hardly time to recoup for a 10-miler on Central Park's toughest course—10 miles of rolling hills and a finish that is a long, steady upgrade to the Tavern on the Green. The Trevira is an hour-plus of unremitting pain—a continuous, desperate but losing effort to keep up with the flow, with little to show for it. My performance at the Trevira never reflects its cost.

Yet each year I stand there with thousands of others, waiting for the starter's gun—all of us impatient to get on with this challenge. Many of us are still hurting from Boston but oblivious to everything else in our lives, completely focused on the race ahead.

Why do we do it? What is there that brings us out week after week in cities and towns all over the country to run these races? Why do we make such demands on our bodies, endure such hardship, go through so much pain?

When Prince Charles, no stranger to arduous and even dangerous activities, was asked why people do such things, he had an answer: "I call it the banging-your-head-against-the-wall syndrome. It feels so good when you stop. But more than that, it makes you appreciate things you have always taken for granted."

The race is a superior way to bang your head against the wall. It is a contest with yourself more than others.

"A contest," writes the philosopher Paul Weiss, "demands that one complete a task. It rarely provides pleasure or fun." The primary emphasis in a distance run, says Weiss, is on struggle and self-discovery.

Three minutes into the Trevira, it is already a struggle. I am totally occupied in maintaining a speed that is just too fast for my chest and arms and legs. I am seeking some compromise between pace and pain. And all the while, I am being passed by a horde of fellow runners.

In those three minutes, I have left an effortless existence and entered one where I am pushing my life supports to the limit.

"The healthy body lives in silence," writes Alexis Carrel. "You cannot hear it, you cannot feel it. Inside deep is the whir of a 16-cylinder motor, and from deep within comes a harmony and peace."

I have left that peace and harmony. That silence has been shattered. I have become a gasping, groaning caricature of the runner who had stood quietly awaiting the gun.

The miles pass without letup. A hill comes, and the groans get louder. Everything temporarily gets worse. I feel the vicelike grip of lactic acid on my legs. My breathing, already inadequate, goes to 60 a minute, and still my whole body is screaming for more air. I am banging my head against the wall and feeling every bang.

I look at my watch. This eternity has lasted 52 minutes. I know then that it will go on for another 12 minutes or more. I have a little less than two miles of suffering left. I have done that innumerable times and know I can do it again—no matter what lies ahead.

I remember I have done it before. But I forgot how terrible it was in the doing. What I have done is only prologue. Now the attrition of those 10 miles, the fatigue and the exhaustion will be added to the pain that has gone on before.

In that last mile I am no more than an animal struggling to reach safety. I am using resources, strength and will and endurance that human beings mobilize only in life-threatening situations. I am reaching for the innermost core that is "I" and no one else—the "I" who is my truth, the isolated essence below and beneath any other "I" that I ever knew.

Somehow I reach that last quarter-mile. I come to that infamous uphill finish and I try to run faster, to pick up my pace. I am running as fast as I can, head back, arms grasping the air. The legs become stiffer and stiffer, heavier and heavier. I am stabbing at the ground. I can't hang on any longer. My body is saying no more, no more, and then I am in the chute. The race is over. The banging has ceased.

It is as Prince Charles has said. It does feel good when I stop. The pain is already subsiding. The breathing has become manageable. The warmth is coming back to my body. I have come back to what was all there at the starting line: a world and a life and friends I took for granted. No longer.

I am now, as the French say, engaged. I do not look; I see. I do not touch; I feel. I do not smell; I scent. I do not taste; I savor. The sunlight has become precious, the breeze a delight. What I was blind to, I now see plain. I know the meaning in a handshake, the treasure in a smile. Being alive has become a mystical experience.

As I lie there on the grass, I know the Kingdom of Heaven is already here.

20

On Inspiring

❝

I am increasingly aware
that I know more than I can tell.
Much of that knowledge comes from my body.
It is the body more than anything else
that contributes to my feelings of certainty,
or self-control, or self-esteem.

❞

"AT ONE TIME, one of the aims of my mind was to know how a man with a massive physique felt about the world around him," wrote Yukio Mishima in *Sun and Steel*, his psychological autobiography. "Then suddenly I was the one with the fine physique."

Mishima, the man of words, had finally become his own body. He had learned what came to be his second language, the language of the flesh.

Sun and Steel, a book Mishima called "a confidential criticism," tells how this process came about. It is a fascinating account of how a puny, bookish boy discovered the importance of his physical being.

It is also, as the book jacket points out, an attempt to relate action to art; an account of one individual's search for identity and integrity and a demonstration of how an intensely personal preoccupation can develop into a profound philosophy of life.

Mishima states that this revolutionary change occurred because of his pondering on the nature of the "I." These meditations on the self led him to the conclusion that the "I" corresponded precisely to the physical space he occupied. He saw his self as the dwelling and the body as the orchard that surrounded it. He resolved then to cultivate the orchard with sun and steel—the sun being the cult of the open air, the steel the weights used in body building.

He entered a new phase in his education. Previously he had concentrated on his genius in writing. He did not understand reality and action and the flesh. Now that had all changed. He was following the guidelines set out by the Greeks, the *paideia*. This was no less than a lifelong process of transformation. The *paideia* was not merely learning; it was the making and shaping of the man himself as a work of art.

The steel led to that transformation in Mishima. It made him a work of art.

"By its subtle, infinitely varied operation," he wrote, "the steel restored the classic balance the body had begun to lose—reinstating it in its natural form, the form it should have had all along."

Muscles seem useless and irrelevant in modern life. They are usually unnecessary from a practical point of view. Mishima admitted this. However, they gave him an entirely new kind of knowledge—a knowledge that neither books nor experience could impart.

William James, in his *Gospel of Relaxation*, thought that muscular vigor also corresponded to the spirit. It lent, he said, a background of sanity, serenity and good humor.

165

Once into his body, Mishima never looked back. He turned to fencing and then to running. Running was a mystery. "It washed away the emotions of the daily round," he reported. "Before long, my blood would not permit me a halt of even a day or two. Something ceaselessly set me to work. My body would no longer tolerate indolence but began instantly to thirst for violent action, urging me on."

His life then became what observers must have considered a frenzied obsession. "My solace," he declared, "lay solely in the small rebirths of the soul and flesh that occurred immediately after the exercise."

It was in the exercise and these rebirths that Mishima found the touchstone of the writer, the ability to translate reality into words. So he did not come back reluctantly to the world of words. These rebirths of the soul and the flesh ensured that he could return to writing joyfully and with a glad heart.

I know this to be true, as I return time and time again from my encounters with my body. When I run, my body is the Good Me. I experience it in a unique and genuine way of knowing that includes perception as well as verbalization.

Running has given me a physical intelligence, a biological wisdom. Previously I was deaf to the body's signals, blind to its illuminations. The body, I have discovered, has a mind of its own.

Other cultures have always known this. There is a Zen saying that in the dark the mind is in the fingers. There was also an Indian chief who once told Carl Jung why white men had wrinkled faces: "They think only with their heads."

I am increasingly aware that I know more than I can tell. Much of that knowledge comes from my body. It is the body more than anything else that contributes to my feelings of certainty, or self-control, or self-esteem.

When I began running, I was 160 pounds. Now I am 136 pounds, my running weight in college. I now occupy the right amount of space. I move with ease and grace and endurance.

Where Mishima became the classic weight lifter, I have become the classic distance runner. Where his body possessed certain qualities, mine possesses others. I too have seen the correspondence between the body and the spirit. But it is my body and my spirit, no other. And it is my intensely individual preoccupation with running that has developed my philosophy in life.

There are times when the all-powerful intellect is only an interpreter, and a poor one at that. It continues to seek truth as the soul seeks the good. The self desires all this and more. The fully functioning and knowing and loving self desires action and sweat and the total use of a playful body.

Mishima said it all: Become the athlete your body has to be.

"Shared suffering," wrote Yukio Mishima in *Sun and Steel*, "is the ultimate nonverbal expression." The pain we undergo with others takes us to an area where language fails and silence begins. It was just that area which Mishima sought. *Sun and Steel* is an odyssey of an artist of the word, a man of surpassing genius in verbal imagery, seeking the representation of experience in purer form. That ultimate expression he found in group pain. In that special union with others, he joined art and action.

He began by becoming an athlete. His body, he discovered, spoke a language of its own. It did not speak Japanese. Next came pain—not the vicarious pain of the writer, but the real and actual proof of consciousness that athletes undergo. And then he underwent that most difficult of conversions for an intellectual and an artist: he became a member of a group.

He came to realize that the use of strength and the ensuing fatigue, the sweat and the blood, could confer the glorious sense of being the same as the others. And so, in the final scene of this book, we see him running in the dim light of morning—one of a group, stripped to the waist in the freezing air.

"Through the common suffering," he tells us, "the shared cries of encouragement and the chorus of voices, I felt the slow emergence, like the sweat that gradually beaded my skin, of the affirmation of identity, of nobility, of being united in seeking death and glory."

Every athlete might not put it quite so dramatically, but athletes know that what Mishima writes is true. My own life as a runner has duplicated his personal journey—first becoming an athlete, then feeling the pain and finally reaching the race. I came to running and became my body. I took to the roads and felt pain. Then I went into the race and knew that here was something unlike any other relationship I had ever had.

Mishima saw that. The group, he contended, has a special language. "Whether it is written down on paper or shouted aloud," he writes, "the

167

language of the group resolves itself into physical expression." This is not the speech of the solitary artist. Mishima the writer knew that. "This is not a language," he says, "for transmitting private messages from the solitude of one's closed room to the solitude of another distant closed room."

The group is concerned with all those things that could never emerge in words: sweat and tears, joy and pain.

"Verbal expression can convey pleasure or grief; it cannot convey pain," writes Mishima. "Only bodies placed under the same circumstances can experience a common suffering."

Unamuno, the Spanish philosopher, makes the same point: "We are united by pity, not by pleasure. We love only those with whom we share suffering." There can be no love without pain.

All of that is felt during the race. And at the finish words again fail us. It is the race itself that is our language. The running is the word made flesh. The group and the suffering speak within each of us. We have been united in a way words can never accomplish.

Each runner in a race contributes suffering and pain and previously unknown energies to a common cause. The race unites the one and the many. It illuminates the paradox of remaining an individual yet identifying with a group.

"I belonged to them," he writes, "they belonged to me; the two formed an unmistakable 'us.' " It was the beginning, he notes, of his placing reliance on others—a reliance that was mutual.

In the race, I feel this same belonging, develop this same trust, come to this same faith. So the race becomes for me what running that morning was for Mishima: "A bridge that once crossed left no means for return."

After I became interested in Yukio Mishima's *Sun and Steel,* a friend questioned me about it.

"I don't know how you can read Mishima," she said. "He was obsessed with death."

She was absolutely right. Mishima was so preoccupied with death that he described life as a rehearsal for his death. *Sun and Steel* makes that evident. In a real sense, this book is a suicide note. In November 1970, the year it was published, Mishima committed *seppuku*—ritual suicide.

To Mishima, the process of becoming his total self, his own perfection, meant becoming uncompromisingly and unendingly the person he conceived himself to be. Mishima was one of those people we regard with amazement. They do not have views; they are views. They do not have opinions; they live them. They do not write about theories; they make them realities. They do not talk about myths; they act them out. They are the heroes.

Mishima was a hero. This does not mean that he was right or rational or to be commended for what he did. It does mean that he lived what he believed. In the course of that life, he did things that were childish and foolish and, from our point of view, incomprehensible. All his decisions and judgments came from inside himself. He was interested in nothing but the ideal life that he had set in front of himself.

Like most heroes, Mishima imposed his will on reality. And further, he saw his will as the will of the universe. He became body-mind-soul the creature he believed his Creator had in mind the day he was born.

No matter how illogical and irrational it may seem to praise this man's book, *Sun and Steel* is filled with wisdom and common sense. Mishima was much like a person with paranoia. Aside from his single delusion, his life was completely sane. Aside from his obsession, his book reads as a text on how to become and develop and love your self. He expressed this union of mind and spirit as few had done before him.

One reason for this is that he came upon the body from another culture. He saw its perfection in much the same way a man blind from birth suddenly sees the world. *Sun and Steel* is no ordinary book on the role of the body in this life, not just another volume of the effect of sport and play on man. It is a testimony by the most ardent of lovers, the truest of believers, the convert who came last to the faith.

I have come to accept Mishima's truth. His "steel" is my running. His discovery of the body parallels my own. Where he translated his intensely individual interest into a philosophy of death, I have been able to translate mine into a philosophy of life.

Mishima modeled his life on a great myth, not a petty success story. He lived the questions and did not wait for answers. He showed the tremendous intensity and enthusiasm we need, and how large a canvas we must use, if life is to take on meaning.

21

On Thinking

"

The athletic life is as mental as it is physical.
Training becomes so automatic
that the mind is free to do whatever it pleases.
The muscles need no conscious direction,
so the mind can occupy center stage.

"

I RECEIVED A PHONE CALL from a man whose son was in trouble in college. This young man had written an essay on "Positive Addiction" describing his experiences as an oarsman on the freshman crew. From what I could see, it was something I had read many times: a recounting of the conversion phenomenon which so many people go through in becoming athletes.

Unfortunately, his professor was unaware of this universal human reaction. He happened to read William Glasser's *Positive Addiction* and assumed that the student had cribbed his theme and material from this book—a book, incidentally, that was written by runners as much as by Glasser. Glasser solicited personal testimony of the running experience from readers of *Runner's World*, and the book was the outcome of those letters. The student says he never read the book. I believe him.

Here, in effect, was simply another contribution to that book. Rather than being inspired by the book, it was very like one of those personal stories from which it was made. The new insight, new life, new sense of self that this freshman presented in his essay were indubitably his own.

I recall in school that the use of the word "I" was discouraged. The personal was too trivial to consider. If one is to be educated, that education must be left to the experts. We were not allowed to live out our own lives or, even more, to consider them important. The common man, despite the influence of Emerson and Thoreau and James, was considered a cipher.

What I see in the indictment of this oarsman is the continuation of that attitude. I would suggest to this professor that he reread his Emerson about the common man. Emerson writes, "What Plato thought, he can think. What the saint felt, he can feel. What happened to any man, he can understand." And then again, "The philosopher spends his life putting into words what the common man experiences."

Long ago, I called a five-mile run "a trip" and suggested it was an addiction, a fix if you would. Long before Glasser, I read a speech by Edwin Land, the inventor of the Polaroid camera, saying that we are all addicts of something. What we need, said Land, are constructive addictions, not destructive ones. That was my first contact with the idea of positive addiction, and I wrote about it in my column six or seven years ago.

All runners have known this addiction, and many of them have tried to put it in much the same words. Any editor of a running magazine can tell you of being deluged by stories which their writers presume to be original, but which are almost the same.

There are only a few truths, a few themes. There is so little to write about. The even greater truth is that these truths occur to everyone and that there are those of us who burn to write them just as if we were geniuses.

I doubt my gift for writing. To further limit any loss of self-esteem, I rarely read live writers. I look on them as competition. I do not want to be derivative. Yet I find myself taking the same theme and frequently using the same words. How can this be?

One answer would be the inadequacy of language. No two individuals, no two experiences, are exactly alike. Yet we cannot express that uniqueness without also expressing its similarity to something else. We cannot make it stand alone. If this young man failed in his essay, it is because everyone fails. No one can tell us exactly why it is different for him. Therefore, in the telling, he tells us what we have ourselves experienced but have never been able to say either. So it lies there between us, almost right but not quite, almost true but not quite.

For those outside the experience, the whole thing is a mystery. Not knowing the truth, they cannot see what went on inside the person and cannot know—however stereotyped the presentation—that it is as true and accurate as one's genius permits.

The athletic experience will be forever a mystery to those who have forgotten their childhood and never again suspect that the good life has its roots in the perfection of the human body.

Train your brain and your body at the same time.

This is not a new idea. It goes back to the original philosophers in Greece who found their best thoughts while walking and thereby attending to their physical fitness. One reads of this phenomenon again and again in the journals of the great thinkers and writers and artists. They were often great walkers as well.

Not only can one train the body while one is using the mind; the mind actually works better when the body is in motion. Take 90 minutes a day, and use half of it or more for a walk or a run or a cycle or a swim. Then come back and put the products of your brain's activity on paper or on canvas or into some new appreciation of your life.

In the beginning, both body and mind will balk. When that happens,

172

force the mind back time and again to consider the subject in question. Whatever you have decided to meditate on before you leave the house, require the brain to consider it. The brain is tireless. Do not let it con you into relaxing your demands. Push it to the limit.

The body, too, will say, "That's enough for today." In the beginning, as with the brain, it will want its own way. Don't give in. Make the effort comfortable as possible, but don't stop or turn back. Each day, ask a little more. In a short time, your work capacity can increase as much as 400 percent.

First develop the capabilities for greater physical and mental effort, then decide what to do with them.

It was late in the question-and-answer period I usually conduct after my lectures when a man stood up and asked, "What do you think about when you are running?"

I liked the question; it made me think. Most questions are routine. They generate routine answers. They stimulate a reflex arc in my brain and produce an automatic response. Partly this is my fault. Every question has something novel about it. There are an infinite variety of people in an infinite variety of situations. The good teacher—and questions are a good teaching device—should always be alert to the lesson in each one of them.

This question broke new ground. I had never before systematized what went on in my mind when I ran. Yet the athletic life is as mental as it is physical. Training becomes so automatic that the mind is free to do whatever it pleases. The muscles need no conscious direction, so the mind can occupy center stage.

How, then, to use this hour of thought? The question opens up the full range of the mind's activities. I can, should I want to, utilize any of the special skills the mind has. For this hour, I can train my mind to perform new feats as I simultaneously bring my body to a higher level of function.

As he stood there, my mind was leaping to categories. I realized my thinking had become mundane. With all the possibilities out there, I had largely limited myself to two basic uses of that training during my 10-mile runs. With rare exceptions, my runs involve either free association or are focused on one subject, one problem that I would like to solve before I get back to home base.

173

The exceptions are the days when my goal is complete absence of thought and all external and internal stimuli are gradually removed from consciousness. Motion becomes my mantra. Through it I gradually divest myself of worry and anger, of fear and depression—and the reasons for them. I can reach a state when time is this never-ending moment and where this place is the entire world. This is the passive meditation of the East. The Self subsumed in the Whole.

There is another type of meditation which is active, involving fantasy and imagination. Psychiatrists sometimes recommend it. When you thrust yourself into such a prescribed setting, the ensuing feelings and events help to reveal your psychological problems.

I never practice it. I have poor visual memory, and only with difficulty can I conjure up the undulating green meadows, the landscapes and vistas that are recommended. I prefer to deal with the thoughts and ideas and concepts that come, invited or not, into my mind.

In fact, that may be the best answer to the question of what I think about when I run: simply whatever pops into my brain. I suit up, go out on the run, and there I meet these unexpected ideas and new insights. The old wine in new bottles. It is all unpremeditated. I know this happens with other runners.

Dr. Thomas Tutko, the sports psychologist, speaks of the same experience. "I can't wait to get out on the roads," he says, "to find out what I'm going to think about." It is all as unplanned, as undirected and as unexpected as that.

I have days when that is true. I come upon an interesting topic and explore it for a while. The hour becomes a stream of consciousness, with one tenuously related idea following another. One thought will suggest the next, and as the association goes on, words and people and events are coupled like so many freight trains, each from different railroad lines and different parts of the country.

Then there are days when I discipline my mind to concentrate on one particular theme. My mind still tends, as it does on other days, to go romping off following other leads. But I bring it back as I would a bird dog who wanted to play instead of hunt. And so the hour passes as I focus this 10-billion cell computer in my skull on the problem at hand.

Mental training can be as exciting and varied as physical training. Both are an act of discovery.

22

On Creating

"

If the opera is loud
and unintelligible and interminable,
get up and leave.
Your art is not there.

"

In my early teens I was taken by my aunt, a music teacher, to a performance of *Aida*. The evening was interminable. Opera, I discovered, was a long, loud and unintelligible bore. I could not wait for it to end so we could head home.

In subsequent exposure to capital "A" Art in other forms, I have had the same reaction. I do not have any grasp or appreciation of what constitutes culture. This is not from lack of trying. I have gone to the Whitney and the Guggenheim museums, sat through concerts at Carnegie Hall, and attended the ballet at Lincoln Center. For all that was happening to my mind and emotions, I might just as well have been riding the subway.

This intimidation by Art disappeared when I became an athlete. I lost the inferiority I felt in the presence of Art, the opera and classical music, painting or the dance. I had discovered the true art, the art of living.

This realization came with a reversal of my role of accepting other people's opinions to one of living my own. The development of the self which occurs with physical training led to that self-expression which I came to recognize as art.

Each one of us is animal, artist, hero, saint. In each of those aspects we have certain abilities and certain disabilities. I knew almost from the first that I would never be the heavyweight boxing champion of the world. What I did not know was that a symphony would never be more to me than a series of pleasant or unpleasant sounds. Nor did I realize that music appreciation was of consequence only to those who appreciated music. I could live long and well and artistically without it.

We have what E. F. Schumaker called "adequatio" for certain mental processes. We are born with them or without them. The knowledge and acceptance of such unchangeable qualities in our makeup can free us to get on with our true vocation, and to such avocations as contribute to the personality that is potential in each of us.

Emerson, my best friend, put me straight in this. "Each individual soul is such," he said, "in virtue of its being able to transform the world into some particular language of its own—if not into a picture or statue or a dance, then into a trade, an art, a science, a mode of living, a character, an influence."

Being an artist is simply discovering the self and then expressing that self in self-chosen terms. Running opened up to me that self and that expression. I found my language. I expressed myself through my body and what I wrote and what I did. No matter that Art is still as unintelligible to me as Chinese.

There is, I now see, an art to everything. There is an art of medicine, an art of selling, an art of child raising. James describes well the art of teaching. It is, he said, the interposition of an imaginative mind between a fact and a pupil. So it is with any art in life.

In a humane society, said Santayana, everything is art. Manners, clothes, politics, conversation. We go around all day being artists if we would but know it. It is difficult at first to see that all my life is an art. Yet every time I read the great thinkers I find this said again and again.

We must express what Emerson called our particular genius. My experiences in both my conscious and subconscious mind are translated into my own individual language. Does this seem too ordinary, too commonplace to be art? Not so. I am now aware of what Ortega called "the wonders of the simple unhaloed hour." I see life face to face and deal with it. I try to put my stamp on every minute and hour and day I live.

So I let my upwardly mobile friends acquire culture and attend the Arts. For those with the "adequatio" to understand and appreciate what they hear and see, this is both a privilege and pleasure. For others it is a waste of time and even a life. They should be in pursuit of their own art and become masters of it.

If the opera is loud and unintelligible and interminable, get up and leave. Your art is not there.

The day eventually dawns when the fact of your age also dawns on you. You discover you are getting old. Physically certainly, creatively to a degree, and mentally quite perceptibly you are going downhill. "Can it be," you ask yourself, "that I have already lived?"

The age varies. Maybe thirty for the fortunate ones. Fifty for most. For Arnold Bennett it was forty. For John Stuart Mill it was twenty-one. But sooner or later we put to ourselves the old questions concerning the intrinsic value of life. What have I got out of it? What am I likely to get out of it? What's it worth?

The urgency for answers increases when you get older. For the first time you see death approaching. The dying and its attendant urgency make the answer easier. Once dying is accepted, you see the overwhelming importance of each day, the futility of living in the past, the absurdity of living in the future. Living now is life itself.

Countless philosophers grasped that truth, reminding us again and again that we must perceive the folly of neglecting to savor the present, the folly of assuming the future will be any different from the present, the fatuity of dying before we have begun to live.

This does not preclude change. It presupposes it. If this is to be our last day on earth imagine how you would spend it. Yet each day could be that final day—or even the hereafter. "Today," said Lewis Mumford, "may be a fair sample of eternity."

No matter how many philosophers have instructed us in how this day should be spent, each person must test it for himself; each person must be a philosopher. We have a protective and profound egoism that prevents us from accepting ready-made answers. What is it to us what Plato thought unless it agrees with our own experience?

We need not read Plato to realize how little we are doing with our potential. What limited ideas we have about our physical and creative and mental capabilities. How little we accomplish with the marvelous powers we have.

So the first use of this sensation of aging is to break with the past. Life must be a process, a continual movement in word and in thought, the expression of our particular genius. That death lies at the end should not deter us; it should lend impetus.

Some see this process as tragedy. André Malraux wrote that it takes sixty years of incredible effort to make an individual and then he is good only for dying. The late Ernest Becker states this dilemma even more precisely. "A person spends years coming into his own," he wrote, "developing his talent, his unique gifts, perfecting his discrimination, broadening and sharpening his appetite, learning to bear the disappointments of life, becoming mature and seasoned—finally a unique creature in nature standing with some dignity and nobility and transcending the human condition; no longer driven, no longer a complete reflex, not stamped out of any mold . . . and then has to go the way of the grasshopper."

Age as they describe it is the culmination of life. In these observations I do not see tragedy, but hope; not an end, but a goal; not discouragement, but incentive. When we feel aged we are receiving the word not about what we are doing right but what we are doing wrong. We need not, indeed we should not, and will not deteriorate physically and mentally and creatively. We should, as these writers have written, grow in wisdom and will and character. Every day I live can add to the person I am. It is my duty to make that happen.

"You learn to use everything that happened in your life, in creating the character you're working on," said Marlon Brando speaking about acting. "You learn to dip into your unconsciousness and make use of every experience you ever had."

I can find no better description of art and creativity. When my life is the work of art, I am creating a character—myself. And I am doing it out of everything I have ever experienced. I am dredging into my unconscious, bringing up everything down to the seaweed.

I am not a motor genius or a mental genius or a creative genius. I am not a spiritual genius. Yet I have what Emerson called my peculiar genius, my personality, which is the sum of those attributes. And no less than Marlon Brando or Picasso or Nureyev or any athlete; artist, hero, saint, I can fulfill that genius. I can become a character and create the self that I am.

Such creativity, says Bill Moyers, who has made a study of the subject, demands that one remain a perpetual child. What creativity demands, it seems to me, is that we have passion. Not a specific passion. Not some great enthusiasm for a certain subject but an undifferentiated passion that is there when we rise and is still with us when we retire at night.

A passion for life itself.

Anyone can have it. One need not be a member of Mensa or a graduate of Juilliard or the schools that train people in the arts. Nor is the eventual expression of that passion important. Once passion is there, the way a person does a thing becomes much more important than what is being done.

Passion itself it not enough. We are also, as Brando says, our experience. The expression of this passion will be limited to this storage-and-retrieval system in our conscious and subconscious minds. It is imperative, therefore, that we learn to see the good in everything that happens. We are our experiences. We are also in an even more important way our interpretation of those experiences.

There are no bad experiences, if you have a sense of humor. If you can see through to the actual meaning and import of an event. Humor acknowledges no logic. Humor knows that life is a problem which admits of no solution.

Nevertheless, we must act as if one did exist. We take this reality, interpose our peculiar genius, and produce our own art. My art is running. It is also writing these essays. But primarily it is the making of my character. I am creating the person I am, just as surely as Marlon Brando creates a person on the stage or in a film.

A good friend wrote me about a seventy-year-old named Lou who was once a professional ballroom dancer. Lou runs all day in a park in Miami trying to become his ideal physical self. Running is Lou's answer to the ever-present opposites of life and death. He is building himself a character, the invisible and permanent profile or marking of himself which can never die.

23

On Competing

"

. . . human nature abhors equilibrium.
There is nothing more boring
than ease and routine.
We cannot stand for long
the slow succession of uneventful days.
We are never quite content with the status quo.
It is nature that aims to achieve stability,
nature that constantly seeks homeostasis.
But human beings will not let things rest.
We must be in motion.

"

FIVE MINUTES BEFORE the Fourth of July 10-Kilometer Pepsi Challenge Race the loudspeakers began to pour out "Rocky's Theme." There was a noticeable increase in movement on the plaza of the George Washington Bridge. Thousands of runners began walking and jogging to the starting line. The race was only moments away. The next half-hour for some, an hour for others, would be what the Greeks called the *agon*, the struggle. Johan Huizinga in his book *Homo Ludens* described it as play. We runners know better. We call it sport.

"The occasion," said Huizinga, "is sacred or festive." Today it was both. We were celebrating a secular feast. It was a day of holiday and history. A day that said all men were equal and all men were free. And we were putting the seal on it by freely taking an oath on the race that was to follow. Giving our word of honor to do our best.

There was a brief silence. Then the anthem. And now we were ready for what was to come. "It is an activity," Huizinga went on, "which proceeds within certain limits of time and place, in a visible order according to rules freely accepted and outside the sphere of necessity and material utility."

We were to proceed for 10 kilometers (about 6 1/4 miles) over the bridge into Manhattan and end up at Baker Field, an athletic facility of Columbia University. We knew the rules and accepted them. Runners are a law-abiding lot. But in the race we accept rules that are generally unenforceable. Cheating is not merely unethical, it is unintelligible. It destroys both the runner and the race.

One reason for this obedience is time. Time matters as much as space. Indeed, the real enemy is the digital clock at the finish line. That clock is the closure, the end, the judgment. And it has, as you can see, no relation to necessity or utility.

In those last moments I can feel the electricity in the crowd. There is a continual stirring. An excitement that leaps from one runner to another. "The mood," wrote Huizinga, "is one of rapture and enthusiasm." I feel that mood fill me. "Enthusiasm" is a strong word for strong feelings. I have them. Passion and daring and commitment to what is ahead. And rapture. I am seized by the whole event. The rest of the world falls away. Up until now I have felt reluctant to suffer, but now that is set aside. I cannot wait for that suffering to get underway.

The gun sounds, and we stream down an incline and spill out onto the bridge. The Hudson is on either side and in front Manhattan and the entire span empty of everything except runners. I am running the first mile too fast as I always do. I am filled with the exultation that Huizinga said accompanied the action. I am carried away by the race and the day and those around me. I feel larger than life and capable of anything.

A brief six minutes and the feeling is over. From now on another emotion identified by Huizinga will dominate—tension. Uncertainty about myself and the outcome will fill the rest of the race. I am in control, yet I am not in control. What will I face and will I be able to face it? I'll be running with that question from here to the end.

We come off the bridge and run upriver past The Cloisters. The going is fairly easy until a steep half-mile hill leading to the toll booths on the Henry Hudson Bridge, the turnaround point. That hill is my moment of truth. I am paying for the fast pace on the first mile. I hold nothing back, but my pace gets slower and slower. People are passing me, and my thighs can take no more pain. This is the race right here.

The top finally comes and then the long merciful downhill. Now I am passing those who passed me going up. I am feeling better than at any other time since the start. The race, I suddenly realize, is mine.

And that was the way it was through the finish. The digital clock read 38:38, my best time of the year. Others had done personal bests also. Baker Field was filled with happy runners in groups talking about the race and how it had been run. All around me it was as Huizinga described it. "Mirth and relaxation follow," he said.

Eventually we went to a small Irish bar a block or so away and sat drinking beer and telling each other what wonderful people we were. Not, of course, in words but with our eyes and our gestures and that bearing that comes with running the best you can on the Fourth of July.

I had discovered what every runner looks for. A race with a small field, a flat course and trophies in my age group. It was a Sunday event in a little seacoast town with less than 200 entrants and only a handful in the fifty-and-over group.

Then I saw him. He was already waiting at the starting line stripped to the waist, wearing a digital stopwatch and the telltale 500 number. He was lean and muscular and built for endurance. And not a gray hair on his head. I had found a race and gotten myself a tiger.

I knew then it would be no different from every other Sunday. The stage was set for the usual drama. Age-group racing does that. The confrontation with runners my own age makes every race a race within a race, a play within a play. Every race is a stage, and I become one of the actors.

The race is always a race against the clock. It is also a race for the best place in the multitude that faces the starter's gun. But when there is a prize for people of my vintage the race becomes pure Elizabethan drama.

In Greek drama it is man against the superhuman. The tragedy results when the hero or heroine sins against the gods. Our current theater is man against the world. The individual interests against the common good. The question is, Which is the stronger, the one standing alone or the one who gives to others? But the Elizabethan drama is man against himself. The plot unfolds and is determined by the flaws and faults of the protagonist. The ambition of Macbeth, the irresoluteness of Hamlet, the jealousy of Othello, make the play.

In the next 30 minutes or so this bare-chested, well-trained competent fifty-year-old runner was going to test me. He was going to search out the flaws in my character. He and I were about to produce, write and act out our own drama. It would be, as George Santayana wrote of athletics, a physical drama, in which all moral and emotional interests are involved. "The soul is stirred," he said, "in this spectacle that represents the basis of its whole life."

You might wonder why at my age I do these things. I could easily have been at the beach or sitting over a late breakfast reading *The New York Times*. I could have been enjoying this summer Sunday like millions of others in this land. But no, here I am with but moments to the start, tying my shoes for the third time, taking the last ounces of my cola, exchanging greetings with those around me.

I have left behind the self and the equilibrium I have established over the years. I have come to the uncertainty and tension and the possibility of disaster that this race represents. I have put myself in a most difficult and trying situation when I could be peaceful and content at home.

Why do I feel this compulsion? Mainly, I believe, because human nature abhors equilibrium. There is nothing more boring than ease and routine. We cannot stand for long the slow succession of uneventful days. We are never quite content with the status quo. It is nature that aims to achieve stability, nature that constantly seeks homeostasis. But human beings will not let things rest. We must be in motion.

184

So I take this hard-won equilibrium, this self that I have made, and then establish a vacuum of deeds not yet done, achievements not yet mine. I say nay to all that has gone before, and I come to the race. I impose another test, another trial, another challenge to be experienced before I can claim to be me.

The playwrights know this sequence well. The equilibrium is first destroyed. Then there are moves and countermoves. There is the clash of wills. The issue is joined. The inevitable then occurs. The flaws of the individual are revealed. And they determine the outcome.

When the equilibrium is restored, what must be done has been done. The play comes full circle revealing what has always been potential in the situation and the people in it. Replay the drama and it comes out the same. Rerun the race and it does also. Only the growth and development of the characters can change it.

There were by now only seconds to go. I stood just behind my rival waiting for the curtain to go up on our private struggle. The gun went off. The play had begun.

When the gun sounded we went off as if tied together. Two fifty-and-over runners oblivious of the rest of the field. What was now of importance in this six-mile race in a little seacoast town would occur between us. The moves and countermoves, the clash of wills which would mark this drama, would be our moves and countermoves, and our personal clash of wills. The exposition, the confrontation, the climax and the denouement would all occur in the less than five yards that would separate us for the entire race. And the new equilibrium we would find at the finish line would come from who we truly were.

The race does what every good drama does. It tells the truth. Each move, each event, is an actual happening. And everything that happens has an effect on everything else. In race as in drama there is no unimportant information. From gun to finish line my every action would reveal the inner man who prompted it.

The stranger who was my opponent and rival would also be colleague and friend. Together we would write and act out this drama. Together we would explore this new experience. Together we would gain a new appreciation of ourselves. Together we would make this struggle an image of our inner struggle to make sense out of our lives.

We went through the first mile in six minutes. The exposition was already taking place. His best pace was my best pace. The issue was now joined. He made the next move. A slight acceleration in pace. He was using the classical strategy in the confrontation between my speed and his endurance. He was trying to break away from me or at the least take the sting out of my kick at the finish.

My tactic was simple. Sit in behind. Let him do the work. Take him at the end. His had become equally simple. Increase the pace until I let him go. The pressure of this speed eventually became unbearable, so I took the lead in an attempt to slow it down. He would have none of that and immediately went out in front once more.

And so went those first few miles. It had become a matter of the body and the will. Emotion can help, but reason is useless. After the first rush the race is a matter of character and talent. One runner rarely out-thinks another. The runner knows what must be done and then musters the courage to do it.

He knew his role; I knew mine. His, a continued striving to leave me behind. Mine, a persistent refusal to allow that to happen. So on I went, the arms getting heavy, the chest desperate for air, the legs now filling with pain. He was calling on his body for even more effort, and I attached to his right shoulder and was paying the price.

This was the perennial struggle between human wills and within individual human wills now seen plain. We had gone through the exposition and the confrontation. Now we were in the last mile. He still led with me a step behind. Neither of us would give an inch. We matched stride for stride. I was running on virtues and values I never knew I had. I just would not give up. Nor would he.

I was now no longer merely racing against him. I was racing against me at my best. That was what he had come to represent. He was my alter ego. The best possible me. And only my best effort would beat him. He was in a similar predicament. He had not been able to shake me. I was still there off his right shoulder as I had been almost from the beginning. It was a signal to do more or less.

We made a turn then, and far down the road I could see the banner over the finish line. My friend mustered his final challenge. His pace went up a notch or two. Mine did also. And we came down that last stretch head to head, chest to chest, like a team of matched horses.

By now he was flat out and so was I. With less than a hundred yards to go we were still neck and neck. When I thought of that later I realized we had both won. We had done what had been asked of us and surpassed ourselves in the doing. This tense struggle of wills and bodies had told us truly who we were.

What happened after that was anticlimactic. With 50 yards to go I pulled the trigger and surged forward. I was running on muscle fibers I had not used and he did not have. Pain and exhaustion and shortness of breath were no longer deterrents. He was no match for this madness. So I won the 50-and-over.

I had beaten him but it really didn't matter. Seconds later we were shaking hands and congratulating each other. We stood there happy and content and more than a little proud. We had made the theoretical fact that we were born to be heroes a reality.

24

On Rewarding

"
The trophy announces
the completeness of the event.
It is the final act that isolates,
encloses and memorializes the race just run.
It need not be something
you can see or feel or place on your mantel. . . .
But there should be *something*
that makes the contest a matter of record.
"

THE NEXT DAY, people kept asking me how I had done. At first, I answered that I didn't finish. Then I began saying that I *couldn't* finish. What I should have said was, "I hit the wall." I should have told them right off that I hit it. Then they might have understood.

In any case, that is what happened. In this 1980 Boston Marathon, I finally hit the wall. After years of reading about it, hearing about it, lecturing about it, I had totally and irrevocably hit the wall. After seventeen years of successful Bostons, I failed to finish. I reached the Prudential in a trolley, not on foot.

Just past the 21-mile mark, coming down the hill at Boston College, I knew I was finished. There had been, however, a hint of disaster all day. I had come to Boston on the strength of my best-ever marathon and was attempting to duplicate it—a dangerous thing to do at any time but particularly with the temperature in the 70s. There was a cloudless sky, so the sun was contributing another 10 to 20 degrees. The following wind virtually eliminated heat dissipation by air conduction.

On such a day, initial pace is of paramount importance. When there is excessive heat stress, speed increases dehydration, elevates body temperature, and, of prime importance, rapidly uses up the muscle-glycogen stores. On such a day, I should have been thinking of running 30 seconds a mile slower than my usual time. Instead I was thinking of running 30 seconds a mile *faster*. I had always prided myself on prudence in such circumstances, but like many other runners I was already thinking about qualifying for next year. Instead of running according to our bodies, we ran against the clock. It was the most competitive Boston Marathon I ever ran.

At around the 15-mile mark in Newton Lower Falls, I began to feel uneasy about the outcome. The long downhill there was much more difficult than in other years. Then, on the upgrade, I discovered I was losing the drive in my legs. There was no bounce. I had no lift. I could hear my foot strike, a sure sign of losing form and coordination. I was like a pitcher who had found there was no steam on his fastball. I was in trouble.

Nonetheless, I negotiated the Newton hills and got past Heartbreak without too much additional difficulty. It was on the long descent past the crowds at Boston College that I began to come apart. My pace slowed until I was running in slow motion. My arms were moving more than my legs. All the way to the foot of the hill, I ran—rather, moved in a grotesque caricature of running—all the while hoping that I would be all right once I got on the flat and could run again.

Going downhill at that point is always bad. The front thigh muscles always protest. Each step becomes extremely painful. I had gone through that before and then recovered to run well to the finish, so I hoped that would happen again when I finally reached the bottom.

"Now," I said to myself, "it will be better." But it wasn't. If anything, it was worse. The pain was still there, and now an overwhelming weariness. The muscles had become lifeless. They had lost not only power and coordination but shock-absorption as well. Every step not only hurt my thighs but was doing terrible things to my knees.

Nevertheless, I persisted. With each step my pace became slower, but I refused to walk. There was simply no question of walking. No matter what happens, I told myself, I will not walk. I had never walked in Boston, and there would be no first time.

I could hear the crowd encouraging me. Some called out, "Looking good." Others yelled, "You can make it." The more perceptive shouted, "Tough it out," and "Hang in there." Now and then, I would hear what seemed to be the rallying cry for this year's run, "Go for it."

It was going for it that had gotten me into this state. Had I run prudently during the first half, I would now be taking it in, running my body and heart out but finishing. Now I was reduced to this private little hell, my eyes fixed on my shadow in front of me, watching this pantomime. I was apparently running but actually not. I was moving up and down, but not forward. I was virtually running in place. And all the while, I was losing any sense of the crowd and the race and where I was. My life became that one thought: keep running.

Then I felt a hand and looked up. There was a friend beside me. She was watching the race and seeing me in this state, she had rushed out.

"Don't you want to walk, George?" she asked. She was a mother talking to a child. By now she had her arm around me, holding me up. I was still running, and there she was standing there holding me up. I was no longer moving forward, but I was not going to walk.

"George, don't you want to walk?" she asked again. She had come out of the crowd to save me from myself. I looked at her standing there, her face full of sympathy and care and love. I knew it was the end.

"Nina," I said, "all I want is someone to take me home."

Then a trolley appeared as if she had summoned it, and she got me on it. When I boarded it, the twenty or so people inside sent up a cheer. That upset me at first.

"Why cheer me?" I asked them. "I didn't even finish."

It apparently didn't matter. Someone came up and offered me orange juice, and someone else gave me his seat. So I rode to the Prudential, beginning to feel good about the whole thing.

The wall, I thought, can be a peak experience.

The awards ceremony was drawing to a close. My partner, Althea, and I were standing just below the officials' box, pressed against the rope controlling the crowd. Peter Roth of the New York Road Runners Club was about to announce the winners of the 120-and-over division of the Trevira Twosome.

The Trevira was then only in its second year, but it had already caught the imagination of runners. Pairing male and female runners, and grouping them according to aggregate age, adds interest and enthusiasm for everyone in the race. Some runners even bypass the Boston Marathon to run the Trevira a week later. The field totals more than 3,000.

I had sought Althea out after seeing her run a fine 10-kilometer in Bermuda and come back the following day with a respectable marathon. Most important, she was 63; we had become the team to beat in our age group. Now we were waiting to see if we had done it.

We must have won, I thought. It had been a tough race. Running 10 miles only a week after Boston had to be tough. I had been walking downstairs backward until two days earlier, but in this race the old moves had come back. My time had been good, too. I had shaved my pre-race estimate of 64 minutes by a few seconds.

Then it had been a matter of waiting for Althea. She had predicted a time of 1:18, and I knew I could set my watch on that. Althea runs like a metronome. A few seconds past 1:18 on the digital clock, I saw her enter the chute. She is a little over medium height, quite thin, with straight gray hair and features that remind me of Amelia Earhart. That moment, Althea looked like a very competent runner.

The ceremonies began more than an hour later. By that time, most of the thousands of runners and spectators had departed. But several hundred waited in the rain for the awards. Here and there were umbrellas,

191

and most of the winners sought refuge under an awning suspended from the Road Runners' van.

Applause went up for the overall winners: Herb Lindsay and Margaret Groos. Both had set American road records for 10 miles. They had beaten the team of Frank Shorter and Joan Benoit. Althea and I were in distinguished company.

More categories were announced. The various winners went up to receive boxes containing huge silver bowls and then departed, taking their friends with them. The rain continued to fall intermittently. The skies gradually became darker. Officials began taking down the finishing chute. The starting-line banner went next. Then the other banners disappeared.

During a lull, a man who appeared to be my age asked what our team's elapsed time had been. I told him.

"We beat you," he said. "I ran 67 minutes, and my wife ran 72."

All that waiting, I thought, and we were only runners-up.

The computer had to dig deep to get winners in the higher age-groups. Peter Roth apologized for the delay. More people left. Then he called out the 100-and-over winner—the husband-and-wife team. I had worried needlessly. I had forgotten to ask how old he was. Althea and I were sure winners in the 120-plus group.

By now there was no one left but Althea and me, her husband and three friends waiting to take me for a beer. There was no evidence left of the run. Central Park Drive was empty. Even the officials' box was empty. Peter Roth had gone to the van to get the final results.

Then the door of the van opened and Peter came out, paper in hand. He strode to the stand, mounted it and faced the nonexistent crowd.

"I want you to hold it down," he shouted. Then he proceeded as if all 3,000 runners were there. He raised his hand, gesturing for order.

"Further," he said, "there will be no storming this stand to congratulate the winners. I'm sure they can give you time afterward. In the 120-and-over category, from Huntington Station, Long Island, Althea Wetherbee, and her partner, from Red Bank, New Jersey, George Sheehan. Their elapsed time: 2 hours, 22 minutes and 2 seconds."

Althea and I climbed onto the box and faced out, seeing the faces of people we had run with, reliving the joy we had felt crossing the finish line—and feeling, too, joy in this marvelous charade.

Peter asked us to say a few words to the multitude, which we did, and then finally he gave us our boxes. They were empty. It was the final twist. Both Althea and I broke up. Everyone was laughing as if laughter had just been discovered.

When we made our way down the steps, two officials who had stayed through the whole ceremony came over. They were wearing Trevira sweatshirts. One took his off and give it to Althea, and the other took his off and gave it to me. Then he went into the van, came out with two New York Marathon slickers, and gave one to each of us. The winners of the 120-and-over division of the Trevira Twosome departed in style, the cheers of the crowd ringing in our ears.

These mornings, I drink my let's-start-the-day coffee from a mug with sea gulls painted on it. It is the most cherished memento I ever won in a race. The house is filled with medals and plaques and prizes from other races, but I rarely look at them. The mug is there every morning to remind me that I am a runner.

I won that mug in a 5-mile race in Spring Lake, New Jersey. There were 1,500 runners in the race, with the first 140 finishers receiving mugs. Without age groups or special divisions to differentiate men from women, the starter fired his gun and the first 140 runners back got mugs. No race could be simpler.

I do not recall a more competitive race. Spring Lake is a coastal town, a resort where every square foot is at sea level. There isn't a hill to be seen. No matter how a course is laid out in Spring Lake, it's going to be as flat as a billiard table.

You would think the absence of hills would have made the race easier. Not so. Hills make it easier to forget the runners in front of you. Hills turn your thoughts to survival; finishing becomes more important than where you finish. A flat course has no such distractions. You are compelled to maintain contact with the leaders for as long as you can. And at Spring Lake this desire was intensified. No one was giving up. No one would let anyone else pass. It was every racer for himself.

We went out, 1,500 strong, at flank speed, trusting that we could hold on to a pace that was too fast for most of us yet commonly arrived at. I heard my split at the end of the first mile: 5:42—my fastest mile of the year, and yet there seemed to be hundreds of runners ahead of me.

After the first blistering mile, it was time to hang on, never give up, pick off a runner now and then, but mostly not to let anyone pass me.

193

And no one did until the 4-mile mark. He was half my age and probably double my strength. But I stayed on his heels, fighting the pain and the weariness through those interminable final minutes. I was even able to sprint the last 50 yards and storm through the finish line, where the officials handed out placement cards. I looked down and read mine: 136. The mug was mine.

Why did I need a coffee-mug trophy? After all, I had the Spring Lake T-shirt and race number to keep. Weren't they sufficient souvenirs of that day? Why another memento of that occasion? I'm not sure myself. I often leave a race without picking up my award. The shirt, the number, the companionship and the competition are memories enough. Yet many sports are synonymous with the prize: hockey and the Stanley Cup, college football and the Heisman, golf and the Masters green coat, yachting and America's Cup. The word "prize" comes from the same Latin root as "price" and "praise." The prize reflects the price the athlete paid for the victory, and the praise from spectators and fellow contestants.

The mug proves I am an athlete. The word "athlete" comes from the root word *aethlon*, which also means prize. The seemingly inconsequential coffee mug is proof of my new existence as a runner. It is evidence of the contest—a contest that is different from a game. It is not fun or pleasurable. The Greeks called such a struggle *agon*, from which we get the word "agony." I have gone through that agony, I have done my best, and now I have the trophy to prove it.

The trophy announces the completeness of the event. It is the final act that isolates, encloses and memorializes the race just run. It need not be something you can see or feel or place on your mantel; it may simply be raising the victor's hand. But there should be *something* that makes the contest a matter of record.

The trophy also acts as a sacrament. It is an outward sign of an inward happening. The trophy asserts that human beings are willing to push themselves to the limit simply to prove they can do it. The prize, the race and human limitations are inextricably tied together in the mystery that is sport. The explanation, therefore, remains unexplainable. There is no logic in illogical acts.

There was also no logic or explanation for the way I acted when I picked up my mug at the officials' table. Holding it aloft to look at it, I savored the feel of the handle under my fingers. Carrying it proudly so all could see, I jogged back to my gear—a victory jog instead of the usual exhausted walk. The mug had become the seal on an event I would never forget.

When I drink my coffee from the "trophy," I remember that race. And there is even more in that memory than the actual happening, more than placing 136th and the good feeling afterward. My mug helps me start the day, ready for whatever comes. Because of that race and other races now almost lost in memory, I know I am good and whole and holy; that what I must do I *can* do, and that the world is filled with people ready to work and suffer and enjoy with me.

The real trophy, you see, is not the coffee mug at all. It is the person drinking from it. My real trophy is the self that running and racing have made me.

25

On Sharing

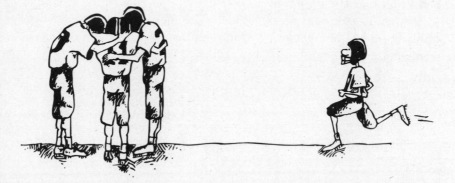

"

**What we are doing is past analyzing.
I know only that I cannot lose
my attachment to my companions.
If I do, I will become once more
a frail individual attempting a task
that is at once irrational and unnecessary.**

"

WHEN WE LINED UP for the race, the field was at least one-third black, another third Hispanic. Not the usual entry for a road race, but then the El Barrio 10-Kilometer in Spanish Harlem was not the usual road race.

I was there because there was no race that Sunday in Central Park, none on the seacoast where I live. I had no choice but to enter what seemed to me to be occupied territory. I had set out for Third Avenue and 100th Street with some apprehension. I was worried about my car and my belongings, if not my person.

I am as prejudiced as any American. We live in a melting pot that has never quite melted. Most of our brotherhood is symbolic, not concrete. We avoid situations that would force us to act upon our beliefs. We are all for brotherhood, but we stay clear of our brothers.

This is in some ways normal. Humanity, says Erik Erikson, is inherently inclined to differentiate itself into various sub-species: race, class, nation, etc. The resultant allegiances, he points out, bring out the best in man in terms of loyalty, self-sacrifice and charity. They also, however, bring out the worst. Outsiders become threats to our basic needs of survival and security, of acceptance and self-esteem. They become expendable.

Prejudice is an adult disease. Nevertheless, its incubation begins in childhood. It doesn't take very long for a child to be taught that other people are different. It doesn't take very many years to establish strata of acceptability. When that happens, childhood is lost.

When I was a kid in Brooklyn, we stayed in our own section. We learned that where there were differences in race and language and ethnic background, there were tensions and even dangers. We knew enough to stay out of what we called "tough neighborhoods." We came to see strangers as threats to ourselves and our property.

Because I still retain the vestiges of that boy growing up in Brooklyn, those feelings—some conscious, some subconscious—were present when I parked my car a block or so away from the starting line in Spanish Harlem.

Third Avenue was already alive with runners and families with children of all sizes. The playground at the intersection was filled with people getting their numbers and officials giving directions. There were tables of T-shirts and entry blanks for future races, and on the side paraphernalia for the party that would follow the race. In the background flowed music with an insistent, catchy beat. The usual movement and excitement and enthusiasm before a race were intensified.

By the time we began that slow walk to the starting line, I felt completely at home. This was the same as any other race on any other Sunday. Ahead of me lay the familiar 6.2 miles that would test my tolerance of pain, my capacity for suffering, the limits of my will, the extent of my tenacity. And as usual, I was about to undergo this trial in community with others, themselves engaged in the same enterprise. I was once more just a runner among runners.

The gun sounded, and within a few strides we were neither black nor white, Irish nor Hispanic. We were simply a homogeneous horde of panting runners. At the mile mark, all I could see around me were fellow sufferers. Pain knows no color; exhaustion has no creed. The language of the body is universal; it speaks to all in the same way.

The race disdains distinctions. Fatigue and discomfort and shortness of breath make us all brothers. They purge us of the fear and the hate and the pride that breed prejudice. The race cleanses us, using a pace we can barely sustain, for a distance we can barely traverse and a length of time that is at the outer limit of our physical ability. We are renewed by being totally spent.

After I finished, I moved with the others through the cheering crowd into the playground, where the party had already begun. I was met there with soda and beer, beans and barbecued chicken. All around were music and laughter and a great good feeling.

You see, there are things that unify us. There are emotions that demonstrate clearly our essential oneness. These experiences bring us, no matter how diverse the expression of our humanity, into an acceptance and trust and belief in each other.

One of them is pain; we had that in the race. Another is sport; we had that in the race, too. Finally, there is celebration, and I have attended few better parties than the one we had after the race in Spanish Harlem.

The awards ceremony came last. There was applause for everyone, and just a little more for those runners who had names like Hector and Carlos and José. The 50-and-over trophy went to an Irishman from a suburb in New Jersey. He told the crowd he had been born two blocks from here and had grown up in Harlem.

"I want to thank the people of *el barrio*," he said, "for an outstanding day in my life."

As we used to say in Brooklyn, that goes double for me.

Two decades ago, no one influential in running or exercise physiology or physical education had any idea that women could run long distances, much less marathons. Women were restricted to the sprints.

"I had wanted to run 20 years ago," I was told by a thirty-nine-year-old woman about to start a Boston Marathon. "But I wasn't allowed to. They thought women were too delicate. We were not permitted to run over 220 yards."

History, however, has proven that women are capable of running a marathon. It is now evident that whatever a man can do in distance running, a woman can also do. As the number of women long-distance runners increases, they present continuing proof that women respond to training the same ways as men. They make the most of what they were given at birth.

When a woman becomes a runner, she develops her own level of competence. Each one is able to establish herself somewhere on that long continuum of men and women who compete together. When I race, there are women ahead of me, women behind me. I see them only as fellow runners. They train as I train. In the race, they make the same effort, feel the same pain, suffer just as much in that drive toward the finish. And afterward they share the same pleasant exhaustion, the same satisfaction. Running and the race have made us, male and female, one.

A woman told me about this new attitude she had discovered in running. "For the first time in my life," she said, "I am considered as another human being rather than a woman doing fairly well at a man's job."

One reason this occurs is that the woman runner feels this way about *herself*. Once a woman thinks she is capable, she is. Once a woman discounts the difference between the male and female athlete, it ceases to exist.

Plato thought much the same way. In *The Republic*, he stated, "Women should take part in all the same occupations as men, both in peace and in war, acting as guardians and hunting with the men like hounds."

199

Women, he said, should be treated the same as men—both mentally and physically—and trained in identical skills.

William James joined in this plea for the full development of physical potential. In his *Gospel of Relaxation,* he referred to the social and educational changes in Norwegian women once they had taken to skiing.

"I hope," James wrote, "that here in America, more and more the ideal of the well-trained and vigorous body will be maintained neck-and-neck as the two coequal halves of the higher education for men and women alike."

Women now know that they have the same enormous endurance capabilities that men have. Once an achievement is seen as possible, it will be achieved. Once a woman believes she can run a marathon, she will run it.

The Establishment is always a step behind these developments. The exercise physiologists, those professors in human performance, are just now agreeing that women are indeed capable of running respectable marathons. The American College of Sports Medicine recently published an opinion paper by experts on this issue. It presents all the current evidence and gives this final opinion:

"There exists no conclusive scientific or medical evidence that long-distance running is contra-indicated for the healthy, trained female athlete. . . . The ACSM recommends that females be allowed to compete at the same distances in which their male counterparts compete."

This is, of course, old news to Plato and James, and to thousands of women marathoners. It will, nevertheless, do some good if it enlightens those educators and coaches and physicians whose present policy is to restrict rather than expand women's participation in sports.

I am standing, waiting for the gun, at a 10-kilometer race in Central Park. On a cold, wet day that normally would deter me from leaving the house, I wait impatiently to attack the 6.2 miles of challenging terrain that lie ahead of me. There are 4,500 runners in this race. The starting line has become a crush of bodies. I am pressed in on all sides. No longer the solitary runner, I have become a member of a mob—one of a crowd.

Whenever I race, I take on the characteristics described by the French psychologist Gustave LeBon in his classic treatise *The Crowd: A Study of the Popular Mind.* When a certain number of individuals gather in a crowd for the purpose of action, he said, there result certain new psychological qualities.

"Visible social phenomena appear to be the result of an immense unconscious working that is a rule beyond our analysis," LeBon wrote.

The race is just such an unexplainable, visible social phenomenon. People can see some practical reasons for running but almost none for racing. That is because what lies ahead is not an intellectual act; it is an emotional event.

Crowds never accomplish deeds demanding any degree of intelligence. Crowds have to do with the unconscious—with instincts, passions and emotions common to all. On the starting line, we are all equal. We may differ markedly in intellect and mental ability—but not in character, not in the capabilities of our unconscious. The starting line is where all these psychological events occur. It is here that each runner becomes part of this new being, the collective "us" about to run this race.

As I stand here, I already possess some of the qualities enumerated by LeBon. The first is the sentiment of invincible power. In this pushing together of bodies, the task before me no longer appears formidable. I draw strength from those about me. Their good cheer, their indifference to the ordeal now only minutes away, fills me with the same overwhelming confidence. I know that my powers are equal to whatever is to come.

The gun sounds. As a horde, we stream down the first hill, then up the next at almost breakneck speed. All of us are caught in the contagion that seizes groups. Reason departs, instinct takes over.

"In a crowd," wrote LeBon, "man descends several rungs in the developmental ladder. Isolated, he may be a cultivated individual. In a crowd, he is a barbarian—that is, a creature acting by instinct."

The first mile is all of this. I am drawn along by the contagion, kept at this speed by my new suggestibility. I believe that this incredible pace is not only necessary but possible, and I hold it—or at least try. But try as I may, I lose some ground. The army that started is beginning to break down into platoons.

It is from this point that the race becomes a transforming experience. The race is an instance of a crowd that has a positive effect on those in it. Too often, we think of crowds as bad or criminal. But a crowd can also be heroic. Great actions, LeBon pointed out, are rarely performed in cold blood.

This race I am in may not be a great action, but what is left after that first mile can only be called heroic. Pain and persistence are now our common experience. We have a common mind which has become a common reflex.

We have focused down to the running of this race. It has become the most important thing we will ever do. Everything else is blotted out of our minds.

"Crowds," wrote LeBon, "are cognizant only of simple and extreme sentiments." We know that. We have no doubt or uncertainty about the extreme importance of what we are doing.

William Barrett, the philosopher, has written about this feeling: "The runner does not doubt the race as long as he continues to strain every nerve and muscle in the effort. If he eases up for a moment, he is likely to see the whole thing for what it is: an absurd and useless display, not worth the effort."

This almost never occurs, Barrett admitted. Writing about the last finisher in the Boston Marathon, he called him an image of the man of faith: "There simply cannot be a question of his quitting."

For me, this "absurd and useless display" is taking on more meaning. For me and those in my platoon, there is no question of quitting. We find strength where there is no strength left. Pain becomes bearable, because everyone else is bearing it. And inside of that pain, we find energies that only agony will release.

We are now moving into areas behind logic and reason. What we are doing is past analyzing. I know only that I cannot lose my attachment to my companions. If I do, I will become once more a frail individual attempting a task that is at once irrational and unnecessary.

I do not allow that to happen. Alone on this day, I would long since have given up. I can do what I am doing only when I am one of this crowd—because I am a racer with my fellow racers.

"Take me in," I say—sometimes aloud, sometimes under my breath, sometimes as a plea, sometimes as a prayer. And they do. They always do.

"Did anything memorable occur during the race?" The questioner at the other end of the telephone was in a Charleston radio station. I was standing in a phone booth wearing borrowed sweats and holding the sixty-and-over trophy for the Cooper River Bridge 10-Kilometer Race.

Outside I could see the remnants of the 2,000-entry field still enjoying themselves and their refreshments.

I searched my mind for something a news reporter would think memorable. Someone hit by a car, or collapsing from the effort. What man had bitten a dog during the race? What incident that would interest those people who spend their days listening to what happens to other people?

The man was patient. He repeated the question. I remained silent. I was still thinking. I did not tell him about the day before. I had been picked up at the airport by a stranger who was also a runner. This morning I was taken to the race by this same man, now a close friend. I had spent less than 12 hours in a strange house I now and forever would regard as another home. I was as comfortable in Charleston as I was in my old running shoes.

I did not tell him about sitting in the car at the starting line. It was too cold this blustery day to warm up. The flags on the *Yorktown*, berthed at the Point, were straight out and flapping. When the race began the first mile was straight into that driving wind, yet the huge mass of runners made it like being in the eye of a hurricane. There was practically no air movement at all.

I did not tell him about the bridge. It loomed up just after we made the hairpin turn at the mile mark. From then on the wind would be at our backs. Never a real hindrance, it became a help. It pushed us toward this narrow ribbon of steel rising into the sky like something in a fairy story.

I have run other bridges—the George Washington, the Golden Gate, the Verrazano. All give the impression of solidity and function. For all their architectural brilliance, those bridges are matter-of-fact utilitarian structures. They are simply there to carry things to the other side.

Not so the Cooper River Bridge. It is a thin double span that crosses two rivers and goes for some two and a half miles to a destination that must be accepted on faith. This bridge carried us up and over and through to some distant land, to a mythical Charleston. It was not a bridge, it was an adventure.

Nor did I tell him about the woman runner. She appeared beside me on the first rise. Her pace was steady, relentless and unforgiving. I knew she would not vary one iota from that stride and speed until the finish line. I gave her the reins and concentrated on just staying with her.

We went together, scudding down the other side and up the second rise, finally spilling out into East Bay Street in Charleston. If there ever was Heaven in a race, this was it. I had shed my hat and gloves and thrown my shirt over my head so I was running bare-chested in this perfect weather. The wind was at my back, the course flat, and I still felt fresh.

Then came the turning into Queen Street, and everyone began to pick up the pace. "How far to go?" gasped a lanky teenager beside me. "A half mile," I said. He took off like a colt who has seen its mother. His tow-head disappeared in the crowd up front.

Then I heard, "On your left . . .," and his place was taken by two runners, George Halman, who is blind, and a companion who was joined to him by a cord at the wrists. Until I saw George I thought I was doing my absolute best. Now I was spurred to do more. I went with him hoping to share in his strength and courage. I drew up to his shoulder and drew on his guts and determination.

We went that way to the end. The digital clock read 39:05, my best this year. Afterward, I stood at the chute for a long time congratulating those who finished behind me, seeing in their happy and contented faces the happiness and contentment in mine. The feeling of being special filled those beautiful Charleston streets.

Then I joined a group of Irishmen surrounding a truck with a keg of beer. Later I wandered down to the ceremony at the Cistern and received my award. It was the perfect end of a perfect day.

The man was still waiting for an answer. "Did anything memorable occur during the race?" he asked once more.

"No," I said, "it was just like all those other races we run every weekend."

26

On Striving

" Winning is never having to say I quit. "

THERE ARE THINGS about myself I would rather not know. My IQ, for instance. I have no idea what it is and no intention of finding out. Either way, high or low, the news would be bad.

I would be distressed if my score was low, because I would rather not know my limitations. A low IQ could dissuade me from reaching for something within my grasp.

On the other hand, if it was high, I would be under the gun to produce more than ever before. There is nothing worse than being told you are quite capable of something that you know will stretch you to your very limit. There would no longer be any excuse for failure.

The IQ test identifies mental prodigies. A test of physical potential is equally disturbing. It identifies physical geniuses. This measurement might be called the "physical quotient," but instead it is known as the maximal oxygen uptake test. This test measures the system's capacity to transport oxygen from the lungs to the contracting muscles during exercise.

The major physiological changes that occur during fitness programs are usually measured in two ways: physical work capacity and maximal oxygen uptake. Work capacity is the ability to finish a distance. It has to do with endurance, not speed. This capacity may improve enormously, while there may be only a minor increase in oxygen uptake. Unless a person starting a fitness program is grossly overweight and completely out of shape, the oxygen uptake values usually do not increase more than 20 percent during training.

Oxygen uptake indicates the ability for all-out effort. In general, the maximal oxygen uptake determines where you will finish in a 5- or 10-mile race. With a high uptake, you'll finish up front. With a low uptake, you'll finish far back in the pack.

Although I have stuck to my decision not to learn my IQ score, I decided to have my oxygen uptake measured. It was a great mistake. It caused me as many problems as would have occurred with the disclosure of my IQ.

Knowing my oxygen uptake means that I now know exactly what times I should run in the mile, at 10 kilometers and in the marathon. I also know the absolute best times I can hope to achieve. This raises two problems: First, there is no excuse to do worse. Second, there is no hope to do better. What I can do is already programmed into my body. My responsibility is to get that performance out of it, fully realizing that achievements beyond are reserved for others more gifted than I.

I don't like living with this type of predestination. I no longer dream of doing better than my maximal oxygen uptake will let me. And I am no longer allowed to feel good about a race time that is just a mite slower than the one in the charts of my oxygen uptake.

Having this information seems to turn my body into a racing car that can do so much and no more, destined to live with my specific level of performance. A footrace seems to become a race between machines with different engine capacities.

Fortunately, winning is never this predetermined. For me, winning is a matter of doing my absolute best on a particular day. It is a matter of enduring pain, never relaxing when I feel good and maintaining contact as long as I can with the runners around me, even those better than I. Winning is never forgetting that I am running against the unforgiving clock—and not against the companions who race along with me. Winning is never having to say I quit.

So the war between my maximal oxygen uptake and me continues. In some races, I equal the predicted times. In others, I am far below them. Sometimes I am upset over the injustice of the fact that I am hurting as much as those who will finish minutes and even hours ahead of me. At other times, I am satisfied that the pain means I am getting the most possible out of this aging, finite body. When I translate the race into minutes and seconds, winning becomes a matter of breaking even. Winning is ending in a tie with my maximum performance potential.

I recall once holding a gasping conversation on this subject during a race in Central Park. One runner said he had a maximal oxygen uptake of 65 milliliters per kilogram per minute. My reading is 56.

"What does that mean?" he asked.

"It means," I said, "that you are dogging it back here with us. You should be a half mile ahead."

That is always my worry: dogging it, not getting the most out of what I have. That is my burden, and a terrible one it is. Every race imposes on me a duty not to cheat on myself, and in every race I must respond.

After an agonizing stretch run at the finish of a race in Van Cortlandt Park, an official came up to me and said, "George, you have guts."

I sat there wearily looking at him, and then said, "But why does it have to be that way in every race?"

Whether I know my IQ or not, my maximal oxygen uptake or not, there is no escaping the necessity to do my best, to fulfill my potential. Whether I am a success or a failure is recognized by every cell in my body.

The Friday night before the New York Marathon I spoke at a spaghetti dinner given by a local running club. Before the talk to the 100 runners and their families I loaded up on the bread and beer and pasta. And I shared in the excitement and enthusiasm and anticipation they all felt. Then in the question-and-answer period that followed someone asked me if I was going to run the marathon. Without hesitation I answered, "Yes."

Until that dinner I would have said "No." For the previous week I had thought of any number of legitimate reasons not to run. Primarily, I had not gotten in the necessary training. The current marathon pretraining programs prescribe a gradual buildup over three to six months to where the runner is doing at least 60 and preferably 70 miles a week. I have always run marathons on a good deal less. In fact I have never run 70 miles in one week and don't intend to. Two to three hours a week of easy running and a weekly race have been my premarathon routine over the years.

But this year my training had dipped far below even my minimum. Travel, colds and injuries had cut into my time on the roads. And when I was healthy I had raced so much I was too tired to train. My mileage in the last month was less than what most runners preparing for this race do in a week.

Then there were the calf cramps. In several recent races I had some ominous warnings in my calves. Cramps that were severe enough to slow me down on two occasions. Suppose I got a cramp (and it seemed like a distinct possibility) in some godforsaken spot in Brooklyn or the Bronx and I had to walk in.

Even if I was able to run without injury it would undoubtedly be in some undistinguished time. In coming months whenever the subject of the New York Marathon came up I would have to apologize for my time. I once ran the White Rock Marathon in Dallas after a long layoff in 3:28. Quite respectable under the circumstances. But few people let me explain the circumstances. So rather than be a bore, I just told them my time and let them think I was over the hill and going through an accelerated phase of degeneration.

I had this all in mind when I rose to speak that Friday night. I had even investigated the possibility of other races that day, a five-miler perhaps or some easy 10-kilometer run. But the closest event I could find was in Richmond, Virginia.

Then as I looked around me at those runners, I knew I had to be in it. One of the worst feelings in the world is that of missing something. The feeling that everything is going on somewhere else. Those people in front of me were what William James calls "the faithful fighters." And they were silently saying to me the words James used on the faint-hearted who declined to go on, or the words of Henry IV when he greeted the tardy Crillon after a great victory: "Hang yourself, brave Crillon! We fought at Arques and you were not there."

That Friday night I knew I wanted to join in the fight. It was easier to risk pain and embarrassment and failure and the possibility of walking home from the Bronx than to miss this great and wonderful struggle.

So on Sunday I was there at Fort Wadsworth with 14,000 others, getting my number verified, fortifying myself with coffee and doughnuts and using the world's longest urinal. All my reluctance had gone. I was impatient to get underway.

The first twenty miles were a delight. You have heard of automatic writing that flows out of the writer from some unapprehended source. Those first twenty miles were automatic running. Almost effortless, the 7-minute miles spun on and on. At 10 miles the digital clock read 1:10:10, and at 20 it was 2:20:10. An almost incredible consistency. Then I passed a sign that said, "Salazar 2:08:13, World Record." It was an inspiration. He had gone for it, so would I.

But from then on it was everything the last 6 miles of a marathon is said to be. Try as I might, my pace kept slowing. My form began to go. I lost the strength and flow that had marked the early going. Now the pain became a constant presence in my legs and thighs. And on the hills it filled my arms and chest.

I was constantly losing time to the clock. With a mile to go I was still uncertain about finishing. But those about me were still running so I assumed that I could and must. By now I was on Central Park South heading for Columbus Circle. The avenue has a slight upgrade with poor footing and was strangely devoid of spectators cheering the runners. I find this stretch always the most trying of the entire marathon. Here pain and exhaustion fuse with an intense desire just to give up. I want to say enough is enough. This whole enterprise is a mistake. It is too much for me.

But then I made the turn into the park and heard the cheering up ahead, and there they were, thousands of people lining the road and filling the grandstands and calling out my name. That was all I needed. I went up that last terrible hill to the finish line as if it didn't exist.

So hang yourself, dear reader, if we ran the New York Marathon and you were not there.

God was watching. If there is any explanation for the 1982 Boston Marathon, that was it. The winner in collapse. Another finishing with a broken leg. A third crossing the line reciting her prayers. Thousands in various stages of dehydration and exhaustion. The medical area at the Prudential Center looking like something out of the Crimean War.

God is watching the Salazars, José Salazar had said before the race, granting prodigious talents and expecting spectacular sacrifice and fidelity in return. That God has called us to great heroism and it is within our power to accomplish it. This world is in fact an arena for heroism, and our main task on this earth is to be heroic.

There are those who would have us be heroic in other ways. The marathon is foolishness. It is not truly important. It is not rational to use it as a setting for talent and sacrifice and fidelity. It is not the real world. Running is not our role here on earth.

Say what you will, we knew God was watching. More than that, we ran as if God were watching. Religion is not dogma and theology; it is not something you enunciate and systematize. It is not even what we think we believe. It is what we do. My religion is my truth. It is not something I have; it is something I live. My life depends upon it.

God was watching Alberto Salazar, and he ran as if his life depended upon it. He totally extended himself. He made the marathon a contest between himself and the all-too-human tendency to excuse one's self and settle for less than one's best. He pushed himself to the limit and set the example for the rest of us. Heroism, so difficult to find in the real world, became commonplace.

God was watching Guy Gerstch, and he ran the last 19 miles of the marathon with a fracture of his thigh bone. Guy had come all the way from Salt Lake City and was not going to stop. That was one reason. Deep in the subconscious was a more formidable one. At the starting line in Hopkinton he had taken an oath. He had given his wordless word of honor to do his absolute best. To be a hero. He was.

God was watching Sister Madonna Buder, and she knew it. "In the last four miles there is such a temptation to break," she said. "I had to keep calling on Jesus to keep me running." One hour and a half behind Alberto, this heroine finished secure in the belief that she was pleasing the very source of creation. She came across the line asking Divine help in this absurd human activity.

God was watching me. His confused and wayward son. The beauty of the marathon is that there is no indecision about what I am supposed to do. At other times I keep asking, "Lord, what will Thou have me do?" and the answer is never clear.

In the marathon, there is no need to ask for direction. All I ask for is the strength and courage to carry it out, and the faith that it need be done. It was hours out and miles to go when I was flooded with that faith, and filled with the courage and strength to endure to the finish. I knew then a very special joy, a joy that for those moments absented me from pain. I knew myself as never before.

God was watching all of us. Consciously or subconsciously those thousands of runners felt that Presence. We are here, said the late Ernest Becker, to use ourselves up. We were meant to be heroes. We did and we were.

That is why the marathon is a serious, important and totally rational activity. It allows us to use ourselves up. To push to our limit. To be heroes. When words fail, as they so often do, it tells us what we truly believe: we have been granted prodigious talents, and spectacular sacrifices and fidelity are expected in return.

27

On Revealing

"

I am a selfish person.
Except, of course, for God,
no one knows more about me
than myself or is more interested.
Whether that annoys others or not is immaterial.
It is an absolute necessity.
The development of the self
is the first and essential step
toward union with anyone else.

"

LATER A NATIONAL MAGAZINE described it as the world's first "Me-In." It was "The Event," which brought together speakers for the various human-potential movements for the largest self-improvement rally ever held. I was there to talk about running.

I got off to a bad start. There was a 10,000-meter race near home that I did not want to miss. So I ran the race and then arrived late for the press conference held at the luncheon break. My colleagues in this extravaganza were already explaining their positions to a skeptical crowd of reporters and writers and cameramen.

Some of the questions were frank: "What do you tell people in Queens who say this is a load of bull?" asked a New York *Daily News* reporter.

Some were snide: "If this is so important, why don't you experts do it for nothing?"

Some were far-out: "Why were the pyramids built in that shape?"

No one asked for a comment on John Leonard's column in *The New York Times*. He had no intention, wrote Leonard, of attending this gala. It was difficult enough, he said, to avoid these people at cocktail parties where they talked about nothing else but their health and their relationships. They were, he declared, graduate students in nothing more than themselves.

The press conference ended without my saying a word. The speakers went back to their chores. Drs. Masters and Johnson led off the afternoon program. I was to follow. I spent their entire session pacing nervously back and forth in the corridor behind the stage. Then my moment came.

I went out on that stage, into those bright lights, before a thousand or more people. The nervousness was gone and suddenly I was at ease. I was ready to think out loud upon the questions I never got to answer—ready to explain to myself and to the audience, to John Leonard and to the people in Queens, what running was all about.

What made it work was Buckminster Fuller. As I looked out over that expanse of faces, I saw him sitting in a separate chair placed ahead of the first row. Not 20 feet away from me, his hands folded in his lap, his face raised expectantly, he sat waiting for me to speak. This beautiful eighty-three-year-old man, whose certainty had given me trust, sat waiting for me to say something worthwhile. And because of him, I did.

213

Each of us is born a genius, he had written. Each of us is born to be a success. Somewhere things went wrong. Somewhere we lost sight of who we were and what we could do. We became consumed either with ambition and anxiety or boredom and depression. We had been changed from being generalists who knew the world into specialists who knew only a small part.

We are not to worry about the world. That was Buckminster Fuller's message. Technology will save technology. Miniaturization will make the world easier and easier to live in. It will be a world that a handful of superbly intelligent people can direct. The rest of us should concern ourselves with our own personal salvation.

But where lay that salvation? Was there someone in this marathon of speakers able to give us that answer? Had anyone among these authors written the ultimate how-to book? Was there anyone whose directions we could follow to a destiny in Paradise?

If there was, I told them, it wasn't me. I was not there, I said, to teach them anything. I was there to make them remember things they had forgotten. Because nothing worthwhile can be taught. The answers to life are not in the back of the book. All the gimmicks and techniques and the how-to books can be a waste of time. Anything that changes your values, changes your behavior, changes your life, has to be self-taught, must be self-discovered. Kierkegaard was one of the first to say that. The doleful Dane told us there is no way to communicate our deeper experiences to another.

I agreed, I said, with the people in Queens. A lot of what would be said today would be bull. The glow felt at this event would be gone by tomorrow. It would last only to the extent it moved us to action. It would be only talk unless we pushed our bodies and minds and souls to the absolute limit. By doing and suffering and creating, we learn—and no other way.

There is no human-potential movement worth the name if that movement does not mean growth. You have to grow to see. You have to grow to understand.

I had found that growth in running. By making running the most important thing in my life, I was able to pull my own strings, become my own best friend and realize my human potential. As I ran, I grew in health, and I grew in truth, and I grew in love.

214

I agreed, nevertheless, with John Leonard. I am a selfish person. Except, of course, for God, no one knows more about me than myself or is more interested. Whether that annoys others or not is immaterial. It is an absolute necessity. The development of the self is the first and essential step toward union with anyone else. To accept another, I must first accept myself. To be able to love someone else, I must first love myself.

Only rarely, however, are this acceptance and concern and love visible. I remain detached, isolated, solitary. I seek a personal perfection that shuts everyone else out. Leonard's indictment seems to stand—and behind his charge, the statement of Norman Cousins: "In our focus on individual identity and uniqueness, we have taught people to become fully involved with self, with a resultant skewing of communal values."

But once more I gazed down at Fuller's happy face and took heart. He has given us the answer. His every movement, his every word, his very presence shouts, "Life is worth living." He has the confidence that he has lived the only life cycle possible to him, has run the good race, has fought the good fight. And the young, who need no less than this faith, can see it and taste it and feel it in his very being, and love him for it.

By now the excitement had gripped me. I was brandishing the microphone, asking the audience to see this same truth. The complete realization of our self is our contribution to the common good—the greatest contribution anyone of us can make, because it is that certainty that our own life was good and true and worthwhile that gives the young what they need most: trust, the trust that they too can reach 60 and 70 and 80 with the same wonder and zest and joy.

I looked down again, and the expression on Fuller's face told me I had crossed the finish line.

A column defending the selfishness of the long-distance runner provoked an answer from my former professor of philosophy. He accepts, in part, my defense of contemplation and the solitary life. He would, up to a point, allow me to work out my salvation alone on the roads. But he insists on the additional need for devotion to the common good.

"We should not belittle one truth," he writes, "in espousing another." Contemplation is needed, he concedes, but so is the taking upon yourself the good and welfare of others. His view coincides with that of Aquinas, who stated that contemplation was one of man's highest

215

activities. The highest, he said, was contemplation followed by implementation of the truths of that contemplation.

In fact, we are ideally suited for one or the other, not both. The religious impulse may well be resident in every man, but its manifestations are individual and even unique. This diversity is nowhere more evident than in the apparent unity of the Catholic Church. Her various religious orders run the gamut of religious expression, from the anchorite, whose mission is silence, to the missionary, whose mission is people.

Although my old teacher would take the middle ground, there is in truth very little middle ground. This is a debate that has gone on from the beginning of time.

"We should not sacrifice one good thing for another," states the professor. I agree. But he is thinking of the common good, and I am thinking of my own solitude. It is the age-old problem of being an individual and/or identifying with a group.

Join few things, wrote Frost—your family and your country and nothing between. But then Frost was also the man who said there was more religion outside the church than in.

So it goes. We are reminded of our attachment to everyone in the universe, and then we find with astonishment how much that is human is alien to us. There is always this conflict between the two points of view: the Renaissance man who says "I" and the man of the Reformation who says "We."

When I am besieged, I call upon Emerson or Thoreau or William James. "Stand apart in silence, in steadiness," counseled Emerson. "You may think I am impoverishing myself in solitude," wrote Thoreau, "but I shall burst forth a more perfect creature, fitted for a higher society."

But perhaps this struggle, and the evident truth on both sides, is most clearly seen in the relationship between James and his protégé, colleague and friend Josiah Royce.

James, in his Gifford Lectures (a series of talks given annually in Scotland by distinguished thinkers), gave his report on the religious experience. These were later to become the justly famous *Varieties of Religious Experience*—written, as he told a friend, because he believed the experience of religion was man's most important function. He also believed in man's private way to his own private truth. He was the champion of rugged individualism. This made for pluralism, the lack of absolutes. Indeed when James died, he left a note. There are no conclusions, he had written, no advice to give, no fortunes to be told.

Royce, who was as much a theologian as he was a philosopher, took exactly the opposite tack. He knew there was an Absolute, and that Absolute was God, and all this could be proven from our natural reason.

"We are saved," said Royce, "through and in the community." Our meaning, the meaning of our life, rested in loyalty—which he defined as "the willing and practical devotion of a person to a cause." Loyalty to loyalty was Royce's guiding star. It unified life, gave it center, fixity, stability.

James's loyalty was to himself, to his own truth—to his egoism versus Royce's altruism. But for all that, Royce had to be answered, and James spent the final years of his life in that intellectual effort.

"Beloved Royce," he writes at one point, "when I compose the Gifford Lecture mentally, it is with the design exclusively of overthrowing your system and ruining your peace."

He then goes on to say, "Oh, dear Royce, can I forget you or be contented out of your close neighborhood? Different as our minds are, yours has nourished mine as no other social influence has."

Royce in return called James "one of the dearest of my friends and one of the most loyal of men." And in a letter to him, he said, "No criticism of mine is hostile. Life is a sad, long road sometimes. Every friendly touch and word must be preciously guarded. I prize everything you say or do, whether I criticize or not."

This great and loving debate still goes on. There is, it seems to me, a James and Royce inside each one of us. One is at times dominant; at other times the other gains control. What we must do is reconcile these two equally positive, these two equally reproductive, drives in our lives.

The essential is that the reconciliation be a true one. It cannot be contrived. Whatever we do must be authentic. What I do must be me.

Thomas Merton once wrote to this point: "He who attempts to act and do things for others without deepening his own self-understanding, freedom, integrity and capacity to love will have nothing to give others."

Oddly, the more this push to the limits, the more the differences between us. Since I have become a runner, I see this clearly. The one thing that James and Royce shared was this demon on their backs, driving them to the best they could possibly be.

217

Each, of course, drove the other. "The prolonged struggle with Royce," observes scholar Ralph Barton Perry, "subjected James to a severe discipline. He had not evaded the issues. He fought them out and in doing so greatly strengthened his intellectual tissues."

And Royce was later to say, "Had I not early in my work known Professor James, I doubt whether any poor book of mine would ever be written."

So there you are. We work out our salvation in our own way, with our own truth and no one else's. The only requirement is that we be what James and Royce were—eagles.

You don't find them in flocks. Like runners, you find them one at a time.

I am a loner. An observer. I am one of Colin Wilson's outsiders. My involvement with other people may at times be deep and sincere, but it is nevertheless transitory. Like Thoreau, my interest and affection for my friends increases the longer I go without meeting them. Again and again, I find myself in the journals of those solitary writers over the centuries. I say the same things to myself that they confided in their notebooks.

It is nevertheless a continuing burden. I am indeed working mightily against this quality in my makeup. Every day, I roll my rock up this hill, conforming to my role in society, being a social animal. I belong to a profession whose aim is to help others. I have fathered children. I am a son and brother to others. I am a husband and part of a household. There is no end to the structures I inhabit and whose harmony depends to some extent on what I do.

Society depends upon these relationships. Tradition is the glue that holds everything in place; authority, the cement that prevents the entire structure from collapsing. There is a way things work, there is a way things are supposed to be, and there is always that second commandment of the two that can replace all others: "Love thy neighbor as thyself." So religion, too, locks me into this daily struggle between my natural tendencies and what is fitting and right and proper to do.

Even so, the self that I am cannot be denied. I see tradition as someone else's truth, not mine, and authority as an attempt to supercede my own judgment on any situation. It is something done in the interest of the community, not mine. Institutions exist because of authority. The individual must be sacrificed to the general good. And I see religion more as the exegesis—or better, the living. Religion is not something you think; it is something you do. In the end what I do may show more love of neighbor than living with them.

The Church, in prescribing celibacy for its clergy, took note of this possibility. And in its Orders, the Church acknowledges this need to be alone. There are indeed Orders whose mission is going out and preaching to all people. But there are others, like the Trappists, where life takes place in what is virtually solitary confinement.

There are deeply moral writers who speak of this ever present need to be free of others.

"I do not want to live among people who say 'we' and to be a part of 'us' to find I am at home in any human milieu, whatever it may be," writes Simone Weil. "I feel it is necessary and ordained that I should be a stranger and an exile in every human circle without exception."

"Necessary" and "ordained" are strong words. They speak of something intrinsic in the personality, the living out as fulfilling one's destiny. Nothing can stand against such a statement. There can be no argument. For Simone Weil, being a loner was being herself, the person the Creator had in mind when she was born. Our common heritage, the axioms of conduct, the accumulated scholarship of the ages, cannot withstand those forces.

You might say that Simone Weil's experience does not apply to ordinary human beings. She was certainly odd and may have been a saint. She took things much too seriously. And she had a penchant for unpopular causes—including, you might say, her own. Simone Weil, I will admit, was one of a kind, a rare bird, a museum piece.

Yet so are we all—would that each one of us could speak out for a life as distinctive as hers, that inner life that has been so suppressed and submerged we may have difficulty recognizing it, our own personal truth ready to be lived.

You may be quite surprised at the result. There are rebels yearning for tradition, revolutionaries whose need is authority. Ram Dass, after a decade of nonconformity, came back from India and announced, "The Ten Commandments is the way the world works." Your thing may be what you have been doing all your life and never fully accepted.

In all of us, there is a need for tradition and authority and religion. But each of these forces must be rooted in the self. They cannot come

219

fully and completely from others. In all things, we must be heretics. We must, in the original Greek sense of that word, be choosers. We must choose the fitting and right true thing for us. The loner has that obligation as much as those who would bring him to the fold.

28

On Believing

"

**The athlete knows
he controls what happens to him.
He blames no one but himself
when things go wrong.
The athlete makes his own luck.
He decides his own fate.
He believes that what he does is important
and, in some odd and mystical way, matters.**

"

"THE FREE MAN," wrote Martin Buber, "believes in destiny and that it has need of him."

More than most men, the athlete is aware of Buber's truth. The athlete knows he controls what happens to him. He blames no one but himself when things go wrong. The athlete makes his own luck. He decides his own fate. He believes that what he does is important and, in some odd and mystical way, matters.

But take us out of sport, and we see ourselves as innocent victims of forces too strong for us to handle. We are transformed from autonomous athletes to human beings completely controlled by our environment. Suddenly bureaucracy, the system, society determines what happens to us. The man who blames no one but himself in his games blames *everyone* but himself in his life.

I offer myself as Exhibit A. Take that 20-mile race in Central Park, when I won the 50-and-over plaque, beating out my perennial rival Bill Coyne at the very end of the race. I took full credit for that. And I lost my White Stag warm-up, along with my eyeglasses and car keys. For that I blamed society, the system, the Parks Department, the officials and whoever was sick enough to steal these things.

It all happened because the Parks Department's usually permissive lieutenants were replaced by some faceless commissar who would no longer let me park near the dressing room at Ninety-sixth Street. For three months I had done that, put my gear in the car and gotten a nonrunning friend to hold the keys.

This time I needed the warm-ups to jog the dozen or so blocks back up Fifth Avenue to the starting line. Now the officials got into the scenario. They offered the trunk of a car for anyone who wanted his gear brought to the finish line. Any rational man would have paused to think about the possible complications. Not I. I was on an ego trip.

Those White Stag warm-ups made me look like the runner I never was. As I jogged to the line, someone yelled, "Sheehan lives!" And then someone told me he had seen me quoted in *The New York Times Magazine* article on the Olympic marathon winner Frank Shorter.

Any playwright could have seen the tragedy unfolding: disrespect for authority, the old pride and then acting without thought of the consequences. No thinking man would let anyone but a blood relative take care of his prized warm-ups, his gold-rimmed Ben Franklin glasses and the keys to his VW. Yet in a few seconds, I reduced myself to long

222

johns, red nylon running shorts, a ski mask and a pair of cotton gloves in a hostile city 50 miles from home.

The race was long and cruel and satisfying. Coyne went out at a pace I was afraid to match, and I never saw him again until I came upon him walking up the last hill. Running against him was like running against your best time. You knew you had to be at your best and accept pain in quantity to win. I did.

At the finish line, I changed my role from captain of my fate to victim. Our sweat suits placed with great care in the trunk had been scattered about on the grass among the crowd at the finish. Mine had disappeared. It was no wonder. Among the debris worn by my friends, the White Stag warm-up must have glittered like a Kohinoor diamond.

The end of a 20-mile race is no place to face such a crisis. The hurting after a 20-miler is sometimes worse than when you are running. This was one of those times. My legs and stomach started to cramp up as I stood there in my wet running clothes in the rapidly chilling February air.

The cramps grew worse as I got to a phone booth with a borrowed dime. They finally forced me to sit shivering on the ground, with the phone barely reaching my ear, as the family hunted for the second set of car keys 50 miles away. Two hours later I was headed home, wishing indignities on the thief and his offspring for at least three generations— and thinking of punishments for the officials and the park commissioner that Attila the Hun would have judged harsh.

Two days later I would read Buber and know that everything was my doing—or else nothing was my doing. You can't have it both ways, and I do treasure that 50-and-over plaque.

The athlete lives what the philosopher would explain. Epictetus said it plainly centuries ago: "If any instance of pain or pleasure, glory or disgrace be set before you, remember: now is the combat, now the Olympiad comes on, no way can it be put off, and that by one failure and defeat, honor can be lost and won."

The race is not play; it is sport. The emphasis is on the martial virtues: discipline, dedication, courage, loyalty. I am there to conquer— if not the world, myself. The race brings to the real world what is not normally in the real world: the tournament, the trial, the test by which we may come to know ourselves.

When I race, I become pure will. The race is my opportunity to suffer and to endure. In each race, I grow. I mature. And what happens in the race, I take back with me to my run. There my intellect tells me what the suffering meant. There I discover the "why" of all this doing.

The run gives me solitude for this meditation. It gives me unoccupied time—time free from people or demands or rules or regulations, time as white and virginal as new canvas, time to be used for the first and only time, time that will hold ideas as large or as small as I make them.

When I run in that time, I sometimes wonder why I race. There is no need, it seems, to go beyond this contemplation. Surely life can hold nothing better than this day-after-day communion with oneself. This is how the artist should work. This is where the writer should come upon his subject and learn how to deal with it.

True enough, I find. But sooner or later, it fails. Sooner or later, there is nothing left to write about. There are no new insights, no new experiences, no new thoughts to put on this pristine canvas. So there is a need to go back to the race, its pain and its people.

Frost said it all: "If you wish to write a poem, have an experience."

If you wish to come upon a general rule, you must first experience the particular that demonstrates that rule. If you wish to find out a quality in you or others, you must first live through an instance where that quality is demonstrated. So the race which is the microcosm of life becomes of supreme importance. If I were to run without racing I would be incomplete.

"To see complete absorption in being," writes the philosopher William Barrett, "only leads to quiescence and boring repetitions." Yet racing without running would be scurrying around, aimlessly accumulating experience without thoughts to their meaning. I would neither be growing nor learning.

Running is being, racing is doing. I have learned that truth lies in the tension between one state and the other. I know whatever stops either the running or the racing, stops the living as well.

"To be converted, to be regenerated, to receive grace, to experience religion," wrote William James in *The Varieties of Religious Experience,* "are so many phrases that denote the process by which a self hitherto divided and consciously wrong and inferior and unhappy, becomes unified and so consciously right and superior and happy."

James wrote at length on how and why these transformations occur, and why adolescents were particularly susceptible to this phenomenon in their behavior.

When I turned to running at forty-four, I experienced just such a conversion. For one thing, I was a forty-four-year-old adolescent. I had much the same feelings as a teenager—the same sense of incompleteness, the same sense of something missing, the same brooding, the same hope I could get through life unnoticed and therefore unpunished by my Creator.

My conversion was aided by two other motivational assets. A sense of physical sin, for one. When you are forty-four, your body becomes acutely aware of being sinned against. Another middle-aged asset is the certain knowledge that you are not doing the best that is in you, the realization that the 11th commandment is "Don't bury your talents."

When the conversion does come, it arrives in two ways. The first is preoccupation with sin. This is conversion due to guilt—my guilt about what I had done to the person I had been. This conversion is conscious and voluntary. It is quite clear what must be done, and I must simply summon the willpower to do it.

In such instances, James wrote, the regenerative change is usually gradual and consists in building the new "I" piece by piece. That "I" is the person I was before I became the person who began running—an "I" that I could no longer accept. I could see my sins and was ready to repent.

There are fitness evangelists who preach physical sin. They have their own ten commandments of do's and don'ts. When they face a smoking, drinking, overweight, out-of-shape audience, you are reminded of Cotton Mather working over his New England congregation. Such revival meetings frequently harvest a bushel of souls ready to run and sin no more.

I go through that conversion every time I am out on the roads. When the sweating starts, I can feel the badness leaving me. I can sense the excess fat being burned off, the training effect on the heart. I am aware of the strength and endurance building in my muscles. I am purging myself of sin, ridding myself of guilt.

There is, however, another and more subtle conversion going on—a conversion that ultimately produces what James called "the state of assurance" and Maslow defined as "the peak experience." By any name, it is the happening that convinces us we are indeed whole and happy and one with the universe.

This conversion is not a movement away from sin. It is a movement toward righteousness, toward the positive ideal we wish to attain, toward the splendor each one of us was created to attain. This is a conversion that is going on in the subconscious, in our subliminal life. It is therefore involuntary. It is accomplished not by willpower, but by relaxation and acceptance and self-surrender.

In this conversion, the impetus is not guilt but shame—shame that I have not taken out of every moment what was there to be done, shame that I have fallen short of my own potential.

Yet this type of conversion is a positive one. I become excited not about my faults, but my excellence, not about what I have done but what I can do, not about who I was but who I will be.

All this requires, said James, an active interior life. I have found that in running. Somewhere in the second half-hour, especially with the wind at my back, I can enter my cell and meditate. Motion has become my mantra, and my subconscious is in ferment. Not that all or most of it surfaces or is plainly seen, but on the infrequent occasions that it does surface I realize what has been percolating in those recesses.

I am out on the roads several days a week renewing my vows, hoping for those signs given the elect.

My conversion is a series of conversions. I must continue with my fight with physical sin; I must trust that my subconscious will continue its path toward my perfection and on occasion permit me a glimpse or two.

James summarized this well. First, that state of assurance. The main characteristic, he said, is the loss of all worry—the sense that all is ultimately well, the peace, the harmony, the willingness-to-be.

Converts, James said, have a sense of perceiving things not known before. The world seems different now. There is a feeling as if everything is being seen for the first time. And finally, there is that ecstasy of happiness produced.

Why, I sometimes ask myself, must all this occur only on the roads? What is it that makes running an essential of this whole phenomenon? Is it the solitude or the motion or both that are the source of this revelation?

Whatever the reason, Emerson was familiar with this sort of occurrence. In *The Transcendentalist* he wrote, "[My faith] is a certain brief experience, which surprised me on the highway and made me aware that I had played the fool among fools—that I should never be fool more. Yet in the space of an hour, I was at my old tricks—a selfish member of a selfish society."

So each time I run, it is to become, if only briefly, the person the Lord meant me to be—unified and consciously right and superior and happy.

EPILOGUE

Beyond Fitness

"Fitness helps you look for
the life you should lead.
Being an athlete means
you have found it."

BEING FIT IS ONE THING. Being an athlete is another. Thirty minutes of movement done at a comfortable pace four times a week will make you fit. The movement could be running, cycling, swimming or walking. Two hours a week will make you fit. But athletes who are runners, cyclists, swimmers or walkers may train those two hours *every day*.

Fitness is the ability to do work. There is a relationship between the time put in and the energy derived from it. Fitness is a scientific, measurable, testable fact. People who want it can be told just how much it will cost. Time and again, researchers have proven the validity of the fitness equation of duration, intensity and frequency.

Being an athlete is something quite different. Fitness is what you pass through on the way to a superior physical and mental and spiritual state. Beyond fitness is also a new and demanding, albeit infinitely rewarding, life style.

Fitness is keeping the commandments. Being an athlete is pushing one's physical capabilities to the limit, getting the most out of one's genetic endowment. Fitness is attention to the minimum daily requirements of the body. Being an athlete is attaining the maximum daily output—and paying what it costs.

Fitness and its maintenance can be programmed. You can allot a half-hour of your daily schedule for the necessary activity. Some run in the morning so they can then concentrate on their work the rest of the day. Most find a time that interferes the least with other more interesting and important activities.

The athlete, on the other hand, looks for a time when other less interesting and important activities interfere least with his or her sport. Play, not work, has the priority.

Being an athlete is not something I do an hour or so a day. It is something I *am*. Being a runner is something that informs my entire day. My 24 hours is lived as a runner. Everything that occurs takes on increased interest and importance in so much as it pertains to my running. My entire environment, internal and external, is monitored in relation to effect on my performance. So I am now runner-doctor, runner-writer, runner-lecturer. I am runner-father, runner-husband, runner-friend. For me, fitness is no longer enough. I must be an athlete.

Fitness helps you look for the life you should lead. Being an athlete means you have found it.

BOOK

2

Running and Being
The Total Experience

DRAWINGS BY NORA SHEEHAN

To Joe Henderson and Rich Koster,
who encouraged when encouragement was needed,
praised when praise was due,
and were silent when that was the kindest thing to do.

CONTENTS

Introduction 237
Prologue 241

INTRODUCTION

"

My design is thin and linear.
I am a nervous, shy noncombatant
who has no feeling for people.
I do not hunger and thirst after justice.
I find no happiness in carnival, no joy in community.
I am one with the writers on *The New Yorker* whom
Brendan Gill described. They touched each other
only by accident, were secretive about everything,
and never introduced anyone properly.

"

GEORGE SHEEHAN is an uncommon man. Doctor. Writer. Runner. He is more than the sum of his visible activities.

Uncelebrated, underpublicized, he is equally unconcerned. He is unquestionably a philosopher, and much of his journalism is both poetic and mystic.

But most of all, Sheehan is himself. Through pain and sweat and honesty, he has discovered who he is and he has become that person. Totally. He is an eloquent, joyful man. Not one, perhaps, for these times —but one who has made himself comfortable in them.

To write of Sheehan is as compelling as it is frustrating. His definition of himself and his vision of the world around him deserve a wider and much more versatile audience than that which currently enjoys him.

But to attempt to interpret, to explain Sheehan is an exercise in inadequacy—if only because he does it so much better himself.

Biographically, George Sheehan is a fifty-nine-year-old cardiologist in Red Bank, New Jersey, a peaceful community fifty miles from Manhattan. He was reared in Brooklyn, the oldest of fourteen children. He has twelve children of his own.

In spite of these numbers, he is and always has been one of life's private people. His wife, Mary Jane, says of him, "He has never needed anyone else. He doesn't find most people interesting, and he's uninterested in the conventional."

Sheehan is a paradox. He is private but he is equally humble. He communicates with the world through his writing: a column called "The Innocent Bystander."

And he communicates with himself on the roads. Running is his essence. Through it, he has discovered the marvel of his own human spirit. He has become himself. He has fulfilled himself.

And from this experience, his running, has come rare articulation, a special, individual prism that is his window to the world. Individual, but far-reaching.

From an ever-mounting stack of Sheehan columns—a major problem was simply staying ahead of a man as relentless in his writing as he is in his running—the following sampler is offered:

On sport and character: "Sport will not build character; it will do something better. It will make a man free. It has this tremendous potential for self-revelation. What we want to know is who we are, and sport can tell us quickly, painlessly and as surely as any other human activity. Besides, I would rather be one than have it."

On the decline of heroes: "Where have all the heroes gone? They've gone with the simplicities and the pieties and the easy answers of another era. Our lack of heroes is an indication of the maturity of our age. A realization that every man has come into his own and has the capacity of making a success out of his life. Of being able to say, 'I have found my hero and he is me.' "

George Sheehan may or may not be his own hero, but he certainly is his own man. He lives life at his own pace, ignoring what he refers to as "the full-court press" which destroys the human game plan of so many of his fellows.

In his sixth decade, Sheehan runs for approximately an hour every other day during his lunch hour. He travels seven and a half miles along a winding, hilly river road, and then "towels off," because "honest sweat has no odor."

He lunches on "Tab and yogurt," does his work in a sports shirt, Levi's and canvas shoes, and is "a great napper. Naps are one of the most neglected parts of modern civilization," he states flatly.

Sheehan ran competitively in school, but then abandoned it for tennis until about fifteen years ago. Now, besides his daily adventures along the river ("I look for answers on the roads. I take my tools of sight, hearing, touch, smell, taste and intellect and run with them. I discover a total universe, a world that begins on the other side of sweat and exhaustion."), he runs in the Boston Marathon, and almost every Sunday he races in New York's Central Park.

"Racing is the lovemaking of the runner," he says. "It's hard to pass up. A runner has few friends, and they are always other runners. The place to meet them is at the races."

Modestly he maintains, "As a writer, I'm like Eddie Stanky, a .230 hitter. My theme is mostly the idea of play. Of bringing back your body, of becoming yourself, a total man. When I write, I tell who I am, what I'm like, what I've discovered running. I'm not embarrassed to expose myself. I don't care what I write as long as it's true."

He was and is a sports fan. But he sees danger in the pervasive spectating of today's America.

Sheehan believes that Americans must "spill out of the TV room after an event, and act on what they have seen." As for himself, he has been known to spill back onto the road for a second run of the day after being stimulated by a televised sporting event.

What George Sheehan is, really, is not any different from the rest of us. But what he does in the common situation, how he sees it and himself, sets him apart.

Sheehan writes, "Fitness is my life; it is indispensable. I have no alternative, no choice, but to act out this inner drive that seems entirely right for me."

Running is euphoria for Sheehan. "But then comes the Hill," he writes,

and I know I am made for more. And by becoming more, I am challenged to choose suffering, to endure pain, to bear hardship. . . .

At first the gentle swell carries me. . . . But gradually the Hill demands more and more. I have reached the end of my physiology. The end of what is possible. And now it is beyond what I can stand. The temptation is to say, "Enough." This much is enough. But I will not give in.

I am fighting God. Fighting the limitations He gave me. Fighting the pain. Fighting the unfairness. Fighting all the evil in me and the world. And I will not give in. I will conquer this hill, and I will conquer it alone.

And George Sheehan will be himself. And, in writing about it, a gift to us all.

Rich Koster
St. Louis Globe Democrat

PROLOGUE

THERE ARE TIMES when I am not sure whether I am a runner who writes or a writer who runs. Mostly it appears that the two are inseparable. I cannot write without running, and I am not sure I would run if I could not write. They are two different expressions of my person. As difficult to divide as my body and mind.

Writing is the final form of the truth that comes from my running. For when I run, I am a hunter and the prey is my self, my own truth. Not only my own truth felt and my own truth known, but my own truth written. Good writing is true writing. A thing written as true as it can be done. And that truth must be sought deep inside of me. "Look into your heart," said the poet, "and write." The hunt, then, is in my heart, my inner universe, my inner landscape, my deepest inner forest.

To reach these recesses, these hiding places below the conscious, I must first create a solitude. I must achieve the aloneness that is necessary for the creative act whether one is a master or a common man like myself. Because nothing creative, great or small, has been done by committee. And having reached this solitude, this privacy, this detachment, I must await the coming of truth and know how I am to write it.

But all of this, of course, begins much earlier. First an idea interests me. Then I put it in my head and allow it to germinate for a while. Each day I take it out and inspect it for substance. If it stands up I go to the typewriter for a day or two and accumulate pages of copy. Thurber referred to this effort as "mud" and saw it as the necessary first step to the finished product.

Next, I try to organize this raw material. Attempt to discover its essence, its true meaning, what it is all about. This is almost always a failure. What I have written until then is only information. It can make me neither laugh nor cry. It has yet to be transformed into something true, something alive. That must wait until I am on the roads. Only when I am on the run does this happen.

What running does is allow it to happen. Creativity must be spontaneous. It cannot be forced. Cannot be produced on demand. Running frees me from that urgency, that ambition, those goals. There I can escape from time and passively await the revelation of the way things are.

There, in a lightning flash, I can see truth apprehended whole without thought or reason. There I experience the sudden understanding that comes unmasked, unbidden. I simply rest, rest within myself, rest within the pure rhythm of my running, rest like a hunter in a blind. And wait.

Sometimes it is all fruitless. I lack the patience, the submission, the letting go. There are, after all, things to be done. People waiting. Projects uncompleted. Letters to be answered. Paperwork to do. Planes to be caught. A man can waste just so much time and no more waiting for inspiration.

But I must wait. Wait and listen. That inner stillness is the only way to reach these inner marvels, these inner miracles all of us possess. And when truth strikes, that brief, blinding illumination tells me what every writer comes to know. If you would write the truth, you must first become the truth.

The mystery of all this is that I must let it come to me. If I seek it, it will not be found. If I grasp it, it will escape. Only in not caring and in complete nonattachment, only by existing purely in the present, will I find truth. And where truth is will also be the sublime and the beautiful, laughter and tears, joy and happiness. All there waiting also.

All this, of course, defies logic. But so does life. We live, then explain things after the fact, and imperfectly. Somehow, perhaps not the way I have said, running gives me the word, the phrase, the sentence that is just right. And there are times when I take a column on the road and it is like pulling the handle of a slot machine. Bang comes down the first sentence. Bang comes down the second, and the paragraphs unfold. And then Bang, jackpot, the piece is finished, whole and true and good.

But writing is never easy. And no matter how well done, never to one's satisfaction. Writing, someone said, is turning blood into ink. Whatever, the idea of suffering is so natural to both writers and runners it seems to be a common bond.

And therefore no surprise when one turns out to be both.

1

Living

“
No athlete ever lived,
or saint or poet for that matter,
who was content with what he did yesterday,
or would even bother thinking about it.
Their pure concern is the present.
Why should we common folk be different?
”

You WIN, the experts agree, if the game is played in your rhythm. You lose if it isn't. Every basketball fan knows that. "We put on the press," a coach once told me, "not so much to create turnovers, but to upset our opponent's rhythm. To get them moving and not thinking." Most basketball fans know that, too.

But how many of us know that the same thing is happening in our lives every day? How many of us see that we are letting someone else set the rhythm of our lives, or that we face the equivalent of the Boston Celtic full-court press when we get out of bed each morning?

The clock is where it all starts. This mechanical divider of time controls our action, imposes our work day, and tells us when to eat and sleep. The clock makes every hour just an hour. It makes no distinctions between morning and afternoon. Aided by electric daylight, it doles out apparently equal minutes and seconds until *The Late Show*. And then, Good night.

The artist, especially the poet, has always known this to be wrong. He knows that time shortens and lengthens, without regard to the minute hand. Knows that we have a beat foreign to this Greenwich metronome. Knows also there is an ebb and flow to the day that escapes the clock, but not us. And realizes that this rhythm, this tempo, is something peculiar to each individual, as personal and unchanging as his fingerprints.

The artists know this. The scientists have proved it. In *Biological Rhythms of Psychiatry and Medicine*, Bertram S. Brown writes, "Rhythm is as much a part of our structure as our flesh and bones. Most of us are dimly aware that we fluctuate in energy, mood, well being and performance each day, and that there are longer, more subtle variations each week, each month, each season, each year."

There was a time when we could sit and listen to these rhythms, but now they can hardly be heard over the din of the mechanical clocks set up by school and business and society. Now we have commuting and TV, three-day weekends and twelve-hour workdays, March migraines and April ulcers, twenty-one-year-old addicts and forty-five-year-old heart attacks.

Is anyone listening to his innards? But then, who listened to Socrates: "Know thyself"; or to Norbert Weiner: "To live effectively is to live with adequate information"; or to the Japanese philosopher Suzuki: "I am an artist at living, and my work of art is my life."

244

But that's what we must do to face that Celtic press every morning. Listen to what our body is trying to tell us. Know ourselves. Get adequate information. Become artists. Otherwise, someone else will control the pace, the game, and the score.

The Celtics are there and the press is on. They make us fit the job. Make us fit the hours. Make us fit the demands. Make us change to their tempo. March to their drummer. All the while, destroying our game plan. Our way of becoming all we are. Choking off what we do best.

They have made us prisoners of their artificial time, their mechanical clock. And all the while, they are planning the final irony. When we retire, they will give us a watch.

"Living the good life," wrote Nikolai Berdyaev, "is frequently dull and flat and commonplace." Our greatest problem, he claimed, is to make it fiery and creative and capable of spiritual struggle.

I agree. Life, except for a favored few, like poets and children and athletes and saints, is pretty much of a bore. Given the choice, most of us would give up the reality of today for the memory of yesterday or the fantasy of tomorrow. We desire to live anywhere but in the present.

I see that in myself. I start the day with an agenda of things to be done that makes me completely oblivious of what I'm doing. I arrive at work with no memory of breakfast and no idea of what kind of day it is. I am in perpetual concern or rumination about the future.

Numbers of people do the same thing in reverse. They avoid reality by living in the past. Nostalgia is their way of life. For them the good old days will never be equaled. Or emulated, for that matter, since these people rarely bestir themselves to any activity.

But for those active in mind and heart and body, the child and the poet, the saint and the athlete, the time is always now. They are eternally present. And present with intensity and participation and commitment. They have to be. When the athlete, for instance, turns his attention from the decision to be made this second and every second, he invites disaster. Should his concentration falter, should his mind wander to the next hole, the next set, the next inning, he will be undone. Only the now exists for him.

And the saint, for all his talk of heaven and the hereafter, knows that everywhere is right here, that all of time is right now, and that every man exists in the person in front of him. He knows that every instant he must choose and continue to choose among the infinite possibilities of acting—and being. He has no time to think on the future.

Nor has the poet. He must live on the alert. Always aware. Always observant. When he does this well, he teaches us how to live more fully. "The feeling of life is in every line of the poem," writes James Dickey of the *Odyssey* by Kazantzakis, "so that the reader realizes time after time how little he himself has been willing to settle for in living; how much there is on earth, how inexplicable, marvelous and endless creation is."

For such a man, Perfection Past is no temptation. Nor is it for the saint or the athlete. Their characteristic fall from grace is in the contemplation of future triumphs. Heaven, perhaps, or a masterpiece, or a world's record. No athlete ever lived, or saint or poet for that matter, who was content with what he did yesterday, or would even bother thinking about it. Their pure concern is the present.

Why should we common folk be different? Are we not all poets and saints and athletes to some degree? Yet we refuse to make the commitment. Refuse to accept our own reality and work with it. So we live in the might-have-been world of the past and the never-will-be world of the future.

What we need is an element of present danger, an intimation of tragedy, some feeling of powerful implacable forces at our doorstep. We need a threat to the commonplace which will suddenly and for all time intensify its value.

Some years ago, that happened to me. I had run a personal best marathon in Oregon, and came home full of what I would accomplish at the Boston Marathon. Five days later, I came down with the flu, and everything of importance fell into place. I no longer cared what I ran at Boston, or indeed if I ran at Boston at all. What I cared about first was health, and then being able to run again. Just to run and feel the sweat and the breathing and the power in my legs. To feel again what it was like to toil up hills and to push through pain. Just that and perhaps that good tired feeling after a race. No past runs or future triumphs would comfort me. I was ready to repent and hear the Good News.

I knew then what every poet and child, every athlete and saint knows. The reason they say this is for all the marbles is because it is always for all the marbles. And the reason they say there is no tomorrow is because there is never, at this very moment, a tomorrow. We are always at risk, always at hazard.

246

* * *

"The trouble with this country," the late John Berryman once told fellow poet James Dickey, "is that a man can live his entire life without knowing whether or not he is a coward." For the burly Berryman and ex-fighter-pilot Dickey, ordinary day-to-day living did not provide the arena for the ultimate test, the moment of truth. For at least Dickey, war is the Big Game.

"Nothing," he writes, "gives you such a feeling of consequence and performing a dangerous and essential action in a great cause."

Where, indeed, can we find those qualities in our nine-to-five existence? "There were a lot of people in the service," says Dickey, "who cried when they were discharged because they knew they would have to go back to driving taxicabs and working in insurance offices." This perception of the heightened life of the soldier is expressed even by the late James Agee. Greatness, said Agee, emerges only under difficult circumstances, and it is war that produces these circumstances.

"The fact is," writes Agee, "that in war, many men go well beyond anything that any sort of peace makes possible for them."

But peace is where courage is. It lies somewhere between the wartime obliviousness to danger and the prudence of intellect that helps us preserve the race. Courage, if we go back to its Latin root, means that the seat of the intelligence is in the heart. That the heart determines a man's action, rather than his reason or his instincts. And if the heart has its reasons the mind does not know, it also has reasons the body does not know.

Our day-to-day living may seem mindless to the mind and of no consequence to the body, but the heart tells us different. The heart is where faith lies. Where we find the supreme act of courage, the courage to be. To take arms against oneself and become one's own perfection.

"Courage," according to Paul Tillich, "is the universal and essential self-affirmation of one's being." It therefore includes the unavoidable sacrifice of elements which are part of us, but prevent us from reaching our actual fulfillment.

In everyday language, this means that if the most essential part of our being is to prevail against the less essential, we may have to give up pleasure, happiness and even life itself. Courage, then, has nothing to do with a single act of bravery. Courage is how one lives, not one specific incident. Just as mortal sin is a life style, not one startling transgression.

Some, like Berryman and Dickey's men in *Deliverance,* still ask for that one supreme test. They go from peak experience to peak experience. Shooting rapids, making parachute jumps, climbing mountains. Looking for fear that can be met and overcome fairly. Looking for something of consequence done for a great and essential cause.

Can day-to-day living provide that? Can day-to-day living become the Big Game? It can if you increase the stakes. Take Pascal's wager that God exists. Even if men had no reason for believing in God, said William James, they would postulate one as a pretext for living hard and getting out of the game of existence the keenest possibilities of zest.

"Every sort of energy and endurance, of courage and capacity for handling life's evils," claimed James, "is set free in those who have religious faith." Religion, he concluded, will always drive irreligion to the wall.

It will because suddenly we are doing something for a great and essential cause. And everything we do is of consequence and demands our perfection, physically and intellectually and psychologically. But always keeping sight of the truth that each of us is unique, each affirming his own self. Therefore we are not submissive. We are not concerned with right and wrong but with verities like good and evil.

So you see it is not as Berryman said. We are, in fact, always being called upon to be whoever we are, hero or coward. The challenge is always there. But it is not the reckless pursuit of catastrophe, it is the acceptance and perfection of the persons we are meant to be. In that perennial process so frequently fatiguing, often depressing and occasionally painful, courage is the bridge between our minds and our bodies.

"There are days when you can't get the ball in the basket, no matter how hard you try," a basketball coach once told me. "But there is no excuse for not playing good defense."

I've known those days. Days when every shot is forced. Every idea manufactured. Days when invention and wit and originality disappear. When nothing is new or bright or wonderful. The air is the same. The people are the same. The problems are the same. And on those days I start to press and everything gets that much more difficult. The feel is gone. And with it the touch, the ease, the brilliance that play brings.

The offense, you see, is play. The defense is work. When I am on offense, I create my own world. I act out the drama I have written. I dance the dance I have choreographed. I sing the song I have composed. Offense is unrehearsed, exuberant, free-wheeling. Offense is an excitement which provides its own incitement. Its own compulsion. Its own driving force. It generates its own energy.

Offense, then, is an art. It cannot be forced. It is a spontaneous, joyful unification of the body and the mind. Therefore there are days it won't happen. The circuits of the brain will not open. The playful right hemisphere remains inaccessible.

Defense needs none of this. Defense is dull, boring, commonplace. It is the unimaginative plodding attention to duty. It is grit and determination and perseverance. It requires—can I use that word?—simply an act of the will. There is never a day you can't play defense. All you need is the decision to put out. To give one hundred percent.

On defense I am another person, the real person. Offense is a showplace for talent and even genius. What defense discloses is character. There effort and energy are a matter of the will. There I am asked, "Will I or won't I have it so?"

So defense is a matter of pride. The determination to be the person I am. The decision to give my word of honor, to take an oath that what has to be done will be done.

I try not to be proud of my offense. My play, my creativity, is a gift freely given and perhaps just as readily taken away. How many poets have turned to drink in an effort to restore that childlike way of looking at things? One has to be superstitious of such feats. The mystic never presses his luck. He accepts the vision, tells few if any, and does not expect to see it again.

I enjoy my play. Enjoy having the ball. But I know that my talent is something I carry. The real test comes when that is absent. When I am filled with fatigue and boredom and the desire to be off on a vacation or a short drunk. We all know this and react differently. In an army survey, sixty-four males averaging twenty-two years of age rode exercise bicycles at fifty-five percent of their maximum oxygen capacity. They were told to ride until it became so discomforting that they felt it necessary to stop. They stopped at times varying from one and a half to ninety-eight minutes.

Defense therefore narrows down to character, the ability to persist in the direction of the greatest resistance. There are teams, and successful ones, that no longer look solely to talent. They recruit on character. It is a long season. There are days on end of giving of yourself, and talent is not enough. Only character can fix my will to the idea that anything less than my best is unworthy of me and the game and the people I play it with. Only character can take defense and make it worth every iota of my mental and physical energy. Only character can make me function when my existence seems to be, as Emerson said, a defensive war.

I know all that, as I suspect you do. But I still play defense like almost everyone else. Knowing that eventually there will be a turnover and I will get the ball. And I dream of suddenly seeing that new idea plain like a man coming open. And I hit him and then see his shot, that long perfect parabola. Knowing that when the ball leaves his hand, like the idea not yet written, it will hit nothing but cords.

But dreams are not the stuff defense is made of. Nor are men, for that matter.

2

Discovering

"

Who I am is no mystery.
There is no need to tap my phone or open my mail.
No necessity to submit me to psychoanalysis.
No call to investigate my credit rating.
Nothing to be gained by invading my privacy.
There is, in fact, no privacy to invade.
Because like all human beings I have no privacy.
Who I am is visible for all to see.

"

WHEN I WAS YOUNG, I knew who I was and tried to become someone else. I was born a loner. I came into this world with an instinct for privacy, a desire for solitude and an aversion to loud voices, to slamming doors and to my fellow man. I was born with the dread that someone would punch me in the nose or, even worse, put his arm around me.

But I refused to be that person. I wanted to belong. Wanted to become part of the herd, any herd. When you are shy and tense and self-conscious, when you are thin and scrawny and have an overbite and a nose that takes up about one third of your body surface, you want friends, you want to join with others. My problem was not individuality, but identity. I was more of an individual than I could handle. I had to identify with a group.

I was not unusual in this. Youth rebels, but rebels into other conformities. Moves from Christianity to Communism. From Brooks Brothers suits to T-shirts and jeans. From meat and potatoes to macrobiotic diets. From crewcuts to long hair. But no one is going it alone. No one is facing just who he is.

We all know this to a degree. We refuse to accept the true self so painfully evident to the young, a self so tragically concealed from the old. "There is only one complete, unblushing male in America," wrote Erving Goffman in *Stigma,* "a young, married, white, urban, northern, heterosexual, Protestant father of college education, fully employed, of good complexion, weight and height, and a recent record in sports."

Anyone who fails to qualify in any one of these ways, comments Goffman, is going to view himself from time to time as unworthy, incomplete and inferior.

I spent the next four decades with these feelings of being unworthy and incomplete and inferior. Combating my own nature. Trying to become someone I was not. Concealing the real me under layer after layer of coping and adjusting and compensating. All the while refusing to believe that the person I had initially rejected was the real me. All the while trying to pass as a normal member of a normal society.

Then I discovered running and began the long road back. Running made me free. It rid me of concern for the opinion of others. Dispensed me from rules and regulations imposed from outside. Running let me start from scratch.

It stripped off those layers of programmed activity and thinking. Developed new priorities about eating and sleeping and what to do with leisure time. Running changed my attitude about work and play. About whom I really liked and who really liked me. Running let me see my twenty-four-hour day in a new light and my life style from a different point of view, from the inside instead of out.

Running was discovery, a return to the past, a proof that life did come full cycle and the child was father to the man. Because the person I found, the self I discovered, was the person I was in my youth. The person who was hypersensitive to pain, both physical and psychic, a nominal coward. The person who did not wish his neighbor ill, but did not wish him well either. That person was me and always had been.

And that person, wrote Dr. William Sheldon in his *Varieties of Human Physique*, was as normal as anyone else. In fact, wrote Sheldon, most people built like me act that way. Function follows structure, wrote Sheldon, and there is a relationship between body build and personality. To act any other way would be foreign to my nature. Sheldon's constitutional psychology was the scientific confirmation of what I had already learned about myself on the roads.

But could he tell me more? I dug into his *Atlas of Men* and there I was. Somatotype 235 (Mesomorphic ectomorphy), the fox among men. (Sheldon used an animal symbol for each body type.) The number 235 is somatotype shorthand for little or no fat (2); a moderate amount of muscle (3); and a predominance of skin, hair, nervous tissue and thin bones (5). (The limits being one to seven.)

Just like the fox, whom Sheldon described as delicate, lean and fast, a brittle, meat-hungry hunter of great speed and resourcefulness and endurance. If cornered, defiant and courageous beyond his real strength, but normally a furtive, secretive way of life. With a little less muscle and aggressiveness, I would be a squirrel. A little more and I would be a wolf.

So who is the 235? Like the fox, he is a defiant loner who makes his own rules. "The 235," writes Sheldon, "is too brittle for direct fighting, too exposed to thrive in the over-stimulation of ordinary social life, but he has a sense of confidence and a subconscious knowledge that he has a long life ahead."

This eventually leads him to a defiant way of life and often to the mental hospital, with now and then a savior emerging from the ranks. Like Prometheus, he sometimes has enough strength and endurance to triumph over the establishment.

I am not all that sure about being a 235. But there are days when I run when I know I am a fox. Days when I feel the Hound in pursuit. When I appeal to all swift things for swiftness and flee Him in the mist of tears and under running laughter. When I am hunted, but I know there will be no kill. Know that in the end, the Hound does run with the fox. He will not take me until I know what I need to know, and do what I am supposed to do.

No practiced eye is needed to distinguish a marathoner from a middle linebacker, and both of these from the nonathlete who would prefer to float around in the water conversing with his companions. Each is built for his task. The fragile, thin and small-boned distance runner can carry his light frame for miles and miles. The athletic and muscular football player is, as Don Meredith once said, hostile and agile and all those wonderful things. And the soft, round and fat swimmer rides high in the water and takes to it like a dolphin. In sports, your body determines your role. Function follows structure.

Life is no different. Our work, our life style, should be like our play. "To maintain one's self on this earth is not a hardship," wrote Thoreau, "but a pastime; as the pursuits of the simpler nations are still the sports of the more artificial." So the dominant component in physique that makes a person a distance runner also determines his approach to people and society, to eating and travel, to education and discipline, to the goals and values and behavior that marks his "good life." It should come as no surprise, therefore, that his "good life" is quite different from that of an aggressive football player and the relaxed socializer.

Yet educators, psychologists, theologians, social scientists and philosophers continue to lump us under that great umbrella, Man. Man, they tell us, using "we" and "our" and "us" and other collective words indiscriminately, should, would, will, ought or must do this or that.

They try to set up an all-embracing system of ethics and psychology. Tell us how to act and react. Lump the marathoner and the middle linebacker and the plump nonathlete into one composite human being.

It doesn't work in sports. It won't work in life. The centuries-old injunction "Know thyself" still applies. And the best way to know yourself is through an analysis of your body structure and the way it moves.

The Greeks were the first to notice this. Aristotle would have diagnosed me by the shape of my nose. Hippocrates looked at the body build and predicted subsequent disease. Later, men were classified by body humors, sanguine, phlegmatic, choleric and melancholic. Through the years men have been the connection between the way a man is constructed and the way he acts. As in all of nature structure determines function.

It wasn't until three decades ago, however, that Sheldon finally made this constitutional psychology a legitimate science. Sheldon saw that we were made up of different ratios of the three primary layers of tissue in the embryo: the ectoderm (skin and nervous tissue), the endoderm (intestines), the mesoderm (bone and muscle). Depending on the ratio and the predominating tissue, he was able to predict physical abilities, reaction to stress, aesthetic preferences, personality, temperament, and appropriate life style.

To read Sheldon is to have a whole new world opened to you. And to accept Sheldon is to accept yourself and your own peculiarities and to learn to live with the peculiarities and to learn to live with the peculiarities of others. To see yourself as normal and lovable no matter how odd you appear. And to see others as normal and lovable also, however difficult that is to comprehend.

Mostly we have gone wrong because we have failed to investigate this relationship between the shape of a man and how he behaves. We have not seen that physique and temperament are two aspects of the same thing. That structure must somehow determine function and with it the laws of each human being and his inner harmony. It identifies, to use Emerson's expression, the music of one's own particular dance of life.

Should his structure be analyzed correctly, a person would discover what kind of a body he has and therefore what kind of person he is. Learn his strengths and weaknesses, his likes and dislikes, how he relates to people and things, and even his appropriate life style. With such an analysis, he would come to know his own individual physiology, psychology and philosophy. ("A man's religion or philosophy," wrote Ellen Glasgow, "is as natural as the color of his eyes, or the tone of his voice.")

He would then perceive whether he is built for flight or fight or negotiation. Whether he was born to dominate his fellow men or socialize with them or avoid them completely. Such a study would tell him his work, his play, and whether he should marry, and if so to whom.

These are the restrictions on our inalienable rights of life, liberty and the pursuit of happiness. Our bodies define and determine that life, that liberty, and the form of that pursuit. Each is different for each person, and the body, writes Sheldon, is the objective record of the person. The task before us, says Sheldon, is to convert that record into speech.

For Sheldon there is no body-mind problem, no conscious versus unconscious, no break between the physical and the mental. He sees only structure and behavior as a functional continuum.

"My aim," he wrote, "is to develop every individual according to his best potential, protecting him from false ambition, the desire to be someone he never can be, and, even more important, never should be."

Without Sheldon you will try to reform yourself or others. Either despising yourself or viewing others as hopeless ruffians or sloppy bores. At least two thirds of the people in the world will set your teeth on edge if you don't understand each body build and the natural way these people act.

Mankind, said Sheldon, is divided into three races. But these races have nothing to do with color or geography or blood types. There is the athletic race, the muscular mesomorphs (the doers); the relaxed and amiable race of endomorphs (the talkers); and the thin small-boned race of ectomorphs (the thinkers).

These races have their special qualities, and harmony between these races is a lot more difficult then you might suspect. Each reacts differently and in ways the others may well find annoying or distressing or even dangerous. The mesomorph reacts to stress by going into action. He is best described by words like *dominant, cheerful, energetic, confident, competitive, assertive, optimistic, reckless,* and *adventurous.* The leisurely endomorph, on the other hand, reacts to stress by socializing. He is more likely to be described as *calm, placid, generous, affectionate, tolerant, forgiving, sympathetic,* and *kind.*

The ectomorph is none of these things. He is *detached, ambivalent, reticent, suspicious, cautious, awkward,* and *reflective.* He finds ideas much more interesting than people. And he reacts to stress by withdrawal.

In a world where concern for one's fellow man is basic, he preserves himself by being uninvolved. Like Einstein, he was made to pull in a single harness. Like Thoreau, he has found no companion so companionable as solitude. And with him, as Kazantzakis said, "People sense I have no need of them, that I am capable of living without their conversation. There are very few people with whom I could have lived for any length of time without them feeling annoyed."

His solution, of course, is not to impersonate the achiever or those who love community. This would be a pseudolife. Even if he succeeds, he fails. He must realize that the life that men praise and regard as successful is, as Thoreau said, but one of a kind.

And let his body lead him to the kind for him.

Who I am is no mystery. There is no need to tap my phone or open my mail. No necessity to submit me to psychoanalysis. No call to investigate my credit rating. Nothing to be gained by invading my privacy. There is, in fact, no privacy to invade. Because like all human beings I have no privacy. Who I am is visible for all to see.

My body tells all. Tells my character, my temperament, my personality. My body tells my strengths and weaknesses, tells what I can and can't do. If I were in a big black box and all you knew about me were my measurements, my lengths and breadths and circumferences, you would still know what kind of man I am.

William Sheldon used just such techniques in his *The Varieties of Human Physique*, describing the dominant temperaments that went with the primary physical components.

Sheldon was saying something all painters, but especially caricaturists, know. Man reveals himself through his body. "When I draw a man," wrote Max Beerbohm, "I am concerned simply with the physical aspect of him. I see all his salient points exaggerated and all his insignificant points proportionately diminished. In those salient points, a man's soul reveals itself. Thus, if you underline these points and let the others vanish, one is bound to bare the soul."

What each of their subject's bodies reveal to Sheldon's tape measure and Beerbohm's pen is the range of human reactions to stress, be it psychic or physical. And the even wider range of pleasures and desires. Yet each must be considered normal for that particular individual. Otherwise, he would be leading someone else's life. In effect, playing someone else's sport. My life is authentic only when I feel, think and do what I and I only must feel, think and do.

This is nowhere more evident than in the thin, detached, introspective, solitary long-distance runner. In an egalitarian, competitive society where there is no excuse for failure, he scores well below the median in need to achieve. He lacks the necessary psychological energy and enterprise and willingness to take risk.

This is a lot to learn, you might say, from one long look. But Sheldon is not alone in this idea. There are many who think that the body, the product of heredity and our genes, is still the dominant force in who we are and what will happen to us. So we hear of type-A personalities having heart disease; and of predicting coronary attacks from body build.

There are many who will not accept this. The Freudians, who think we were born with a clear slate and then childhood and our parents did us in, see this as an aberration. So do the dreamers of the American Dream, who say we can be anything we want to be. They see Sheldon's theories as deterministic, a threat to freedom.

I see it differently. My body shows me what I am free to be. It does not set a boundary but shows me a fulfillment. And liberates me from a depressing past and an impossible future.

Who are you? Take a look.

I am a runner. Years ago that statement would have meant little more to me than an accidental choice of sport. A leisure time activity selected for reasons as superficial as the activity itself.

Now I know better. The runner does not run because he is too slight for football, or hasn't the ability to put a ball through a hoop, or can't hit a curve ball. He runs because he has to. Because in being a runner, in moving through pain and fatigue and suffering, in imposing stress upon stress, in eliminating all but the necessities of life, he is fulfilling himself and becoming the person he is.

I have given up many things in this becoming process. None was a sacrifice. When something clearly became nonessential, there was no problem in doing without. And when something clearly become essential, there was no problem accepting it and whatever went with it.

From the outside, this runner's world looks unnatural. The body punished, the appetites denied, the satisfactions delayed, the motivations that drive most men ignored. The truth is that the runner is not made for the things and people and institutions that surround him. To use Aldous Huxley's expression, his small guts and feeble muscles do not permit him to eat or fight his way through the ordinary rough-and-tumble.

That he is not made for the workaday world, that his essential nature and the law of his being are different from the ordinary and usual is difficult for everyone, including the runner, to comprehend. But once it is understood, the runner can surrender to his self, this law. And become, in the puritan sense, the "free man," the man who is attached only to the good.

In this surrender, the runner does not deny his body. He accepts it. He does not subdue it, or subjugate it, or mortify it. He perfects it, maximizes it, magnifies it. He does not suppress his instincts, he heeds them. And goes beyond this animal in him toward what Ortega called his veracity, his own truth.

The finished product is therefore a lifetime work. This giving up, this letting go, the detachment from attachments, is an uneven process. You should give up only what no longer has any attraction to you, or interferes with something greatly desired. That was Gandhi's rule. He advised people to keep doing whatever gave them inner help and comfort.

I have learned that also. Whatever I give up, whatever innocent indulgences, ordinary pleasures or extraordinary vices, I do so from inner compulsion, not in a mood of self-sacrifice or from a sense of duty, I am simply doing what comes naturally.

For the runner, less is better. The life that is his work of art is understated. His needs and wants are few, he can be captured in a few strokes. One friend, a few clothes, a meal now and then, some change in his pockets; and, for enjoyment, his thoughts and the elements.

And though he's on the run, he's in no hurry. Concerned at times with tenths of a second, he actually responds to the season, moving through cycle and cycle, toward less and less until body and mind and soul fuse, and all is one.

I see this simplicity as my perfection. In the eyes of observers, however, it appears completely different. My success in removing myself from things and people, from ordinary ambition and desires, is seen as lack of caring, proof of uninvolvement, and failure to contribute.

So be it. A larger view of the world might include the possibility that such people are necessary. That the runner who is burning with a tiny flame on some lonely road does somehow contribute. And while a world composed solely of runners would be unworkable, a world without them would be unlivable.

3

Understanding

“

I am who I am and can be nothing but that.
'Do not mistake me for someone else,'
said Nietzsche. Do not mistake me for a
listener or citizen or friend. And when I
get that look in my eye that says I'm going 'away,'
do me a favor. Let me go.

”

WHEN I RUN THE ROADS, I am a saint. For that hour, I am Assisi wearing the least and meanest of clothes. I am Gandhi, the young London law student, trotting ten or twelve miles a day and then going to a cheap restaurant to eat his fill of bread. I am Thoreau, the solitary, seeking union with the world around him.

On the roads, Poverty, Chastity and Obedience come naturally. I am one of the poor in spirit who will see God. My chastity is my completion in the true Eros which is play. And the Ten Commandments are the way the world works.

But off the roads, that all changes. Anyone who has lived with a distance runner knows that. They see in him what was said of Moses by the advisers of an Eastern king. Looking at his picture, they said, "This is a cruel, greedy, self-seeking dishonest man." The king was puzzled and asked Moses, who said the experts were right. "That's what I was made of," he said, "I fought against it and that's how I became what I am."

Unfortunately, I am a long way from that final victory. And, like most distance runners, I have all the bad features of a saint without any of the redeeming ones. Pity the family and friends who have to care for us.

"Caring" is the word, because the average distance runner is a helpless creature who can with difficulty change a light bulb. He is unable to fend for himself in a competitive world and has long since given up trying. From long experience, he expects that things will be done for him. Meals provided. Laundry done. Errands run. All of the amenities taken care of so he can do his thing. And do it to his heart's content.

So my poverty is not poverty. My needs may be little, like Saint Francis. But unlike him, the little I need, I need very much. The little I want, I want very much.

My breakfast is simple. But it must be perfect. Do not cut my English muffin with a knife or I may not talk to you for the rest of the day. My clothes may be rejects and hand-me-downs, but lose them or even have them in a laundry at the wrong time and my day may be ruined. And so it goes from shoes to yogurt, everything has to be just right or the day becomes dark and dreary. And not only for me, but for the people around me.

If I do resemble Assisi, it is in the matter of money. I never have any. I expect others to take care of me. Pay my entry fee. Take care of my lunch. Only in absent-minded moments will I reach for a check. Rarely through the years have I been caught with enough change to buy a chance for charity.

And if poverty is still a battle, what about chastity? Even more of a struggle. Like thousands of scrawny, pinch-faced Irishmen, I have fought my body since my First Communion. Known that the body belongs to the Devil. Read Joyce or O'Casey or even Yeats, who wrote in his diary that he set these things down so other young men might not think themselves peculiar.

So, off the roads, chastity comes from the highest form of fear—the fear of eternal damnation. "Others, I am not the first," wrote Housman, "have wished more mischief than they durst." Only beyond such restraint is the reconciliation of body and soul and then the true Eros and the love of friends and, finally, the agape where in the giving we receive.

And finally, what of obedience? Discipline in running, discipline in training, comes easily. Discipline in real life is another story. The mind and the will and the imagination are not as easily controlled as the legs and the thighs and the panting chest. Running, of course, helps. The art of running, as Eugene Herrigal wrote of the art of archery, is a profound and far-reaching contest of the runner with himself. And that contest should lead to his perfection.

When I was young, I was afflicted with what my aunt called "convenient deafness." I still am. I have the ability to tune out what is going on around me. It is normal for me to retreat inside myself and become less and less aware of my surroundings. If I am in a group and not talking, do not suppose I am listening. I am "away." I am off in another world. Off in my natural habitat, my mind.

Being "away" is the true freedom. I escape to where I want to be, thinking what I want to think, creating what I want to create. Wherever I am, whomever I am with, it doesn't matter. The greatest bore in the world may be holding the stage, but I am untouched. I am, as Yeats once said, like a child in the corner playing with his blocks.

And being "away" from making a fool of myself. When I am with people I am always saying too much or too little. Something better left unsaid, or stupid, or soon regretted. If it takes me ten hours to write a six-hundred-word essay, how could I possibly say something out of hand that I would ever care to have repeated?

I am a descendant of similar people of the mind. Men like

Kierkegaard and Emerson and Bertrand Russell. Those who saw themselves early as different and, at first, disastrously so. "I was a shy, solitary prig," say Russell. Ungenerous and selfish, cautious and cold, was how Emerson described himself. Kierkegaard made much the same analysis. "Ideas," he wrote, "are my only joy, human beings an object of indifference."

Such people, according to Ortega, have very little knowledge of women, business, pleasure and passion. They lead an abstract life, he said, and rarely throw a morsel of authentic live meat to the sharp-pointed teeth of their intellect.

The way out of that abstract existence is to go out. If not to other people, at least to the body. And so they became great walkers, outdoor people. Emerson's journal has a reference to a forty-mile walk from Roxbury to Worcester, and Russell wrote of his pleasant relaxation after his twenty-five-mile walks.

And that, I suppose, is why I run and find there the authentic life. "First be a good animal," said Emerson. And in running I am that animal, the best animal I can be. Doing what I am built to do. Moving with the grace and rhythm and certainty that I seem to have possessed from all time.

And there I find joy. Kierkegaard was mistaken in that. There is no joy in ideas. Joy comes at the peak of an experience and then always as a surprise. I cannot have joy on demand. At best, I go where I have felt it before. And that is mostly on the river road, moving at a pace I could hold forever and my mind running free. So that I am in this alternation of effort and relaxation, of systole and diastole. And then I have that fusion where it all is play and I am capable of anything. I become a child.

It will not surprise you that the thinkers believe that our true journey is back to our childhood. One mystic wrote that man's perfection and bliss lay in the transformation of the bodily life to joyful play. Norman Brown declared that man is that species of animal which has as its immortal project the recovering of its childhood.

I will not apologize, therefore, for an activity that makes me a child. An activity that takes me away from women and business, pleasure and passion. An activity that is its own meaning. An activity without purpose.

So I run in joy and even afterwards there is a completeness that lingers and is even restored in the long hot shower. I am "away," not in the mind but in its warm, relaxed, tingling happy body, the feeling of running still in my legs and arms and chest. I am still enjoying who I was and what I did that hour on the road.

Some of you may wonder that a life can be felt so completely in the absence of other people. I wonder at that myself. It goes against everything I have been taught. Everything that went into the preservation of our culture.

But I am who I am and can be nothing but that. "Do not mistake me for someone else," said Nietzsche. Do not mistake me for a listener or citizen or friend. And when I get that look in my eye that says I'm going "away," do me a favor. Let me go.

The distance runner, I have observed, is usually a secretive person. I am one myself. There was a time before I came to running when I rarely looked anyone in the eye. Even now I am reluctant about it. Some, I am sure, think me shifty-eyed and not to be trusted. And to an extent they are right. I am shifty-eyed. I avoid that direct gaze. I prefer to neither see nor be seen.

Seeing, looking into another's eyes, can be a total revelation. The look, wrote Ortega, is an act that comes directly from an inwardness with the straight-line accuracy of a bullet. Erving Goffman described it as "the most direct and purest reciprocity that exists anywhere."

The look, then, is in the present tense. It has nothing to do with past or future, with were or will be. The look is now. It is direct. Like a poem it must not mean, but be. We look through, not with, our eyes. Our eyes, therefore, are what we are. My eyes are me.

The eyes, then, reveal and in revealing appeal for revelation. Richard Avedon, the photographer, says of himself and his subjects, "We are there eye-to-eye, completely open, naked to each other." He is there, he says, asking them to give and they are trying to give, to demonstrate themselves. And when that ultimate revelation is achieved, he says, "Thank you." Then the strangers again become strangers. Eyes then glaze over. Looks become unfocused. The connection is broken.

The look, then, tells no less than who I am. It says, "This is the real me." It tells truth in the sense the Greeks used the word: to bare. The look, that subtle yet tenacious look, does just that. It bares me down to the submerged inner landscape of my soul.

In times gone by I was ashamed of that truth, ashamed of the self I supposed myself to be. And, being ashamed, avoided other eyes. There was a time when I could not abide with that soul or that inner landscape. I sought only to hide it. I lived then in an either/or world. If you were not one thing, you were the other. I was always the other, the unacceptable, the sinner, the outsider. And it was all there in my eyes. One look straight into my eyes and the observer would know me for what I was. One who cared little for his fellow man. One who viewed the Other, if not as an enemy, at the very least as a threat.

In one unguarded unequivocal gaze, one sharp straight line from one heart to another, I would be illuminated like a countryside by a lightning flash. All my embarrassments, my mistakes, my playing the fool. So I learned to protect myself. To wear a mask. To talk into the air. To control others' access to me. To keep intruders away from my real self or who I thought my real self to be.

In those days the worst command I could hear was "Look me straight in the eye and tell me that." Then inevitably the truth would come out. I would be caught in the lie. "Never let them get your eyes" was the motto of a famous New York detective. If you did they knew you. In that instant all deception was over. My eyes revealed in those seconds what I have buried for years. Exposed scars and opened wounds I thought long healed.

Running has changed all that. Given a new perspective to that inner landscape. I accept my ups and downs, my ins and outs, my uncertain being and becoming. I do my best. I remain patient and enjoy. And most of all I make no judgments except about effort. There I demand the most and more.

So my look is no longer furtive. No longer unfocused and shifting over the surface. No longer directed three inches to the left of the listener's ear or just over the speaker's left shoulder. I am able to show myself to another human being, desiring to give my love and receive theirs. I no longer need to avert my gaze from anyone.

But I do. I am still the secretive runner. My looks are still for those who are like myself. Those who share my truth, my feelings, my perception of the world as happy and sad. When I lecture to runners I go from one face to the other speaking eye to eye, mind to mind, heart to heart. And I am moved as I move them.

At races it is much the same. Not so much, perhaps, before the race, when we are a little frightened and worried about the future. At that time I sometimes exhibit a spurious ease and a false assurance to mask that fear.

It is afterward that we see inside of each other. It is after we have survived a desperate thirty minutes that there is pride and happiness and union in the looks we exchange.

There even poetry fails. Poetry, said Eliot, is the best possible words in the best possible arrangement. Yet it is still less than the nonverbal that provoked it. Poetry is only the putting into words of what my eyes and yours have said.

I have always felt uneasy in the presence of authority. The sight of a police car in my rear-view mirror is enough to paralyze me from the waist down. Any legal-looking document in the mail can ruin my day. And one word from someone with a title or uniform and I snap to attention like a Marine in boot camp. My world, you see, is filled with drill instructors whom I avoid as much as possible.

Every once in a while I fail. A dozen or so years back, I made a U turn in our main street after picking up the morning paper. When I completed the turn, I was looking right into the face of the chief of police. He knew me immediately for what I was. A man who hated rules but was afraid of those who enforced them. "Don't ever do that again," he said. I never did and I never will.

But human laws are minor. Human authority can be either avoided or heeded with little change in everyday living. Nature cannot. Nature's laws can be either major or minor, but they cannot be ignored. Nature, I have found, can lean on you more than any human being. It is one thing to avoid principals and bosses and policemen, but quite another to avoid the laws that govern the universe.

Human law is soft and kindly and forgiving compared to the ones that run the cosmos. Traffic tickets and felonies, and income tax evasions and legal suits are easily negotiable compared to gravity and the laws of motion and thermodynamics. Laws, incidentally, that are omnipresent and unavoidable. I can evade a clash with my head, but not with the rules that make the world work.

That clash begins when I get into the car in the morning. It may or may not start. Either way, the car is obeying rules that govern energy and its transformation. Rules from which there is no appeal. There is no

266

letting you off just this once, no probation, no leniency. And neither prayers nor curses will revive a dead generator.

Should I try to circumvent this need for mechanical conformity by getting a push, I only dig the hole a little deeper. Now other regulations, about force and vectors and torque, come into play. The bumpers lock.

What good pleading extenuating circumstances? Temporary insanity? A defect in toilet training? The day has barely begun and I am in the hands of tyrants, controlled by a dictator.

Should the car start, this unfeeling oppression continues. As I accelerate, my cup of coffee previously resting securely on the open door of the glove compartment falls to the floor. The coffee splashes my freshly cleaned Levi's and the books and papers on the seat beside me. I brake and the deceleration covers the floor with a fine mixture of coffee and correspondence. Before the trip is complete I have experienced the adverse effects of gravity, centrifugal force, friction and any number of other laws in nature that can wreck your day.

At those times, I think of heaven as the place where all those laws can be broken. Coffee never spills no matter how carelessly I place it down or how quickly I shift. And everything stays in place no matter how fast I take the turns. And should I forget and leave something on the roof of the car, it will remain there until I get to my destination. And I will be preserved from the violence and interference of laws both human and natural.

Actually, it is the other way around. Law preserves me from violence and interference. Because my neighbors obey policemen and legislators and bureaucrats, because my coffee and car obey the precepts of physics and science, I live in a stable world. And because of that, I am able to rise above the law and become a free man. The least I can do is obey the traffic laws and learn how to drive a car.

Generosity is not one of my faults. I have no impulse to spread my money around. No temptation to give until it hurts. I treat my neighbor as myself. Which means to use it up, wear it out, make it do. And ask for separate checks.

I wasn't brought up that way. My father made a point on entering a restaurant with a party to see the waiter immediately to make sure he got the bill. He viewed any effort by others to change this arrangement as a personal insult. In the days before the expense account and the charge card, he was the quickest draw with a wallet I ever saw.

Being a slow man with a buck is therefore not a matter of training. It seems to relate to body build and is apparently characteristic of weak, small-boned people like myself. It is an especially common finding in lonely long-distance runners. Also like myself.

Race directors know this only too well. Should they raise the entry fee a quarter, they get complaints from all sides.

And if they neglect to give out free meals or complimentary T-shirts, they will draw protests even from affluent road runners. It is not unusual, despite their dependence on their organizations, for most runners regardless of financial status to try to compete without shelling out a few dollars for an AAU card. And almost to a man they have to be dunned for their Road Runners Club dues.

You may look on this as being stingy or miserly, think of our habits as to sharing costs and helping others as un-Christian, even immoral. But that is because you are you, and we are quite different. My nickel-and-dime approach to life comes from deep inside of me. It is part of the person I am, part of the body I inhabit, part of my peculiar union of flesh and spirit.

And it is not only instinct. It is also external evidence of a personal austerity, a self-imposed mortification, an attempt at simplicity and poverty and the childlike attitude that Bernanos said was the only defense against the Devil. Against, you might say, his Devil, not yours. Except that his Devil seems to be my Devil. The distance runner's particular Devil.

Part of our problem is other people. People who, as Russell Baker wrote in his *New York Times* piece "The Summer of '39," used to hold us upside down by the heels to prove how strong they were. That was our outer world then. And we still live in a world controlled by the people who hold us upside down by the heels to prove how strong they are. It is a world primarily of money. A world of mortgages and life insurance and down payments and grocery bills. A world that is easy pickings for those who learn how to move around in it; and torture for those who don't.

I have never learned how. And never will learn how. What I have learned is to get outside the world. To need less. To reduce my wants. To be satisfied with essentials. I have learned that possessions get in my way. That money and what it can buy are distractions. I have learned that simplicity starts when income exceeds outgo.

If I were a world class runner in my age group my body fat would be less than six percent. Instead it is twice that and always will be. The reason? I am a natural-born, died-in-the-wool, nothing-can-be-done-about-it freeloader. Hungry or not, I will eat anything that is free. Last month, for instance, after a fifteen-kilometer run in which I absolutely wasted myself and went to the point of exhaustion and beyond, I nevertheless accepted and finished a postrace box lunch of orange drink and fried chicken. Yes, fried chicken.

Hand me a box lunch and, however indigestible it is, I'll gobble it up. Hand me a meal ticket and regardless of appetite I'll get on line. When all desire for food has vanished offer me anything edible and I'll manage somehow to get it down. Inside of me, as in every thin man, there is a fat man saying "Eat." And my fat man is adding "Eat, it's free."

You may not have noticed, but there are free meals not only at races, but everywhere. Everywhere, that is, if you see as free any meal that you don't pay for right there on the spot. So home meals and free access to the kitchen at night are really meals offered gratis. At those times the inner voice saying "Eat, it's free" is just as loud as when I am accepting the traditional beef stew after the Boston Marathon. I'm a freeloader in my own home.

Fortunately this tendency to eat when it's free is counterbalanced by an equal and opposite tendency not to eat when it isn't. I can go heroic lengths of time without food if I have to buy it myself. Although I look on this as being frugal, there are some places where I am thought to be a cheapskate. I will admit that I am reluctant to break a dollar, but only because there is soon very little left of the original buck. And I do fortify this reluctance to spend money on food by having no money on me to spend. There is no better way to control impulse shopping.

Buying food never did make sense to me. When I finally spend some money I prefer to have some permanent evidence of the expenditure. Doing it on something that is immediately consumed leaves me feeling cheated. For much the same reason, I suppose, I have never smoked. Buying something and then setting it on fire is incomprehensible.

So for long periods during the day I am protected by this natural miserliness or what I prefer to think of as natural austerity. When I lunch it is usually forty cents' worth of yogurt and tea, and back to work. It is only later when I arrive home that things begin to go badly.

From then on I eat as if I were a digestive athlete. I clean my plate just as I did when my mother first told about those less fortunate starving children who could live a week on what I left behind. Later I go through the kitchen like some TV-game-show winner given free access to a supermarket. During the first two commercials I can use up my five hundred calories earned so dearly with five miles on the roads. Unless somehow restrained I will go through the breadbox, get involved with the pretzels, succumb to the cheese crackers, and do away with any remaining ice cream. And still have an hour to go before the nightly news.

The answer, it seems to me, is to turn the home into a commercial establishment. Eliminate the free meal. Put everything on a pay-as-you-go basis. When I get home at night I should be faced by a menu with everything à la carte and quite expensive. And no credit cards, only cash accepted. Once I start computing cost per calories and watching the right-hand side of the bill of fare I'll quickly get back to my normal penurious self.

And for the after-dinner period there should be a checkout counter in the kitchen. Then the trip through that larder will take a lot longer as I reluctantly part with my well-worn dimes and quarters. And I'll get back to the TV room with only the best buys of the day.

On that great don't-come-and-get-it day, I'll have an answer to the fat man inside of me: "Shut up, you dummy, they're charging money for it."

The way to argue against drunkenness is not to tell lies about it. Alcohol can take you places the sober man may never see. Sobriety, wrote William James, diminishes, discriminates and says no; drunkenness expands, unites and says yes. "The sway of alcohol over mankind," he concluded, "is unquestionably due to its power to stimulate the mystical faculties of human nature."

This is what alcohol can do: Can give you a glimpse of yourself in your own particular world, of you as part of the cosmos. Drink also reveals the person you are. Whether you are the solitary schizoid, thinking great thoughts and living in fantasy. Or the gregarious manic-depressive who wants to be part of a warm and eternally friendly group. Or the muscular paranoid, ready to settle any disagreement with his fists.

270

What alcohol cannot do is bring these insights into purposeful action. Having glimpsed the person he is, the drinker must now find an alternate and fruitful path to his truth. To do this, he must first disentangle himself from alcohol, and then rescue himself from the lies of his daily living. So it is frequently the ex-alcoholic, who has been there and back, who experiences the new birth. It is the former lush who finally unites his divided self. It is the reformed drunk who accepts the person he is without reservation. And pursues that perfection however mediocre or even abnormal it may appear to someone else.

Becoming an ex-alcoholic, however, is not easy. Drink may be futile and ultimately degrading, but only the fortunate drinker discovers this. And it is the even more fortunate one who then comes upon a new and healthy path to the summit of his physical and mental powers. Before the liver goes, the heart enlarges, and the brain begins to deteriorate, he must get the message that there is a better way to experience himself and the universe.

My own drinking habits changed because of two such fortunate events. Back in those days when I was living it up on Saturday nights, I had always supposed that drink made me brilliant. I thought that someone should be writing down everything I said, preserving these great ideas and clever bon mots for posterity. Then, one night, someone took fifty feet of home movies of me under the influence. What I saw on the screen looked like the Missing Link rather than the intellectual I imagined myself to be. Here was photographic evidence that when drunk I was incapable of thought, much less of expressing it. Because of that film, I quit serious drinking. Not so much to become the person I was, but simply to rejoin the human race.

Distance running, my next discovery, was a positive factor and the decisive one. Negative injunctions never work. Lives are changed by do's, not don'ts. And if one is to stop drinking permanently, one must be actively involved in becoming what one is. Distance running did that for me. It reintroduced me to my body. And my body, I found out, had a mind of its own. It would no longer accept anything less that the best. Having gotten into trim, it refused to be tampered with. Having reached the peak of its powers, it dragged my mind and my will along with it.

Now the hour a day on the roads began to provide the altered states of consciousness that alcohol supplied so fleetingly. Running, I learned, gave me a natural high. What happens in those moments I am not sure.

Andrew Weil, the author of *The Natural Mind,* calls it the integration of the conscious and unconscious spheres of our mental life. "This integration," he states, "is essential to the wholeness (health) of body and mind."

I'll give him no argument there, but this I know: whatever it is, it starts with the body. By first reaching a fitness which reveals the real person inside my body (just so does the sculptor find the statue inside the stone). And then through this body, this mirror of my soul, this key to my personality, this telltale of my temperament, I see myself as I really am.

I don't drink much anymore. I am never the life of any party. The hostess who invites me knows within the first five minutes she has made a mistake. I usually wander into the kitchen for a cup of coffee and then find a large book and a quiet place to read until the festivities are over. I have found out who I am. And I have no intention of impersonating anyone else.

Some people liked me better when I was drinking.

4

Beginning

❝

**If you think that life
has passed you by, or, even worse,
that you are living someone else's life,
you can still prove the experts wrong.**

❞

THE PEOPLE WHO THINK they know say that given a second chance a man will make the same mess of his life he did the first time. Playwrights and novelists over the years have never given us any hope that reliving our lives would have any different result the second time around. Our scientists and psychologists seem to agree. Even such disparate thinkers as Bucky Fuller and B. F. Skinner are together on this. "We shouldn't try to change people," writes Skinner. "We should change the world in which people live." It is a thought Fuller has often expressed.

Some, of course, take an opposing view. The people who deal in Faith, Hope and Charity seem to think that one day is as good as another for changing your personal history. Philosophers since recorded time have recommended it. From Pindar to Emerson they have told us to become the thing we are; to fulfill our design; to choose our own reality, our own way of being a person. What they didn't tell us was how to do it; or how difficult it would be. When Paul said to put on the New Man, he reminded us of the unlimited potential of man; but the lives we lead constantly remind us of the obvious limits to this potential.

Clearly the Good Life is not as accessible as the books say. And yet it is not from want of trying that we have failed. We start our new lives with almost as much frequency as Mark Twain gave up smoking (thousands of times) and with about the same success.

Can tomorrow be the first day of the rest of our life? And can that life be completely different from the mess it is today? The answer, of course, has to be yes, or all those great men wouldn't have said so. But how do you go about it?

The first thing to do, it seems to me, is to retrace your steps. To go back to that period of your life when you were operating as a successful human being (although you most likely weren't aware of it). To go back to those times when your soul, your self, was not what you possessed or your social standing or other people's opinion but a totality of body, mind and spirit. And that totality interacting freely with your total environment.

Somewhere past childhood that integration of self and that response to the universe began to dissolve. We came more and more to associate who we were with what we owned; to judge ourselves by other people's opinions; to make our decisions by other people's rules; to live by other people's values. Coincidentally, or maybe not so coincidentally, our

274

physical condition began to decline. We had reached the fork in the road. We took the well-traveled path.

One who took the path overgrown with weeds and rarely used was Henry David Thoreau. The world knows Thoreau as a man of intellect, a shrewd observer, a rebel against conventional values. What has not been emphasized was that he was an athlete, and a fine one. He was, of course, a great walker. This kept him in prime physical condition. "I inhabit my body," he wrote, "with inexpressible satisfaction: both its weariness and its refreshments." It would not be too much to say that Thoreau's other activities derived their vitality from the vitality of his body. That the self that was Thoreau depended on being as physical as he could be. And that no life can be completely lived without being lived completely on a physical level.

If Thoreau was right, the way to find who we are is through our bodies. The way to relive our life is to go back to the physical self we were before we lost our way. That tuned-in self that could listen with the third ear was aware of the fourth dimension and had a sixth sense about the forces around it. That tuned-in self that was sensitive and intuitive, and perceived what is no longer evident to our degenerating bodies.

This may come as a surprise even to physical-fitness leaders. Physical-fitness programs have long been based on the desire to lead a long life, to forestall heart attacks, to feel better generally or to improve your figure. No one ever told us that the body determined our mental and spiritual energies. That with the new body we can put on the new person and build a new life, the life we were always designed to lead but lost with the body we enjoyed in our youth.

Now, common sense will tell you that you'll never see twenty-eight again, but the facts on fitness show that almost anyone can reach levels of vigor and strength and endurance equal to most of the twenty-eight-year-olds in this country. Given the good fortune to find an athletic activity that fits him, a man can recapture his youth and a second chance to listen to what his total self held important at that time.

If you think that life has passed you by, or, even worse, that you are living someone else's life, you still can prove the experts wrong. Tomorrow can be the first day of the rest of your life. All you have to do is to follow Thoreau. Inhabit your body with delight, with inexpressible satisfaction; both its weariness and its refreshments.

And you can do it if you'll just go back to that fork in the road.

* * *

If you are seeking the solutions for the Great Whys of your creation, you will have to start with the Little Hows of your day-to-day living. If you are looking for the answers to the Big Questions about your soul, you'd best begin with the Little Answers about your body. If you would become either saint or metaphysician, you must first become an athlete.

Study the lives of those who sought their own meaning and the meaning of the cosmos. Or read the works of the saints who lived the questions and waited for the answers in the hereafter. The common denominator of these people is asceticism, which comes from the Greek *ascesis*, meaning rigorous training, self-discipline and self-restraint.

The ascetic is no oddball recluse; he is someone seeking his optimum, his law, the life he is to lead. And asceticism is practiced by weight lifters, football players and distance runners as well as by saints and philosophers.

"First be an ascetic, which means gymnastics," wrote Kierkegaard. "Then bear witness to the truth." And he took his own asceticism into walking and there he thought out and composed his philosophy. Kant was another great walker. His neighbors could set their clocks by his passage through town.

For Thoreau, the length of his walk made the length of his writing; if shut up in the house, he did not write at all. The mind and the body, wrote Huxley, another advocate of fitness, are organically one. Motion and meditation are apparently a unity. "Sit as little as possible," wrote Nietzsche. "Give no credence to any thought that was not born outdoors, while one moved about freely—in which the muscles are not celebrating a feast, too."

But for your muscles to celebrate, and you to move about freely, you have to pay attention to details like diet and climate and training. How can one play and think and find truth when stuffed with jelly doughnuts? Nutrition is still a very controversial subject, but few will argue that we get into more difficulty eating than fasting, and that our intake of salt and refined sugar is unnatural.

Climate is something about which we don't have too many options. Some are luckier than others. When Green Bay trained in Santa Barbara for the first Super Bowl, one of the Packers asked a reporter, "What have these people done to deserve to live here?" Others have to live in their own equivalents of Leipzig, Venice and Basel, which Nietzsche found disastrous to his physiology.

Still, exercise covers a multitude of dietary and meteorological sins. The acclimatized athlete adjusts to his environment and begins to use altitude or heat or humidity to make him stronger. And his diet, through some inherent body wisdom now being allowed to operate, begins to conform with his needs, his nature.

Attend, then, to the little things, to the commonplace of diet and climate and your own form of play and sport. "I myself am my only obstacle to perfection," wrote Kierkegaard. The athlete has always known that. The athlete and the child at play have that same perception. That all things are possible and that I alone am master of my fate.

True, we must render unto Caesar. There are the forty hours we must contribute to the common good and the preservation of ourselves and our families. But beyond this door is freedom. The effort to make work more than the key to this door may not succeed in our lifetime or, indeed, in future lifetimes. But that should not bother us.

Even now work seems to distress psychologists and psychiatrists and sociologists more than the workers themselves. They have found the wisdom to accommodate to it. And they have not allowed its obvious physical, spiritual and psychological inadequacies to affect them.

Today's work does not make us the persons we can be. Work is simply the price to be paid. Having earned our daily bread, we can turn to our daily play. Having paid our dues for survival, we can pay attention to the more serious business of living. Having taken care of our bank accounts, we are now ready to take care of our bodies and the minds that go with them.

Wisdom, it says here, begins at 5 P.M.

"Is there a doctor who has the time," wrote a seventeen-year-old West German to the medical ministry, "to tell me how to live healthily?"

I'm not sure there is a doctor who would touch that question even if he had the time. Living healthily is a question few physicians seem ready to tackle. Living healthily is nothing less than arriving at old age and, in Erikson's words, "accepting one's one and only life cycle as that something that had to be and that, by necessity, permitted of no substitution."

To live healthily, therefore, is to become what one truly is and to work at it. To become in fact, as Ortega said, what you are in design. This may be a routine or rare accomplishment depending on how you view it. For myself now wandering around in my middle years seeking answers, it is like waiting for what happened to Saul on the way to Damascus.

The young, however, may get the same revelation through sport. That is one area of human activity in which they can taste of perfection. And even should they fail in that there is no better way to self-knowledge.

The athlete cannot fake it. He is a highly visible example of man maximizing himself. Or failing in the attempt. In this age of the phony and the upward failure, the athlete remains an example of excellence, grace and purity. Or at the least an honest effort to achieve those attributes.

But succeed or fail, the true athlete makes no excuses. He recognizes himself without pride or prejudice. He knows what he can or cannot do. He has found what he does best and is happy with it regardless of where he is listed in the standings. He has discovered himself, understood his strengths and weaknesses, and accepted them.

"To change the fundamental patterns of constitution and temperament is beyond our powers," wrote Aldous Huxley; "with all the best will in the world all that anyone can hope to do is to make the best of his congenital psycho-physical makeup [the particular personality associated with a given body build]."

The athlete already knows that. So he makes the best of it. Seeks fitness through positive goals rather than negative restrictions. The athlete doesn't stop smoking and start training. He starts training and finds he has stopped smoking. The athlete doesn't go on a diet and start training. He starts training and finds he is eating the right things at the right time. In just such a way other things fall into place. His sleep habits adjust. He automatically rests after eating and practices on an empty stomach. He warms up thoroughly and is satisfied with progress however slow.

He has discovered fitness and the fine line between peak performance and disaster. He becomes alert to his body signals. Palpitation, a sore throat, lightheadedness on arising, some minor joint pains, or awakening in the middle of the night—all these have meaning and alert him as a breaking twig would alert a deer in the forest. They tell him he has gone as far as he can go.

Where fitness ends, self-discovery starts. The athlete who is in complete command of the skills of his sport comes to understand the person he is through his attachment to his particular sport and his response to the stresses and strains that arise within it. He finds out what he is made of. What his true personality is.

Charles Morris in his *Varieties of Human Values* suggests there are three basic components to the human personality: Dionysian, the tendency to release and indulge existing desires; Promethean, the tendency to manipulate and remake the world; and Buddhistic, the tendency in the self to regulate itself by holding in check its desires. In psychological shorthand these components come out as dependence, dominance and detachment.

It shouldn't take all that long for a physically fit seventeen-year-old to find his or her sport and the appropriate life style to go with it. Detached, dominant, or dependent; Buddhistic, Promethean, or Dionysian.

It might even work for us aging worriers who are not at all sure that we are living, as Erikson said we must, our appropriate and only possible life cycle.

The formula for greatness, wrote Nietzsche, is *amor fati,* the love of fate, the desire that nothing be different, not forward, not backward, not for all eternity. And not merely to bear what is necessary, but to love it as well.

Offhand the statement would seem to have little application to the ordinary person, to you and me. Greatness and necessity and fate and eternity are words that thinkers tend to use, ideas that have little relation to our realities.

But when we read Keats and the poet's view, we move another step into this necessity and into our own reality. Keats saw the world as a "Vale of Soulmaking," but said we humans are not souls until we acquire identities; till each is personally himself.

The only man who truly lives, Ortega stated, is the one who follows his inner voice which says, "You are able to be whatever you want; but only if you choose this or that specific pattern will you be what you have to be."

The question, then, is not the presence of this necessity nor even its acceptance. We will certainly do that when faced with such a truth. The question is how to discover it, how to hear this voice, how to find our pattern, how to know the identity of our soul.

Our problem, then, is not the possibility of this necessity but the probability that we may never know it. That we may finish our lives without actually having lived it. That we may come to the end never having experienced it; never having heard the call. Our tragedy may be an unused soul, an unfulfilled design.

Fortunately, Nietzsche had some suggestions on what we should do to avert such a catastrophe. Attend, he said, to the little things. Take care with your nutrition. Watch your diet. Be careful about where you live and the air you breathe. Do not commit a blunder at any price in the choice of your recreation. Develop an instinct for self-defense. Make your life a matter of play.

Know that these small things are inconceivably more important than everything one has taken to be important so far. Great tasks, he concluded, depend upon small things, things which are generally considered to be matters of complete indifference.

Our salvation, then, is in the day-to-day living of what is surely the athletic life, the life committed to fitness, the life of one who knows the importance of attention to the little things, to the supposedly minor details of everyday living. The athlete is aware of all the points Nietzsche makes. Knows the response to training and diet and relaxation. The effect of tension and other people, of energy wasted on situations and relationships which make him merely a reactor. And the athlete knows more than most how one can find himself in play; and can accept himself who he was, is and will be.

Those who have found this play and with it their bodies know that life comes down to the usual matters of tasting, touching, hearing, seeing, breathing. "Our bodies are us, us," writes John Updike in discussing immortality, another grand idea. And then goes on to suggest that the only Paradise we can imagine is this Earth; the only life we desire is this one.

Fitness, then, is an imperative. How it is to be done is an individual matter, a matter, I might say, of necessity. But whether it is jogging or scuba diving, tennis or mountain climbing, its performance will involve attention to the details Nietzsche outlines. And in following this prescription we will begin to uncover the person inside, to burnish and polish and scrape away and let ourselves take shape.

Surely this is the way we must go if we are to find ourselves, know self-respect, accept our fate. Fitness can be our formula, if not for greatness, at least for the self-knowledge necessary to live a full life. Which is the most all of us, great or small, can expect.

The weakest among us can become some kind of athlete, but only the strongest can survive as spectators. Only the hardiest can withstand the perils of inertia, inactivity and immobility. Only the most resilient can cope with the squandering of time, the deterioration of fitness, the loss of creativity, the frustration of the emotions, and the dulling of the moral sense that can afflict the dedicated spectator.

Physiologists have suggested that only those who can pass the most rigorous physical examination can safely follow the sedentary life. Man was not made to remain at rest. Inactivity is completely unnatural to the body. What follows is a breakdown of the equilibrium. When the beneficial effects of activity on the heart and circulation and indeed on all the body's systems are absent, everything measurable begins to go awry.

Up go the girth of the waist and the body weight. Up go the blood pressure and the heart rate. Up go the cholesterol and the triglycerides. Up goes everything you would like to go down, and down goes everything you would like to go up. Down go the vital capacity and oxygen consumption. Down go flexibility and efficiency, stamina and strength. Fitness fast becomes a memory.

And if the body goes, can the mind be far behind? The intellect must surely harden as fast as the arteries. Creativity depends on action. Trust no thought arrived at sitting down.

The seated spectator is not a thinker; he is a knower. Unlike the athlete who is still seeking his experience, who leaves himself open to truth, the spectator has closed the ring. His thinking has become a rigid knowing. He has enclosed himself in bias and partisanship and prejudice.

He imagines himself self-sufficient and has ceased to grow. And it is growth he needs most to handle the emotions thrust upon him, emotions he cannot act out in any satisfactory way. Because he is, you see, too far from the athlete and participation in the effort that is the athlete's release, the athlete's catharsis.

He is watching people who have everything he wants and cannot get. They are having all the fun. The fun of playing, the fun of winning, even the fun of losing. They are experiencing the exhaustion that is the quickest way to fraternity and equality, the exhaustion that permits you to be not only a good winner but a good loser.

Because he cannot experience what the athlete is experiencing, the fan is seldom a good loser. The emphasis on winning is therefore much more of a problem for the spectator than for the athlete. And the fan, in losing and being filled with emotions that have no healthy outlets, is likely to take it out on his neighbor, the nearest inanimate object, the umpire, the stadium, or the game itself.

It is easier to dry out a drunk, take someone off hard drugs, or watch a three-pack-a-day smoker quit cold turkey than to live with a fan during a long losing streak.

And should a spectator pass all these physical and mental and emotional tests, he still has another supreme challenge to his integrity. He is part of a crowd, part of a mob. He is one of those the coach in *The Games* called "the nothingmen, those oafs in the stands filling their bellies." And when someone is in a crowd, out go his individual standards of conduct and morality. He acts in concert with his fellow spectators and descends two rungs on the evolutionary ladder. He slips backward down the development tree.

From the moment you become a spectator, everything is downhill. It is a life that ends before the cheering and the shouting die.

5

Becoming

"

My fitness program was never
a fitness program. It was a campaign,
a revolution, a conversion. I was determined
to find myself. And, in the process, found my body
and the soul that went with it.

"

I PROPOSE TO YOU that human enterprises succeed because they are absolutely rational or because they are just as absolutely absurd. Science is a success, but then so is religion. Knowledge succeeds, but so does faith. We usually act when something can be proven. But we act with equal frequency when it cannot. *"Credo quia absurdum,"* said Saint Paul.

Just so are there two types of successful fitness programs. One is rational, practical, physiological; the other nonrational, mystical and psycho-
logical. One is obligatory; the other voluntary. One aimed at changing the person to fit the life style; the other aimed at changing the life style to fit the person. One is utilitarian; the other creative. One is work; the other play.

The first is successful because it is concerned with the result; the other because it is concerned with the process.

In one instance, the exercising person is satisfied with Dr. Cooper's minimal daily requirements; in the other, he is dissatisfied with his own maximum daily capabilities. In the first, there is a purpose, the product, which is fitness, but little or no meaning in how it is attained. In the second, there is meaning in every movement, but no purpose beyond the action itself; fitness is merely a byproduct. The first pursues an ambition; the second pursues a dream.

The first program is for unfit, out-of-shape people with their backs to the wall. They know what they want to do, but are no longer able to do or enjoy it. They have finally and irrevocably had enough of how they feel and look and live out their lives. They are now ready to repent of past physical sins. Willing to obey the Ten Commandments of fitness. Anxious to follow the path of rectitude, provided vigor and energy lie at the other end.

You would think that such sensible decisions come easily. Nothing could be further from the truth. People just do not do things because they are good for them. And are even less inclined to do so when they enjoy doing the opposite. People accept the rational, practical, physiological only when it dawns on them that life any other way is a waste. Only then will they agree to a program which to them is a mindless, inconvenient and boring use of their time.

The other program is for unhappy people who find that it is life that is mindless, inconvenient and boring. Common-sense programs are of no help here. Only something that is nonrational, mystical and psychological can benefit them. Only something that is spontaneous and creative and playful will be effective. These people are looking for no less than an alternate way of living. Looking for a leisure-time activity to involve them completely and give them a new life style. Looking to become a true believer, to be struck like Paul on the road to Damascus with a new passion to replace the old one.

That passion of profession or career had changed, as Jung predicted, first to becoming a duty and now to being a burden. Life had become, as James Michener suggested, a falling away, a gradual surrender of the dream. What is left? "To live one's days," writes Bill Bradley, "never able to recapture the feeling of those few years of intensified youth."

Such pessimism is unwarranted. This fifty-eight-year-old man who has rediscovered play and sports can attest to that. It was simply enough for me to ask the question "You have one life to live. How do you want to live it?" and then come up with an absurd answer: "As a distance runner." With that decision, I awakened that passion, relived my dream, recaptured my youth. I re-entered my life through re-entering my body.

And so my fitness program succeeded because it was absurd. It was nonsense for someone my age to decide to become an athlete. Purely preposterous to concentrate the intensity and involvement that I once felt for the life of a physician into the life of the distance runner. Ridiculous to make running my vocation and medicine my avocation. But then my fitness program was never a fitness program. It was a campaign, a revolution, a conversion. I was determined to find myself. And, in the process, found my body and the soul that went with it.

For me, medicine was an illusion that had failed. I was seeking a new world, where I could live and create my own drama, and not play with the meaning of life. I found it in running.

So when you see a jogger out on the roads, you can never be quite sure what is going on in his or her head. Whether the reason for running is reasoned and practical and altogether a matter of just getting it done. Or, on the other hand, whether this childlike foolishness is the focal center of the runner's day. And running is the answer to the crucial question: How do you want to live the rest of your life?

A Canadian observer, John Sansom, has come up with a new solution to the physical-fitness problem. Religion. He suggests that we need more than a commitment to physical fitness for its own sake. We have to act on our religious beliefs (or a belief in a practically achievable Utopia) that regard bodily fitness as an essential part of life style directed toward a single all-important goal.

Will this be the answer? Jogging to eight-o'clock Mass? Cycling to temple? Doing circuit training before the Unitarian services?

I think not.

Every man is religious. Every man is already acting out his compelling beliefs. Religion is not something you belong to, or accept, or think. It is something you do. And you do it every waking minute of every day. Religion is the way you manifest whatever is urgent and imperative in your relationship to yourself and your universe, to your fellow man and to your Creator. Every act is a religious act.

That act may begin in dogma, but it ends in the deed of a unique, unprecedented and nonrecurrent individual. Religion or agnosticism or atheism may speak authoritatively to us about our bodies, but, whatever our persuasion, we will practice it only according to our inner compulsions and outer design. We are made for happiness and joy ("To miss the joy," said Stevenson, "is to miss all"), but we must pursue it in different ways. Fitness may not be one of them.

My design is thin and linear. I am a nervous, shy noncombatant who has no feeling for people. I do not hunger and thirst after justice. I find no happiness in carnival, no joy in community. I am one with the writers on *The New Yorker* whom Brendan Gill described. They touched each other only by accident, were secretive about everything, and never introduced anyone properly.

I am an intellectual. This does not mean I am intelligent, but that ideas are more important to me than people. My world lies inside of me, as it does with most people with my slight build. And that world and its completion depends on my physical fitness. In the perfection of my body lies my own perfection.

Fitness is my life; it is indispensable. I have no alternative, no choice, but to act out this inner drive that seems entirely right for me.

A majority of my readers will, I suspect, never feel that necessity, that urgency. The happiness, the joy they are born for, can be attained without it. They belong to one of the other two great races of men. Races with fundamentally different bodies and different temperaments, different life styles, and different religious expression.

The first of these races are strong, muscular people who are aggressive and insensitive to pain, both in themselves and in others. They find fulfillment in action, and seek to control people and events and things. Once athletic, they no longer need their bodies for their eyeball-to-eyeball confrontations. Where once they settled arguments with their fists, they now use their irresistible energy and moral courage. Physical fitness is no longer a priority.

The middle third are the round, pleasant people who love to have their arms around each other. They are generous and affable and quite close to being fat. Their bodies are for eating and drinking and company and family gatherings. Kierkegaard, another loner, once described such a man: "The ideal Christian is happily married, looks like a cheerful grocer, and is respected by his neighbors." For this race, fitness is irrelevant.

So I won't talk to you about fitness if you promise not to give me the kiss of peace or a membership blank to the Holy Name Society.

I gave a lecture on physical fitness recently at the Carrier Clinic, a psychiatric institution near Princeton. In the discussion that followed, one of the staff asked me, "Will jogging prolong your life?" I looked at him, my colleague in medical orthodoxy, and answered, "Will psychiatry?"

The answer was unpremeditated. A backlash against being required to answer a question I consider both irrelevant and immaterial. What runner cares whether running will prolong his life?

Will it? I don't know and I don't particularly care. On the other hand, running certainly does something to my body. But what exactly does it do? A few years back, I decided to find out. I went to a local community college for a fitness test. My maximum oxygen capacity, it turned out, was fifty-four volumes percent, considered excellent for a twenty-eight-year-old.

Apparently, running has given me an exceptional level of fitness. But what else? Has it prolonged my life? Pure absurdity. My physiology may be that of a twenty-eight-year-old, but I still have a fifty-eight-year-old body. I have my vigor, both physical and psychic, but the body ages relentlessly. My hairline recedes. My eyesight diminishes. And no one can persuade me that I have, at this date, a twenty-eight-year-old heart or blood vessels.

Yet something good is happening. Checking out as a twenty-eight-year-old must mean something. It does. It means that despite my years I am still an athlete. That running has gotten me to my lean body weight and to my personal cardiopulmonary best. Taken me to my physical peak. Because of my running, I am living at the top of my physical powers.

Now, to some that may mean that life will also be prolonged. Not to me. We are born, I suspect, with a built-in longevity quotient, which we can diminish but not increase. We are born, it seems to me, with an appointed time when noise will develop in the signals sent by our messenger RNA. When the song the molecules sing will no longer be heard by the cells. Disease, disintegration and death follow.

We can apparently hasten the process, but not retard it. Medical progress has gone through its finest hour and has had little impact on our life span. It is interesting that the Italian painters of the Renaissance had a life span of sixty-seven years, only a few less than medicine can produce in this nuclear age.

So let us forget about longevity. Get away from the idea of prolonging life. Let us realize the truth of Thurber's dictum "There is no safety in numbers—or in anything else." Despite exercise, diet and abstention from all the vices, we will die in our appointed time. That should not concern. It is what happens from now until then that is important.

Now rephrase that question. "Can running, or any strenuous form of play, improve my life?" This allows an answer. An answer which is clearly affirmative, if only because running concentrates on positives rather than negatives, emphasizes doing rather than not doing, and above all makes the person responsible for what he is doing.

The medical profession would like nothing better than to have all of us acting responsibly, taking a part in our own fate. The scientists think they can do better only if we do better. "The next major advance in the health of the American people," says Dr. John Knowles of the Rockefeller Foundation, "will result only from what the individual is willing to do for himself."

When I run, I am willing to accept that responsibility. But I also discover that to be responsible implies the ability to respond. To take care of my body, I must be able to listen to it, and to hear what it says.

In this continuing dialogue between me, the runner, and my body, I become more and more healthy-minded. I become eager for more training, more discipline, more self-control, seeking inside of me the person George Leonard called the ultimate athlete. All the while knowing, as Leonard suggests, that I am playing the ultimate game, which is life.

And in life, you remember, it is not how long you lived, but how you played the game.

A daily jogger has written to me in frustration because medical science has failed to come up with conclusive proof that jogging will prevent heart disease. Why jog, he asks, if there is no definite evidence that jogging will thwart a heart attack?

The answer, it seems to me, is that we should do so for more important and urgent and compelling reasons. We jog, play tennis, cycle, swim, hike, hunt, ride horses, or whatever because they have to do with the quality of our lives than the quantity. "I know only two things," a student said to Rollo May. "One, I will be dead someday; two, I am not dead now. The only question is what I shall do between those points."

Sport and play and exercise are essential to that doing, that being, that becoming. They are concerned with physiology, not disease; with health, not heart attacks; with fitness, not the lessening of hypertension, strokes or other human ills.

Sport and play and exercise are therefore vital to the process of maximizing ourselves and reaching the top of our physical powers.

We should not underestimate the importance of this in the full life. Training the body was an essential part of Plato's prescription for education. Education, he said, should train the body and mind as one. Only then can the body which is the source of energy and initiative be put in harmony with the mind which is reason. "The body," wrote Ortega, "is the tutor and the policeman of the spirit." It is the fit body, the body at the height of its powers, the body with range and daring matched with maturity that is the best teacher, the best disciplinarian.

Jogging or whatever our sport, therefore, is the way we move from actuality toward our potential, toward becoming all we can be. At the same time it will fill us with uneasiness, with what Gabriel Marcel called inquietude, the recognition that there is work to be done to fulfill our lives. And it allows us to see, as Theodore Roszak has recently suggested, that our most solemn, and pressing, and primary problem is not "original sin" but "original splendor," the knowledge of our potential godlikeness. "We grow sick," writes Roszak, "with the guilt of having lived below our authentic level."

Can we reach this level or even attempt to reach it without sport and play and exercise? Can we hope to have the necessary energy and reason, the harmony and imagination without training and disciplining and enjoying our bodies? That is for each of us to decide.

For myself, the usual arguments for exercise are pathetic representations when placed beside this holistic approach to the human condition. "My troubles are two," sang the poet Housman. "The brains in my head. The heart in my breast." It is the day-to-day living with these troubles that makes us realize the importance of health and fitness. Not perhaps with making it easier. In fact, it makes living more demanding. The athletic individual can be more conscious of choice, more aware of the dangers of freedom, more awake to what the French call *difficulté d'être*.

Each of us must face this difficulty in being every conscious moment. And it is for each of us to discover how best we can handle this encounter. And here it comes down to whether you are an Aristotelian who sees the law outside himself or a Platonist who would look for it within. Should you wait for proof, or act out what your internal message tells you?

The message I get from consulting myself is clear. First I ran from instinct. Later I was forced to exercise in Phys. Ed. Even later I came to run and exercise because it was prescribed by authorities. But finally I have come to run because it is the right and true and just thing for me to do. In the process I may be helping my arteries and heart and circulation as well, but that is not my concern.

My true aim now is a state of fitness prior to and unrelated to sickness or disease. My true task, to live at my authentic level. My true goal, to reach my original splendor.

Run for my life. You had better believe it.

6

Playing

"

**Run only if you must.
If running is an imperative that
comes from inside you and not from
your doctor. Otherwise, heed the inner
calling to your own Play. Listen if you can
to the person you were and are and can be.
Then do what you do best and feel best at.
Something you would do for nothing.
Something that gives you security and
self-acceptance and a feeling of completion;
even moments when you are fused with
your universe and your Creator.
When you find it, build your life around it.**

"

SHAKESPEARE WAS WRONG. To play or not to play: that is the real question. Anyone with a sense of humor can see that life is a joke, not a tragedy. It is also a riddle and, like all riddles, has an obvious answer: play, not suicide.

Think about it for a minute. Is there a better way than play to handle "the slings and arrows of outrageous fortune," or take up arms against a "sea of troubles"? You take these things seriously and you end up with Hamlet—or the Nixon Gang, who came back from World War II, wrote Wilfred Sheed, "talking about dollars the way others talked about God and sex."

Neither of these ways works. Neither will bring us what we are supposed to be looking for, "the peace the world cannot give." That is also part of the riddle. You can have peace without the world, if you opt for death. Or the world without peace if you decide for doing and having and achieving. Only in play can you have both. In play, you realize simultaneously the supreme importance and utter insignificance of what you are doing. And accept the paradox of pursuing what at once is essential and inconsequential.

Play, then, is the answer to the puzzle of our existence. The stage for our excesses and exuberances. Violence and dissent are part of its joy. Territory is defended with every ounce of our strength and determination, and moments later we are embracing our opponents and delighting in the game that took place.

Play is where life lives. Where the game is the game. At its borders, we slip into heresy. Become serious. Lose our sense of humor. Fail to see the incongruities of everything we hold to be important. Right and wrong become problematical. Money, power, position become ends. The game becomes winning. And we lose the good life and the good things that play provides.

Some of those good things are physical grace, psychological ease and personal integrity. Some of the best are the peak experiences, when you have a sense of oneness with yourself and nature. These are truly times of peace the world cannot give. It may be that the hereafter will have them in constant supply. I hope so. But while we are in the here and now, play is the place to find them. The place where we are constantly being and becoming ourselves.

Philosophers have hinted at this over the centuries. Now the theologians are taking a hard look at the thought that we must become as little children to enter the Kingdom. If so, there is nothing more characteristic about children than their love of play. No one comes into this world a Puritan. If there is anything children care less about, it is work and money and power and what we call achievement.

We watch and envy as they answer the call "Come and play."

What happens to our play on our way to becoming adults? Downgraded by the intellectuals, dismissed by the economists, put aside by the psychologists, it was left to the teachers to deliver the *coup de grâce*. "Physical education" was born and turned what was joy into boredom, fun into drudgery, pleasure into work. What might have led us into Eden led us into a blind alley instead. And simply changed our view of the universe.

A universe where we are to play and enjoy ourselves and our God is one thing; a universe that is a large, forbidding place where we have to fight for everything we get is quite another. A universe where it is either "us" or "them" will certainly make us seek peace in another world. Life under those circumstances is just as Samuel Beckett described it. "A terminal illness."

Play, of course, says otherwise. You may already have found that out. If you are doing something you would do for nothing, then you are on your way to salvation. And if you could drop it in a minute and forget the outcome, you are even further along. And if, while you are doing it, you are transported into another existence, there is no need for you to worry about the future.

When Dean Caldwell and Warren Harding reached the top of El Capitan a few years back, the nation breathed a sigh of relief and turned to other matters. Why anyone would spend twenty-seven perilous days climbing 3,400 feet of perpendicular rock is beyond the comprehension of even ordinary humans, much less those of us who get vertigo hanging curtains.

"Why climb mountains?" is a question which, it turns out, cannot be satisfactorily answered even by mountain climbers. Everyone, of course, attempts an answer. But all freely admit that the whole truth is not there. The whole truth, they imply, cannot be captured.

Participants in the "blood sports" are equally unsure. Forget about Hemingway's moment of truth. It doesn't even enter into novelist James Michener's explanation of why he ran with the bulls at Pamplona. Two men met death within feet of him. Yet he made himself go back a second and a third day. Why did he and the crowds with the rolled-up newspapers (to touch the bull—and claim the touch) come to Pamplona?

Because, Michener claims, throughout history a certain kind of man has wanted to test himself against the most demanding experience in his culture. Michener characterizes this motive as idiotic, jejeune, unrewarding and senseless. But notes that you frequently find that it is the best men who insist on taking the risks. "In our age," he says, "you can climb Everest, fly to the moon, or run with the bulls of Pamplona."

For those of us who are "endlessly catching trains," the thought of testing ourselves against the most demanding experience in our culture can be a new and exciting idea. But the streets of Pamplona are as distant to us as the Sea of Tranquility, and even the mention of Everest causes nausea. Paradoxically our intuitive urge to expand ourselves, to test our limits, is blocked by our instinctive reaction that the way of Michener and his Spanish friends is not our way.

What our instincts (and athletes and sports psychologists) tell us is that sports and athletics will show us how to satisfy the main urges of this generation: to possess one's experience rather than be possessed by it, to live one's own life rather than be lived by it—in fine, to become all you are. Up until now that has always meant your brain. No more.

"As Prometheus (sometimes called the Greek Christ) sought to stretch the capacity of mankind," writes West Coast psychologist Wilfred Mitchell, "so do athletics."

One who has found sport stretching his capacity is Joe Henderson, the running editor of *Runners' World.* Henderson feels he can't answer the why-I-run question any better than others. But he tries. "I write," he says, "because the thoughts inside have to be put in more visible form. I run because it's inside pushing to get out."

Running is a total experience. That which some of us do best just as others find their satisfactions and fulfillment in skiing, mountain climbing, bicycling, snorkeling, pitching or what have you.

The experience is one that proceeds from one level to another. It can be merely physical fitness (which is like taking up painting to improve the strength of your arm). Or distraction: "I think" said Tug McGraw, "the reason I like baseball so much is because when I come into a game in the bottom of the ninth, bases loaded, none out, and a one-run lead, it takes my mind off all us screwed-up people." Or religious: "Surfing is a spiritual experience," says Michael Hynson, one of the world's top surf-ers. "When you become united with a wave, you lose your identity on one level and make contact with it again on a higher plane."

At one end of the spectrum you find a former college cross-country runner stating that the "opportunity to encounter and deal with pain is one of the aspects that makes the running experience ultimately so satisfactory." At the other, you hear Dick Cavett, a dedicated snorkeler, report, "Snorkeling is a rebirth. You just hang there in liquid space like an irresponsible fetus. For me it combines the best features of sport, sleep and religion."

This quiet revolution is spreading over the land. The rarity of the true dropouts should not fool us. For each ski-bum who belongs to the moun-tains there are thousands who already know that's where they come alive. For every runner who tours the world running marathons, there are thousands who run to hear leaves and listen to rain and look to the day when it all is suddenly as easy as a bird in flight.

For them, sport is not a test but a therapy; not a trial but a reward; not a question but an answer.

The first and basic commandment for health and longevity is the following: Pursue your own perfection. No one will have difficulty with this dogma. But as usual with dogma, we begin to have dissensions when the theologians start interpreting it. Then we become schismatics and heretics and start religions of our own. In health, the main problems with orthodoxy are with the word "exercise."

I am ready to start a new religion, the first law of which is, "Play regularly." An hour's play a day makes a man whole and healthy and long-lived. A man's exercise must be play, or it will do him little good. It may even, as we see regularly in the press, kill him.

I have scientific support for my position. Recent studies in both England and Ireland have shown that hard physical work did not change the coronary-risk factors or heart disease in more than thirty thousand men. However, in the same group, hard physical activity during leisure time was accompanied by a significant reduction in risk factors and heart attacks. Not by hard work, but by swimming and running and heavy gardening, and by tennis and squash and handball, and other forms of play, these men achieved health and a long life.

So it is not effort that reduces heart attacks and degenerative disease.

If it were only effort, then effort on the job would do the trick. So it is not running, but running that is play, that is necessary. Exercise that is work is worthless. But exercise that is play will give you health and long life.

Exercise that is not play accentuates rather than heals the split between body and spirit. Exercise that is drudgery, labor, something done only for the final result is a waste of time. If I hated to run and ran only for longevity and was killed by a truck after five years at the sport, I would have a right to shake my fist at Providence, or at the doctor who advised it.

It is not the runner, but those impersonating the runner, who is at hazard. Those with the "hurry sickness." Those aggressively involved with achieving more and more with less and less time. Those who are always competing with or challenging other people. "Only the sick man and the ambitious," wrote Ortega, "are in a hurry." It is these people who use jogging to escape from death who find it taking them to their appointment in Samarra.

What, then, should you do? Run only if you must. If running is an imperative that comes from inside you and not from your doctor. Otherwise, heed the inner calling to your own play. Listen if you can to the person you were and are and can be. Then do what you do best and feel best at. Something you would do for nothing. Something that gives you security and self-acceptance and a feeling of completion; even moments when you are fused with your universe and your Creator. When you find it, build your life around it.

"Therein lies perfection," said Marcus Aurelius, "to live out each day as one's last." That is why I run and will always run. I have built my day and my life around it.

There is no better test for play than the desire to be doing it when you die.

as yes is to if, love is to yes

—E. E. CUMMINGS

If sport had a feast day, it would be Christmas. It is the day that speaks to man the player. Homo ludens is what Johan Huizinga called him. To differentiate from Homo sapiens, man the thinker, and Homo faber, man the maker.

296

Christmas tells us once again that play is a proper activity of man. It reminds us that fun is something philosophers cannot explain or understand, and insists that life is a game in which all can be successful.

A lot of this is not new. Plato in his *Laws* says, "Life must be lived as play, playing certain games, singing and dancing." This idea was also prominent during the Renaissance. But those enemies of man and his body, moral zeal and intellectuality, moved in during the Reformation, and with them a decline in play.

The nineteenth century and the Industrial Revolution were even worse. "All Europe," writes Huizinga, "donned the boiler suit." Utilitarianism, efficiency and educational aspirations almost wrecked the play spirit.

But there is hope. We still have the poets, the children, the athletes. And sports.

The intellectuals who look at sport start with the assumption that it must serve something that is not sport. They see its useful functions of discharging surplus energy and providing relaxation, training for fitness and compensation for other deficiencies. What they don't see is that play is a primary category of life which resists all analysis.

Play, then, is a nonrational activity. A supralogical nonrational activity in which the beauty of the human body in motion can reach its zenith. Just as the supralogical feast of Christmas confirms man's unique value and destiny. So the intellectuals are probably as upset with play as the theologians are with Christmas. Men having fun is as mystical and supralogical as the Word made flesh.

Fortunately, mysticism doesn't come hard for the common man. "History unanimously attests," wrote G. K. Chesterton, the master of paradox and therefore the master of Christmas, "that it is only mysticism which stands the smallest chance of being understood by the people."

Philosopher Jean Houston has observed, "We tend to think of the Faustian man, the one who fabricates, manipulates, seduces and ends up destroying. But the new image will be man the creator, the artist, the player."

The first Christians told us all that. The game plan had been changed. When the angel said, "Rejoice, be not afraid. I bring you good news of great joy," we knew that everything was going to be different. The world, which had moved from "if" to "yes," was now moving on to love.

The game would be for everyone. And the arena would be the world.

And the good news is that man will eventually triumph. All of us for this once are going to be on the winning team. And not only that. All of us can be great players.

The first Christmas says with Shakespeare, "What a piece of work is man. How noble in reason! How finite in faculties! In form and moving, how express and admirable!"

Homo ludens knows this. Oh, what pieces of work are Muhammad Ali, Jimmy Connors, O. J. Simpson and Kareem Jabbar! No sports fan needs to be educated about man's potential. Or the irrational elements that go into the intensity of the game. Or about the community of the crowd.

The sports fan knows all this and suspects that there is nothing more spiritual than the human body. Knows that nowhere is every man given his dignity as he is on the playing field. And instinctively feels that somewhere here is the news of the first Christmas.

Those of us weary and discouraged by the front-page tragedies caused by Homo sapiens and the ecological disasters of Homo faber can turn for uplift to the sports pages and know that there every day is Christmas. A Christmas foretold in the Book of Proverbs:

"I was with Him forming all things, and was delighted every day, playing before Him at all times; playing in the world. And my delights were to be with the children of men."

Who speaks for play? These days, almost everyone. The physiologists and the physicians, the psychologists and the psychiatrists, the economists and the sociologists all champion play.

Play and sports and the use of the body are becoming respectable. Play is good for losing weight and reducing our risk factors. For relieving stress and returning us to work relaxed. Play maintains our health and promotes our longevity. Compensates for needs not met at work, and provides a harmless way to vent antisocial emotions. Play, the experts say, is a necessity in a leisure society.

But these acceptable and respectable reasons for play are not the real reason we must play. The reason for play is much more radical than the scientists and thinkers presume. The reason for play is to be found in our reason for being. And, therefore, with the problem of God.

The problem of God has moved from the ancient question "Does God exist?" past the medieval inquiry, "What are his attributes?" to our present dilemma, "Why did He create the world?" Our difficulty now is the inability to explain the existence of the world and therefore ourselves. We are unable to define our purpose, to show how we serve, to demonstrate our usefulness.

The best answer, it seems to me, is to consider Calvin's thought that the world is *"theatrum gloria Dei."* We are here, therefore, to glorify God. And that we do this by glorifying the God who is Himself a player. Who created in joy, in play, in sport.

Calvin, the Sunday bocce player, may not have thought of it this way, but it does answer today's question. We are in this world to give glory to God and rejoice in our own and God's existence. And we do this in play.

Children, who are athletes and poets and saints and scientists all in one, do this naturally. They seldom question themselves about purpose. Rarely wonder whether or not they are useful. Practically never consider service and respectability. These latest arrivals from Paradise are nevertheless examples of pure unity of heart and soul and brain united with a body which is almost always in action. And that action is play.

What the child lacks is wisdom. Undirected action is not enough. When we become adults, we realize this. "Fight, do not pray," advised Plutinus. "Play, do not pray," we might say. But first we must know our fight, our action, our play. The child does not yet know the role he plays in his own drama. We must find that without losing the gift childhood provides, the gift of play. Without becoming what Erikson defines as an adult: "a commodity-producing and commodity-exchanging being."

The aim of education is to avoid this. It is to help the child become an adult but at the same time to find the secret of allowing the adult to remain a child. We should be children grown but children grown wise and discovering the significance of our peculiar union of flesh and spirit. Children grown wise and knowing that the answer to the question "What are we doing here?" is "I am."

The center of that existence is my play. From it springs all other activity. Sport and play are the stuff bodies are made of. They are also the stuff that makes the person and the self. My running enables me, as Norman O. Brown wrote, "to live instead of making history, to enjoy instead of paying back old scores, to enter the state of Being which is the goal of Becoming."

True, running does not fill my day. But it influences the rest of what I do and how I do it. From it comes my role and the style in which I play it. In it I find myself and my design. I start in play, use myself increasingly, and end in joy.

You may notice that play can be painful and strenuous and dangerous. It can demand endurance and suffering and perseverance. It can ask the most that a person can give. It presupposes an absence of greed and vanity and the appetites that remind us we are mortal. Play, you see, can be more difficult than work, and no easy task for an adult.

It is, however, worth every effort. What better to be than a player in the hands of a playful God?

I love them all. Love every Buck, every Celt. Love Kareem and Oscar and Mickey Davis; Perry and Warner and Bobby Dandridge. Love Cowens and JoJo and John Havlicek; Silas and Chaney and Baby Face Nelson. I love Tom Heinsohn and Larry Costello. I love them all. Because these men, doing what they do best and doing it superbly well, proved to me that sport is the eighth art. Made me realize how precious is the thing they do, how priceless is the thing we watch.

No one can say after watching the Buck–Celtic playoff that sport is an inconsequential thing. That play is simply recreation for the players, a diversion for the spectators. Huizinga, who said that the imperishable need of man is to live in beauty, went on to say, "There is no satisfying that need except to play."

And this was beauty and play at its best. The fascinating Kareem who is so good at what he does, you are put off by the ease and simplicity with which he makes the most difficult look easy.

And Robertson, the complete basketball player, with his slow-motion fakes. Oscar lives in another time frame, where he can wait and wait and wait some more; and finally comes the release of that soft shot tracing a perfect parabola to the net. The Bucks were without Lucius Allen, but they had Dandridge with his quick hands, the menacing Warner, and Mickey Davis looking like some kind of mad king who had come off the throne to play with his jesters and by royal fiat had declared that all his wildly impossible shots would go in.

Against them, the Celtics had brought champions of equal strength and speed and skill. The tireless Havlicek, who was everywhere he was expected to be and everywhere he wasn't expected as well. And Nelson, the Knick Killer spelling Silas after his incredible leaps under the enemy basket. And forever joined in the battle was the bullyboy Cowens, who could be as soft as silk from the outside.

And making the team move through space in patterns as intricate as Balanchine's were imperturbable White and Chaney, before the impulsive Westphal inscribed his signature on the final outcome.

It was, as Santayana said of athletics, "a great and continuous endeavor, a representation of all the primitive virtues and the fundamental gifts of man." It was also a work of art. It certainly satisfied the first half of Santayana's definition of art: "manual knack and professional tradition." We are unlikely to see the manual knack and professional tradition displayed by the Bucks and the Celts surpassed by anyone but the greats in art and music and dance.

Santayana further defined art as having a contemplative side which he described as pure intuition of essence. I am not sure what he meant by that, although I suspect it has to do with knowing the inner meaning of what you are doing. I also suspect that the Bucks and the Celts were doing whatever Santayana was trying to describe.

It is usually true that philosophers try desperately to put into words what is familiar experience to the man in the street. "The poet," said Emerson, "is in the right attitude. He is believing. The philosopher, after some struggle, has only reasons for believing."

I am a believer. What I saw during those games was good and beautiful and therefore important. I may get an argument from those who are more likely to spend their afternoons on Madison Avenue than at Madison Square Garden, who see their art in the Met and not in the Mets, who find their joy in colors and shapes and nature, not in knack and tradition and essence.

Still, I can take heart from something Hilton Kramer said about Ansel Adams' exhibit. "For myself," wrote Kramer, "the look on the face of Georgia O'Keefe—in the 1937 photograph—is worth all the views of Yosemite Valley ever committed to film."

And I'll take the look on the face of Oscar Robertson, or any other Buck or Celtic.

Mr. Kramer has told us what we always knew. That we really know a lot about art. Primarily because we know what we like and what brings us joy. Pure joy, said Santayana, when blind is called pleasure, when centered on some sensible object is called beauty, and when diffused over the thought of a benevolent future is called happiness.

It is possible that sport and play do all these things. That having found our sport, as the Bucks and the Celts have found theirs, we will feel its pleasure, know its beauty and live happily ever after.

But that is philosophers' talk. Let them try to explain what I already feel. I love them all. Every Buck, every Celt.

7

Learning

"

'Thank you, God, for school!'
Somewhere, an astounded Creator clapped his
hands. One of His creatures has understood His
creation. Had realized he was born to be a success
in a successful universe. Had discovered what a
wonderful thing it is to be a human being.
Had found himself lovable and his friends
and teacher loving.

"

I REACHED MY PEAK in creativity when I was five. I could draw and paint and sculpt. I could sing and dance and act. I possessed my body completely. And with it became completely absorbed in a life that was good and beautiful and joyful.

I examined and tested and explored. I could not bear to watch. My every day was filled with the creativity that Rollo May defined: "the encounter of an intensely conscious human being with his world."

I do not confuse creativity with talent. I never had talent. Few do. But I was aware and responded and I responded totally. And I had what in older people is called purpose or dedication. At five, I was creative and authentic. At five, I did it my way. At five, I was like most five-year-olds, a genius without talent.

That genius came from energy and effort and taking risks. I would not know for years that Thoreau had commended arduous work for the artist. "Hard, steady and engrossing labor," he said, "is invaluable to the literary man."

And I would not read until even later that the Greeks had no word for "art" or "artist." That they never separated, any more than I did, the useful from the beautiful. For them, either a thing was useful and therefore beautiful or it was sacred and therefore beautiful.

The five-year-old does not yet know sin, but he may well know what is sacred. Poetry and painting and music are, according to Blake, "three powers in man of conversing with Paradise." The five-year-old sees that Paradise correctly, not in technology but in the fairy story, in the great myths that control and guide our lives. And myth is meaning divined rather than defined, implicit rather than explicit.

At five I had that intuitive, instinctive faith that my cosmos, my family and the world were good and true and beautiful. That somehow I had always been and always would be. And I knew in a way of a five-year-old that I had worth and dignity and individuality. Later, when I read Nietzsche's statement that these are not given to us by nature but are tasks which we must somehow solve, I knew him to be wrong. We all had them once.

We lost them when we substituted watching for doing. When we saw the lack of perfection as a reason not to participate. When we became specialists and learned to ignore what was the province of other people.

For me, this meant no further interest in how things worked, in construction and making things, in crafts of any kind. I lost control of my

304

life and in time became helpless in front of any malfunctioning machine. Now, if left to my own devices, I could not house or feed or clothe myself. Were I a castaway on a desert island, I would not know how to apply the efforts of all the scientists since the time of Archimedes. I would have to live as if they never existed. As if their talent and the products of their intense encounter with the world had never occurred.

And this all because my encounter, my absorption, my purpose and my interest and intensity had never occurred. I had changed from a genius without talent into the worst of all possible beings, a consumer.

The consumer is passivity objectified. Where the five-year-old finds the day too short, the consumer finds the day too long. I had lost the absorption of the five-year-old and gained boredom. I had lost my self-respect and gained self-doubt. Being middle-class, I had neither the need to use myself physically to survive, which poverty imposes, nor the absolute freedom to complete myself physically that wealth allows the aristocrat.

The five-year-old is just such an aristocrat. He seeks his own truth, his own perfection, his own excellence without care for the expense. He could well be a millionaire in his lack of concern for money and the family bank account.

But the five-year-old is more than an aristocrat; he is the worker Thoreau commended. He is the artist the Greeks saw no need to define. He is the athlete we all wish to be. And the saint we will never be. Every five-year-old is a success, just as every consumer is a failure.

The road back for a fifty-nine-year-old consumer is a long one. But there must be untapped resources of enthusiasm and energy and purpose deep in me somewhere. Somewhere I have the same creativity I had when I was five. I suspect that it is hidden under my clean, neatly folded and seldom-used soul.

In the kindergarten class my daughter teaches, it is customary for the children to say a short prayer before the juice and cookies. They take their daily turn expressing gratitude or directing requests to their Creator. Last week, a pupil who has been a constant joy to her took his opportunity and exclaimed, "Thank you, God, for school!"

Somewhere, an astounded Creator clapped his hands. One of his creatures had understood His creation. Had realized he was born to be a success in a successful universe. Had discovered what a wonderful thing it is to be a human being. Had found himself lovable and his friends and teacher loving. And was using his tools, his sight, smell, touch, taste, hearing and intellect for creation, growth and self-discovery.

"Thank you, God, for school!" How I envy him that prayer. That sense of knowing who he is, and, even more, the sense of knowing why he is. His awareness of his infinite potential. School can do that. School is simply the unfolding of ourselves to our consciousness, a harmonious growth of our person and personality in our environment. And for us adults, this is attained in leisure.

What is school for the student, wrote philosopher Paul Weiss, is leisure for the mature. A time when we devote ourselves to detecting who we are and what we can do; a time to understand the world and how it works; a time to loaf and invite the imagination to full activity; a time to exhaust ourselves in play and dance and celebration.

"Mortals are most like gods," wrote one Greek commentator, "when they are happy, which means when they are rejoicing, celebrating festivals, pursuing philosophy, and joining in music."

Others from Aristotle to Cardinal Newman to Eric Hoffer have said much the same thing. The Greek word *schole* means leisure. Newman's writings on the university originated the idea of the liberal arts, studies undertaken for their own sake and enjoyment. Hoffer suggested dividing the state of California in half: northern California for those who wanted to go to school for the rest of their lives; southern California for those who preferred to work and support them.

These ideas have not done well in the marketplace. School has become more and more vocational, a place where one learns his life's work, then settles down to a quiet existence and a restful and eternal reward in heaven.

Leisure has become recreation time which revitalizes the worker, allowing him to return to work and higher productivity. Instead of being ends in themselves, school and leisure have become means to a designated "good life."

When one fools Mother Nature that way, terrible things are bound to happen, and they have happened. Our failure to see life for the great playful game it is has resulted in serious physical, psychological and spiritual disease. The world, since my day in school, has passed through three periods the psychiatrists are now calling the Age of Repression, the Age of Anxiety and our present era, the Age of Boredom.

If all the words spoken between the psychiatrists and the patients afflicted with these ailments were laid end to end, they would reach to the outermost galaxy. But not quite to their Creator.

To reach Him, and cure ourselves, we must return to the wonder of childhood; to the intensity of play; to the love of ourselves and our bodies, to growth and creation and self-discovery. We must return to school and leisure.

Only in leisure, that occasionally disorderly and disorganized pursuit of my being, of finding my thing and doing it, can I mature, can I become a man. Without it, life makes no sense. Without it, death is intolerable. Without it, I will never in this life or the next know who I am and who I could become. Without leisure, I will not be perfected.

But what about work? Isn't that an ever present necessity? It is, and somehow it has to be dealt with. There will come a time when technology will merge with art, when work will become play. Until then, work must be approached with a sense of humor, an understanding of how it can be used to make us more human than less.

To do this, we need the perspective otherwise available only to poets and philosophers and to children saying their prayers in kindergarten.

A juice-and-cookies break might be the first step.

I don't know if anyone ever said, "You can take the boy out of the city, but you can't take the city out of the boy." No matter. It's true. I've always felt the pull. When the kids are grown, I used to say, we'll go back to the city to live. Partly because that meant living where, as Paolo Soleri says, the institutions that make our civilization survive and develop. Living in what Peter Goldmark calls "our main learning device." Living with, in Henry James's phrase, "accessibility to experience."

But the city is, or was, more than that. In my time, it was an asphalt playground. Now they call it an asphalt jungle, but in those days it was a giant all-weather playground stretching block by block from Van Cortlandt to Bay Ridge.

The playground city is linear. And the games of the linear city are linear. The baselines straight along the curbs in boxball, or diagonal in stickball, banked off the curbs and ranging from sewer to sewer. And the final enclosures made by chalk, an indispensable item for growing up in the city. Not just for baselines and bases and out-of-bounds, but also for the box scores, which set each afternoon's contest in history, if only until the next rainstorm.

The squares and diamonds and box scores marked the mathematical precision of the city games. We learned that there was a certain dignity in losing by ten or fifteen runs, as long as it was recorded on the street next to home plate, inning by inning. We had rules for every eventuality. Many called, for some obscure reason, Hindus, which gave you a replay of your time at bat.

One thing alone was unforgivable: losing the ball over the roof. We learned what the city was to forget, that control comes before power.

In those days, the automobiles had not yet taken over the city. It was possible then to have a playing field of two sewers without a car parked its entire length. Few cars would ever drive through the street to interrupt the play. But later they marched onto our block and sat there twenty-four hours a day. If one left, another took up the vigil. Beneath them, the football fields, the hockey fields, the boxball and stickball fields lay unused. And the city died. Killed by Ford and Chrysler and General Motors.

Now we are being told by Barry Tarshis, in *The Asphalt Athlete,* that the city is still a playground. But he is not writing about our street, our block, the home of our platoon. He is writing about schoolyard playgrounds.

Now, playgrounds are all right, but they are a compromise. They are neutral ground. There is no sense of belonging there. Your block was your block. Your block was your territory. No playground could duplicate its singularity.

One might as well try to substitute Shea Stadium for Ebbets Field. We knew our block. Knew how to play the caroms off the brownstone fronts and the stoops and the areaways. Knew which steps to get pointers in stoop ball. Knew where to push the ball past the third baseman in boxball so it would go down some basement steps for a double.

Our block was like no other. We knew it and ourselves. And we watched the seasons pass as surely as any country kid in Iowa. Touch football, which was really "association," then roller-skate hockey, the cycle went. Then came spring, and the Spalding High Bouncers would appear, and with them boxball and stoop ball and the game of them all, stickball.

308

In stickball, no matter what your ability, there was an occasional miracle when broom met "Spaldeen" and the ball would go high and far up the block for an unbelievable distance. It would be a memory never quite erased by past or subsequent failures. In all our games, this held true. Strength and power were almost never dominant. Grace and control and anticipation made the play in the city games. It was a world in which every bounce was true and the short hop came easy even for the tyro.

There are some who say that this city of the short hop and the three-sewer home run will never come again. That this city I knew as a boy is not only dead, but deservedly so. Many believe with theologian Jacques Ellul that the city is "a specific evil, independent of its inhabitants." And see no hope for better.

"Let there be no confusion," says Ellul. "There is no use expecting a New Jerusalem on earth."

I disagree. Mainly because the boy in me provides hope.

The city, I grant, is lying moribund—maintained like some person kept alive by machines after his heart and brain have given up the ghost. But it is dying because architects and politicians and ordinary citizens have forgotten that the city must primarily be a playground. And a playground is just what it isn't. "In my neighborhood," writes Joseph Lyford of the Fund for Peace, "every adult is a dead child."

Those children will continue to die until the block again becomes the block. The block without cars. The block with neighbors who know each other and walk to shops and work and school. The block where seasons will be marked by the games that its children play.

The block will be the measure of the new city, perhaps of the world. Arnold Toynbee thinks so. The new city, he says, will be a world of streets and houses. We will have an immense number of units on the scale of those planned by Doxiadis for Karachi, or the "quadros" designed by Costa for Brasilia. Then once more we can be children and neighbors and men and women on our own block.

When that day comes, I'll be an expert. I know just the length and heft you need in a broomstick and where to get a Spalding High Bouncer. And don't worry about the chalk. I always carry some, just in case.

* * *

309

If I were a college president, I would recruit athletes, not scholars. I would give grants-in-aid for sports, not for academic achievement. The scales in education have been tipped too much in favor of the intellectual. It is time to raise our level of consciousness about the importance of sport and play.

Scholars will make their way whether we support them or not. We live in a knowledge society and they are the elite. But there are clouds in the future. The computer has an unrivaled intelligence quotient, and those it won't replace are coming to see their positions as white-collar facsimiles of the blue-collar assembly line.

Society needs a few geniuses, if you believe Bucky Fuller, or thousands of mediocrities, if you support the hypothesis of Ortega. In any case, most of us should be educated in the good life and how to attain it.

In that, the athlete provides a much better model than the scholar. The athlete restores our common sense about the common man. He revitalizes old truths and instructs us in the old virtues. However modest his intellectual attainments, he is a whole person, integrated and fully functioning. And in his highly visible pursuit of a highly visible perfection, he illustrates the age-old advice to become the person you are. Simply by being totally himself, the athlete makes a statement that has profound philosophical, psychological, physiological and spiritual implications.

Philosophically, the athlete gives us back our bodies. No matter what the Cartesians say in the classrooms, the playing fields tell us we do not have bodies, we are our bodies. "I run, therefore I am," says the distance runner. Man is a totality, says the athlete, and forces us to deal with that truth.

Psychologically, the athlete affirms the necessity of play. I should say reaffirms. We always knew the necessity of play. We knew it from the Scriptures and Plato and the Renaissance educators who gave athletes an equal share of the curriculum with the classics and ethics.

But somehow we forgot about play and sacrificed it and sport to the demands of our overgrown material civilization. We made play a means, not an end. Athletes show us that sport and play are essential to the good life. To consider their function as simply the cultivation of bodily vigor with a view to longevity is, as Santayana said, "to be a barbarian."

Physiologically, however, the athlete's vigor and longevity are immediately apparent. The athlete provides us with a new normal man. He

310

shows us that those we previously considered normal were spectators heading for a premature old age. Normal man is man at the top of his powers, man reaching his maximal metabolic and cardiopulmonary steady state.

From the athlete, we learn that health is not merely the absence of disease, any more than sanctity is the absence of sin. Health, the athlete tells us, is a positive quality, a life force, a vital characteristic clearly recognizable in those who have it.

The athletes, then, can be a tremendous force for good on campus. We may not be able to teach virtue, but it is no small thing to demonstrate it. Nor is it inconsequential to have excellence in any form in clear view. Education, said William James, is a process by which we are able to distinguish what is first-rate from what isn't. Sport, more often than not, shows us the elements of what is first-rate.

It does this because it is the long-sought moral equivalent of war, not as an outlet of aggression and violence, but as an arena where man finds the best that is in him, a theater that reveals courage and endurance and dedication to a purpose, our love for our fellows and levels of energies we never knew we possessed. And where we see, if only for moments, man as he is supposed to be.

In these moments, the athlete makes a contribution not only to his classmates singly, but also to the entire college community. Because then, in these great spectator events, he provides celebration and adds to the myths that help us survive.

And the greatest of these is that man is born to be a success. We believe that only when we see him at play.

DEAR MARK,

Your father tells me you are worried about giving up time from your studies in order to run cross country. You wonder whether devotion to a sport might endanger your college career. Whether running and learning are compatible.

I can assure you they are. For you and me and others like us, running is the way we learn. For us, in fact, there is no better way to insure academic success than by running an hour or so daily. I discovered this in college, as I am sure you will. My marks paralleled my running. When I was running well and enjoying it, I studied with interest and profit and this was reflected in my grades.

But education is much more than that and so is running. Part of education is learning the fundamentals. Getting the tools for your life's work. But the more important part is to see life as a whole and the world as a whole and to come to your full potential as a complete human being. "We are not," says Pascal. "We hope to be." Education is the way we start toward that fulfillment. By taking what we are told, what we hear and what we read, and then experiencing it. By testing it through our body and mind and soul and by thus filtering out our own truth, our own reality.

We are taught collectively; we educate ourselves individually. Education, said Socrates, was the winning of knowledge out of yourself. Yet the activity of the classroom and the lecture hall is to homogenize people. To present every one with the same facts, the same data, the same information, even the same truth. What we must do is take it elsewhere as a dog does a bone to worry it until we get to the marrow.

This activity starts with the body. A healthy, well-working body. A body that is all it can be. Which implies dedication, desire, hard work, discipline. And requires a self-renewing motivation for physical activity that occurs only in play. The body desires play just as the mind desires truth and the soul desires good.

For you and me, running is our play, so we are well started. And because running operates at all levels, during our hour run the road is at once a gymnasium, a laboratory, a classroom, even a temple. In this gymnasium, we find fitness. And with it, our own uniqueness. We do not need to be told that each one of us is like no one else before or after in this universe. And in that hour on the roads, we so use our bodies that we actually become our bodies. And in them see the possibilities of other perfection.

The road becomes a laboratory where we subject what we have been taught to the test of this visible, experienced universe. Where we use our own senses to evaluate the textbooks. And thereby give them new meaning.

But more than anything, that hour on the roads is for ideas and principles, for meditation and contemplation. We runners think in congruities and incongruities. We do not remember through organization, but by relationships, and we have to wait for these to glide by. We cannot force our brain to our bidding. Running is the key to this lock. Somehow in the relaxation, the letting go, we arrive at a state which Heraclitus described as "listening to the essence of things." We open ourselves up to the world.

And what of the soul? This hour allows, as does no place else, the freedom of seeing yourself as you are. Where better to examine your life, or your conscience, or to say your prayers? In that hour, every vice, every weakness, every shortcoming is seen and accepted. There is no confession you would withhold from yourself.

And yet you can accept yourself as you are, because at that very moment you see doors open and glimpse possibilities for yourself you never imagined. And you know you are indeed finite and imperfect, but you are also, like David, fearfully and wonderfully made.

Because of moments like these, moments of sudden illumination which come effortlessly and without trouble, this will become the most valuable hour of your day, and a most necessary part of your education. The educated man who does not move through the countryside with his own thoughts as his companions is in danger of never making the real discovery. Who he is.

All the best,
Doc

If you would learn how to defraud the consumer, observe the educators. They imprison their audience; set up delusionary goals called success and happiness; sell inadequate means called science and the humanities; and disparage their competitors the body and the spirit. And when they fail, they blame the pupils, not the teachers. Blame us, not themselves.

In the final analysis, however, their indictment is correct. We stand guilty as charged. Not because we have failed as scholars, but because we have failed as people. Because our education has not led to our own self-development, our own self-fulfillment. That is our own responsibility. As with everything else in life, if you would be educated, you must do it yourself.

Fortunately, the natural course of the human mind is from credulity to skepticism. And there comes a time in every person's education when, as Emerson wrote, he arrives at the conviction that envy is ignorance, and imitation is suicide. "When none but he knows what that is which he can do, nor does he know until he has tried."

Yale's Kingman Brewster, in an introduction to *Dink Stover at Yale*, described this growth as a progression from arrogance to self-doubt, to self-pity, to rediscovery and finally to mature ambition. For Blake it was the succession of innocence, experience, rebellion, and finally Vision. When our view of man is limited, when we see ourselves as IQs, SATs, or Graduate Record Exams, we end this journey early. Even our best intellectuals, as Robert Coles has confessed of himself, can end in arrogance. Some are becalmed in doubt, others unable to move beyond self-pity. For more than a few, rebellion is enough.

The necessity is to see ourselves totally. To know that we also have a physical and aesthetic intelligence. Without them the IQ is just another pretty face. Education proceeds only when we realize that the body and the mind are indissolubly one. When we are our bodies, and play and sport are integrated in our minute-to-minute pursuit of our perfection.

Only the athlete in us knows this. Only the athlete, as philosopher Paul Weiss points out, pushes himself toward the state where he so accepts his body he cannot without difficulty distinguish himself from it. Sports, writes Weiss, are a superb occasion for enabling young men to be perfected; there is no better agency for helping them mature.

Nonathletic educators reject this truth. They would educate us in their own image. In Dink Stover's day that meant, as his friend Bockhurst said, "developing the memory at the expense of the imagination." Now, if the Yale alumni are to be believed, it is an even more fundamental error. At their fall convocation the highest per capita income producers among American college graduates complained that the body had been sacrificed to that success.

These men have come to know the frustrations of false ambitions. There are, after all, at any one time only five or six supremely intelligent people on earth, those half dozen whose discoveries could pay, as Bucky Fuller claims, to educate all the rest of us. We are, Yale graduates included, only deckhands. "Not one man in a million," wrote C. P. Snow, "granted all the training in the world and with total dedication, would be likely to make a significant contribution to theoretical physics."

The last men of thought to make a difference, according to Kenneth

Clark, were Freud and Marx. A tiny few, therefore, actually merit education as potential contributors to society. The rest of us are entitled simply by being our unique selves. We deserve to be included in what William James called the stringent never-ending search for wisdom and freedom.

Yet the educators would close us out with our board scores. Check our SATs for verbal and math and decide whether or not we are educable. It is easier to teach those who need not be taught. Easier not to be threatened by a completely different kind of intelligence. Easier to label as primitive what may be the future and not the past.

Picasso had trouble with arithmetic. Terry Bradshaw, someone said, has a twelve-cent brain. Intelligence is never mentioned in the Bible. Nor is it, we are told, the hallmark of a poet. We are carnal creatures with an incarnate God. The artist, and athlete, the saint and the poet know that. The educators alone remain ignorant.

The people they are defrauding may be themselves.

Graduates of Downstate Medical School, families, friends and faculty:

Your dean said it was an honor to have me as a commencement speaker. That you were about to hear from a distinguished cardiologist, philosopher and an expert on fitness. That remains to be seen. But those are not the reasons I am here. The real reasons are quite simple. Your student body president, who extended the invitation, said they were looking for an alumnus, someone who would keep people from falling asleep, and they had no money. He hoped that would not matter. It didn't. At fifty-seven, I am willing to talk to anyone who will listen.

I will not deny I am a cardiologist. But I don't consider that important. Like most specialists, I am not intelligent enough to be a family practitioner. And of all the specialists, cardiology is the simplest and the safest for someone who is ambivalent and indecisive. In common with most heart specialists, I am a Hamlet who is always wondering what to do. Fortunately, the patient improves or is even cured during the soliloquy.

I also admit to being a self-taught philosopher. There is no other way for us physicians, for surely we must be the worst-educated of professionals. We go through medical school in college to prove we can cope with medical school in medical school. We are never taught the

315

humanities or their importance. Scientists, you see, need know nothing about yesterday. It is already incorporated in today's technology.

But to be human, to be a person, you must start with the Book of Genesis and work forward. You must always be on the alert to find the giants, the writers, the thinkers, the saints, the athletes, who speak to you. Those who reflect your instincts, your temperament, your body, your mind, your tastes.

I do plead guilty to being fit. But only because at forty-four I became bored with medicine. When I applied for the faculty at Rutgers Medical School, citing that boredom was my only qualification, the application was rejected. I then turned to a higher ambition. To become a forty-four-year-old miler. And, in an absolute, unreasonable, single-minded dedication to that absurd project, discovered my body, my play, my vision and eventually a new life. I found my truth.

I stand here now hoping to transmit some of that truth. But even more, I don't want to lie to you. "The old lie to the young," said Thornton Wilder. And never more than in commencement addresses. All over this land at this time of the year, there are speakers talking about hard work. Of the need for continuing study. Of the necessity of becoming men and women. They are urging graduates to succeed, to give service, to dedicate their lives to others.

I am here as an advocate for other values. I am here to speak not for work, but for play. Not for the mind, but the body. Not for becoming a man or a woman, but remaining a child.

I am here to tell you that in your success will be the seeds of your failure. That in giving service, you will eventually do a disservice to yourself and your family and your patients. That in your dedication to others, you may die without actually having lived.

My experience has taught me that you must first and always seek the person you are. And this becoming unfolds through the intensity with which you use your body, through your absorption in play, and through the acceptance of the discipline needed to be an athlete. At all times, you must protect your Self. Maintain a childlike wonder. Acquire if you can the ability to be careless, to disregard appearances, to relax and laugh at the world.

If you are to succeed, you must always be on the alert. Establish priorities. Keep one hour a day inviolate. A full sixty minutes in which you retire from God, country, family and practice. And there must be

316

one day a week that is yours alone. Learn self-esteem, self-acceptance. Know that you can be a hero.

It won't be easy. There are people out there waiting to kill you with their demands. They will want an eighteen-hour day. Then a twenty-four-hour day. A thirty-six-hour day if possible. The song tells you, "They will kill you if you let them. Don't let them. You have a friend."

But you have no friends. Those who call you by your first name are the worst. They will call you any time, day or night, and especially on your day off.

You are your only friend. The only protector of your body and its beauty. The only defender of your play and its delights. The only guardian of your childhood and its dreams. The only dramatist and actor in your unique, never-to-be-repeated living of your life.

Rise to that challenge. Live your own life. Success is not something that can be measured or worn on a watch or hung on the wall. It is not the esteem of colleagues, or the admiration of the community, or the appreciation of patients. Success is the certain knowledge that you have become yourself, the person you were meant to be from all time.

That should be reward enough. But best of all is the fun while you are doing it. And, at the very least, you will heal yourself.

8

Excelling

"

'Williams,' wrote Updike,
'is the classic player on a hot August weekday
when the only thing at stake is the tissue-thin difference
between a thing done well and a thing done ill.
Because he was one of those who always cared,
who care about themselves and their art.'

"

AT MY AGE, I am no longer intimidated by the opinion of others. I no longer respond when told what book to read, what movie to see, what side to take in the Middle East, or why I need an antiperspirant. And I have had it up to here with being told I shouldn't enjoy the things I do enjoy. With people who are trying to give me guilt feelings because sports are a major part of my life.

But this is a new age. A time when we should be trying to communicate with each other. Explaining man to man. Explaining those of us who are really into sports to those who are not. Those who could watch football or some substitute fifty-two weeks a year to those who say if you've seen one game you've seen them all. And for the sake of that communication, it's time to set the record straight on sports being boring, repetitious, a waste of time, and a meaningless pastime to which serious things are in danger of being sacrificed.

Boredom, like beauty, is in the mind of the beholder. "There is no such thing as an uninteresting subject," said Chesterton. "The only thing that can exist is an uninterested person." That puts the critics in the dock. If you are not interested in football, it's because you don't understand it. Be bored, you pundits, but know it to be your own inadequacy. If you don't enjoy the Super Bowl, it's your fault, not the game's.

That, of course, works both ways. I may have difficulty comprehending the grasp that music has on its enthusiasts, but I see that as a deficiency in myself, not the music lovers. When a musician tells me Beethoven's Opus 132 is not simply an hour of music but of universal truth, is in fact a flood of beauty and wisdom, I envy him. I don't label him a nut.

And being a city kid, I may be slow to appreciate the impact of nature on those raised differently, but, again, I regret that failure. And when Pablo Casals said, as he did on his ninety-fifth birthday, "I pass hours looking at a tree or a flower. And sometimes I cry at their beauty," I don't think age had finally gotten to old Pablo. I cry for myself.

And if like many scientists I have trouble grasping the meaning of poetry, I see that as a measure of my want of imagination, not the poet's. When a critic like Randall Jarrell writes, "If you ask me, 'What can I do to understand Auden or Dylan Thomas or whomever the latest poet is?' I can only reply, 'You must be born again.'" Then and only then can I estimate the effort it takes to know, really know, what makes other people come alive. What brings them joy.

It is that effort that the cool, dispassionate uninvolved critics won't make. So for them the Super Bowl is three hours of yawns. But what of the fans, the losing fans who feel pain; and the winners, who are stirred to frenzy? Does the boredom of the critics make their emotion less legitimate?

Now, some would think that pain is the opposite of joy. It isn't. Numbness, apathy, lack of feeling and caring are. Caring is the operative word, the central emotion of the fan. It is by a nice coincidence a very theological word. I must care. The players must care. Together, like actors and audience, we must make each other care. Together, we make athletics, as the philosopher George Santayana said, a physical drama in which all the moral and emotional interests of man are involved. "Watching a football game," he wrote, "the whole soul is stirred by a spectacle that represents the basis of life."

No need to tell me that, or the average fan. No need to tell the players either. To what vocation do men bring such effort, such ability, such excellence?

All share to some degree the skills and virtues of Ted Williams. A player who brought to the plate, John Updike wrote, a competence that crowds the throat with joy.

"Williams," wrote Updike, "is the classic player on a hot August weekday when the only thing at stake is the tissue-thin difference between a thing done well and a thing done ill. Because he was one of those who always cared, who care about themselves and their art."

That is why sport is never boring, never repetitious. Why Santayana, a Harvard professor, could take time to write an essay replying to those who asked him, "Why do you go to games; why do you waste your time upon the bleachers?"

Politicians may say it, theologians may write it, Americans may even believe it, but it has taken sport to prove that race, creed, color and country of national origin are only incidental qualities of a human being. It is of little moment in sport whether you are black or white, Catholic or Protestant, whether you are Italian or German, Israeli or Arab.

Sport eliminates these divisions and substitutes new ones. It demonstrates that we are divided by more fundamental differences which cannot be transcended. Sport shows that mankind is divided into three basic groups, and that these groups have identifying physical and physiological and psychological characteristics.

This is not a new concept to philosophers and theologians. They are continually trying to reconcile the unity of our goal with the variety of ways of attaining it. The *Bhagavad Gita,* for instance, outlined three paths to union with God: the way of works, the way of knowledge, and the way of devotion. Which path a person took was determined by his essential nature, his constitution and his temperament.

In sport, it is the football player who works out his salvation through works. He is the man of action. His body, his personality, his temperament demand it. And his zeal and enthusiasm and courage give us a glimpse of why these same men occupied with lesser loyalties like race and creed and country completely disrupt the world.

Unfortunately, adherence to such causes can be easily manufactured. This is another lesson derived from sport. Fans are made by such incidentals as what high school they attend, what town they live in or what college they graduated from. Sherif, the social psychologist, used a boys' camp to show how easily loyalties and friendships could be developed and destroyed simply by rearranging team rosters. The exaggerated importance of such superficial attachments is a phenomenon which is highly visible in any sports-minded community.

This passionate identification is also highly visible in the international community where these direct, bold, adventurous men act in the name of patriotic interests of various countries. They are, however, identical, except for the flag they wave and the cause they support. Like Sherif's campers, if moved to another country, another continent, they would joyfully fall in to fight their former friends. And meanwhile, the rest of us suffer and wonder what to do about these militants. Wonder how to enlist these marvelously courageous and dedicated people to a higher cause.

It has always been this way. The world looking for some way to harness and utilize this energy. "Civilization," wrote Aldous Huxley, "is a complex of religious, legal and educational devices for preventing these extremely muscular individuals from doing too much mischief, and diverting their irrepressible energies into socially desirable channels." William James spoke in much the same vein. He sought a moral equivalent of war. Some demanding activity, some cause of peaceful nature that would occupy these people, and turn them from destructive pursuits.

James saw war as a source, however unacceptable, of many good things like fitness, manliness and instances of the highest sacrifice man can make. It provided for many the way to perfection.

It is instructive that the Catholic Church in attempting to perfect her adherents gave them a choice of Orders corresponding to these divisions of man, including the man of action. One could join a meditative order like the Trappists, or fulfill himself in the ritual of liturgy of Benedictines, or go out and change the world with the Dominicans. In the Church, they did not let incidentals of birth and geography get cluttered up with more fundamental differences.

Similarly, sport does not care whether you are a Democrat or Republican, capitalist or Communist. Sport goes to the essence. It reminds me of an encounter group I once attended. In the first exercise, the person next to me asked me again and again, "Who are you?" When I answered successively with the conventional identifications and relationships, my neighbor kept repeating, "Thank you, but who are you?"

Eventually, you get down to basics that have nothing to do with flags or slogans, political campaigns or fund-raising dinners, where you come from or what you do for a living.

Such exercises do not give solutions. But they do show how shallow and trivial most of our allegiances are. The answer to "Thank you, but who are you?" is available to any athlete who has found his sport.

A world record always reassures me that author Teilhard de Chardin was right. A 3:49.4 mile convinces me "that man is still moving along his evolutionary trajectory." The breaching of another physical barrier makes me certain that "like a multistage rocket, mankind is now visibly starting a fresh forward leap."

I can see in this external perfection, this economy of energy and space, a sign of internal perfection, an indication we are getting better and better. We are, as Teilhard said, seeking not simply to enjoy more or know more, but to be more. And evolving in love toward the perfection of man and the universe. The Omega Point. The divine milieu.

This is not a popular view with the experts. Not many see man as essential to God's plan. Not many more see any hope for the future. One prominent exception is the athletes. While everyone around is crying doom, the athletes are caught up in Teilhard's "continually accelerating vortex of self-totalization." They are telling us that nothing can prevent man—the species—from growing still greater, as long as he preserves in his heart the passion for growth.

And there is nowhere better to watch that growth than the mile run. The runner has three great challenges, and the greatest of these is the mile. The others are the dash and the marathon. Taken together, they comprise all of exercise physiology. They correspond to the three major sources of muscular energy, and they call on man in his various guises as body, mind and spirit.

The dash is raw speed powered by high-energy phosphates. The marathon is the unerring test of endurance and the use of oxygen. But the mile is all these, plus a third force, anerobic metabolism, the use of sugar in the absence of oxygen, and the ability to clear the body of lactic acid.

The dash is pure body; the marathon is pure mind. The mile is body, mind and spirit. "The mile remains the classic distance," wrote Paul Gallico, "because it calls for brains and rare judgment as well as speed, condition and courage." And its searching third quarter requires the leap of faith that what you are doing is worth the effort.

What better place, then, to observe mankind evolving, to look for the ultimate in human performance?

John Walker, the current ultimate, is the athletic descendant of another outstanding New Zealander, Peter Snell. At six feet, one and a half inches and 185 pounds, Walker compares to Snell's five feet, ten and a half inches and 175 pounds. Like Snell, he is a four-hundred-meter man coming up to the mile. And like Snell, he is driving the smaller man into longer races.

His record run was unbelievably easy. But so are most world records. When they come, they appear easy, expected, even inevitable. But why they happen still confounds our traditional scientists. Despite the detailed and accurate statistics of track and field, the scientists consistently underestimate the human body and its potential.

They do, of course, figure in factors of better food, better training and better equipment. What they fail to calculate is the human factor, the multitudes of people engaged in this struggle who are constantly producing better individuals and better community. They do not see that man is a process, not a product.

323

Genes and numbers and passion for growth will produce not only new records, but also a new world. The mile, then, is a minor but very evident part of this common enterprise. From it, we can take heart that "far from reaching his ceiling or even slipping back, man is at this moment advancing with full vigor."

Teilhard and John Walker and every athlete who has put on a track shoe, indeed all those who have tried to become the best they could be, keep telling us this. We have yet to see the true marvels of mankind and the universe.

"Man is so made," wrote La Fontaine, "that whenever anything fires his soul, impossibilities vanish." No one in our lifetime has shown this more clearly than Vince Lombardi. Lombardi was a practical demonstration of the power of emotion, will and, finally, prayer and meditation to unleash the untapped energies of man.

I suspect that not a few intellectuals are distressed by the fact that a football coach and his players should provide such an example of the unlimited capacities of man. (When *Commonweal*, a liberal Catholic weekly, put down pro football and the Super Bowl a few years back, an irate reader wrote that Lombardi was forming at Green Bay one of the few truly Christian communities in the country.) But others now recognize sports as one of man's major endeavors.

Among them is philosopher Paul Weiss, who classifies sports with politics, art and religion as relating to issues of fundamental importance. Weiss might also agree that no political leader, artist or even religious figure has had the positive impact of Vincent Lombardi on the nation's thinking.

The impact was partly the result of the fundamental importance of sport that Weiss mentions. The personality, character and beliefs of Vincent Lombardi did the rest.

What is the source of immediacy and vitality of sport? Denison, in his *Lives of Children*, writes of the look of children in games: "the brightness of their faces, the vivacity of their faces, the swiftness of their intention, the accuracy and drollery of their observations." Add to these priceless qualities the miracles of dexterity (occasionally performed ourselves) and the achievement in becoming all we are; that is what sports is all about.

Becoming all you are was the Lombardi credo. Religion is not something you believe; it is something you do. For Lombardi, born into a world of Original Sin, a world of imperfect men to be endured while en route to heaven, that religion became one of the perfectability of community, and the overwhelming importance of the present. Football was not merely important to living the good life. It was the good life.

No more revealing story about this conjunction of life and football has been told about him than the one about Leroy Caffey loafing on a play in a practice session. "Caffey," said Lombardi, "if you cheat in practice, you will cheat in a game." This is where most coaches would stop, but Lombardi went on: "And if you cheat in a game, you will cheat for the rest of your life. And I will not have it."

The failure to live up to potential was the supreme tragedy to Lombardi. Like the New Theologians, he preached the importance of the body. And he saw the Good News that God loves men no matter what they do as making the short passage through time and life crucial. Death, writes Leslie Dewart, is the termination of the possibilities open to human nature and life. For Lombardi, those possibilities had to be tried and improved and worked on every waking moment. Let death and heaven and hell take care of themselves.

So Lombardi was a disciplinarian, but not for discipline as discipline. Sonny Jurgensen, for instance, said Lombardi was the first coach who didn't mention his weight. He merely told him that he expected Jurgensen to be ready to play his best. To give one hundred percent, to love one hundred percent, Lombardi found, was impossible without a discipline that was more than discipline. It was a belief. That sort of belief which is commitment without reservation. It was a commitment without reservation that Lombardi demanded and got both from himself and from his players.

How did he do it? Others—Lombardi was not the first—had these ideas. Held these beliefs. Sought to motivate men. Why was Lombardi successful?

Many of his friends and associates, players and politicians, have tried to tell us who and what Vincent Lombardi was. But when the final word is written and the last story of his dedication to football is told, the one thing that will stand out about Vincent Lombardi will be his vocation.

Not the restricted sense of vocation as a football coach, but his vocation as a man. The vocation that theologians define as the strong sense that one's life and responsibilities must always tend toward evoking a sense of God's presence for one's self and one's fellow man. And it comes only to a man of prayer.

It was this third element, prayer, that made Vincent Lombardi a man of great emotions and great willpower, able to do the impossible. Also to be, as Willie Davis said in his eulogy, "All the man there is."

Amen.

"Can you really see Christ as a professional football player?" a professor of philosophy asked me recently. We were discussing a criticism he had written of football and the men who play it. "Programmed violence," he called it. "The joke," he said, "was on those who cultivate the illusion of eternity in time, of perfection in trivial things, of camaraderie of violence, synthetic hatred and relentless dedication to bloody, competitive victory."

The joke, I suspect, is on the professor. He is in the ought-to-be of the intellect which is telling him weird things about what are essentially physical experiences. The football player is in the has-to-be, arising from the deepest regions of his being. He is following a call which is almost as mysterious to him as the game he plays is to the professor.

Yes, I can see Christ the football player. Just as I can see Christ the plumber, Christ the artist, or Christ the carpenter. The Good News he brought two millennia ago is that the body is holy, the world is sacred and nothing human is alien to Me. When He became Man, we became men. The message of Bethlehem was not simply that all men were created equal, but that all men were created unique. And they would succeed or fail in the way they fulfilled the possibilities of this uniqueness—the one authentic life each one should lead.

Unfortunately for the professor, this starts with the body, the temple of the Holy Ghost, as our professor of surgery used to say very carefully before he began his lectures. What do we in the intellectual pursuits really know about the body? What do we professionals with the clean white hands know of the world of Christ the linebacker? What would we know of the world of Christ the plumber? Or of Christ the carpenter?

What do we know of the sound of a nail hit true, the smells of the different woods, the feel of the grain and the planed surfaces, the easy grip on the hammer and the smooth expert use of the saw? Cannot the carpenter find his eternity in contemplating his completed house, his perfection in apparently trivial things?

326

Undoubtedly, the waste of a mind is a terrible thing. The waste of a soul is worse. But it all begins with the waste of the body.

"Our first concern," says Carlos Castenada, whose experiences with the Mexican sorcerer Don Juan have made him a folk hero, "should be with ourselves. I can like my fellow man only when I am at the top of my vigor and not depressed. To be in this condition, I must keep my body trim."

This care of body, says Castenada, must be impeccable, because the body is an awareness with which we know the world and ourselves. This is not too far from the thought of C. G. Jung. The great psychiatrist felt that there were a number of separate centers in the body, called chakras, each capable of human thought. A Taos Indian chief had once told him that white men were covered with wrinkles because they were crazy. And they were crazy, the chief said, because they thought only with their heads.

Of course, in our present culture, the head is paramount. Success, which is money and fame, comes easiest to the brain worker. People are graded to the extent they use their hands (blue collar) or their minds (white collar). In our system, professors of philosophy are light-years ahead of pro football players in status.

But isn't the linebacker the one who is living authentically in his own world, his body impeccably tuned in, believing in himself and what he is doing? "Work," wrote Mark Twain, "is anything a body has to do. Play is anything a body doesn't have to do." By those standards, the professor might be a slave and the football player a free man.

The unlived life is the real threat. And because we don't understand ourselves and our prejudices, we are in danger. How can I find the has-to-be deep inside of me if I am already persuaded by my society that working with my hands is second-class work? How can I follow my vocation if that is a vocation supposedly fit only for the uneducated?

"Have we at last," I asked the professor, "found in football the one occupation of the twenty-eight thousand open to man that the Lord would not have for his own?"

The truth is, we know many jobs fit for the Lord, but not his children. It happens whenever genius and talent are replaced by that worst of heresies—good taste.

* * *

When I was fifty-two and no longer interested, I learned the secret of all hitting games. While watching a TV program about racquet ball, I suddenly grasped the principles of hitting a ball. I saw the basic physics of translating my power into an object's velocity. I knew at that moment how to hit a ball, any ball.

Who at that age, seeing how it should be done, would not mourn over a lost youth? Who would not dream of three-sewer stickball home runs, or a tennis game of serve and volley and smash, or even using an eight iron for the second shot on a par-four hole? Who would not want to relive his life as a hitter?

I wouldn't, for one. At fifty-two, I had learned the real secret of all hitters. They are born and not made. And I was not one of them. Technique is essential, but it cannot stand alone. No amount of timing and rhythm and biomechanics will make a hitter out of a person lacking the physical and mental and emotional equipment.

The hitter is born with the hitter's physique, and the hitter's psyche. Technique will not make a hitter out of a nonhitter. It will merely make the hitter a better hitter.

TV also told me this: Close observation of baseball players, golfers and tennis players revealed a common structural characteristic. Power. Their muscularity is evident from all angles. No one makes it in those sports who is not that type of person. The number of golfers who are ex-football players or who could easily be taken for ex-football players alerted me to this. Even apparently slender athletes have an underlying bone structure that belies their slight build. Fred Patek, for instance, the vest-pocket shortstop of the Kansas City Royals, has arms as big as my thighs. And his wrists are enormous.

There is where the hitter is to be found. The wrists give him away. They are the evidence of his power and his willingness to use it. If you become a wrist watcher, you can pick out the natural athlete, the person with the potential to succeed in these competitive sports.

You will also be able to recognize those with the potential to succeed in this competitive personal life. Those who will bring to their job or profession or career that same aggressive, energetic and direct approach.

Some, like Patek, are deceptive. To see them in clothes, you wouldn't imagine the inner strength they have, the courage and willingness to mix it up. But one glance at the wrist and you know you are prey facing a predator.

I am a wrist watcher myself. When you have the thin, delicate wrists of a nonhitter, noncombatant in life, you have to be. So when I check my fellow man, I check his wrists. Other aspects may change. The waist may enlarge and recede. The double chin come and go. But the wrist is unchanging. And it tells me about the inner man and how he is going to respond. I know then who comes to each day tough and ready for whatever comes.

With the proper technique, I could impersonate this hitter, but I would never be one. At fifty-two, I realize this. My philosophy has ripened, as Aristotle had predicted so precisely, at the age of fifty-one. I passed the crisis that comes to all men who find that their machismo must lie in other, presumably less masculine activities. Who find that they are not designed for confrontation and assertive action.

I passed the crisis that comes when you realize that Rollo May was wrong when he said the myth of competition was dead. (Arthur Miller's *Death of a Salesman,* said May, showed that competition was outmoded and that cooperation would be the new myth of our lives.)

I suspect that May's wrists are no bigger than mine, and that he would like to think competition is finished. The way I see it, competition is alive and well and flourishing in sports and in corporate America. And no one is going to make it to the top without the wrists to do it.

Some critics have called sports the religion of America. I think not. Religion is an unprovable assumption about the experienced universe. It requires a construct too comprehensive for sports to provide. But there is a good case to be made that sports is the basis of our present culture, providing common values that men of all religions can live by.

For a culture to be passed along, Santayana wrote, it is not necessary that people read certain books, but simply that all people read the same books. And if by books we mean the literature of the day, then sports has indeed become the basis of our culture.

The literature of this day is journalism, and the authors of this day are journalists, whether they are called novelists or playwrights or essayists or reporters. Our daily reading is journalism because our novels and plays and essays and newspaper scores are clearly reports on the personal observations of actual events and people, even if more times than not the people observed are the authors themselves.

329

And the heavyweights in these writing fields are writers to whom sports are always important, or sometimes the whole ball game. Mailer, Marianne Moore, Updike, Roth and Dickey, to name a few, have found in sports the analogies to explain what happens elsewhere in life.

When Mailer had his fiftieth birthday party and Fifth Estate fiasco at the Four Seasons, he said the failure was not without some compensation; he could now write intimately, he said, "of the after-sensation of being called out on strikes in the last of the seventh when there are men on base and you never take your bat off your shoulder."

The game was just as important to Miss Moore, who wrote in her review of George Plimpton's *Out of His League* that the book should earn Plimpton the triple crown for poetry, biography and drama. And also as important to Updike, who wrote: "A game can gather to itself awesome dimensions of subtlety and transcendental significance."

The root of this subtlety and transcendence is the body. We proceed to these almost mystical heights through a reality common to us all. The body is where all religion, all culture, all literature must start. The body is where all writers must start, and few do.

"Literature does its best to maintain," wrote Virginia Woolf, "that its concern is the mind; that the body is a sheet of glass through which the soul looks straight and clear, and (the body) is null and negligible and nonexistent. On the contrary, the opposite is true. All day, all night, the body intervenes."

Writers who know sports and play never make that mistake. And having started with this deep regard for the body, they are able to go off in diverse and wonderful ways to praise men and their games. They have shown again the old truth: The deeper the belief, the more various the ways it can be expressed.

"Marianne Moore, Pulitzer Prize winning poet and a baseball fan extraordinary," read the wire service report last weekend, "died yesterday at her Manhattan home. She was 84."

The ex-left fielder of the Carlisle High School girls' baseball team, poet laureate of the Brooklyn Dodgers, and watcher of three television sets in season had, in one of her favorite expressions, "run out of room."

The teacher of Jim Thorpe, lover of Bach and Elston Howard, Stravinsky and Floyd Patterson, admirer of birds, animals and athletes, had taken her penetrating vision to another and because of her presence more lively and interesting place.

And I had lost one of my saints.

She had appeared, as saints usually do, when she was needed. Needed to provide acceptance and to champion the faith, the myth, the guiding fiction of my life. Not only to give it social and intellectual respectability, but also to give me assurance that the truth I dream is true.

Back in the thirties, the attack was, "Religion is the opiate of the people." And I was there when Peter Viereck said, "Anti-Catholicism is the anti-Semitism of the intellectuals." In those days, my saint was G. K. Chesterton, a man of talent, wit and humor who took on and defeated all comers. Chesterton, the master of the paradox, was the right person at the right time not merely because he was a thinker and writer equal to any of his opponents, but because he spoke what the common man felt. What we felt but could not express.

"The common man," he once wrote, "may be as gross as Shakespeare, or as garrulous as Homer; if he is religious, he talks almost as much about hell as Dante; if he is worldly, he talks nearly as much about drink as Dickens." And we can now add, if he is philosophical, he will think as much about baseball as Marianne Moore.

Miss Moore was the saint I needed for sports. The answer to "sport is the opiate of the people." Her genius was in observation. She saw everything vital and fresh and new as if for the first time. Her interest was in the common things in life. She did not write on eternal things or infinity. "I'll talk about them," she said, "when I understand them," and she wrote about Jackie Robinson and Campy and Big Newk instead.

She became a baseball fan at the age of sixty-six. A friend had taken her to a Dodger game and there she caught the fever. Not from a spectacular play, a memorable catch or a clutch hit, but from a conference on the mound.

It was the sight of Roy Campanella out there calming Karl Spooner down, the big mitt resting on his hip, his mask pushed back on his head and his earnest look—zest, she called it—and how he imparted encouragement with a pat on Spooner's rump, that captured the poet, who appreciated not only the skills but the emotions as well.

Marianne Moore knew the skills ("I don't know how to account for a person," she said, "who could be indifferent to these miracles of dexterity"). And although her favorites were Howard and Campanella, because they were strong, lumbering quarterbacking catchers, she also liked what she called the precision positions, third base, pitcher and first base.

She knew what they were trying to do. When Mike Burke asked her to throw out the first ball in 1969, she told a reporter that she had been instructed to throw it high for the benefit of the photographers. "But," she said, "I'm going to keep it low and outside where you're supposed to."

Earlier this poet, whose work is said by T. S. Eliot to form part of the small body of durable poetry of our time, whose poems were praised by Ezra Pound and pilfered by W. H. Auden, wrote in her poem "Baseball and Writing": "Your arm too true at first can learn to catch the corners, even trouble Mickey Mantle. They crowd him and curve him and aim for the knees."

Her poems were like that. Never the fat one down the middle. She worked the corners. No rookie from Tidewater was she. Reading her is going against the speed of Koufax, the accuracy of Seaver, and the assortment of Preacher Roe.

"Pitching," she said, "is a large subject." And so is her poetry. Full of sliders, slips and slants, but marvelous in its compression, its control.

To her, it was like baseball. You can never tell with either, she wrote, how it will go or what you will do; generating excitement, a fever in the victim—pitcher, catcher, fielder, batter. Athletes for her were exemplars of art ("You cannot see art off in a corner," she said, "and hope for it to have vitality, reality and substance"). And she and the athletes had this in common, that they see as opportunity what others feel as menace.

So the artist-athlete carves out his own drama, provides the pauses, determines the action on the field. He is not choreographed by Balanchine or playing someone else's music or reciting some playwright's lines. He is there, forcing his own identity on the game.

He is also contributing some no-nonsense virtues that Miss Moore always admired. Like patience, courage, loyalty and independence. And perhaps some of what she saw in the athlete, in this case Floyd Patterson, what she called "the age-old formula for results in any kind of work, profession, art or recreation—powerful feeling and the talent to use it."

Baseball gained stature from the stature of this admirer. Intellectuals might marvel that a "poet of extraordinary discrimination, precision and restraint" (Randall Jarrell), who "like Poe, Hawthorne and Henry James had a passionate predilection for the genuine" (R. P. Blackmur), would concern herself with baseball. Yet when she was leaving for Boston to receive her Doctor of Letters from Harvard ("By finding joy in earth and sky," read the citation, "she has stirred our hearts"), she remarked sadly that her schedule would not include the Red Sox game at Fenway Park.

Now this saint is dead. This kind, gracious, unpredictable woman is gone. But not before she had given the lance to "sport is the opiate of the people;" not before she had taught us the importance of the physical, and the attention we must give to every moment, every object, every animal, every human in what he says and does.

"Whatever you do," she said before she left, "do it with all your might."

I'll try, Miss Moore, I'll try.

9

Running

> The best most of us can do
> is to be a Poet an hour a day.
> Take the hour when we run or tennis or
> golf or garden; take that hour away from being
> serious adults and become serious beginners.

EVERY MILE I RUN is my first. Every hour on the roads a new beginning. Every day I put on my running clothes, I am born again. Seeing things as if for the first time, seeing the familiar as unfamiliar, the common as uncommon. Doing what Goethe said was the hardest thing of all, seeing with my own eyes that which is spread before me. Bringing to that running, that play, the attitude of the child, the perception of a poet. Being a beginner with a beginner's mind, a beginner's heart, a beginner's body.

There is no other way to run, no other way to live. Otherwise my runs become dull, uninspired interludes. The running becomes routine, becomes part of the humdrum apathy and indifference which the poet John Hall Wheelock called a shield between us and reality. It becomes a chore, becomes habit. And habit kills awareness and separates us from ourselves.

My awareness begins with my body, my beginner's body. Each day I discover how to breathe. Taste the air. Feel it move through my lungs. I learn to exhale totally and groan and grunt, marking my passage through the fields and trees like some animal.

Each day I search out how to run. Feeling the thrust of the hamstrings. Letting the foot drop below the knee. Arriving at the form the child adopts naturally. The body, a little stronger perhaps, certainly more durable, must come upon these ideas as fresh as if newly thought. And then concentrate on this beginning and bring to it the beginner's joy in doing this tremendously simple yet tremendously complex thing so well.

From then on it becomes more and more difficult. It is relatively easy to return to basics with the body. But to have a beginner's heart and mind is a different matter. To take sight and smell, hearing and touch and become a new Adam in a new Eden is tough going even for a poet. Even for those who live more and participate more in their own existence. And yet like them I must listen and discover forgotten knowledge. Must respond to everything around me and inside me as well.

Poets do this naturally. A really good poet, wrote James Dickey, is like an engine with the governor off. And it's no good for people to say that life should not mean that much to a poet. The really good poet, said Dickey, has no choice; that's the way he is.

The best most of us can do is to be a poet an hour a day. Take the hour when we run or tennis or golf or garden; take that hour away from being a serious adult and become serious beginners. Take an hour away from what Shelley called a life of error, ignorance and strife, and introduce love and beauty and delight.

Those good things began in my beginning. When I was not afraid to respond to my feeling. Before I was taught not to cry. Before I learned that humor had a time and a place and deep emotions had best be concealed, that passion be left unfelt.

When I run I go back to those better days. Now no emotion is foreign to me. I express myself totally. My body and heart and mind interact and open me to the infinite possibilities only a beginner can envision. And I relive that moment in the beginning of things when, as Yeats said, we understand more perfectly than we understand until all is finished.

And what of that finish? "It is development, improvement and completion that means the deterioration of the creativeness," wrote Berdyaev, the Russian theologian, "the cooling down of the creative fire, decay, old age."

I will have none of that. So each day I take to the roads as a beginner, a child, a poet. Seeking the innocence of the beginner, the wonder of the child and the vision of the poet. Hoping for a new appreciation of the landscape, a new perspective of my inner world, some new insights on life, a new response to existence and myself.

There are times, more often than the good times, when I fail. I never do pierce the shield. I return with a shopping list of things to do tomorrow. The miraculous has gone unseen. The message has gone unheard. I have had one of those loveless days on a lovely day for love.

Still, there is always the chance I'll have beginner's luck. And this run, this hour, this day, may begin in delight and end in wisdom.

I am a noonday runner. In the past, and still from time to time, I have run in the morning or evening. But almost always these days, I run in the early afternoon.

You might think this choice of when to run simply a matter of convenience. Of fitting it in when time becomes available. Most people believe that running is running, regardless of when it is done. But I know this is not so. There is a time, as Ecclesiastes wrote, for every purpose under heaven. There is a time for running. Mine is midday. I run at midday because I must. I run at midday because my body and soul tell me to.

336

My body is at its best in early afternoon. My circadian rhythms at their crest. Like the sun, my energy is at its zenith, my fields of force at maximum. Whatever I do, I do best at this time of day.

But midday has more than physiological importance. When I run at noon, I run at the sixth hour. I run at an hour that has significance that goes back through the history of the race. An hour that reminds me I am participating in an ever-recurring mystery, seeking and making a self I will never fully know. An hour that brings me back to myth and ritual and a feeling for the holy.

In the sixth hour, I am in a time that is recurrent and symbolic. A time that Eliade wrote of as circular, reversible and recoverable. A time that tells me I am a child of the universe born for more than is visible in this world.

Daybreak and sunset have similar implications. The morning run speaks for rebirth and the new life. Just as morning prayers praise the Lord, sing the earth, tell of renewed purpose. And the evening run is for those who have fought the good fight and now desire only the peace an hour's run at a slow, steady pace will give them. When I run in these closing stages of the day, I am a philosopher. I accept life, death, the self, what I have done. I am content.

From this perspective, the morning run is my youth. Running in the morning is to wear the bright morning face. It is for health and fitness and making the team. It is accepting discipline, obeying duty and acquiring self-control.

Midday is adult. The run is in pursuit of goals, the making of the self, the looking for something to leave behind. You must say it is in the Catholic tradition, linking goodness to beauty and proportion and achievement.

If so, the evening run is toward the East, toward that ancient acceptance of things as they are. That mature wisdom with which we see a world that has order and sense. And we know, as Erikson said, that our one and only life cycle was something that had to be and, by necessity, permitted of no substitutions.

One thing we runners know. There is no substitute for running. No matter what age we are. No matter what time we do it.

My fight is not with age. Running has won that battle for me. Running is my fountain of youth, my elixir of life. It will keep me young forever.

When I run, I know there is no need to grow old. I know that my running, my play, will conquer time.

And there on the roads, I can pursue my perfection for the rest of my days, and finally, as his wife said of Kazantzakis dead at seventy-four, be mowed down in the first flower of my youth.

The fight, then, is never with age; it is with boredom, with routine, with the danger of not living at all. Then life will stop, growth will cease, learning will come to an end. You no longer become who you are. You begin to kill time or live it without thought or purpose. Everything that is happiness, all that is excitement, whatever you know of joy and delight, will evaporate. Life will be reduced to a slow progression of days and weeks and months. Time will become an enemy instead of an ally.

When I run, I avoid all this. I enter a world where time stops, where now is a fair sample of eternity. Where I am filled with excitement and joy and delight, even with the intensity and inner fire and never-ending search for self of a Kazantzakis. I enter a state that will be man's most congenial environment.

"Play, games, jests, culture, we affirm," wrote Plato, "are the most serious things in life." And for the most serious of all reasons, what Kierkegaard called "choosing one's self." Or, to use Plato's thought again, to recapture our original state of perfection.

But isn't that perfection, or at least the bodily part of it, only resident in youth? Not if you persist in your sport, persevere in your play. True, we delight in our bodies in our youth and envy the young as we grow old. But this need not be.

We can continue to keep our bodies in beauty and competence until death claims us. We should know that the fit die young in body as well as in mind and heart. That, like Kazantzakis, whatever their age they will be mowed down in the first flower of their youth.

Running has made me young again. I run now as I did at twenty. I have the same health, the same vigor, the same sensations of power and grace. And I have the strength and speed and endurance of those years younger than me. Not because I am exceptional, but because I do what I do with my whole self. My running is an incitement to energy. It is an outpouring from the very center of my being. It is a vital force that takes me to the peak of my powers and there opens me to myself and to the world and to others.

Running gives me a body and mind and heart willing to follow my own vision, to break the mold, to choose a new course, even perhaps to become the hero that Ortega said we all carry within us. This is a lifelong task. A lifelong of saying, as did Ortega, "That's not it, that's not it." And therefore a life that must be very young and eager and full of enthusiasm, full of sport and play, full of running.

If you would not age, you must make everything you do touched with play, play of the body, of thought, of emotions. If you do, you will belong to that special class of people who find joy and happiness in every act, in every moment. Those to whom leisure is the one thing valuable. Those whom Ruskin called "the proudly idle."

My running and your play may be idleness to those of another mind. But it is the self-awareness, the consciousness, the intensity, that is important, however inconsequential the activity. "Come into the kitchen," said Heraclitus. "The gods are there, too." And out on the roads, and whenever you play, there is fitness and self-discovery and the persons we were destined to be. There is the theater where we can write and act out our own dreams. Having first, of course, gotten down to bone and muscle, and then come to some understanding of the unique once-in-an-eternity person each one of us is.

Running reminds me that any age man is still the marvel of creation. With the passage of time, there is little deterioration of our physical or psychic powers, little worth thinking that is lost. The only important issue, as Rollo May tells us, is not whether a person is twenty or forty or sixty, but whether he fulfills his own capacity of self-conscious choice at his own particular level.

That's a game the playful person almost always wins.

Is running an art and the runner an artist? The best answer is that of Picasso. When asked, "What is art?" he replied, "What is not?"

So running is an art along with everything else we do. When I run, I know this to be true. Running is my art and I am an artist however ordinary my performance. Running is for me what the dance is to others. The oldest and highest of the arts. My ancestors ran before they danced. And it is running, not dance, that gives me a perfect conformity of form and matter.

Running also fulfills Herbert Read's definition. Art, he stated, is an escape from chaos; movement ordained in numbers; mass confined by measure; matter seeking the rhythm of life. You could almost believe Read was watching runners while he wrote.

Where better to escape chaos and find order? Where more is movement numbered, in steps, in breaths, in minutes, in miles? Where more sharply is space and mass defined; the runner lean, the road unending? Where else, for me at least, to seek the rhythms of life, to listen to the body, to hear it speak of my soul?

And because body becomes soul, soul becomes body, running is a total experience. It is art and more than art. In itself it provides the thinking and abstractions that precede other arts. "I need hours to read and think about what I've read, to synthesize and be alone," one painter said. "The time spent at the canvas is minor compared with that."

The runner, on the other hand, is always at his canvas. He is always observing, feeling, analyzing, meditating. Always in the process of raiding the preconscious that stores past preconceptions. The preconscious that stubbornly refuses to illuminate the present with what we experienced in the past. And beyond and before it the runner explores his instincts and emotions and even dips into what can only be called mystical states.

Where the runner fails is as an artist. He may be able to express these feelings, these insights, and perhaps does, but no one sees them. He fails in the prime function of the artist, to transmit the understanding of the emotions he has experienced. The spectator sees little of this inner life. Even the poet, tuned to see life at various levels, sees the runner in almost one plane.

"Alone he emerges/Emerges and passes/alone, sufficient." Loneness, motion, sufficiency is the runner. The world knows no more about him.

In time this will change. Running is an old art but only newly resurrected. We are still learning how to develop a total response. In traffic I may be as expressionless as Buster Keaton, but on lonely roads and in empty woods the inner man is becoming visible. There I respond to grass and dirt and fallen leaves. My running is part of sun and shadow, wind at my face, wind at my back. If you saw me, you would see elation, mastery, struggle, defeat and despair. There I reveal sorrow and anger, resentment and fear; fear of dogs and men and high places, fear of the dark and of being lost and alone.

But what matters whether we can be understood by someone else? By someone who is not a runner? Not certainly to induce them to try it

340

themselves. But rather to encourage them to seek their own art, to become their own artists. To listen for that inner voice calling them to their own way of being in this world. To what they must be.

The runner knows this necessity. I know that although I am free to be anything I choose, I must be a runner. Ortega put it this way: "You are able to be whatever you want to be; but only if you choose this or that specific pattern you will be what you have to be."

When I run, all that Ortega says falls into place. I have found my specific pattern, heard the voice that calls me, found my art, my medium to experience and interpret life. Nor do I worry that running will be inadequate to the task. I know the truth of what William James once said of a young man learning about himself and his instincts and emotions: "Sport came to the rescue and completed his education where real things were lacking."

The distance runner is the least of all athletes. His sport the least of all sports. That he does it at all, either well or ill, implies that he can do nothing else. He has by the process of elimination come to the level of his competence, which is little more than survival.

Nor does he survive in ways we might admire. By challenging his environment, for instance, for conquering his enemies. He performs no feats of skill or strength or agility. He is no Crusoe who would build a new house, a new town, a new city, even a new civilization. He does nothing more than this: bring his body to the performance of a minor art, and attain an inconsequential type of perfection.

And being the least of all athletes, he appears to be the least of all men. A lonely figure on a lonely road, he seems to have no past, no future, and to be living in a present that has no rational meaning.

He performs with perverse intensity an action which has no marketable value. And is completely engaged in what is not only impractical, but even unintelligible to his fellows.

Still, this apparently witless and homeless creature, this most ordinary, most commonplace, this least of all men, has a message. A message we all carry, but sometimes fail to hear.

The distance runner is a prophet. Like the poet, he is the antenna of the race. Like the poet, he does what he does with his whole being. And like the poet, he gives thanks for his "fabulous possessions, his body and fiery soul." Like the poet, he sees himself as a question to himself.

And seeks the answer by seeking to be, by creating himself. And again like the poet, he suggests that each one of us has this revelation, this Truth; and that we must find it through our bodies, through experience, and always in the present.

Most of us think of religion as something out of the past that promises something about the future. We ignore the primacy of the present. We forget that the opposite of the present is not past or future; it is absence.

The distance runner who accepts the past in the person he is, and sees the future as promise rather than threat, is completely and utterly in the present. He is absorbed in his encounter with the everyday world. He is mysteriously reconciling the separations of body and mind, of pain and pleasure, of the conscious and the unconscious. He is repairing the rent, and healing the wound in his divided self. He has found a way to make the ordinary extraordinary; the commonplace, unique; the everyday, eternal.

What he does begins in play, moves through suffering and ends in delight. And tells us that we must do the same. That we who began in play as children and move toward a heaven where we will have nothing to do but play will find our revelation and ourselves only in play.

The distance runner has found his play. And with it, he purifies his body. He does not, as the early Fathers suggested, kill his body because it kills him. He accepts it and perfects it and then seeks out suffering, and finds beyond the suffering the whole man. Not at first, of course. At first he explores the possibilities of letting the suffering pass. Of trying every diversion to remove the pain. But in the end, he grasps it and holds it and welcomes it.

This may be an odd way to find the meaning of life. And the distance runner is certainly an odd person to be demonstrating it. But the meaning of life is beyond reason. Genius upon genius has told us so.

The meaning of life is found in revelation, a revelation that is present in each one of us. To be found where our blood and flesh whisper to our unconscious. The distance runner, the least of all athletes, the least of all men, is continually taking his daily encounter with his universe on that inward journey.

Consider your body, he tells us. Not in the memory of past pleasure. Or in anticipation of a glorious future. But for this present moment when you might indeed be in Paradise.

* * *

As soon as the race results are in the paper, the usual comment I hear in the hospital corridors is, "I see you let a girl beat you." The statement is wrong on all counts. Wrong in what it says. Wrong in what it implies.

For one thing, she is not a girl, but a woman. Anyone who has had their consciousness raised knows better than to call a woman a girl. You use "girl" where if it were male you'd use "boy." And it is about time everyone learned that. Further, she is not only a woman but a runner, and a good one. Women runners can be more than just competent. They have less percent body fat than most men. Their maximum oxygen uptake can be amazingly high. And their slow and fast twitch muscle fiber ratios are identical to men runners' in other events.

I have discovered in races and in training that women runners have the same spectrum men have, from very good to very bad. I have been beaten regularly by the best and have had some head-to-head struggles with those not quite good. And I have trained with some whose cruising speed left me speechless and gasping to keep up with them. So there is no question of letting a woman beat you. Some do. Some don't. As with all runners, it depends on who is best that particular day.

But mostly I am upset with that statement because it implies that there is something wrong about women in sports and particularly in men's sports. There is the suggestion that the whole thing is somehow unnatural.

And in the sense of the orthodox, it is. In becoming a runner, the woman gives up her appearance of completeness. She becomes less and less of a mystery. She relinquishes her power, the intimidation of being a woman. Running removes what Ortega called her "perpetual self-concealment." And in this surrender, she finds who she actually is and reveals that self to others. The woman who comes to know herself to be truly a runner has discovered not only her body, but her soul as well.

People who see only the differences between men and women do not understand this. Their herd-thinking cannot conceive that sport has something to offer women, who, after all, need nothing but children, church and kitchen. They cannot imagine any benefits from men-women competition. And their emphasis on the biological and social perpetuates the war of the sexes.

The truth is that sports, and that includes men running against women, may well be the salvation of the men-women relationship, the answer to our marriage problem, the solution of the eternal discord between what is masculine and what is feminine.

You may find this theory farfetched. But consider this first and primary thought: Nature works for the herd. She has us breed toward the middle. Opposites are attracted to opposites, and produce the average, the mediocre, the commonplace. "The decisive factor in a nation's history," wrote Ortega, "is the common man." Our herd's future, the future of the race, has always depended on its innumerable mediocre men.

This is fine biologically and even socially, but not psychologically. Each of us wants to be an individual, a thoroughbred, whether it be a quarter horse or a Clydesdale. The herd would have us marry for what we lack. We should marry for what we see of ourselves in others. Our aim should be, as Plato said, to find our other half.

This cannot be done unless each is revealed, body and soul, to the other. And where better can this be done than in sports? In those arenas where a person finds his or her moment of truth. Knows what she or he has been from all time. And, in that knowing, reveals it to others.

Nature would rather avoid this revelation. Rather the woman remained a mystery. Rather the masculine in women and the feminine in men went unrecognized. So men and women are attracted at an early age in the interests of forces that are unconcerned about their personal fulfillment. Originality, individuality, creativity and personality are sacrificed. And all of this has gone unnoticed because, as H. L. Mencken once said, a man can be happy with any number of women. And Mencken could have added: women continue in situations that cry for vengeance on heaven.

But in our overpopulated world, the herd is no longer that important. Leisure and free time now make the psychological problems of such marriages more evident. In 1976 for the first time, divorces in the United States exceeded one million. Our affluence and forty-hour work week have allowed for communication. And, as Ogden Nash once wrote about your conscience, you should have a good communication or none at all.

Eventually, love, marriage, communication, good conversation or good silences depend on a total meeting with someone who is most like ourself. So that, as Berdyaev put it, we are "united in one androgynous image, overcoming our loneliness."

That, of course, is the ultimate. Creating union, knowing the other, overcoming loneliness, bringing together two solitudes.

Sport is the key to this undertaking. Athletes who know themselves in their body know when they differ from others. But even more, they know when they are alike. When they are simpatico.

When I see women running, I see a new world coming. Not perhaps for girls who are as soft and as pink as a nursery, but certainly for those who wear sweats and running shoes and train thirty miles a week.

10

Training

"

**Nature, as T. H. Huxley has told us,
never overlooks a mistake
or makes the smallest allowance for ignorance.**

"

IF YOU WANT to run a marathon you must train six miles a day. If you are looking for that natural high that distance runners talk about, you must do the same. And if you would prefer to die of something other than a heart attack, the daily six miles is physiological magic.

But know this: Disaster will pursue you to the very gates of heaven unless you do the Magic Six. These are exercises designed to counteract the bad effects of daily training—the muscle imbalance that contributes to overuse syndromes of foot, leg, knee, and low back. Without the Magic Six you will soon become an ex-runner, no longer able to accept five thousand footstrikes an hour on a hard flat surface with a foot constructed for sand or dirt.

Training overdevelops the prime movers, the muscles along the back of the leg, the thigh, and the low back; they become short and inflexible. The antagonists, the muscles on the front of the leg, the thigh, and the abdomen become relatively weak. The Magic Six are necessary to correct this strength-flexibility imbalance. Three stretch the prime movers; three strengthen the antagonists.

The first stretching exercise is the wall pushup for the calf muscles. Stand flatfooted about three feet from the wall. Lean in until it hurts to keep the knees locked, and the legs straight, and the feet flat. Hold for ten "elephants." (The time it takes to say "One elephant" is about one second.) Relax. Continue for one minute.

The second is the hamstring stretch. Put your straight leg, with knee locked, on a footstool, later a chair, and finally a table as you improve. Keep the other leg straight with knee locked. Bring your head to the knee of the extended leg or toward the knee until it hurts. Hold for ten elephants. Relax. Continue for one minute.

The final stretch exercise is the backover for the hamstrings and the low back. Lie on floor. Bring your straight legs over your head and try to touch the floor with your toes until it hurts. Hold for ten elephants. Relax by bringing your knees to your ears for ten elephants. Continue for one minute.

The first strengthening exercise is for the shin muscles. Sit on a table with your legs hanging down. Suspend a three- to five-pound weight over the toes of one foot. Flex the foot upward. Hold for six elephants. Relax. Continue for one minute.

For the quadriceps assume the same position with the weight. This

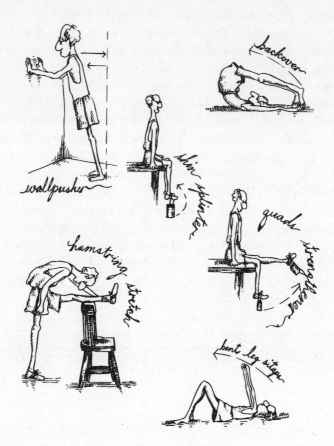

time straighten the leg, locking the knee. Hold for six elephants. Relax. Continue for one minute.

The final exercise is the bent-leg sit-up. Lie on the floor with your knees bent and your feet close to your buttocks. Come to a sitting position. Lie back. Repeat until you can't do any more or until you've reached twenty times.

It takes a little over six minutes to do the Magic Six. Done before and after running, this means just twelve minutes a day to keep you in muscle balance and counteract stress fractures and heel spurs and Achilles-tendinitis and shin splints and runner's knee and sciatica and all those other terrible things that happen to runners.

* * *

Is your second toe longer than your first toe?

If so and you are an athlete you are in for trouble. If you haven't already had it. The long-second/short-first toe, called Morton's foot, is probably the most disabling of the common congenital defects in the architecture of the foot which cause it to fail with overuse.

Until Dudley Morton noticed it, the long-second/short-first toe was considered no more important than a large nose or a square jaw. No one had thought about what constitutes a normal foot. Morton changed all of that. In 1935 he published his classic, *The Normal Foot,* which for the foot was what Harvey's *De Motu Cordis* three hundred years earlier was for the heart and circulation.

The function of foot, wrote Morton, depends on two factors:

1. Structural stability, supplied by the 26 bones and the 112 ligaments which bind these bones together. Any abnormality in the bony architecture or laxity of the ligaments, Morton said, can end in weak, painful and inefficient feet. Further, these biomechanical problems can cause more remote difficulties in the leg and the knee and even the groin and the low back.

2. Postural stability, maintained by the short muscles of the foot and the long muscles of the foot and the leg. Imbalance caused by a short heel cord or strong inflexible calf and thigh muscles, he claimed, puts additional stress on the foot and the arch.

The most frequent cause of structural instability in the foot is Morton's foot. It is a biomechanical absurdity. The two-millimeter or more shortening of the first metatarsal distorts the normal weight-bearing tripod: the heel, the head of the fifth and the head of the first metatarsal. The foot adapts by either (a) bearing most of the weight on the head of the second metatarsal, thereby causing a stress fracture; or (b) pronating the foot (rolling over the inside) and opening up a Pandora's box of overuse injuries.

The most prevalent of these injuries are evenly distributed among the foot (the heel spur), the leg (the stress fracture) and the knee (runner's knee, or chondromalacia).

If you are an athlete and have suffered from any of these illnesses it is possible, I could say probable, that no one has observed whether or not your second toe is longer than the first. Or whether you have any of the other more subtle structural flaws that can cause foot difficulties.

Morton's discovery has been forgotten. It was taught to one generation of physicians and then discredited. Many people had Morton's foot without symptoms. So when it appeared in those with complaints, it was thought a coincidence.

The truth was that people were just not using their feet that much. It wasn't until after World War II that athletes upped their practice time fivefold and the overuse syndromes of foot, leg, knee and back became the major concern of sports physicians. By that time Morton's book had disappeared from the libraries and the curriculum. And with it his theory of structural and postural strain which was the answer to these mysterious ailments.

For many who are on their feet very little, Morton's theories are just that. For the practicing athlete his theories can be the difference between being active and being on the injured list—indeed, the difference between being an athlete and being an ex-athlete. When the basketball player spends hours on the court daily, and the runner increases his mileage to fifty and sixty miles a week, and the tennis player makes it a twice-a-day thing, then we begin to hear about Butazolidine and cortisone shots and whirlpool treatments.

But we never hear about Morton's foot and structural stability and postural stability.

I wonder why.

"At this late date in the history of sport," writes Paul Weiss in his *Sport, a Philosophic Inquiry*, "we still do not know much about what an athlete ought to eat before he engages in a grueling contest." This ignorance, of course, extends further. At this late date in the history of mankind, we still do not know much about what any of us ought to eat before we engage in work or life, much less play. The human intestinal tract, its physiology, and its diseases remain a mystery.

Fortunately the experts are confessing their ignorance and thereby liberating us from relying on their diets and treatments. The cause of duodenal ulcer, states a recent editorial in *The Lancet,* a British medical journal, remains poorly understood, and "the logical basis of treatment completely escapes us." It also escapes the task forces on gastrointestinal research commissioned by the National Institutes of Health. The reports of these groups, assigned to various parts of the digestive system, come to one general conclusion: Most of our firmly held ideas about digestion and digestive diseases are either untrue or unproven.

350

What are we to do while the experts suck their thumbs? The best answer is to go back to the three rules of digestion known since antiquity:

1. Eat foods that agree with you.
2. Avoid foods that disagree with you.
3. Don't go to bed mad.

One thing the investigators are discovering is that the foods we said agreed with us agree with us. And the foods we said disagreed with us disagree with us. Their high-powered sophisticated technology is confirming what patients have told their doctors over the centuries: certain foods give them heartburn or indigestion or cramps or diarrhea, other foods do not. Only now the people in the laboratory are finally finding out why. Learning why certain people have trouble with certain foods and others don't. Why foods that should be good for you can cause wholesale trouble.

Milk is a prime example of a food that should be good for us but frequently isn't. Some people are allergic to milk, but many more cannot handle the milk sugar lactose because of an enzyme deficiency. It seems likely now that if you never liked milk you shouldn't drink it. It may be the perfect food but not for you.

Each of us has particular foods that we know are not for us. Foods that cause heartburn or a variety of gut symptoms. Each of us is, therefore, an experiment-of-one in finding out what foods we can handle and what foods we can't. There is no sense appealing to the books, or the experts. The body will not listen. Eventually we will get a scientific explanation for what is happening. For the time being we must accept the reality.

One such reality is that if we go to bed mad we are likely to wake up with a riled-up stomach. If I go to bed with fire in my eye, I will wake up with fire in my stomach. It is not only food but emotions that act on the intestinal tract.

When I become an athlete, emotion becomes even more important. Pre-game tension, pre-race apprehension, can stop the stomach from emptying. Food that would ordinarily get in and out in four hours may sit undigested for six or more. Then I add the effect of strenuous exercise which is to increase spasm and propulsion through the bowel. Emotion and exertion are why the athlete has one additional rule:

4. Always compete on an empty stomach and an empty colon.

Otherwise the athlete and his food are soon parted. He will either throw up or have diarrhea, or both.

Follow the rules, however, and you can come up with your own answer to your pre-event meal. Liquid or semiliquid, with little fat and not too much protein, so that it will be easily digested and quickly out of the stomach. And composed of foods you take every day and know you can handle.

Here, as in all things related to health and to well working and to functioning at our maximum, we must listen to our bodies. Fortunately the gastrointestinal tract speaks in a loud, clear and unmistakable voice. When we make a mistake we know it.

Even slow learners get the message if they lose their lunch or have to retire from the fray for a bowel movement.

Life is the great experiment. Each of us is an experiment of one—observer and subject—making choices, living with them, recording the effects. "Living," said the philosopher Ortega, "is nothing more than doing one thing instead of another."

But that doing must be total. We must live on the alert and perform at capacity. "From my point of view," Ortega declared, "it is immoral for a being not to make the most intense effort every instant of his life."

When these conditions of conscious choice and maximum effort apply, we find that nature has set up the best of experiments, simple and controlled, solving questions one at a time. When we study ourselves in motion, under stress, trying to be all we can be, then, and sometimes only then, our deficiencies become apparent in unmistakable ways. If we would be artist or scientist or philosopher or saint, we soon learn what makes us more human or mortal than those who succeed. But we learn even quicker when we are athletes.

And of all athletes, the endurance athlete—the distance runner, the swimmer, the cross-country skier—is the researcher's dream. When my mind and heart turned to the marathon, my body could do nothing but follow. I became willing to accept any schedule, any training, any diet in the promise of better times, in the hope of breaking the three-hour barrier. And so I became one of the observers and subjects in the great carbohydrate-loading experiment.

The program is simple. One week prior to the marathon you take a long run, preferably about ninety minutes. The following three days you limit your diet to meat, fish, cheese, and eggs, staying away from carbohydrates. During this time you continue training. The final three days you stop training and eat mainly carbohydrates.

This dietary sleight-of-hand first depletes the muscle sugar, or glycogen, then supersaturates the muscles with the same glycogen, which is the major source of energy in marathons. Original experiments in Sweden showed that work capacity could be increased anywhere from one hundred to three hundred percent. That means that running time in an eighteen-mile race could be improved as much as fifteen minutes. No wonder marathoners all over the world have become carbohydrate "loaders."

You can now see the great carbohydrate-loading experiment taking shape. Given these large numbers of runners training maximally and eating much the same diet, the variables are reduced to those inherent in each runner's muscular system, in his intricate metabolic and biochemical and enzymatic reactions. It is here where nature conducts the most instructive of experiments, where the lack of just one of thousands of enzymes can be shown to cause serious difficulty in body function.

And so it is with carbohydrate loading. For most of us the results were marvelous. The last quarter of the run became less and less of a nightmare. If, perhaps, the three-hour barrier remained unbreached, at least the times were much faster. Paul Slovic's studies of carbohydrate loaders (*Nutrition Today*, 10:18, 1975) showed an average improvement of eight minutes and thirty seconds, which translates to twenty seconds, or one hundred yards, a mile.

However, nature had more to tell us. One of Slovic's loaders met disaster and ran one hour slower than his predicted time. Here and there we heard of other runners who had developed leg cramps or fatigue and had been forced to drop out very early in marathons.

What these unfortunates had in common was muscle breakdown and an increase in myoglobin in the blood sufficient in some instances to clog the kidneys and cause renal shutdown. These events are most likely set in motion by the first three days of low carbohydrate intake and continued training, rather than the three-day binge of carbohydrates that follows.

And so it goes. The marathoner who cannot load has discovered (as I did when I found I was tone deaf, and as all of us do in some fashion) that life is unfair. But he has also learned what everyone performing this great experiment of life must know. That nature, as T. H. Huxley has told us, never overlooks a mistake or makes the smallest allowance for ignorance.

The party line of the scientists is that we catch colds. We become infected with one of the numerous rhinoviruses and in short order come down with the familiar sore throat, cough and runny nose. And it will be only a matter of time, they assure us, until research will produce a vaccine or antibiotic and the common cold will be just a memory.

I don't believe it. The way I see it, the common cold will last as long as the common man. We have those rhinoviruses in our systems and always will. Usually they lie dormant, but when our defenses are lowered, then somehow the barriers are breached, the cold develops.

You don't catch colds. Everyone from Plato to our sainted aunts has told us that. They are caused by pride and stubbornness and arrogance, three qualities the Greeks put together in one word: *hubris*. As soon as we put ourselves over ordinary men, as soon as we aspire to be better and better, as soon as we risk going beyond our capabilities, just as soon do we risk what the Greeks called coryza and catarrh.

The runner who is a modern-day Greek knows this all too well. Like the Athenian, he is trying to live each day at the top of his powers. And always looking to the day when he will suddenly break through into a greater source of energy. A day when he will be filled with strength and speed and feel no fatigue. The runner knows with Sophocles, "The best is to live without disease;/To have that most sweet power to win each day the heart's desire."

But in reaching for this, in the training and the racing and, yes, in his pride and stubbornness and arrogance, the runner would be more than he actually is. And it is then that he begins to come apart, his defenses fold, the rhinovirus strikes, and he gets the common cold. And then, if only for a week, he agrees with another thought of Sophocles, "Never to have lived is best."

How to avoid this, how to reach for it all and not fall into the pit?

Plato had some rules for athletes: Don't drink. Avoid Sicilian cooking. Stay away from Corinthian girl friends. Abstain from Attic confectionery. But giving up beer and pizza, groupies and chocolates is not the real answer. Plato knew that also. The athlete in training, he said, is a sleepy creature and the smallest deviation from his routine leads to illness.

The runner is aware that this deviation from routine is racing. It is in the race that he challenges himself to his limits. And instead of husbanding his strength and hunkering down, instead of waiting for spring and the fulfillment of his year, he tries to become everything he is right now in this Sunday race and next Sunday's race and the race after that. Few can resist the call to test themselves to the limit today, here, on these hills. Few runners are ruled by reason when autumn and cross-country are here.

And unfortunately when the running is going well, the runner must be most alert. He is on a collision course between his heart's desire and the common cold. He should know that just beyond this workout—if run too hard, or this race—if too demanding, lies disaster. And he must be prepared to break off when he loses his zest for training, or a race leaves him fatigued for days afterward.

Just recently I ran three very tough races in seven days, the last ten thousand meters over hills at Holmdel Park. According to my family I looked worse at the two-mile mark than I did finishing at Boston at the marathon. My son even had ideas of tackling me to get me out of the race. When I finished, I lay motionless for five minutes, asking for someone to take my shoes off.

That should have been it for the cross-country season. Unfortunately it wasn't. The National Masters Championship was the following week at Van Cortlandt Park, another grueling ten-thousand-meter run. I could already feel the rhinoviruses preparing to charge. There was nothing to do but rest. I took the whole week off, hoping I had one more race before the barricades came down. I did. I ran my best race of the year. The next day I came down with the cold.

The goal of the runner is not health. His objective is the fitness necessary for maximal performance. Health is something the runner goes through on the way to fitness. A way station he hardly notices in his pursuit of the twenty to thirty percent of capacity that lies untouched.

355

And health, therefore, is what he risks in training to do his best. Because just beyond fitness and a personal record lies staleness, and with it fatigue and exhaustion and depression and despair.

I have gone through this sequence many times over the years. In reaching for my peak at distances from the mile to the marathon I have discovered that disaster is only a hard workout or an all-out race away. I have gone through the runner's version of being overtennised or overgolfed, of leaving my fight in the gym. I have become stale. I have reached that state where, as Lombardi once said about fumbles, "there is nothing to do but scream."

My task then is to reach this fine line; and not go over. To reach a state where training runs are what I live for and racing is the supreme experience; and not to go over the cliff that awaits just ahead.

In such a project in this exploration of my absolute limits, I would like as a motto that of another explorer, Roald Amundsen, "Leave nothing to chance." But the science is just not there. Staleness is something the physiologists know very little about. I must seek my own ways of knowing when I am in danger, when I must limit my training. When I must avoid races. When I must stop all activity and rest.

Over the years I have come to believe in two rules about training. The first: it is better to be undertrained than overtrained. The second: if things are going badly I am undoubtedly overtrained and need less work rather than more. This is in line with Bill Bowerman's belief that a bad race almost always indicates too much work. For this reason Bowerman has always recommended hard-day/easy-day schedules to avoid overtraining. Most runners and coaches, of course, take the opposite view. For them a bad race is an indication to double the training rather than cut it in half.

But must you wait for a bad race? Is there some way to guide yourself more precisely? Yes. First, by listening to your body. Second, by keeping a fitness index.

Your body is always trying to tell you where you are. Listen to it. Beware when you become tired and listless, when you lose interest in workouts and approach them as a chore rather than a pleasure. Back off when you become lightheaded on arising or notice an irregularity in your pulse. Slow down if you get a cold or sore throat or feel as if the "mono" is coming back. Be on the alert if you develop depression insomnia (ease in getting to sleep but repeated awakenings during the night) or remain unrefreshed after a night's sleep. Take it easy if your attention span diminishes and you can't concentrate. Listen well to these things. Your homeostasis, your equilibrium with training stress is breaking down.

The method of keeping a "fitness index" is simple and can be charted, which makes it more satisfactory to some than listening to your body. When you awake in the morning, lie in bed for five minutes, then take your pulse. To do this, grasp your Adam's apple between your thumb and your index finger. Then slide the fingers back about an inch or more until you feel the carotid arteries pulsating. Now count for sixty seconds. Also check your weight and breathing. Then chart. Do the same later in the day after training. Take your pulse immediately and then fifteen minutes later.

As you record these figures over the weeks you will chart your course through health to fitness. You will see a weekly improvement until you plateau out at your basic heart rate, usually around fifty per minute. Now you must be wary of any sudden rise. If the morning pulse is up ten or more beats, you have not recovered from the previous day's training. Practice therefore should be eliminated or curtailed until the pulse returns to normal.

Such attention to pulse taking may make a hypochondriac or a neurotic out of you. But more than likely the "fitness index" will give you better control of your running life rather than less. At present writing there is no better early-warning system for the proximity of overtraining. No better way to avoid staleness, the catastrophe on the other side of fitness.

The race should be the ultimate test of my running ability, the stopwatch the final judge, but I never really believe it. I always feel I could do better, that I have not yet exhausted the limits of talent and training. Most of all, I fear I have not given a full one hundred per cent.

So I went to Indiana to find out the truth, to spend a day with David Costill, Ph.D, in the Human Performance Laboratory at Ball State University in Muncie.

I had all the exercise physiology tests given our Olympic distance-running candidates earlier in Dallas—vital capacity, percent body fat, muscular strength, maximum oxygen intake, running efficiency, and a

357

calf muscle biopsy. All this to tell what my potential is and whether I am running up to it.

I soon learned that to Costill and his crew, human performance meant maximum human performance. I hardly had time to rejoice over having only 5.3 percent body fat when I was being pushed to my limit and beyond. Every test was accompanied by a constant stream of encouragement to do more, to try harder. And every test was repeated until I was doing worse instead of better. They had to know they had pushed me as far as I could go.

A few hours later, while doing the maximal oxygen uptake test on the treadmill, I knew they had. I had first run a mile at an eight-minute pace, then one in seven minutes, and finally one at 6:40, which is approximately nine miles an hour. All with a short rest to towel off, get my breath, and then resume.

But now it was time for maximal effort. I had the electrodes for the electrocardiogram reapplied to my chest, the plastic helmet holding the oxygen apparatus readjusted, and the mouthpiece fitted. Then suddenly I was off at a 6:40 mile going up a four percent grade. They were to increase this grade to six percent after three minutes and then an additional two percent every two minutes until I couldn't go any farther. When I felt I had only thirty seconds of running left I was to give a hand signal.

The first half hour required a noticeable increase in effort, but I felt in command. It was hard work, but I was getting accustomed to the peculiarity of the treadmill, of staying in one place, and of always having people just feet away urging and cajoling and imploring me to do my best.

When they raised it to six percent, I knew I was reaching my limit. My legs began to get heavy. The helmet became cumbersome and started to flop around. The mouthpiece was a distraction. I was barely able to keep up. And then they raised the grade to eight percent.

A mounting wave of fatigue and pain went over my body. My chest and legs were in a relentlessly closing vise. More people had wandered in to watch my final agony. They began to take up the chant: "Push!" "Harder!" But the struggle between me and the machine was coming to a close. Six minutes into the test and one minute at the eight percent grade, I gave the hand signal.

I had waited too long. I was finished and still had thirty seconds and

130 yards to go on this infernal, unforgiving apparatus. It was an eternity in time, an infinity in space.

Fifteen seconds to go and there was Costill just inches away. "Hang on!" "Hang on!" Then ten seconds. How slowly time goes. Five seconds. How could five seconds last so long? Someone was counting: four, three, two, one. The treadmill stopped.

I took out the mouthpiece, gasping, "Oh, God! Oh, God!" The physiologists were poring over their figures. They were delighted. "He went over the hill," said one. I had peaked and gone down the other side, reached my maximum and gone past it. I had done what they wanted me to do.

The pain had receded. I sprawled out on a chair, content, trying to think of an equivalent maximum human performance.

"How soon," I asked, "can I see the baby?"

No one heard. They were on the way to prepare for my muscle biopsy.

11

Healing

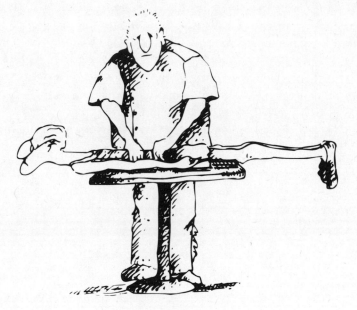

"

**When I am ill I become a skeptic.
What has hitherto been a certainty becomes
perhaps; what was perhaps becomes maybe;
and what was maybe becomes probably not.**

"

THE JOGGER has three natural enemies: drivers, dogs and doctors. The first two are easily handled. Motorcars are part of the logical technology we have learned to live with. In fact, cannot live without. Running against traffic allows the runner to be in command. Anyone who is alert and agile should be able to stay alive.

Dogs are even less difficult. The dog is, after all, just another animal like ourselves who reacts to aggression, seizure of his turf and other inroads much the same way we do. He is simply more spontaneous and uninhibited in expressing his feelings. As the jogger becomes more runner, more body, more animal, he finds that a dog can be more a friend than an enemy.

Not so the doctor. Doctors are human. And to be human is not to be logical like a machine, or predictable like an animal. To be human is to be gullible, to have opinions that thereby become truths, and worst of all to become altruistic. And doctors are for the most part altruists. They are accepted into their profession because of their altruism, for their selfless dedication to their fellow human beings. And unfortunately when a man does a thoroughly stupid thing, as Oscar Wilde pointed out, it is usually done from the noblest of motives.

The jogger is continually having to cope with this nobility and stupidity. He is constantly reading stupid articles about the dangers of his sport, written by noble, high-minded physicians whose only desire is to help him.

Jogging has recently been described as one of the most wasteful and hazardous forms of exercise. And its followers have been told they can expect a myriad of illnesses ranging from hernias to ruptured discs, from sagging breasts to varicose veins.

What is the truth? Is jogging hazardous and wasteful? Or is it, as joggers insist, the most economical, least dangerous and most satisfying of physical-fitness programs? Do joggers get more hernias, back troubles, female pelvic problems and floating kidneys than nonjoggers? Or are these conditions a matter of individual susceptibility, deficiencies in the protoplasm from which we are constructed, and therefore independent of the running and jogging? Is the fifteen to sixty minutes a day spent jogging a danger to health? Or is what we do the rest of the day that is preventing our enjoyment of life and leading to disease and an early demise?

We joggers have one set of answers, the doctors another. Those who are uncommitted and undecided might do well to consider what jogging actually is. Better yet, they might try it.

Jogging or running is the most efficient and natural way for the body to move. When it is done correctly, the jogger flows through his environment using his largest and most powerful muscles. He is propelled along smoothly with the least of impact. The body from the hips up being used merely for balance. The abdominal muscles occupied only with breathing.

His footstrike is heel first, with the foot under the still bent knee. This keeps him from bouncing up and down, and his shoulders are thereby kept parallel to the ground. The overall effect is one of smoothness, a physical activity done at a pace at which the jogger can maintain a conversation with a companion, an activity without stress or strain.

When injuries come, and about two thirds of joggers report injuries, they are due to weak feet and to muscles that become too tight and overdeveloped while their antagonist muscles are becoming too weak. Both problems, the one structural, the other postural, are easily corrected. The feet with arch supports, sometimes individually made. The muscle imbalance, with daily preventive exercises.

In seven years of writing a medical-advice column for runners, I have yet to hear from an injured runner who regretted his jogging. The jogger's main concern is the "dark night of the soul" he experiences while he is unable to run.

Those well-meaning articles about the dangers of jogging serve little purpose except to expose the inadequacy of orthodox medicine when faced with a human being trying to be all he or she can be. Nevertheless, the proper care for these "diseases of excellence" is available. What needs to be known is exactly where to find it.

Until the doctors do, they will remain one of the jogger's natural enemies. And, like cars and dogs, best be avoided.

One way for a doctor to acquire skill, said Plato, was to have knowledge of medical science and a wide acquaintance with disease. But the best way was to have experienced in addition all kinds of disease in his own person. And to this end, he thought that doctors should not be of altogether healthy constitution. Such a liability would not, of course, keep them or any Greek from being an athlete. Everyone in those days was urged to train both body and mind. And thereby to arrive at the proper harmony between energy and initiative on one hand and reason on the other.

Like it or not, I have followed the Platonic prescription. I am a runner-doctor with a defective constitution. And my diseases are a lengthening litany ranging from head to toe, from dandruff to athlete's foot. At one time or another something in every section of me has gone awry.

My respiratory tract, for instance, is noticeably defective. My sinuses refuse to empty. My Eustachian tube is forever closing off. My ears ring. My tonsils are out. And a postnasal drip is a constant companion.

My circulation is little better. My electrocardiogram is abnormal. I have peculiar heart sounds, a pulse that occasionally goes into a conga rhythm, and a worrisome ache in my chest when I think on these things.

All the while, there is hardly anything right going on in my abdomen. How could it with a hiatus hernia, a duodenal ulcer, an absent gall bladder, diverticulosis and two sizable inguinal hernias?

From my hips down, I am a battleground of the war between me and my running. Feet, legs, knees, and sciatic nerve all have been the sites of major skirmishes, and now exist relatively pain–free in an uneasy truce.

All of this has turned out to be, as Plato suggested, an extraordinary learning experience. And I now know, as every teacher should know, the truth of Ortega's statement "It is not desire that leads to knowledge but necessity." When illness strikes I suddenly develop an immediate and urgent need to learn, an interest in books that would delight my former teachers.

But with it comes also the almost certainty that there is no answer. And I approach this ready-made knowledge, as Ortega suggests, with caution and suspicion, even assuming in advance that what the book says is not true. I suspect, and often rightly, that my problem, my specific and unique and desperately important problem, has never been answered.

When I am ill I become a skeptic. What has hitherto been certainty becomes perhaps; what was perhaps becomes maybe; and what was maybe becomes probably not. I realize that most regimens for disease are proposed not because they are effective but because there must be a standard operating procedure for every illness. And in this process I discover that I need such things as disease and doubt, failure and defeat, to make me wise. Anyone can follow the book. Only someone who has fallen on his face and started over can write one.

Being an athlete introduces another decisive element. The runner-doctor knows that health has nothing to do with disease. Health has to do with functioning and wholeness and reaching your level of excellence. My health has to do with my life style, with moderation of the soul and the body. It is a matter of discipline of my total person. And my health can be maximized even when disease is present. There is, I find, a healthy way to live your disease. Disease may change or modify my excellence, but it does not remove excellence as a possibility.

Disease, then, is one of those bad experiences that turns information into knowledge and knowledge into wisdom. The bad experiences that make you love yourself and your body and the world. And make you know you are in a game that has to have a happy ending.

At the age of fifty-six, when faced with the choice between the book and the body, between reason and instinct, between learning and intuition, I go with doing what comes naturally. The experts, of course, advise otherwise. Human beings, they say, are born defenseless and must learn how to live in this world. And that will be by our wits, not our reflexes.

But when I get down to the basic questions of stress and survival, when, for instance, I am gasping for breath, it is my body, not the physiology text, that tells me the right thing to do. This act of inhaling and exhaling, an act which symbolizes life itself, has occupied the wise men since the beginning of recorded time; but none seemed to have analyzed it by pushing himself to his own limit, and beyond. I have.

I have spent twelve years in distance running. Twelve years in various states of air hunger. Twelve years of panting training and gasping races. Twelve years seeking how to get the most oxygen with the least amount of effort. Twelve years of going to the point where my only thought was self-preservation. Twelve years that qualify me for a bachelor's degree in respiration, a master's in labored breathing, and a doctorate in dyspnea.

What has it all taught me? What have I learned from the animal inside of me? That when man rose on his two feet when he stood upright, he forgot how to breathe. Belly-breathing, which is natural when we are on all fours, fades from memory when we become, as Milton wrote of Adam and Eve, "Godlike erect."

Yet belly-breathing, all the authorities agree, is the proper way to breathe. The white-coated wizards who deal in vital capacity and tidal volume and expiratory reserve all recommend the bellowslike action of the diaphragm for maximum oxygenation. Even those geniuses whose field is the human spirit have made this type of breathing an essential of the practice of yoga.

But as rapidly as they teach, just as rapidly their pupils forget. The masters have not understood why this fundamental and innate ability has been lost. They have not discovered that it is Man on all fours, Man prone, Man prostrate, who breathes correctly. I have. And I discover it anew at the end of every race.

Relieving that incredible postrace shortness of breath is the crucial experiment. When my respiratory rate goes to fifty a minute and it still isn't enough. When I am literally fighting for air and consciousness, I yield to impulses older than history and go down on my hands and knees. And finally find the position, the only right position, with my head and shoulders and hands on the ground. No longer Man "Godlike erect," but Man the supplicant. Only then do I have any confidence that I will someday rise to run again. Only then does the air on this planet become adequate.

It is this posture that makes me belly-breathe. Not education, or knowledge, or enlightenment, or wisdom. Once I start to lean forward, my belly goes out and my diaphragm comes down when I breathe in. And this is most likely the reason why people with asthma are better at swimming and cycling than at running; and why they often obtain relief by getting on all fours.

Posture has a remarkable effect on respiratory capacity.

Why this has remained a secret is no secret. Our researchers believe they are studying the new Adam. But they have accumulated vast amounts of data on a creature who is not the new Adam and never will be. They are examining Man sedentary, in repose, and slowly deteriorating. They should be observing Man gasping and panting his way toward the day when he will truly be "Godlike erect."

If they do, they'll rewrite the book.

* * *

If, as Eric Hoffer claims, man's most useful occupation is play, then the care of the athlete must be medicine's most important duty. Yet the athlete who consults a physician often wonders what goes on in medical school. He begins to question the priority of disease and disaster; the emphasis on crisis and catastrophe. His own problems of health and preventive medicine, of maximum performance and day-to-day living, seem to have been ignored.

Physicians who handle emergencies with éclat, who dive fearlessly into abdomens for bleeding aneurysms, who think nothing of managing cardiac arrest and heart failure, who miraculously reassemble accident victims, are helpless when confronted by an ailing athlete. They are even less able to counsel the athlete and his never-ending questions about health.

Health is what makes the athlete medicine's most difficult patient. It is as simple and as complicated as that. Health, said Chesterton, is the mystical and mysterious balance of all things by which we stand up straight and endure. Athletes want that mystical balance by which they can do all things. They want that mysterious harmony of body and spirit which they have come to know as fitness and feel as an all-encompassing rightness. And because no one man can give them that, because no one man can specialize in health, which is to specialize in the universe, the athletes overwhelm any physician who presumes to treat them.

The athlete needs a medical team to treat him. A team composed not only of physicians but also of professionals from all the health-science fields. The physician educated in isolation from these colleagues is usually unaware of the contributions these people can make; and is unwilling to give them authority and autonomy in caring for patients. The physician still sees himself as a member of an elite group in which some members are more elite than others.

A recent poll taken by Professor Stephen Shortell of the University of Chicago makes this perfectly clear. Physicians who were asked to rate the status and prestige of 41 professional categories in the medical health field ranked no other professional group above any of the medical specialties. They gave first place to the thoracic surgeons and listed 22 more varieties of doctors before coming to dentists (24). The physicians seemed particularly ignorant of the importance of podiatrists (40), who were placed below nurse's aides (39), or osteopaths (37), who were given a niche just above practical nurses (38). The result is, as the British therapist James Cyriax points out, "huge numbers of relievable disorders in otherwise healthy people are not relieved, not because nothing can be done but [because] there is no one to apply knowledge already there for the asking."

Who is there, then, who will save us, the athletes and the potential athletes? Who is there to bring these specialists up and down the Shortell list together in one complete team dedicated to the nation's health?

I nominate the family practitioner. He is the one man who could orchestrate the whole of patient care, the one man who is close to patients and colleagues, the one man who could come to know the contributions of the other medical health-care professionals. The one generalist among all the specialists.

The physicians place the family practitioner (22) at the dividing line between their medical establishment and the professions they consider subordinate to them. I find it a happier concept to see this primary-care physician as the one man who can unite the medical profession and the others in the health sciences. He alone can go anywhere on this 41-category scale to get help. Freed from the ego problems of the experts whose reputations depend on success, he can advise and counsel and let others take on the onus of the specialist's infallibility.

In time such a man will come to resemble the athletes he treats, caring little for the status and prestige Professor Shortell would publicize. But simply seeking truth and accepting it wherever it appears, and turning medicine into play.

The athlete is medicine's most difficult patient. His pursuit of perfection is an unprecedented challenge to what Cannon called "homeostasis" and Claude Bernard termed the "internal milieu," the body's inner harmony with its external environment. His desire to run faster and jump higher and throw farther is causing injuries and illnesses the medical profession is unprepared to treat. And in his attempts to reach his potential he is aiming at goals not in the medical texts. And using methods that are at times unorthodox, and not infrequently heretical to medical dogma.

Yet the athlete is no different from the rest of us, except in degree. He is simply trying to get more out of himself than we are. By definition an athlete is someone who is trying to get the most out of his

(1) GENETIC ENDOWMENT
    through
(2) TRAINING
    in his
(3) ENVIRONMENT.

This is the prescription for maximal performance. It is also the equation which limits it. The athlete's difficulties start (as do ours) with the person he is. They begin with the stuff he is made of. His basic material. And the pattern he is cut from. His body type, his bone structure, the way he inhabits his body. All these things are crucial to his susceptibility to injury and illness. As are his peculiar differences in other functions, cardiac, pulmonary, metabolic. And his own unique response to stress. Each athlete has (as do we) a built-in weakness for certain disorders. Inherited defects in the germ plasm. His DNA and RNA carry the seeds to his destruction. Breeding and bloodlines do count.

He then takes this weakness, this susceptibility, and subjects himself to training, to stress which Selye defined as any demand for vital activity. Overtraining then becomes relative. It varies from person to person. Used correctly, training and stress lead to the ultimate in fitness. Used incorrectly, they lead to disaster. And the physician who must know the athlete's inherited strengths and weaknesses therefore must also know how he trains, and how much. How long he sleeps. How much he rests.

The physician cannot stop there. He must also know the athlete's environment. This includes anything taken into or externally affecting the body. Heat, cold, altitude, diet, drugs, the equipment he wears, the implements he uses. Nor can the social and psychological climate be ignored. Stress, we now know, is not only physical.

Let us consider these factors in the relatively simple matter of a leg injury in a distance runner.

Unless the doctor uses this holistic approach, genes, training, and environment, he is almost certain to have an ex-distance runner as a patient.

To begin with, the slightly built fine-boned runner frequently has been born with a Morton's foot (which is peculiarly prone to injury and to causing leg, knee and low-back problems). And he may also have minor but significant anomalies of the lumbosacral spine. The physician

368

who does not look for these abnormalities and treat them will fail his patient.

In addition, the runner's training leads to tight, inflexible prime movers which cause even more stress on the Morton's foot and the low back. At the same time the antagonists are becoming relatively weak and are inclined to pull or become tender and swollen (shin splints). Hence the saying "When an athlete trains three things happen to his muscles, two of them bad."

But even having treated all these, the negative genetic endowment, and the imbalance induced by training, the physician may fail if he is unaware of the athlete's environment, in this case his shoes. The doctor who is unfamiliar with the inadequacy of most running shoes is treating his patient in the dark. A shoe with no shank and little shock absorption can lead to injury as certainly as the presence of Morton's Foot or the lack of remedial exercise.

This simple problem shows how the athlete's care calls for the integration of numerous specialties (in this case trainers, coaches, podiatrists, physiotherapists, osteopaths, orthopedic specialists and even shoemakers). As we get into other systems, cardiac, pulmonary and others, this interaction of exercise with health and disease becomes much more complicated.

The principle, however, remains the same. The material we are made of, and the stress our exercise and our life style and environment put upon it. Our genes and how we treat them produce our diseases. Or our personal bests.

This New Medicine is as old as Bernard and his "internal milieu." We were just put off the track by his contemporary Louis Pasteur and the discovery of germs, obviously the cause of all disease. It might be well to recall that on his deathbed Pasteur said, "Tell Claude he was right."

The prevention and treatment of athletic injuries could easily be considered human engineering. These injuries are caused and can be corrected by consideration of stress, strain and torque applied either acutely, as in trauma, or chronically, as in the overuse syndromes of the foot, leg, knee, thigh and low back.

Such overuse syndromes constitute the majority of athletic injuries in this country. Trauma may occupy the press, the medical journals and the TV screen, but the majority number of injured athletes participate in the noncontact sports.

Until recently, the ever-increasing demands of training were thought to cause these injuries. Hence the term "overuse." Stress fractures, both metatarsal and fibula, heel spur, Achilles tendinitis, posterior tibial tendinitis, shin splints, hamstring pulls, and sciatic neuritis, among others, were thought to be due to the enormous number of footstrikes occurring per hour of practice, be it track, tennis, basketball or soccer. This is calculated to be approximately five thousand footstrikes on each foot per hour.

However, it is now evident that the "overuse" is simply the precipitating agent. The overuse searches out any biomechanical weakness in the athlete and results in the symptoms.

This biomechanical instability can be either congenital or acquired, structural or postural. It is usually, as will become evident, both. The congenital or structural biomechanical weaknesses are:

1. *Weak feet.*

   Here the untutored physician, like myself, should look for the Morton's foot or the eversion of heel. These indicate a neutral position of the foot which decompensates with each footstrike. The pronating or flattening foot sets up stresses and torques which cause near and distant injuries.

2. *Lumbosacral abnormalities.*

   A high percentage of sciatic-pain patients have abnormal lumbosacral X rays.

3. *Leg-length discrepancy.*

   This causes a variety of biomechanical adjustments which place stress on the foot and pelvis. Foot, leg, knee adductor and sciatic pain can result.

The acquired or postural biomechanical abnormalities have to do with muscle strength and/or flexibility imbalances. These relative muscular inadequacies come as a direct result of the volume of training. They can be divided into:

1. *Inflexibility of the prime movers.*

   Tightness of the posterior tibials, gastrocs, soleus, hamstrings

370

and ilio psoas. This inflexibility below the knee puts further stress on the inadequate foot and this feeds back to cause Achilles, calf and knee problems. Above the knee, this inflexibility causes forward rotation of the hips, lordosis and sciatic symptoms.

2. *Weakness of the antagonists.*

The anterior antigravity muscles, those of the anterior chamber, the quadriceps and the abdominals, are the critical structures involved. These weaknesses contribute to skin splints and other anterior-compartment syndromes, quadriceps pulls and lumbo-sacral-sciatic syndromes.

In analyzing overuse syndromes, the role of shoes and surface should also be recognized. Many athletic shoes have no support whatsoever through the shank and, therefore, should be avoided. Even wearing good shoes with proper supports, the runner with congenital and acquired susceptibility can be at hazard from the slant or camber of the road. This slant tends to pronate and stress the uppermost foot. Running against traffic stresses the right foot; running with traffic stresses the left.

Once the injury has been diagnosed, treatment must proceed along biomechanical lines.

1. Evaluation and correction of any biomechanical problem in the foot is a must. Faulty weight bearing on the first metatarsal must be corrected and the neutral position maintained.

2. Strength-flexibility must be evaluated and corrective exercises prescribed. (See Figure 1.)

3. Recommendations as to foot gear, surface, training methods and running style should be made.

4. Above all, treatment should be directed to the cause, not the effect. Heel spurs, Achilles tendinitis, shin splints, and chondromalacia, all point to a failure of the entire foot-leg continuum. Use of Butazolidine, steroid shots, and surgery have no place in the human engineering required in the treatment of overuse syndromes.

Treating overuse syndromes requires a thorough biomechanical analysis of the runner's foot, low back and musculoskeletal system and a knowledge of his training conditions. Unless the underlying biomechanical weaknesses are corrected, treatment will not succeed.

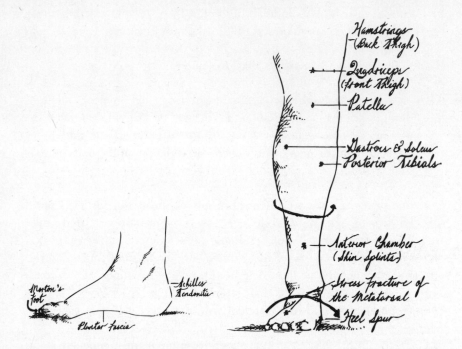

Subsequently, a return to running will inevitably result in a return of symptoms. Pain-free running awaits proper analysis and appropriately integrated treatment.

SUMMARY

Most athletic injuries of the lower extremity are not due to trauma, but to overuse. Underlying these illnesses are: (1) congenital biomechanical instability of the foot and the low back, and (2) acquired biomechanical instability of the muscles. Additional environmental factors, including shoes and surface, contribute to the stresses producing symptoms. Treatment, to be successful, must take all these factors into account.

12

Racing

"

**But even at the end there is strategy.
It is not enough to have the speed. Not enough
to give your all. That sprint, that giving, must be
done at the right time, at the precise moment that
allows no adequate response.
It must be checkmate.**

"

YOU MAY FIND it difficult to believe, but the distance runner is a one-man track team. The ambivalent, indecisive, forgetful, absent-minded, manually inept daydreamer is not merely a runner. He is also his own coach, manager and trainer; positions which he is incapable of handling. He is never quite sure what type of practice he should do; is liable to show up at a race a day late; and is always lacking some essential piece of equipment.

The runner fails as a coach, manager and trainer because he is a feeling, thinking, completely absorbed human being. The man you see running down the road is in a world of his own. He might at that very moment be taking a victory lap after winning the 1992 Marathon at Barcelona. With such an exciting inner world, is it any wonder the runner forgets such things as shirts and shorts and starting times and first-aid supplies? And the only remedy for his dreamlike state is the ditty bag.

Into the ditty bag goes everything a runner might ever need, no matter what the emergency. Its supplies should be all-weather, all-seasons. Perennial and universal are the words for the ditty bag.

All this may seem ridiculous to you. What, you may ask, could a runner need besides the minimum he wears while running through towns? Until you've been through a season of road running, you could never guess how many things a runner needs and how these needs multiply.

Take shoelaces, for instance. Breaking a shoelace shortly before a race can cause a panic state equaled only by lining up your first deer. Paralysis, hope, despair, a sense of the time accelerating make for a moment you will never want to relive.

Tape is another item. For blisters and the blister-prone areas. If there is anything worse than running the last six miles of a marathon, it is running these last six miles with a blister. For this problem, ordinary tape won't do. It is too stiff. And Band-Aids tend to slide, which is worse. So Zonas tape is the tape to use.

Next is the Vaseline. To coat you when the wind-chill factor is in the twenties. And for the chafed areas. But tape your feet first. Once you have Vaseline on your hands, the tape becomes unmanageable.

Then come the gloves and the ski mask. There are days you just won't finish if you have to run without them.

And for the summer, there's the handkerchief. By using knots in the four corners, you can fashion a cap for the head and cut down on solar radiation. If you keep it wet during the race, it dissipates the heat on those August run days.

And don't forget the nail clipper and the felt pads to use as heel and arch supports. Or the pins for the number and an extra buck for the entry fee. And the nasal spray, the antacid tablets and the APC's. Remember also the ballpoint pen and the pad to record your place and number.

At one time or another, I have forgotten one, some or all of these essentials. In fact, I have arrived at a race with nothing at all. Not even my running gear. So now I have developed a foolproof solution. I put on my running clothes at home and then check out each article in my ditty bag.

I did that for the Heart Fund race in Jersey City. I dressed at home. No problem. Then I checked the bag. Money, pins, tape, Vaseline, ski mask, gloves, shoelaces, nail clippers, nasal spray, antacids, APC's, pen and pad, extra turtleneck sweater (in case it turned cold), the plastic wrapper that comes on clothes from the cleaners (in case it rained), the entry blank with the date and the starting time, some extra sugar cubes and a can of soda for after the race. All present and accounted for.

On the way up, I was relaxed, knowing I had prepared myself for any eventuality. But when I walked into the dressing room in the basement of the Stanley Theatre, I had the feeling I had forgotten something.

I had. The ditty bag.

In common with most distance runners, I have to get psyched up for practice, not for a meet. For athletes who go head to head with their opponents, the opposite seems true. They use the dominant emotions, hunger and rage and fear, to dominate their foes. From such extraordinary excitements come extraordinary efforts. I once heard a lineman relate how he would get into the right mood for a game by imagining his house had been burned down by the opposing tackle.

I have no need for such imaginings. Before I even park the car, I can feel the adrenalin flowing. The sight of runners warming up sends a rush through my bowels. The smell of the dressing room sets my pulse to racing. The track under my feet makes me break out in a cold sweat. And then comes the yawn that Darwin first described as the accompaniment of fear.

So I have no need to psych myself up for a race. Sight and sound and smell will do that unbidden. And this reaction must be curbed, not encouraged. I have no need for short-lived bursts of superhuman energy. My game is endurance. My object perfection. My race is a product of training, determination and reason. Strong emotions often contribute nothing but stupidity. It is the fired-up, psyched-up runner who runs the most irrationally placed races.

It would be equally irrational for me to view the other runners as my enemies. They are not. They are there to help me do my best; to make this event the culmination of all my training. Anger against them will only dissipate my energy; it will not increase it. I know this to be true, because I have experienced it.

Who, then, is the enemy? I have found my enemy and he is me. The runner's confrontation is with himself. And this confrontation begins and ends in practice. My struggle is not in my race with my friends, but in my day-to-day battle with myself. And for that battle I need all the emotions, the excitements, the feelings that others seek just prior to the big game.

In practicing, it is truly psych up or psych out. There, doubled and trebled, are all the difficulties I face in a race. There I must deal with doubt and discomfort and fear. Not once, but continually. There I reach the barrier where pain is at its worse. Not once, but repeatedly. There I must overcome the desire to quit, to break off, to leave until tomorrow. And do this daily.

And there in practice I must convince myself that there is no substitute for hard work and discipline, all the while looking for an excuse from this drudgery, an escape from this tedium. And I must believe that the payoff comes from this day-to-day commitment. Even while pushing further seems absurd and I am regretting the things given up and the time lost.

But where can one find emotions that support such punishment? When I park the car for practice, I feel no surge of adrenalin. The sight of the empty track does not cause the juices to flow. And when I get out on the track, I am filled with great reluctance rather than anticipation of things to come. Should I yawn, it would be from boredom rather than fear.

Yet there is an excitement in practice. Perhaps the greatest of all excitements. The discovery of who I am. Alone with myself and my

376

stopwatch, I learn who I am. I find out what I can do. The race may subsequently confirm this, but it cannot deny it. I am first what I am in practice, and only after that what I am in a race.

Knowing that potential is there to be gained or lost can incite anyone to strong emotions. And there are times when I become my own Lombardi and I go to the whip. I turn my anger on myself. And on such occasions where I have described my character and my ancestry in words I have not used or even heard since leaving the Navy, I have finished practices I would have thought beyond my energy.

Whatever your game, you can always spot a pigeon. When I warm up for a road race I can usually tell at a glance the newcomers to the sport. When I am estimating how high I will finish, I find it reassuring to see groups of my fellow contestants sporting fancy sweat shirts, or dressed in all-white, or wearing their numbers on their backs. These are all signs of the pigeon.

An expensive warmup suit marks the runner as beginner. The suit is almost invariably a present from a friend in recognition of this new pursuit. But having arrived at this first race the recipient is immediately aware that the fashionable togs are out of place. Fortunately in due time the warmups are stolen and the runner quickly acquires some less obtrusive outerwear. And is on the way to becoming a veteran.

The all-white costume, plain white T-shirt and white shorts, is another giveaway of the neophyte runner. The all-whites indicate no previous experience. Plain white is the uniform of the embryo, the about-to-be-born. The runner in plain white is a maiden, has yet to break the novice.

There is a definite possibility that this is the runner's first race. And the chances are good that the distance will be too much, the race misjudged, or any one of a thousand things from shoes to shoelaces will go wrong in this first race.

If the number is pinned on the back it may not be the runner's first race, but I know it is the runner's first road race. And therefore I am dealing with a runner I can safely ignore if the distance is over five miles. I have occasionally been fooled by the fancy warmups and a few times by the all-whites, but never by the number on the back. It is an infallible sign of a tyro at road racing.

I recall years back when I arrived at a ten-mile race in Westport,

Connecticut and noticed that every runner had his number on his back. I was suddenly struck with the thought that at forty-seven I was about to win my first road race. And win a trophy legitimately, not because of my 1918 birthday.

My certainty increased as the starting time approached. This was to be my day. Then five minutes before the gun was to go off (and they are always on time at Westport) my hopes were dashed. Eight members of the St. John's cross-country team arrived. They were shortly followed by Attila Mattray, one of New Jersey's best distance runners. He was visiting in the area, heard about the race and showed up.

I finished tenth behind the nine latecomers, but I beat all the others. The first law of distance runners, "Never worry about a runner who wears his number on his back," was put in the books that day.

But the pigeon remains a pigeon for only so long. The next race, the runner has the number where it belongs. The fancy warmups disappear, to be replaced by something less gaudy, less obtrusive. In a short time the runner becomes one of us, a T-shirt freak.

I have thirty or more T-shirts myself, and the longest preparation for any race is the selection of the shirt. These run from high school (a year I spent coaching) through college (old loyalties die hard) to clubs, those I've belonged to and others I run with in my travels. They are a record of road runs, some obscure, some famous, and of marathon after marathon. Some were won, most came with the entry fee. Whichever way, they were paid for in the race. Each one represents a racing experience.

The why of the selection I find difficult to explain. Somehow the T-shirt must go with my mood, the event, my fellow runners. But more often than not I try to be the runner who has come far. When I run in Central Park or at Van Cortlandt I wear my Oregon Road Runners shirt or the beautiful white nylon of the West Valley Track Club. Then when I run at Golden Gate Park I wear the Jersey Shore Marathon or the classic running shirt of all time, the NYAC, the simple white with narrow shoulder straps and the red winged foot.

So by the T-shirt you know them. No longer rookies, no longer apprentices, the pigeons have become Hawks.

Now they are looking around for runners with fancy sweats, dressed in all-white with their numbers on the back.

*　*　*

I am not a runner who suffers in silence. When I am hurting, every-one around me knows it. If I am in pain during a race, and I almost always am, the runners in my vicinity are all too aware of it. And even alone on the roads when I feel distressed by hills or speed, I'm likely to fill the air with groans and sighs and Oh Gods.

One reason is that I have a pain threshold at the level of a firm handshake. I am hardly into a race, therefore, when the pain arrives and in quantity. I am like a novice nun who suddenly realizes she is not made out of the same stuff as Saint Teresa. Or a seminarian who now suspects he is not another Ignatius. But there is no going back.

So I feel the pain early and often. This is natural for me. It is equally natural for me to react to it. "Let the parts harmed by the pain give an opinion of it," wrote Marcus Aurelius. I agree. If I am my body and my body is in pain, let it speak. No animal would repress the wail, the groan. Why should I? Am I not first a good animal? Why not, then, do what is normal and natural?

I am also Irish. I come from a complaining race. We are civilized but not domesticated. Especially my people, the little black men from the bogs. Those who feel pain and sing those sad songs. Two generations of attempting to be gentry is not enough veneer to conceal what goes against our grain.

The result is what I am. A method runner. A runner who reacts totally, letting the pain become visible in my face, and audible over the countryside.

This is not the way I was taught. In my childhood my heroes were those who withstood pain without flinching. The Spartan youth who un-complaining allowed the rat to eat away his stomach. The Indian brave who impassively watched his own torture. Everywhere in my reading I was encouraged to be a stoic. Given as models those who were silent in the face of suffering, those who went to their deaths with a smile on their lips.

I have tried it that way and I can't handle it. When I come apart, the disintegration is total. I come apart all over. And with a loud noise. So I subscribe to Ken Doherty's holistic approach. The former Penn coach always espoused the idea of a total body-mind-spirit reaction. It takes extra energy, he stated, to maintain a passive expression when you're hurting inside. Don't do it, he said. Be yourself. Accept the pain, show it

379

and then you will be able to use it in a positive way. You will be able to relax.

One of the great British runners, Gordon Pirie, was of the same mind. The stiff-upper-lip philosophy, he wrote, costs the runner and prevents him from reaching his greatest heights. Better to react completely and use it in the running. "The free relaxed runner shows in his face and gesture that it is torture and agony to give his last ounce of energy," he wrote. "How silly to pretend it is not."

Anyone who runs near me knows that I am in agony. Knows that I am ready to give my last ounce of energy. If indeed I haven't already done so. So disturbing is this to some that they have written to me complaining about the experience. Apparently they did not want to say anything during the race for fear I was actually about to collapse.

One colleague sent a note asking that I please not run within two hundred yards of him in the future. He also added the hope that I would desist from calling upon the Deity. Another, younger runner wrote that he had a phobia about running near me. "Your constant wheezing," he wrote, "drains my energy. I feel as if my lungs are a reserve tank for your breathing." Nor was that all. My sighs were shattering him. They contained, he felt, all the despair in the universe. "My mind quickly leaps," he wrote, "to why finish? Why race? Why are we here? Why exist? Please stay away from me."

I sympathize with them. It has to be disturbing to have an elderly man hanging on at your shoulder, using your pace, being carried along in your draft; all the while wheezing and groaning and sighing as if every breath will be his last, and continually asking his Creator to take notice of what is going on.

It has to be even more disturbing when this aged suffering soul noisily takes off in a long sustained sprint and beats you to the finish.

But then Percy Cerrutty could have told them that would happen. Conscious control, determined maintenance of proper style and decorum of facial expression was, he said, "a concept of weakly men."

You have to let it all hang out. Which is no problem for a thin little Irishman with a low pain threshold.

I am at my best nearing the finish of a race. Until then I am just another mediocre distance runner. Just one of the many run-of-the-mill competitors well back in the pack. Just one more old man trying to string together six-minute miles and not quite succeeding.

But with the finish in sight, all that changes. Now I am the equal of anyone. I am world class. I am unbeatable. Gray-haired and balding and starting to wrinkle, but world class. Gasping and wheezing and groaning, but unbeatable.

My running friends have come to know this. A few years back in a handicap race at Van Cortlandt Park, I sprinted the last three hundred yards to beat out someone straining at my shoulder. All I knew was that his name was Tom, because he had a number of people urging him to catch me. Afterward I discovered it was Tom Siggins, a Quantico Marine who only a year back had been captain of cross-country at Manhattan College. He came up later and said to me, "If I had known you wanted it that bad, Doc, I wouldn't have tried to catch you."

Wanting-it-that-bad comes from training. I was trained by a coach of the Herb Elliot ("The only tactics I admire are those of do-or-die") school. He taught me to run one way. Give everything. Hold nothing back. The race you can walk away from was not worth running. It became easier to run myself into oblivion than face him after a race.

The ability to sprint, to kick it in, on the other hand, comes from breeding. I was born with half-miler's speed, and the half mile is still my best distance. With a quarter mile to go, I have the best part of my race still in front of me.

These two together, speed and the willingness to push myself to collapse, will win most of these last-minute duels. Other things being equal, the runner with the kick will beat his opponent. It allows me to run from behind, sit in the other man's draft, judge him for strength or fatigue, and decide when to make my move. It gives me control of the situation.

But even at the end there is strategy. It is not enough to have the speed. Not enough to give your all. That sprint, that giving, must be done at the right time, at the precise moment that allows no adequate response. It must be checkmate.

This last I have learned with age. A thousand races have taught me when and how to make my move, when to accelerate and in what manner. A thousand attempts to beat someone so far back neither of us will remember the next day where we finished have made me a grandmaster at this end game.

There are two primary bluffs in closing minutes. The first, that I am much more exhausted than I actually am. The second, that I am much less tired than I actually am.

The former I use in the fake-pass/late-sprint gambit. This is particularly effective against a strong, obviously fresh younger runner who is a sure bet to beat me.

I first make a tentative move to pass him. This must be done slowly, otherwise he may take off with a rush and I will be hanging on for dear life like a sailor with a harpooned whale. No, slowly does it, and with much audible travail and agony indicating this is about my last gasp.

I then let him draw away quite easily, thereby confirming I am no real threat even though I remain only a few steps behind. And then, with about thirty yards to go, I pull the trigger. I pass him as if shot from a gun. By the time he reacts, it is too late. When he does pass me again, I will be over the finish line.

The I'm-not-as-tired-as-you-are bluff works best on runners my own age. Here I make my breathing as quiet as possible, my footstrike almost unheard, and I pass them swiftly and with élan, exuding confidence. And I make my move earlier than they think sensible. The lead I gain is often enough to allow me to slow down briefly and then gather myself for another dash to the finish.

Once in the lead, I never look back. There is no greater spur to a tired runner who is about to give up and coast in than seeing this over-the-shoulder distress signal. So I never look back. I reach for the man in front of me no matter how impossible it seems for me to catch him.

Hills are great levelers. If there is anything that can cut a runner down to size, it is a reasonably long hill with a fairly steep grade. And particularly if it is placed near the end of a race. Hills make all men brothers. Coaches who use them for training swear by them. Runners who find them sources of suffering swear at them.

The runner's world, you see, is divided into two worlds: the world of the hills and the world of the flats. In the hills, the runner must move vertically as well as horizontally. It is a simple matter of physics. A body of known weight moving at a certain speed up a specific grade for a given distance. A simple matter of physics, but one that causes physiological results that can be close to unendurable.

The pay-as-you-go effort of the flat is transformed into the I'll-pay-you-later-if-only-I-survive struggle of climbing the hill. The runner working on oxygen he has not yet received arrives at the summit, his lungs bursting like a swimmer who has been held underwater; his leg muscles screaming for him to stop, his entire body a dead weight.

Such tortures are common. If the ecstasy of distance running is felt in those periods of rhythm and grace when everything is easy and flowing and natural, then certainly the agony of the sport is in the disrhythmic, graceless tortured movement up the hills. If the heaven of this distance running is in the moments when the runner and his running seem to reach toward infinity, then assuredly its hell or purgatory is in the hills that expose him as failing and inadequate and finite.

And if running on the flat is the world of those optimists that William James called the once-born, running the hills is for the twice-born, those of morbid mind who see and accept the evil in the world.

Some hills are, of course, worse than others. On the East Coast we have some well-known monsters. Heartbreak Hill in the Boston Marathon. Cemetery Hill at the four-mile mark of the five-mile course at Van Cortlandt Park. The final three hundred yards uphill to the Du Pont Hotel in the Caesar Rodney Half Marathon in Wilmington. And, closer to home, the last quarter mile at Garrett Mountain. There is hardly a major race that doesn't have a strategic hill to make the event memorable for the runner.

I have run all of these. And on them reached areas of pain unmatched at any other time in racing even in flat-out finishes or in marathons where I had to quit from exhaustion. But the worst hill of all was in a fifteen-mile race at Greenwich one August.

The heat and the mileage had taken their toll and I was nearing the finish when I reached this hill, which seemed the longest and steepest I have ever had to climb in a race. Going into the hill, I was some ten yards behind another competitor and well ahead of any pursuit. Up on top of the hill, a teammate yelled encouragement to me: "Go get him. You can get him."

Twenty yards up the hill, I had slowed perceptibly. The runner in front began to pull away. "Pick it up, pick it up," came the cry from the top. By now I was leaning forward, making groping movements with my hands but very little forward progress. My friend would not give up. "Keep moving," he yelled. "Keep moving."

It was no use. I was running in place. And now the others behind me were catching and passing me. The runner who was ahead of me had reached the crest and disappeared.

Then from the top of the hill came the best advice of the day: "Walk fast," he shouted. "Walk fast."

I did, and I passed two men who were running.

You frequently read that a runner would have done better if he only had someone to push him during a race. Perhaps so. But for me and probably most others the need is for a pull, not a push. I need someone to pull me along, to stretch me out. I do best following the pace, sitting in behind the leader. Running easiest drafting at another runner's shoulder. And then at the end I can always reach back for the little extra that is there if I look for it.

You might think that a mile is a mile whether you are in the lead or back in the pack. That the energy expenditure per quarter mile is the same for the leader as it is for those who follow in his wake. But you should know that leading a race costs. It costs in overcoming air resistance and, for most runners, costs in loss of efficiency. Running in front may be good for your ego but it is a severe drain on your physiology. Leading is a lonely and often stupid business. The leader should know that he requires more effort to do the job than those running behind him. They are shielded from air resistance by his body; and free from the tension and anxiety and mental effort of setting the pace.

The energy cost of air resistance has been investigated by the English physiologist L. G. C. Pugh, who found it to be on the order of 7.5 percent of the total energy cost at middle distance. Having established that, Pugh discovered that a runner by staying within a meter of the leader and directly behind him could eliminate eighty percent of this oxygen cost. This would give the second-place runner or someone back in the pack six percent advantage in utilizing his maximum oxygen uptake. A figure which further translates into as much as four seconds a lap and certainly not less than a second a lap.

So running in someone's lee pays off in ways a physiologist can measure. It also pays off in ways they have yet to measure but eventually will. In concentration, in relaxation, in rhythm, in harmony, in efficiency. When I follow a leader I no longer have to worry about pace. No longer have to concern myself with continual judgment and analysis of how fast I'm going. No longer have to worry about distance, the race, victory or defeat. That is all for the man in front. He is the stroke of this crew. The race is now his responsibility and I can simply key off him. Use him. And so I become lost in the running, lost in its rhythm, lost in its music. My mind and will are at rest. They leave my body alone, letting it do what years of training and conditioning have taught it to do so well.

I had this happen to me two years ago when I set a United States age-group record in the two-mile at Peddie School. You should know that except for that day I have never before or since in my fourteen years or so of running gone under eleven minutes for that distance. My only real competitor in the race knew it and set his pace accordingly. He ground out thirty-three seconds a lap on the Peddie ten-lap track hitting exactly 5:30-mile pace as if he had been programmed by a computer. And just three feet back I was in another world.

Given a pacemaker who had zeroed in on the perfect pace, I reached a state of blessedness that I have rarely equaled. I was for those minutes completely and utterly relaxed, unconcerned about the outcome, yet completely absorbed in what I was doing. I was in what has been described as a cocoon of concentration, absolutely involved, fully engaged in running. Not racing or winning but simply running. Everything was harmony and grace. Everything was pure. Effort had become effortless.

These things are much easier to experience than to describe. But at those times I think of running as Emerson did of poetry, that it was all written before time was. And I was trying to reach that original perfection. I was at the edge, to use Merton's phrase, of a great realization and was trying to get out and get lost in it.

And so it went. I felt incredibly fresh the whole race. And later it seemed to have been run without reference to real time or real space. Space and time had narrowed down to him and me and the running. It was almost as if I had taken some hallucinatory drug that altered my perceptions. Then there were only two laps to go. I gunned past him, increasing my lead with every stride. And finished still fresh in 10:53.

So there it was, my personal best by following the leader. Letting him do the work. Letting him pull me through that air. Letting him establish the pace. And all the while letting myself go. Letting myself get inside the running and become the running itself. Letting my body do what it does best.

Racing physiology is simple. Except for some early speed, the runner should find his maximum steady pace for that distance and hold to it. Racing tactics are even simpler. Follow the rule of the great Tom Courtney. He never took the lead, he said, unless he wanted to do something with it. Either to slow the pace down or speed it up.

The final answer to top performance, then, is evident. Find someone to set that pace for you. Then you can lock in behind him and run carefree until those last few yards when it is everyone for himself.

13

Winning

"

**I was moving in a sea of lactic acid,
lifting legs that no longer understood what made
them move. My breathing came in short, inadequate
gasps, but my body no longer cared.
I had broken through a barrier just as surely as I
broke through the tape at the finish.**

"

WHEN I WAS IN SCHOOL, I ran from the day classes began in September until they closed the doors in June. Now I run from the beginning of the year until its end. The Road Runners Club schedule on the kitchen bulletin board has over 140 races extending from January to December.

So distance running is the sport for every day of my life. There is no need to pack my gear until running starts again. It begins every day. And every time of year is a time for running. I love all of that ever-recurring cycle of the year.

But, like the lover who loves the girl he's near and clings to the kiss he's close to and fancies the face he faces, the season I love best is the one that's here. Soon I will see winter as Paradise, then spring as another Eden, and later summer as the Promised Land. But for now, autumn is my season in heaven.

The October air does that. Crisp, clear, invigorating. Carrying every sound. Demanding attention. And the weather perfect for running. The runner is as sensitive to the weather as a Stradivarius. And it is autumn that makes me go best. I am living the life my youth had promised me. Living at the top of my powers. No wonder that Yeats, who saw spring as youth and summer as adolescence, saw autumn as manhood.

And autumn is heaven because there are races to do that best, to run at that peak, to manifest that manhood. And make no mistake, it is in action that we are in heaven.

Heaven is not quiet, said Yeats. There the lover still loves, but with greater passion; the rider still rides, but the horse goes like the wind; and the battle goes on. The runner still races.

And for now, in this forever that is autumn, cross-country is the best of all races. That is where I began. In autumn with cross-country. It was my first taste of running and it is good to taste it again.

Cross-country is free running at its best. Just me and the land. Me and that crisp air. Me and the leaves underfoot. Me and the silent hills. That's cross-country. Just me and the breathing and the leaves crunching underfoot on those silent hills. Nature has given up the ghost. Everything around me is dead or dying and I feel reborn. I am at my best.

And it is a best, a rebirth that I experience alone. Nature is the only spectator. In other seasons, in other races, there are people to cheer and encourage or just to watch. Curious onlookers. But not in cross-country. Within minutes, I am alone with my fellow runners. Minutes later and I am separated even from them. Yards ahead or yards behind, they are out of my line of thought, beyond the horizon of my mind.

I am alone on the back hills of Van Cortlandt. And the course which tested me as a teenager is testing me again. And again I suffer on hills that made me suffer when I was eighteen. Again I fly down hills I flew down in bygone years. And again I come out of those hills facing an all-out fight to the finish with any runner close to me.

And that was the way it was at Van Cortlandt last week. Nine miles, three times over those back hills. The first three-mile loop oddly the most painful. Then the second loop not quite as bad. And finally the third time actually running at the hills and conquering them. So that when I came out on the flat, the man I had to beat was only thirty yards ahead.

Only in another autumn, in another season in heaven, will I relive that finish. An impossible quarter-mile sprint and then holding on to the man I had just beaten so I wouldn't fall down. Hearing his heart pounding against my ear and my own beating in unison. Knowing only that and a world suddenly filled with friends saying nice things to an aging man who felt ageless in autumn.

The note he put on our kitchen bulletin board finished Tim McLoone. It was there when I came down for breakfast Monday morning. "The Great Sheehan," it read, "is in trouble in the Takanassee handicap race tonight." It was signed "The Phantom."

McLoone the piano player had gone too far.

I had put up with losing three weeks in a row to this keyboard artist from a Fair Haven bistro. Had put up with the hordes of runners he had led across the line ahead of me. Had even put up with finishing so far back I was left out of the newspaper summaries, and people had asked me whether I had retired.

But the note was too much.

So, OK, he was an 8:53 two-miler at Harvard. That was two years ago, and any in-shape fifty-year-old worth his entry fee should be able to take a guy two years out of college at anything requiring skill, hard work and intelligence. Given weight for age, that is. And that was what I would be getting at Takanassee that night. McLoone, I thought, will get his comeuppance.

There was a time when all was different at Takanassee. The fields were small and incompetent. The runners a mediocre bunch of incoming high-school freshmen, out-of-condition upperclassmen and a few over-weight collegians. In those good old days, I was usually in the first twenty and sometimes in the first ten. I was, I assure you, treated with respect.

Takanassee itself was part of an idyllic existence. The lake forms a three-quarter-mile loop which is rimmed by an asphalt road with just enough give to make it fast yet comfortable. The road has a sharp turn at the ocean end which gives you a quick glance at your pursuit without having to turn your head and letting them know you've about had it. And then after the fourth loop, the five thousand meters end with seven hundred yards of gradual downhill slope which has to be the best way to finish a race.

And don't forget the weather. The ocean is only yards away, so the evenings are cool. And when there is no wind and the air is dry and the sun is still bright in the west, it seems the best of all places to be. Maybe even more so when the race is over and you've run well and are still wet with sweat on the ride home. Then there's time to stop for a lemon ice and a dip at North End.

Into this Eden came the piano player and his friends, all 4:30 milers and sub-ten-minute two-milers. In came the guys who made running heartbreakingly easy, who cruise out of sight when your chest is bursting in an all-out effort. And for the first three weeks the only runners I passed had young spectators yelling, "Come on, Daddy" to them.

The time had come to convince McLoone that I had just been loafing up until now and was just about ready for a big one. But first I had to convince myself. Memories of other elders who had suddenly faded at age fifty-two raced through my mind. Was fifty-two the end of the trail? What was needed, obviously, was strong medicine.

First, the haircut. Streamlining your head has absolutely no effect on your speed in a five-thousand-meter race. Your brain says that—but not your gut. Your gut knows you are ten or twenty seconds faster right there. You know that. And McLoone would know it later, when he saw me. "That guy looks faster," he would say to himself. Then a shot of B_{12}. It always fakes a guy out to hear you've had a vitamin shot. He knows it won't help, but his gut doesn't. His gut says, "This cat has got to be stronger."

The real psych comes with the track shirt. My best is the "Caesar Rodney Half Marathon Wilmington, Del." shirt. Because just remembering you were able to finish that course does wonders for your morale. On this shirt I pinned my number saved from the Boston Marathon, and then I put on my racing Tigers. They were the same shoes, modified by the same Colombian shoemaker, that Mejía wore in winning the Boston.

I was ready. What was even better, I knew it and McLoone knew it.

There was a moment of apprehension at the line. The race director and handicapper had seen fit, in his wisdom, to give me a three-minute head start instead of the hoped-for four. But by this time I was completely psyched. I knew McLoone was through, and with three minutes I could beat anybody in the race.

And I did, except for two. A fourteen-year-old with a choirboy's face and the legs of an Apache messenger who had conned the handicapper out of six minutes, and a gutsy young redhead who started on the line with me and never gave me an inch. We kept picking up the larger handicap runners, and the little glimpses at the turn never showed a strong threat from the rear. Coming into the finish, I ran at the redhead. I was really hurting now, but knowing that the way to keep from getting caught from behind is to try to catch the fellow in front of you.

That was the race. The photographer took a picture of the first five finishers. We were weekly also-rans who had put together our best effort of the year. But no one had run really badly, and you could feel that warm Takanassee feeling settling over the pleasantly tired runners. And then McLoone came over and said some nice, extravagant things about my running.

It was the good old days all over again.

It was thirty-two degrees with a fifteen-mile-an-hour wind driving into our backs when we lined up for the start of the beach run. The beach stretched to the north, deserted for as far as the eye could see. The jetties were interrupting the white sand every two hundred yards or so, pushing ribbons of rock and concrete out into a blue ocean. The water was at low tide, calm and forty-five degrees, and there was a frigid wetness most of us would experience before the race was over.

Almost fifty runners waited for the gun, some drawn to the unusual event by the trophies and medals. Others addicted to the sport came like the gambler to the crooked roulette wheel, because it was the only game in town. A few of us who would be running our own race within the race came because sand and wind and ocean might bring another dimension to the running experience. That would be Bob Carlson, Tom Baum, Paul Kiell and myself.

Take Carlson, for instance. Carlson is the Brick Township mailman who has run the Pike's Peak Marathon, the most grueling race on the calendar, and can't wait to take a shot at Mount Washington, which he proudly declares "has the worst weather in the whole country."

Tom Baum is five years younger than Carlson and may yet outstrip him in seeking suffering. Baum, the director of the Jersey Shore Marathon, called me a few days before the beach race to predict that the event would be held in horrible weather. In a voice radiating joy he said, "I think we'll have a snowstorm with high winds and freezing temperatures. It will be an experience we will never forget."

The beach run was to be an experience that forty-three-year-old psychiatrist Paul Kiell would never forget. Kiell was to describe the race as a terrible dream all tied up with guilt and the ambivalence of weather we want to escape or be caught and punished. But that would come later.

At the start, he was off with the rest of us. The usual order of finish of this group was Carlson, Sheehan, Baum and Kiell, with an occasional change due to disordered physiology or lack of sleep. Carlson already had entered his excuse. Extra deliveries and the holiday drinks offered along his route had done him in.

What did him and the rest of us in was the sand.

I had once run at Ventnor and the sand was hard and packed, hard enough to use spikes and to maintain your usual form and speed. But this was the opposite. Soft and crumbling where it was dry. Soft and squishy where it was wet. On every step, we sank deeper and deeper into its yielding surface. Starting off with the usual rush, we found ourselves in distress and struggling within the first hundred yards.

Up ahead, Carlson, with his powerful, thrusting stride, was in early trouble, and soon he was left floundering in our wake. His style apparently unsuited for the mushy going. But the rest of us were having equal difficulty. We reached the mile mark, midway on the northward leg, and heard the time, 7:43, just two minutes slower than what we would expect for the effort, the breathing difficult, the legs heavy.

But on we slogged, running sometimes ankle deep in heavy, soggy sand at the water's edge, and then losing even that slim purchase on the sand rises built up on the south side of the jetties.

The intense effort was broken by the hard, sure step on the concrete, only to be followed by the tricky descent on the north side as we jumped from rock to rock. This usually ended in a final flatfooted jump to the level beach, forcing us to resume the running stride from a complete standstill. Frustration followed frustration.

And with this struggle came a new menace—Tom Baum. He suddenly appeared at my elbow and passed me as I turned for home. And with that shock came an additional one. Going north had been difficult, but now we would be going back against the wind and would have to climb the jetties instead of jumping off them.

Two miles to go and somewhere close behind us was Carlson, who had modified his stride, a discovery I had still to make. Kiell was farther back, deep in his dream of being chased. We all have that dream. In attempting to run, our legs feel heavy, we keep falling back and sliding, he said later.

Baum, all 170 pounds and six-foot-three of him, seemed to have had little difficulty guiding his size-thirteen shoes to adequate footing. It was taking me more and more effort to stay with him, and, with about a mile to go, he gradually began to draw away. I felt like a passenger on a boat watching another boat disappear upriver.

It was then I noticed his technique. He was running as if on a bicycle. His back was straight up and he was in a sitting position with his knees bent and rising up and down as if to follow the motion of the pedals. His size thirteens acted like snowshoes, with the result that his foot struck the sand for a minimum length of time, and while he was weight-bearing, the entire sole of his shoe was on the sand.

I mentally mounted my ten-speed bicycle, put it in low gear and went after him. Baum's ten-yard lead vanished, and I was on his shoulder as we climbed the last jetty.

After almost four miles, we had found out how to cope with our beach environment, found out how to live with the difficulties. The weather was no longer a physical thing. Our energy output had brought us to a humid tropical land. The wind we could no longer feel. The sand and its requirements had been met and defeated. But we refused to accept this as victory. There was the question of other energies, other insights as yet unknown to us, and whether we could escape to another level of consciousness.

So Tom Baum and I started to sprint on that unsprintable sand. Form and technique no longer mattered as we became the ache that was our legs and chest. The whole world was on that beach and getting smaller as we drove for the finish line. And for a long moment, the whole world was inside of us.

Then, once again, it was thirty-two degrees with a fifteen-mile-an-hour wind and we were hoping for the worst January 9 in history.

The Eastern Two-Mile Championship for fifty-and-over held on Cape May was no different from any other two-mile race I have ever run. The first mile was smooth and rhythmic, the second a painful agonizing effort to maintain the pace of the first mile.

I had run the first mile in 5:28, cruising along in the stead wake of New Zealander Bob Harmon, and both of us about fifty yards astern of Browning Ross, one-time king of the forty-and-overs, now in his first over-fifty race. But as we turned for home I began to feel the heaviness in the legs, the aching muscles and the breathing getting difficult.

And then as Harmon made his move to pull up on Ross, I was faced with the choice. Accept the challenge and maintain contact, or settle for a respectable third place. It was the moment that decided the race.

Some say races are decided beforehand. Depend on the runner's motivation. If so, I would be a loser. Prior to the start, I had conceded to Ross and Harmon and was hoping to beat the rest of the twenty-five-man field. But motivation, it seems to me, rarely stands up to pain. No matter how determined you are, that determination is conceived in a pain-free atmosphere. It has no relation to the real world that comes into being shortly after starting the second mile.

Still, if motivation enhances performance, task aversion, the psychological response to the discomforts of lactic-acid accumulation, the anticipation of future agonies, certainly diminishes it. Where motivation paints the future in unnaturally rosy hues, task aversion pictures it in somber grays and funereal blacks.

Task aversion is not new. Even the God-man asked that the cup might pass. We all have the tendency to give up. Army physiologist R. A. Kinsman reported that subjects working on a bicycle ergometer at fifty-

394

six percent of aerobic capacity had quitting times ranging from one and a half to ninety-eight minutes.

When Harmon made his move, I was battling all three elements of fatigue: motivation, lactic acid and task aversion. If I went with Harmon, if I maintained contact, it would mean the escalation of effort in trying to catch the supposedly unbeatable Ross, and, even worse, the possibility of actually catching up to him and then having to sprint, God knows how, to the finish. What that would mean to my already suffering body was too cruel to contemplate.

But, cruel or not, I chose the race. And, having made the decision, concentrated on Harmon's shoes. And while I sat in behind him, using his draft, focusing my attention on his feet, narrowing the whole world to just him and me, we reached Ross and passed him.

Now the pain and the tension and the apprehension became unbearable. My great desire was not so much to slow down as to sprint. To sprint and get it over with, no matter how painful it might be.

And that was the way it was. With almost a full quarter to go, I took off. Not because I could stand the pain better than the other two, but because I couldn't. And because I wanted to control my own fate. Set my own pace and not accept theirs.

This much-too-early move took them by surprise and they waited, and that was fatal. By the time they came back at me, I was beyond catching because I was beyond pain.

I was moving in a sea of lactic acid, lifting legs that no longer understood what made them move. My breathing came in short, inadequate gasps, but my body no longer cared. I had broken through a barrier just as surely as I broke through the tape at the finish.

Fatigue, you see, does depend on motivation and lactic acid and task aversion, but it also depends on something else. Man's limits are not simply in his cells or even in his brain. You can measure lactic acid and stimulate brain areas with an electrode and make a person's arms and legs move. But there is no place in the brain where stimulation will cause a person to decide. No substance in his blood that will cause him to believe.

That choice, that act of faith, is made in the mind. And in answering the great question "Will you or won't you have it so?" we find the energy that conquers fatigue and conquers ourselves as well.

*   *   *

I am now fifty-nine years old, which is an awkward age to define. At fifty-nine, I am no longer middle-aged. I have, after all, no 118-year-old elders among my acquaintances. Yet I could hardly be called elderly.

An awkward age, then, to define, but a delightful one to live. I am aging from the neck up. Which means I am elderly enough to have attained a look of wisdom; middle-aged enough to have a body that allows me to do what I want; and a face that lets me get away with it.

You know that look. My hair is short and graying, the face is just skin and bones, the general impression of an ascetic who began the fight with the Devil in the garden, decided it wasn't worth it and walked away. My latest picture, in fact, looks a little like Teilhard de Chardin. The look of a man with ideas so heretical they bothered the Devil even more than they did the Pope. Preaching the perfectability of man might not get you banished from Rome, but it certainly would get you thrown out of hell. And the look, too, of a man who forgave God, and then his fellow men, and finally himself, and then was free.

Well, you know I am not yet old enough to look even remotely like that. But fifty-nine leaves quite a bit of time to go. Years that could be as exciting as any that have gone before.

What will always remain an excitement is the race. At fifty-nine, I am still the benchmark of performance for any number of runners. Over my fifteen years of running, I have consistently year in and year out been at the junction of the upper and middle thirds of runners finishing in a race. I have become the pass-fail mark for my fellow runners. If they beat me, they go home satisfied. If I beat them, they hope to do better next time. For my group, then, I am the top gun, the man they call out for a showdown.

I am no easy mark. I could give most readers of this book, whatever their age, a five-minute head start and run them down in twenty or thirty minutes. I also have guts, which is simply the decision to stand pain.

Some think guts is sprinting at the end of a race. But guts is what got you there to begin with. Guts start in the back hills with six miles still to go and you're thinking of how you can get out of this race without anyone noticing. Guts begin when you still have forty minutes of torture left and you're already hurting more than you ever remember. Fortunately, guts seem to increase with age, rather than decrease. I may not want to wrestle with the Devil, but I am willing to wrestle with myself. And while I am beating myself, I usually beat others as well.

Newcomers are usually easy to handle, although I may have to pass them twice. The first time anyone is passed by someone my age, the natural reaction is disbelief and a sudden sprint to regain the lead. However, the next time I pass they usually give in, resigned to the fact that they are not yet ready to take the old man.

Some are injudicious enough to rile me up. This summer, I was passed at the halfway mark of a six-miler by someone who said, "I've been waiting to do this for three years." I passed him back about a mile down the road and now he'll wait another three years before he gets near me again.

Of course, I have that same effect on others, although I never say anything to upset anyone. This year, for instance, at Westport in a ten-miler, with about a mile to go, I closed in on a running friend, a twenty-five-year-old, whom I had never been near before in a race. With about two hundred yards to go, there were only fifteen yards and three runners between the two of us. As we entered the shopping plaza for the finish, the other three runners passed him and he did nothing. He was, as far as I could see, dead in the water. I cranked up, and with a hundred yards to go I blew past him. It was early, but it seemed safe. Did I neglect to tell you I am also dumb?

I was about ten yards ahead and apparently home free when I heard this groaning, grunting animal coming up on me. He drew even and as I glanced over I could see him, wild-eyed, spittle all over his face, and his face the picture of agony. Then he was gone.

Later he told me he had recognized the bald head and there was no way I was going to beat him.

So it is not age that is threatened by youth, but the other way around. Youth is threatened by age. From where I sit the fifties look great, and I suspect the sixties will be even better. I may not yet look like Teilhard, but there's always this: I will never again look like my high-school picture.

14

Losing

"
I have seen death plain
in a September surf, and it was all
wrong for me and I escaped. I have seen death
symbolically in a marathon and know certainly that
is the way I must end:
finally coming to a stop and falling apart,
like the wonderful one-horse shay.
"

LATER, after the hot tub had soaked some of the pain out of my legs, I hobbled to the bed and stretched out, enjoying being horizontal. Downstairs, John, our number-six son, put it to the rest of the family watching the Lakers-Bucks game. "If he's going to feel that bad," he asked, "why does he do it?"

Upstairs, I was asking myself the same question.

Why suffer this way? Why run marathons when nine out of ten of them end in a contest of the human will pushing the human body beyond endurance? This one had been no different. The first ten miles to Sea Bright had been a lark. Moving steadily along the coast with that strong south wind at my back was a fine way to spend a Sunday morning in January. Past Sea Bright, I had even picked up my pace, still feeling good and full of running.

The first hint of disaster came at the turnaround in Sandy Hook Park. The fifteen-mile-an-hour wind, hardly noticed as an ally, became a constant alien presence. Reducing my speed and increasing my effort, it would give me no respite for the next two hours. Still, the legs felt fresh, the breathing good and the form under control. Sea Bright reappeared and disappeared in my wake.

Then, as quickly as it takes to write this, the cramps came. They started in both calves, then spread to the thighs, cutting my stride in half and making each step a painful decision. It was ridiculous, I told myself, to even think of finishing with seven miles to go. No one who knew how I felt right now could expect me to finish.

But I kept going. My progress getting slower and slower as I tested a variety of running forms that might permit movement without torture. Nothing helped, but the thought of quitting gradually receded from my mind. When the pain was particularly bad, I would breathe, "Oh, God"; more a statement than a prayer. And I took to counting my steps. Counting by ones seemed the highest mental activity I could perform. It also reassured me that I was moving and would after 4,500 or thereabouts steps arrive at Convention Hall in Asbury Park.

Somehow in all this torment, Allenhurst came and went. Deal Lake appeared, then the Convention Hall and then three of the longest blocks in the world to the finish. Three hours and forty-five minutes after it started in ecstasy, the agony ended.

The marathon, I thought, as I lay there feeling warmer and healthier by the minute, is just not my race. True, I had not trained adequately for this one. Had not run over ten miles in one stretch since April and the last Boston. It was foolish to expect a good one on that amount of work. In the old days, maybe, but now, with age coming on and the desire dying, it might be best to let the marathon go.

There were times in the beginning when the marathon, any marathon, seemed an impossible dream. When any race over five miles was beyond my imagination. My goals were more immediate (a five-minute mile) and practical (physical fitness).

Subtly, insidiously, running became much more. Became, as exercise did for Oliver Alden, George Santayana's Last Puritan, a necessity. "To go a single day without two hours of rigorous outdoor exercise," wrote Santayana, "was now out of the question. It would have meant physical restlessness and discomfort indoors and the most horrible sensual moodiness in the inner man."

For Alden, the two hours of sculling or horseback riding brought him into genuine communication with nature such as he never found in either religion or poetry. And was able to turn him for the moment, Santayana declared, into the gladdest, the most perfect and yet the most independent of people.

Couldn't that "escape, that wordless religion," be enough? Why get into twenty-six-mile runs with the certainty of bone-weary fatigue and the possibility of the ignominy of walking to the finish line? Wasn't the marathon equivalent to Alden's Puritan ethic, from which he escaped only when rowing on the Charles or galloping his horse on a brisk New England day? Another mindless duty, another needless challenge, another unwanted privilege. All demanding success and achievement.

Downstairs, Kareem Jabbar was not looking to escape. He had engaged Wilt Chamberlain in hand-to-hand combat and was revealing what Fordham's Charley Yelverton once said was the principle of being an athlete—"the principle that makes you dig your guts out no matter what kind of game you're in."

I still don't know. "You can very well afford to dangle about enjoying the fresh air and admiring the sunset," the captain of the Harvard crew had told Alden, "but we've got to train. We're not in the crew to have a good time, but to win the Yale race."

But perhaps you could have both. Perhaps what I needed was more marathons, not fewer. Needed the pain, the torture, the indescribable fatigue of a marathon in February and another in March.

400

The Boston in April would be a breeze, another of those daily afternoon runs when you know who you are and where you're going. And I would come to the finish as I would come to my back door, warm and relaxed, still strong and full from running, enjoying the fresh air and admiring the sunset.

Now, where was that February entry blank?

You may have seen my name in the Shore Marathon summaries on Monday. It was there in the agate under "Other Area Finishers": "69, George Sheehan, Shore A.C., 3:18:32." Not bad, you might think. Not bad for place, with 235 starters. Not bad for time, about midway between my best (3:02) and my worst (3:33) serious efforts. You might think that. And you would be wrong.

Because it was a marathon without tears, without pain, without distinction. It was a marathon that I am ashamed of; a marathon I would like to forget. It was a marathon that proves there is a point where prudence becomes timidity, where caution becomes cowardice, where respect becomes fear.

The 26:22-mile distance tends to make all runners prudent, cautious and respectful. "Anyone," said the great Percy Cerutty, "can run twenty miles, but only a few can run the marathon." That extra six miles changes the game from penny-ante to table stakes. Your entire physical bankroll can dissolve in a matter of minutes.

We are not quite sure why this happens. Some physiologists suggest that at twenty miles the body exhausts its available sugar supplies and must switch over to another form of energy metabolism. Maybe so, but, whatever the cause, the runner knows that no matter how he feels at any particular stage of the race, disaster may be waiting for him at the twenty-mile mark. This makes the marathon a chancy and risky business, where the initial pace can be all-decisive. Too slow and you have a poor time; too fast and you may not finish. So those even more timid sometimes use the first seven miles to warm up, and thus change the marathon into an ordinary twenty-mile road run.

That is just what I inexcusably did. I had the mileage to go all out. Long runs with my Shore A.C. friends, and a fast ten-miler (sixty-two minutes) the week before when I beat them all. But within a mile after the start of the marathon, my quartet of friends were minutes ahead of me and my warmup pace. A pace I kept at not just for seven miles, but for the entire outward leg of 13.1 miles.

A mile and a half from the turnaround point, they passed me going the other direction, heading for home. Three miles and twenty-four minutes ahead of me, they were giving the race and the course and the weather (it was a perfect forty degrees and little wind) all they had. They had accepted the challenge. They were making themselves vulnerable, opening themselves to the possibility of great achievement or a wipeout.

Meanwhile I was sliding. That's what Ed Gentry, the get-through-the-day man in James Dickey's *Deliverance,* called it. "Sliding is living antifriction," he said. "It's finding a modest thing you can do and then greasing that thing. It is grooving with comfort."

But even groovers and sliders sometimes get religion. I did at the halfway point. The fact that I was back in 154th place may have helped a little. Provided some additional incentive. But whatever, I set out at full throttle for my colleagues up ahead. I went through Sea Bright like the Blue Comet and highballed through Long Branch passing seven or eight runners each mile.

With five miles to go, I caught struggling Paul Kiell (who was to finish in his best time ever and qualify for Boston), and a quarter mile from home I passed Gene Minor, now walking. Up ahead, Tom Baum had finished in 3:03 and Pat Barrett had become the tenth-fastest woman marathoner in the world with a 3:04.

The people at the finish line said some nice things to me. The time wasn't all that bad and I had run a hell of a last 13.1 miles. But I knew where I should have been. Up with Baum and Barrett, or walking. I had chosen the middle way, the way of the lukewarm. And afterward, when there were awards for almost everybody, I didn't wait around. I wanted no memento of that race.

On the way home, I recalled Nikos Kazantzakis, in *Report to Greco,* asking his grandfather's ghost for a command. His grandfather answered, "Reach what you can, my child." But Kazantzakis refused that command and asked for a more difficult, "more Cretan" command. The ghost then thundered, "Reach for what you cannot."

I may put that slogan on my running shirt. If there is a better rule for a marathoner, I have yet to hear it. If you want to be all you can be, you have to expect a failure from time to time. Finding the limits of your ability will almost certainly end eventually in a walk to the finish line.

Which is why you can never tell from the agate who is a failure and who is a success; who is simply out there grooving and who is reaching what he cannot. Who is a twenty-miler and who is a marathoner.

Only God and the runner know that.

"Pain and wrong and death," wrote William James, "must be fairly met and overcome, or their sting remains unbroken." Prosperity is not enough, he said, if we expect to possess life excellently and meet best the secret demands of the universe.

Psychiatrist Viktor Frankl was another who spoke of the need to confront this "tragic triad of human existence": guilt for our past, pain in the present, and death in the future. These realities, they both warn us, must be neither ignored nor evaded, but squarely faced and conquered.

But where can this encounter be sought? Where can pain be found on demand? Where can we meet guilt head on and cleanse ourselves? Where can we experience death and then return?

The best answer, it seems to me, is sport. Sport is where an entire life can be compressed into a few hours. Where the emotions of a lifetime can be felt on the acre or two of ground. Where a person can suffer and die and rise again on six miles of trails through a New York City park.

Sport is a theater where sinner can turn saint, and a common man become an uncommon hero. Where the past and the future can fuse with the present. Sport is singularly able to give us peak experiences where we feel completely one with the world, where all conflicts are transcended as we finally become our own potential.

For me, these remarkable events occur almost every cross-country race. Every race begins in hope. Every start is filled with the joy that is hope in a physical form. I can feel it in my body and in those around me. It is a confidence, an anticipation, a unity which makes the race a celebration, a holiday.

Every race begins, then, in that optimistic state James called being "once-born," of treating evil by ignoring it. Two miles later, I am in the hills and I know differently. Life is no longer neat and cozy and comfortable. In the hills, it is short and painful and dangerous. My body is now crying for oxygen. And I have come to know pain that people otherwise know only in childbirth or disease or catastrophe. And I know it not once, but many times, because there is hill after hill after hill. And each more terrible than the last.

Once past, the hills are still in my body. Because the past is always incorporated into your body. Each cell contains the past. Either the hills and pain fairly met, or the hills and pain evaded. Either pain or guilt, but usually both. I am always sure I could have done better. Certain that somewhere I eased off and avoided the total commitment. Positive that I failed myself again, as I have done so often in the past. I come out of the hills filled with pain and guilt, looking for some way to make it worth the effort. Looking for a good place or a good time or a good finish.

And all around me, runners are doing the same. The race begun as a community in celebration is ending like an army in rout. Everywhere now it is friend against friend, as the quiet, tolerant nonaggressive runners become the tigers we are inside. Now there is a race for every place and the leader is the man in front of me, whether he is 45th or 86th or 203rd, just as long as I am one place behind.

And we go down that last stretch head and head, each demanding the other do more. Each giving until there is no more to give. Until there is nothing left but the "I." I am beyond pain and guilt. I am where I have never been or seen or touched in daily life. In those final yards, I am near the state described by the dying patients of Dr. Elizabeth Kubler-Ross, of floating out of the body and having a feeling of peace and wholeness. I feel just seconds away from being outside my body watching myself finish, just a moment away from the accomplishment of my task and the total peace that goes with it.

So there it is. Football, said Red Blaik, is the game most like life. What he meant, of course, was that life is the game most like football. Every athlete feels that way about his sport. He knows that sport is where he lives. Where he can best meet and overcome pain and wrong and death.

Life is just a place to spend time between races.

When death comes, we should have had time to fulfill the demands of Pythagoras: build a house, plant a tree, sire a son and write a book. There is the conventional wisdom about a subject where there is no conventional wisdom. Strike the Pythagorean bargain. The best revenge is to live long and well.

But what of the young who die? What of the athletes? How can we

404

accept the deaths of the Israeli Olympians and of men like Brian Piccolo and Chuck Hughes? Is it possible that the athlete is better prepared for death than the rest of us? And for reasons more persuasive than "outrunning one's fame," which is the theme of Housman's poem "To an Athlete Dying Young"?

The answer, it seems to me, is yes. The athlete for very compelling reasons has found a way to live to his absolute limits and has reconciled himself to his own mortality; which is a way of saying the athlete has developed a sense of time, an acceptance of pain, an appreciation of relationships, and a happiness that so completes him that death becomes simply another experience.

The athlete's time emphasizes his mortality. Others of us may drive this thought from our minds. We do not like to think life is short and man corruptible, two obvious facts to the athlete. For him, as Ortega suggests, this fact compresses and intensifies his life, and gives it urgency, imminence and the need to do his best at every instant.

That instant, peculiarly enough, becomes one with the past and the present and the future. In each contest the athlete brings with him the sense of time which we associate with certain primitive people. Indians, for instance, who have only one word for past, present and future. An idea primitive yet so sophisticated as to be accepted by a great thinker like Einstein. Writing of a lifelong friend who had died, Einstein said, "He now has gone a little ahead of me. This is of little significance. For us believing physicists, the separation of the past, present and future has only the meaning of an illusion."

The athlete adds to this perception of time extending behind and ahead of him the realization that hardship and pain and discomfort must be met and overcome. Or else he will, as William James suggested, go through life suspecting that he is not really inside the game. That he lacks the great initiation. That initiation, meeting the terrible fatigue and exhaustion and suffering demanded in sports, can lead a man, thought James, to a profounder way of handling the gift of existence.

Many of us don't realize that gift of existence until it is already taken from us. Psychologist Abraham Maslow, who had suffered a severe coronary attack and almost died, spoke of his life thereafter as his postmortem life. "Everything," Maslow wrote, "gets doubly precious. You get stabbed by the very act of living, of walking and breathing and eating and having friends. Every single moment of every day is transformed."

Every moment of every day has been transformed for eight-year-old Jenny Bagwell, who received a kidney transplant from her mother. "Jenny," says her mother, "sees the flowers open their throats to sing in the morning. . . . She talks to the stars."

Maslow, now deceased, and Jenny alive and well and athletes the world over live in close relationship to nature. They do not want to find out, as Thoreau feared, that they have not lived life at all. For them at least, damnation will not be an unused soul, as Bernanos suggested.

But, for all that, athletes would be incomplete if they weren't happy. This is, however, a characteristic of athletes and one way you can pick one out in a crowd. For them, everything else is work.

Yet this happiness is not simply pleasure, a sensual experience. Happiness is an energetic act, a real effort. Ortega, writing thirty years ago in an article printed in *Sports Illustrated* recently, made this point. Happiness, he declared, using hunting as a model, may include hardship and discomfort, but a man remains immersed in them, the whole present fills him completely, free from nostalgia and desire. Opposite to the life that annihilates itself and fails (the life of work), he builds a plan of life successful in itself, a life of delight and happiness.

Could Ortega be serious in suggesting that all this was possible with sports? No question. "What does a man do when he is free to do what he pleases?" he asks. And supplies the answer. "Raced horses, competed in physical exercises, gathered at parties and engaged in conversation."

The Ortegan proposition appeals to me. It has to do with being. The Pythagorean injunctions relate to having. The athlete becomes more and more as he has less and less. He is obsessed with being all he can be. And in the course of this becoming, he has already died the little deaths. Has learned how to accept the inevitable. Has even taught himself what death will be like when it comes.

For Olympians, death has no sting. They have had the great initiation.

Why mourn Peter Revson? He died doing what he did best. Died at thirty-five before the prudence of advancing years could prevent the full use of his skill. Died quickly and surely as the driver expects to die. Died happy as the philosophers say all men should die.

"When a man dies," wrote Charles Peguy, "he dies not from the disease alone. He dies from his whole life." For the Grand Prix driver to whom racing is his whole life, death in action is the true death. It was for Revson.

"I know Peter led the life he wanted to live," said his friend George Lysle. "He wanted to excel in his own way in his own universe." And Revson died at the height of his excellence. The race driver reaches his highest performance in his early thirties. Before that, he lacks the skills to be the complete driver. After that, he becomes too cautious.

And the event itself is to the driver almost nothing. "I'm not afraid of it [death] for myself," said Jackie Stewart. "I don't think any driver is, because it can't hurt for very long."

Stewart is typical of all topflight race drivers. They are willing to explore openly the possibilities of danger and death. The typical race driver, it has been found, is tough-minded, extraordinarily dominant, aggressive, with a high need to achieve.

Far from being a neurotic seeking death, the driver has a below-average need to feel guilt, blame himself or punish himself. He is a hard-nosed, unemotional, poised human being.

In a book Revson wrote before his death, he explained a tendency to see mistakes not as death-dealing but as something that is, as he says, "going to penalize me in a race. I'm going to lose time. I'm going to lose. Understand this: losing really hurts. To fail in a race is the most painful thing imaginable."

Revson put failing in a race above life itself. Ecclesiastes, who said the most—and the least—about death, would agree with him. Everything is vanity and chasing the wind, said Ecclesiastes. Driving race cars, running governments, amassing wealth, building cities: all this is vanity and chasing the wind.

But, said Ecclesiastes in an about-face, whatever you put your hand to, do it with all your might. He answers to life: It is not the inconsequential things that you do but how you do them that magnifies the Lord.

Doing is, of course, more obvious in those of the same temperament as those racing drivers. Men of action. They have no thought of death. They would die, if it had to come, *in medias res;* taken from life at maximum activity. But their fate is not to go over the guardrail at Indianapolis; they will be cut down by heart attacks or strokes, the hazards of the nonsports world.

A man, Peguy is telling us, is responsible for his own death. It should be in character. Done in one's own style. I have seen death plain in a September surf, and it was all wrong for me, and I escaped. And I have seen death symbolically in a marathon and know certainly that is the way I must end: finally coming to a stop and falling apart like the wonderful one-horse shay.

For people like me, with long histories as silent losers, there comes a time when there is just nothing left. There comes a time when death is welcomed; you just cannot take another step. And then, freed of both guilt and ambition, you can ride the bus back to the finish.

On occasions when I have done that in a marathon and passed runners struggling and suffering on the final miles, I viewed them as if I were already a member of the Church Triumphant, beyond such mortal interests.

The best we can do, it seems to me, is to die proper. There may be more to life than driving racing cars, or running governments, or amassing wealth, or building cities, or even running marathons. But not in this life. So we must pursue these vanities and chase the wind.

And do it with all our might, like Peter Revson.

15

Suffering

**Not to yield says it all.
The enduring, the surviving, does not stop
with age. We may even grow more skillful at it
as the years pass. So we do not envy youth.
We ask no quarter of life. We accept no favors.
We are men following virtue and knowledge.**

In 1964, when I ran my first Boston Marathon, the race was little more than a club. We were 225 strong. But many of us were present only because of a dare or as a joke. Some were overweight and out of shape, attired in gym suits and tennis clothes. Others wore sneakers instead of running shoes. And, I recall, either that year or the next, a runner who led me all the way to Framingham wore a derby.

That first year at Boston, I finished ninety-sixth in three hours and seven minutes and because of this considered myself one of the top hundred marathoners in the country. Now, with nearly the same time, I am not even in the top five thousand. Back then, there were about seven marathons a year; now there are over two hundred. The Boston field has swelled to 9,600 and those are runners who have met qualifying standards to get there.

Where have all these people come from, and why do they do it? How did this mania arise, and what keeps it multiplying among the populace?

I can only answer for myself, and even my answer changes from day to day. For this day, then, I will tell you what I discovered in running. Then why I eventually came to run marathons. And finally, what the continuing fascination of the marathon is. Runners, you see, do not run one marathon. They run them again and again. They are much like surfers seeking the perfect wave.

Why I began running is no longer important. It is enough that it generated a desire to run. Then the running itself took over. Running became a self-renewing compulsion. The more I ran, the more I wanted to run.

One reason was the energy. "Become first a good animal," Emerson said. I did. I came to know my body and enjoy it. Things that previously exhausted me were no longer an effort. Where once I fell asleep in front of the TV set, I was up roaming the house looking for things to do. I was living on a different level of performance.

Then I discovered, or rediscovered, play. Running, I found, was fun. Running became an hour of play and enjoyment away from my daily routine. And in that hour of play I discovered, or rediscovered, myself. Finally, after forty-five years, I accepted the person I was.

It would seem that this should be enough—the fitness, the play, the self-acceptance. But it wasn't, and never will be. I wanted to be chal-

410

lenged, wanted to be tested, wanted to find my limits and then surpass them. Merely running and enjoying and creating were not enough.

From here on, I think more of the answers will be found in the philosophy of William James than anywhere else. However I phrase it, it comes down to one of the Jamesian expressions: "The nobler thing tastes better. The strenuous life is the one we seek."

James was not a writer for those who would simply cope, for those who would groove through life. He believed in effort. He thought the decisive thing about us was not intelligence, strength or wealth. Those are things we carry, he said. The real question posed to us is the effort we are willing to make.

And that available effort is always, he kept saying, much more than we suspect. We live far below the energy we have and therefore must learn how to tap these reservoirs of power. For this, he said, we need a "dynamogenic agent," a "moral equivalent of war." Like war, this would provide a theater of heroism, an arena where one could demonstrate courage and fortitude, a setting where one could be the best one would ever be.

For me and others like me, that is the marathon. We are all there in the works of William James. He is the psychologist who tells us we can be more than we are. The philosopher who appeals to everyone who values his own experience. The thinker who saw happiness in the struggle and found the meaning of life in the marriage of some unhabitual idea with some fidelity, courage and endurance. Which is as good a definition of a marathon as you are likely to find.

I tell you all this, and still you might not understand. What is so special, what is unique about this 26-mile-385-yard distance? Why this and not some other race?

The answer is the wall, the physiological breaking point that comes at the twenty-mile mark. Runners claim that at this mark the marathon is only half over, that the last six miles are equivalent to the twenty that went before. It is nearer the truth to say that the twenty-mile mark is where the marathon begins—there at the wall.

The miles that have gone before are just the foothills to this Everest. The wall is where the runner begins to come apart. Either as suddenly as it takes to write this sentence or slowly and inexorably as the final miles turn into a cauldron of pain.

Any reasonably fit runner can go a twenty-mile race. Were I to get up

411

next Sunday and see in the *New York Times* that there was a twenty-mile race in Central Park, I would be likely to pack my gear and go. But if that same morning I discovered there was a marathon in town, I would draw a bye. I would not be prepared to go that extra six miles, to handle the wall.

Exactly what happens there is not known, even to the experts. Is the exhaustion, the seeming impasse, due to low blood sugar or lactic-acid accumulation? Is it due, perhaps, to dehydration, or high body temperature? Is it the result of a loss of blood volume or, as many runners suspect, depletion of muscle glycogen?

No one seems quite sure. Whatever the reason, the runner's homeostasis, the equilibrium of his internal milieu, begins to break down. And the final six miles must be accomplished in some way unexplained by medical science. From the wall on, the runner goes it alone.

One exercise physiologist, Dr. David Costill, director of the Ball State University Human Performance Laboratory in Muncie, Indiana, ran the marathon as an experiment because he did not think the wall existed. When he came to that point, however, he said, "The sensations of exhaustion were unlike anything I had ever experienced. I could not run, walk or stand, and even found sitting a bit strenuous."

So there it is. It begins with running. Until one day you progress to where you want to be challenged by the marathon. And then you meet the wall. No matter how many times you attack it, you always think you can do better, find more energy, more fortitude, more courage, more endurance. You always think this time you will be the hero you were meant to be.

Fifteen years and fifty marathons later, that's the best explanation I know.

If you would be a marathon runner, study William James. Technique and training can safely be left to lesser teachers. You will soon find the proper shoes, know what to wear, how to eat, what exercises to do, how far to run. What you need most is to know it is possible, possible for you, possible for any common man.

And then you must learn it is not only possible, but necessary. And that there are ways to make what is possible and necessary, however difficult it appears, a source of joy and happiness.

James is the man who teaches this. He is the psychologist who speaks to all who would be more than they are. He is the philosopher who appeals to everyone who values his own experience. Everyone who suspects there is more to each one of us than meets the eye. He is the thinker who said that how to gain, how to keep, and how to recover happiness were the certain motive of all we do and are willing to endure.

James is the scientist who dealt in happiness. He went beyond science into the human heart, into those recesses where lie our values and ideals and with them the energies needed to accomplish them. For James, life was meant to be a struggle. Life, he said, was built on doing and suffering and creating. Its solid meaning was the same eternal thing —the marriage of some unhabitual idea with some fidelity, courage and endurance.

Sweat and effort and human nature strained to its utmost and on the rack, yet getting through alive, he wrote, are the sort of thing that inspires us.

"Man must be stretched," he wrote. "If not in one way, then another."

The marathon is one way. Running twenty-six miles is a feat that truly stretches a human being. At the twenty-mile mark, someone has said, the race is half over. Almost anyone can run twenty miles, but the last six are the equivalent of twenty more. Here the runner finds himself pushed to the absolute limit. And therefore needs to call on those hidden reserves, to use all the fidelity and courage and endurance he has.

Would James have considered the marathon an absurd waste of these energies, of these great human resources? I doubt it. Indeed, who better than James to speak to marathon runners? He always championed the life of sanctity or poverty or sport. He was always caught up with the athlete or the saint, whom he saw as the athlete of God. He always admired the ascetic way of life, which is no more, as the original Greek word would have it, than athletic training. "Asceticism," he stated, "is the profounder way of handling human existence."

This type of discipline, he thought, would allow us to live to our maximum. And find in ourselves unexpected heights of fortitude and heroism and the capability to endure suffering and hardship. To discover, if you will, the person we are. Reaching peaks we previously thought unattainable.

And how better to reach this state than by the rules of habit formation that James suggested? To lead life well and attend to the major things, we must, he said, make as much of our daily activity as possible simply habit. Otherwise we will consume both energy and time making decisions.

The marathoner who would be successful can learn how to get the correct habits from James. Put on the right course, his training will be no problem. The thirty to fifty miles a week he needs to run a respectable and suitably painful marathon will be a matter of course. He will suit up and get out on the roads without agonizing about wind or cold or weather. Or about more attractive things. Or the priorities of family or society.

Begin, said James, with firm resolve. Start with high hopes and a strong and decisive initiative. Do not permit exceptions, he warned. Unraveling a string is easier than winding it up. Practice must become an inviolate hour. Nothing should come between the runner and running.

Next, seize every opportunity to act in the direction of this habit. Further, do not talk about what you are going to do; do it. And finally, he said, keep the faculty of effort alive by a little gratuitous exercise each day.

The marathoner schooled by James comes to the Hopkinton Common on Patriots' Day at the height of his physical powers, willing to pay the price in pain and even agony the marathon demands. But James also wrote on other things that occupy the runner on the way to Boston: mystical states, the primacy of religion, and the problem of truth.

And in the end, when the race is half over, when there are six miles to go, because he is mind and soul as well as body, the runner will find new ways of looking at himself and his God. "Experience," said James, "is a process that continually gives us new material to digest."

And for the marathoner there is no greater experience than the marathon. And no better companion on that run than William James.

James Joyce took the ten years of Homer's *Odyssey* and compressed them into a Dublin day. He looked into the mind and heart and body of the hero Ulysses and created Leopold Bloom, who is everyman. And saw in the lotus-eaters, Cyclops, the gift of the winds, Circe, Hades, the Sirens and even the nymph Calypso, those inner and outer events that happen to everyone, every day. And then he put all of it into the waking-to-sleeping day of his Irish Jew. It takes eighteen hours.

The Boston Marathon does it in three.

Like many sports, the marathon is a microcosm of life. The marathoner can experience the drama of everyday existence so evident to the artist and poet. For him, all emotions are heightened. Agony and ecstasy become familiar feelings. The journey from Hopkinton to Boston, like the journey from Troy to Ithaca, reveals what happens to a man when he faces up to himself and the world around him. And why he succeeds or fails.

Ulysses succeeds not because he is a superior athlete, although he is. He can build a boat and sail it. He can wrestle, run and throw a discus. He can flay, skin, cut up, and cook an ox. But all these skills do not explain his eventual success. His secret is that he endures. He takes life as it comes and says yes.

This trait is so commonly displayed at Boston, it seems universal. I believe every human must have this capacity and could find it if he tried. And there is no better place to discover it than a marathon. For the truth is that every man in a marathon is a survivor or nothing, including the winner.

Winning is, in fact, unimportant. "Brief is the season of man's delight," sang Pindar in his ode to an Olympic winner. And many a winner has learned the truth that his laurel is indeed, as Housman wrote, a garland briefer than a girl's.

There is, then, no happy-ever-aftering for a marathoner, no matter what his age. Tomorrow is another race, another test, another challenge. And then there is another race, and another.

What, then, of Ulysses? Was he content to live as an aging and idle king? Others besides marathoners have thought not. Dante saw him calling on his old comrades, urging them to further adventures. "Consider your origin," he tells them. "You were not formed to live like brutes, but to follow virtue and knowledge."

Such pursuit would be in action. The Greeks developed the whole man. They saw no happiness in creature comforts, no wisdom in meditation.

We aging marathoners already know that. We learned it at Boston. And so, when Tennyson takes up Dante's idea and has Ulysses speak, we hear ourselves: "And though we are not now the strength which in old days moved earth and heaven, that which we are, we are—made weak by time and fate, but strong in will to strive, to seek, to find, and not to yield."

415

Not to yield says it all. The enduring, the surviving, does not stop with age. We may even grow more skillful at it as the years pass. So we do not envy youth. We ask no quarter of life. We accept no favors. We are men following virtue and knowledge.

"Though much has been taken," wrote Tennyson, "much abides." We will live and endure. We know, better than others, "how dull it is to pause, to make an end, to rust unburnished, not to shine in use."

I do not intend to pause, or rest, or rust. Descendant of Ulysses, brother of Bloom, I will survive.

There is no easier running for me than the first few miles of the Boston Marathon. I come to that race at my peak. I am lean and fit and ready. And the excitement of the day lights a fire. So I am almost pure energy when the gun goes off at high noon on the Hopkinton Common.

The start is all laughter and talking and wishing people well. The pace is a pleasure. Smooth and comfortable and little more than a trot. I move at a speed just above that of my warmup ("In the beginning always hold something back," Adolph Gruber, the Austrian Olympian, once told me). So these miles are like no others in any race.

Down the long hill out of Hopkinton and through Ashland and over the gentle slopes to Framingham, I coast along. The running is automatic. I feel nothing but the elation of being in this company. The miles pass as if I were watching them out of a train window.

But miles change, somewhere the holding back must end. I pass the ten-mile mark and enter Natick. The miles no longer effortless become an effort that comes easily. My style remains sure and smooth and economical. I increase my speed, but it is still well below the six-minute miles of those cruel ten- and twelve-milers in Central Park. I try for maximum efficiency. Careful to push off my toes and get those extra few inches a stride that make the difference in a three-hour run.

Soon I am at Wellesley, the halfway point. The miles again change. Now each mile is running at my best. It is now becoming hard work. Not disagreeable, but an exertion not previously felt. I am still surprisingly fresh and moving well. Better now than I have moved before or will move later. Still, the body is beginning to tell me this is no lark. No longer child's play. Not just a long run in the sun.

And now at the seventeen-mile mark come the Newtown Hills, a two-mile stretch which includes the four hills that make up the world-renowned Heartbreak Hill. I will take these on the grass divider behind the crowds that line the street.

The grass dampens the shock on my lower legs and thighs. And I shift to shorter steps as a cyclist would shift to a lower gear to maintain the same work load. Even with grass and ministeps, miles over hills are most difficult.

Quite suddenly, what in the beginning seemed like something I would accomplish with ease and even distinction comes down to survival. A question of whether or not I can keep moving. These two short miles seem interminable. And then, just as suddenly, I am at Boston College and it is, as the crowds insist, all downhill from there.

Downhill or not, we marathoners know that at Boston College the race is only half over. I am quite a different runner from the one who stood on the line at Hopkinton. The steady pace has used up my muscle glycogen, my precious fuel supply. The Newtown Hills have built up my lactic acid and the heaviness in my muscles. The downhills in the early going have inserted icepicks in my thighs. My blood sugar is getting low. And although I have drunk everything in sight, I have not kept up with my fluid loss.

Descending the hill from Boston College, I feel these inner events for the first time. And I know again that the last six miles at Boston will be the worst six miles I will ever run. From now on, pain is a constant companion. The slightest downgrade is a torture to my thighs. My legs get heavier and heavier.

The same effort that made a romp of a seven-minute mile outside of Hopkinton barely gets me through a ten-minute mile on Commonwealth Avenue. I experiment with strides and body positions to see if there are any muscles still willing to respond.

By now I can see the Pru Tower, and then come the unkindest miles of all. Miles where I must will every step toward a goal that never seems any nearer. I spend a mile in agony and bring that tower not one inch nearer. Minutes pass, and the Pru and with it the finish and the relief from pain and my chance to get into a hot tub seem just a mirage.

But somehow I reach Beacon Street and I know I have made it. Like a horse who smells the barn, I am suddenly refreshed. The last mile brings with it a joy, an elevation of the spirit, that makes everything that went before worthwhile.

And worth doing again next year. One mile at a time.

* * *

Like most distance runners, I am still a child. And never more so than when I run. I take that play more seriously than anything else I do. And in that play I retire into the fantasyland of my imagination any time I please.

Like most children, I think I control my life. Believe myself to be independent. I am certain I have been placed on this earth to enjoy myself. Like most children, I live in the best of all possible worlds, a world made for running and racing, where nothing but good can happen. And, like most children, I am oblivious to all of the work done by other people to make it that way.

This is more than faith. Faith is the Breton peasant praying for rain and then taking an umbrella with him when he leaves the house. Faith is a nun friend of my grandmother's who periodically herded thirty to forty orphans onto a train at Poughkeepsie and set out for Coney Island without a penny in her purse. "God will provide," was her motto. That's faith.

Faith is an act of the will made by an adult. The child acts before will and reason and dogma. He simply knows. And the child in me knows that I am in a game that will always have a happy ending. That I can enjoy the anxiety leading up to the race, and the tremendous challenge in the running, and the sweetness or bitterness of the ending, knowing that, whatever happens, I am already a hero, a winner. Knowing that in the end, whatever the crisis, there would always be someone to take care of me.

I hadn't realized this (although it may well have been evident to my family and friends) until the 1976 Boston Marathon. The official temperature on Patriots' Day was ninety-two degrees, a level listed as dangerous for livestock and death-dealing to runners. Any thinking adult would have sat this one out. But there I was with 1,800 others dressing at the Hopkinton High School gym.

Then, walking to the starting line, I passed a gasoline station with a thermometer on the wall. It read 116 degrees. I passed by undeterred.

At the starting line there were hoses to fill our cups, to douse our heads and caps and the shirts we wore. The family of man was already operating. The people were already taking care of their children.

And that was the way it was. The whole thing was absurd. The race should have been postponed or set for later in the day. There was no way for a runner to go those twenty-six sunbaked miles to Boston relying on official help. Yet I set out knowing I would get whatever help I needed. Knowing I would survive.

For one thing, Boston Marathon crowds are special. I recall my first Boston and how astounded I was that people called me George all along the way. They stood in groups with one person picking the names out of the *Globe* so that when I got to them there would be cries of "You can do it, George," or "George, you're looking strong," or, in the late stages, "Keep it up, George, there's only three miles to go."

What that can do to a childlike runner previously known only to his own family is unbelievable. I felt capable of anything, even completing the Boston Marathon.

This year the crowd outdid itself. Within two miles we were running in the rain. It was ninety-two degrees and a cloudless sky, and we were running in a rain provided by hose after hose after hose. There was water everywhere. Mile upon mile of people and children offering water to drink and pour on me. Swarms of young boys giving out Gatorade, with the same enthusiasm they had shown an hour before supplying the leaders. Others with buckets of ice. Some with the traditional orange slices, many of the children just holding out their hands to be touched by the heroes passing by.

From Ashland on, there was nothing but applause and cheers. Then came the reception from the girls at Wellesley, and farther on the children in the Newtown Hills outdoing each other to get us ice and water. And there I saw this solemn four-year-old, just standing with a tiny cup, hoping someone would stop. I did and drank the two ounces and told her, "You're my honey." Boston is like that, a voice, a face, a child that you remember forever.

I was in Boston now and should have been home free. I wasn't. I was running a poor marathon, and when you run a poor marathon you not only hurt, you hurt longer. I had been out on the roads longer than any time in my fourteen years of running. But through all the pain and not knowing whether I would finish, the dragging out those last terrible miles, I always felt safe. I knew I was surrounded by friends and family and those who would take care of me no matter what happened.

And knowing, too, that if I stopped they would say, "You gave it your best, George." Knowing that whatever I did, I would not disappoint them. There would always be a meal and a soft bed and a good day of running tomorrow.

Only the child still lives in a world where such days are possible.

The year my daughter entered college in Boston, she came to see me in the marathon. She was, she told me later, the only calm and rational person among those thousands that jammed Prudential Center.

They cheered and yelled and applauded every finisher. They cheered the young, cheered the old, cheered those from Harvard, cheered those from California. And they cheered even more wildly when someone they knew came into sight. Through it all, she stood as quiet and as staid and withdrawn as an Episcopalian at a revival meeting.

Then I arrived. I made my turn into that long wide plaza, which at that moment was completely empty except for me and the cheering group. The finish line was still an eighth of a mile away, but it didn't matter. The race was over. The crowd's cheers told me that. I had made it. And this was my victory lap. Almost an hour behind the winner, having nailed down 312th place, I was suddenly renewed and refreshed. I was running my home run home, and every stride I took revealed my joy.

Then I saw a figure break out of the crowd into the white expanse that lay between me and the officials at the finish. It wasn't until another fifty yards that I recognized who this yelling, waving, cheering person was. My daughter.

The finish of any marathon can be that kind of emotional experience. Somewhere along the way the runner has been challenged. He has met pain fairly and overcome it. He has had a real deliverance. And at the end of that ordeal, both runner and spectator are aware that something very special has happened.

Sometimes this awareness is expressed in ways that neither runner nor spectator will ever forget. For me that occurred in Boston. For a friend of mine the setting was the Scottish Games at Grandfather Mountain. The marathon there is one of the most difficult in this country. Its 26.2 miles through mountainous country test a runner as almost no other race does.

My friend survived that test and ultimately conquered the course. And when he came to the last climb where the finish was supposed to be, he heard the sound of bagpipes. Now, as everyone knows, the skirling of bagpipes stirs passions and emotions inaccessible in other ways. So my friend, already overcome by reaching the end of this ordeal, was in tears when he breasted the hill.

And now he saw he was on a great plain encircled by the camps of the various Scottish clans. And each sent up a great shout as he passed them.

What place he took, he sometimes forgets. But he will never forget when time stood still on that plain atop Grandfather Mountain and all around him were happy cheering people and the sound of bagpipes.

All this has, of course, nothing to do with winning and losing. Winning and losing is what you do in team games. The runner is not in a game; he is in a contest. And that is a word whose Latin root means to witness or testify. The other runners are witnesses to what he is doing. And therefore, anything else than all he can give is not enough. When you race, you are under oath. When you race, you are testifying as to who you are.

The distance runner understands this. He is the mildest of men. Quiet and even-tempered and rarely given to argument. He avoids confrontation and seeks his own private world, but in a marathon he becomes a tiger. He will go to the end of his physiology to find who he is and what he can do. Put himself deeper and deeper into a cauldron of pain. What is necessary becomes possible, however absurd the effort may be.

But such interrogations, if they are to mean anything, should be infrequent. If the marathon is to measure a man, it should synchronize with the cycles of his growth. Maturity is an uneven, discouraging process. Becoming who you are is not done on schedule. There are years when nothing seems to happen.

But one must still say that marathons can make memories like no other event in your life. And that could be an argument for running one every month. When rocking-chair time comes, you'll be all set.

Somewhere east of Wellesley, past the church tower at the halfway point, the Boston Marathon ceases to be a race and becomes an experience. Forgotten now is the camaraderie of the gym; the banter at the starting line; the ease of the 7:30 pace through Framingham and Natick. All that was preparation for the encounter the runner will have with himself and his world as he heads for the Newtown Hills.

Those hills and the miles beyond will challenge everything he holds dear, his value system, his life style. They will ask nothing less than his view of the universe.

Yet he moves toward this meeting unhurried, relaxed, in complete tune with his body rhythms. He is rediscovering that precious reward of countless hours of training—those moments when he and the running are one. He becomes the running as the golfer becomes the swing. To reach this mystical place, time must be ignored. He must act as Zorba said he always did: "As though I were immortal."

Past Wellesley, then, the runner moves toward the action he is performing, gradually becoming more and more the action until he is the running. And then he reaches even further into these mysterious areas. Like the swimmer who becomes one with his world of water and sky, the runner finds a total relationship with earth and air and wind and rain.

These events are difficult to describe. "Truth and fact," wrote William James, "well up in our lives in ways that exceed verbal formulation."

And almost always this truth occurs in action. When the philosopher Herrigel went to study Zen, he was told to learn archery and use that as the way to wisdom. We learn through our muscles. We learn through the perfecting of our bodies, and stretching them to the utmost. "There are thresholds which thought alone can never permit us to cross," wrote Gabriel Marcel. "An experience is needed."

The Boston is just such an experience. The runner passing Boston College and seeing the last six miles flat before him has reached an understanding he could not gain through his brain alone.

The runner who started in Hopkinton competitive and independent now nears the finish with a sense of dependence and community that is almost overwhelming.

One runner spoke of this feeling between the runners and the spectators as a family. "I know now," he wrote in a letter to the *Boston Globe,* "that the Boston is more than a race, and more than a club. It is a family and I'm proud to be part of it."

The runner is coming to know, or will know if he runs enough Bostons, that it is more than a family. He knows, or will know, that the universe is the smallest divisible unit. And he will know that Assisi is right, that Christian ethic is livable. It has failed because we have regarded our neighbor as Other. As separate. But no one is separate going down Commonwealth Avenue.

The runner has gone beyond the golfer and his swing, beyond the swimmer and his world. The runner has joined common humanity, the seas of anonymity moving toward Pru Center. He has reached the consciousness the Buddhists call Metta, the absolute identification with another suffering human being. He sees a weary, tiring runner and addresses him, if only mentally, "Oh, myself."

Fantasy? Perhaps. Sentimental nonsense? Maybe. But before you write it off completely, read Joyce Carol Oates's wonderfully optimistic essay "New Heaven and Earth."

"Instead of hiding our most amazing, mysterious and inexplicable experiences," she writes, "we must learn to articulate and share them."

Even more to the point is her suggestion that we are coming to a transformation of America. "Our minds," she writes (echoing the early Church Fathers' "The multitude of the faithful have only one heart and one soul"), "belong to a collective mind and the old boundary of the skin is no boundary at all but a membrane connecting the inner and outer experiences of our existence."

The runner relaxing in a shower at Pru Center senses he has united these two existences (his own and the world's). He has a new and radically altered relationship with other people, the earth, the universe.

That's the sort of thing that can happen almost any Patriots' Day somewhere east of Wellesley on the way to Boston.

They gave me the business at Mort's Corner the next morning. "Why don't you write about the human-interest stories in the Boston Marathon," someone asked, "instead of a column that no one will understand, including yourself?"

It was a good question, but it held its own answer. Because there are two Boston Marathons. One is the outer event. The Boston of the sports writers. The World Series of distance runners, attracting athletes and characters from all over the world. The Patriots' Day event filled with funny and odd and touching happenings all the way from Hopkinton to Boston.

The other Boston is an inner event. It concerns itself with what these thousands of runners are looking for. The search, whether they know it or not, for one's "true gravity." And that is already, as they say at Mort's, something no one understands, including myself.

The first I had learned of "true gravity" was in a remarkable book I had read before leaving for Boston, *Golf in the Kingdom,* by Michael

Murphy. Shivas Irons, the golf professional who takes Murphy on this extraordinary golf round, is a disciple of Pythagoras and says we must know the world from the inside; that we can come to know the deeper structure of the universe only through our own body and senses and living experience.

With a shillelagh and some primitive golf balls Irons teaches Murphy to find his "inner body." To forget his images of disaster, the hook, the ever present rough, the familiar curses and excuses. So that, in Murphy's words, he "played the remaining holes in this state of grace," and, as he put it, "those final holes played me."

Somewhere past Wellesley, the halfway point, I suddenly found that Murphy had written something that had an equal application to running and especially to marathons.

This marathon had begun no different from other Bostons. As usual, the weather was bad. The bright Hopkinton sun told of midday heat farther on. The course would run long and slow today. Nine Bostons had made me a realist. And a realist in a hot Boston will wear light clothes, and a handkerchief to shield his scalp from the sun. He will drink everything handed to him and pour what's left on his head. He will run well within himself for seventeen miles, take the hills as best he can and let it all hang out in Boston.

That's the way it went. I started near the leaders (one year I stayed at the back and it took me over a minute to get to the starting line after the gun went off). And at least eight hundred passed me in the first ten miles. My pace, however, was just right for me and I had survived an anxious moment in Natick at the first Gatorade station, which was empty when I got there. For a hundred yards the street was filled with discarded-Gatorade cartons. I noticed an upright one and picked it up. It had some Gatorade left. So, stopping here and there and now and then, I left Natick almost fully revived.

By Wellesley I knew it was going to be a good one. Not in time, perhaps. The three-hour marathon would have to wait another year. But it would be good for this heat.

And then it happened. After nine agonizing Bostons, nine Patriots' Days of worrying about pace and time and even finishing, I finally found, if only for a few miles, what running was all about.

Now, people will tell you why they run. And the reasons will change from day to day, because it is like peeling an onion. They get down to deeper and deeper reasons but always failing to reach the essence of the running experience.

But now, heading out of Wellesley toward Lower Newton Falls and the beer drinkers at Mary's Bar, I suddenly found what must be the essence of running. I was thinking then of Murphy's golf game. I would, I said to myself, just concentrate on finding the perfect running form. I would find the pace at which I could run forever. Then let my inner body take over.

I ran then oblivious of the other runners. Only half hearing a nine-year-old philosopher sitting on the curb who shouted, "Smile and it won't hurt as much." Still looking, of course, for every orange slice, every cup of water. Still touching the children's outstretched hands. But in a world of my own where my running became me. I have on occasions in practice been lost in thought, oblivious of my surroundings but oblivious, too, of the running, so that I could not recall how I got to where I was. But this was entirely different. I was entirely occupied with this magic thing I was doing. I was one with what I was doing.

Past Boston College and through Brookline I went, full of running. The course, as Murphy had said, was now running me. Three blocks to go and the crowds were building up to the ten thousand waiting at the Pru Center. Two blocks to go and there were my daughter and her college classmates giving me a reception even Ted Williams would have acknowledged.

It was too much. The day. The run. And now this. Suddenly I had the handkerchief off my head and I was twirling it in the air. I ran laughing past those girls toward the finish line, still twirling the handkerchief like Zorba the Greek telling those wonderful affectionate Bostonians that in some way I had found what running and the Boston Marathon were all about.

Mort, I'll have the coffee black and no chatter.

16

Meditating

**In this ease of movement, this
harmony, this rhythmic breathing of life into life,
I am able to let my mind wander. I absent myself
from road and wind and the warm sun.
I am free to meditate,
to measure the importance of things.**

"SINCE PAIN AND BOREDOM are the chief enemies of human happiness," wrote Schopenhauer, "Nature has provided a protection against both. We can ward off pain by cheerfulness; and boredom by intelligence."

Unfortunately most of us are equipped to handle one but not the other. The cheerful people are those who need people. They need people to love or be friends with or to help or master or rule. For them life without other people would be pure boredom, the ultimate torture. Solitary confinement, the supreme punishment. A monk's cell, a slice of hell. They look on loneliness as a disease and find "unoccupied leisure," Schopenhauer said, "altogether unendurable."

Others, like myself, see things the opposite way. We are rarely if ever bored but feel pain at ranges imperceptible to most people. I feel pain as a dog hears sound. I am an early-warning system for discomfort, a mass of nerve endings, a being dominated by my nervous system. And this intolerance is not only to physical pain but to psychic pain as well. The real pain in everyday life.

On the other hand, I like being alone. I enjoy my own company. I am satisfied running the roads far from any other human being. For me loneliness is the desirable state. Solitary confinement, a touch of heaven. I am never bored. People and the pain they cause are what I cannot stand. The pain of relationships made and broken. The pain of leaving. The pain of being left.

I am built to be alone. I am an intellectual, which I suppose is what Schopenhauer meant when he wrote "intelligence." But being an intellectual has really nothing to do with intelligence, it simply describes the way I think. My mind works through association rather than logic or reason. When I run those miles over the roads there is all the while a stream of consciousness, a torrent of ideas, coursing through my brain. One idea after another goes hurtling past like so much white water. Giving me here and there a new insight, a new intuition, a new understanding. Each in turn soon replaced by yet another thought, still another idea.

At those times I can believe Erich Segal's story of wanting to dash up to a house and ask for a pen and paper to write a thought down. For he knew as surely as I that the thought, however clear, would soon be forgotten. And since there is no logical progression, no amount of reasoning would bring it back.

By that rushing stream I come alive. The world's thinkers have known this and blessed this solitary state. The yardstick of a human being, said Kierkegaard, is his ability to bear being alone. You can find similar passages in Emerson, Nietszche, Schopenhauer and many others. But for myself it is sufficient to justify myself, not to put anyone else down. Either everyone is normal or no one is. The people who need people, and the people who don't need people. Where I do well, some do badly, but the opposite is also true.

The intellectual does badly as a lover and almost as poorly as a friend. It is the payment I must make for a life free of boredom. The price I must meet for my precious stream of consciousness, my river of ideas, and the growth that goes with it.

Love, you see, dams this torrent, obstructs this flow. Love is, among other things, abnormal attention. It is attention to one person, one idea, and I cannot have that. "What happens to a person in love," said Ortega, "is to isolate on one object and remain on it alone, fixed and paralyzed like a rooster before a hypnotic white line." It was therefore, to that Spanish intellectual, "an inferior state of mind and a form of transitory imbecility."

Nor am I better with friendship. For one thing, anyone who would accept me is suspect. Of any friend I feel like Santayana when told that William James had a high regard for him. "If he knew me better," he said, "he would like me less." With me it works both ways. As soon as I reach friends' limits I am gone. As soon as they no longer contribute to my growth I must leave.

Emerson was on to this. "A man's growth," he said, "is seen in the successive choirs of his friends." Jung made much the same observation. He was saddened, he said, by the friends he had to abandon, but there was nothing else to be done. When they no longer were in his orbit they had to be left behind. "As soon as I had seen through them," he said, "the magic was gone." An odd way to live, you might say. And truly it is. Never boring, to be sure, but frequently depressing and filled with pain and an aching emptiness. And there are times when that rush of white water bubbling through my brain doesn't seem worth the people it costs me.

Perhaps Jung felt the same. "I need people to a higher degree than others," he said, "and at the same time much less."

Let me take that idea and run on it.

You come, too.

* * *

The distance runner, I have said, does badly as a lover and almost as poorly as a friend. It is the price I must pay for my stream of consciousness, my river of ideas. It is my payment for the growth that goes on in my brain, for the knowledge I have yet to attain. I cannot attend to anything that would obstruct that flow or keep me from those goals.

On the road I become a philosopher and follow the philosophers' tradition. I affirm my own existence and no one else's. I am occupied with my own inner life. I am constructing a system which will justify my own way of being in the world. And discovering, as Emerson said, that there are thoughts in my brain which have no other watchman or lover or defender than me.

So I have no time or attention or energy to throw away on anything else, be it person or cause or country. I have no time for love; nor do I have time for hate. Hate, you see, takes the same attention and time as love, and even more energy. When you hate, energy flows out of you toward the hated person, the hated cause, the hated country. Nothing burns one up faster than hate and anger and revenge. There is no quicker way to be drained of emotion and energy.

And hate no less than love stops my stream of consciousness. It prevents my exploration of myself, my passage through my inner world. It takes time of which I have so little, and none to waste. There is no deadline more insistent than the riddle of life.

So hate is something I do as little as possible and never with relish. I will not be forced into that state. Cross me and I will put you out of my mind. Injure me and I will drop you out of consciousness. Vex me and you will no longer exist. Insult me and I will not respond.

You might see this failure to react as making me a pacifist. To an extent you might be right. I am ready to flee at the slightest indication of violence. Under no circumstances will I fight, and I seldom argue. Like Galileo I say to myself, "It is so nevertheless, whether I say it or not."

But I am no pacifist. Pacifism is just another cause. Another object that requires attention and time and investment of myself. What I am is neutral. I reserve the right never to take sides. I continue to deny, to doubt, to analyze, to suspend judgment. In me you see the epitome of the neutral, the outsider, the uninvolved. I am not interested in either sin or the sinner, unless it is my sin and I am the sinner.

When I run I am a neutral. My road is a neutral zone. It is an area no one violates. A territory everyone respects. No one bothers me. No one asks me for an opinion, or a contribution. No one wants me to sign a petition or stand up and be counted. No one asks for love, or deserves hate.

During fifteen years and thousands of hours on the road I cannot recall being angry for any length of time. Or indeed spending any of those miles thinking of revenge or experiencing envy or jealousy, or whatever might alienate me from other humans. On the other hand, neither can I remember many times I have thought of other people except for their ideas.

My involvement, like it or not, is all with myself.

I devote all my care and endurance and intensity to my own thoughts and imagination and self-analysis. My temptation is delight in thought itself, in the intricate dance of my mind. The pleasure in the process that might stop me from reaching the End. My danger is not that I will fail my fellows (I have already done that); or in making the world work (which doesn't interest me.) My danger is that I will fail to reach my limits and find God.

But here my body helps. Running is an awareness and a perfection that I find unrivaled. Nothing else, mental or physical or spiritual, do I do as well. And it is that feeling of being totally whole and satisfied in my body that keeps me dissatisfied with what I think. I cannot accept less from my mind than the perfection that I experience in my body.

And since that perfection is not to be gained this side of the divide, I keep running and seeking the truth which lies beyond love and hate. And I accept the paradox philosophers know only too well: My unity will be found in division from my lovers and friends.

The first half hour of my run is for my body. The last half hour, for my soul. In the beginning the road is a miracle of solitude and escape. In the end it is a miracle of discovery and joy. Throughout, it brings an understanding of what Blake meant when he said, "Energy is eternal delight."

I always start in optimism. For one hour I feel capable of being a hermit, an anchorite. On the road I can seek my own desert, my own mountain, my own little cell. I am alone and away from the world, in an area, a pace and a silence that allow me to be myself. More than an hour might be too much. Few of us, and certainly not I, have the self-discipline and control to fill the hermit's day—with prayer and reading and meditation.

But for that hour I am a solitary. And I begin with that same discipline and control, now needed for the strong, steady pace against the headwind and the hills along the river road. In that first half hour I become my body. My body is me and I am my body. And I know that only in its fullness will I be all that I will be. I delight in my energy, my strength, my power as I pass by the freshly greening fields. In a world coming alive with the energy in spring, I feel myself come alive, come back from being split and splintered, and becoming whole. I am a total and perfect runner.

And in this perfection, this ease of movement, this harmony, this rhythmic breathing of life into life, I am able to let my mind wander. I absent myself from road and wind and the warm sun. I am free to meditate, to measure the importance of things. I am purified by the effort that has gone before, drained of pride, filled with childlike grace and innocence; the energy of my body becomes an energy of the mind. An energy that becomes delight, however, only to the degree I understand what Bernanos warned about: the impotency of power, the ignorance of learning, the idiocy of machination, the frivolity of being serious.

But those are the insights of a free mind. Thomas Merton, another solitary, understood that. The beginning of freedom, he wrote, is not liberation from the body but liberation from the mind. We are not entangled in our own body, we are entangled in our mind.

I am now turned from home. I am going downwind and in those miles I become unentangled. I move out of thickets that have constrained me. Out of underbrush that has reduced me to futile plans and more futile action.

I move beyond ambition and envy, beyond pleasure and diversion. In those miles downwind, I have a new vision of myself and the universe. The running is easy, automatic, yet full of power, strength, precision. A tremendous energy pours through my body. I am whole and holy. And the universe is whole and holy and full of meaning. In the passion of this running, truth is being carried, as the poet says, alive into my heart.

So in those final miles meditation becomes contemplation. What has been a measuring of things becomes an awareness of the sacred. The road now becomes sacred ground, the temple the word contains. There

431

are cars and traffic, noise and exhaust, but I am past sight and sound, past this disturbance. I know or, better, I experience the whole of what Blake said.

Man has no body distinct from the soul. Energy is the only life and is from the body; and reason is the outward circumference of energy. And energy is indeed eternal delight.

So as my run ends I am back in my body. The energy I felt at the beginning of the run gradually filling my mind and soul, gradually creating a unity, a wholeness, a peak feeling of being one with myself and the universe. What they call "in zen," satori. And if at that moment I still don't know the answers to the last dramatic questions of my existence and yours and the existence of the universe, at the very least I know now these answers do exist.

And tomorrow I will be out on the roads seeking them once more.

Today I took Truth and ran with it on the ocean road. I do that every day. For one hour, it is yesterday, today and tomorrow. At eight minutes a mile, I am, I was, I will be. On the ocean road, I experience what I cannot know. Because for me and you and the common man, revealed Truth must be experienced. Only the giants can come to know through reason what Moses brought down from Sinai. The rest of us must learn with our bodies.

So we begin in fear, which is the beginning of wisdom, and seek understanding. And our bodies, our senses, teach us that law is how a thing works. That the Ten Commandments describe how the universe works. And we discover that the closer we become to just being, the closer we come to understanding "I am who I am."

This is probably not true about everyone, but the runner would agree. He possesses himself in solitude and silence and suffering. He is gradually stripped of desires and attachment to things. As I run, I get closer and closer to requiring nothing more than life supports, air and water and the use of the planet. I surrender to something greater than my will. My design? His will?

Such moments do not come easily or for the asking. Running is a serious thing and must be taken seriously. I will not find truth in something I use to avoid it. I will not find it, either, in something I do as a means and not an end. To use running to become fit or lose weight or calm my nerves would lead not to truth but to heresy.

So I take that hour and run as if my life depended on it. I run into being and becoming and having been. Into feeling and seeing and hearing. Into all those senses by which I know the world that God made, and me in it. Into understanding why a Being whose reason to exist is "to be" should have made me to His image.

Am I operating at too low a level this too physical body? I can only answer that is the way I know. And whatever happens, revealed Truth must be experienced Truth. If not through intelligence or some special ability to alter consciousness, then through hard work and effort, however mediocre. Through desire and determination and qualities accessible to every man.

The body does all this. The body which is the stumbling block to the philosophers. The body they have separated and discarded. That body brings the messages.

It lets us see that the New Testament, which changed the law to love and made the Word flesh, is a hymn to the body. The blind see, the lame walk, the deaf hear, the dumb speak. People are hungry and thirsty and indulge in sex. There is color and sound and wind and water. There are tempests and droughts. And a climax of pain and suffering and torture and death.

This is something the runner in me understands. I start with the guilt and doubt and despair that possess most of us. But I am soon exploring the limits of my body, of my sensory powers. I run in complete touch with myself. I can tell you the wind speed, the temperature, the humidity and whether I'm on a grade and how steep it is. I take the universe around me and wrap myself in it and become one with it, moving at a pace which makes me part of it.

And then I add the sound of wind and the changing pitch of my footstrikes as I go from surface to surface. And I take in the sight of light and shadows and the road itself, the road that Bernanos called a miracle of solitude and escape. "The man who has not seen the road in the early light of morning, cool and living between two rows of trees," he wrote, "does not know the meaning of hope." But then Bernanos was one who believed that man must possess himself in solitude and silence before he is of any use to society.

The runner need not break four minutes in the mile or four hours in the marathon. It is only necessary that he runs and runs and sometimes suffers. Then one day he will wake up and discover that somewhere along the way he has begun to see order and law and love and Truth that makes men free.

It could happen to you or me on the ocean road.

"Do you believe in personal immortality?" a Unitarian friend asked me at lunch the other day. Not an everyday subject, but if you have Unitarian friends (being nonjudgmental, they are the best kind) you become accustomed to such questions. Even at lunch. Unitarians, it appears, are ready to discuss the Eternal Verities any time, day or night. In fact, my friend assures me, they would rather go to a discussion about heaven than to the actual place.

This time I was ready for the hard question. Just the previous day personal immortality had changed for me from a childhood belief and an undergraduate theory to actual fact. It had become a reality. On my afternoon run I had suddenly overreached the confines of time and space. I had become the perfect runner moving easily and surely and effortlessly toward infinity. My ten years of almost daily running had brought me to an area of consciousness, a level of being, that I never knew existed.

For the runner, running has always been a form of contemplation and meditation; an activity with the saving grace, as Santayana said, of football, of purging, rinsing and exhausting the inner man; a time when the movements of his body in concert with his mind and heart gave him an appreciation of what was good and true and beautiful. But it is now evident it can do even more.

Running that day became for me, as I'm sure it has for others, a mystical experience. A proof of the existence of God. Something happened and then, in the words of a recent letter writer to *Harper's*, "One simply knows, and believes, and can never forget."

There is no way of documenting this. Such states are difficult to describe and impossible to analyze. Conversely, there is no use denying them. "Mystics," wrote William James, "have been there and know." The mystic, James declared, is invulnerable.

He is also, for the most part, unchallenged. Although we may not have been there ourselves, we suspect what he says is true. We simply do not know how to make it true for ourselves.

That way now seems open. Where once it was so that not more than a thimbleful of meditation was going on in America, we are now becoming a nation of meditators. And in our newfound leisure we are discovering the salvation and liberation that exist in play. For it is sport that is finally giving the common man a true picture of himself. Freeing him from authority and allowing him to find and fulfill his own design. For the runners this meant the realization that solitude is the staff of life and not a mark of failure. That, for him at least, community is a myth. He became able to pursue his asocial ways. To change his life to accommodate to his inner reality.

(When a psychiatrist-marathoner friend asked me recently, "What was it like before we started running?" I could not remember. If there had been a life before running, it was imperfect and unfulfilled.)

Play is truly the answer. "There are many routes," wrote poet Jonathan Price, "in fact, any way the serious world calls play." So it is running for those who are runners. Other forms for other people.

What route you take depends on yourself. I cannot bring visions of immortality to a nonrunner by dragging him along on my afternoon runs. What you do must absorb you utterly and intensely; and to do that it must be your game, your sport, your play. "How we play," writes George Leonard, "signifies nothing less than our way of being in the world."

For the dancer, the dance brings this feeling for life, this intimation of immortality. ("When a jump works," says Jacques d'Amboise, "it feels like forever. I'm riding on top of time.") Others get the same sort of experience from skiing, surfing, karate, golf, football or what have you.

How long it will take is another story. One must go through discipline to get to freedom. Be assured it does not occur to beginners. Only when how you do a thing surpasses the thing you are doing can you break through the barriers to these levels of consciousness, your own inner depths.

But then when they ask you the real question that is bothering everyone in this age, "Is this all there is?" you can answer, "You've got to be kidding."

17

Growing

"

**I am in that first Paradise,
the Paradise given. The danger is that
I will be content to stay there.
That I will never reach for the Paradise
that must be won or lost.**

"

RUNNING IS a dangerous game. At one pole the danger is contentment. Running becomes so addictive physically, so habit-forming psychologically, that it takes willpower for me not to run. And it has a solitude so satisfying that I sometimes wonder if the hermit isn't the supreme hedonist.

So there is this absolute contentment. This willingness to absent myself from everything else. To see little else as worth the effort. When I run I take the risk of that contentment. Of becoming what Updike described as the contented man, "an animal with clothes on."

Running can do that. When I run I am completely content. I cease growing. I live just for those moments on the road. After all, what else do I do as well? Where else do I feel as invulnerable? How else can I know such peace?

So I know this contentment all too well. The road becomes my place to hide. There I withdraw from the world. I retreat into a universe bounded by my line of sight, the sound of my footsteps, the feelings of heat and cold, of sun and rain and wind. I narrow the cosmos to this hour, this road, this running. Naught else occupies me. I am content.

This is one pole. If I am not Updike's animal, I am a child in running gear. I am in that first Paradise, the Paradise given. The danger is that I will be content to stay there. That I will never reach for the Paradise that must be won or lost. The danger is that I will never move on, never grow up.

But that movement, that growing up, is even more dangerous, perhaps the most dangerous thing a human being can do. And that is precisely what happens when running becomes a meditation. When I become a thinker and leave the freedom of childhood; and, in my hour on the road, begin the lifelong journey whose goal is self-knowledge.

When a person thinks, he inevitably separates himself from prevailing opinion. And, by hidden and secret ways, will eventually end, according to Ortega, in some secluded spot filled with unaccustomed thoughts. Thinking will put his stable universe in peril. He will be alone with no one else to help him.

I know this to be true. When I run and meditate, I forsake the shelter I had in the pure simplicity of running. I abandon the certainties built into my everyday life. I leave in my wake my ancestors, my traditions, my church, my society, my family, my friends, everyone and everything I hold important to me. I jettison everything I have not made authentic by my own experience. Everything, as Thoreau said, I have not learned by direct intercourse and sympathy. I put all this at stake in that seemingly playful carefree hour on the river road.

It is a gamble I must take. No one can substitute for me in deciding for myself, in deciding on my life. No one can think for me. Nor needs to. Of the common man, Emerson said: "What Plato has thought, he may think; what the saint has felt, he may feel; what has befallen any man, he may understand."

This is my ball game to win or lose. And what I must deal with is not luck or chance, but choice. It is choice that is omnipresent in life, not chance. What I can see and feel and almost taste is choice. Choosing my self, my values, my universe. Choosing my own drama, my own life, my own heroism. Seeking through imagination and reason and intuition that unique something that I, and no other, am here to do.

No one ever said it was easy or safe. We have no contract with life. But neither are we here simply to avoid pain and enjoy pleasure. At some time or other, I must leave my childlike existence. However reluctantly, I must chance it and risk the contentment; knowing that to be reborn I must first be ejected from Paradise.

And knowing also that I may never come back. That I may wander forever in search of a self I will never find. Yet never being able to return to the easy theologies, the painless salvations I left behind.

I want no other choice. In this game, the only sure way to lose is to sit it out.

I am a lonely figure when I run the roads. People wonder how far I have come, how far I have to go. They see me alone and friendless on a journey that has no visible beginning or end. I appear isolated and vulnerable, a homeless creature. It is all they can do to keep from stopping the car and asking if they can take me wherever I'm going.

I know this because I feel it myself. When I see a runner, I have much the same thoughts. No matter how often I run the roads myself, I am struck by how solitary my fellow runner appears. The sight of a runner at dusk or in inclement weather makes me glad to be safe and warm in my car and headed for home. And at those times, I wonder how I can go out there myself, how I can leave comfort and warmth and that feeling of intimacy and belonging to do this distracted thing.

But when finally I am there, I realize it is not comfort and warmth I am leaving, not intimacy and belonging I am giving up, but the loneliness that pursues me this day and every day. I know that the real loneliness, the real isolation, the real vulnerability, begins long before I put on my running shoes.

The real loneliness begins with my failures as son, husband, father, physician, lover, friend. The real loneliness begins when those other gods have failed, the loved ones, the career, the triumphs, the victories, the good life.

The heartbreaking loneliness begins when I realize that no one can think for me; no one can live for me; no one can die for me. I can count on no one for help.

The true loneliness, then, is me seeing that nothing I do is true. Me and this inner emptiness, me and the abyss, me and the false me I am with other people, me being what I do, what I accomplish, the clever things I say. Me and that living of a lie, a long, lonely lifetime lie.

When I'm about overwhelmed by all this, I take this loneliness out on the roads, there to find my true self, to hear my own message, to decide for myself on my life. But most of all, to know certainty, to know that there is an answer even though I may never find it.

All this is not new. Hell may be other people, but the final enemy is within. "Will I always torment like this?" wrote Gide. "I worry from morning to night. I worry about not knowing who I will be: I do not even know who I want to be."

And then hear R. D. Laing, the psychiatrist: "Whoever I am is not to be confused with the names people give me or what they call me. I am not my name. I am a territory. What they say about me is a map of me. Where O! Where is my territory?"

When you see me, that lonely figure out on the road, I am looking for my territory, my self, the person I must be. There I am no longer the observer watching myself think and talk and react. I am not the person others see and meet and even love. There I am whole; I am finally who I am.

And there I encounter myself. That encounter is a deep place totally isolated which cannot be understood or touched by others, a place that cannot be described as much as experienced, a state that philosophers could define as solitude. It is no longer me and the abyss; it is me and my God.

But of course this is only the outline, the game plan. In actuality, it is not that easy. Like all pilgrimages, this one is filled with stops and starts, with peaks and valleys, with pains and pleasures. There are periods of depression and elation, times when I overflow with joy at this conjunction of action and contemplation. Other times when I am so tired I must stop and walk. But in that hour I know certainty. I know there is an answer to my odd union of animal and angel, my mysterious mixture of body and consciousness, my perplexing amalgam of material and spirit. And if for now that answer is only for the moment and only for me in my lowest common denominator, me the runner, it is still enough.

By abandoning myself to this, as Emerson said, by unlocking my human doors, I am caught up in the life of the universe. Then, finally, loneliness is dispelled. I know I am holy, made for the greater glory of my Creator, born to do His work.

Which for this day and this hour is running, a lonely figure on a lonely road.

When I became a runner, it seemed a small step to go from a sound body to a sound mind. Altogether natural that muscular strength be converted into virtue. That the ability to handle pain and fatigue would allow me to come to grips with guilt and anxiety. It seemed inevitable that the well-working body would become the well-working of the mind and the heart. And somehow necessary that the maximal steady physiological state should have its quickly attained psychological counterpart. Physical fitness, I thought, would give me back not only my body but my soul as well.

It never happened. As I became sound of wind and limb, as I neared my physical perfection, I became more and more aware of my mental imperfections. I was not normal, healthy and happy. I was, on the contrary, confused, angry, ambivalent, blaming others, denying responsibility. As my pulse slowed and my heart became more efficient, I knew my character to be a lie and my life style a shield from my own reality.

As my endurance increased and my performance improved, my day-to-day living became an ordeal of guilt and anxiety. Instead of life becoming routine and automatic and secure, I found myself unable to cope and adjust, and know now I never will. The normal life, I discovered, is for others, not me.

Meanwhile, my body went blithely on its way. I still run close to five minutes for the mile. At other distances, I am usually within a minute a mile of the winners. I sleep well and can eat anything this side of a bathtub stopper. My bowels are regular and I rarely have a headache or a muscle pain. My energy level is high enough to do anything I like to do for as long as I like to do it. My body is at the top of its powers. It is tuned to an exquisite clarity and has a wide range of perception.

But all this does nothing for my mental health. In fact, it probably helps destroy it. Mental health disappears when we see ourselves as we are. And my level of fitness has made me see myself as I am, warts and all. The intensity of my physical life tells me all the old sayings are true.

Sin *is* the failure to reach your potential. The answer to life *is* more life. You must seek the limits of the possible and then go beyond. Guilt *is* the unlived life. When I became fit and lean and uncompromising in my running, I saw myself as I really was without disguise or defense. I could no longer accept the person I had pretended to be. And I was unprepared to deal with the person I really was.

All of which means there are interesting years ahead.

There is at least one thing to be said for being a neurotic and living with guilt and anxiety: it is never boring. It may, in fact, be exasperating, especially for those around me who had to put up with my irrational discontent. The search for self-esteem, for the heroic action, by anyone as disorganized and transfixed by choice as I am, can occasionally push friends and family to verbal abuse. But there is no epithet I haven't already used on myself.

Still I know, and they should, that I will eventually find in real life the unity I feel during my hour's run on the roads. There I am in the palm of God's hand, running with my angel. And at those times I know what Yeats meant when he wrote: ". . . my body of a sudden blazed/And twenty minutes more or less/It seemed, so great my happiness/That I was blessed, and could bless . . ."

And then in the race I go through the penance of a three-mile run, accepting the painful grip of lactic acid and knowing what going without oxygen does. And at the end is the absolution, free from fear, free from anxiety. The marathon is much the same. A purgatory of mile on mile and then at the finish the peace beyond understanding. A time when even death becomes acceptable.

Those hours, those races, sustain me. The rest of the day, I am caught in my own inadequacy. So it seems that being sound of body does not automatically make you sound of mind. It may even delay the process.

But in the end, it is vital to the synthesis of body and mind and spirit that makes the whole person.

Until then, I am like Nijinsky. I am kept alive by movement. When I am immobile, I risk all that I am. Even my sanity.

My friend Tom Osler, who is a fifty-miler and teaches math at a state college, says that depressions are a part of life. The runner, he says, must expect them; even welcome them. They are just as normal, just as inevitable and just as necessary as the happy times.

And now in the depths of my semiannual, or is it quarterly, depression, I am inclined to agree. Periodically, no matter how I try to avoid it, I run myself into this growing inner discontent. Every six months or so, I develop this feeling that every task is too difficult to do and not worth the effort anyway.

My running suffers most. In fact, it is the first indication that things are amiss. I no longer look forward to my daily run. And should I ignore this lack of zest and run anyway, I tire easily and don't enjoy it. But the running and this loss of enjoyment are only part of it. My emotions, my moods, my concentration, my attention span, my attitude toward myself and others are all affected. Instead of battling anoxia and lactic acid and muscles depleted of sugar, I am in hand-to-hand combat with dejection and dependency, with rejection and self-pity, with guilt and loneliness. I am truly in the dark night of the soul.

In the real night, I awaken repeatedly for no apparent reason. And in the morning I am not refreshed or ready for the new day. I would like to pull the covers over my head and wait for this terrible state to pass over.

Is all this something inevitable, as Osler states? Or is it simply because I have run myself into some temporary physical state? And could I not, with a little prudence, avoid all these unnecessary sufferings?

I think not. Such periods are inescapable. Ecclesiastes was right. There is a time for everything. A time for running. A time not to run. Human nature frowns on prudence. It demands that we maximize ourselves. That whatever we do, we do it with all our might. And, predictably, this means periodic exhaustion, periodic failure, periodic depression and, as happily, periodic reevaluation.

I am now in those days of Ecclesiastes. "The fine hammered steel of woe," Melville called this book. I believe it. Now words cannot describe the weariness of things, and days give me no pleasure. And now it does

442

seem as it did to him that "all effort and achievement come from man's envy of man."

The peculiarity, as Ecclesiastes noted, is that these depressions occur not when things are going badly, but when they are going well. Not in times of failure, but in times of triumph. These depressions are not preceded by tragedy, but by celebration. Not by the worst race I have run, but by the best.

Less than two weeks ago, I ran a taxing and courageous and outlandishly fast ten-miler in Central Park. I ran to my limits, met the challenges of several runners who might normally have beaten me; and then ran the last five miles faster than the first, never giving an inch to those trying to catch me. It was an hour and four minutes and fifteen seconds of being as good a runner as I could be.

Later, as I sprawled on a chair in the parish hall of the Church of the Heavenly Rest, watching my fellow runners fill up on coffee and doughnuts, I felt warm and tired and satisfied. I turned to a friend next to me and said, "George, right now I could pull the sword out of the stone."

Today, if I said that, it would be presumptuous. I have lost what Yeats called "radical innocence." But I know there is and there always will be a time of running. A time when running is enough. When it is enough to race the same races, run the same roads. Enough to live out the cycle upon cycle of the running year. And thereby to fulfill myself in the many ways I do when running is the focal point of my life.

But there is also a time of not running. Time to see that the good can be the enemy of the best. That it is not merely the trivial that clutters up my life, but the important as well. I have, as Anne Lindbergh wrote, a surfeit of treasures. And it is time for me to answer the question of Ecclesiastes, "What is best for men to do during their few days of life under the sun?"

If it were not for the depression, I would have thought that unanswerable question answered. But now I know that running is not enough. The answer "Sheehan's my name, running's my game" is not enough. There are more ways to understand life, it now appears, than running.

Or business or politics or the arts or the sciences, for that matter. I am reminded that Bernard De Voto once said to Robert Frost, "You're a good poet, Robert, but you're a bad man."

Perhaps he was and perhaps he wasn't. To me, it seems that could be almost anyone's epitaph, including my own. And my periodic depressions make me realize that life may well be a game, but God judges the player, not the performance.

Not the race, but the runner.

The enemy, as always, is within.

It is Christmas morning. The day the Word was made Flesh. The birthday of the Incarnation. The day of Joy to the World, peace on earth, goodwill toward men. And I am running my river road, celebrating my flesh, rejoicing in my nativity, experiencing my incarnation. I am finding my peace in the rhythm of my thighs and lungs and pulse. Discovering my joy bounding over hills of virgin snow.

Elsewhere, people of goodwill are exchanging gifts, going to worship, preparing feasts. The day wears a halo of compassion and love. This is the day of the family of man. A day no one should be alone. A day that reveals your view of yourself and your universe and your fellow man.

I am alone and happy with myself and my view of the universe. I occupy my body with delight. And the universe is not only the message, it is my medium. My body is made to accept the message, to create in the medium. I am slim with good legs and a small trunk, a social introvert but a biological extrovert. I resemble Martha Graham's description of the new dancers.

"They are built," she said, "more for air, swiftness, than for argument." And through the dance they discover themselves.

I am discovering myself on this run. Beginning again at the beginning. Beginning with my body; the body that Coventry Patmore called "creation's and Creator's crowning good . . . So rich with wealth conceal'd that Heaven and Hell fight chiefly for this field."

I begin to sing myself and hope, like Whitman, not to cease till death. And hoping always to find what others have and I have not, a faith in love.

Love requires muscles I have never used. It is not easy to make feeling somehow transcend itself to emotion and then further to tenderness and sometimes love.

It is even more difficult if you lack the buoyant enthusiasm so common in most people or the courage obviously resident in others. My dominant quality is neither enthusiasm nor courage; it is the power of relinquishment, of withdrawal, of doing with less. I avoid risk, and making myself vulnerable. I am unwilling to stake anything on anyone else. I live in a fantasy world shut off from other people.

Yet where I am now is no fantasy. It is beautiful and real and a delight. The snow crunches underfoot. The pure light of the sun flashes off the white surface, the sky is high and blue. The air is dry and clean in my lungs. My senses are filled with these realities, with the sound of my breathing, the soft noise of my passage. I am living time and I am living space. The time and space Blake described, when a pulsation of an artery is equal to six thousand years and where a space no bigger than a globule of a man's blood opens into eternity.

But it is a time and a space into which I will admit no other. I am still alone, not daring to let my solitude join another solitude. Still not having the patience, the forgiveness and the acceptance that living with and loving other people demands.

So, for this distance runner at least, the holidays are too much. When socialization and celebration are at their height, I am most miserable. When, in addition, gifts and in them the secret knowledge of the Other are exchanged, it becomes too much. I am inclined to rise in defense of Scrooge. Leave us alone in our misery. Let us work out our own salvation.

This Christmas morning, I run far from family and friends, hoping to see my path to what they already have. All the while knowing a freedom I would exchange only for the whole truth. Feeling a delight that I would risk only if there was a promise of eternity. Living with a peace that perhaps no one else can share.

Like other solitary men who concentrate on thought and imagination and self-analysis, I am afraid to invest myself in anything less than perfection either in an idea or in a person. Like them, I have a great need for affection, but cannot give it. I am fearful of not being loved, but even more frightened of having to love.

When I think on that, the running is not enough. I am alone and lonely running the river road.

I am in debt to anyone who can make me cry. To anyone who makes me know joy. I owe for those moments when I see the world beyond this world. And know that I am not a biological animal or a social animal, but a theological animal. That the answer to my existence must somehow contain God.

I met such a person last week. Miss Emily Dickinson. Or rather Miss Julie Harris as Miss Emily Dickinson. And for an hour and a half was in her company. A short way into those ninety minutes, I had given up any pretext of composure. I had stopped holding back the tears. I sat with handkerchief in hand, keeping Miss Harris and her Emily from becoming a blur on my TV tube.

"I know it is poetry," Emily had said, "if I feel physically as if the top of my head were taken off." My ways may be different, but they are just as physical, just as uncontrollable. When I am in the presence of poetry and genius and the real world we came from, I know it. When I see clearly life is not a biological game or a social game or a political game, but a theological game, I know it, too. And know it with every blood vessel and nerve ending and muscle fiber in my body.

Emily played that theological game. Reduced the world to herself, her family, nature and God. The longest trip she took all day was from her bedroom door to the head of the stairs. Others have also taken that narrow focus. Rodin, for instance. He once told Rilke that he had read *The Imitation of Christ* and that in the third chapter wherever the text had the word "God" he had substituted "sculpture." It read just as well, he said.

So Emily took poetry and played her game with God. Emerson put it this way: "Take what you want, God said, and pay for it." But better would be to take what you want and play for it. The stakes? Your soul, yourself, your life. "I'll tell you what I paid," she wrote. "Precisely an existence."

And in the end she won, of course. She won the game with the "burglar, banker, father." She accepted Him and apologized with tongue in cheek "for Thine own Duplicity." She challenged, complained. Yet she knew that in heaven there would be a new equation. Somehow it would all be even.

But her answer here was to become as good at her game as God was. To approach His perfection by perfecting her imperfections. She knew all along that God is Himself a poet.

The runner knows God is a runner. "Some keep the Sabbath going to Church," Emily wrote. "I keep it staying at home." I keep it in company with some hundreds of others, running races in Central Park.

We congregate at the Ninetieth Street entrance, just north of the Guggenheim and across the street from the Church of the Heavenly Rest, our postrace meeting place. And we stand around like so many souls waiting in an antechamber while somewhere else the process of birth is about to happen.

446

The gun goes off. I have prepared for this race, known the ordeal to come. But it is always worse than I had imagined. Only a mile or so out and I wonder why I ever started.

I have sacrificed, denied appetites, fought desires, avoided pleasures for this? I am not only in pain, but I know it will last until the race ends. And, despite the effort, being passed and passed, continually losing ground. Can this possibly be the thing I do the best?

And then, a mile or so farther, a worse temptation. To quit. No one will know. Quitting does not mean stopping. It means giving just a little less than my limit. Slowing the pace to where I can breathe without pain and where the legs (is it possible?) feel comfortable.

And then it is over. The last stretch is survival, a counting of each step, head down, not daring to see how far it is to the finish line. But when I finish, I know what it is to race 6.2 miles in thirty-seven minutes and eleven seconds. What it is to go to the absolute limit. What this biological theological animal can do.

I have made my move. I await His. I am with the others in the Heavenly Rest. Purified. At peace. The appetites no longer appetites. The desires no longer desires. Tea is enough. And the Other becomes someone to touch and embrace and congratulate. The body becomes a person, my neighbor.

A very small life, you might say. So was Emily's. Yet so full I can but envy her. Others, of course, see it so empty they can feel only pity. She saw no moor. Saw no sea. Saw few people. The few she loved died. But all the while, she played her game with God. Put out the pieces every day and took her position. Made her move and waited for His.

And for me on the way home, the Turnpike clouded with my tears, Amherst, Massachusetts, a century ago seems but minutes away.

I have raced and I will be back next week. This week coming, I will be a sinner. I will know food. Give in to the body. Ignore beauty. Forget truth. This week, God will be burglar, banker, father.

But come Sunday, He will be my friend and lover, and runner. And I will beat Him at my game. And I'll know it if I do. Because I will end in tears. I will know joy. And I will feel as if the top of my head were taken off.

447

18

Seeing

**And in those moments
there is a light and joy and understanding.
For a time, however brief, there is no confusion.
I seem to see the way things really are.
I am in the Kingdom.**

WE WERE NOT created to be spectators. Not made to be onlookers. Not born to be bystanders. You and I cannot view life as a theatergoer would, pleased or displeased by what unfolds. You, as well as I, are producer, playwright, actor, making, creating and living the drama on stage. Life must be lived. Acted out. The play we are in is our own.

There are reasons, of course, to observe others. To learn how something is done. And to see the human body or soul or intellect in its perfection. We watch others so that their skill becomes our skill, their wisdom becomes our wisdom, their faith becomes our faith. But eventually we must go it alone. Find our own skill, our own wisdom, our own faith. Otherwise we will die without having learned who we are or what we can accomplish. And we will die without having an inkling of the meaning of it all.

I look for those answers on the roads. I take my tools of sight, hearing, touch, smell, taste and intellect and run with them. And I leave behind whatever I own, forgetting whatever I thought valuable, whatever I held dear. Naked, or almost, I come upon a new world. There on a country road, moving at eight miles an hour, I discover the total universe, the natural and the supernatural that wise men speculate about. It is a life, a world, a universe that begins on the other side of sweat and exhaustion.

I am purified by that sweat. I am baptized in my own water. I move again through a new Eden. I am fallen man restored, not yet knowing he will fall again. For now, at least, I am a child at play, at home in a home made for me. I am saturated with the goodness of the world, filled with the sight and the sound and the smell and the feel of the land through which I run. I sing with the poet Hopkins, "What I do is me; for this I came."

But then comes the Hill, and I know I am made for more. And by becoming more, I am challenged to choose suffering, to endure pain, to bear hardship. And in that becoming, I must live the mysteries of Sin and Free Will and Grace. All this I feel as I leave the beautiful endless time of running on the flat to risk everything on the ascent of the Hill.

At first the gentle swell carries me. At that level, nature is a help. The same nature which Bucky Fuller says is so prepared for us that whenever we need anything we find it has been stockpiled from the beginning of time.

But gradually the Hill demands more and more. I have reached the end of my physiology. The end of what is possible. And now it is beyond what I can stand. The temptation is to say, "Enough." This much is enough. But I will not give in.

I am fighting God. Fighting the limitations He gave me. Fighting the pain. Fighting the unfairness. Fighting all the evil in me and the world. And I will not give in. I will conquer this hill, and I will conquer it alone.

Of that moment, Kazantzakis tells a story: When God was asked when he would forgive Lucifer, He replied, "When he forgives Me." Kazantzakis in *Report to Greco* made his own Ascent, leaving, as he said, "a red track made by drops of my blood." And finding in the crucifixion the strength to persevere.

I cannot live the life of this genius. My Hill is but a mound to his mountain, my pain a shadow of his torment, but the human mystery is still there.

And still striving for that impossible summit. I forgive God. I accept the pain. I pass the crest. And for the briefest of eternities, I am God's child, brother to Christ, filled with the Holy Ghost.

The world belongs to those who laugh and cry. Laughter is the beginning of wisdom, the first evidence of the divine sense of humor. Those who know laughter have learned the secret of living. Have discovered that life is a wonderful game.

Crying starts when we see things as they really are. When we realize with William Blake that everything that lives is holy. When everything is seen to be infinite and we are part of the infinity. Tears come when we are filled with the joy of that vision. When we finally and irrevocably say yes to life. When we reach past reason and logic and know that the test of what we do and how we do it is delight.

For most of us these feelings are long in coming. We fail to touch or hear or see the real world. "Anything can make us look," writes Archibald MacLeish; "only art makes us see." Art and other things, but more of that later. We do not see because we are occupied with the doing and the getting and the spending. With Blake's unholy things, the lethargies, the cruelties. We fail to love. We lack passion. We feel no urgency. We have no intensity. We possess no enthusiasm.

This is as evident from our faces as our souls and intellects. George Burch, the cardiologist, once remarked that watching the expressions of the people on the street made him pessimistic about the medical profession being able to help them in any way.

Yet each of us, if Blake is right, has the faculty of seeing things as they really are. The visionary faculty is a natural gift. But this perception must be cleansed, otherwise we remain in the world of reason and mortality. This cleansing, it seems to me, must start with a cleansing discipline, a purifying effort. And for me, that means running, distance running.

Running keeps me at a physical peak and sharpens my senses. It makes me touch and see and hear as if for the first time. Through it, I get past the first barrier to true emotions, the lack of integration with the body. Into it I escape from the pettiness and triviality of everyday life. And, once inside, stop the daily pendulum perpetually oscillating between distraction and boredom.

But most of all, running gives me that margin Colin Wilson spoke of in *The Outsider*. There is a margin, he wrote, that can be stimulated only by pain and inconvenience, but which is indifferent to pleasure. It is only after that pain and inconvenience, after that challenge, that occurs the momentary and passing clarity in which things are seen as they eternally are.

Of all this, Blake is the great reporter. When asked if he saw the sun as a great red disk, he said: "Oh, no, no. I see an innumerable company of the heavenly host crying: "Holy, holy, holy, holy is the Lord God Almighty." No wonder his wife, when asked about him, said she never had much time to talk to him. "Mr. Blake," she said, "is almost always in Paradise."

For me such moments come more easily now. Goodness and truth and beauty suddenly possess me. I am surprised by joy, filled with delight, and there is nothing to do but exult in tears. And I think of Housman, who said he was careful not to think of a poem while shaving, lest he cut himself. And I must be careful while in company not to think on my dear dead friends who wrote so truly and so beautifully of what moved them to tears, lest I be thought senile and childish sitting there weeping.

On my runs, I am not so constrained. They have become shameless hours with tears streaming down my cheeks. I am now one with Nietzsche, who wrote of being unable to leave his room for the "ridiculous reason" that his eyes were swollen. "I have wept so much on my walk the day before," he wrote, "not sentimental tears, but tears of joy. I sang and cried out foolish things. I was full of a new vision."

Such tears cannot be manufactured, neither in myself nor in those who wrote for me or for you reading this piece. "If you would have me weep," wrote Horace, "first you must grieve yourself." Only someone who has wept in joy and truth and beauty, who has had the vision, can make us weep also. Only those who have gone through the cleansing and purification in a long apprenticeship of discipline and effort can speak to our innermost hearts.

The total process is perhaps best described by poet John Hall Wheelock. "The long lonely effort and the self-discipline," he wrote, "are the poet's prayer that he may be the instrument of that voice [the voice of the race or the unconscious in all of us]. And thereby to speak words and wisdom beyond his own scope and clairvoyance."

The world belongs to those who make this effort. Those who laugh and cry, who sleep with the angels and, like Blake, are almost always in Paradise.

"Time and freedom," wrote Nikolai Berdyaev, "are the fundamental and most painful of metaphysical problems." But he reserved his most disturbing observations for the problem of time. "It is the child of sin," he states, "of sinful slavery, of sinful anxiety." And, in his way, he agrees with the words of Buddha: "As long as you are in time there's suffering."

But suffering we can take. It is the swing from boredom to anxiety, from depression to worry, that exhausts and defeats us. The sure knowledge that we can be much more than we are frustrates us.

But how does one get out of time? How does one escape from this slavery, this anxiety? How does one find his creativity? If the experts don't know, what are we common folk to do?

Well, I don't know about you, but when I have a problem, I run with it. And so on this clear October day I am heading north toward the Hook on the ocean road. Ready to live the questions. Trying to find answers. Searching for a new response to the human condition. For insights I am sure will not come through my senses or rational mind.

But at first the day floods my senses. The sky is as high as heaven. The bay and the ocean on either side are a deep blue to the horizon. I am framed in the bright whites and the clean colors that sea and sun and sand possess in the fall. There is a breeze at my back and the sun is warm between my shoulder blades. I am already bathed in pleasant sweat.

But now I begin to get beyond this sight and sound, of observing the road ahead and the water to the side. The running alone occupies me. Fills my awareness. I am a steady flow. I am pure involvement. Total concentration. I am comfortable, calm, relaxed, full of running. I could run like this forever.

And during all this I narrow my consciousness to the immediate moment. I am moving from time measured to where time stands still. I am giving up past and future for this now. I am leaving the linear time where my footsteps are a metronome, my pulse and respirations are in harmony, and every eight minutes I move my body one mile.

And for a while I alternate. Briefly, I return to sweat and movement and sun warm between my shoulder blades, the sight of sea and sky. Then once again I am in the now, the eternal present where literally nothing happens. I am suspended, content with the nothing. And the peace that comes with it.

And that perhaps is the essence of the running experience for me, and any number of different experiences for other people. The lack of anxiety, the complete acceptance, the letting go and the faith that all will be well. In running, I feel free. I have no other goal, no other reward. The running is its own reason for being.

And I run with no threat of failure. In fact, with no threat of success. There can be no consequences to make me worry or doubt. I am secure whatever happens. And in that security I reach a wholeness that I find nowhere else.

I have moved that little more out of the nothing into the now, the present moment that Aldous Huxley said was the only aperture through which the soul can pass out of time into eternity. That may or may not be. I do think there is aperture and when I run I move through it into fields of words and thoughts, of ideas and concepts I was never conscious of before. And I plunder the past of my race in this place which is outside of time.

And when I once again feel sweat and movement, once more see water and sky, I am a quarter of a mile farther on. My body is always on time and it stays on course. But somewhere on the way to the Hook, I

453

have escaped guilt for the past and boredom in the present and anxiety for the future.

I have, as the poet Blake sang, held infinity in the palm of my hand and eternity in an hour.

For most of us, the meaning of life will remain obscure this side of the resurrection. Until then, what we do know or believe must be conceived in contemplation and born in action. It must be given substance by our bodies. Fleshed out by our flesh.

It has to be a total intellectual and spiritual and physical reaction to the human predicament. Which is no less, as Ortega said, than the perpetual surprise of existing without any previous consent on our part, castaways on an unpremeditated globe.

These reactions are sometimes thrust upon us. When we are in danger, for instance. When we are, as the Spanish saying goes, "between the sword and the wall." G. K. Chesterton reported on such an experience in a runaway hansom cab. "I had, so to speak," he wrote, "five religions in as many seconds." He went, he said, from pure pagan fear to what he hoped was Christianity.

But all such revelations need not begin in fear. Need not be set in action by the thought you have only a minute or hour or day or six months to live. They may, as I have discovered, occur in the course of an afternoon's run.

Before I run, I am a Cartesian. The body is simply a machine. I must take it for a run and tune it up. I must improve my body so that I can fulfill my real purpose, which is to think. It isn't until I get on the roads that I know again, as I have known for fifteen years, that I am my body and I am my soul, and I exist as a totality.

At first, however, I am all body. Where finally I hope to become aware of the surrounding universe and the self and finally my place in the scheme of things, I am now completely occupied with my body.

Finding rhythm and speed. Making adjustments for wind and hills, for heat and humidity. Attending to the sensations from feet and joints and muscles. I am a thinking animal using my brain instead of my mind.

Then, quite mysteriously, I am in the second wind. Like a jet suddenly settling into cruising speed after the surging of the takeoff, my running becomes easy, automatic. It has become play. And I have moved from being animal to being a pleasure-seeking adult. A castaway enjoying what he can.

But that euphoria, that glow, passes. The running asks for effort. It is no longer easy. The next quarter hour will demand more and more. I will be tempted to turn and head back to town. Being human, it seems, is more than enjoyment, more than pleasure. Life is also pain. And because of that, it is perplexity, essential and continual perplexity.

Some of that perplexity clears when I reach the third wind. The second wind is physiological and has to do with the heart and blood vessels and core temperature. The third wind, which comes after half an hour, is psychological, and has to do with the mind and the spirit, with joy and peace, with faith and hope, with unity and certainty.

Sometimes, this state, this awareness, comes at the best part of my run. I am at the crest of my hill, looking down on my river and seeing in the distance my town, where people are right now working and sustaining life, theirs and mine.

And now that hill becomes every hill, the river every river, the town every town, and the people all humanity. And in those moments there is a light and joy and understanding. For a time, however brief, there is no confusion. I seem to see the way things really are. I am in the Kingdom.

Just once, I have gone beyond this. My running became my offering. A dozen years of training and discipline, hours upon hours of perfecting the art and purifying the artist, came to this: I was a child before his Father, offering what I did best. Asking that my Father be pleased. That I be accepted. And I found myself, this little child, with tears streaming down my face, running the river road back to town.

A happy few have known it all. Have known that acceptance. Hear the words of Aquinas, who said all his work was straw. And the words of Pascal: "From about half past ten in the evening to about half an hour after midnight. Fire. God of Abraham. God of Isaac. God of Jacob. Not the God of philosophers and scholars. Absolute certainty; beyond reason. Joy. Peace."

We begin in the body and end in the Vision.

The flight home was depressing. The weekend in Crowley, Louisiana, had been a peak experience. Had been, in fact, a climax of my life as a runner and as a writer, and perhaps as a person. I had worn the number

455

"1" in the National AAU Championship Marathon and finished in the top third of the field.

Before the race, runner after runner had come and shook my hand, saying, "Dr. Shee-han, I loved your book and just want you to know it." One said he had given eighteen copies as Christmas presents. All weekend, they sought me out to tell me how much I helped them.

Later, at the awards dinner, I was given a plaque. I was, the inscription said, the outstanding distance runner of the year. A similar plaque the previous year had said the same thing about Frank Shorter. I was being classed with the immortals. And then, as a final gesture of esteem, I was permitted to talk.

The talk was more than a talk. It was a love affair. I spoke to each face in turn. And saw in each a reflection of my feeling for them. I told them of the beauties of our bodies, and how we needed play. I told them we were all to be heroes in some way and if we were heroic enough we would see God.

And when I finished, I was in tears and so were they. And then we all stood and applauded who we were and what we had done and the feeling that was in that great room.

And now I was flying away from all that. Flying toward what? Where was I to go from here? What was there to reach for that would surpass where I had been? Where would I get the size and strength and presence to be more than I was that day?

Life, I saw again, was a problem that will never be solved. At no time is this more evident than when we are close to the solution. No time more evident than when we succeed. When we have come far, but not far enough.

The wise men have spoken of this. For every hundred men who can handle adversity, they concluded, there is but one who can handle success. Flying home, I knew I was not that one. My elation had disappeared. I was fearful of the future. I had exhausted my potential and could see nothing ahead but repeating what I had already done. Doing the few things I did well over and over again for the rest of my life.

The man next to me was a runner who had completed his first marathon. "What do I do now?" he asked, echoing the thought in my mind. His answer would be my answer.

What do I do now? More of the same, only better. Run another and learn that much more about myself and the world and Who made me.

Run another and another. Bathe myself in pain and fatigue. Reach for energies I have yet to use. Run another and another and another. Make my truth out of that experience, out of what happens.

What do I do now? No matter what I have done, there is still more to do. No matter how well it has been done, it can still be done better. No matter how fast the race, it can still be run faster. Everything I do must be aimed at that, aimed at being a masterpiece. The things I write, the races I run, each day I live. There can be no other way.

I thought then of the ancient Egyptians who believed there was a judgment after death and the initial step was to weigh the heart. It seems so true. The heart is the measure of our energy, our courage, our intuition, our love. It is the measure of our days, of what we have done, of who we are.

Was I ready, then, to have my heart weighed? Was this as far as I would go? Was I ready to rest, to obey the commandments and await my reward?

The plane was bringing me back to earth. Without thinking, I took my pulse. A slow, steady forty-eight, and only a day after a marathon. And I knew then, as every runner knows, my heart is capable of anything. All it asks is the time to do it.

When I have run my best marathon and written my best piece and done my best deed of love for myself and my neighbor, I know the cry will still come from my heart: "There is more, there is more. I Who have made you know." What else is a heart for, then, but to be uneasy, to ask for what seems impossible, and never be satisfied? So my heart will be restless until it finds its final rest.

Then they can weigh it.

B O O K

This Running Life

DRAWINGS BY MONICA SHEEHAN

To my readers
who have thought what I have thought,
felt what I have felt,
and already know what I attempt here
to put into words.

CONTENTS

PART

The Body

IN THE OLDEN DAYS of radio a famous show called "Duffy's Tavern" featured a bartender-philosopher named Archie. One of Archie's patrons was Finnegan, an amiable, simple-minded character, who would greet Archie with the question: "How are things in the world, Arch?" The reply, from a man who knew men and had seen all kinds, was "Your world or ours, Finnegan?"

In a sense, each of us is Finnegan. We each occupy a different world, a world that is separate and distinct from any other. "No two men," writes philosopher Maurice Friedman, "are ever in the same situation." Each brings a unique body-mind-spirit totality to his decisions about life's values and his own various options.

Three decades ago, psychologist William Sheldon developed a system for classifying human differences. According to Sheldon, each person could be pinpointed on a chart in relation to three physical and three closely related psychological components. Sheldon gave the physical components the names of *endomorphy* (predominantly soft and rounded), *mesomorphy* (hard, big-boned and strong-muscled) and *ectomorphy* (slender and small-boned with stringy, weak muscles).

The endomorph leans psychologically toward *viscerotonia:* love of food, ceremoniousness, childhood and family, sociability and people. The mesomorph's temperament is *somatotonic.* He loves muscular activity, is aggressive, indifferent to pain, courageous, competitive and needs action when in trouble. The ectomorph is *cerebrotonic.* His world is mental. He wants to live and let live. He is nervous, shy, moody, inhibited. He hates loud noises and the bellowing of the mesomorph, and has no patience with the endomorph's love of luxury and ceremony.

Basic Temperamental Traits

Viscerotonia- endomorphy (Circular type)	Somatotonia- mesomorphy (Triangular type)	Cerebrotonia- ectomorphy (Linear type)
Dependent	Dominant	Detached
Relaxed	Assertive	Tense
Calm	Confident	Anxious
Kind	Aggressive	Considerate
Love of comfort	Love of risk	Love of privacy
Extrovert of affect	Extrovert of action	Introvert
Extensive rapport	Enduring rapport	Intensive rapport
Cheerful-depressed	Even-explosive	Hypersensitive- apathetic
Self-satisfied	Self-assured	Self-centered
Soft-tempered	Quick-tempered	Gentle-tempered
Complacent	Irascible	Reflective
Amiable	Talkative	Reserved
Warm	Active	Cool
Affected	Reckless	Suspicious
Tolerant	Energetic	Inhibited
Generous	Enterprising	Restrained
Forgiving	Outgoing	Precise
Needs people when disturbed	Needs action when disturbed	Needs solitude when disturbed
Stress on being	Stress on doing	Stress on perceiving
Lets things happen	Makes things happen	Watches things happen

Yet daily we endomorphs, mesomorphs and ectomorphs ignore these differences, and insist on asking other people how things are in our own private, personal, never-to-be-duplicated worlds. We are told the absolute, immutable truth in sports, politics, religion and art by people who never warn us: "Your world or ours, Finnegan?"

These same people guide us into mess after mess. We find ourselves at a play we dislike, a movie we can't stand, reading a book that puts us to sleep or secretly enjoying a game that others consider a waste of time. Even with recognized masterpieces, the range of public reaction may extend from one pole to the other, from adoration to repulson. Yet, oddly enough, the people with similar body builds have similar reactions.

Of course we need experts. There is too much to see and know without the help of experienced observers. But we must choose them well. There are times when I'm convinced that if you don't pick a rabbi, priest or minister with your own body statistics, you may end up wishing you were an atheist. That if you don't choose a movie critic with your own bone structure you'll miss the two pictures a year worth seeing.

"Life," wrote Ortega, "is a desperate struggle to succeed in being in fact what we are in design." Design is the word. What we are in design—bone, muscle and gut—determines our temperament and even our values.

In *Varieties of Human Values*, William Morris reports on a study in which different life styles were offered to students of all races and cultures. Surprisingly, he found that those people sharing the same body builds—whether Japanese, Danish, Indian, American or Canadian—opted for the same values. This suggests that the ectomorphic American distance runner relates much better to his foreign counterparts than to his nextdoor neighbors.

Me? I'm five feet, ten inches, weigh 135 pounds and have the bones of a chicken. That's the world you'll read about in this book.

1

The Design

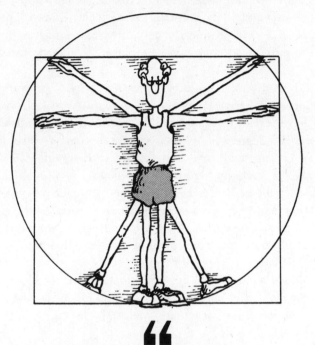

"

'Who is one truly,'
asked Abraham Maslow,
'if not first one's own body,
one's own constitution, one's own functioning?'
And how else is this to be learned
but by hearing those inner signals,
those directives from within,
the voice of the real self?

"

I WAS BORN A COWARD and by any normal standards still am one.

Function follows structure, says the rule of biology, and I don't have the structure to fulfill the function of the red-blooded American male. We all know what that function is: to face up to bullies, look your enemies in the eye and never retreat. Americans are supposed to work thirty hours a day, eight days a week; know what teamwork means; and rise from office boy to president. The United States of America expects you to be a hero, to stand up and be counted, to show the stuff you are made of.

I know the stuff I am made of: pipe-stem bones, an overbite and a long, tender nose. I have poor teeth, one slightly crossed eye, am tone deaf and have a pain threshold at the level of a firm handshake. I am constructed 180 degrees out of phase with the pioneer spirit, the daring do, the raw courage and the adventurousness that made America great.

Since man is a totality, a physical psychological whole, I have other drawbacks. I jump at loud noises, and when younger perspired if a girl entered the room, and was known to vomit if sent to the principal's office. I found early on that standing up to bullies meant either a blow to the nose, sending me into a black pit of indescribable pain, or a shot to the mouth, leaving my upper lip full of teeth.

We are built, wrote physiologist Walter Cannon, for fight or flight. I was built for flight, and nature never intended me to do anything else. I fulfill the function of my particular structure by taking to my heels when trouble brews.

But what American boy would accept that, or what American parent? Is it possible that someone can find contact sports painful to the point of nausea, get faint at the prospect of tackling a runner in the open field and still be all any American can be—a hero to himself? The answer is yes.

Take my operation, for instance. A gallbladder operation is an elective, clean, soft-tissue operation involving only minor trauma. Mr. Average American with his high pain threshold usually can breeze through the hospitalization part of gallbladder surgery—the part I don't want to talk about or even remember. The pain of those few days was beyond my imagination. I never knew such agonies existed. While others were grumbling about being kept in the hospital, I was still struggling to get out of bed.

Where I finally triumphed was during my post-operative recovery.

That's where being thin and bony came to mean something. That's where I outdistanced those muscular heroes who were packing their bags three days after leaving the operating room. That's where I found that physical cowards can handle pain—as long as it is self-inflicted. We can suffer and endure as long as the enemy is ourselves.

Ten days after my surgery, I started jogging. Less than three weeks after the surgery, I ran 35:01 in a five-mile race over very tough hills at Van Cortlandt Park. Within another month, I had brought that seven-minute-a-mile average down to 6:30 in a nine-mile race on the same course, my best time in three years.

Each race was as painful as any I can remember. The hills were almost unbearable. There were miles and miles of groans and gasps, interspersed with appeals to the Almighty. But that is something that happens almost every weekend in a runner's life. It is the kind of pain he can handle—and others can't.

Some muscular surgeons called my post-operative recovery "fantastic," but it was no odd or wonderful thing. It was just an ordinary accomplishment for thousands of distance runners who are constructed like I am. We would rather run twenty-six miles into a near-coma than be hit on the nose or even have someone threaten to hit us on the nose.

For runners, as for others, the first rule is to know that you are normal. To find this normal, you can use some rules suggested thirty years ago by anthropologist Earnest Hooten.

"The body," wrote Hooten, "will guide us most rapidly and unerringly to the mind and personality. Body structure affords the safest and most accessible takeoff for the exploration of individual personality."

Translated, this means that if you have a weak little body fit for running from fights and altercations, you should do so. Your body tells you who and what you are. If you listen well, you can be a success, perhaps a hero, even though no one else may be aware of it.

Just remember, function follows structure—and so does fulfillment.

"Know yourself."

What was written on the temple of Apollo, we must now write in even larger letters where we can see it every day. Know yourself, so you may live that life peculiar to you, the one and only life you were born to live. Know yourself, that you may perfect your body and find your play. Know yourself, that you are not only the patient but also the therapist. Know yourself, that you may accept that knowledge.

For the Greeks, the time for this discovery was leisure—a time that also included activities like health, self-expression, character formation, personality and self-adjustment. Included, of course, were play and the training of the body. We are, wrote Plato, playthings of the gods and life must be lived as play. The body, in Plato's opinion, was the source of all energy and initiative.

Therefore, we must know our body, its strengths, its weaknesses, its likes, its dislikes. Socrates stated that a sensible man should know what is good or bad for him better than any physician. And later, Tiberius said that anyone who had lived for twenty years should be able to take care of himself without a doctor.

We are, then, to become experts in ourselves. I should learn not from books or from others, but from my own experience. I should understand myself by self-study rather than by consulting the professional. The body is here to be seen. Visible, measurable, it delivers its message. Stripped down before a mirror, it reveals to me who I am.

Similarly, I can know my own temperament—that level of my personality where I express my desires and motivation and interact with other people. Here again, I am as circumscribed as I am in my body. I have a particular mixture of traits which I can change only in a very narrow range. Like me or not, I am what I am.

"My purpose," says sports psychologist William Beausay, "is to help the individual athlete improve performance through the knowledge of his own psychology and the way to get the most out of it."

That certainly sounds as if Professor Beausay is on the side of the angels. He is going to help us jocks "to know thyself" (Plato); "to be what thou art" (Nietzsche); "to be the self one truly is" (Kierkegaard).

The professor has tested middle linebackers and Indy 500 drivers, and has found them cut from the same cloth. They are nervous, depressed, dominant, hostile, aggressive and impulsive. They also perform beautifully. Beausay is nonjudgmental about these qualities. He is a pragmatist. The only way a linebacker can improve his dominance, hostility and aggressiveness is to be more dominant and hostile and aggressive. Beausay shows them how.

It is only when he turns to distance runners that he reveals his failure to grasp the true role of psychology. Distance runners, he reports, score surprisingly low in hostility and dominance. "Most runners," he states, "seem to be passive, submissive followers." But instead of developing these traits and making distance runners more of what they are, as he has the football players and race-car drivers, he would change them. He would give them the psychic attitude of the Indy drivers. "When that happens," he says, "the world mile record will come down a full 10 seconds."

I am sure that Professor Beausay believes this to be progress. Distance runners just have no business, he thinks, being tolerant and submissive. And so we are faced with the age-old problem where men of conviction, either religious or scientific, would populate the world with people who fit their idea of what is good or normal or successful.

Making runners hostile and aggressive (or football players passive and tolerant) is unnatural and completely counter to their temperament and personality. It is bound to fail. It would be easier to make a rabbit a killer. Unfortunately, this self-evident truth has escaped psychologist Beausay and indeed most of the scientific community. Its members continue to ply us with books explaining man as if he were some homogenous composition of traits and values instead of the infinite variety he is.

In the past this sort of thinking insisted on a single way to theological salvation. Now, it insists on a single way to social salvation. Beausay would have runners turn hostile and aggressive to break world records. Harvard Professor Richard Herrnstein would have them be hostile and aggressive to save our social structure.

Society, according to Herrnstein, thrives on our socio-economic competition. Should our disparities in wealth and status be eliminated we would, he predicts, have prompt social and economic disaster.

We distance runners certainly don't want Dr. Herrnstein's and our society to fail for want of aggressive, dominant, confident, adventurous and courageous men (and I'm sure it won't), but we shouldn't be expected to change our behavior to suit anyone's theory. And all those who delight in large family gatherings and love an evening at the theater should not be offended if we would rather spend those hours with a good book or on a solitary run.

We runners are not built for the rat race or the community of men. Turning distance runners who are made for flight and thought into fighters or socializers goes against nature.

475

* * *

Near the end of my hour's run on the river road is a long, steep hill. On certain days I see it in the distance, and remember its length and height and slope. Then, I think of the effort it will take and how I will feel at the top, and I wish I were already back in town, the run over, doing other things.

On those days, my mind is in command. I am a reasoning, calculating human being. I have forgotten I am also my body and that my body accepts such challenges. My body wants to be stretched as far as it can go and then stretched even further. I have forgotten that the body wants the best and the true just as much as my mind and heart do. It will not be satisfied until it has reached its limits. On those days, I am not a runner. I am a mind.

On other days, I gratefully accept the challenge. I run at the hill with all my might. I spend ninety seconds or more at flank speed with all systems at go. I let my body take control. Once having willed the action, I am content to receive the messages from the feet and legs and thighs, to hear from the heart and lungs and brain, to listen to why my body tells me, to listen but not to interfere.

It has taken years to reach this stage, to become a listener, to learn from my body and teach myself not to inflict my ignorance on it, to allow my body to seek its own perfection.

It takes that long to learn the craft, develop the technique, submit to the discipline. "What tedious training, day after day, year after year, never ending," wrote Emerson, "to form common sense." But after tedium comes enlightenment. Where the unaided intellect fails, the body now reveals. As I race up that hill, I am a pupil, an observer. My body is my tutor.

It is, after all, the finite body, my imperfect body, which is trying to express the infinite my soul would have me be. And it is the finite body which is the first to tell me who I am. Therefore, the mind's first step to self-awareness must be through the body.

"Who is one truly," asked Abraham Maslow, "if not first one's own body, one's own constitution, one's own functioning?" And how else is this to be learned but by hearing those inner signals, those directives from within, the voice of the real self?

In that long, painful surge as I attack that hill, I experience those signals, those directives, those voices. Now, instinct is in command, not reason. I am listening to a body which has taken complete control. On those days, I am not a runner. I am my body.

For a good part of my day, I am no more than a robot. My actions are pure reflex. My body is on automatic pilot. It is programmed to take care of the demands of my outer world while I escape to my inner one. For the better part of my time, I am like a captain who has given control of the ship to a junior officer and retired to his cabin to read his favorite author. I have made routine things in my day so routine that they get done without me being aware I am doing them. Unfortunately, things also don't get done, or are done badly, or done in the wrong place at the wrong time.

Some would say that this inattention to the ordinary requirements for maintenance and survival is due to my upbringing. It is true that I was spoiled by my parents. I have, in fact, never had to take care of myself. I went through my entire education, including college and medical school, without leaving home. Then, there was the Navy and officer quarters, and finally marriage.

I am, therefore, in terms of ability to survive, still an infant. My natural habitat is in someone's protective arms. I suspect, however, that even if I had taken to backpacking and become a mountain man, I would still be plagued by the effects of this retreat into the mind. I would right now be standing somewhere wondering how in the world I had gotten there and where in the world were those vital paraphernalia I had in my possession just a moment ago.

Whatever the reason, nature or nurture, my waking time is filled with excursions into the recesses of my mind. In the outer world, I am a reluctant citizen. I am continually breaking laws, both physical and social. When I am with my dear, dead friends in my head, I often pass my live ones with glazed eyes and not a sign of recognition.

My family has grown accustomed to this. My absentmindedness is now part of our tradition. I am expected to forget errands and birthdays and phone messages and the like. It causes no comment when I have no money for gas, or the restaurant bill, or the turnpike tolls. They are not surprised when I forget the names of their friends or even their own. They are not upset when I ask them to repeat a question. Hence, I am given only the simplest of tasks, the minimum of responsibilities. My family has arranged for life to go on, not without me but around me.

This works well until I get away from home. Away from home, I am a disaster. Every attempt, of course, is made to minimize what is in any case inevitable. I am sent off with a manilla envelope containing flight number and destination and the names of who will pick me up and who will deliver me, with all the correspondence about the meeting and the program which I had been meaning to read but never got around to. It also contains an absolutely essential piece of information—the title of my speech. As I enter my car, I am a sixty-year-old version of the first-grader going to school with a note pinned to his jacket.

The manilla folder works no better than the note. Before I sit down to read it, I must first get to the airport. That becomes a problem when I am leaving from Kennedy or LaGuardia because my body always drives to Newark. Having gotten to the correct airport and the right airline after another wrong turn or two, I may have to return to the car in the parking lot for my ticket, wallet or glasses, or all three.

One weekend, I went to Indianapolis with a physician friend from South Africa who is thirty years my junior. We were to do a sports medical clinic, and then go to Muncie to visit Dr. David Costill and his wife, Judy. By the time we reached Indianapolis, he had begun to assess the situation.

"George," he said, "from now on, I will be in charge of the tickets."

That took care of the tickets, but when we unpacked at the Costills' I was already missing my glasses and one yellow sock. By nightfall, I could not find a T-shirt I had received as part of the clinic and also the *Runner's World* shirt I had lectured in. Something odd was happening and I began to wonder about the Costill house. I was reminded of a home I stayed in at Crowley, Louisiana. When I reported a shoe missing at breakfast, I was told I would never find it. "This house," my hostess said, "eats things."

In the morning, I discovered it was me, not the house. The shirts were in a drawer. I had broken the basic rules of ineffectual losers on the road: One, do not unpack; and two, if you do, under no circumstances put things in drawers or hang them behind the door in the bathroom. Otherwise, instead of bringing home a memento, you will leave one.

Then, the glasses fell out of the shirt, so I was in good shape except for the yellow sock. I told Judy Costill about it as we left for a ten-mile run.

It was a tough ten. No reflex here. I went to the lead and resisted any

478

attempt to pass me. I was no longer reading in the cabin; I was at the helm. I was in charge. This was the type of survival that claimed my full attention, the kind of maintenance worth my total participation. I was in touch with myself and everything around me in that bright early-morning sunshine.

We came into the final quarter of a mile, running abreast now, still flat-out but feeling good. The gym came into sight and then a tiny cluster of people at the finish point. Right in the middle was Dave Costill, waving what appeared to be a victory flag. As I got closer, I could see what it was: a last-minute behind-the-bathroom-door find by Judy Costill—my pajama pants.

The yellow sock? It was in one of the shoes I had worn while speaking in Indianapolis. I found it when I got home.

2

The Fitness

"

Exercise to lose weight.
Run to lower your blood pressure.
Bicycle to reduce your cholesterol.
Swim to increase your cardiac function.
Play tennis to help your breathing.
Golf so you'll sell more clients.
Do calisthenics to clear your brain.
All those things are good.
But beyond all this fitness is
the discovery of who you are.

"

WE ARE BORN with a seventy-year warranty. Some of us, for genetic reasons, are slated for significantly longer lifespans. In any case, it would appear that this longevity quotient is predetermined. So why exercise? It is not going to change our life expectancy. It is time-consuming and frequently boring. It is, in a word, a bother. So why bother?

There are, it seems to me, a variety of reasons. Exercise may not lengthen our lifespan, but it will certainly combat the problems that are said to shorten it: hypertension, obesity, addiction to nicotine, high cholesterol. What we are coming to know is that the insurance against these risk factors is almost always diet plus exercise.

Dr. Ralph Paffenberger has reported evidence that 2,000 calories a week spent on some sweaty activity will significantly lower the risk of coronary artery disease. Weight loss, salt restriction and exercise are also the primary ways to control hypertension. Similarly, most drug-dependent diabetics can stop medication with weight loss, exercise and a complex-carbohydrate diet.

Exercise, therefore, takes you a long way toward realizing your total longevity quotient. In addition to its effects on such measurable things as weight, pulse, blood pressure, blood sugar and cholesterol, exercise has a psychologically beneficial effect on the desire for cigarettes and food. It substitutes a positive addiction that tends to build the body for a negative one that tears the body down.

But if you talk about life expectancy being altered by exercise, you can still get an argument. There is just not enough evidence to satisfy the scientist—enough, perhaps, for practitioners who mix art with science in treating patients, but not enough for those who understand statistics, programs and the necessity for conclusive experiments. Proof positive is still lacking.

If, however, by "life expectancy" you mean *what you expect out of life today*, there is no contest. Anyone who exercises regularly can attest to their increase in energy. In addition, there are physical and psychological changes that enable us to live life in full, to live at the peak of our powers.

That should be our aim: to live each day totally; to live it, as Marcus Aurelius said, as if it were to be our last.

Exercise, particularly exercise that is play, allows us to do that. Not only does it enable us to become totally fit, but it is accomplished in a playful activity which we would be willing to do on the day we die.

When exercise becomes play, it becomes a self-renewing compulsion. It becomes part of each day, part of your life. The fitness that ensues is simply a bonus. In fact, if fitness remains the primary purpose and the play is never discovered, in all likelihood the fitness program will fail. Only people with the proverbial gun in their ribs will persist. Only those under doctor's orders—because of a prior heart attack or some disease requiring exercise—will persevere in an activity that they find boring, mindless and time-consuming.

Play, of course, is quite the opposite. It occupies us totally, and time passes without our noticing it. Play is one of those peak experiences described by Abraham Maslow. It is the priceless ingredient in exercise. We should be like children at play.

Suppose you accept this thesis, acknowledge the need to play and the benefits of the exercise that comes with it. How would you find your play?

First, you must discover what you do best, which means analyzing your body structure. Function follows structure, so the body usually reveals how it functions best.

Having done that, you must analyze your temperament to see how you like to play. Are you built for flight, fight or negotiation? Is your tendency under stress to withdraw, to socialize or to become aggressive? Is your nature predisposed to detachment, dependence or dominance?

All of us have a little of each tendency in us, but one force is dominant and usually decides whether we prefer to play sports as a loner, or part of a highly social activity, or want to go head-to-head physically with an opponent. Fortunately, our structure usually goes along with these choices.

The solitary individual usually is thin-boned, stringy-muscled and equipped for endurance sports. He finds running an intensely satisfying exercise-play which indeed can become part of his life style.

The socializers may not be natural athletes. If their bodies possess neither strength nor endurance, they can still enjoy sports like golf, doubles tennis, cycling, skiing, skating and running. They are particularly good at aquatic sports. But the primary and engrossing part of their play-exercise is other people.

The hitters, on the other hand, need other people not as companions but as opponents. They play the big game in tennis, tend to increase the suspense in golf by betting and often become engaged in activities such as the martial arts, weight lifting and hitting the heavy bag.

Having begun with the question, "Why exercise?" we find that the answer is to be found in yet another question: "Why *play?*"

When we begin an exercise program, it is almost always for the wrong reasons. We seek physical fitness because we believe we *have* our bodies and want to do something to them, not because we *are* our bodies and wish to find out who we are.

It is an understandable error. Historically, society—the church, the school, the corporation—has taught us an abnormal view of the body. The preachers have warned us against the excesses of the flesh; that the body is an instrument of the devil, something to be disciplined and denied. The intellectuals have taught us that the body is a mere conveyance, a mundane vessel for the triumphs of the mind. Keep the body in repair and it won't bother our essential function, which is thinking. And what of businessmen? They have perceived the body as a machine, a tool. Fitness makes us better workers, improves our output.

The body, then, has been treated as a second-class citizen. Anyone who would think otherwise must develop his own rules, come to a different view of the universe. He must question what he hears from the pulpit, wonder how his childhood teachers could miss the point, and look on the laws of supply and demand as necessary only for the preservation of the herd. He must somehow discover that his body is equal with his soul.

Oddly enough, this unity occurs most readily in play and sports, and in those exercise programs where the magical and the mystical have taken over from the practical and the pragmatic. We should know, as Ortega said, that life demands two different kinds of effort—one stemming from sheer delight, originality, creativity, vitality, spontaneity; the other effort ruled by compulsion, obligation, utility. The former is sport, the most important part of life. The latter, work or labor, ranks second.

Ortega concludes, "Life . . . resides in the first alone; the rest is relatively mechanical and functioning."

The millions who get into exercise programs will succeed or fail, therefore, inasmuch as they move beyond the details of fitness—beyond tables and charts and schedules—and into the vital, creative area of play. Beyond fitness itself, everyone is a child—a child at play but also a child, as Blake said, grown wise.

The truth is that play is where we live. In running and climbing and swimming, in hunting and fishing, in riding horses and playing games we become ourselves and open ourselves to experience. There, we find an inward calm and peace. There, thinking and feeling have a clarity that occurs almost nowhere else. And there, we discover a wholeness, a completion and an integrity that makes us want to celebrate our being. Away from daily life, away from politics and religion, from economics and science, we see the universe and ourselves as being much more than logic and reason have taught us.

Exercise to lose weight. Run to lower your blood pressure. Bicycle to reduce your cholesterol. Swim to increase your cardiac function. Play tennis to help your breathing. Golf so you'll sell more clients. Do calisthenics to clear your brain. All those things are good. But beyond all this fitness is the discovery of who you are.

The written word must be suspect. If you are denied truth firsthand, however, make sure the truth you get is no worse than secondhand. If you are going to rely on an expert, let him speak directly to you and not through someone else. If you read about something outside of your experience, be sure you read the original and not the commentary.

One instance where the commentary missed the truth of the original was the press treatment of an article on running that appeared in *Physician and Sportsmedicine.* Written by Dr. William Morgan, a psychologist, the article was titled, "Negative Addiction in Runners." That title, which conveys less than half the story, caught the attention of the press. What followed was a nationwide warning about the dangers of running.

The *Chicago Tribune,* for example, led off its review of the Morgan report in this fashion: "A growing number of joggers and runners are becoming so addicted to their foot-pounding pursuits that they are developing the same kind of problem as heroin users."

After this opening came a litany of the disorders caused by the search for a running "fix," as well as a list of withdrawal symptoms which occur when these addicts are unable to run.

But as I read the original research report on what the newspapers would have me believe is self-destruction, I saw only the positive aspects of running. By the time I had finished reading "Negative Addiction in Runners," I was convinced that running is a *positive* not a negative addiction. Reading between the lines, I perceived running as an affirmative discovery of the self.

Morgan, you must understand, was not out to condemn running. His previous research had convinced him of the beneficial effects of exercise, especially on depression. All of his earlier studies had been positive. This treatise was simply about runners who tended, in his opinion, to carry running a bit too far. But then, we always have been aware of this tendency. Man is a maximizer, ripe for excesses and exuberances. When life becomes a celebration, we are likely to over-celebrate.

Let's look more closely at what Morgan has to say before forming a judgment.

"I would like to suggest that running be viewed as a wonder drug." Morgan takes his stand immediately. Running is good for you. It is one of the great scientific breakthroughs of the century. It can be a panacea not only for the body but for the mind as well. But as with all therapy, you must tailor the dose, beware of abuses, avoid the bad reaction. Then, running not only restores your health; it adds to it.

"Exercise makes people feel good. No wonder they get addicted to it." That is, of course, the addiction we need—a positive one, a self-renewing compulsion to do what is good for us. The difference between running and drugs is the absence of fantasy. The good feeling in and from running is no delusion. It is an accurate perception of what is actually taking place in our whole being—body, mind and spirit.

"We begin running just to stay in shape, but soon we are seduced by the sense of clarity, energy and self-esteem accompanying the daily run." This is the good news. A true clarity, energy and self-esteem, not a false one, is available to us out on the roads. What we are seduced by are the negative addictions which destroy our bodies, and our minds and souls with them. Running is a purifying discipline.

"The running experience should not become an end in itself, because at this point runners may lose perspective, internalize questionable priority systems and place self above everything else." Runners, of course, see it differently. Running is an end in itself, as well as a means. It does

change our perspective. It does give us the sense of humor to see ourselves as we never have before. And it does drive us to adjust our priorities toward our own truths and rules and roles, not those thrust upon us.

We do move inwardly, but only so we can later move outwardly toward union with others; so that the self we destroy is the false one we have been carrying all these years, the one that is no longer necessary.

Thoreau went into the woods because he feared that when he came to die he would discover that he had not lived. He wanted to live deeply and suck the marrow out of life. Each of us has the same fear, the same desire. And we also know there are experiences that are, as Thoreau said, "indescribable, infinite, all-absorbing, divine, heavenly pleasure."

But Thoreau also wrote, "I looked to books for some recognition of kindred experience, but strange to say I found none."

The printed word rarely matches the experience.

"Exercise addicts," wrote William Morgan, "give higher priority to their daily runs than job, family and friends. They run first, and then if time permits they work, love and socialize."

But surely that is the correct sequence. First come fitness and play, energy and self-discovery. We must first be made whole. Then, we can return to the busy world of affairs. We must first go back to being a child before we can do those adult things.

Still, the runner's attention to self bothers Morgan. "As the runner becomes more aware of the self," he warns, "there is less interest in vocational achievement."

The key word here is "vocation." What indeed is my calling? And if I am responding to that call, am I capable of meeting the demands it makes?

Chances are, the runner's search for self will also reveal which work will be a witness to that self. The chances also are that running will lead to true achievement in whatever that field is. It will, if nothing else, lead to looking at all day-to-day activities from a new point of view.

"Genius," said William James, "is just another way of looking at things." Running develops our particular and peculiar genius, and gives us the audacity to put that vision into action.

When Bill Rodgers was teaching school, he ran during most of his free time. One day, the principal called him into the office. "Bill," he told him, "you will have to make a decision. The time has come to concentrate on your vocation." Rodgers took his advice. He quit teaching. He had arrived at a point described by Morgan:

> Monetary rewards become irrelevant to the exercise addict, who has moved in an inward direction, become quiescent, at terms with his environment, at peace with himself. Such a point of view may not only limit professional growth, but it can actually jeopardize one's employment.

But personal growth must precede professional growth. What you do in your profession is a function of the person you are. That must, therefore, be your top priority.

What is personal growth? I like something Robert Frost wrote in his account of an all-star baseball game. What those athletes demonstrated, he said, were the four attributes needed for any achievement: prowess, courage, justice and knowledge.

Running is my means to those ends. Training gives me the prowess, the race gives me courage. And then I begin to see what justice means —being true first to myself, extracting every ounce out of every talent I possess, and then being true to others and to my profession. I know that job, family, friends will wait while I run. In fact, they must await the outcome of my runs. And that outcome depends upon the lifetime that is in every day of running.

So there it is. Can anything have a higher priority than running? It defines me, adds to me, makes me whole. I have a job and family and friends who can attest to that.

It was inevitable that we would see articles in the magazines and the press taking a negative view on running. The pendulum always swings. Each action provokes a reaction: The "outs" become the "ins," the rebels become the Establishment, ripe for attack.

In the beginning, when running was first catching on, the press was filled with enthusiastic articles extolling the virtues of the sport. Journalists are sensitive to enthusiasm. They have antennae that pick up any electricity being generated in the community. They could sense a new idea developing, so they made running the darling of the media.

But every enthusiasm provokes an inescapable backlash. Innovation which generates sympathy becomes orthodoxy which stimulates criticism. The sport for the lonely long-distance runner became the sport of the masses. It became fair game, and also interesting reading to knock its hat off.

The journalists at both ends of this process, and also those who read them, miss the point. Running, which was originally praised for the wrong reasons is now damned for shortcomings most runners would see as only incidental problems.

Journalists, you see, are much like trial lawyers. They are forced to become instant experts in the subject at hand. They acquire masses of information. Then, they have to digest this data and process it into readable prose. The end result is the map, not the territory. It is the menu, not the meal. It is truth secondhand.

We will never discover truth secondhand. If I am to write the truth or know it when I read it, I must first live it. I must touch it, taste it, smell it and hear it. I have to sense it, become aware of it, give it my unmixed attention.

We cannot delegate that instruction to anyone else—not to the journalists, not even to the experts. I cannot understand something I have not gone through myself. I must live my own causes and then experience my own effects. This is a never-ending, ever-changing process. Whatever conclusion I come to today, I will undoubtedly modify tomorrow. I can never make the absolute statement.

Journalists, like trial lawyers, want none of that. They want to simplify, not amplify. They want yes-and-no answers. They are looking for the nonexistent final and definitive word on the subject. So, no matter how sincere, how open, how willing to present both sides, the journalists are bound to fail. They truly do need "inside" information.

I had a reporter call me for help in writing an article about running a marathon. While talking to him I realized it was an absurd situation. I should have been writing the article, not him. Eventually, he would have to edit my words, then filter my experience through his own experience, and he could not do that.

Knowledge, the philosophers say, is a function of being. There has to be a change in the being of the knower for there to be a change in the nature and amount of knowing.

Emerson said it plain: "What we are, that only we can perceive."

488

If I wish to understand running and runners, I must first become a runner myself. I must go through at least the minimum of the sensations and the excitements and the fulfillments of the runner's life. I must live with some program involving effort and discipline, fatigue and pain. I must experience the "feel" of running.

How, then, can we evaluate critical articles on running, or indeed on any human activity? Most important is to be sure the writer is writing from inside the subject rather than outside.

3

The Cures

Peguy, the French philosopher,
said that we die of our entire life.
We live of it, too.
Everything we do is important,
and even more when we are living with a disease.
For then we especially need that
background of sanity and serenity and good humor
conferred on us by vigorous exercise.

"

A FRIEND IN DALLAS gave me a watch. I had gone without one for more than a decade and had done nicely. I had handled my day without a watch and felt no need for one. I had, in fact, lost my watch while raking leaves one day and had not raked leaves or worn a watch since. I believe, you see, in signs.

Nevertheless, I took the new watch. He is a good friend and was quite insistent. He actually took it off his wrist and put it on mine. So I let it stay. Besides, it is a marvelous instrument—one of those modern-day wonders of miniaturization and circuitry. It not only tells time; it is a stopwatch that can give me lap times as well. Further, it has an alarm to warn me, for instance, when my time is up during a speech. It also gives the date.

When he gave me the watch, I told him I could see the value of all its functions except the date. When I run, I do not have a clock in my head. I usually have no idea what time I am doing, so a stopwatch can come in handy during a race or in training. And I do have a habit of speaking too long. It is not often a man my age with a large family gets a chance to speak for any length of time without interruption. Once I begin to interact with an audience, I forget time and need something or someone to bring me back to reality.

But the date—who needs that? Why all these additional elements in the watch just to tell me the date? The date, it seemed to me, was overkill. This Japanese watch had one capability too many, one function that was unnecessary.

"Irving," I said to my friend, "one thing I do know is the date."

Now, I don't know the date. The watch knows the date. I am a victim of what I have come to call the "Japanese Watch Syndrome." I have allowed technology to come between me and my perception of the world.

I can operate without knowing the date. It is, in fact, a desired state for anyone who wants to be a child, an athlete or a saint. Knowing the date more often than not indicates a preoccupation with the past or future that is hostile to genuine living. Knowing the date is rarely accompanied by feelings of joy.

When I am concentrating on the date, the odds are that I am concentrating on nothing else that is important. Chances are, I am missing out on those experiences which occur only when I am in a timeless state where past and present and future come together.

I would like, however, when I finally come back to reality after those mystical moments, to have some idea of what day of the week it is and even what month without referring to that infernal watch. My aim in this life is to be as independent as possible. The watch continually reminds me of failure. I am, if anything, becoming more dependent and must fight this tendency every day.

If you look, you can see this dependency all around you. The machine (or the expert behind the machine) monitors our acts, replaces our instincts, substitutes for our intuitions, acts as judge for our insights. The machine tells us what to do. In the process, our instincts are no longer heard. The animal in us is caught and caged, and no longer has to live on the alert.

Our best course demands exactly the opposite. If I am to be a good animal, I must live on the alert. I must develop my instincts. I must be able to hear and interpret what goes on in my body. I cannot be a blind and deaf tenant of my body. I cannot relax and sit back without sacrificing yet another function and capability of my body to technology.

Technology must be seen for what it is—both good and bad. It frees us, certainly. It liberates us from work that is drudgery. It shortens the work week. It transforms society and gives us leisure which is simply, as the Greeks knew, a school for becoming oneself.

At the same time, technology has removed physical stress, atrophied our legs and bodies, and allowed us to gain weight as only affluent societies do. It has taken over the decision-making process in our day-to-day living. Computers now tell us what to eat, how to sleep, what shoes to wear, how hard and how long to exercise. We merely establish what we want done, and the experts can program us for it. No need to use, for instance, our inborn power to perceive exertion; they will do that for us with a treadmill. No need to trust the signals we are getting from our body; they will run a printout of eighteen tests which will tell us exactly how we feel.

When this happens to me, I become no more than a guided missile, my life's trajectory already plotted out. I lose the chance to be me. I am now ruled by clocks, calendars, schedules, agendas; living in an environment that is self-correcting and almost void of physical stress.

Abraham Maslow spoke of "subjective biology" or "experiential biology" where we are aware of the inner signals in the body. He saw the great need to hear these "voices of the real self," to know what and whom one likes and dislikes, what is enjoyable and what is not, when to eat and when not to, when to sleep, when to urinate, when to rest.

My Japanese watch is a symbol. I may not have a real need to know the date, but there is no question that I no longer know it. Technology can do that. Our task is to use technology without being enslaved by it. It must help us become more human rather than less.

It was Williams James who spoke of saints as being athletic, and athletes being "secular saints." For James, who was a constant seeker after man's potential, the coexistence of bodily and spiritual perfection was not a coincidence.

This theme—that saints are athletic and that athletes are, in some measure, saintly and that the common man can aspire to be both—never received the attention it deserved. Theologians viewed sin rather than sainthood as the normal state of man. Physicians, preoccupied with disease, considered the athlete a physiological freak.

But times are changing. Both professions are becoming as interested in the here and now as in the hereafter, and are investigating man's capabilities for good rather than analyzing his faults and diseases. For the physicians, this means the emergence of sports medicine as a new and major specialty.

A result of this work is the *Encyclopedia of Sports Medicine.* It runs to 1,707 pages and is culled from just about as many manuscripts, filled with fact and unfortunately a great deal of speculation.

"Probably 50 percent of the topics," said the editor, the late Albert Hyman, "lack solid research data." Such refreshing honesty doesn't obscure the fact that what is contained shakes many long-held theories in medicine.

One of these is the danger that athletics, if taken in large amounts, can lead to the development of the dreaded "athletic heart." The "athletic heart" describes a condition in which the heart muscle enlarges beyond the capacity of the heart's arteries to sustain it. This condition, according to Oklahoma City physician Dr. Dale Groom, does not exist, and he has the Tarahumara Indians to prove it.

For the Tarahumara, who lives in northern Mexico, running is the principal sport. It is at the same time his livelihood, his recreation and his criterion for success, since he hunts a deer by the simple method of running after it relentlessly for a couple of days until the animal drops from exhaustion. He also catches wild turkeys by pursuing them until they can no longer rise from the ground in flight.

But at play, the Tarahumara performs even more prodigious feats. His "kickball games," played by teams of men kicking a wooden ball about the size of a tennis ball, extend for distances up to 150 miles. This is no relay; each man runs the route.

The Indians examined by Groom ranged in weight from 114 to 135 pounds and were between five feet, two inches and five feet, six inches tall. They were all lean and fit (what else?), having almost no perceptible body fat. But most important was the finding that all these men with a lifetime of prodigious endurance activity had normal-sized hearts on X-rays, and normal electrocardiograms as well. On questioning the Indians, Groom could find no instance where anyone had dropped dead or became fatally ill from any of these almost interminable running sessions.

"Obviously, more questions than answers have been raised by this work," writes Groom. Where, for instance, do the Tarahumaras get the 11,000 calories needed for such a long race? Physiologists had already established that this is beyond the limit that can be expended by the body in a twenty-four-hour period. Have the Tarahumaras, asks Groom, received a special dispensation from some of the human limitations known to us?

If they have, I suspect it is because these limitations are artificial. They have been based upon our imperfect knowledge of what man can and cannot do.

"The phenomenal feats of these primitive Indians," concludes Dr. Groom, "afford convincing evidence that most of us brought up in this sedentary, comfortable civilization of today actually develop and use only a fraction of our cardiac reserve."

We are now coming full circle. Man, who originally lived or died on the basis of his bodily skills, is faced with this same predicament again. His life expectancy—living each day at the top of his powers rather than longevity—depends on getting the utmost out of his body.

Like most runners, I have become an endurance animal. I have attained the body composition, the cardiopulmonary function and the internal economy one would expect of an animal in the wild. I have reached training levels far beyond those needed for our current culture and have developed the body to match.

Looking at me, you would hardly suspect this. I look no different from most nice, ordinary, sedentary people you see every day. It is only when I go for a physical examination and have laboratory tests done that it becomes clear I am very different—or very sick. Almost every test done on me shows changes indicative of a disease state.

Since I am no different from thousands and thousands of other runners, the annual physical has become the annual fiasco. The animal is hardly back in its habitat when the phone rings and the doctor suggests some more tests or a short stay in the hospital.

One fifty-eight-year-old runner from Maine, who was averaging fifty miles a week, had not missed a day's work in years and felt like a young colt, was told he had the liver and kidneys of a seventy-year-old alcoholic.

Conditioning, you see, changes "normal" values. When we train, we can no longer use the standards established for spectators. There are laboratory findings that tell us we have gotten the most out of our bodies and give numbers that go with excellence. Unfortunately, these are also in many instances the same changes that doctors associate with disease. So we runners are told we are ill or about to become ill.

The truth is, of course, exactly the opposite. Dr. Joan Ullyot once told me she could predict how a runner would do in a marathon by the tests. If they were normal, she was sure the runner would do poorly. I feel the same. Whenever my blood tests are normal, I figure I'm not training hard enough.

What are these tests that confuse the doctor and frustrate the patient?

• *Blood count:* The blood count of the distance runner frequently shows a low hematocrit (39–42) and a low hemoglobin (12.5–14). Does this mean anemia? Not at all. In fact, the runner has more circulating hemoglobin mass than his inactive physician. There is, however, an even greater increase in blood volume, so the blood is slightly diluted.

• *Urine:* Runners frequently have blood cells and protein in their urine. This is normal and will clear in three to five days if the doctor can think of any way to get the runner to stop running that long.

• *Bold urea nitrogen (BUN):* Although this is usually elevated in runners, it does not indicate kidney disease. There is simply an increased turnover of waste products, and the kidney does not quite keep up.

• *Liver enzymes (SGPT):* These are elevated as much as two to three times normal. These levels do not mean liver disease, and will come back to normal if and when the running is stopped.

• *Heart enzymes (CPK):* Again, these enzymes may reach very high levels and are not indicative of any heart damage or disease.

• *Muscle enzymes (LDH):* As would be expected, these can rise to quite high levels with heavy training. Again, they are of no clinical significance.

(The tremendous elevation of heart and muscle enzymes, often occurring simultaneously, is alarming to the physician. Doctors find it difficult to conceive that a running program could result in such profound alterations of these tests. For this reason, runners are cautioned on the need for further study of the heart, liver or kidneys. All of the tests are, of course, unnecessary.)

• *Cholesterol:* Here, the runner is told of a negative change. The cholesterol level remains the same; therefore, it is said, the running isn't doing any good. In fact, the good thing that is happening is in the ratio between "good" cholesterol (high-density lipids) and "bad" cholesterol (low-density lipids). HDL protects against coronary disease and is invariably elevated in an adequate running program. Total cholesterol correlates better with weight loss than fitness.

• *Bilirubin:* An elevated bilirubin is almost always present in distance runners. It is probably due to breakdown of red cells in the body. Again, it is not a sign of liver or blood disease, just part of the normal physiological changes with high mileage.

• *Uric acid:* This is a test that gets better when you run. Heavy-mileage runners lower their uric acid levels rather than raise them.

• *Enlarged heart:* The endurance animal has a larger heart than the animal that is domesticated or in captivity. The same thing happens with athletes. The largest hearts are found in professional cyclists, cross-country skiers and distance runners. This is a physiological response to training, the development of a capacious filling-type heart that can drive gallons of blood through the circulatory system. Spectators have little, shriveled-up hearts.

There are dozens of interesting ways in which the athlete differs from the spectator. This new breed of animal needs a new breed of doctor to examine him.

Most diseases are self-limited. If left to their own devices, most bodily ills will take their departure within forty days—if not sooner. Unless agitated by treatments and medicines, they have a natural life-expectancy of three to six weeks.

In the days before wonder drugs, this was part of our conventional wisdom. It was the consensus of the ancients, certainly, that we should treat disease with respect and not try to fight it. When fought, an illness was more likely to stand its ground and last a good deal longer.

Mark Twain had a unique response to sickness. It was his custom when ill to give up smoking and drinking and swearing. Soon afterward, the disease would become discouraged and go away.

You can read similar advice in Plato and Plutarch, in Galen and Montaigne. The way to go is the Twain way. Just hunker down and wait it out. Diet and rest, climate and light activity were the prescriptions of Hippocrates. Only when they failed would he wheel up the heavy artillery of drugs and surgery.

We should not regard this information as trivia. Neither drugs nor surgery will hasten the convalescence of most illnesses. Despite the wonder drugs, it still takes six weeks for a fracture to heal, to recover from a heart attack or go through a bout of rheumatic fever. It still takes, and always will, six weeks to recover to your preoperative work tolerance after major surgery.

What the natural history of disease tells us is to be patient. There is no sense rushing. We are lifelong athletes. Whatever seems of paramount importance today must always be evaluated from that very long-range view. There will be plenty of time to enjoy our sport and improve our performance. There is always another race.

Hippocrates said it all: "Life is short and art long; the crisis fleeting, experience perilous and decision difficult."

The impatient patient only makes it harder.

There is a healthy way to be ill, a healthy way to deal with disease, a healthy way to live with a sickness.

There is an old saying that the way to live a long life is to get a chronic disease and take care of it. It is simply a matter of following the golden rules of health, and making the effort to tap those energies and capabilities we have left untouched. There is no reason to take an illness lying down. Strength, stamina and vigor are still there for those willing to work for them.

To understand this, we must see the difference between disease and illness, and between curing and healing. A disease is a biologic event. It is an interaction of a pathologic process with our cells and organs. The curing of the disease is the removing, reversing or retarding of this process. Curing is the science of medicine.

Illness, on the other hand, is a *human* event. It is my reaction to my disease. Healing is the decreasing of my symptoms and the enhancing of my sense of physical and psychological well-being. Healing is the *art* of medicine.

Illness, then, is the way I perceive, experience and cope with disease. I have two choices: to delegate authority for its management or to accept it myself. I can watch the doctor or assume command; see the doctor as the all-knowing doer or as a teacher and companion in this cooperative venture—health.

Health, as I see it, cannot be conferred; it must be earned. I must make a personal decision. I must do more than wish or want health; I must *will* it. I must take the responsibility.

Both doctors and patients find this move toward the personal in medicine a difficult one. Patients are sometimes incredibly passive. My father once told me a story about a patient he had examined who then asked him, "How do I feel today, Doctor?"

Even more absurd is the doctor who isn't interested in how his patient feels. He treats lab tests, electrocardiograms and computer writeouts rather than a living, breathing, frightened, depressed human being. The physician who feels guilty when his science doesn't work must realize that the real enemy, as one patient said, is not death but inhumanity.

Health is the reverse. It is an affirmation of humanity. It is the determination to follow Thoreau's dictum: "The whole duty of man may be expressed in one line—make yourself a perfect body." Health comes from that active determination of my life style that perfects me whether I am sick or handicapped or disabled.

I am not saying that all of this will affect the disease itself. Exercise may not give me an extra day of life. It will, however, give extra life to every day. If it doesn't improve my vital capacity, it will improve my capacity for everything vital.

Peguy, the French philosopher, said that we die of our entire life. We live of it, too. Everything we do is important, and even more when we are living with a disease. For then we especially need that background of sanity and serenity and good humor conferred on us by vigorous exercise.

Specialists intent on tests and pathology often fail to see this. They don't particularly like things that can't be measured, felt or put on a slide and examined under a microscope. They demand hard facts and proof of cure. Therefore, they miss the fact that the patients have healed themselves.

I place in evidence some reports:

• *Item:* Sixteen asthmatic children ages twelve to fourteen were given a vigorous exercise program for three months. Only a few were already participating in sports, yet fifteen out of the sixteen tolerated the program well. The results showed no gains in oxygen transport, and the authors of the report concluded that the exercise was "unlikely to have longterm benefits on underlying asthmatic disease."

I ask, can we measure the health residing in play?

• *Item:* In a Mayo Clinic study, eight men with coronary heart disease were put on a year-long exercise program. No changes were found in their coronary artery X-rays or their left heart function. All, however, had a decrease in pain, an increase in self-esteem, and a more positive attitude toward their work and their disability.

My comment: Exercise has to do with physiology, not disease; with health, not heart attacks. These men had become men again. They had been healed.

• *Item:* A thirty-seven-year-old man with a past history of polio, now paralyzed in both legs, was examined because of a slow pulse due to his physical training. His daily program included several hours of walking exercises on crutches, then one hour or more of swimming and gymnastics, followed by two hours of crawling on the beach! The disease was unaffected; there was no improvement in paralysis.

I say, how can we hope to measure this man or be his equal in living?

* * *

A reader who had returned to running marathons after a bout with cancer wrote, "There is nothing more certain than the defeat of the man who gives up." And, I might add, the victory of one who will not.

I was speaking at a meeting of heart specialists when the question was raised: "Is exercise the best treatment for coronary artery disease?" My answer was immediate, direct and unqualified. "There is only one treatment for coronary artery disease." I said. "Surgery."

Coronary artery disease is a narrowing of the arteries that carry the blood to the heart muscle. This obstruction is organic and fixed. It cannot be altered; it must be circumvented. Blood must be detoured around the blockage. That is precisely what coronary artery bypass surgery does.

This does not mean, however, that surgery should be used routinely. It should, in fact, be the last alternative the physician considers. The doctor's first rule has always been to treat the patient, not the disease. Without altering the coronary obstruction, the cardiologist can do much to diminish its impact on the patient's body and psyche. Without increasing the blood flow through those arteries, the doctor can remove most of the physical limitations and the emotional stresses this disease causes in a patient's life.

To do this the physician must employ a subject generally ignored in medical school, exercise physiology. The study of the effect of exercise on the body. The science of human performance. Exercise physiology teaches us the process of health just as pathology teaches us the process of disease. To minimize the effects of disease we maximize the benefits of health.

Physiology helps everyone sick or well to mobilize his total energies. "The plain fact remains," said William James, "that men the world over possess amounts of resources that only exceptional individuals push to their extreme use. We have a habit of inferiority to our full self. Compared to what we ought to be we are only half awake."

Fortunately, coronary disease does wake people up. It does motivate. It does make them receptive to the discipline that exercise physiology demands. The coronary patient is ready to accept a personal responsibility for health. To follow Emerson's rule, "Look not outside yourself for strength or truth."

The physician, once more the teacher, can now say, "This is your problem, not mine. This is what you must do, not what I will do for you." The patient must act, not be acted upon. The prescription is not drugs but effort; not medicine but exercise and diet and a change in attitude. And the best model the patient can use is the athlete.

The athlete model has the additional advantage of being familiar to all of us. Further, unlike most advice dispensed by physicians, athletic practices make sense. They should. They use the application of the best that is known in exercise physiology, the fruits of the research designed to get the most out of the human animal.

The first step is the process of getting into shape. Observing the athlete we learn that this is done quite slowly. The athlete goes to a training camp in order to be in peak condition when the season starts. So too with the coronary patient. At first the stress applied must be minimum, both in time and intensity and frequency. Then each factor is gradually increased.

The athlete also has to diet. The overweight athlete is a target for ridicule. Leanness is the most obvious characteristic of athletes, particularly of the distance runner. In fact, as a group they appear weak and undernourished, even haggard. There is good reason for this. The oxygen delivery system is based in part on our body weight. Each pound of body fat we lost increases our available oxygen 1 percent or more. A genuine weight loss where diet is accompanied by exercise can improve our efficiency enormously.

There are other athletic practices that are also instructive. Not eating before a race, for instance. So too the coronary patient. Effort should be done on an empty stomach. And then the warmup, essential to the heart patient.

The athlete learns to avoid smoking and curtail drinking; the heart patient learns much the same thing. And so it goes down the line. The more the life style of the coronary artery patient approximates that of the athlete the better.

Other good things are happening during this process. The personality changes for the better. Signs of the hurry sickness diminish. Attention to deadlines becomes less obsessive. Self esteem improves. The patient begins to feel more at home, more in control of what is happening from day to day.

These changes are generated by the maximally functioning athletic body. And that is necessary whether we have coronary artery disease or not. Life itself, as Beckett said, can be a terminal illness. We can go either way. Succumb to fear or anxiety or depression, retreat into a sedentary defensive existence. Or extend ourselves to our limitless limits and thereby make actual all that is potential.

Once motivated the execution of such a plan may be quite simple. Witness Kierkegaard's advice. "Above all, do not lose your desire to walk; every day I walk myself into a state of well being and walk away from every illness; I have walked myself into my best thoughts and I know of no thought so burdensome that I cannot walk away from it."

The cardiologists were waiting for a final word. "Before you begin to treat a patient's arteries be sure you have bypassed the patient's previous existence. Before you take the patient to surgery be sure you have taken the patient to the playing fields."

Only when becoming an athlete fails should we treat the disease itself.

I was cruising along the river road, locked in on automatic pilot, when disaster struck. Not all at once, of course; first there were some premonitory symptoms. It was not discomfort I would normally attend to, but then the back of the mid-thigh is not a place a distance runner usually has trouble.

I presumed it was nothing. But the nagging increased, and on the long downhill to the bridge just about six miles out, I thought of walking. Halfway across the bridge, the pain exploded into a searing sensation that brought me to a halt. I had to phone home and have someone come and get me.

My first reaction was fear. This had to be a very serious condition. Something dreadful was evidently going on in that thigh muscle. I was initially immobilized by the pain, then I became immobilized by fear. Might I never be able to run again? Once a hamstring pull, the saying goes, always a hamstring pull.

In the next few hours, it became evident that this was indeed something that was going to last. It was not just a cramp. I could not tolerate any pressure on the back of my thigh. Even sitting down was painful. That night, I drove to New York and gave a clinic on sports medicine. As I answered the questions I had to limp from one side of the stage to the other. The doctor had become the patient.

502

I soon discovered that I was just like every other patient. I wanted help, I wanted it right now, and I was willing to try anything. I was suddenly at odds with the physician inside of me. For years, I had been dealing with runners and their injuries, answering their questions logically, rationally, pointing out the uselessness of drugs when the problem was the postural and structural imbalance of the body. These injuries, I had told telephone callers from as far away as Johannesburg, are not acts of God. They are due to the weakness or inflexibility of the muscles. No amount of boiling or baking or drugs or vitamins will help. You have to go back to basics and restructure the body.

But now I was the one in pain. I was the one hobbling around. And now I knew logic and reason are not enough. You can't trust a doctor, I told myself. Shaw said that every profession is a conspiracy against the laity. When you become a patient, you remember William James and his dictum, "Truth is what works."

Was there a chance the whirlpool would work? I was in it. How about ultrasound? Lay it on me. Would Butazolidine help? Give me a handful. What about vitamins? You never know. I was there taking them by the hour—first the C, then the B, then the rest of the alphabet.

A week before, I had received a letter from a runner whose leg cramps had yielded to vitamins C and E. At the time, I had given him high grades for self-hypnosis. But now, I was in them up to my hips. By noon, my urine was a bright saffron. The B-complex was at work. The last time I had taken that many vitamin tablets was when I was recuperating from hepatitis. I took so many that my urine actually became fluorescent, a reaction that startled even the doctors at the Rockefeller Institute who reviewed my case.

At night I would retire to a hot tub with some cracked ice in a plastic wrapper, and every so often would take the damaged limb out of the water and rub it with the ice. As I sat there, I would think of yet more remedies for this catastrophe.

Oddly, things seemed to be getting better. I was far from well and a long way from running, but I began to hope. And with hope came prayer. I began to dun heaven, to appeal to my lost saints. I prayed to everyone including the tooth fairy. I left nothing to chance.

Something was working—perhaps the Butazolidine, or maybe the C, more likely the hot tub and ice. It may have been just the passage of time. Whatever it was, my hamstring pull was beginning to clear up.

With the improvement came the resolutions—soon to be forgotten, of course. My reform would last only until I was running pain-free, and then I would forget to do all those things I promised. But for now I was resolved to stretch before and after running and each night before I went to bed. I would never allow my hamstrings to get that tight and short and inflexible again.

Two weeks later, I received a letter from a runner with a hamstring pull. He wanted to know about drugs and vitamins, about the whirlpool and ultrasound. Was there a chance, he asked, that massage and manipulation would work? By then, I was no longer a patient. I had become the doctor again. Reason and logic again held sway.

All that was just first aid, I told him. He must find out why it happened, discover what balance exists in his body structure and in his muscles. There is no real evidence, I pointed out, that any of these other treatments are of value.

Still, I said, you never can tell. Try whatever you want, and if it works let me know. Medicine, you see, is not only a science: It is an art. But that is something you have to be a patient to know.

In 1973, we celebrated the 500th anniversary of the birth of Nicholas Copernicus. We honored the man who first said the earth revolved around the sun, the man who wrote, "If we face facts with both eyes open, finally we will place the sun himself at the center of the universe."

That same year, a meeting was held in San Francisco proposing a theory no less revolutionary. The foot, said this convention, is the cause of most athletic injuries. The athlete, claimed this convocation, revolved around his or her foot. Treatment must begin there, or there would be no beginning at all.

In the early 70s, sports medicine was still a surgical specialty. The typical patient was one of Saturday's Heros. The typical injury was the damage resulting from a split-second collision of irresistible force and immovable object. The typical treatment was surgery.

"The sports medicine meetings I attend," a team physician told me at that time, "are really surgical conferences."

The emphasis on surgery to the detriment of orthopedic medicine had been deplored by the surgical leaders. In 1951, the president of the American Academy of Orthopedic Surgeons had issued this warning: "Because operations are spectacular, our residents often complete their

504

training with distorted views as to the importance of surgery in orthopedics. They enter practice with but a vague view of the application of orthopedic principles."

This condition still has not changed. Recently, I talked to a young orthopedic surgeon with a professional team who told me he had learned more sports medicine from a baseball trainer than he had in all of residency or practice.

"Before that," he said, "I had taken the traditional approach: Make the diagnosis; select the appropriate operation."

But even then, the handwriting was on the wall. There were no longer any appropriate operations. We had gone from the sports medicine of trauma to the sports medicine of overuse. The typical patient became a common, garden-variety human being engaged in a running sport—jogging, tennis, handball, basketball or the like. The typical injury was the result of innumerable repetitions of the same action. The typical treatment was medical.

The problem now was too much conditioning rather than too little, overdeveloped muscles rather than underdeveloped ones. The basic cause was a structural weakness in the foot rather than an act of God in the momentary cataclysmic reaction between two opposing forces.

So orthodoxy failed. Standard practices were not enough. The athlete began to look elsewhere. "It is a well known fact," wrote South African physiotherapist C. Pilkington in 1970, "that a great number of sportsmen lack confidence in the medical profession and turn to quack treatment for a rapid cure." I felt the same way myself.

I began running fifteen years ago, before jogging became respectable. And it cost me days and weeks of injuries to learn that I, a physician, knew nothing, and my colleagues knew nothing. In my years of running, I have never been helped by anyone with M.D. after his name. I learned about feet from a podiatrist, muscles from a gymnastics coach, the short leg syndrome from a physical education teacher.

The roads became my teaching laboratory. I learned to use different shoes, different surfaces, arch supports and exercises. I discovered that running on the other side of the road could help, or running with my toes floating or even pigeon-toed. But I never put it all together, never saw that it all came down to maintaining a neutral position of the foot from stride to take-off.

That final illumination came from a most courageous human being, an ex-marine who ran in what he called "essentially agony" for two whole years with chondromalacia patella, or runner's knee. He had gone through the usual treatments—drugs, cortisone shots, casting—and had experienced no relief.

Such lack of successful treatment was the common experience of athletes who suffered from irritation of the undersurface of the kneecap. An editorial about that time in the *British Medical Journal* had said of chondromalacia patella: "The exact cause of this syndrome remains a mystery." And therefore the treatment remained problematical. The orthopedic surgeons who had taken control of sports medicine on the basis of treating one injury of the knee, the torn cartilage, were about to lose control due to failure to handle chondromalacia of the kneecap, the most frequent overuse injury.

The ex-marine was finally cured, but not by the surgeons. He developed some pain in his arch and consulted a podiatrist friend who made an orthotic, or support, for his foot. And that support not only cleared up the foot pain but, *mirabile dictu,* the knee as well.

Sports podiatry had been born.

The 1973 San Francisco convention on "The Role of the Foot in Sports Injuries of the Lower Extremity" met not to announce a new miracle drug or a new miracle operation. It met to announce the birth of sports podiatry.

The cry at San Francisco that year was body engineering, body mechanics, body physics. Butazolidine and cortisone were dead. The foot mold would replace the scalpel. Exercises would take the place of machines. Othopedic *medicine* would occupy the center of the sports medical world. The sports podiatrist and the physiotherapist would become the central figures in the athlete's care.

All these were set in motion when runner's knee was cured with a foot support. We learned then that an abnormal foot strike can cause trouble with the knee, and we realized that the way to treat a knee was simple: Ignore the knee and treat the foot.

If this is so, then drugs and shots and operations and even exercises aimed at the knee will predictably fail. And if a foot support can help the knee, what else can it help? We soon found out. An odd foot strike can cause trouble at three levels: (1) the foot itself, with stress fractures, metatarsalgia, plantar fasciitis and heel spur syndromes; (2) the leg, with stress fracture (this time of the tibia and fibula), shin splints, achilles tendonitis and posterior tibial tendonitis; (3) the knee, with tibiofibular arthralgia and, of course, runner's knee. All begin with a biomechanically weak foot.

So the sports podiatrist who could diagnose and treat these peculiar feet became the new leader. Orthopedic medicine, the non-surgical side of orthopedic care, was in the ascendancy. But the podiatrist and the physiotherapist would lead the way. They would fill the void that the surgeons had chosen to ignore.

As late as 1975 Dr. Paul Lipscomb, president of the American Orthopedic Association, saw this as a continuing danger. "What can we do," he asked his colleagues, "to prevent orthopedic surgeons from becoming technicians with little or no responsibility for preoperative diagnostic evaluations, or postoperative rehabilitation, and for the management of the 80 or 90 percent of patients who do not require surgical procedures?"

My own feeling is that the present way is the best. Orthopedic surgeons should be surgeons. Surgeons are born, not made. They have a particular personality: dominant, energetic, competitive, courageous, optimistic. It would be boring and out of character for them to occupy themselves with the routine medical care of the athlete.

We must allow every specialist to do what he does best, be it podiatry, physiotherapy, osteopathy, chiropractic or orthopedic surgery. There is a place for everyone on this team. The only requirement is that they be effective, and that the treatment be directed at the reason for the injury, not just the result. Nor should we waste time with treatments that have proven time and again to be ineffective.

We must accept, however unpalatable, however unexplainable, the therapy that is successful. "Truth," said William James, "is what works." And the truth is that sports podiatry works.

4

The Aids

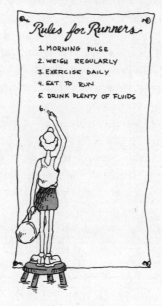

"

You are an experiment-of-one.
Establish your own schedule;
do not follow anyone else's.
Listen to your body,
Train, don't strain.

"

TRIED AND TRUE RULES of the road for runners:

1. *Keep a record of your morning pulse.* Lie in bed for a few minutes after you awaken and then take your pulse. As your training progresses, it will gradually become slower and after three months or so it will plateau. From then on, should you have a rate ten or more beats higher than your morning norm, you have not recovered from your previous day's runs, races or other stresses. Take a day or more off until the pulse returns to normal.

2. *Weigh regularly.* Initially, you will not lose much weight, and getting on and off the scales will seem a bore. Subsequent losses should be in the area of one half to one pound a week. This equals 250 to 500 calories a day in output of energy over intake of food. What you lose in fat you will put on in muscle. Running consumes one hundred calories a mile and there are 3,500 calories to a pound, so you can see weight loss will be slow unless you do heavy mileage.

3. *Do your exercises daily.* The more you run, the more muscle imbalance occurs. The calf, hamstring (back thigh) and low-back muscles become short, tight and inflexible. They have to be stretched. On the other hand, the shin, the quad (front thigh) and belly muscles become relatively weak. They must be strengthened. There are specific exercises geared to strengthening these muscles.

4. *Eat to run.* Eat a good, high-protein breakfast, then have a light lunch. Run at least two, preferably three hours after your last meal. Save the carbohydrates for the meal after the run to replenish muscle sugar.

5. *Drink plenty of fluids.* Take sugar-free drinks up to fifteen minutes before running. Then, take twelve to sixteen ounces of easily tolerated juices, half-strength "ades," tea with honey or sugar, defizzed Coke, etc., before setting out. In winter, that should be all you need. In summer, take an additional ten ounces of fluid every twenty minutes during the run.

6. *Run on an empty colon.* Running causes increased peristalsis, cramps and even diarrhea. Having a bowel movement before running and particularly before racing prevents these abdominal symptoms.

7. *Wear the right clothes.* In winter, this means a base of thermal underwear followed by several layers of cotton or wool shirts, at least one a turtleneck. Wear a ski mask and mittens. Use nylon, Gortex, lycra,

or polypropylene if necessary to protect against wind and wet. In summer, the main enemy is radiant heat. Remember to wear white clothes and use some kind of head covering.

8. *Find your shoes and stick to them.* Heavy people do better in tennis shoes and basketball sneakers. High-arched feet do better with narrow heels. Morton's feet (short big toes, long second toes) may need arch supports in the shoes. If a shoe works, train in it, race in it and wear it to work.

9. *The fitness equation is thirty minutes at a comfortable pace four times a week.* Your body should be able to tell you that "comfortable" pace. If in doubt, use the "talk test." Run at a speed at which you could carry on a conversation with a companion.

10. *Run economically.* Do not bounce or overstride. You should lengthen your stride by pushing off, not by reaching out. Do not let your foot get ahead of your knee. This means your knee will be slightly bent at footstrike. Run from the hips down with the upper body straight up and used only for balance. Relax.

11. *Belly-breathe.* This is not easy, and must be practiced and consciously done just prior to a run or a race. Take air into your belly and exhale against a slight resistance, either through pursed lips or by a grunt or a groan. This uses the diaphragm correctly and prevents the "stitch."

12. *Wait for your second wind.* It takes about six to ten minutes and a one-degree rise in body temperature to shunt the blood to the working muscles. When that happens, you will experience a light, warm sweat and know what the "second wind" means. You must run quite slowly until this occurs. Then, you can dial yourself to "comfortable," put yourself on automatic pilot and enjoy.

13. *Run against traffic.* Two heads are better than one in preventing an accident. Turn your back on a driver, and you are giving up control of your life. At night, wear some reflective material or carry a small flashlight.

14. *Give dogs their territory.* Cross to the other side of the road and pick up some object you can brandish at them. Never try to outrun a dog. Face the dog and keep talking until it appears safe to go on.

15. *Learn to read your body.* Be aware of signs of overtraining. If the second wind brings a cold, clammy sweat, head for home. Establish a

DEW line that alerts you to impending trouble. Loss of zest, high morning pulse, lightheadedness on standing, scratchy throat, swollen glands, insomnia, palpitations are some of the frequent harbingers of trouble.

16. *Do not run with a cold.* A cold means you are overtrained. You have already run too much. Wait at least three days, preferably longer. Take a nap the hour you would usually spend running.

17. *Do not cheat on your sleep.* Add an extra hour when in heavy training. Also, arrange for at least one or two naps a week, and take a long one after your weekend run.

18. *When injured, find a substitute activity to maintain fitness.* Swim, cycle or walk for the same time and at the same frequency you would normally run.

19. *Most injuries result with a change in your training.* A change in shoes, an increase in mileage (twenty-five miles per week is the dividing line; at fifty miles per week the injury rate is doubled), hill or speed work or a change in surface are all factors that can affect susceptibility to injury. Almost always there is some associated weakness of the foot, muscle strength/flexibility imbalance, or one leg shorter than the other. Use of heel lifts, arch supports, modification of shoes and corrective exercises may be necessary before you are able to return to pain-free running.

20. *Training is a practical application of Hans Selye's General Adaptation Syndrome.* Stress is applied, the organism reacts, a suitable time is given to re-establish equilibrium, then stress is applied again. Each of us can stand different loads and needs different amounts of time to adapt. You are an experiment-of-one. Establish your own schedule; do not follow anyone else's. Listen to your body, Train, don't strain.

Once our consciousnesses have been raised, our expectations are raised as well. Once I knew I could be a runner, I expected to be a good one. I expected to improve and to improve at a constant rate. I soon learned that such was not generally the case. Improvement is not automatic. When it comes, it is likely to be in cycles. There are soaring peaks, it is true, but there are also long and depressing valleys.

Almost every runner has suffered at one time or another from this Failure-to-Thrive Syndrome. It is an ailment that has three different clinical pictures.

1. There is the runner who just never improves; he is virtually stuck at day one.

2. Then, there is the runner who gets better but then hits a plateau; there is no further progress.

3. Finally, there is the runner who does well, builds up to a peak, sees excellence on the horizon and then takes a nose-dive; this runner gets worse and worse rather than better and better.

The most difficult to treat of these Failure-to-Thrive Syndromes is the first. It is also the most difficult to explain, and for the runner the most difficult to endure. No matter what he does, he seems unable to get up to any acceptable speed or mileage. While others are proclaiming gains in pace and distance, he is trapped at a performance level that is almost embarrassing. He is still trying to go four laps around the track without stopping when others who began at the same time are already talking about marathons.

A significant part of this difference is probably due to innate ability. Many people are taking on physical activity for the first time in their lives and have no idea of their inherent capability. In some instances, this may be limited. One way to find out is to use Dr. Kenneth Cooper's twelve-minute performance test.

This can be done quite conveniently by going to a high school track with a stopwatch, a whistle and a friend. First, warm up for ten minutes or so by walking and jogging. Then, have your friend start the watch as you begin to run the longest possible distance in the next twelve minutes. At that point, your friend will blow the whistle and stop the watch. The accompanying chart will tell you your relative ability.

Predicted Maximal Oxygen Consumption on the Basis of Twelve-Minute Performance

Distance (miles)	Laps (1/4 mile)	Max. Ox. Con. (ml/kg/min)
1.0	4	25
1.25	5	33
1.5	6	42.6
1.75	7	51.6
2.0	8	60.2

Levels of Fitness Based on Twelve-Minute Performance and Maximal Oxygen Consumption

Distance (miles)	Max. Ox. Con.	Fitness level
Less than 1	Less than 25	Very poor
1–1.25	25–33	Poor
1.25–1.5	33–42	Fair
1.5–1.75	42–51	Good
1.75 or more	51 or more	Excellent

Runners who enter with a low maximal oxygen uptake are likely to make one of two contrasting errors in training. They either go too fast or too slow. Therefore, they have difficulty satisfying the three elements in the fitness equation. The running, it states, should be of a specific intensity, for a specific length of time, done a specific number of times a week. The aim is to do thirty minutes four times a week at a pace somewhere between easy and hard. This is necessary to achieve the training effect.

The difficulty is finding this correct pace. If the pace is too slow, it does you very little good. On the other hand, a fast pace is self-defeating. I have a friend who was in much this situation.

"I can't run more than a half-mile," she told me. "No matter what I do, I'm finished at that point."

A few days later, I went running with her, and we ran a mile and a half without the least difficulty for her.

"Oh!" she said, "I never run that slowly."

That was the answer, of course: slow enough to chat and still get that nice, warm sweat; slow enough to run for twenty minutes and then for thirty; yet fast enough to get better and better, fast enough to get that 25 percent improvement in maximal oxygen uptake that occurs with most running programs.

Runners must also be patient. They must not look for improvement too soon. Most studies show that the major increase in oxygen uptake and physical work capacity takes as long as twelve to sixteen weeks.

The essential, Ken Cooper says, is not to despair. Eventually, things will work out. Millie Cooper, his wife and the author of an aerobics book for women, says it took her a year before she could run a mile without stopping.

Like most runners, I always want to do better. I am constantly after myself for eating too much and training too little. I know if I weighed a few pounds less and trained a few hours more, my times would improve. But I find the rewards not quite worth the effort. My resolutions, so firmly made the night before, dissolve with the dawn of the following day.

I am forced, therefore, to do the best with what I've got. I must get my speed and distance from the most efficient use of my body. This means, I have discovered, paying close attention to the three B's of running form: *big toe, buttocks* and *belly.*

I learned about the basic three by watching those who run the best and seeing how they differ from the rest of us. At a casual glance, most internationalists not only differ from us; they differ from each other. On closer inspection, however, you will find that from the hips down most world-class runners look quite alike. They can only be distinguished from each other by what they do with the upper body.

We can tell them apart by characteristics that have no particular effect on running itself. Think a minute and you will realize you tell one celebrated runner from another by the attitude of the head, the position of the shoulders, the carriage of the arms, what they do with their hands.

But it is what goes on from the chest down that makes for economy, efficiency and maximal performance. What they do from the chest down allows them to get the most out of what they've got. That is their secret.

We are beginning to learn what this secret is. The kinesiologists who

514

study them think it has something to do with their increased use of the ankle. Dr. Richard Schuster, who has treated many of these athletes, has noted that their shoes are worn out under the big toe. My initial discovery, then, was my big toe. As soon as I emphasized the use of my big toe, I sensed an increase in power, a stronger pushoff, a longer stride.

I had learned the significance of a slightly longer stride some years back. I finished a twenty-mile race almost forty minutes behind the winner, only to be informed by an observant friend that the winner and I had taken the same number of strides per minute. What separated me from glory, he told me, was the ridiculously short distance I was airborne.

Not long after, I had another instructive experience about being airborne. I was watching the long jump of the IC4A Championships. The second-place jumper came down the runway, hit the takeoff board perfectly, but fell inches short of the leader. He had given it his best shot and failed—or so it appeared.

His coach came over and pointed out that he had reached for the board. His body had been slightly behind his foot. That almost infinitesimal check had cost him the necessary distance.

The jumper went back. He hit the board perfectly again, but this time there was no checking action. His body was over his foot. He won the event.

So there it is: You increase your stride by *pushing off*, not by reaching out. Never let your foot get ahead of your knee. Expend no energy in slowing yourself down. Save your major effort for your big toe. The big toe automatically brings the buttocks into the action. The harder I push off, the more likely I am to feel those big muscles around my hips come into play. The faster I run, the more evident is the post-training tightness in that area. A series of in-and-out 220s causes spasms in the buttocks that I never feel in a casual ten-miler.

What is happening is that I am becoming a sprinter. I am using my anti-gravity muscles and increasing my ridiculously short airborne distance. I am also stabilizing the pelvis, keeping my back straight. It is the straight back that gives the thrusting leg the leverage for maximum stride. As the pelvis tilts forward, the runner becomes less and less efficient.

This, however, is only two thirds of the "B" axis. The belly also has a major contribution to make. When I belly-breathe, I add to the stabilization of the pelvis and the straightening of the back. I assume the running posture that marked Bill Bowerman's runners during his years of coaching at the University of Oregon.

As you read this, it may all seem disjointed. In practice, it is a composed, rhythmic movement. I begin with the thought that I will wear out the shoe under the big toe. This action automatically increases the range of motion at my ankle and then enlists the full power of the quadriceps (the group of muscles on the front of my thigh). The buttocks and belly now act as stabilizers. They keep the spine straight, the pelvis in the correct position.

I am still a little overweight, a trifle undertrained—but I'm moving like a champion, getting the most out of what I've got.

Every genius brings a message. Every champion teaches us something. When a person breaks a world's record, there is almost always a lesson to be learned—a new truth or a reaffirmation of an old one. What Sebastian Coe, former world record-holder in the mile, has done is to bring back relaxation.

Coe has all the other attributes of an outstanding miler. Like Peter Snell, he can run a fine quarter-mile and set the record at the 800 meters. He is light, less than 130 pounds, but has extremely powerful legs. With Coe, the footplant is not emphasized; it is the thrustoff that propels him that extra distance that separates him from the others.

But more than this lower-body power, the Coe characteristic is upper-body relaxation. Coming down the stretch in his record mile, his facial expression ranged from the casual interest of a passenger looking out of a train window to the serenity of a runner on a country lane at dusk. From time to time, he gazed over his shoulder—not in apprehension, but in curiosity about where everyone had gone. Then, his attention turned elsewhere. Never was there any indication that he felt the need to use his chest or arms or face to increase his speed.

Behind him, the best in the world were doing just that. They were beginning to tie up, the shoulders rising, the arms tight, the face assuming that "risus sardonicus," the smile in lockjaw, finally reaching that terminal state where they were using the neck muscles to assist the breathing.

I have a photograph of much the same scene in the Tokyo Olympics. This time it was Peter Snell, a smile on his face, driving completely airborne through the tape. Some fifteen yards behind him, spread across the track, was a phalanx of the world's best, each with a foot firmly planted flat and forever on the ground. It was the footplant that told as much as the tension in the face and arms and body. The runner's enemy, "rigor mortis," was setting in.

Coe was still doing what a runner must do to prevent this. He was running from the hips down. The upper body has two functions, balance and breathing. Motion of the upper body responds to and counterbalances the driving propulsive movements from the hips down. The arm carry has nothing to do with forward progress; it keeps the runner in balance. The arms, therefore, should be completely relaxed, moving just enough to compensate for what is going on below.

Breathing should be with the diaphragm. You fill the belly, then the chest. There should be no need to use the shoulders or neck muscles. Many runners do, of course. The result is not only wasted energy but also difficulty in breathing, development of chest and arm pain (the ubiquitous "stitch") and a general loss in performance.

After a race, a young runner came up to me complaining of difficulty in breathing during the race. He said he just couldn't get his breath and felt that he was overbreathing. He suspected he had "hyperventilation." He did. Hyperventilation is an excess amount of breathing in relation to oxygen needs. He was breathing more than was necessary for what he was doing. Usually, hyperventilation occurs at rest, but it can also happen while running and particularly while racing.

I gave him a suggestion: Pretend you are riding a horse, I told him. The lower body from the hips down is the horse. Just sit loose on that horse, using your upper body for balance. At the same time, concentrate on breathing with your belly and exhaling with a groan. The upper body, I pointed out, should simply respond to the hips and legs. It has no more to do with the running than the rider does.

When I was finished, he said, "I dig you, Doc. I'm a jockey." When I saw him the following week after the race, he told me he had noticed a definite improvement in his breathing and his performance.

The relaxation that we see in Coe—and that I recommended to this runner—is nothing new. Coaches have always promoted the idea of upper-body relaxation. When the educator-architect-designer Buckminster Fuller was at Harvard, he ran cross-country and was coached by Alfie Shrubb, a dedicated advocate of relaxation. "Stop running with your hands!" he would yell to Fuller. Then, Fuller would notice he was running with his fists tightly clenched.

I am aware, as you are, that to have someone say "Relax" often has the opposite effect. Try as we may, we find it most difficult to do this apparently simple thing. When this happens, it might be helpful to try doing the opposite. Instead of relaxing, tighten your hands and arms and shoulders and chest as much as you can for as long as you can. Soon, you will find you have achieved that relaxation you are searching for.

Paradoxical intention works in other disorders—insomnia (try to stay awake), for instance, and stuttering (try to stutter more). It may be an effective technique when your hands and shoulders and chest interfere with your running. You can, of course, always pretend you are riding a horse—or take another look at Sebastian Coe.

We probably would have grown to be adults with fewer food problems if our parents had not forced us into certain food habits which they thought were good but were later proven bad.

Young children are like animals; if not pressured, they will do what is right for their bodies. I once worked at a rheumatic heart clinic, and we were told to restrict the activities of the children. We never restricted those kids; they restricted themselves. They did what they could, until it became unpleasant; then they stopped.

The same would be true with food that is unpleasant to them. Milk is a case in point. People who do not like milk when they are kids never like milk. If they take it, something often goes wrong. I have ulcer patients who actually get worse by taking milk. People who come to see me with ulcers usually have been to other doctors. One reason they still may have problems is that the medication they take lasts only three or four hours, so by two o'clock in the morning their stomachs begin to secrete acids which again cause pain. First, they need a medicine that will last eight to ten hours. Second, they may have been put on milk, which they cannot tolerate.

I had one doctor call me recently because his son's ulcer was not getting better, despite their using the standard treatment—milk diet.

I asked, "Does he like milk?"

"Oh, no," the doctor replied. "He hates milk."

We took him off milk, and soon the son's ulcer symptoms disappeared.

Parents worry that their children will develop calcium deficiencies if they don't drink milk. Actually, it is very difficult to become calcium deficient, particularly if you follow a varied diet. Numerous cultures throughout the world do not drink milk, yet are not short on calcium. They obtain it from sources other than milk. In Cyprus, for instance, yogurt is a popular food. In India, it is ghee. Individuals who have problems digesting milk often have no such trouble with cheese, a milk product which contains the same basic nutrients.

One way to determine whether or not you have a food intolerance is to keep a food diary. Otherwise, it is very difficult after you have had some sort of reaction to remember exactly what you ate three weeks earlier when you had a similar reaction. If something unsettles you—diarrhea, nausea, headache or some symptom which makes you feel terrible for a while—you should suspect your diet as a contributing agent.

If it is something that happens intermittently, independent of your stress loads, milk or grain probably isn't to blame. It may be something you don't eat as often as those two staples. At the Mayo Clinic, they automatically remove from your diet shellfish, chocolate, strawberries and other suspicious foods. There are also skin and blood tests for detecting allergies. If you keep a food diary, you may be able to spot recurring symptoms each time you eat a certain food.

The way the food is prepared may also create a problem. For instance, raw eggs probably cause more trouble than hard-boiled eggs. Recently, I took an injection of flu vaccine, and it caused a tremendous localized reaction. Considering the composition of the vaccine (it is grown on eggs), this indicated I must be allergic to eggs, chickens or feathers. But I continue to eat eggs, except the morning of a race when the extra stress might be sufficient to cause reactions.

I have bacon and eggs almost every morning for breakfast. I don't know if everybody should do that, but it works fine for me because I don't have cholesterol problems. Maybe if my father had died of a coronary at age forty-two and no other male member of my family had lived past fifty, I would eat something else. That diet doesn't bother my system, and it sets me up for the day.

You get all your amino acids in two eggs. Perhaps I'm getting too much salt with the bacon and should take steak like the Australians do, but if you have bacon and eggs in the morning you won't have any blood sugar problems the rest of the day. (Hypoglycemia, low blood sugar, affects huge numbers of people.) By praising bacon and eggs, I am sure to get a lot of letters telling me what poor advice I am dispensing. But if you go back to 1900, people were eating this way and had nowhere near as many coronary problems as we have today. Poor health is more often related to lack of exercise than to diet.

You have to be very open-minded about diet, because people all over the world have so many different ideas about it. You should tailor diet to suit yourself. If you are the type of person who has high blood pressure and eats bacon and eggs for breakfast, I would say you're crazy. You probably cannot handle salt too well and should be on a salt-free diet. If you have a family history of heart disease, you probably should avoid these foods. But if you have a family and personal medical history similar to mine, I see no point in observing those restrictions. Why shouldn't I enjoy myself in areas that are relatively harmless to me?

Bertrand Russell once said about philosophy that it occupied a no-man's-land between science and religion. I like to think that diet occupies a similar no-man's-land.

Dr. Henry Cabot, who was one of the great men of American medicine, claimed that when the final judgment is sounded and we know all the answers, the thing that the medical professions will be most embarrassed about is the diets prescribed for our patients.

And on that day of judgment, the cultists—the vegetarians, macrobiotic people and the like—will be similarly embarrassed because of the diets they've subjected themselves to in the belief that good health requires it. They sacrifice much time and money on their diets. If they do it because they enjoy it, that's fine. But if their motive is a desire for longevity, they are like the people who run solely to prevent a heart attack—only to be struck down on the street by a truck. They wasted all that time when they could have been playing a cello, seeing a movie or sailing a boat.

Almost no one doubts that alcohol has redeeming social value. It is by far the best means for breaking the ice at any social gathering. But does it have redeeming physiological value? Does alcohol impair or improve immediate performance? Does it have an effect the day after? And what are the limits of daily intake that will not cause any permanent damage to the body?

First, we must understand that alcohol is not only a drug but also a food. It provides seven calories per gram, calories that need no digestion because alcohol goes right through the wall of the stomach and small intestine. So at blood levels below 200 milligrams, a level that impairs heart action, alcohol is fine. Two beers an hour can provide a stimulus and a potent source of ready calories.

• *Item:* Runner reaches Boston College, the twenty-mile mark of the hottest Boston Marathon ever run. Says later he was near collapse. Is given, why no one knows, some vodka and water. Finishes in style, passing some seventy runners on the last six miles.

• *Item:* Runner in New York Marathon, his second in eight days, nears sixteen-mile mark in noticeable difficulty. Given twelve-ounce can of beer. Rejuvenated, he virtually sprints the last few miles.

What do such anecdotes prove? Nothing, scientifically. But they do suggest alcohol may not be all bad and that its use in athletics could stand more investigation.

But even conceding that alcohol in judicious quantities can provide both energy and fluid, what about the morning after? How about running with a hangover? What happens after a night on the town with little sleep and a couple of quarts of beer? Anecdotes here are as frequent as those about taking spirits or brew immediately before or during a race.

I recall a teammate in college who was carried home after a night-long beer blast and rose the next day to win a two-mile championship.

I have heard much the same story of a well-known runner who was poured into bed the early morning of a national championship and later that day won going away.

These were, of course, athletes who might have been able to win in any condition. But I have spoken with an exercise physiologist who tells me that runners have actually tested out better on his treadmill the day after a night of beer drinking. It is enough to boggle my middle-class mind.

And what of the longterm effects of six to nine beers a day? You're not going to believe this, but the literature suggests there may not be any. If your intake of alcoholic calories is below 15 to 20 percent of your total caloric needs, you are presumably safe.

If you run ten miles a day, this would add 1,000 calories to your basic requirement, or a total of about 4,000 calories. At 115 alcohol calories to a twelve-ounce can of beer, this would allow you to go up to at least six cans of beer. Prudence, however, suggests that four cans might be a better number. That corresponds to a pint of wine. Oddly enough, eight cans of beer are the equivalent of the liter of wine the French say should be the limit.

Having arrived at these conclusions, I decided in the interest of science to try them out. One Saturday night, I drank six beers, then ran a good six-mile race the next day. After a day off, I again drank six beers the following night. The next day, I thought about running but went home and took a three-hour nap instead.

5

The Trials

66

I struggle with the breathing.
I am gasping fifty times a minute,
and it's not enough.
My groans fill the stadium. The legs refuse to move.
Four of these are enough. But I am hearing
the still small voice asking the Jamesian question,
"Will you or won't you have it so?"

99

"THERE IS NO SELF-MASTERY without discipline," wrote Simone Weil. "And there is no greater source of discipline than the effort demanded in overcoming obstacles." It is necessary, she went on to say, that we hamper ourselves with obstacles that lead us to where we are to go.

My self-mastery comes from the discipline and the effort demanded by my personally invented obstacles—interval quarter-mile runs. Running has helped me in other ways. The long training runs, for instance, make me grow. Long, slow distance is long, lovely distance. Those miles are miles of thought and creativity. My ten-milers are no chore. When I finish, I feel ten feet tall.

I am using my body with intensity when I run long. I am reaching levels of energy that previously seemed impossible. I also am running with an absorption in my thought processes that puts me into another reality. I am listening to a debate which has, as William Gibson says, been going on since the day of my birth.

Discipline is another thing entirely. It is not a matter of being a good animal, of being a child grown wise; not something sprung full grown out of instinct or intuition. Discipline is not talent or intelligence, not strength or beauty. Discipline is the cement that holds all of these things together. Discipline comes from following what William James called "the still small voice," and thereby doing the ideal action—the action against the line of the greatest resistance.

I can't think of any action against greater resistance than repeat quarters, nor any time when the still small voice is stiller and smaller in my ears. Just the thought of interval quarters—a measured hard run, then a brief jog, then repeat, again and again—makes me willing to be a quitter and a coward. I approach the high school stadium with dread. I try not to think about what is ahead of me. When I do, I use the philosophy of Alcoholics Anonymous. I am going to handle them one at a time and not think about the next one.

I give myself the first one, hold my speed in check, look for seventy-five seconds on the clock. I stride through it, holding form through the finish. It's the last one that will be easy.

Two minutes later, I am at it again. The initial turn is faster. I feel good through the backstretch, but I have difficulty holding form at the end. Still, a relatively easy seventy-three seconds.

I jog around for two minutes. Then, back to the line and into the sprint. This time, I feel it at 220 yards. I have to go back to basics.

Relax. Run from the hips. Breathe with the belly. I reach back for strength I never tap except in a race. The last few yards are in slow motion. Another seventy-three.

This time, recovery is much slower. I lean on the fence, catching my breath. I stretch a little. Oddly, stretching is getting easier. The speed seems to lengthen me out. Despite my resolve, I think ahead. I'm getting near the limit. From now on, they are going to hurt real bad.

The fourth does. Only the first hundred yards come easy. From there, I am holding on until the finish. I try to maintain my pace and keep my form from falling apart. The homestretch seems a mile long. Then, I am over the line. The watch reads seventy-three once more.

I struggle with the breathing. I am gasping fifty times a minute, and it's not enough. My groans fill the stadium. The legs refuse to move. Four of these are enough. But I am hearing the still small voice asking the Jamesian question, "Will you or won't you have it so?" The two minutes are up. The debate is over. I start my fifth interval quarter.

Again, I am a hundred yards out when I begin receiving distress signals. They come from all over my body—arms, legs, chest. Every organ, every cell is reporting overload. Doing seventy-three seconds is going to be a world-class achievement. I am breathing so rapidly that the air seems to get no further than my larynx and then come out again. I am out of the last turn and headed for the finish. But I can no longer coordinate my legs. I begin to stagger. There is no way I can last until the finish. I focus down to one step at a time, counting when my right foot hits the ground. Where it hurts, I make it hurt more. I try to concentrate the pain into one circumscribed unbearable ache and so leave the rest of my body alone.

Now, with the finish still yards away, I am reliving the agonies of other runners before me. No better description has been written than by W. R. Loader telling of his quarter-mile leg in a relay race against Cambridge.

"Dear God," he writes, "the weight of the legs, the revulsion of the tortured body for this punishment. These were no longer limbs that were being moved. They were inanimate projections, hard and massy as metal."

Still, as Loader recalls, there was no thought of stopping. "Remote in its eyrie, the mind cared nothing for the plaints of the body. Keep moving. Let's have no nonsense like throwing back the head and thrashing about. It never helps."

So it is with me—the same revulsion, the same will standing in judgment and insisting I go on, the same graceless finish, my face now contorted in that terrible grin seen only in lockjaw and at the end of races, my shoulders joining in the breathing just as in terminal pneumonia.

The pain is more than I can stand, and then I am over the line. I throw myself on the grass. My chest is heaving, trying to pay back the monumental oxygen debt I have incurred. I lie on my back and find the breathing gets worse. I settle for the knee-chest position, my face on the grass, my butt high in the air. Enough, I say to myself. No more. There is no way I will finish another one. I'll collapse. No more. Don't make me do it.

I finally get a look at the watch. Again, it is seventy-three seconds. I reset it and try to get up. Eventually, I get to my feet. There are thirty seconds before "go." I think of every reason why another 440 is unnecessary and irrational and even harmful. But my thirty seconds are up. I've reached the line. I start the watch and get into stride.

The first hundred yards feel easy. I'm trying not to think of what lies ahead. . . .

We had a five-mile race in our town. It was a hot, muggy day with a bright sun, little cloud cover and virtually no wind—a day to make use of every trick I knew about handling heat.

Many runners, I am sure, did not even think of the day as hot. For them, the temperature of sixty-nine degrees was seasonable for a day in mid-June. However, it was the humidity that was important. At 79 percent, it was high enough to elevate almost any temperature to a dangerous level.

When the potential for heat stress is that great, almost any race is a long race. Two years earlier, we had three runners hospitalized with temperatures over 106 after a five-mile race. All three had been training and were apparently acclimatized to heat.

The key to heat stress is how much fluid your body loses in sweat in a given period of time. The body adapts to heat by sweating and the cooling effect of its evaporation from the skin. The amount of sweat can be almost unbelievable.

A friend of mine who dropped out of a very hot Boston Marathon at the fourteen-mile mark discovered that he had lost twelve pounds, or five quarts of sweat. He was fortunate not to have suffered an acute heat syndrome. Loss of 5 percent water weight can lead occasionally to catastrophe.

The object, then, is to minimize this loss—to take plenty of fluids before the race, as well as during it. The most important ingredient is water. Only secondarily should we worry about what is in it.

For an hour or so before our five-mile race, I drank fluids, water at times, but mostly iced tea in quantities that eventually made me urinate. Only that way could I be assured I was in my normal hydrated state.

By now it was about fifteen minutes to go, and they began giving us the instructions for the race. There was to be, they said, one water station. It would be at the three-mile mark.

They were wrong. There were to be two water stations. One was on the starting line. Right there, I took six ounces of water and six ounces of iced tea. I was now ready for the first three miles—more ready, I suspected, than anyone else standing there awaiting the gun.

The race was the hot one the temperature and humidity promised. Fortunately, we ran on tree-lined streets and were in the shade almost the entire way, so radiant heat was not a factor.

At the halfway mark, I was struggling to stay with a group that was ticking off six-minute miles. Nearing the water station, I could feel them drawing away from me. I was beginning to lose ground to them and to the clock. Then came the hose and the tables with the cups and people handing them out. Most of those ahead of me took a quick drink, hardly more than a gulp, and went on. Some never even looked as they passed by.

When I reached this relief station, I stopped and stood there drinking. I downed two six-ounce cups, doused another over my head and then set out in pursuit. They had gained over fifty yards on me. But if the rules of physiology held up, I would catch them before the finish.

Water not only saves, you see, it also insures maximum performance. Keeping your fluid level normal also keeps your blood volume normal. That is what allows you to run efficiently. Passing up the water not only sets you up for a heat stroke, it does something worse; it makes you run badly.

And that was the way it was. Coming into that last mile, I made up the fifty yards I had lost. I was back in the pack and knew now I was the strongest among them. It was just a matter of being tough on that hill, and then I sprinted home with no one near me. My time was just over thirty-one minutes for the five miles, which was comparable to my cold-weather times.

Two minutes later, a runner half my age crossed the line and collapsed. He was taken to the hospital, given two quarts of fluid by vein and subsequently a quart by mouth before his circulation came back into the normal range.

What had happened was that he had taken no fluid before the race. He had heard, he said, conflicting stories about taking water. So he had rinsed his mouth out and then run the race. Had he stopped at the water station? "Just for a mouthful." So he had run a five-mile race in heat and humidity with the protection of one ounce of water. The result was near-disaster.

It was also instructive that he had felt no thirst. And that at no time had he suspected he was in difficulty. Heat is really a silent killer. The victim is down for the count before any warning comes.

The deficit in water begins at the gun, and for that reason we must begin to make it up in advance. Playing catch-up is not a game that works in hot-weather running.

Still, as my race demonstrated, there is a way to make hot-weather running safe, efficient and even enjoyable.

Running has always been a sport where effort pays off. Training has time and again made up for limited talent. It is also a sport where intelligence counts, where physiology works, where science is helpful, and where understanding what is happening to your body can make the difference between talking about heat stroke and having one.

Once I am underway, I enjoy running in winter weather as much as any other time of the year. The cold doesn't bother me. Once I am warmed up, once my core temperature has risen that necessary one degree, once I have reached my second wind, I run as comfortably as I do in May or September. The drivers, who pass by wondering why I am torturing myself, are no more cozy, snug and warm in their cars than I am in my running gear.

Running in cold weather is not torture; it is fun, invigorating, life-giving fun. All I need to do it is a little will power and some common sense. The will power is that extra push that gets me out the kitchen door. The common sense I have acquired through numerous experiments is dressing for winter running. I have learned through experience the rules that govern the choice of clothes for a run on a cold winter's day.

The best way to keep heat in is to use several layers of light material. Such "layering" allows the air between each layer to act as insulation. I like to have cotton next to my skin, then wool if it is cold enough outside, and finally a nylon mesh T-shirt which is both water-repellent and wind-repellent. I use nylon shorts for the same reason.

So I begin with cotton longjohns, then follow with a cotton turtleneck shirt. This covers the arteries in my neck. For me, this protection for my neck is essential. No matter how warmly I dress, if my neck is exposed I feel cold.

The lesson I learned quickly was not to overdress. When I do, I sweat so much the clothes soak through, and I immediately lose heat and rapidly feel cold. It is amazing how little clothing is needed on a frigid day. The experts estimate that the amount of clothing needed to sit around in seventy-degree temperatures is sufficient for running at 45 degrees Fahrenheit. Some runners prefer to wear clothes made from Gortex, lycra and polypropylene.

One way to avoid wearing too many clothes is to use some temporary insulation which can be discarded after the run or race is underway. I frequently use newspapers under my T-shirt for this purpose. As soon as my body warms to its task, I get rid of them. Meanwhile, my overdressed colleagues are stuck with several extra items of outerwear.

Another method of temporary heat conservation is to use the plastic covers that come on clothes from the dry cleaners. I cut a hole for my head and arms, and wear it. This is especially effective in difficult wet-cold conditions, those days when it is about thirty-five degrees and sleeting with winds of fifteen to twenty miles an hour.

Covering the head and covering it well is essential. I am told we lose 40 percent of our heat through our head. I believe it. For me, running without a ski mask is next to impossible. The mask warms the air I breathe, and then my exhaled breath keeps my face warm. In fact, one of the most enjoyable things about winter running is being inside that mask. It is also the answer to that frequent question about freezing the lungs.

The experts tell us there is no such thing as freezing the lungs. All the air that is inhaled is filtered, warmed to body temperature and completely saturated with moisture long before it reaches the lungs. Still, the mask is what makes me believe what they say.

After the mask come the mittens, not gloves. Gloves separate the fingers, allowing heat to escape. I like wool mittens, but when the thermometer starts to hit bottom I switch to down mittens with a nylon cover. On occasion, I have used heavy wool socks either alone or over mittens and found them to work well.

Oddly, with all this attention to other target areas, my feet have given me little trouble. Tennis anklets seem to be enough. However, I do use leather running shoes which may give me added protection.

That about does it for my clothing. There is, however, another staple item in my ditty bag which I find indispensible in cold weather: Vaseline. I apply it liberally to my face, cover my ears, then work on my hands and use what is left over on my legs. Even where body areas will be under layers of clothing, I use Vaseline and have the impression it helps a great deal.

There is one other thing I must remember to do before I open the kitchen door: I have to remove my wristwatch. It has a metal band and can become so cold it is painful to wear. On a long run, I usually end up taking it off and holding it.

Now, I am ready for the road. I have enough layers of clothing artfully arranged to handle the weather outside. I have taken into account the temperature, the wind-chill factor, the presence of rain, snow or sleet.

What remains to be determined is which way to run. Shall I go north or south, east or west? At other times of the year, direction is chosen by whim. Here, it is by *wind*. The rule in winter is to go out against the wind and come back with it.

In running, as in life, if you follow a few simple rules, half the battle is won.

When I first came to Red Bank, New Jersey, to practice medicine, it was a sleepy little town. The newspaper was a weekly. It came out on Thursday and was read word by word until the next issue. The stores closed at 5 P.M., except on Wednesdays in the summer when closing time was 1 P.M. There were no Sunday sales except for necessities. Travel was by train, and then only to New York and back.

This may sound like the turn of the century, but it was only thirty years ago. Late-night TV was not yet here. The twenty-four hour day in sales and services and manufacturing was still in the future. Air travel, particularly across the continent and trans-world, was for the few.

In those days, we lived according to our circadian rhythms (from the Latin *circa dies*, meaning "about a day"). We followed the time kept by our biological clocks. We worked, ate and slept on a schedule synchronized with preset oscillations in our physiological functions.

Now, technology has changed the world. Everywhere, including Red Bank, the pace has quickened. Our schedules vary; Our days have become dysrhythmic. We are asked for peak performance when our body functions are at an ebb. We baffle these marvelous internal mechanisms by continually altering our time and environment.

This can be done, as it has been by many, by slipping into a life style that makes the night the major period of wakefulness. Mainly, however, it occurs through necessity in two ways—jet travel and shift work.

Each of these messes up our body clocks—the one by crossing time zones in a plane, the other by crossing time zones in our own home town. In other words, the shift worker can get permanent jet lag and never leave home. It is simply a matter of sleeping days and working nights, having to be active when every cell in the body wants to rest.

Jet lag has become almost as common as a hangover. Every day thousands upon thousands of professional people working for government or industry shuttle back and forth across the country displacing their twenty-four hour cyclical functions. The result is impaired judgment, slowness in recall and difficulty in making decisions. And when the problem affects a professional quarterback, the disastrous results may be viewed by millions of Americans.

In the case of jet lag, fortunately, the problem is relatively transient. No matter what happens, you are home soon and back on your own time. Pilots have learned to minimize this change in body rhythms by staying on their home time, and maintaining the same schedules of eating, sleeping and exercising.

In shift work, this cannot be the solution. The biological clock must be made to tell a new time and the body made to follow a new schedule. This is not easy, and shift workers are easy prey to fatigue, gastric upsets, duodenal ulcers and sleep difficulties. Researchers in the field tell us that the shift worker is less contented than the day worker. The

531

most prevalent attitude is one of resignation and acceptance rather than adaptation and enthusiasm.

I have had fairly extensive correspondence with runners in shift work, particularly the graveyard shift. They complain most about frequent changes of shifts which make complete adaptation impossible.

One runner wrote to me about the effects of changing shifts every three weeks. "I feel like I'm commuting from New York to Honolulu," he said. "My mileage, which was 25 miles per week, is down to ten."

Other runners have reported much the same experience. "Rotating shifts is a disaster," wrote one. "Trying to change your cycles is a losing battle," said another. Even those with permanent night shifts have had to make some compromise in their training programs. They usually settle for lower mileage and less racing.

In resetting the biological clock and developing a new circadian rhythm, each shift worker does what seems best in getting the inner pacemaker to synchronize with the external time-setters. Some run right after work. Some take a nap, then run, then go to sleep again. Some wait until after a good sleep and then take their daily run. In this way, they divide into the "morning" runners and "night" runners we are familiar with in the usual day/night working world. No shift worker who has written to me, however, runs during his lunch hour. Running at 4 A.M. must be too dangerous or unpleasant even for the dedicated runner.

Two important elements in the adaptation to shift work are eating and sleeping. The sleep of shift workers is almost always poor. Special effort should be taken to minimize light and noise, and to reverse the usual social pattern.

Eating during shift work becomes a learning process. "The secret that I keep telling anyone who will listen," wrote one shift worker, "is eating only when you are hungry."

That is good advice for anyone. So is the suggestion that understanding the body clock is essential to all of us, whether or not we are on shift work or log high mileage in jet travel. We excel when we match our functions with our metabolisms.

While I was warming up for a race, the local runners kept warning me about what was ahead. I was in Denver, two time zones away and 5,200 feet straight up from my home course at Takanassee Lake. I had run this same 10,000 meters during our summer series at the lake in 38:40, a

6:15 average per mile. Now, I was being told that such a pace was out of the question.

"It took me five months to get back to my sea-level times," one man told me. Add a minute a mile, was the common advice. Only one person out of five in Denver was born there, so most of the people in the race had gone through this same adjustment. Now, they came over one by one to caution me. In this beautiful park filled with evergreens and bright sunlight, I was hearing nothing but bad news.

There is always a home-team advantage. Visitors have difficulty with the natives wherever they go. This is particularly true in Denver. On the ride to the park, we had passed the Mile High Stadium where the Broncos are almost unbeatable. The Denver Nuggets, who were sponsoring this "Go for the Gold" race, had a winning record at home which was remarkable even in a sport where the home-court advantage means so much.

Visiting teams had come to dread their trips to Denver and the routine defeats they seemed bound to suffer. They had tried many different tactics to beat the local champions, but none seemed to work. Some had used oxygen on the bench. Others had experimented by arriving at Denver at different times, just before the contest or several days in advance. Denver still prevailed.

My approach to the time-zone problem was the same I always use: Fool my body. Stay on New York time. Sleep and eat and work out according to my watch, not theirs. Then, get out and run before my body knows it has left home, the sooner the better.

I had learned from practicing medicine and running marathons that the body takes about thirty-six hours to react to adverse conditions. I have run marathons with distinction after being up all night in the emergency room. The sleep that counts is the night *before* the night before you run.

I had arranged the same sort of schedule for Denver: Arrive late Friday. Give the clinic Friday night. Race Saturday morning. Before my biological clock knew what was going on, it would be all over. So the time zones would not matter. It was the 5,200 feet that would make the difference. As the Denverite saw it, the altitude was the only problem. They hadn't even considered the time-zone dysfunction. The jet-lag effect was minor in relation to what altitude would do to me.

I had read as much as I could on just what altitude was going to do to me and how I could cope with it. Most physiologists agreed that adverse effects started around 4,000 feet. At the mile-high mark in Denver, I could expect anywhere from a 6 to 10 percent drop in maximum oxygen uptake, with an almost equal drop in performance.

A well-known British authority, L. G. C. E. Pugh, had done some very interesting research in this field on athletes at Mexico City. He had reported an immediate drop of 15 percent in their maximum oxygen test at that level (7,500 feet). One month later, the athletes still tested about 10 percent below their normal ability. Times ranged accordingly.

All I had to counter this ominous information was the same strategy I used for time-zone changes. Get in and get out. I had heard somewhere that if you are going to race at altitude, be sure you get there no earlier than twenty-four hours before the race. If you do, you will run better. Not well, just better. It was the only positive thought I had when the gun went off.

There were 800 in the race, and I stayed back in the pack, trying not to get caught up in the early rush. Even at altitude, the tendency is to run the first mile too fast. I aim for a pace I would be happy with if I were finishing. I ask myself, "Is this the pace I usually run toward the end of the race?" If the answer is affirmative, I stick to that speed no matter how many runners go rushing by. It is always best to run an even pace in a race. At altitude, it is absolutely essential.

In Denver, this tactic worked. I had figured the altitude should cost me about thirty seconds per mile. I could handle, I reckoned, a 6:45 average. At the mile mark, I was moving at a pace that my body approved. I felt really good, and then I heard the split: "6:35." I then settled down to holding that same speed for another 5.2 miles and having the confidence I could do it.

Then, I noticed for the first time how thin the air was. My legs felt fine and I was full of running, but the air was not adequate. It was as if I had ordered a milkshake and had been given skimmed milk instead.

Still, I kept it around that same pace all the way. At five miles, I was just ten seconds over the 6:30 average and even ready for a drive to the finish. What held me back was not pain, although there was enough of that. What stopped me was fear. I was willing to stand the pain, but I just did not know what would happen if I tried harder. I had seen world-class runners collapse at the finish of distance runs in Mexico City, and

534

now I began to think of that possibility. Had they gotten any warnings? I didn't know.

So I kept it steady through that last mile. I came through the finish line hearing my time, 40:18. I had strung together successive 6:30s. I had astounded the natives. I had, as the gamblers say, beaten the spread, finishing less than two minutes behind my time at sea level. It was a personal triumph.

An hour later, I began to pay for the triumph. The stomach cramps came first, then the nausea and then the fatigue. I was wiped out, unable to enjoy the hospitality of my Denver friends. All the Italian food and the Guinness and the good talk went to waste. I slept on the plane home, but it was three days before I felt myself again.

Denver, I decided, is a great place to live, but not to visit.

PART 2

The Play

SOME CHRISTMASES AGO, the school where my daughter taught kindergarten had open house. I visited her classroom. The entire room was covered with drawings of angels, but angels only a child could see and no theologian had ever imagined. They were of every shape and size, every color of the spectrum, uniformly joyous.

I thought, "Please, don't let them grow up."

An impossible plea, of course. We all grow up. We lose the wonder and imagination and trust that come with childhood, and then pass as childhood passes and are lost forever.

Or so I thought, until in France I went to see the Matisse chapel in Vence. Entering that chapel was like re-entering that kindergarten —only better. Here was the final, glorious manifestation of those childhood visions. Here was the work of, as Blake wrote, "a child grown wise." Here was all that joy, all that certainty and trust done by a master's hand. Matisse had transformed a room not much larger than my daughter's kindergarten into a world of flowers and light.

When Matisse wrote about the chapel, he said it was the fruit of a huge, sincere and difficult striving—not a labor he had chosen, but rather something for which he had *been* chosen. He had succeeded because he had learned the secret of aging. It is to become once more a child.

Later, when I visited the Matisse Musée, I was struck by this same progression in his work. The museum is on the outskirts of Nice, a villa in a small park. Immediately in front of it is a children's playground with brightly striped booths, a May Pole, and a small platform for games and dancing. I could sense already what I was to meet inside.

In the first rooms, I saw Matisse becoming that accomplished artist. There were the usual nudes, the still lifes and the landscapes done impeccably well. Then, gradually, I could see the bold line taking over, the reduction to essentials, childlike drawings done by a genius. The master expressed the uninhibited energy, passion and perception of the child. The complete control of his art allowed him to play, capturing everything in a single line and the simplest of colors.

This, surely, is what Picasso meant when he said it takes a long time to become young. The advantage of age is that you can become that child again, and better—for now you are a child who has the tools, a child who has been twice born, who has seen the worst in the world and yet who, like Matisse, is able to go beyond to the real world.

The young-old see the miracle that each day represents. True aging occurs not in retirement but in rebirth, in a new kindergarten, a new making of angels, a new chapel to a new and understanding God.

6

The Age

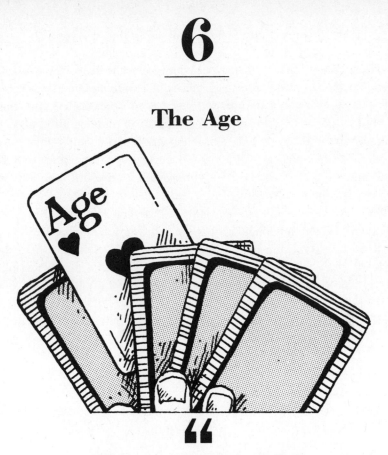

What can my aging body do?
Almost anything if I want it badly enough.
Given the dedication, the courage and the persistence,
a sixty-year-old can become an athlete
—and a good one.
In fact, if you are twenty-eight and watching TV,
you'd better not get up and look out the window.
You'll see any number of elderly men and women
who are training to beat you at your own game.
Youth.

DURING A VISIT TO DUBLIN, I had occasion to run with Noel Carroll, the former Villanova middle-distance star and ex-Olympian. Carroll, then thirty-seven, had never stopped running. At 175 pounds, he was almost twenty-five pounds lighter than when he ran for Jumbo Elliott at Villanova. He had the hungry look that is the mark of a champion. He was a completely functional unit of bone and muscle. For him, running was a fluid, incredibly easy motion. But underneath, you could see the power and strength he had available.

That day, he was doing in-and-out 200 meters. He carried us along, me and a half-dozen younger runners, mostly students at the University. He would jog down the backstretch, accelerate into the turn and then gradually draw away from us down the stretch. After crossing the finish line, he would slow to a trot until we caught up. We would do twenty fast 200s in all, he said.

Five was enough for me. I stopped to watch as Carroll kept turning them out. Presently, I met a runner my age, and we headed for a meadow and a few easy miles. When we came back, they were still at it. The students were looking weary and were barely hanging on. Carroll was bathed in sweat, looking stronger than when he started. He was now giving glimpses of what he could do when pressed. He pushed the last repetition and left the other runners gasping far down the track. Then, he jogged up to me.

"Tomorrow," he said, "we'll do an hour over some beautiful Wicklow hills."

It was a remarkable demonstration by a remarkable athlete. But is Carroll really a one-in-a-million phenomenon? Does the fact that he ran a 1:52 half-mile at the age of thirty-seven make him an unlikely model for the rest of humanity? Or is he showing us the potential we have available but have never used?

I favor the latter. Noel Carroll is demonstrating what an international-class runner can do if he keeps training, keeps competing, keeps believing in himself and his body and what he can accomplish. Right now, putting the stopwatch aside, Noel Carroll is better than he was in his prime. But even in absolute terms, he is living proof of the extremely slow deterioration of physical performance with the passage of time.

Age-group world records compiled by *Track & Field News* lead to the same conclusion. From those statistics, we would expect Carroll still to retain about 95 percent of the ability he had in his prime—which is indeed what he is doing.

The facts, as *T&FN* presents them, are simple. When we plot speed against age, we find that speed improves up to twenty, is at a maximum between twenty and thirty, then gradually lessens beyond the age of thirty. Using world records as 100 percent, we see a slow fall in performance: down to 93 percent at age forty, 84 percent at age fifty and 74 percent at age sixty.

Still, you might say, these are world-class athletes, world-record-holders. What about the common folk? What relation does this have to us?

Amazingly enough, these statistics for world-class runners gave the same results as similar studies of large numbers of run-of-the-mill people in endurance races in Sweden and in the marathon at Boston. In both groups, there was a reduction of 7 percent in performance for every decade past their prime. Whether you are an Olympian or a housewife, you can keep very close to what you did in your twenties as the years go by.

I take myself as an example. At the age of twenty-two, I ran my best mile, 4:17 on an indoor track in New York. At the age of fifty, I ran a mile in 4:47. This was only 12 percent behind my time set nearly three decades before.

When I began running again in my forty-fifth year, I didn't have an inkling of what would happen. I was embarking on an expedition without a map or a destination. No directives were available for a middle-aged male searching for what his body could do.

At that time, there were only a few distance runners, and most of them were in New England or California. They were not ordinary men; they were giants—already legends in their time. I saw them then, and still do, as a breed apart, not common folk like myself. Most of them had never stopped running, yet here I was starting from scratch after twenty years off.

When I came back to running, I was the only runner in my town who was not a high school student. So, for companionship and competition and coaching, I joined a high school team.

What happens to a forty-five-year-old when he tries out for high school cross-country? In my case, I made the jayvee team. The varsity was too tough and the freshman a mite too easy. I had learned something: A forty-five-year-old in training could become the equal of a capable fifteen-year-old. I could push back the clock. The question became, how far?

It was a year before I dared think of running a marathon and another six months before I finished midway in the field of 200 at Boston. I had learned something else: A forty-five-year-old in training could run a respectable marathon. I could push back the clock, but the question still was, how far?

At sixty, I'm still working on that question. I have reason to think I am not that much worse than I was fifteen years ago. Depending on how much I am willing to hurt, I think I could make the jayvees again or, at worst, the freshman team. At the Boston Marathon, I finish about midway in the field. My time is only a minute or so slower than my first Boston ages ago.

Now, of course, I am no longer an experiment-of-one. These days, runners number in the millions. Collectively, we are finding what the aging body can do. We are gathering evidence on the natural history of the aging process. We are showing what is inexorable and what is not, what can be delayed and what happens regardless of the work we put in.

Prior to the fitness boom, all studies on aging had been made on sedentary people, those the medical profession used as "normals." Then, Dr. Herbert DeVries, a University of Southern California physiologist, noted that reports on the effects of aging made no allowance for fitness. It seemed to him that we had been given a false picture of the inevitable loss of function with advancing years. He decided to see what training could do for elderly people.

Dr. DeVries went to a retirement community and recruited sixty-two card-playing, TV-watching bench-warmers for a fitness program. He set up a one-hour-a-day, four-day-a-week schedule of stretching, calisthenics and walking/running in an attempt to make these people into athletes.

These subjects with a mean age of sixty-nine significantly improved and maintained cardio-pulmonary endurance. Testing after the exercise program showed improvement in work capacity up to 35 percent. DeVries proved that the sedentary sixty-nine-year-old can improve by the same percentage as the sedentary twenty-eight-year-old when enlisted in a suitable training routine.

This experimental evidence has been corroborated by studies done at two major endurance events, the Vasa cross-country ski race in Sweden and the 1978 Boston Marathon. The fifty-four-mile Vasa hosted 7,625 male skiers with large numbers in every age-group, including the over-sixty category. The Boston run had 4,762 entrants and, again, had sufficient finishers in every age-group to make a credible statement about performance related to age.

L. E. Bottiger, who analyzed the Vasa results, came to these conclusions: The best mean time was turned in by the thirty- to thirty-five-year-olds. There was a decrease of 5 to 10 percent in performance for every additional ten years of age (actually, the fifty-five to sixty time was only 15 percent behind the leaders).

The Boston report was quite similar. However, in a foot race the younger age-groups always do better. In the marathon, the best mean time was set by the twenty- to twenty-five-year-olds at 2:51. With each five-year increment in years, the time got progressively slower. But the thirty-six to forty group still finished in 2:59, excellent time and remarkably close to runners fifteen to twenty years younger. My platoon, the fifty-six- to sixty-year-olds, had a mean time thirty minutes slower than the winning group. This figures out to only a 16 percent loss in thirty years—an amazing figure.

What can my aging body do? Almost anything if I want it badly enough. Given the dedication, the courage and the persistence, a sixty-year-old can become an athlete—and a good one. In fact, if you are twenty-eight and watching TV, you'd better not get up and look out the window. You'll see any number of elderly men and women who are training to beat you at your own game. Youth.

When I turned sixty, I reached what *The Amherst Student* in a congratulatory letter to Robert Frost called "that advanced age." Frost, of course, would have none of it. In a reply, he said he considered sixty no achievement at all. Advanced age, he stated, was somewhere around ninety, no less.

The World Health Organization, however, seems to agree with the editors of *The Amherst Student*. When I became sixty, according to the WHO, I was indeed elderly. For that institution, and I presume scientists around the world, sixty is a decisive year—a time to be excused from active duty, a time to retire, a time that marks the end of my effective participation in the activities of the herd.

No one—and certainly not I—wants to be elderly. You are, they tell me, only as old as you feel. Feel young and you stay young. I personally will have none of that message. How I feel depends on the time of the day and how long it has been since my last cup of coffee. Now, and for as long as I can remember, I awaken in the morning feeling like Methuselah. If feeling old means it is difficult to get out of bed, even more difficult to get to the bathroom and almost impossible to bend over the sink, I have felt that way since my youth. Only the smell of breakfast, the bacon and the coffee, has kept me from collapsing back under the covers.

I have learned to distrust feelings. When I feel my worst, I do my best. I have learned to push past the barrier of ennui and boredom, of lethargy and listlessness, learned that how I feel has little significance to what I can do.

The Pollyanna approach to old age does not satisfy me. Either I can hack it or I can't. Don't tell me about feelings, tell me about performance. Tell me what a sixty-year-old can do, what a seventy-year-old can offer, and tell me what's in store at eighty. Tell me about creativity. Tell me about my capacity to handle things like oxygen and boredom and stress. Don't tell me about being young; tell me about being old.

Despite being elderly, I am also an athlete, a distance runner. I know I am as old as what I do. What I need to know is, what is my physical scope? What is age going to do to me mentally? Only when those questions and other practical considerations are answered will I be able to accept all this poetry and mysticism about my coming of age at sixty.

What I need and want is a standard—something that can be clocked, recorded, seen, read, somehow quantified. Feeling is not enough. I want my time and place and how far I was behind the winner. Tell me what I can do and how well I can do it.

Now that I have reached the age of sixty, I have also reached a fundamental conclusion about my life: There's hardly anything I don't do better as I age.

That statement might not get too much argument from writers or artists, but those who keep sports record books are not going to believe it. An aging individual, to their mind, just cannot stand up to a younger person in an athletic event. The stopwatch is an unfailing instrument in establishing the difference between the young and the middle-aged, the elderly and the aged.

But what I am writing about is not a specific time or place in a race, although even there I am still doing well. There are days when I know I am a better runner than I have ever been in my life.

The truth is that every day I am born afresh. Every day, I recapitulate and add to and enlarge the person I was the night before. Age teaches me that. Each day, I learn more. Each day I run, I spend time listening to what my body is telling me. Each day, I am taught by the greatest of all teachers—the living, feeling, moving, tasting, hearing, seeing human body.

No wonder that in past cultures age was revered. Before technology, it was experience that was important. There were no shortcuts to the wisdom only the elders had, because experience could come no other way than by growing with the years.

Now, in the leisure conferred by technology, the aging athlete has become a new patriarch. Endurance runners with graying hair, wrinkled skin and birth certificates going back to World War I have become the darlings of the exercise physiologists. Scientists are endlessly testing middle-aged and elderly distance runners, and publishing their results.

What they have discovered, I already knew. My body can perform within 15 to 20 percent of its physiological prime. And I know from others I run with that I can expect only a gradual decline until I am in my seventies. Like most other runners my age, my body fat percentage is less than half that of the ordinary citizen. I also am able to take up, transport and deliver oxygen as well as any sedentary twenty-eight-year-old. My work capacity and physical performance is as much as 75 percent higher than untrained men my own age. All in all, I am operating at a level about twenty-five years younger than my chronological age.

Yet, for all of this, I am not special. I am a runner of sixty years who is simply getting the most—or nearly the most—out of his body. I am like all athletes of my age who are doing, not watching; growing, not aging.

Part of this ability to stand up to time is technique. When I run, I use biofeedback in its most sophisticated form: not with wires, gadgets and machines, but by letting my body teach me the most economical way to do what I am doing. This is the original biofeedback—listening to the body.

The conventional wisdom is against this approach. Either you are a natural athlete and do things perfectly without thinking or instructions, or you have to be taught from the ground up. I find both of those approaches wrong.

The natural athlete, as swimming coach Doc Counsilman discovered, usually doesn't know what he is doing. When Counsilman asked his world-class swimmers about their technique, they gave him answers which subsequent underwater photography proved all wrong.

The same thing happens with young baseball pitchers. When they first come up to the Major Leagues, they are *throwers*. They overpower the batters. Only later, with maturity, do they become pitchers. In the beginning, it is all talent. With age, they add the wisdom of their minds to the wisdom of their bodies, and only then reach their full potential.

I run my own peculiar way, my body's way. I try to experience the running and let my body direct the motion—with awareness of what is happening but without too much interference from the brain. I let my body self-correct. I let go, so I can feel what it is like to do it right. This teaches me to let go when I am doing it wrong.

I listen to my body in other ways. I treat heat and humidity, hills and headwinds with respect. I consult with my body when the elements become a factor. I have learned, for instance, that the best way to run hills is the way my body wants to run them.

I see age as an asset. Not a day passes when I don't learn more about my craft. Perhaps I don't learn enough to compensate entirely for the loss of strength and endurance that occurs inexorably each year—but enough so that everything except the stopwatch tells me I am now running better than I ever have.

There are even times, regardless of what year it is, when I beat the watch. I've been running since I was forty-five, but I ran my best mile (aside from my schoolboy times) at the age of fifty, my best marathon at fifty-five.

More often, however, I have days like the one at the New York City Marathon just before I turned sixty. It was a perfect day for an aging runner—hot Indian-summer weather with no cloud cover. Instead of

548

running my planned 7:00-a-mile pace, my body held me to 7:30 throughout. But that was enough to carry me past hundreds of younger, more talented runners who had started too fast.

The time of 3:17 was okay for a fifty-nine-year-old. But now I'm sixty and expect to do better.

When Emerson was sixty-one he wrote in his journal: "Within, I do not find wrinkles or a used heart, but unspent youth." I am now sixty-one and know exactly what he meant.

Yet I'm not sure what led Emerson to make that entry, just what it was that alerted him to his continuing potential for growth. For me it was the announcement of the qualifying times for the 1980 Boston Marathon. Specifically the stipulation that runners over forty must better 3:10 in order to enter. There were no further provisions for age. No exemptions for those over sixty. No indication that the committee realized the toll that years take on the body.

My initial reaction was outrage. I had not run under 3:10 in three years and did not expect to do it ever again. I was content to be, and indeed deserved to be, emeritus. I was entitled to privileges and prerogatives that went with that status. I had run in Boston since 1964 and should be allowed to run there as long as I pleased. Asking me to turn back the clock was ridiculous.

Other sixty-year-olds were taking the same position. One of my aging friends had written a long letter to Will Cloney, the head man, asking for leniency. Pleading that Cloney make an exception for the old timers. Otherwise some grand old men, he said, would be excluded.

This grand old man felt the same way. When I read the letter I thought, "Right on!" It was unseemly to treat us heroes that way. We had paid our dues. We had been there and back. Yet here they were asking us to re-enlist and do it again. At sixty I was through with combat. I wanted out. Just give me a standing ovation. Then a quiet corner where I could put my feet up, drink some beer and give advice. At sixty everything is or should be settled. No more tests. Behind, the best I could do; ahead, the enjoyment of having done it. Suppose I could even beat 3:10; why should I? What would that prove?

Eventually it was the thinking that did me in. I began to see that the Boston people were right. They were, in fact, doing me a favor. Offering a challenge, and given the proper response, an opportunity for rebirth rather than retirement. They were forcing me to face the crisis of the sixty-year-old, which is no less than a third adolescence.

The feelings I had were much like those I had experienced at twenty and again at forty-five. Of being capable of more, but being afraid to try. Of being capable of more, but shrinking from the necessary hard work and discipline. And above all dreading being told what I was capable of because then I had to go out and do it.

The third adolescence is as difficult as the other two. The young fear failure. The middle-aged have come to doubt success. The elderly know both are false and it is effort alone that counts. For the elderly adolescent the major problem is getting geared up to go out again. It doesn't seem worth it. The lesson, then, is never give up. So I knew it would not be just for this once but again and again. People may retire you, but life never does.

Emerson, of course, had no doubts. A year later we see him going full tilt into the future. "When I read a good book" he wrote in the journal, "I wish that life was 300 years long. The Chaldaic Oracles tempt me. But so does algebra and astronomy and chemistry and geology and botany."

So I yielded to the Boston group. I accepted their unfair standard. I knew then this goal was good for me. It would make me the best marathoner I could be. It would lead me through this crisis to a new flowering, a new growth.

My first try was the New York Marathon. I ran well, placed well, won the sixty-and-over. But my time was 3:14, still not good enough. Two weeks later I was in Washington for another attempt, this time the Marine Corps Marathon.

Looking back now it is remarkable how easy it was. The course was flat, the weather perfect. A little band music before the start. The *Festival* Overture of Shostakovich, then the "Battle Hymn of the Republic" followed by the National Anthem. I had to be restrained from jumping the gun.

There was no need. I breezed through the first mile in 6:30. Then found a young medical student named Victor who claimed to have a clock in his head. "I am going to run seven minutes a mile," he said, "until I come apart." He turned out to be a metronome. And his pacing was all I needed.

There were a few anxious moments at the twenty-three mile mark when I thought I might be hitting the wall. Then they passed and I was in control the rest of the way.

The last mile was against the wind and the final 600 yards uphill, but I never had any doubts of the outcome. I crossed the line 783rd in a field of more than 7,000. My average time for the mile: an unprecedented 6:54. After sixteen years of running and fifty or more marathons, I had run the Marine Corps Marathon in Washington, D.C. in the time of 3:01:10, an all-time personal best.

The next day I gave a lecture on running at a college in upstate New York. Shortly into the question and answer period someone asked me what I thought of the qualifying times for Boston.

I stood there gazing around at the audience of students and faculty and townspeople. Surveying this assemblage of adolescents, some twenty, some forty, some sixty. Looking out at all that unspent youth.

Then I drew myself up and stood as tall as a sixty-year-old can without appearing arrogant.

"Eminently fair," I said.

After Montaigne read Cicero's essays on old age, he wrote, "He gives one an appetite for growing old." I have developed the same appetite, but not from reading Cicero. It is distance running that makes me want to grow old.

This desire to be a year or two older is common among competitive distance runners. Alone among our contemporaries, we await with anticipation what are supposed to be our declining years. For myself, I found my competition in the fifty-and-over division too much for me. I wanted to be sixty and king of the hill.

That's the way it has always been. I moved into another classification, and I go from losing to winning. A birthday can change my post-race duties from giving congratulations to accepting them. A date on the calendar can convert me from an also-ran to world class in a new age-group. Add a year to my age, and I go from pursuing to being pursued; from simply rounding out the field to becoming the one to beat.

It is all there in Masters track, the world of the forty-and-over, the fifty-and-over, the sixty-and-over, even the seventy-and-over. This program takes into account the inevitable reduction in ability that occurs with age. It recognizes that small but significant decline of 7 percent per decade that takes place in running performance. It allows us to grow old with dignity and even delight.

The essence of living is wanting more life; not staying where you are but wanting to move on into the future.

Now, I've found asylum among my elders in the sixty-and-over group.

7

The Fun

Play is the answer
—the answer to the unsuccessful fitness program,
the answer to the unsuccessful life.
Once you've found your play,
all else will be given to you.

WHEN I BEGAN RUNNING in the early 1960s, I made two discoveries.

First, I discovered my body. I found my body was a marvelous thing, and learned that the ordinary human body can move in ways that have excited painters and sculptors since time began. I didn't need to be told that I was a microcosm of the universe, and indeed its greatest marvel.

I also discovered play. The great discovery was that this wonderful body was made for play. The books on fitness ignore play. They tell us "how to," not "why." They remind me of Bobby Kennedy's remark about the Gross National Product. Those figures, he said, tell us everything about America except why it is wonderful to live here. The books on fitness tell us everything about fitness except why it is wonderful to live at the top of your powers. That reason is play.

Play is our first act. If we are lucky, it will be our last. "The child's toys and the old man's reasons," wrote Blake, "are the products of the two seasons." We begin in play, and in our wisdom return to it. Play is a taste of the paradise from which we came; a foretaste of the paradise we will enter.

I discovered that play is an attitude as well as an action. That action is, of course, essential. Play must be a total activity, a purifying discipline that uses the body with passion and intensity and absorption. Without a playful attitude, work is labor, sex is lust, religion is rules. But with play, work becomes craft, sex becomes love, religion becomes the freedom to be a child in the kingdom.

What, then, is play? Perhaps even more difficult than discovering play is defining it. George Dennison in his *The Lives of Children* states that play is the perfect learning environment and then describes it:

> Let it be an environment that is accepting and forgiving; and let there be real pressures, and let it make definite and clear-cut demands, and yet let the demands be flexible; and let there be no formal punishment or long-lasting ostracism; and let there be hope of friendship and hope of praise; and let there be abundant physical contact and physical exertion; and let the environment offer a sense of skills and a variety of behaviors that lead to greater pleasure . . . and greater security; and let the rewards be immediate and intrinsic to the activity itself.

But that setting doesn't define play. We know play instinctively. Play is a peak experience, the feeling of "that which was, is and ever shall be." When we play, really play, it is unmistakable. Then, we become children and see things as they do, in their essences. Then, the present alone is true and actual. The moment becomes all time, the place we are in becomes the whole world, and the person we are with is everyone in it.

I have known these moments. There are times, for instance, when I come home from running a race in Central Park, and I don't know who won or where I finished or what time I ran. My family wonders, then, why I went, why I spent the day coming and going and endured the cruel hour on those rolling hills. I have no logical answer. I simply know that for that hour I was whole and true and living at my peak as a human being. That hour was life intensified.

Others are discovering the same thing, so the current popularity of running and other sports is understandable. What we are seeing is a revolution of play. Play tells us we are our bodies. It teaches us that all revolution must begin there.

Play is the answer—the answer to the unsuccessful fitness program, the answer to the unsuccessful life. Once you've found your play, all else will be given to you.

Some fifteen years back when the field for a distance run was usually less than a hundred, I ran in a marathon in New York where five of the runners were fifth grade grammar school students. They were members of a team called the River Rats which had been formed at the Tarrytown Grammar School.

At about the halfway point, one of the River Rats, his teeth gleaming with braces, went by me and soon disappeared up ahead. Fortunately, I was able to outlast the other four.

I learned then what I was to read in the texts later: The ten-year-old is one of the best endurance animals in the world.

The heart/body ratio of a ten-year-old, according to a German physiologist, is equal to that of a professional cyclist or an Olympic runner.

A later report comes from a Canadian, Roy Shepherd, who reviewed 9,000 tests of maximal oxygen uptake reported in the medical literature and made an interesting discovery. The maximal oxygen uptake, the best-known test for endurance, peaked for U.S. males at the age of twelve, an age coinciding with graduation from grammar school.

We have no need to worry, therefore, about children this age running races and even marathons. There is no more danger for them than for any healthy athlete. Heat is their only enemy, as it is ours. Proper attention to protection from heat syndromes is essential, but otherwise there is no danger in children running.

There are, to be sure, always the doomsday people. Now that fears about the heart and circulation have been put aside, there has been a lot of talk about orthopedic problems. Growth will be stunted. Other difficulties are postulated.

I myself see nothing that isn't transient or wouldn't have happened had the youngster not run. Runners grow or don't grow the same as children have always done. In fact, the runners who tend to do poorly later are those who develop too much and lose the physical characteristics that made them good at ten or eleven.

And if running is good for a youngster physically it is even better psychologically. Running which produces improvement in endurance and stamina and strength does the same psychologically. It improves the self-image and self-esteem and gives the child the opportunity to do something of value and even something heroic.

These are of primary concern to the child. It is these concerns that make children such a trial. They are continually comparing the attention they are receiving with the attention paid to others. They are in a never-ending battle to be number one.

They are, you might say, no different from the rest of us. They need to feel good about themselves. They need to be successful.

For many children, running offers the best chance to do that. Running is the right food for a healthy narcissism, the narcissism that says, "notice me, love me, value me," and then earns that recognition by being and becoming. Otherwise we have the unhealthy narcissisms of the real world which we feed by having and getting, a solution that always breeds failure.

Running is a positive sum game in which everyone can be a winner. It is especially productive of experiences where children can feel good about themselves. It is essential, however, that the children enjoy it. Running must above all be play. It must be an end in itself. It must provide for the child that magic moment where the world falls away. It must provide those experiences which are truly wordless. As much as possible, training and practice should be fun and should vary so that opportunities are given for runs in groups or alone as the child desires. Pain and fatigue, which can also be part of transcending and uplifting experiences, should be reserved for the race.

Too often I have seen these simple rules violated. I have seen, for instance, large numbers of freshmen come out for cross-country and then never come back. Their goal-oriented coaches were too demanding. There was not enough fun and play so they looked for some other pursuit their sophomore year.

Running is a low-key sport with many advantages. It allows everyone to participate. In running no one need sit on the bench. Every child who wants to run can run. And children quickly discover that the next best thing to running and winning is running and losing.

In a few minutes after a race it would be difficult to know who placed ahead of whom. It would not be difficult, however, to tell just who in the crowd felt good about what they had done. Everyone with a scant few exceptions.

What then is the problem with children running these long races? Simply that they will be turned off this wonderful sport and so lose what could be a lifetime of health and growth and happiness. We have seen it happen in other sports. We know of the tennis parent, the ice-skater's parent, and the problems in Little League and Pop Warner. And perhaps the worst of these is swimming.

I recall one Boston Marathon when I ran the last mile or so with a thirty-five-year-old dentist who told me he had been a swimmer at Ohio State. I asked him why he wasn't swimming instead of running. "I've never been in a pool since I graduated," he said, and I know that that is not an unusual occurrence among swimmers.

I'm always afraid of that with young runners. Will some parent or coach push them until they lose all the love of running and grow to hate it? Or will they lose interest and stop before they learn how much it has to offer?

We are a breed that crossed continents on foot. We were born to be in motion and in motion for inconceivable lengths of time. And what we can do, our children can do also.

We are also of a breed that has an inevitable drive toward the heroic.

Each of us wants to prove that he or she is of value. Each one of us wants to prove his or her self. Children want no less.

Those who would prevent them must know something I don't know.

From what I remember of our block on Brooklyn, it wasn't exactly a melting pot. There were no blacks and no Jews, but we did have Irish, Germans, Italians, Armenians and one or two Poles. And we did have divisions, but those divisions had nothing to do with ethnic or racial or religious differences. It was whether you were a talker, a doer or a thinker.

In those days, these differences were evident every day after school when the gang gathered for the afternoon game. One group stood out immediately. They were the talkers. They had little interest in the game except as a means of socializing. They could spend the entire afternoon discussing what to play and choosing up sides. Talking was their real game. Should the game actually get underway, they still found the most enjoyment in conversation. In fact, the talkers would be just as pleased if the games were never played. Being together and gossiping was all they really cared about.

While they passed the time on the brownstone steps, the doers would already be in action. They were the real athletes trying to get the game underway, but in the meantime horsing around, bumping each other and generally trying each other out. For these doers, the day would not be a success unless they hit something or somebody. Football was their game, but they hung in there the rest of the year getting pleasure from flinging the ball against the stoop or whaling a pitch three sewers in stickball.

That left the third group, the thinkers, waiting quietly but impatiently for the game. Talking and horseplay didn't appeal to them. The game was everything to this group, which found in it the ease and assurance so difficult for them to reach elsewhere. This was a chance to lose themselves in a new and different world where they were competent and brave and excelled in something where it was worth excelling.

Those were the groups on my block—not based on the accidents of birth, but on the traits that really divide men and yet unite them as they did the players on my block.

Some, perhaps most, of us have come no further than that block in Brooklyn. We had people who wanted to settle an argument by punching you in the nose. They still do. At their best, these doers can be heroes. They are courageous, resourceful, adventurous, energetic and loyal citizens. At their worst, they are bullies and bigots.

The easy-going style of the stoop-sitters has carried them through the years, healing wounds and making the irreconcilable reconcilable. At their best they are friends with everyone, comprising a group affectionately recognized as the "salt of the earth." At their worst, they have become corpulent and sodden with food and honor and money.

The thinkers, always searching and never certain, have shattered false idols and ridiculed false gods. They have made everyman look closely at his own beliefs. But at their worst, they themselves have believed nothing, and have lost their loyalty to country and man and even God.

It is much easier, I think, to be black or Irish or Catholic or Jewish than to be a man.

"Man," wrote Schiller, "is never more human than when he plays." Play is the path to self-knowledge, the way to self-acceptance. If you would know yourself and then accept that knowledge, you must first find your play, and learn how to play it.

We knew that once. When we were young, we had no difficulty playing. We had sports for all seasons. Whether we were good at them or not, they filled our hours with interest and absorption and delight. We knew then what Chesterton meant when he said, "If a thing is worth doing, it is worth doing badly."

Unfortunately, we forget all of this as we age. I came upon my forty-fifth year no different from millions of others. I had forgotten the child I was. I was trying to be someone I wasn't. I asked the authorities, the experts, those with infalliability, just what I should do and how I ought to do it.

Fortunately, the knowledge of the true self is not far from our consciousness. It is just that we won't accept it. What I had to do was to go back to play, to the doing of something that came naturally. When I began running, all of this came back to me. I ran like the ectomorph and cerebrotonic I am—enjoying solitude, delighting in reflection, finding peace in privacy, feeling satisfaction in the detachment that has come to mark almost everything I do.

Running, therefore, defined the person I am. It filled in the picture of the real me. It made me understand that I was normal. That personality is not a matter of charm and agreeableness, but simply self-acceptance.

Running can do the same for almost anyone. It is a universal sport. Anyone can do it. Anyone can enjoy it. I know there are some who say running is a bore, some who must hit something or somebody when they play. I have heard, for instance, of a rugby player who said he would play tennis if every third or fourth game he could jump over the net and beat the crap out of the other guy. And a headmaster of a prep school once told me they had lacrosse in the spring for kids who like to hit each other.

But still the fact that we are aggressive or tolerant or withdrawn has a great deal more to do with *how* we play rather than the game itself. Running can be made to satisfy these competitive, explosive instincts. Training must be hard and exhausting, and competition frequent.

For those who are more social, running must have social values. Training must be done with others and at a comfortable pace. Racing should be an event and it should be marked by good fellowship. Run-for-fun meets or only incidentally competitive races are needed. Group running can be decisive in the success of such a program.

Find the kind of play that fits you. Remember the saying: You can never beat a man at his own game.

In my running beginnings, I thought of myself as a member of a running elite. I saw myself as one of those happy few who were born to run. I pictured myself as the perfect runner: loner, interested in ideas, content to cruise the roads, living inside my mind, thinking myself inadequate for aggressive and competitive activity, supposing that I had little need for companionship. Function follows structure. I was built for running and little else.

To some extent, this was true. Running is the place where we born runners can delight in our own ability, be surprised by our own competence and find joy in a momentary excellence. But running does more. It makes runners into whole persons who accept competition and confrontation, into fulfilled persons who enjoy being there with others.

My running made me grow. It taught me to accept the paradoxes of the human condition, experience my own truth and act out the inner man. We embody truth, said Yeats, but we cannot know it; we must live it. To do that, we must become the persons we really are.

Running is basic training for that process. It is the sport for all reasons. It is play, it is exercise, it is thought and meditation, it is competition, it is community and neighbor, it is the self and the other. Running is not pure physiology although it can be, not purely psychological although it is at times, not purely religious although in certain circumstances that is its essence.

Running, therefore, is the sport for everyone. No matter what element dominates our temperament, constitution or personality, running provides an outlet. It satisfies that demand, and at the same time allows us to define our weaknesses and make them strengths. It supplies those missing attributes that diminish us and keep us from functioning fully. It makes us whole.

In the beginning, and perhaps even continually for some, running is not a pleasure. The discomfort and boredom of running are the price for the physiological marvels that result from it. For those who live by law and order, by gratification deferred, who see a desired fitness at the end of the road, this can be accepted. Commitment, self-control and hard work are part of their nature. For them, running is one of those purifying disciplines that the Greeks thought made you the sort of an individual a god might be willing to inhabit.

Others who have never been athletic, whose play has been in coming together with friends, can find in running a sacred hour that brings communion with others. For them, running succeeds because it is done in concert.

But for everyone, regardless of the original inducement or the primary motivation, running becomes a ready means of self-completion. This is a state which philosopher Paul Weiss described as "the ability to master other realities while remaining yourself." It occurs most readily, he said, in sports. Running is the perfect sport.

The Mennonites belong to a Protestant group known for its emphasis on plain ways of dressing, living and worshipping. When you think of Mennonites, play is the furthest thing from your mind. The Mennonites are hard-working, no-nonsense people. They neither drink nor smoke. They are exiles by tradition and still see themselves as outsiders. In this fight for survival, play would seem to have little place.

Yet there I was, the guest of honor at the dinner celebrating the sixtieth anniversary of the Mennonite Hospital in Bloomington, Illinois, telling close to a thousand of these prairie conservatives about the importance of play.

Later, one of the chaplains would come up to me and say, "As I looked at the banner behind you, I thought to myself that we have done everything well these past sixty years except play." Later, too, everyone would seem happy with what I had said.

But when I had risen to speak, I was not sure how my talk on *homo ludens*—man the player—would be received. I had not been invited to speak about play. I had been invited as a spokesman of the 1970s to speak about fitness. I had been invited, the letter said, because of my preeminence in the field of physical fitness; because I had become a leader in getting people to take care of their bodies. I represented, the letter went on, one of the most significant health trends of this decade. Individuals were developing a renewed and heightened responsibility for their health and their bodies, and achieving new levels of health through personal fitness programs.

I did not deny these good things were happening. It was just that I had nothing to do with it. I was there, in fact, as a *representative* of those people—not as a pioneer or a leader. I was just another also-ran making fitness a way of life, just one of millions who had discovered play and with it all the good things the letter of invitation had talked about.

Ten years earlier in the same room at the fiftieth anniversary dinner, the Mennonites had honored Dr. Charles Berry, the physician for the space program. He was a representative of the space age. He spoke for the man of that decade—the man of machines and technology, *homo faber*, man the maker. As the sixties closed, we put a man on the moon and with him the promise of victory over all our other problems. Technology was about to save man.

That promise was never kept. Technology did not fail—but it did not succeed, either. The machine was not enough. Man had to enter into his own salvation, a salvation that had to begin with his becoming as healthy and fit as possible.

There had been a real fitness movement in the sixties. The program had been devised by a former Air Force doctor, Kenneth Cooper, who had even qualified to fly jets. It was fitness by numbers, a product of an age of diagrams and equations. It was absolutely correct physiologically. But despite that, it had only a limited success.

Man, it appears, cannot be programmed like a space shot. *Homo faber* knew the value of exercise but would not do it. Cooper's program, after an initial surge, lost most of its converts. People were content to sit back and enjoy technology. They agreed to let these scientific marvels do their living for them.

The seventies changed all that. The seventies turned our attention from outer space to inner space. The outer-directed sixties became the inner-directed seventies. Our problems, we discovered, were not so much in the world around us as in the world inside us. But this trip to inner space proved to be infinitely more difficult and dangerous than the one to the moon. The Sea of Tranquility turned out to be considerably easier to reach than that innermost core of tranquility we all seek.

What saved us was play. To get into outer space, one must escape gravity. We get into inner orbit the same way—by getting free of gravity and seriousness, by returning to play. The fitness that comes from play becomes the external sign of the child within. When you see fit people, you see people who have again become children, who have once more discovered play.

The Mennonites paid close attention. They knew about holistic medicine, the treatment of the whole person. Their hospital was affiliated with a health center staffed by an equal number of physicians, mental health professionals and pastoral counselors. It was a thriving clinic with constant cross-referrals. The Mennonites knew the body and the mind and the spirit were one.

It was a small step from there to suggest to them that the mind and the spirit enjoyed play as much as the body, and that play was a natural appetite of adults as well as children.

8

The Run

Running, then, is my discipline,
my specialty, my secret.
The golden days of perfection on the road
are the wholeness that results.
But it is a physical wholeness
that fills my mind and soul as well.
In those moments, my philosophy becomes,
"I run, therefore I am."
And on that basis, I view all creation.

"

WHEN IT COMES TIME for my hour run, my body can't wait. It will accept no excuses. It interrupts my thoughts, interferes with my thinking and will not let me be. Once that feeling arises, everything, however important, must be put aside. Like a dog going for its leash or scratching at the door, it badgers me until I give in.

My body wants out, and I don't blame it. During the working day, my troubles are psychosomatic. My body is reacting to my mind, and my mind is reacting to the innumerable aggravations and upsets and embarrassments which go with living with people and deadlines and goals and obligations. My body is the victim of the tension and guilt and anger that go with failing to meet the demands of others and, even worse, myself. Before the sun is at noon, my autonomic nervous system is in disarray, and my visceral brain is about to throw in the towel.

Anything from a late start in the morning to a yet-to-be-opened letter from a lawyer affects that poor body. What I forgot to do or don't want to do or did badly is constantly reflected in the reactions of my body. The knowing observer can see it all: the shifty eyes, the hang-dog expression, the meaningless smile, the body hunched, the head tucked in, the slouching walk.

I know it in other ways. My hands are clammy, my head aches, and my sciatic nerve sings with pain. I am beginning to hear from my intestines. The belches are here, and I sense the stomach filling with acid. Lower down, the colon is in spasm. No wonder my body wants out. It has had enough of manning the barricades.

So the moment I suggest a run, my body goes crazy. It starts jumping up and down (inside, of course) and making joyous sounds (inaudible, to be sure). It begrudges the time needed to get ready. I have, on occasion, been known to start undressing in the car on the way home. My mind and will are little more than onlookers of this dash to freedom.

Still, once out the door my body accepts the leash. It is willing to wait for the second wind. So I trot that first mile, deliberately making it very easy. I allow myself to savor the initial feeling of release, to experience that sensation of escape. And then I am on the river road, away from traffic, alone on that silent road. I slip the leash and let the body go.

The Swedes call it *fartlek*, which means running play. It is simply the body running for fun, running how it pleases, running at the speed the body wants—easy or hard, fast or slow, jogging or sprinting, dashing up one hill and coasting down another, racing from one telephone pole to the next and then barely moving through the grass, feeling it soft and springy beneath my feet.

The body is in command. The mind can do nothing but follow. My soma is healing my psyche. If you saw me now, you would call out, "Looking strong, Doc, looking strong." I feel that way, too—strong and competent and a little proud. For once this day, I am doing what I do best and doing it well.

William James had it right: "To make life worth living, we must descend to a more profound and primitive level. The good of seeing and smelling and tasting and daring and doing with one's body grows and grows."

I can feel that good growing. My body and I go for a long ten-miler every other day now. Listening to it has convinced me that anything every day is too much. There were days, you see, when I took my body out whether it wanted to go or not. It was like dragging a reluctant pooch by the neck. But my body loves those tens. Even a mile from home, when you would think it would slow down and just enjoy, I find my body accelerating.

When I say, "Hey! Slow down and think of tomorrow," what I hear back is, "That's your problem. Tomorrow is my day off."

When I returned to running, I had quite modest ambitions: a mile or so on the ten-laps-to-the-mile track I had marked out behind my house. But that mile became five, and then I began to venture out on the road. The five became ten, and then I discovered the races.

With my first entry blank, I entered a new world. Before me was a cornucopia of excitement and achievement extending from the mile to the marathon. What started as a minor aberration turned into a monomania.

Man, we know, is never content. The jogger who is able to run previously unthinkable distances at previously unthinkable speeds wants to do better and better. The person who thought three miles an incredible distance and ten-minute miles an incredible pace is no longer happy with either accomplishment. The entry blank changes all that. Once a newcomer enters a race, there is a new set of standards, a new set of values. Play becomes sport, which is play raised to the highest degree in its demands and its rewards. Sport is play taken seriously. It asks for the individual's best and will commend nothing less.

Racing was an education for me. I quickly learned the facts about two new variables: place and time. I discovered that place was not that important. It would vary with the number of people in the race. The bigger the field, the more people who would beat me and the more people I would beat. Place was secondary.

It was time that mattered. It was those minutes per mile that I carried home with pride or disappointment. It is minutes per mile that bothers almost every runner. That statistic leads to the Failure to Thrive Syndrome, the runner who hits a plateau and cannot seem to improve. The complaint now is, "I've gotten this good. Why can't I get any better?"

When I failed to improve, it was not that I was training too little. It was that I wasn't doing the right kind of training. I needed the long, slow distance to build up my endurance. But I also needed training of the anaerobic kind for speed and for stamina. This is energy produced in the absence of oxygen. It is the ability to go into oxygen debt and not develop too much lactic acid. The best way to teach my body that ability is to do interval 440s or 880s at the pace I set as my goal.

When I finally accepted that truth, I joined a high school track team and began to do speed work two days a week with the milers. Five years after I began running, I ran my best mile of 4:47, and 10 years after I began, I ran my best marathon of 3:01.

What I discovered, and you should know, is that improvement is not linear. It is cyclic. I also discovered that training is not like money. You cannot put it in the bank and save it. You have to go out continually and fight again and again for the desired improvement. If I am to run a five-minute mile again, it will mean a lot of "bottom" work and a lot of painful "sharpening" work as well.

I spoke of that with Roger Bannister, hoping he knew of an alternative. I asked him about racing a few more five- and 10-milers or doing stadium steps, or perhaps some real long runs.

"George," he said, "you are avoiding the truth. Interval work is the only answer."

The worst-tasting medicine always works best. But like all cures, it must be taken only as directed.

* * *

I have a love-hate relationship with hills. I hate running up hills, but I love the feeling of accomplishment I get when I reach the top. I hate the pain going up, but I love the relaxed sprint down. I'm always looking for a flat course so I can run my best time, yet I look for hills, too, because I want to meet the greatest challenge.

Hills come in all heights, lengths and grades. Their impact depends not only on their shape but also on their location along the course. No matter where they are, they tend to separate runners rapidly. A group tightly bunched going into a hill is likely to descend in single file a half-mile farther on.

There are some awesome hills at the beginning of races. The worst I have ever run on was in Wheeling, West Virginia. After the gun went off, we took a little quarter-mile tour of downtown Wheeling, and then came the hill. It was a mile-and-a-half long with a relatively steep grade. Halfway up, I had forgotten about the race. It was just me and the hill, just me and the space of ground between where my back foot pushed off and my forward foot landed.

A limited focus always helps. The mountain climber's rule is "Don't look down." The runner's rule is "Don't look up." One upward gaze and I am overcome by the immensity of the task. The attention must be all inward—to monitoring the pain, correcting the form and living in that little area. I cannot live in the future that is the top of a hill.

In a race on a flat course, I have to maintain contact with the runners around me. I cannot ignore anyone passing me. On a flat course, I am running all-out from the gun to the finish. It is as close as running can come to being *mano-a-mano,* an eyeball-to-eyeball confrontation. Hills make for a different race. All runners differ in their ability to take hills. So the hill becomes my competitor, not the other runners. I pay no attention to whom I'm passing or who is passing me.

When I train on hills I use a trick the weight lifters use. They find the weight they can lift just ten times. If they can only lift it nine times, it was too heavy. If they can lift it eleven times, it was too light. I find the pace that just gets me to the top without stopping. If I have to quit on the way up, it was too fast. If I am able to keep going past the crest, it was too slow.

One time when I was hill training using this method, I came to a hill and gauged it just right. I ran completely out of gas right at the top. Only it wasn't the top. There was another rise that I could not see from below. I refused to stop and continued up, gradually getting slower and slower. When I finally reached the top, only I knew I was running. A passing motorist might have suspected I was shadow boxing.

When the finish of a race is uphill, it seems as if the effort and any consequent pain is doubled or trebled. The worst of these uphill finishes for me is the Cesar Rodney half-marathon in Wilmington, Delaware. One year, I came to that final torment a yard or two behind a fierce rival of mine. He was, we both knew, in twenty-first place. This fact was to determine our finish. There were, we both also knew, only twenty prizes. So there was nothing at stake at that point except one of us beating the other. I charged by him, took a dearly-bought ten-yard advantage and beat him handily. He told me later that he saw no point in battling to death over twenty-first place, so he eased in.

At the post-race ceremony, the meet director announced that they had somehow come up with one more trophy, so I got an award for twenty-first place. God loves runners who refuse to quit on hills.

I was on the third and final lap of a twenty-mile race in Central Park when I said to my running companion, "Well, at least we only have to run that 110 Street hill once more." He answered, "Doc, that's what we're doing best."

It struck me that he was right. The length of the race had led us to adopt a nice, steady pace. When we came to a hill, we simply maintained the same effort and ignored the slowing of our speed. I noticed that I was taking the same number of strides, but I had decreased my stride length considerably.

Somewhere, I had read that climbing stairs was nine times the effort of walking on the flat. Running up a hill was much the same. To keep the effort constant, I had to take very short steps. I was doing the same as a cyclist who shifts gears on a hill, again using the same effort but sacrificing a significant amount of speed. What we had done was to shift into such a low gear, and the hill had been virtually eliminated.

Since this breakthrough, I have come to learn a lot more about hill running. One indication that I am still using too much effort is a discomfort in the thighs. This is due to lactic acid buildup and indicates, among other things, that I have passed the anaerobic threshold. When this happens, I am using muscle glycogen wastefully. There is a good chance I will come up short in a long race. At the least, I will be running tired and hurt with the lactic acid accumulating in the muscles.

One friend of mine uses this discomfort to gauge his pace uphill. He increases his speed until he gets this sensation and then holds it there. I prefer to back off from that point and try to hold the effort just below the anaerobic threshold. The main difficulty with settling for this constant painless effort was the hordes of runners that passed me. There are any number of runners who pour it on going uphill, increase their effort and even escalate their pace. The worst thing about hills for me had been this feeling of incompetence as these people charged by. I finally learned to ignore them, and things brightened considerably. I now let them run the hills any way they want. I attend to my own business, not theirs.

My own business is running downhill. I always knew how to do that. I learned it in high school: Get up on the balls of my feet, lean forward, let go. Downhill, I'm a demon. Runners who thought they had put me away going uphill are surprised to find me at their shoulder, then past them and still going. Downhill, I let gravity take over. My legs are flying. Yet all around me are the strong runners who passed me on the uphill, now using more energy checking themselves than I am in going by them.

I used these tactics through college and then put them away for more than two decades. When I came back, I learned about distance running from an old-timer who was a bear going uphill. When we came to a grade, he would accelerate. He always took the hills in high gear with me struggling in his wake. Then, we would take it easy on the downside, landing on our heels and gradually recuperating from our surge up to the crest.

This style fitted him perfectly. He had heavy, powerful legs. He was a good climber but had no speed. He could not let out going downhill. I was, of course, the exact opposite and still accepting his way as best. It took a lot of years and a lot of races before I saw the truth. I was built to go uphill slowly and then race down.

I have tried to become a better uphill runner. Even though attacking hills in a race is reserved for the final stages, attacking hills in practice must be routine. That is the only way I will get any better in races where hills are a factor. Hill training develops my quadriceps, and the state of my quads frequently determines the level of my performance. Further, hill-work is what physiologists call "resistance training," which provides strength and endurance that can be gained no other way.

There are even more important reasons for running hills in practice. I can come to a hill and see in it everything bad in me. The hill is every duty I have avoided, every chore I have left undone, every decision I have put off making. The hill is my chance to rectify that, to do penance, to straighten out my account, to make a fresh start. That's what a hill is for.

When I run that hill with that in mind and heart, I am for a short while a new person. Good things have, of course, happened to my maximum cardiopulmonary steady state, but even better things have happened to my psyche.

At such times, I reach down and get energy available under no other circumstance. My body keeps going because I will not allow it to stop. My hands are clawing the air. My head is tilted to the side. Pain is everywhere. My legs are leaden stumps. The foot once planted seems immovable. Yet inside I am running. I will not stop running.

Once, as I toiled up a hill on a training run in ninety-degree heat, I came upon one of my townsmen standing by the curb. "Masochism!" he called out. "It's nothing but masochism."

Whatever it is, it's what I do best.

A reader told me about a peculiar experience he had on a ten-mile run. "At the 8½-mile mark," he wrote, "it was like I'd just gotten a jolt of morphine, a warm rush all over. I felt like I could run all-out forever."

"What was it?" he asked. Does that feeling have a physiological basis? Of course it does. On that day, and during those miles, he had reached his physiological peak. He had enjoyed for that brief time his maximum steady state of heart and lung and muscle endurance. Stress sought and applied and responded to had created this transient perfection.

I, too, have had such days—days runners dream of, days when I can do no wrong, days when the challenge of time and distance evaporates before my strength and stamina, days when I feel I can run forever and at any pace I choose.

One such day came after an Atlantic City Marathon which I had finished still full of running. Two days later, I went to a high school cross-country meet and ran successively in the freshman, jayvee and varsity races. I could have run until night fell.

Another time a few weeks after a Boston Marathon, I had a similar occurrence while running interval halves—surely the most demanding of workouts. But this time, instead of continually deteriorating, my times improved. In the final half-mile, I broke through some sort of barrier and ran my best time of the day.

All athletes know such moments, those times when they are at the top of their game and everything falls into place. Every athlete sooner or later has these occasions of putting it all together, of knowing the sensation of suddenly and surely being integrated with the sport and the environment—all conflicts are resolved and all doubts cease.

Why this mysterious fusion, this knowing you are one with what you are doing, this being for one hour the complete athlete?

For me, it began with believing I was a runner. When I was younger, my sport changed with the seasons. In our youth, we are available to every experience. Life is still an experiment, so we keep ourselves fluid in everything—work, friends, sport, life style, belief. Eventually, we must choose. We must concentrate on becoming who we actually are. We must grow. We must mature. We must follow our instincts.

I chose running. From then on, it was simply a matter of accepting the demands of becoming a runner. "Life," wrote William James soon after he had given up the idea of suicide, "must be built in doing and suffering and creating." I could see the foundation of doing and suffering and even the creating in running.

In addition to this discipline, I had the feeling of being special. Not everyone can get out of bed and run twenty-six miles of a morning. Those who have that ability feel special. We need that feeling if we are to go it alone. We need the support of self-esteem, of feeling our own worth.

Running also became my secret—another necessity for anyone who seeks his own way in this world. The individual, said Jung, needs a secret to support him in his isolation. So running and its mysteries are my secret. No matter how many times I write about it, the whole truth will never be told.

Running, then, is my discipline, my specialty, my secret. The golden days of perfection on the road are the wholeness that results, or at least the part of my wholeness that is physical. But it is a physical wholeness that fills my mind and soul as well, a physical fitness that anticipates psychological fitness. In those moments, my philosophy becomes, "I run, therefore I am." And on that basis, I view all creation.

9

The Race

> **The desire to run comes from deep within us
> —from the unconscious, the intuitive, the instinctive.
> And that desire becomes a passion
> when the runner learns to race.
> Then the race becomes all
> —the lovemaking of the runner.**

I HAD JUST FINISHED the Battle of Monmouth five-mile race, and was standing near the finish line shouting encouragement to the long line of runners following me. Where the race ended, there was a large digital clock so the runners could see at a glance what their final time was. From where I stood, however, a few feet before the finish line, the clock was not visible to them. I was there to alert them to their times.

"Come on!" I yelled to one runner. "You can break thirty-five minutes!"

Then later, "Take it in, you're 39:30!"

And even later, to an aging and overweight and very tired athlete who then broke into a broad smile, "Way to go, you've got forty-five beat!"

If you are a runner, you know how important it is to break those seven- and eight- and nine-minutes-per-mile barriers. If you are a runner, you also know that for me and the 300 other runners this race was not play; it was sport. We tend to use the words interchangeably, but there are essential differences.

Running is play; racing is sport. Play is the preparation; sport is the performance. My training is play; my race is sport in its purest expression.

You can see two of the basic elements of sport in the finish line and the digital clock. Sport proceeds within certain limits of time and space. In sport, there is an ending and then a score. Winning and losing are secondary to this absolute need for a final outcome.

In most things in life, there is no score, no objective, tangible, clear-cut measure of success. Ambiguity and doubt cloud day-to-day living. It is not enough to be told how good one is at writing or doctoring or lecturing. There is something inside me that wants figures and statistics and facts. For that, nothing can beat the race. The race is the supreme reckoning: a mark down to tenths of seconds, an exact place among hundreds of entrants, a course verified for accuracy, records for comparison, age-group prizes. Who could ask for a better ending?

This finish also guarantees another start. There is always another race and another and another, each pure and complete in itself. Sport is the perpetual second chance. If I fail this week, I may succeed the next. If this digital clock does not give me the desired answer, perhaps the next one will.

Play is only the preliminary to this world of quantifiable excellence. Play has no closure, no urgency, no rules. Play is doing a leisurely ten miles on a country road. Play is suffering through a set of interval quarters, or sprinting to one telephone pole and jogging to the next. Play is five miles of conversation with a plunge in the surf at the end. Play is freewheeling, uninhibited, with no boundaries of time or space.

Sport is, of course, altogether different. When I race over a previous training route, I am now aware that every step matters. A grade unnoticed during a creative reverie now presents a critical test of my pace. A hill not seen as a challenge becomes a pass-fail situation. Long stretches of scenic delight on a boardwalk are now miles of barely tolerable pain.

It is in this encounter with time and space that the runner is forged. The race makes me that athlete. All my potential becomes actual. I leave nothing behind, nothing in reserve. There is only the now, the here and me in the unity of this effort. Like most common people, I become uncommon only in my sport.

The nervousness and self-defeating tension that accompany many precision sports are rarely felt in distance running. Where skill and strategy and chance are prime factors in the outcome, a player is likely to choke. Running, however, is not that type of a sport. In running, effort alone is the measure of each competitor.

The danger in running is worrying too little rather than too much. I frequently come to the starting line with little thought of what lies ahead. The race is a festival. It is meeting old friends and making new ones. The exchange of gossip and entry blanks for coming races fills the available time from dressing until the race starts.

So I forget the warmup, I neglect the stretching, I fail to get psychologically prepared for the challenges only a few minutes away. Then, the gun goes off, and I am overwhelmed by the sudden demands on my body —the swift onset of discomfort, the immediate aloneness that comes with every race.

When I get on the line, I realize that the issue is 90 percent settled. My recent training, whether I am over or under or at my peak, the state of my health cannot be helped. These factors are out of my hands. They are behind me. I need no longer worry about them. I have to remember only two things: one, not to do anything stupid and two, not to quit.

My aim in those few minutes before the start must be to create physiological and psychological readiness. The physiological preparation is simple. Ten minutes is usually enough. It takes me just six minutes of easy jogging to get my second wind. I then break out into a light, warm sweat. That means I have raised my body temperature one degree, and most of the blood is going to the muscles and skin the way it must for all-out running. I then do a few spurts at close to full speed, a few minutes on stretching, a minute concentrating on form and belly-breathing, and I am physically ready for the gun.

The psychological preparation is just as simple and to the point. The essential is solitude, a brief period alone with myself. First, I go over the course mentally, deciding where the bad spots will be. Then, I concentrate on what is really at stake here. I am in this race to do my best on this course, on this day. It is at that moment just before the gun sounds that I make those resolutions men make before going into battle. I accept what is to come with full knowledge of what it may contain.

Once into the race, I try to do the best with what I have. There is an old baseball adage: "Don't beat yourself." I must be careful not to run the first mile too fast. The race must be run evenly. Too much speed in the beginning and I will pay dearly at the end. I listen to my body, not the watch. After that first mile, I know exactly what I can do. I push to the pain threshold and hold the throttle there.

There have been races where this pace has been so slow and painful I have felt like quitting. I have wondered if there would be a way to drop out without anyone noticing. When this happens, I say to myself, "George, it is not your fault. You are doing the best you can." When I can identify with effort instead of performance, there is no need to quit.

I recommend this attitude. Over the years, I remember winning and losing races, but mostly I remember giving the race my best shot. I will not deny that my few virtuoso performances have helped tide me over some barren stretches. But I know that some of my best races where those in which I ran poor times. It is an old story: We hate to suffer, but afterward we are glad we did.

* * *

One reviewer has written that Tim Gallwey's *The Inner Game of Tennis* is no less than a new approach to living. If used successfully, it could eliminate anxiety, self-consciousness and self-defeating apprehension. By applying your inner game of tennis to your life, you would redefine success, purpose and ambition, and you could satisfy desires that seem insatiable.

I'm sure that was Gallwey's purpose. His main interest, of course, is tennis. Tennis is his play, as mine is running. But he also sees tennis as a laboratory where he has learned much about himself and life. His book is as much an instruction on living as it is on tennis.

It all starts, however, with the outer game. For Gallwey, this outer game is "played against an external opponent to overcome external obstacles to reach an external goal." This obviously applies equally to running and other sports.

The outer game is talent, technique and training. It is the development and application of skills. Over the years, I have done that with my running. It is a skill my body has acquired.

I know how to run uphill, how to run downhill, how to breathe, how to carry my arms. I have learned what to do with my hips and my thighs and calf muscles, what is right for my ankle and even my big toe. I have found that tightening any muscle above the hips is useless, and that the upper body is used only for breathing and balance.

The outer game is a matter of achieving the greatest speed and the greatest endurance with the least effort, running the best race at the least cost, reaching as close as possible to that point where there is nothing left, neither ignoring nor being deterred by pain.

But then the inner "me" intrudes. My mind enters the race. The real race takes place in the mind, and here the obstacles are more formidable. Here, the opponent is not the runner next to me but myself, not the pain now but the pain to come, not the pain felt but the pain feared. Here, I am my own enemy.

The inner game, then, is an encounter with the doubts and indecisions that prevent me from being myself, from reaching my potential. The inner game is a contest with my inclination to do less than my best.

We all have that inner voice that says, "I think I can't." It must be stilled. The first thing I must do is to accept the commitment of the race, to determine that I will finish no matter what. This alone is a tremendous help.

That is, however, only part of the answer. The full answer, says Gallwey, is relaxed concentration. I agree. To do my best, I must concentrate, focus down on each step, on every yard. Yet I must not interfere. This is the relaxation, the acceptance.

Such concentration and relaxation can be obtained in tennis by concentrating on the ball. Gallwey suggests that the player say "bounce" every time the ball hits the ground, then say "hit" each time it strikes either racket.

When my inner game falters and my outer game goes with it, when my concentration wanders, I use my own running version. I say "bounce" each time my left foot hits the ground and "hit" when I drive off with my right. This little practice brings me back to that five feet or so I travel with each racing stride. It erases the worry that if I feel this bad now, what will I feel like three miles from here? And it allows me to view with almost clinical detachment the fact that the water tower at the finish line seems no closer than it did ten minutes ago. I can focus down on each yard like a wide receiver who sees only the football while knowing full well that he will be clobbered after he makes the catch.

My mind will have none of this nonsense. My mind knows how much I hate to suffer, knows I have always taken the easy way out. My mind recites a litany of my faults, my limitations, my imperfections. It suggests that I slow down, take it easy.

But oddly, I never do. And neither do those around me. I have beaten many runners, but none because they quit. We have mastered the inner game of running, and we are all winners. For a sweet hour or two, it seems we have also mastered the inner game of life.

The desire to run comes from deep within us—from the unconscious, the intuitive, the instinctive. And that desire becomes a passion when the runner learns to race. Then, the race becomes all—the lovemaking of the runner. The feeling after a ten-miler run truly is something beyond his previous experience. But that heightened feeling is just an overture for the marathon.

Eventually, every runner begins to hear that tune, the marathon singing in his head. From then on, the marathon is background music. From the time I began to enjoy running, I heard that theme. From the time I could run five miles and think it nothing, the marathon was an urgent rhythm in my body. From the time I raced ten miles and knew the benediction that followed, I knew I would not rest until I met the challenge of the absolute distance. The music swelled and became insistent in my ears, a melody of craft and courage, of weakness and power, of being alone and vulnerable and naked and helpless, and yet finally of overcoming.

In time, I have come to know my craft and come to know my body. I now see time and space in a special way. I am concerned with seconds and minutes and hours as are few others. I am interested in bones and muscles and heart beats; in oxygen taken in and sweat passed out; in all the things the body does that can be measured and charted and analyzed. I have learned about lactic acid and muscle glycogen and how aerobic differs from anaerobic metabolism.

But most of all, I have studied how to run a marathon: how to train (ten miles Tuesday and Thursday, and a race on Sunday); what to do before the race (rest for three days and eat carbohydrates); what shoes to wear (training shoes; what you lose in weight you gain in support and shock absorption); what pace to start at (my easy training pace); when to accelerate (at five to seven miles, reach for your best pace); and the proper attitude (concentrate on each step; know every minute you are running a marathon).

I became ready for the part of the marathon that is pure body. But the marathon is much more. It is, to use Yeats' description of poetry, "blood, imagination and intellect brought together." The marathoner becomes the total person, the total runner running the total race.

When I run a marathon, I put myself at the center of my life, the center of my universe. I know my life is not my body or mind or heart. It is what I do and why I am doing it. For these hours, I move past ideas of food and sleep and shelter and sexual fulfillment and my other basic drives. I bring my life and its meaning down to this struggle, this supreme effort which I must do myself without help from anyone.

But because the marathon is allegory and myth and history, I am not alone. At the very time when I assert my own self and achieve a solitary state, I join my fellow runners, become part of the people who run with me, accept identification with others. And why? I'm not sure, but it probably has to do with the story of the people. What we do must not be ignored just because we are not great men. Each marathon is part of our present and becomes part of our past. It is embodied in the memory of those who ran, and those who saw or heard, whether they know our music or not.

The music of the marathon is a powerful martial strain, one of those tunes of glory. It asks us to forsake pleasures, to discipline the body, to find courage, to renew faith and to become one's own person, utterly and completely. And then it asks us to give up that prize and join the whole human race.

Near the twenty-three mile mark of the New York Marathon, the course turns off Fifth Avenue into Central Park. The runners face a short but fairly steep and demanding hill, and then the course follows the undulating road through the park toward the finish.

I entered the park in the grip of the inexpressible fatigue that comes at that stage in the race. I was once again engaged in the struggle between a completely exhausted body and a yet undefeated will. I ran toward that hill, realizing that finishing was still problematical, fearing that I might still have to walk, and knowing that no matter what happened those final twenty-five or more minutes would constitute my most painful experience this side of major surgery.

I ascended the hill past a small group of onlookers. One of them recognized me and called out, "Dr. Sheehan, what would Emerson have said now?"

I had to laugh, even in that pain. It was a particularly deft shot at someone who had used other people's words to express his own truth—and I was now in a situation that clearly no one else could describe. But the question also went to the question of why I run marathons.

The case for distance running cannot be stated simply, even by its adherents. No matter how often I'm asked, even in more favorably circumstances than the twenty-three-mile mark of a marathon, my answer is always inadequate.

I am not alone in this inadequacy. At that same marathon, a questionnaire was distributed asking the entrants why they ran. The series of suggested answers had been made up by scientists of the body and mind. There were fifteen possible choices, the last one being, "Don't really know." The range of answers indicated the researchers' own indecision, their inability to put their fingers on their personal motivations.

I think it instructive, however, that only three of the answers—"Improving physical health," "Improving sexual capacity" and "Acquiring a youthful appearance"—had to do with the body. All the others (except the final disclaimer of not knowing at all) were psychological benefits. Runners apparently take as a given truth that physical health is a by-product of running but not the real reason they run.

I am aware of that also. I am my body. What I do begins there. But I am much more besides. What happens to my body has an enormous effect on my heart and mind. When I run, I become of necessity a good animal, but I also become for less obvious and even mysterious reasons a good person. I become, in some uncanny way, complete. Perhaps it has something to do with a sense of success and mastery over this art of running.

The scientists tried to express this in their suggested answers. Do I run, they asked, to relax, to relieve boredom or to improve my mental health? Is it possible, they inquired, that I do it to achieve recognition or to master a challenge or to find an additional purpose in life? Perhaps running, the questionnaire went on, is something I do for friendship and association, or because I am unhappy and unfulfilled without it.

What we were being asked was the familiar "either/or." Is it process or product that pushes us? Is it what happens while we run or what we achieve through running that motivates us? Is running for the body or the spirit?

My running is not either/or. It is all these reasons and more. Running is indeed product. It is done for the goal—the ability to run a marathon, the having done it. But it is the process as well. Training is not only a means; it is an end in itself. The achievement is not the whole reason. There is also what goes on before the attainment of that achievement, what goes on before the mastering of the challenge, what is gone through in finding an additional purpose in life.

My running is both process and product. Sometimes, it is all meaning and no purpose. Other times, it is all purpose and no meaning. Sometimes, it is work, other times play, and there are even times when it is an act of love.

We who run are different from those who merely study us. We are out there experiencing what they are trying to put into words. We know what they are merely trying to know. They are seeking belief, while we already believe. Our difficulty is in expressing the whole truth of that experience, that knowledge, that belief.

So I wish Emerson had run marathons, and somewhere around the twenty-three mile mark a friend had asked him, "What's it all about, Waldo?"

PART 3

The Work

WHEN HERBERT HOWE was preparing for his doctorate at Harvard, he learned he had cancer. Radiation and chemotherapy were begun. That was his physician's reaction, the scientific one. Howe's reaction was the intuitive one. He became an athlete. With an 80 percent chance he would be dead in five years, he committed the greater part of each day to sports.

"I swam an hour a day," he reports, "furiously punched the heavy bag and ran consistent six-mile miles over a twelve-mile course."

Eventually, he took up skateboarding, hang-gliding and scuba diving. Shortly after the chemotherapy ended, he completed the world's longest one-day canoe race. When he finished the seventy-two miles, he collapsed and spent three hours in the emergency room.

Why all this? Why, faced with pain in the future, seek more pain now? Why, faced with death, take the chance of hastening it? Why push on and struggle when he could take the time to enjoy life?

Howe sees no incompatibility between pain and joy. For him, they coexist. "I had to believe that my body was not decaying," he writes. "I had to believe I was winning."

Then, he quotes Michael Novak on winning as "a form of thumbing your nose, for the moment, at the cancers and diseases that, in the end, strike us all down."

To keep from decaying, to be a winner, the athlete must accept pain—not only accept it but look for it, live with it, learn not to fear it.

Herbert Howe decided to do more and more, to work harder and harder no matter how much it hurt. He then found that perseverance and pride became synonymous. Significantly, he notes, "I gained new confidence." Confidence and, of course, faith and trust grew out of the new man. He had reached a point where his experiment and experience had earned him self-certainty, self-trust, self-reliance.

Howe plunged on. He had come to see his chemotherapy and his doctoral dissertation as two marathon events. Since, he says, pride lasts longer than pain, he pushed on harder than ever before. He was supported and sustained in this by the discipline and absorption of his athletics. He was made whole by the fact that he had gone out to meet pain and grasped it, and having defeated his self-doubts about his physical condition he was ready to face the uncertainty that lay ahead.

Herbert Howe had discovered the athlete's secret, a secret they all share and cannot really express. For one thing, pain is always personal. One's pain cannot be felt by another. No matter how earnest the desire to communicate it, the effort falls short. We can almost, but not quite, understand the total reaction of the protesting body, the undecided will, the questioning reason, the hopeful and courageous heart.

Because it is personal, private and secret, pain is a subject that has baffled theologians, frustrated philosophers, sent psychiatrists to other psychiatrists and caused thinkers to wonder how much the mind can explain. Somewhere inside of pain and suffering is the mystery of existence.

Most of us can see the biological necessity of pain. It protects us, keeps us out of harm's way. Pain is nature's early-warning system.

Very few of us, however, can imagine pain as a logical necessity. Josiah Royce, almost as much a theologian as a philosopher, wrote of pain that way. Through our suffering, he declared, God suffers. God must suffer to be whole and just, and so must we.

Royce's theory is unique, as far as I can see. It is much more common for people to see evil and pain as the expressions of a bad body, due to Original Sin. There are others who see pain simply as a bad joke.

For the athlete, pain is neither of these. His life is good, and to live it well is to suffer well. He recognizes his pain as necessary.

"Live in the uncomfortable zone," a man once advised me, "and when you die you will have no regrets."

For one thing, you will have lived, tried everything, discovered your limits. And there is always the chance that you will do what Herbert Howe did: combine pain with joy, and discover that you and your life have no limits.

10

The Effort

"

**At some point the final drive the the finish,
the running is willed but no longer controlled.
My body is running from memory.
Running has become a reflex
maintained only by a stubborn, unyielding, illogical
determination not to stop.**

"

THERE IS A GENERAL FEELING that people who have reached sixty should take it easy; they have paid their dues and are entitled to relax. Nothing could be further from the truth. There is never a time to take it easy, never a time we can relax.

Whether you are eighteen or eighty, the age-old enjoinders still apply: Know yourself, repent and renew yourself, renounce yourself, perfect yourself. Whatever the command, it holds from the cradle to the grave. It never gets any easier to save your soul.

Robert Frost emphasized this fact of life when answering the letter the *Amherst Spectator* wrote him on his sixtieth birthday. He put aside the whole idea of aging and wrote instead on the difficulty in saving one's soul. "Or if you dislike hearing your souls mentioned in a public meeting," he said, "say your 'decency' or your 'integrity.' "

Saving one's soul or decency or integrity is a never-ending task. Life is ever reduced to this: making one choice instead of another. At sixty, I am still living that day-by-day decision. Choice is still being presented, effort is being demanded. But in one way I am more fortunate than when I was younger. The pattern of my life is beginning to emerge. I have found what I do best, and now I can devote my time to doing it with all my might.

You seize control only by growing in truth and purpose and direction. For me, that began with my body—when I discovered the athlete resident in that blurred, out-of-focus body I was before I began running. Once I became conscious of the integrity of my body, I was on the way to that whole integrity of myself. I was running in the pursuit of those goals which have echoed down the centuries.

There is no book on this—no prescription on becoming a better person, the person you were meant to be, your own best friend. What has to be done is to live—to live fully and dangerously, to take chances. If there are rule, they are these: Use your body with intensity, play with utter absorption, accept pain and discipline and suffering as part of the game.

Pain is a large subject. I once spent an entire morning with a reporter in Seattle discussing where pain fit into the running life. He could not understand why pain was necessary. By the end of the morning, I wasn't sure myself.

In training, pain is something I usually avoid. I want the long, pleasant afternoon runs to be pain-free. Pain suppresses any creative mood, retards thinking and dams the stream of consciousness.

Yet there are days when pain is part of training. I challenge the hills; I do interval quarters. Sometimes, taking care so as not to pull a muscle, I sprint from one lamppost to another. And with each sprint, I strive to take as much pain as I can before I am forced to slow down.

It is not pain I seek. Pain is simply the symptom of lactic acid accumulating in my muscles, and I have to teach my body to handle lactic acid in races. You could as much say that I like lactic acid as suggest I like pain.

Pain is to be used. At times, it warns me I am doing something wrong. At other times, it signals I am doing right. If I am driving for the finish of a race and there is no pain, I know I have not yet pushed my body to its absolute limit. On the other hand, there is pain that commands to go this fast and no faster.

The runner is not a masochist. The runner does not enjoy pain. But between the runner and a personal best lies pain in quantity, both in training and in the race. And the pain, once endured, comes to have a value of its own. I do not seek suffering, but once it has been experienced I feel somehow the better for it.

There is only one answer to pain: Go out to meet it; plunge into it; grasp it as you would the nettle. There is always the chance that you will push through it into an area as calm and peaceful as the eye of the hurricane.

Pain has become my companion. For more than fifteen years, almost weekly and never less than twice a month, I have raced. I have gone where pain is and met it in races where pain is simply a constant like the wind or the rain or the footing.

At some point the final drive to the finish, the running is willed but no longer controlled. My body is running from memory. Running has become a reflex maintained only by a stubborn, unyielding, illogical determination not to stop.

The terrible tendency is to cheat on myself. Cheating in a race is making the effort tolerable. I am not here to make the race tolerable, or life either, for that matter.

Someone, probably a Russian, has written, "Go at once and seek suffering, accept it and bear it, and your heart will find comfort."

If you are looking for that suffering and that comfort, you can find them in running.

"The athlete," wrote one observer, "is a fanatic and an ascetic. A hard-driving, self-punishing, very special kind of human being utterly absorbed in a world that is out of this world." You will find no better example than Yukio Mishima. His psychological autobiography, *Sun and Steel,* traces his progress from a weak, frail individual with an inferiority complex about his physique to just such a person.

"In the summer of my 30th year," wrote Mishima, "I discovered the discipline of weightlifting." Thus began his search for himself through his body. From that beginning he went to boxing and then to Kendo, the modern version of samurai swordsmanship. The novelist, poet, actor became a superbly conditioned athlete. He developed not only the athlete's body but the athlete's mind and spirit as well. And made what he considered his most important discovery. Pain and the physical courage to deal with it.

Mishima brought a special perspective to the problem of pain. His was a new eye, a new ear, a new voice. He came from a world of art, not action; a world of fiction, not facts; a world of imagination, not flesh. In that world he had escaped pain in his own body. He had felt it in others; not himself. All that, he now saw, was a matter of coming in contact with shadows. "I lacked the physical courage," he wrote, "to seek suffering for myself, to take pain unto myself."

His encounter with his body changed that. First he felt pain; then he realized how important it was. Pain became an essential aspect of this new experience. "I perceive," he declared, "that the only physical proof of consciousness was suffering." Gradually, he said, there was born in him a tendency toward the physical acceptance of pain.

"During the past 10 years," he wrote, "I have learned strength; I have learned suffering, battle and self-conquest. I have learned courage to accept all with joy."

Being the writer he attempted to put this transformation and the causes of it into words. He tried taking the athletic life as it is lived and extracting the meat out of it. "Men by now have forgotten the profound inner struggle between consciousness and the body that exists in physical courage," he claimed.

"Consciousness (mind) is generally considered to be passive, and the active body to constitute the essence of all that is bold and daring; yet in the drama of physical courage, the roles are, in fact, reversed. The flesh beats a steady retreat into the function of self-defense, while it is the clear consciousness that sends the body into self-abandonment."

It is, of course, the athlete, that fanatic ascetic, who accepts pain and then charges past it. The athlete lives with pain. Pain is the guide on the ascent to an athlete's perfection. The barrier to that same attainment. Pain guards that final goal. It surrounds the athlete's personal summit.

Pain, therefore, is the only way to know when you are nearing your best, approaching your limits. Pain is the teacher. It gives true marks. It is the true measure. And in following pain the athlete is following human nature. Pain is part of the ascetic instinct. We place no value on anything we get cheaply, and rightly so; the more effort, the more discomfort, the more hardship, the happier we are. When we think on it, asceticism seems quite the best way to live one's life. William James thought so. Now a modern philosopher seems to agree with him.

"The ascetic impulse," wrote William Barrett in *The Illusion of Technique,* "is much stronger than we think and forms a not inconsiderable part of the sense of discipline without which life would cease to have meaning.

"The frenzies of asceticism, which may seem mere aberration and abnormality to our minds, are in fact the inevitable means by which the human animal is driven to give meaning to his existence. We create by denying ourselves. So long as we drive ourselves in the toil of some discipline, we cannot believe that our life is meaningless."

So pain puts the seal on consciousness, gives meaning to life and at the same time refutes Descartes: "The body is but a fiction of my mind." Pain makes us answer affirmatively to Maslow's question, "What is one truly if not first and foremost one's body, one's constitution, one's own functioning?"

No athlete thinks otherwise. When I began running and discovered my body, I also discovered pain. It was there in every race. At the mile mark if I had chosen my pace carefully. Much sooner if I had not. And in training it was anywhere I chose. At the crest of every hill. Or the space between two telephone poles. Whenever I pushed myself enough I could fill my body with pain. At any given moment I could have a collision with my limits.

I too learned that pain defined my "I." I began to see the Self, divided then whole. Pain revealed what the Will is. Not determination about the future. Not a decision about what is to be done. Will is the acceptance of the Now, the painful, suffering, exhausting present in which I now exist.

The race told me most. It is life intensified. The possible and the impossible not yet purely defined. The race is a fierce struggle in which I am my own competitor. "If you want to win a race," Bill Rodgers has said, "you have to go a little berserk." It is the best advice I have ever heard.

If you want to win anything, a race, your self, your life, you have to go a little berserk. If you want to make a leap in consciousness, or personal growth, or self-esteem, you have to go a little berserk. You have to have a new vision. You have to become utterly absorbed in another world, in what James called a new and greater reality. Where you exist as your true and perfect self, the once and future king.

When I am in pain and hating it, I remember what Emerson said: "What would you have; quoth God; Take what you want and pay for it." When the prize is the self, the payment is pain.

I am not at all sure I am a fanatic, ascetic, hard-driving, self-punishing person, but I am ready to meet that price.

One summer I had a lingering leg injury and could not run for about two weeks. I swam instead. Long distance in the ocean. Interval sprints in the pool.

I would do the length of the pool, about fifty yards, at close to top speed. Then climb out, walk back and do it again. Fifty yards swimming is roughly equal to 200 yards running on the track. An all-out fifty yards in the water takes just as much out of me, and possibly a little more since I am a runner, as a 220-yard sprint.

The sensations are much the same. With each one there is a gradual buildup of pain. Discomfort first, then the leaden ache in the arms and legs, finally the whole body screaming. And each successive interval raises the base line of that pain a notch or two higher.

One day I was in the final stages of such a workout, feeling and, apparently, showing the ordeal I was putting myself through. A woman who had been watching came up to me.

"Dr. Sheehan," she said, "I hope you are writing all this down somewhere."

She found the entire episode incomprehensible. Yet at the same time she realized that there must be something here that had value. There must be something worth all this effort and suffering.

There are, of course, physiological reasons for running interval sprints. These sharpening techniques are the final preparation for my assaults on my best times at almost any distance. Intervals raise my anaerobic threshold. They enable me to cruise at a higher speed. Interval quarters done once a week will improve my times noticeably within a month.

But such inducements are not what keep me doing just one more, and then another, and another, testing myself again and again. The physiological formula doesn't require those final two or three. The more painful they become, the less need to do them. So why do I continue? What is actually happening when I do these interval workouts?

As I see it, interval training is as much for the will as it is for the body. I am getting my will ready for the race. I am, in fact, running the race in advance. I am trying to reach that interval quarter which will feel exactly the same as the last lap of a race. And then be able to deal with it mentally as well as physically.

In interval quarters the will is paramount. The will makes me finish one interval. It calls up the energies to do another. William James, who was a student of the energies of man, wrote much on this. He was vitally interested in how we could mobilize the forces which we contain deep within us.

For James this effort was the measure of man.

"Effort," he wrote, "is the one strictly underived and original contribution we make to this world." Everything else is given to us. Health, strength, talent, abilities of all sorts, whether spiritual or mental or physical. Effort is the only element we can add. "He alone is happy," James wrote, "who has will. The rest are zeroes. He uses, they are used."

Otto Rank, who was Freud's protégé, also wrote extensively on the same subject. Like James, he was concerned with the heroic and the exuberances of man. For him as well, the will was all. The will was our only real resource in dealing with life, which Rank viewed as an irrational situation from which there was no escape. We have to deal with the fact that we have been given this will to immortality, despite the reality that we must die.

We all respond to this paradox in our own way. We ignore it, explain it away, find security in belief in the hereafter, or deal with it at a personal level. This last, said Rank, depended on the will. A person, he thought, experiences his individuality in terms of his will. His personal existence is identical to his capacity to express his will in this world.

I know of few better ways to reach this primitive level where will and effort combine than interval quarters. The answer to life's question becomes simply, yes or no. There is no place for explanations, qualifications, excuses. Will I or will I not continue until I know this is truly the last lap?

I remember one time running interval quarters in a high school stadium during football practice. There were fifty or more football players on the field going through drills. They took no notice of me as I did one repeat quarter after another. That day as always the laps gradually became more and more difficult. After each successive interval my distress became more obvious. The gasping more noticeable. The groaning a little louder.

Finally I collapsed on the grass, knowing there was only one more quarter in me and then only if I could force myself to do it.

I lay there for the longest time. The two minutes had almost expired when I finally raised myself, got to my hands and knees. Then I noticed that practice had stopped and they were watching me, curious to see what I would do. It was as if I were an animal hit at long range and they were waiting to see if I would get up and trot off into the woods.

Then I did get up and started jogging slowly to the starting line. Behind me I could hear this cheer ringing, and then someone shouting, "Way to go, Doc."

I will not last forever, but I am damn well going to know I have been here. That day, so did they.

There is a tendency these days to see mental pressure as something to be avoided. We view mental health as a state in which we are free from the feeling that there is something wrong with us; free from the need to become more and more; free from the tension between what we are and what we should be. Mental health, we are led to believe, is to be once and for all free from pressure.

Actually, it is quite the opposite. Mental health comes with the ability to live with these feelings, these needs, these tensions. These pressures are as essential as they are unavoidable. They are our way to salvation.

It is, appropriately, a salvation that requires religion. William James pointed this out in his *Gospel of Relaxation.* Religion, he stated, was the sovereign remedy for worry. The really religious person, he said, is unshakable and calmly ready for any duty the day might bring forth.

We common folk know this. There is an expression we use about people "getting religion." We apply it when people finally realize their sport or study or project requires hard work and discipline and dedication, and that it is likely to be filled with failures and false starts. Yet knowing this, they discover the will to decide, and the strength and energy and faith to persevere. They know you've gotta believe.

Religion generates the same attitude as play: the certainty that whatever happens, things will be all right; that there is no final defeat in this world, and within the rules and the rituals we can be as free and inventive as we please.

Play in a sense anticipates religion. It takes us past our basic needs, beyond being fed and housed and kept warm. Play can give us self-knowledge, although in the process we may get cold and wet and go without food. Play is also a theater of heroism. In play, we become capable of facing what must be faced, of enduring what must be endured and somehow coming through in the end.

William Faulkner, in accepting the Nobel Prize for Literature, said, "man will not merely endure: he will prevail. He is immortal, not because he alone among creatures has an inexhaustible voice, but because he has a soul, a spirit capable of compassion and sacrifice and endurance."

That is my project—that this person, however weak, however cowardly, however fearful, however anxious, should somehow not only endure, but prevail. But first, I gotta believe.

"What strikes me about this whole scene," said my friend who is a playwright, "is how gentle everyone is." We were standing at the finish of the Berkshires Masters Ten-Kilometer Run watching the runners stream by. Beyond the grass homestretch on the soccer field was a small grandstand packed with cheering friends and families. Now and then the applause would rise to another peak as a woman or older man dashed the final yards to the finish.

Only moments before I had come through that finish line wrapped in that silent struggle with myself, deep in the private torture that occurs in

597

the last stages of a race. I had gone through those final six or seven minutes where just maintaining my pace is a notable act of courage. I had heard the same applause. Gotten my time and number. Shook hands, touched others, been embraced. And now stood filled with those wonderful sentiments that fill my soul after a race.

And as I looked into myself and looked at those around me, I realized my friend was right. Gentle was the way to describe it. Gentle and perhaps one word more. Peaceful. A poet friend of mine had used the word. She had never, she told me, seen a face more filled with peace than mine after a race.

The peace is a positive quality. It is not merely the absence of stress or strife or conflict. It is a peace that is active. A peace that is strong. It is a peace that has certainty. A peace that tells me that I am good and holy and complete.

It is also a peace that is rare. All other acts carry within them a counterreaction. There is the depression that follows exultation. The sadness that comes after ecstasy. Not so with the race and the peace that follows. This peace is the fruit of the race. Something born of that suffering, that testing, that exhibition of character, that attainment of class.

And with it comes the relaxation, the elimination of desires, the end of craving, the death of ambition. For a time pettiness and the lesser appetites and all the meanness are wiped out. I have put on the new man.

Earlier I had been more concerned with records and performance. While I was warming up a runner came up to me and said, "You'll set a new record, for sure." I thought not. It was my third race in a week and within that week I had been forced to slow to a walk at the three-mile mark in a training run because of fatigue.

As I had jogged up and down the soccer field where the race was to start and finish, I felt my thighs rubbing together, a sure sign of exhaustion. I stopped thinking then about records and concentrated on the thought of doing my best. I was going to do poorly, I knew, but whatever it was it must be my best.

I need not have worried.

It turned out to be one of those days when everything went well. It was an easy out-and-back course with no hills. The weather did its part;

the day was one of those beautiful, dry, clear days in New England, the sky an uninterrupted blue.

Right from the start I felt good and began to feel even better after the first mile. On the way back I felt so strong it was a matter of controlling my speed lest I sprint the entire last three miles. I had my age group won and was beginning to think about the record.

The sequence was much like one a psychiatrist-runner had outlined in a letter to me, describing a half-marathon. "As I started the run," he wrote, "I recalled the lines from Wordsworth's 'Happy Warrior.' By the time I had reached halfway I thought of Kipling's 'If.' By the ninth mile I began praying. That carried me until close to the finish, when simple physiology became dominant."

I was reliving that experience along with everyone else in the race. The first half was the Happy Warrior, "playing in the many games of life the one where what he dost most value must be won." Then as I neared the last few miles it became Kipling and the task of "filling every minute with sixty seconds of distance run."

By this time I had the record in hand, but I could not back off. It was no longer my record, it was everybody's record. I was no longer running for myself. I was running for the 430 people in this race and every runner who would look at what a sixty-year-old had done and feel proud. Despite the pain I had to break that record by the greatest margin possible.

Then as I searched desperately up ahead for the final turn into the soccer field, it was prayer. The usual prayer of the runner: "Let this cup pass." In the end, of course, it was the body gradually reducing its function, but the will refusing to accept anything but collapse. Trying, in fact, to make the finish and the collapse coincide.

Out of that common experience came the scene that was unfolding before us. This spontaneous meeting of bodies and souls as runner after runner came from that common ordeal. There is no purer embrace, someone once wrote, that than of the vanquished and the victor on the battlefield.

Here was its equivalent, except there was no vanquished. All of us were victors. All of us had gone through levels of effort, levels of pain and hence levels of performance which were, by standards of our everyday existence, superhuman. All of us were record breakers. We embraced as equals.

The race is the key. The race and everything that happens in it. Mostly that is pain. Pain that is in time and therefore never ending. Pain that is the negative eternity Hegel wrote about. And because I have lived with this pain and accepted it and offered it for all my fellow runners I have gained this peace. The peace that is Hegel's positive eternity. The peace that is outside of time and therefore unending.

The last finisher was in and it was time for the food and the awards. We stood in line for chowder and beans and franks and got our soda and beer. Then we sat at long tables eating and drinking and exchanging stories of the race we had just run and others we could remember.

And a gentle peace filled that Sunday afternoon in the Berkshires in New England.

11

The Stress

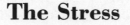

William James spoke of what he termed
the most generally useful precept in one's self-discipline.
It was the rule that bid us pay primary attention
to what we do and express,
and not care too much for what we feel.
Action and feeling go together James declared,
and by regulating the action,
which is under the direct control of the will
we can indirectly control the feeling
which is not.

77

STRESS IS A NECESSITY. We must not avoid it. If not present, we must seek it out. This is especially true in a matter of physical stress, which has become voluntary.

We are no longer obliged to use our bodies. So physical stress must be sought and accepted, applied and endured if we are to become fit. And further, our stress must be of sufficient intensity and our rest periods of adequate duration to build us up rather than tear us down.

What each of us must do, it seems to me, is become an athlete: pick our sport, decide on our event, undergo training, learn technique. No matter that we are the worst in the world at what we do. We must do it. Only in that way will we bridge the gap between what we were born to be and what we are now.

The effect of athletic training, the application of measured amounts of stress separated by suitable periods of recuperation, is easily seen. The difference between the me who began running almost two decades ago and the me who runs thirty miles a week now is the difference between two worlds.

In the first, I did no more than exist. I was able to do what I did for a living and very little more. I fell asleep regularly before the TV set at night. Whatever I did followed the path of least resistance. Anything physical required a push. I was, in a word, a vegetable. Technically, however, I was in good health. I had no active disease. There was no disability that kept me from my daily rounds. What I did not have was true health, zest, enthusiasm, an enjoyment of living. I did not have the capacity to live twenty-four hours a day with the ease and grace and endurance appropriate to the human animal.

Now, I enjoy those things the exercise physiologists promise anyone who would become an athlete—the fruits they guarantee to anyone who would give up the distractions of an affluent society, the rewards for returning to the trials and hardships of another day, the benefits available to those who eat only when hungry and sit only when legitimately tired.

Your heart, the experts say, will become larger and more efficient. You will have a slower pulse and a higher work capacity. Your vital capacity will also increase, as will your ability to take in oxygen and get rid of carbon dioxide. Further, your capillaries will increase and so will your blood volume. The net effect of these changes will be better function of the body at every level down to the tiniest cell. If you train, the scientists say, you will become normal, which is to say the best there is.

I confirmed for myself the claims the researchers made. I underwent a series of tests in a Midwestern medical school. Everything they said would happen did. My fitness scores would be considered excellent for someone thirty years my junior. My endurance capacity was that of a man near his prime.

My first thought was that I was a superior being. My physiologist friend, however, said no. My oxygen intake, he said, was almost all due to a training effect. I was just an ordinary sixty-year-old using stress to the limit and reaping the rewards. He viewed my results as nothing special—just what could be expected from the common, garden-variety human body when stressed correctly.

There are some who think as I once did that athletes are extraordinary people, that athletes are somehow different both physically and psychologically from non-athletes. If so, it is only because the non-athlete has not yet discovered the joys of stress, not yet found the delightful and engrossing and fulfilling process of becoming the person he is.

Everyone is an athlete. The only difference is that some of us are in training, and some are not.

It occurred to me while running that there must be an equivalent training program for the mind. "A sound mind in a sound body" implies that physical and psychological fitness must proceed from the same principles, in fact from the same source.

The basis of the sound body is, of course, stress—stress applied in measured and constantly increasing quantities with suitable intervals of time between to allow the body to adapt. What makes this process work, however, is play. What makes us fit must be sport, or we won't participate. What makes us healthy must come from a self-renewing inner compulsion, or we won't persist in it. What makes us athletes must become an essential part of our day, or our bodies will rebel against it.

If play is the answer to our physical life, should not play be the answer to our psychological life as well? Does not our mental health depend upon play as surely as our physical health does? Will not the play that made us athletes also make us saints?

I put it to you that it does. There is no question in my mind that the best way to handle psychological stress is play. The surest way to develop a sound mind is through humor. How better, then, to deal with stress than with humor?

Humor allows us to tolerate the intolerable, to accept the unacceptable, to bear the unbearable, even to understand the incomprehensible. Humor gives us the capacity to live with ambiguity, the courage to take chances, the strength to go forward without solutions.

What humor does is reduce life to the game that it is. It allows us to take a long look at the real world and all that is evil about us, yet to know that it is somehow part of the plan. Only a sense of humor can help each of us face those great unanswerable questions: Why was I born? Why am I here? Why must I die? What must I do to make my life a triumph?

Long before stress had become our major problem, decades before those who doctor our physical and social ills had recognized its importance, almost a century before authors and publishers had found it to be a profitable and inexhaustible subject, William James had made it a central theme of his lectures.

James was a Boston Brahmin—an aristocrat by birth, position and intellect. He had known stress first-hand. He had been exposed to what must be our greatest danger—security. His initial response had been to contemplate suicide. Rejecting that, he had gone on to develop his own universe. It was a world filled with uncertainty, choice, hypothesis, novelty and possibility. It was an incomplete world, a world in the making, in which man was the most important ingredient. It was a world which demanded no less than his best, a world which required the strenuous life, and was filled with challenge and stress.

In 1900, when James was writing, life was not easy except for the privileged few. Over one third of Americans were farmers. Two thirds of the remainder had manual jobs requiring considerable physical effort. Even the white-collar workers did a considerable amount of walking during the long hours of their work week.

Now, of course, all is changed. Technology has freed all but 3 percent of us from the farms. It has reduced and in most cases removed the manual labor of almost half of the work force still in service jobs. The result is that only about 5 percent of Americans are at jobs that keep them physically fit. The rest of us are gradually succumbing to this new leisure economy. The privileged few have become the privileged many. The common man has become an aristocrat.

Now, challenge and insecurity must be sought. They are not thrust upon us. We have to go back to fundamentals. We need to feel danger, chase after conflict, seek stress. Our aim is "a sound mind in a sound body." Stress is simply the resistance we encounter in seeking that health for our body and truth for our soul.

James said all that at the turn of the century. Every one of us, he thought, needs muscular vigor not to fight the old heavy battles with nature, but to furnish a background of sanity and serenity and cheerfulness to life.

Today, only the athlete knows that feeling. Only the athlete feels the inner peace and confidence that James said wells up from every part of the body of the well-trained human being. James, the intellectual and aristocrat, saw clearly the importance of the body. He knew it was the substrate upon which every other value, mental or spiritual, must take root.

In his commencement address to the women graduates of the Boston Normal School of Gymnastics, William James spoke of what he termed the most generally useful precept in one's self-discipline. It was the rule that bid us pay primary attention to what we do and express, and not care too much for what we feel. Action and feeling go together, James declared, and by regulating the action which is under the direct control of the will we can indirectly control the feeling which is not.

He said we should act cheerful, and act as if we were brave, and force ourselves to say genial things. Then, we would indeed be cheerful and brave and even feel kindly toward those who might annoy us. Whatever stress we were faced with, we could *will* the needed action and hope that our feelings would follow.

This necessity of having the correct attitude has been emphasized recently by the world's expert on stress, Dr. Hans Selye. The way to handle stress, he said, involves taking a different attitude toward the various events of our life.

"Adopting the right attitude," he said, "can convert a negative stress into a positive stress." (For this positive stress, he has coined the term *eustress*, implying good effects.)

The word "attitude" is apt, for it implies more than a point of view, although that in itself is terribly important. In a sense, my attitude is no less than my view of the universe; how I am in the world and what I intend to do about it.

What James and Selye are championing is that we take this word in its positive meaning—that we come, as the athletes say, to play. Such an attitude sees the world as good, and it will somehow be the better for me living in it. It is the conviction that life is a game and that I am a real part of it; I have a role to play. It is the trust that whatever happens, I need have no apprehension about the outcome.

When I see life that way, as the game it is, I am in a position to accept stress. In sport, stress is welcomed. The worse the going is, the better. Obstacles, hardships, the most terrible of conditions only make the game more exciting and rewarding. There is no thrill in an easy win or beating someone weaker. Competition is welcomed because it brings out the best in me.

Do not for a minute think play is not serious. Play is more serious and demanding than anything else I will do. Play is a true measure of how I value myself and what I am willing to do to become the person I am.

Plato saw this. "Life," he said, "must be lived as play—playing certain games, singing and dancing. Then will man propitiate the gods, defend himself against his enemies and win the contest."

12

The Rest

''

'The athlete in training is a sleepy creature'
wrote Plato in *The Republic*. 'Haven't you noticed how
they sleep most of the time
and how the slightest deviation from their routine
leads to serious illness?'

''

MY FRIEND TOM OSLER, who is an ultra-marathoner and teaches math at a state college, says that depressions are a part of life. The runner, he says, must expect them—even welcome them. They are just as normal, just as inevitable, just as important and just as necessary as the happy times.

I am inclined to agree. Periodically, no matter how I try to avoid it, I run myself into a growing inner discontent. Every six months or so, I develop the feeling that every task is too difficult and little worth the effort anyway.

My running suffers most. In fact, it is the first indication that things are amiss. I no longer look forward to my daily run. And should I ignore this lack of zest and run anyway, I tire easily and don't enjoy it. But the running and this loss of enjoyment are only part of it. My moods, my concentration, my attitude toward myself and others are all affected. Instead of battling anoxia and lactic acid and muscles depleted of sugar, I am in hand-to-hand combat with dejection and dependency, with rejection and self-pity, with guilt and loneliness.

Such periods are inescapable. Ecclesiastes was right; there is a time for everything. Human nature frowns on prudence. It demands that we maximize ourselves, do whatever we do with all our might. Predictably, this means periodic exhaustion, periodic failure, periodic depression and, happily, periodic reevaluation.

"The athlete in training is a sleepy creature," wrote Plato in *The Republic*. "Haven't you noticed how they sleep most of the time and how the slightest deviation from their routine leads to serious illness?"

Athletes have not changed since the time of the ancient Greeks. We still are people who require much sleep and many naps. We still get ill whenever our routine is changed. But mainly we are still distinguished by our almost total collapse when we overtrain. This is probably as it should be. The penalty should fit the crime. To the Greeks, pride was the greatest sin. And what is training but pride?

When I train, I am pushing myself to the absolute limit. I am testing the furthermost reaches of my body's integrity. I am trying to go beyond anything I have done before. I am seeking the breaking point of my physiology. Should I pass that limit, I should get more than a slap on the wrist. I should get appropriate punishment, some clear signal that I have

608

exceeded my capacities. And I do. It is called "staleness" and consists of a variety of symptoms which add up to remind me that I am mortal.

When I get stale, I accept this reminder of my finitude. I relax and vegetate. I eat and sleep and nap. Instead of running an hour a day, I take a nap for an hour a day. This routine usually proves to be sufficient penance, and in a week or ten days I am back running at a suitably lower level.

However, there are runners who find that eating and sleeping and napping are not enough. For them, the fatigue persists, the depression goes on, the zest will not return, the curse will not lift. For these runners, days become weeks and weeks, months—and still running is a chore, and performance is never quite the same as before. They are in the dark night of the soul.

Brendan Foster, a world-record-holder from Britain, once described a distance runner as a person who went to bed tired at night and got out of bed even more tired in the morning. I think he was wrong. That is the description of a distance runner headed for trouble. When that state occurs, it is time for rest and reassessment.

Plato said we needed a more sophisticated form of training. It is time we heeded his advice.

In running, as with everything in life, there can be too much of a good thing—too much training but especially too much racing. It is extremely hard to resist the excitement and challenge of a race. So the runner can become overraced just as the tennis player is overtennised and the golfer is overgolfed.

My mail is filled with letters about this phenomenon: high school seniors who have never achieved their sophomore promise, college runners now unable to get back to what they did in high school, club runners who are getting worse instead of better, runners everywhere wondering why their bodies are breaking down.

It is a mystery, this state of staleness—the heavy legs, the rapid pulse, the frequent colds, the loss of zest, the poor performances. There is no specific test that can pin it down. Nor is there any test that will warn me when I have reached my peak, and the next race or hard workout will send me over the cliff into a state of fatigue and depression.

That knowledge is just what we need. The runner who is in peak condition is only a razor's edge from catastrophe. A personal best time is, to be sure, an occasion for joy and celebration, but it should also make the runner quite cautious about trying to better the performance immediately. I have come to the conclusion that the proper response to running an outstanding race is to take a week off to savor it.

Intelligent runners tend to do that. In fact, the winner of one fifty-six-mile Comrades run in South Africa took *six weeks* off before resuming training. Few of us, however, have that common sense. Few of us read our bodies that well. A great race, we are inclined to think, is evidence of an even greater race inside. With a little more speedwork and some time on the hills, who knows what marvelous things can happen? The marvelous things, however, often turn out to be those dismal complaints.

The clearest warning of impending staleness is a bad race. Nine times out of ten, this slump means the runner is overtrained, but the impulse is to go out and train harder. That only digs the pit deeper. The proper approach to this all-too-human problem is to recognize the wisdom of Ecclesiastes, which says there is a time for everything. There is a time to race, a time not to race. There is a time to be elated, a time to be depressed. There is a time to be king of your hill, a time to be at the bottom of the heap. There is a time to train, a time to nap.

When you restore the Biblical rhythm to your days, you will be able to accept staleness. And when you do, it will disappear.

When William Jones spoke on "The Gospel of Relaxation" to the women graduates of the Boston Normal School of Gymnastics, his theme was the vital necessity of the fit and relaxed body to mental health.

Fitness comes first, of course. In saying this, James was echoing the Greeks. In their society, gymnastics was a crucial component of each citizen's life. So James was delighted to address these women athletes. Already, he declared, they had gained that general sense of security and readiness for anything that might turn up. They had discovered, he was sure, the benefits of energy and initiative and independence. But to make the most of these new-found capabilities, they must also learn, he said, to relax.

No statement would be more in character. James was one of the originators of the James-Lange theory of emotions. He believed that emotions begin in the body, not in the mind. We become excited or aggravated or sad or tense *after* our bodies become excited or aggravated or sad or tense, not before. The overtense, excited body, therefore, keeps us in an overtense, excited state of mind.

"It is not the nature of our work that accounts for our breakdowns," he told the graduates, "but those absurd feelings of hurry, of not having time, that breathlessness and tension, that solicitude for results, and that lack of harmony and ease by which the work is accompanied."

This analysis is echoed in some current views on stress. Dr. Meyer Friedman has described the type-A behavior of coronary patients in almost identical terms. "Such behavior," says Friedman, "is an action-emotion complex exhibited by individuals engaged in an incessant struggle to achieve more and more in less and less time."

Friedman sees such behavior as accelerating certain components of the autonomic nervous system, thus causing cardiac damage. These victims of the "hurry sickness" are not deterred by warnings of another heart attack. They must be shown, says Friedman, that they are cheating themselves—that in being totally absorbed in obtaining the things worth *having* they have stopped doing the things worth *doing*.

The Greeks told us that. James told us that. Now, Dr. Friedman is telling us that. Perhaps we ought to listen.

Running is my relaxation technique. When I run, I relax. When I run, I meditate. Instead of becoming immobile and closing my eyes and repeating my word, I take the opposite course. I run and open my eyes and move into inaccessible areas of my mind and soul.

Movement is the key. Movement is the mantra that opens up my mind. It is the rhythm that leads to relaxation. The need for movement is basic to our nature, to our physical and mental health. Our well-being, our adaptation to stress literally depend upon moving about.

Nietzsche told us, "Never trust an idea you come upon sitting down."

And Thoreau, whose inspiration came with walking, said, "Methinks that the moment my legs begin to move, my thoughts begin to flow."

Compared to running, other relaxation techniques seem to me like so much first aid. I use them for rest, recovery and restoration of energy. But motion is vital. Contemplating my navel is of no use unless both I and my navel are in movement. Nor does descending into the subconscious make sense unless I am going to look around when I get there.

Running brings everything together. What running does is increase my receptivity, raise my consciousness, heighten my perception. What follows is simply a temporary stay against chaos, a brief glimpse of beauty or perfection that helps me to face the ever present stress and uncertainties of my life.

When I run, I know as you do that nothing is ever settled. There will be no answers until there is no need for them. We live in an open-ended world. There are, as William James said, no conclusions.

In ways I only dimly understand, running encourages me to live with my uncertainties. It enables me to view the future not as ominous but full of promise. Indeed, there are days I feel as if I was, am and ever shall be—which is about as relaxed as you can get.

13

The Results

"

We are much like the corporation.
We rely on external aids rather than organic growth.
We, too, use some tricky bookkeeping
to prove that we are as good as we ever were.
We, too, reach a time
when we must grow out of our own resources
—a growth that is a day-to-day progress and,
simultaneously, the building up of new energy,
a new vision, a new person.

"

I HAD COME TO PHOENIX to address the top employees of a giant conglomerate at their annual business meeting. The pattern of these get-togethers is familiar. First, everyone is congratulated for a successful year. Then, they are told that much more is expected of them in the next twelve months. They did great, but they must do better.

The scenario reminds me of a story about Vince Lombardi when he was coaching Green Bay. The Packers had won this day and were filing out of the stadium through a cheering crowd of spectators. One of the fans leaned over and yelled to Jim Taylor, the hard-hitting fullback, something about playing a great game.

Taylor turned to him and said, "By the time Lombardi gets through with us in the locker room, we'll think we lost this game."

What football players learned under Lombardi and what employees learn at annual meetings is that the game is never over, the contest never ends. The company is not interested in past successes. It is not interested in retirement and Florida condominiums. It is terribly and vitally interested in performance, the day-to-day doing of routine things well and ordinary things better.

This meeting was no exception. The president spoke about growth. Their company, he said, had grown enormously and competently through the acquisition of other companies. Now, that period was over. They would no longer take over other companies. From now on, their growth would be internal, not external.

This growth, he went on, must of necessity come from their own resources. It could not be someone else's strength, someone else's assets, someone else's know-how, someone else's initiative. And it would have to be a true growth, not some bookkeeping sleight-of-hand.

Such a program, he concluded, would leave no room for complacency. They could not rest on what they had done. This was not the time to hunker down and be content with where they were. He was sure, however, they would be up to it. It took him about an hour to give them the bad news.

As I sat there, I thought to myself, he is giving my speech. He is talking about corporate fitness in the way I was going to talk about individual fitness. The individual also comes to a time where growth must be internal.

When I rose to speak, I told them the good news. The company would grow, and they would grow with it. First, they had to see where they were, then they could see where they were going. We are much like the corporation. We rely on external aids rather than organic growth. We, too, use some tricky bookkeeping to prove that we are as good as we ever were. We, too, reach a time when we must grow out of our own resources—a growth that is a day-to-day progress and, simultaneously, the building up of new energy, a new vision, a new person.

I was not there, I told them, to sell fitness on the basis of longevity but on performance, not because it reduced risk factors but because it contributed to growth. I could see, I told them, that a vibrant, growing corporation must have vibrant, growing employees. So corporate growth depends upon individual growth; corporate performance rests upon individual performance, and the fitness of the corporation hinges upon the fitness of the individual personnel.

In parting, I told them about a friend of mine who had been a swimmer in college. When he joined this company, he started swimming during his lunch hour so he would outlive all the other executives. In the process, however, he outworked them, outthought them and outcreated them. He outdid them in everything connected with his job. When he finally came out of that pool, he was the president.

There came a time last year when I was fed up with conducting medical clinics for runners. That weekend, as so often in the past, I was on a program with Dr. David Costill. My role was to discuss injuries. His was to show how the exercise physiologist could help the runner.

When I saw Dave, I told him, "There must be something better we can do with our time than saying the same old things one meeting after another."

Dave looked at me, smiled and said, "George, they're hungry out there."

He's right. They are hungry. Distance running is more than a sport. It is a way of life. And the running life requires more and more knowledge of the workings of the human body. Distance runners are hungry for any information they can get. I should not need to be reminded of that. Runners ask more questions than a three-year-old. Their questions are just as basic and just as difficult. I'm as hungry as the next one—and just as likely to be at Dave Costill's lecture, taking notes.

Dave has the last word on physiology for me. He is one of the few scientists I have been associated with who has a complete grasp of his subject. When Dave says, "I don't know," I realize nobody knows. Most runners feel the same. For us, Costill has become the Answer Man.

Costill also is that rare academic individual—the exceptional scientist who is also an exceptional teacher. When he takes his six feet, one inch, 162-pound frame up to the podium, he commands a quality of attention you rarely find in school. People who last attended classes only under duress vie for frontrow seats. Students who never were true students can be seen busily checking their notes. Others who cut more classes than they attend eagerly follow Costill's intricate and sophisticated outlines of body functions.

Costill didn't come to this level of acceptance by accident. He has gilt-edged credentials as an exercise physiologist. If there were an exercise physiology hall of fame, he would make it on the first ballot. The literature is filled with significant work that has come out of his laboratory at Ball State University in Muncie, Indiana.

His standing with his colleagues is indicated by his election as president of the American College of Sports Medicine and his recent medal for the application of science to sport. This regard reflects not only his professional competence but his modesty as well. He is the academic counterpart of Bill Rodgers. He is so unself-conscious about his achievements and takes them so lightly, you begin to wonder whether this relaxed person in front of you is really the number one running physiologist in the country, if not the world.

When I first met Dave, I was overwhelmed by the range and depth of his knowledge. He moved around the Krebs Cycle, for instance, like I moved around my own home. So for some time I restricted my conversation to "yes," "no" and "Where's the bathroom?" It wasn't long, however, before I discovered that like most "biggies" (as he calls those he admires) Dave was more concerned about his own ignorance than mine. He treats everyone as another searcher after truth with something to contribute.

There is another reason why we distance runners admire Costill and flock to hear him. What he offers is practical. It works. We can take it out the next day and use it. In this sense he is a throwback to the clinical professors I had in medical school. Unlike the academics, these men were actually in the day-to-day practice of medicine. What they taught could be applied to the next patient.

Costill is a clinical exercise physiologist. When he performs a biopsy on a muscle, it is a runner's muscle. When he studies the emptying of a stomach, it is a runner's stomach. When he tests a replacement solution's effect on rectal temperature, it is a runner's rectal temperature.

And the truth is that Dave Costill is as hungry to teach as we runners are hungry to learn. Perhaps that is why Dave and I still go around the country giving clinics, saying the same things time and again. It isn't often that you face students as eager to be taught as you are to teach.

For almost as many years as I have been writing, I have been making periodic phone calls to Joe Henderson to tell him I am through, washed up; I will never again write anything worth reading. And for just as many years, he has reassured me that all will be well. He has reminded me that I have passed innumerable such crises before, and this one too shall pass.

I go through the ritual because Joe is the only person I trust when it comes to writing about running. If I have one sentence, even one word, that is weak or exaggerated or untrue, he will catch it immediately. If the writing is a fraction off-key, a hair out of tune, his eye and ear will detect it. When it comes to running-writing, Joe has perfect pitch. So if I write anything that passes his editorial scrutiny, I know I need not care about anyone else's opinion.

When I look for the truth about running, I read Joe Henderson and those writers who have passed his editorial standards. What he demands is not sincerity alone; every runner-writer seems to have that quality. It is not enough to want to tell the truth; the revelation has to go deeper and use just the right words in doing it. What Joe asks for is veracity, which is a product of sincerity, plus discipline, hard work and the desire to use yourself up completely. Veracity has a clarity that sincerity can only strive for.

Joe brings that clarity to his writing. He is a deceptively simple writer who makes it look easy. His instinct and intuition about the running experience give him complete control, complete confidence. As you read his work, this control becomes evident. There is the leaving unsaid of things that need not be said, the avoidance of pretense about things he doesn't know.

617

What he knows is enough. Henderson once referred to running as a thinking person's sport. Subsequent events have proven him correct. Running has attracted and continues to attract individuals of all temperaments, but none more strongly than those who live in the mind.

Joe is of similar bent. What he felt was felt by those of us coming after him. What he saw we were led to see. What delighted him eventually delighted us as well. Reading him confirmed our own experience and allowed us to anticipate what would happen next.

During his years as its editor, *Runner's World Magazine* took on the unique character it still has. It became a magazine for the participant, not the spectator; a journal for those who would be heroes rather than hero-worshippers. It became a monthly written by and for the runners themselves. You had a voice in it as long as you told the truth about running.

Joe Henderson is now getting the recognition he deserves, but this will never change him. He is the most modest writer I have ever met, the gentlest and most understanding editor. It is sufficient reward to him that he has a talent, and a passion and an opportunity to use it.

What he is uncompromising about is his writing time. He writes as he runs, seven days every week. He gave up editing the magazine when it began to cut into this time. He now writes and edits other runner-writers' books in his small workshop on the Monterey Peninsula of California. His books are the product of that daily writing and running, those excursions into his inner and outer worlds.

Joe's book have encouraged every runner to think of him as a friend. I sometimes think of him as more than that, more like a twin. Once, for instance, I called him to suggest an outline for a brochure we had planned.

"I've already written it that way," he told me.

I think of my relationship with Joe as being unique, but I'm sure it isn't. Others also see him as their alter ego—the me without my faults, the best I could be. Others also call him and get reassurance that all is well. Others also have that faith in his ability to determine what is first-rate and what is ordinary, and find in his approval an unshakeable confidence in themselves and their writing.

Joe Henderson, in his quiet way, has given us and our sport credibility. His writings have validated the running experience. But he has also demonstrated an even more important truth: Once you have decided that winning isn't everything, you become a winner.

The three of us—my friend Mel, who is also my agent, myself and the man from the beer company—were sitting in the upstairs lounge of an east side athletic club. It was one of those places where you have to wear a jacket and tie. Mine, which matched neither each other nor the rest of my clothes, I had borrowed from the man who checked the coats. But it was the talk that made me more uncomfortable than the clothes.

The beer man had flown in from Missouri to induce me to write a brochure on running. He had read, he said, that I drank beer during races and had written to this effect in my column. I had, in fact, recommended beer as an excellent source of both fluid and energy. And now, with my help, this company would like to put out a pamphlet on running which contained some favorable reference to beer—not their beer, any beer.

The man was very persuasive. He said his company believes in sports, sports are good for America, and what's good for America is good for his company. The interest in running is just the kind of an activity the company wants to aid and be associated with.

So do a lot of companies, I thought. Running has become a major industry. Shoes, clothes and races are bringing business and advertising into the running scene. That was the rub. It appeared that everyone was in it for the money—including me.

For a dozen or more years, I had written because I had wanted to. I was doing something I would have done for nothing. I had discovered a job that wasn't work. And, in fact, I was getting almost nothing to do it— a ten-spot a week from the newspaper, and until a few years ago not even postage for conducting a question-and-answer service and column for the magazine. I never complained; I knew that I would have paid to have it printed.

Now, the money was coming in like it did at Sutter's Mill. Everyone wanted to pay me for something—to endorse, recommend, wear, attend, speak, write—you name it. It was no longer a question of counting the money. It had to be weighed.

The time had come to get my bearings, to set rules and follow them. There is nothing wrong with money. "I don't actually like money," Joe

Louis said, "but it does ease the nerves." The idea is not to get nervous about making it, not to see it as an end in itself but as a by-product.

"Would Paul White have written this brochure?" I asked. If it wasn't unethical or immoral, it did nonetheless seem slightly unprofessional. Doctors, after all, do not write broadsides for beer companies. For life insurance companies, perhaps, or Blue Shield; maybe for a drug house, and even, now and then, in praise of wine. But beer was reaching a bit.

"Would Paul White have written this brochure?" The question hung up like a slow curve ball ready to be hit out of the park. I was asking for a reason to write it. Prove to me that a physician of any stature would write this pamphlet.

The man from the beer company leaned forward. "Doctor," he asked, "why do you write these columns?" He had ignored the doctor and addressed himself to the writer. He had made the right move.

"To be read, of course." Every writer writes to be read, to remind people he has been here, to be remembered, to leave something behind.

The beer man had me, and he knew it. He waited another second or two, and then launched the harpoon.

"We are prepared," he said. "to print a half-million copies of this pamphlet."

The struggle was over. He had landed me. Paul White would have written a brochure on running that reached that many people—a half-million waiting to listen, to be instructed. And any writer would burn candles for that many minds and hearts to reach.

I said, "Okay, I'll do it."

Doing what is right is easy once you decide what is the right thing to do. The first rule in making that decision is, "Never do anything just for the money." Now, I can tell my friends at the beer company that I would have done that brochure for nothing.

Back before running became a phenomenon and Jim Fixx was still at work on his *Complete Book of Running*, he came to interview me. We talked about running and my writing, and he brought up the success of my own book, *Dr. Sheehan on Running*. Why, he asked me, had the book sold so well?

It was his idea that my book had something of the quality of that perennial best-seller, Izaak Walton's *The Compleat Angler*. People who have absolutely no interest in fishing continue to read this discourse on

620

"The Contemplative Man's Recreation." They are simply caught up by the author's enthusiasm and encyclopedic knowledge about what many would consider a trivial subject.

In retrospect, it is clear that Fixx's book is the present counterpart of *The Compleat Angler*. His book is a compendium of all the information you would ever need to become a runner. Fixx is a fine journalist and has in addition a personal involvement, a bias, a zest that journalists are not supposed to have—or at least not show. He is an enthusiast, a true believer, a worthy successor to Walton. His book will stand.

The success of my book (I would include *Running and Being* as merely a logical extension of the first and this current book as a further development) is due not to facts but to feelings. The enthusiasm is there, God knows. I am also a true believer. But all the research, all the information is concerned with one individual: myself.

My book is not journalism; it is a journal. It is about the *feel* of being a runner, the feel of growth, the feel of control, the feel of being at home in what I am doing.

Everything we experience, we should be able to put into words. How often have we said that an event, an encounter with ourselves or others was indescribable —and then found that someone had described it? How often have we had sensations, feelings and emotions for which we could not find adequate words—only to come across their perfect expression while browsing through a book?

Only by putting feelings into words can I possess them. Only by finding the absolutely right words can I transmit the feelings to the reader. I try to express the actual experience as clearly as I can, and hope the reader can feel the reverberation.

Remember that I, too, am a reader, and I know when a writer has bent himself out of shape in a desperate effort to capture those moments of being and becoming. When finally the best words emerge in the best order, the writer and the reader are joined. There is no more intimate relationship. What began as a writer talking to himself now becomes a dialogue with the reader.

Thoreau, who walked alone, now takes daily walks with me. Emerson, who was so reserved in conversation that he drove his friends into a fury, opens himself willingly in my company. Other loners freely admit me to their most private thoughts.

These are the writers who stir me up, give me hope, make me aware of life. They awaken me to my past and raise my consciousness to my present potential. Then, day by day, layer after layer, they lead me to the discovery of myself.

I read Emerson as he read others—sentence by sentence, year after year. Each year, I underline some thought that unbelievably I missed the year before. It is the underlining that gives it away. It is not the sort of underlining I did in school, marking passages most likely to be asked about in a quiz. No, this underlining is done because the writer has illuminated my life just as a bolt of lightning illuminates a landscape. There is a shock of recognition, a realization that this is exactly the way it is.

A book can never be written so badly, said Mark Twain, that someone won't still claim it saved his life. The letters I receive suggest that my book, despite the quality of its writing, has indeed had an impact on some people's lives. If nothing else, it has offered a validation of their own experiences. My pilgrim's progress has been matched by the progress of every pilgrim among my readers.

When someone asks me to sign one of my books, and I find it dog-eared and underlined; when a runner tells me that reading my book is like looking in a mirror; when someone says that whole paragraphs of the book had been written in his mind before he saw my words in print, then I know happiness. I have a feeling that I must write another book to express.

On a promotional tour for an earlier book, my life became a series of TV talk shows, radio interviews and luncheons with book critics. It seemed as if every minute I was asked a question. And since the people I met are good at what they do, the questions were usually probing ones.

"Why another book on running?"

"Why a book so full of quotations?"

"Why a book at all?"

Sometimes, I just smiled and said, "You're right," and ordered a beer. But that is not what book promotion tours are for. So mostly I gave the answers which apply to this book as well as my others.

My book is a "why" book on running, not a "how" book. It is filled with other people's sentences because they have already said that particular thought incomparably better than I could. It is filled with contradictions because life is filled with contradictions. It is not a book at all.

It is a journal—a series of dispatches from the front lines, a pilgrim's progress written, appropriately, on the run.

My book, you see, is not about running. It is about doing your thing. It is about what happens when you do your thing. My thing is running. You could take this book and substitute your thing, and it would read just as well.

The trouble with most books is that they try to prove something. They present a theory, and then proceed to give logical and rational reasons why it is so. The book then ends by giving you the final answer. It exhausts the subject, at least until the second edition.

No wonder when Frank Shorter was asked if he had written a book, he answered, "No, when you write a book you are finished."

Mine is not yet a book. It has no conclusions. There are no answers, no solutions. It is filled with my characteristic ambiguity, my pervasive ambivalence, my sudden enthusiasms and equally sudden defections.

When a reviewer complains that my book is filled with contradictions, I am pleased. A book still in the writing, like a life still in the living, should be filled with contradictions and uncertainties, evasions and half-truths. But it should also be filled with the sudden illuminations, the most personal of disclosures, the utterly revealing confessions.

I write about the only subject on which I am an expert: myself.

"The self that lives in my body," wrote D. H. Lawrence, "I cannot finally know."

What I must do, however, is try with all my might, even though I know that major questions will go unanswered.

Giving a lecture is like running a race. I am never sure how well I will do. I always have a slight feeling of dread, the nagging worry that this one will be a disaster. So I approach every talk as I would a race. I fast. I warm up. I get myself psyched. When I get up to speak, I want to feel lean and hungry and loaded for bear.

I eat lightly that day and not at all during the three or four hours before the lecture. If I am the after-dinner speaker, my meal goes untouched. Food and drink slow my synapses ever so slightly. I seem to be on a one-second delay. I lose the quickness of mind I need once the speech gets underway.

Another essential in this preparation is an hour's run. Coleridge once said that you will never fail in a talk after a ten-mile walk. I know what he meant. This warmup run reaches beyond the second wind of my body to the third wind of my mind. After a half-hour or so, I begin to see the theme of my talk and the direction it will take. Then this sketchy mental outline becomes fleshed out with examples and experiences that gradually surface in my consciousness.

"In any man's head," writes William Gibson, "the voices of the past are infinite, the undigested odds and ends of his lifetime, a bedlam of sights and sounds and touches of the world since his first breath."

Gibson is right. The place where I find that treasury is running on the roads. Then, I use it for my talk.

You would think I could give the same talk each time. I would like to, especially when I have had one go exceptionally well. But it's impossible. Memorizing never works.

I had a high school teacher who told me, "You can't think and remember at the same time." If I try to duplicate a past triumph, I am reduced to the D in public speaking I earned in school.

So I speak without a prepared text. I need no notes, no cue cards, no aids when I am on stage. The run has filled my stream of consciousness with all the odds and ends, sights and sounds relevant to my theme. I am now so filled with my subject I just have to get it out.

Sometimes as I enter the hall before the talk, a person will come up to me and say, "I'm very interested in hearing what you are going to say." And I will reply quite honestly, "So am I." When things go well, that is just the case. I am as interested in what I am going to say as I hope the audience is. In fact, my interest ensures theirs.

A few minutes before I am to be announced, I slip out and begin pacing the corridor, trying to get back into the stream of consciousness of the morning run. It is usually then that the full realization of what is about to come finally emerges.

One reporter who saw me in this state before a talk in Boston told me she had thought to herself, "He'll never be able to speak." Yet it seems true that the more alarmed I get, the more uncertain I become, the better I do.

Even so, beginning is always difficult. On one occasion, my mind went completely blank, and the memory of that feeling of panic still haunts me. I am also a person known only to runners. Most of my listeners have no idea who I am or what I do. All they see is a nervous, scrawny-looking sixty-year-old who is about to use up some of their valuable time.

I have a defense against this. First, I admit I am nervous. This gets their sympathy. Then, I suggest that I should have brought my American Express card. That gets the first laugh. Then, I admit that jogging is boring. That gets the second laugh. From then on, it is the audience lifting me and I am lifting the audience. The more they respond, the more relaxed and digressive and original I become.

There are times when so many new and interesting ideas fill my head, I hang the talk on imaginary pegs about fifteen feet in the air off to my left and promise to come back later. Then, I pursue some interesting anecdote or incident to its conclusion. I find that I am able then to think out loud or even have long periods of silence as I follow one line of thought after another.

The audience is a partner in this enterprise. A great deal depends upon them. Give me salesmen any time. They are listeners by profession. They also have a disdain for facts and an appreciation of rhetoric. Although they carry catalogs and samples, what they really deal in is human nature. When they talk to a prospect, they are already anticipating his reply. Give a good talk to a convention of salesmen and they will escalate it into something even better.

Technical people are a different breed. When I say something to a group of technicians, it just lays out there and they look at it for a quite a while. In the beginning, this terrified me. I thought I was doing poorly. Now, I know it is just their way.

I am able to size up the audience and know how to give the talk. Again, it is like a race. I run differently over hills and against the wind. There are some talks that are just like that.

Every once in a while, things fall into place. I have caught the absolute attention of the crowd. My timing is perfect. Every illustration I use is new and exciting. I feel virtuoso. I am willing to go on and on—and the audience wants me to. In the end, I am never sure what I have said. All I can recall is the enthusiasm and the exhilaration. I know for forty minutes or so these people and I have entered each other's mind and hearts.

Then comes the applause, surely one of the most positive affirmations any creature can give another—and then, every once in a while, that strange and wonderful and spontaneous union of performer and audience, a standing ovation. For that, there can be only one fitting reaction: the clenched fists over the head indicating that we are all winners. Then, I give the audience a standing ovation.

Unlike the race, they are not spectators. They are part of the performance.

PART

The Spirit

I WAS IN THE FINAL MILE of the cross-country race when I heard him coming up on my shoulder. We were part of a rather small field, perhaps eighty in all. Only a few were accomplished runners. Most had only lately come to see the benefits of running. For them—and I'm sure for him—a five-mile race was a new experience.

When he came abreast of me, I could see he was a young lion—my superior by two inches of height and forty pounds of bone and muscle.

As he went by, I called out, "Way to go! You're looking great!"

I tried then to hang on, to stay on his shoulder and use his pace. It was no use; he was too strong. But what I did get was an impetus to try harder. Until he challenged me, I had been running to survive, thinking I was doing the best I could do.

Now, I discovered reserves I had not suspected were there. When I finished, far behind him, I was clocked in my best time of the year.

Such encounters are the rule rather than a rarity in running. They embody the essence of the racing experience. The young man, nevertheless, found my encouragement almost incomprehensible. Later, he told my son that I had blown his mind. The idea that an opponent would urge you to beat him seemed an impossibility. He became so psyched up, he said, he ran better than he had thought possible. Runners, he decided, were marvelous people.

He is right, of course. We runners *are* marvelous people. But we weren't marvelous before we began running. We were like everyone else. We wanted to get things for nothing. We had the tendency to blame others when things went wrong. We saw life as a negative-sum game where there is only one winner, where it is you against me.

I wasn't a runner long before I began to see that I had it all wrong. When I became a runner, I stopped expecting anything for nothing. I discovered that I could go just so far (about one block) without training.

Now, I am in control of what I do. What I do is me, no one else. In a race, my performance is my concern, not yours. I wish you well. In fact, the better you do, the better I will do as well.

That, I have come to see, is the true nature of competition. The Latin root of the word is *petere*—to go out, to head for, to seek. The *com* is doing it together, in common, in unity, in harmony. Competition is simply each of us seeking our absolute best with the help of each other. What we do magnifies each other, inspires each of us. The race is a synergistic society where what accrues to one accrues to all, a society in which everyone can be a winner.

When I live in such a society, if only for five miles, I learn that winning and losing is a process going on inside me. I find it unintelligible to cheat anyone or to be diminished by the performance of another. Compensation is the law of the universe. Pick what you want and pay for it. Don't ask for anything; earn it. There are no alibis.

What makes this easier is that the race is a contest. When I came to understand this, I realized how running could take me, a quarrelsome, contentious, selfish, unsympathetic human being, and make me fairly acceptable to my fellows and myself.

Contest, you see, is also a word that has a Latin root. It means "testify with." The other runners in a race are witnesses to what I do. The corollary of that statement, however, is that I am under oath. I am pledged to do my best.

In the final analysis, it is the oath that makes the difference. It makes me resist the tendency to cheat on myself, to trim the least bit, to slow down before the finish. In the last stages of the race, when along with everyone else I am wondering *why*, I remember I have given my word of honor. I am reminded that each of us shares a common oath.

That is why there is so much support in the ranks. We are all seekers, going toward a common goal; not opponents but witnesses.

At the 1978 Falmouth Road Race, after Bill Rodgers had led for the first three miles, the second-place runner said, "Bill, you're doing all the work. Let me lead for a while."

If the world was a race, it might work.

14

The Self

“

I am—just as you are—
a unique, never-to-be-repeated event in this universe.
Therefore, I have—just as you have—
a unique, never-to-be-repeated role in the world.
Mine is a personal drama
for which I am at once author, actor and director.

”

A READER WHO ALSO RUNS wrote to me of his concern about my focus on self.

"The danger I see in this," he said, "is that unless prodded further, one's growth can end there. We can become a 'healthy animal' but an incomplete human being; have a fitness state of 100 and a social I.Q. of zero. The truth is that we *owe*. If we give an hour or two of the day to self, we clearly owe meaningful time to others in our work and social relationships."

This runner sees running as the beginning and the maintenance of life. But for him, complete living requires interacting with and serving others. He presented the hope that, as surely as we have evolved as runners, we will also evolve as social beings.

There are others who have taken the same view of the selfishness of runners. James Fixx, writing in *Newsweek*, said much the same thing. Runners, he wrote, are incorrigible loners who, far from being troubled by their solitude, revel in it. Fixx conceded the inevitable physical improvement, and he agreed that runners become more stable emotionally, more confident and self-sufficient. But it is this very self-sufficiency which he considered "the opposite of commitment to the human community, which is the heart of the religious impulse."

That may be the conventional wisdom: Love thy neighbor, or at the very least treat everyone as if he were your brother-in-law. For most people, it would seem that religion involves other people. We must work out our salvation with and for the people who surround us.

But there are other ways to look at it. William James defined religion as "the feelings, acts and experiences of individual men in their solitude, as they stand in relation to whatever they may consider divine."

Aldous Huxley pointed out that we work out our salvation in different ways. There are, he said, three paths to salvation: the path of devotion, the path of works and the path of knowledge. Which one we take depends upon, and indeed is determined by, our own peculiar temperament and personality.

Running is not a religion. It is, however, a way of becoming an adult. It is a path to maturity, a growth process. Through it, I am prodded to go further, to grow more, to become a complete human being. I have not yet —and perhaps never will—come to where I can let my life depend on works and devotion. Mine depends on knowledge, which begins with knowing myself.

I am not a joiner; I will not become involved. It is not that I don't want to contribute; I simply must be allowed to contribute in my own way. That way is alone—either alone on the roads or at the typewriter, or alone on the stage separated by that immeasurable distance between the podium and the first row of spectators.

That is normal for a writer and a runner. "Like many writers," someone described a novelist, "he was a cold man."

I am in many ways a cold man. I am secretive and withdrawn, no matter how open I appear in my writing and speeches. William Gibson speaks of that paradox in his *A Season in Heaven.*

The writer can be, and at close quarters often is, unfeeling in his relations with his fellow citizens—and yet simultaneously possesses in a measure beyond any of them the social tact to move their hearts.

We each have a role to play—our own. The contemplative, even a minor-league one, has a place. Aquinas made a point of that. "It is necessary for the perfection of human society," he wrote, "that there would be men who devote their lives to contemplation."

Huxley said of the mystic, "By instinct, he remains solitary, and in the contemplation of the infinite feels himself absolved from duty to his neighbor."

The neighbor, however, may not feel the same. My running is not easily understood by those who are "people" people—those with a natural amiability and care for others. They want and give affection freely, and express their emotions without embarrassment. They are generous and kind, and for them salvation has more to do with their relationships with others than with their own destiny.

I understand these "people" people and know how important their works are. But I am not one of them. That's why I feel most at home and at peace when I run.

I am—just as you are—a unique, never-to-be-repeated event in this universe. Therefore, I have—just as you have—a unique, never-to-be-repeated role in this world. Mine is a personal drama for which I am at once author, actor and director.

Unfortunately, this perception comes late in life. It was something I knew as a child—not clearly, of course, but nevertheless with certainty. My life as a child was my own. It was filled with the play and invention, the energy and intensity, the humor and intelligence that becoming the person you are demands.

But all too soon, we become members of the herd. We learn herd rules, herd regulations, herd morality, herd ethics. We become part of society. Society must be preserved, so we accept the obligations it imposes.

Others have raised questions about this necessity. "Are we sent here," asked Thoreau, "to do chores and hold horses?" The answer, says society, is yes. Work has to be done. And if work is not available, then make-work has to be devised. We must be kept busy. The idle mind begins to think, the idle body begins to play, and that is dangerous for the herd.

In such moments, those childlike moments, we may see ourselves as we are and recognize the life we should live. Some happy few have these revelations early. But most of us submit to the herd with little resistance. We behave docilely until we have fulfilled our obligation to procreate, until we have used our productive years in support of the institutions that keep society on an even keel.

But then what? The forties have arrived. The herd no longer needs us, nature no longer protects us, the race no longer cares. We are on our own. We have served our purpose.

What then are the prospects? Wonderful! Perhaps even better than wonderful. We can now return to the play and invention, the energy and intensity, the humor and intelligence we knew as children. The pressures that made us supportive of the herd are dying out. Each of us is feeling the urges that make us different rather than the same. Each of us is sensing the infinite varieties of body and mind, of values and temperament that make us unique.

And with that comes the knowledge that the chores are over. There are no more horses to be held. We know now about the herd. We need no longer be bound by those rules, need no longer act out those roles. Somehow, we will find the strength and the courage and the insight to make our own rules, to act out our own drama.

That is the paradox. In what others consider the twilight years, we will be more than we ever were before. At a time when we are supposed to take to the easy chair and be content with serenity and a large book, we are transformed with energy. We have a vigor and a toughness youth cannot match, and for the first time since our childhood we know how to play.

Why must this all wait until we are forty? It need not, I suppose. It just happened that way in my case, but I am a slow learner and a creature of habit. For you, it might be different. Lightning may strike when you are twenty-one or not until you are seventy. Today may be your day to leave the herd.

Just before the halfway point where we were to turn for home, he passed me. I knew than I was beaten. The Marcellus Gorge 10,000-Meter Run goes out and back on the same road. The race is easy going out, being mostly downhill, but then gets very difficult coming back because of the uphill stretches.

"The first five kilometers may be the fastest you will ever run," my friend Tom Homeyer had told me. "The second five kilometers will probably be the slowest."

This runner had beaten me at my best, running downhill. There was no way I could take him going back. There was a chance, of course, that he was not in my age-group. He was fifty for sure, but maybe not yet sixty. The first over-sixty I knew was Arnie Briggs, an old-timer I'd run with for years. He was in his first race since some Achilles surgery months back, and his leg was still a little shrunken. Arnie was safely far behind me.

This unknown of unknown age kept moving away from me as we went home against those hills. I never gave up. I kept him in sight. There was even a point a mile from the end when he seemed to falter and I got within striking range. But then came the finish. I had done my best, but he had done better.

When they posted the results, I saw that he was fifty-five. So it had not mattered. I would get the beer mug with the gold medal for the sixty-and-over category after all. Then, I looked at my name just a few places down and saw they had gotten my age wrong. George Sheehan, fifty-eight.

I was studying this mistake when Tom came up and told me about the fifty-five-year-old who had beaten me. He was the local fifty-and-over champion and a great favorite among the runners. He had trained for the past three months for this race and for the possibility of beating me.

Tough luck, I thought. I could straighten this out quickly enough. Just a matter of seeing the meet director. Then, I would point out the error to the officials, tell the local hero he had beaten an old man no longer in his division and take the sixty-and-over beer mug away from Arnie.

I had just enough class to keep my mouth shut—not enough, however, to keep it shut permanently. An hour later, driving back to the hotel, I told Tom. "They had my age wrong, you know. I'm sixty." I had to get it out. But earlier, I had been in a situation that asked the question, "What is this racing about?" and I had given the right answer. I had been given an opportunity and seized it.

There are moments like this when I feel I possess that elusive quality known as class. More frequently, I am certain I don't. But I am aware that it is always available to me. Anyone can have class. It's character is nonetheless elusive.

In talking about class and in trying to define it, one runs the risk of sounding silly and snobbish. For one thing, not only is class difficult to define, it is much more evident in its absence. Since part of class is not boasting about it, the no-class people stand out. For every class athlete you see, you can name any number of spoilsports, showboats, alibiers and cheaters.

Some say class is simply grace under pressure. Others extend it to mean those qualities Frost wrote of after an All-Star game: prowess, justice, courage and knowledge. There are some people, they say, who go through life the way DiMaggio played center field.

The Greeks have a word for it. *Arete* means the best. *Arete* also contains the idea of something, whether it be an object or a creature, doing exactly what it was made for. *Arete* means being the absolute embodiment of what it was designed to be. It is not being better than something else; it is the best of what it is. *Arete* is me being the best possible George Sheehan.

From *arete* comes the word aristocrat. It was the aristocrat who fulfilled in every respect the human design. The Greeks, who saw themselves as the playthings of the gods, were uncompromising on that issue. They settled for no less than a totally integrated person. Harmony of body, mind and spirit was their notion of class.

The important thing about actions is not what you do but the way you do it. "Every calling is great," said Oliver Wendell Holmes, "when

636

greatly pursued." It is the old refrain all over again. Have no care for the outcome. Play the game to the hilt. Show a little class.

The great ones, whether they are mechanics or cardiologists, waiters or housewives, always do. They have all those virtues and qualities that go with class. They also have faith—faith in themselves, faith in what they are doing, faith in those they do it with. They believe the way they do something matters, and in the long run that is all that matters.

The distinction between life lived as a success and life lived as a failure, as I see it, is a matter of class. And though that word is frequently abused, I believe it does touch on something important in both the value and style of a runner's life. Class is a product of body and mind and spirit. I suspect that for me it begins with an all-consuming desire to do my best, a compulsion that everyone has felt from time to time for different activities. My task is to extend it to everything I do. I am, for instance, highly motivated in my writing and my running, but not nearly as much in my other roles and functions.

In my early days as a writer, I wrote my weekly column Tuesday night after supper. It usually had been percolating in my head for about a week, but the actual writing took about five to six hours. This meant that some member of the sports staff would be sitting late into the night, waiting restlessly for my copy. Finally, he would say, "C'mon, Doc. Everything doesn't have to be a masterpiece."

He was wrong. I want everything I write to be a masterpiece. "The true function of a writer," said Cyril Connolly, "is to produce a masterpiece, and no other task is of any consequence."

Of course, it will be my kind of masterpiece, to be compared only with my best previous effort. And this goes for my races and my encounters with other people. They should all be masterpieces. Every day should, in fact, be a masterpiece. It is the realization of this, the enthusiasm aroused by this possibility, the exhilaration when it occasionally happens, that is at the root of class.

I saw it in a race. I ran in a two-person, six-mile relay at Lake Takanassee. The race was eight laps around the lake, which is three-quarters of a mile in circumference. We alternated, doing four laps each, going at a pace which in effect made each loop of the course a separate race.

The teams were picked out of a hat, so each group had a wide range

637

of ability. This disparity became immediately evident, and by the time that my partner Susan had touched me off the second time, the runners were spread almost completely around the lake. Another leg, and it was impossible to tell which of the fifty teams was leading and which was last.

Each runner was now in a private little hell that interval three-quarters become, and only our partners and God cared where we were or how fast we were running. Yet as I stood there each time Susan came in, I could see in her face—and in the face of every runner making the relay exchange—an absolute and total involvement in this painful effort. There wasn't a runner there who hadn't accepted the commitment that goes with the notion of class: Do your best, knowing full well, of course, there was little chance to win or receive any recognition for your efforts.

It would have been easy to trim, to ease off, to take advantage of the fact that no one was observing you. But class will not be bought off.

15

The Others

"

My fellow runners support me
by liking me, even loving me
—at the least, wanting me to run my best.
They join with me in a common identification,
a common interest, a common experience.
In the race, we are members of one body,
each of us pursuing his individual goal
but in a state of synergy where
what is good for one is good for everyone.
Whatever any runner does magnifies us all.

"

I LIKE RUNNING because I am in control. I control the pain. I control the stress. I can endure, it seems, almost any amount of pain as long as I am in charge.

My difficulty begins when I lose that control, when other people enter my environment. They are the primary source of my external and even internal stress. To effectively deal with them, my own resources are not enough. I must seek situations that contain support and affiliation and cohesion. What I need, as do all of us, is care and affection, assurance of my value, my worth. I need the feeling of belonging. I need to act in concert with others.

Like most runners, I seek that support and affiliation and cohesion in myself or my books or a single friend. No matter how many people are around, I am a hermit still, but like Emerson, I have come to know this is not enough. When his wife and family were away for a few days, he found the solitude tedious and dispiriting.

"Let us not wrong the truth and experience," he said, "by standing too stiffly on this cold doctrine of self-sufficiency."

When self-sufficiency is not enough, when people are necessary, I turn to the race. There, the people become *my* people. They turn the race into what Hans Selye calls "eustress," a stress which has good effects rather than bad.

My fellow runners support me by liking me, even loving me—at the least, wanting me to run my best. They join with me in a common identification, a common interest, a common experience. In the race, we are members of one body, each of us pursuing his individual goal but in a state of synergy where what is good for one is good for everyone. Whatever any runner does magnifies us all. The slowest contributes equally with the fastest.

Take, for instance, the day I ran in Central Park with 6,000 other people in the Bloomingdale-Perrier 10,000-Meter Run. As I strolled with my family across the sheep meadow toward the start, a middle-aged woman in a warmup suit ran up to me and exclaimed, "I love you, Dr. Sheehan."

What she really loved was running, the runner she had become, the person she had found herself to be. She loved me because I had tried to put into words what she felt, yet could not quite express.

From time to time, other runners would stop stretching and jogging to come over and express similar sentiments. We lovers of solitude had discovered we really did like each other.

In the race, there was more good fellowship. We took time from the business at hand to offer greetings, good wishes, encouragement, advice, even congratulations. In the course of the race, when I found the going tough, a runner one-third my age said, "Relax, Dr. Sheehan, relax."

I did. It worked a minor miracle. I soon left him behind and began to pick up one runner after another, more often than not getting an encouraging word: "Looking strong," "Keep it up," "Take it in, Doc." Some, of course, were silent, lost in their own problems. But no one saw me as a threat or a measure on his performance. The well-wishers were simply letting me know how they felt about a fellow runner.

My world of running—and my wonder in it—must open to include other people. It means a loss of control, but I am willing to take that risk, willing to chance chaos, because once in a while the magic is there. For a brief time, we are all lovers and friends, if only for a 10,000-meter race in Central Park.

A spectator kept me from quitting the three-mile race at Takanassee Lake. I was struggling through the final yards of the third three-quarter-mile lap when I heard someone shout, "You'll never feel any worse than you do now."

I immediately took heart. My body felt as bad as ever, fighting for every breath, arms and legs clad in lead, unable to move with speed or coordination. Yet suddenly I knew I would finish that lap, and even the fourth and final loop around the lake would be manageable.

My friend, whoever he was, had convinced me. He could have yelled something stupid like, "Come on, move up!" or "Go get them!" or something logical like, "Relax!" or "Use your arms!" But he knew exactly what I felt and what I feared. He was the perfect spectator: kind and interested and competent, speaking from his heart as well as his head.

The perfect spectator is, in a sense, a hypnotist. Under the relentless stress of a race, the runner may actually reach a state that approaches hypnosis. Communication on a rational level is not always possible or even desirable. Orders, if received, most often achieve negative results. Efforts to influence actions which are reflex and automatic can be counterproductive. The runner needs most of all to relax. But a "relax" shouted as a command from the sidelines will rarely be of any help.

The spectator should talk to the runner as you talk to a child: Let him know you know; praise; reassure; give hope; be realistic but confident.

I heard my man and found the strength to go on. He was right. The fourth lap wasn't any worse. I had reached a plateau of fatigue and pain and exhaustion. I even passed two runners, and two other runners passed me. We were all in the same extremity. We had reached the limits of our physiology. What served us best now was any device that helped conserve energy.

We runners need people who generate a feeling of belief and confidence and hope, who know the right thing to say at the right time. This time, it was, "You'll never feel any worse than you do now."

I was sprawled on the floor of the B. M. C. Dirfee High School gymnasium along with the 350 other runners and their families and friends. The first annual Fall River 10-Mile Run was now history. The awards ceremony was about to begin, and, as usual, I hoped to be one of the winners.

I noted with some apprehension that there were only a dozen or so trophies to be presented. Still, I had finished fortieth and run a good time on a course with two very tough hills. Surely there is medal up there, I thought, for a sixty-year-old who did that.

I am, as you can see, a pot-hunter, a sixty-year-old adolescent with a lust for trophies. If there is anything I like better than running a good race, it is running a good race and then capturing a trophy to prove it.

In the sweet afterflow of that painful struggle to the finish, there is nothing more pleasant than hearing my name called out for a prize, nothing more satisfying than making my way, with just the right mixture of pride and nonchalance, through the crowd to the awards table, and then modestly accepting my trophy.

You might think that fifteen years in the sports world would have made me more mature and sophisticated—or at least more jaundiced—about these rewards for performance. Not so. It is true that I now save only the plaques, and recycle the trophies to other meets and races. But I take that inscription plate and mount it on the dashboard of my car so I can see it daily. There, it takes its place along with other mementos of such races as the 1974 Pernod Winter Series, the 1978 Atlanta Mini-Marathon and the 1979 Asbury Park Polar Bear Meet.

Up on stage the Fall River trophies were disappearing at an alarming rate. The first three went to the winner and the two fellows who followed him. Then came the first woman, who accepted the trophy and the applause with beaming face. She was a high school student, and trophies were still new to her.

I recalled a race on a Fourth of July weekend in Dennisport on Cape Cod. The high school auditorium stage was a smorgasbord of trophies and alternate selections of merchandise contributed by town businessmen. There were transistor radios, barbecue sets, alarm clocks, pottery, and any number of attractive prizes. Yet when the younger runners were called to the stage in the order of their finish and allowed to make their own selections, they headed straight for the trophies.

Our presentations continued—one for the first male Fall River runner to finish, then one for the first female Fall River runner to finish. The prizes were dwindling down to a precious few.

"First runner over forty years of age," the meet director called out. I waited hopefully while they consulted the results sheet. It was not for me. A forty-six-year-old had beaten me by over two minutes; no way I could have taken him. That knowledge helped. I might have blamed myself had it been only a few seconds. I always try my best, but when a trophy is at stake, I can sometimes summon up a little extra.

That brought to mind a race two years back where they had 140 coffee mugs as prizes for 1,000 runners. No categories, no age groups, nothing for being a woman; just fire the gun and the first 140 back get mugs. I have never run in a more competitive race. No one would give an inch the whole way. It was five miles at flank speed. I swung into the last mile addressing my body in the third person, warning it of the consequences should it bring me in 141st. I lasted to the finish, desperately reaching for the card the official was holding out to me. Then, I looked at it and saw the number 137. For that one moment, I was the happiest man in the world.

"The first doctor." The announcer paused, glancing at his notes. This was my last, best chance. But the name he called was not mine. A young cardiology resident had taken me by just over a minute.

There had been a time when I was the class performer of the medical profession. My first year in Boston I beat the two other physicians in the race and the *New York Times* gave me the "Golden Scalpel Award." Now, I am simply one of thousands of doctors who have discovered running.

There were only two trophies left on the table. But trophies or not, I consoled myself, the weekend would stand. I had spoken to the runners the night before, discussed our responsibility for our own health, talked about our duty to squeeze the best out of what we were born with, lectured on my obligation to become the best possible—whoever I am. Running did that the natural way through joy and struggle, I assured them. Through happiness and suffering, we come to love this playful purifying discipline.

The announcer was reading the inscription on one of the two remaining trophies. "The youngest finisher," he called out. A proud eight-year-old marched up to the table, received the award and then marched back to an admiring family.

There was only one left. I suddenly knew what the category was to be, and knew also that I wanted no part of it. I squirmed down in my seat, trying to get out of sight.

I heard the words, "The oldest finisher." There was a pause, and then the winner was announced—a man of fifty-seven years. Someone off to the side disagreed. "Dr. Sheehan is at least sixty," he protested. "He should get the trophy."

The correction was made. I had won by being born in 1918, by starting and finishing. I had finally won a trophy I didn't really want.

Then, I recalled a question Satchel Paige used to ask: "How old would you be if you didn't know how old you were?" And I knew the inscription on the trophy meant nothing. They had been conned by my age into giving a trophy for old age to one of the youngest runners in the room.

16

The Faith

“

**'Run into peace,'
wrote Meister Eckhart, the fourteenth-century mystic.
'The man who is in the state of running,
of continuous running into peace,
is a heavenly man.
He continually runs and moves and seeks
peace in running.'**

"

I WAS ON A RADIO SHOW discussing exercise with a woman who did not exercise. "The spirit is willing," she told me, "but the flesh is weak."

I had, of course, heard the excuse many times before. But for the first time, it occurred to me that the opposite was true. The flesh is willing; it is the spirit that is most often weak. Our bodies are capable of the most astounding feats. But the horizons of our spirits do not reach beyond the TV, the stereo and the car in the garage.

The flesh is not only willing; it is eager for action. The flesh is filled with everything our spirit lacks: strength and energy, endurance and stamina. We come from a breed that crossed continents on foot and trekked from pole to pole. Even now, we see housewives running marathons, stockbrokers in Outward Bound, retired executives climbing Everest.

We are of a flesh that asks for more and more challenges, that seeks one frontier after another. What is missing is not physical energy. The fuel is there, waiting to be ignited. We need some spark to light the fires, something to get us into action.

From the moment we wake up in the morning, we cop the plea that the spirit is willing but the flesh is weak. We lie abed as the alarm clock, the radio and the family take turns trying to get us up. Still, we remain immobile until the last possible minute. Yet how many calories does it take to overcome inertia and get out of bed? Whose bodies are so exhausted that they can't get their feet on the floor? I can plead that I'm in a semi-coma, not yet ready for coordinated action, but similar scenarios recur throughout the day. The body is ready, willing and able, but the spirit is becalmed. Where there is no emotion, there is no motion, either.

What is missing is the spiritual energy called *enthusiasm*. It is from lack of enthusiasm that the failures of the spirit multiply during the day. When we are enthusiastic, we develop a determination to equal the endurance of our muscles, a fortitude to match the courage of our hearts and a passion to join with the animal strengths of our bodies.

To succeed at anything, you need passion. You have to be a bit of a fanatic. If you would move anyone to action, you must first be moved yourself. To instigate, said Emerson, you must first be instigated. I am aware of this every time I lecture. For an hour before the talk, I can be seen walking alone, muttering to myself, gradually building myself to a fever pitch so I will find it completely natural to end a talk standing on a table with nothing on but my Levis—and with the pants legs rolled to my knees.

But the spirit has more to offer than just this excitement. It gives us the motivation when the excitement is missing. The spirit is what gets us through when everything else fails. As Oxford professor Ralph Johnson points out in his paper "Factors in Human Endurance," a person's ability to survive often depends on the qualities of his personality.

The mind-body relationship is particularly striking in the historical accounts of explorers and mountain climbers, people in extreme situations and stretched to their limits and beyond. The explorer, Captain Scott, writing of one of his men, commented, "Browers came through the best. Never was there such a sturdy, active, *undefeated* man." Of Scott himself, one of his companions wrote, "Scott was the strongest combination of strong man in a strong body that I have ever known—and this because he was weak. He conquered his weaker self and became the strong leader we went to follow and came to love."

Behind the enthusiasm, behind the inspiration, behind the passion, there must be the will. We can choose. We can decide. We can *will* to do it our own way. When we do, nothing can prevail against us.

Otherwise, we are merely wishing, idle dreamers in the world of the flaccid spirit. We must want something and want it badly—want it with the zeal and passion and enthusiasm of a Don Quixote or a missionary. Then, we will suddenly find ourselves in motion, with a clear focus on our goal. Once moved, the spirit and the flesh are like a matched team of horses, each asking more of the other. Fused by the will for that brief and wonderful moment, the flesh and the spirit become one.

When Viktor Frankl was in a German concentration camp, he made a pact with another prisoner. Every day they would tell each other a funny story. Every day they would find a joke in their experience in that hell that was Auschwitz. Incredible as it seems, they were able to do just that.

What Frankl and his friend instinctively knew, and psychiatrists have come to believe, is that humor is one of the best ways to cope with stress. George Valiant in his *Adaptation to Life* describes eighteen basic coping mechanisms. Of all these means of preserving our psychological equilibrium, he rates humor the first, the most effective, the most mature. Unfortunately, as Valiant points out in his study of Harvard graduates, it is rarely possessed and rarely used. Even the best and brightest are lacking in this seemingly basic human capacity.

That is surprising for if we Americans take pride in anything, it is our sense of humor. Criticize anything about me, and I am likely to agree. However unattractive you consider my features, however puny you regard my body, however unsuitable you judge my dress or companions, I will make no rebuttal. Disagree with my diet, claim the time I spend on running is absurd, say I am self-centered and penny-pinching and a poor citizen, you will get no argument. But tell me I have no sense of humor, and be prepared for a battle.

Yet I suspect Valiant is right. A sense of humor is a gift that is enhanced with age. It is the refined product of years of life's bad jokes, the result of the never-ending failures and defeats that mark the aging process. The older we get, the more likely we are to become aware of what is important and what is not, to know what is first rate and what is trash. We become able to see things and people and events for what they are.

Genuine humor is like genius and play and creativity and religion. It is simply another way of looking at things. Humor scales things down to their real significance. Humor is for the most part deflating, which is good, and humbling, which is important. But it also speaks our own truth, which is essential.

That truth is an ability to see oneself in a very special way. Humor is not only to see myself as others see me. It is even more than seeing myself as only I can see me. It is seeing myself and my circumstances as God sees me. Humor is seeing myself and my life in relation to the eternal.

Humor, therefore, is a sense of proportion and perspective. Humor is the way of wisdom, and wisdom comes only from experience. Humor is the gradual discovery of who one is and what one believes. The vision that goes with humor, then, is the vision of experience. It is seeing not only reality but that "greater reality" as well. And the older you get, the more this humor enters into everything you do. A sense of humor is no more than a sense that life is a great and glorious game and I, you, we know how to play it.

Only humor, as Frankl showed at Auschwitz, allows you to call a spade a spade. It permits you to focus on what is too terrible to be borne and still endure. But it comes only when you have a childlike hope and trust in the human condition, and a faith that does not lie about life and death and reality. And when it comes, it is a sign of growth.

George Valiant does not miss this paradox. "Hans Selye is wrong," he states. "It is not stress that kills; it is the effective adaptation to stress that permits us to live."

In that successful adaptation, we attain the fitness of the body that is health, the fitness of the mind that is wisdom and the fitness of the soul that is humor.

If I were to suggest that creativity is a major requirement for playing this game of life successfully, I suspect most readers would feel the game was already lost. Creativity seems to most of us a rare commodity, a gift given only to exceptional people.

The truth is that each one of us has this creativity. It was more evident when we were children and playing, because creativity is playful and depends on a faith in ourselves and what we are doing. It is associated, therefore, with those adjectives we use to describe children's play—spontaneous, effortless, innocent and easy.

"Almost any child," wrote Abraham Maslow, "can compose a song or a poem or a dance or a painting or a play or a game on the spur of the moment." So, I assure you, can we.

Creativity is a different way of looking at things, a different way of looking at ourselves. When we are creative, when we are at play, when we really believe in ourselves, we open ourselves to our own experiences. We discard preconceptions. We finally become aware. We begin to live.

Creativity, therefore, is a matter of seeing the ordinary as unusual, the commonplace as miraculous, the transient as eternal. It is seeing the new in the old, looking at things as if for the first time.

Not only the child and the saint, but also the athlete takes this creative view of what would strike us as routine. The spectacular things are the routine things done every day, consistently. Mainly, creativity takes the routine and makes it important, makes it worthwhile.

Joe DiMaggio, they say, never threw to the wrong base in his entire career. Was that merely reflex? Of course not. To accomplish that record, each individual throw had to be made with the intensity, fervor and freshness of the very first throw. DiMaggio transformed an activity that could have become routine into a creative challenge.

Andrew Wyeth was another man who had a creative response to familiar things. "I'm not much for the new thing or the new object," he said. "I like to go back again and again, because I think you can always find some new things. I'm actually bored by fresh things to paint. To make old things seem fresh is much more exciting to me."

If Wyett can discover more in the everyday and the familiar, so can we. For myself, I now see that there are innumerable opportunities for creativity. All I need is the faith, the confidence, the ability to let go, and the attitude of play. Then, I can create—when I come together with my family or friends, when I write, when I run, or when I just sit on the beach and look at the sea. The most routine, the most simple act can be a creative event.

"Run into peace," wrote Meister Eckhart, the fourteenth-century mystic. "The man who is in the state of running, of continuous running into peace, is a heavenly man. He continually runs and moves and seeks peace in running."

Now, one should not take the writings of a mystic too literally. They usually tell their good news in analogies and similes and other figures of speech. In this passage, I am sure Eckhart was using running as a metaphor. It represented the soul in motion. He was saying in his own way, "He who seeks God has already found Him." As had many early preachers, he was using running to help us understand the religious experience.

But Eckhart, at least for me, wrote more truly than he knew. I have discovered that "run into peace" can be understood literally as well as figuratively. For me, running is a religious experience. When I run, I actually run into peace. On my river road thirty minutes from where I began as a fallen, finite, sinful creature, I approach Eckhart's vision of the heavenly man.

By that time, I have taken the bad me and gradually stripped myself of anything that keeps me from the physical good. Running is the purifying discipline that the Greeks sought so their bodies would be fit for the gods to inhabit. When I run, I am purged. I am cleansed. I take this beautiful body entrusted to me and perfect it. I become a good body.

The mystic proceeds methodically. His progress is from purgation to illumination to union. And so it is for me in the running: purgation in movement and effort and sweat; and in that cleansing I discover myself becoming whole physically, and allowing for the possibility of further movement toward illumination and union. Because running is not only the movement of the body but is also the movement of the soul.

That movement of the soul is the essence of the religious act. That was the conclusion William James came to in his monumental work, *The Varieties of Religious Experience.* All religions, he pointed out, consist fundamentally of two parts: (1) an uneasiness, and (2) its solution. The uneasiness stems from the sense that there is something wrong with us as we naturally stand. The solution is the recognition that we are saved from wrongdoing by making connection with a higher power.

What happens, said James, is that we not only see the bad in ourselves but the good as well, and we then establish that good as our real self. We realize there is a "more" in us, a better part, and then we reach toward the supreme *more* operating in the universe.

Such description allows, according to James, for all the various religious phenomena he catalogued in his book. It allows us to understand conversions and backsliding, saints and sinners. It accounts for the exteriority of the helping power yet also our sense of union with it. And finally, it fully justifies our feelings of security and joy.

In all of this, it is the progression past purgation that becomes difficult. What we are seeking is an altered state of consciousness, a return to a wholeness that we have not had perhaps since childhood, a crossing over into the universal. To do this, we must somehow divert the rational processes. We must dispense with the having and the getting, the planning and the analyzing, the ambition and the anxiety.

Mystics do this with prayer. Meditators do it with the mantra. Researchers do it with a repetitive word. It is this repetitive word, this mantra, this prayer, William Gibson tell us in his *A Season in Heaven,* that puts a veil between us and the things of the world. And so we enter a cloud of unknowing where and only where we can encounter Him directly.

When I run, motion becomes my mantra, movement becomes my prayer. Running puts me into another reality, a world where truth can be felt but not defined. Running is the way I alter my consciousness, suspend disbelief, ascend to a new perception. But even then, the individual illumination, the experience of union cannot be programmed. We know those moments are rare and wonderful. Once experienced, however, you can never again deny their existence.

* * *

A reader who is also a poet wrote to me commenting on my answer to the question, "Can running be a religious experience?" The question that occurred to her was "Can *living* be a religious experience?"

Cannot everything we do, she asked, be a religious experience, every breath we take, every act of love, of awareness, of stretching, whether we are running the roads or in bed or in the middle of a Brahms symphony?

Having defended running, I'm inclined to agree with her. Every human act, every act that is not simply reflex or automatic is a religious—or an irreligious—act. When it is considered and voluntary and purposeful, every act is a statement about me and my universe, a confirmation of how I view my existence.

"Religion," William James said, "consists in the belief that there is an unseen order, and our supreme good lies in harmoniously adjusting ourselves thereto."

That this is available to all was pointed out by James. "The solid meaning of life," he wrote, "is always the same eternal thing—the marriage namely of some unhabitual ideal with some special fidelity, courage and endurance; with some man's or woman's pains"—and whatever or wherever life may be, there is always the chance for that marriage to take place.

Whatever we do or wherever we do it we can take that occupation and make it a vocation. We can do it in a way we will always be remembered. Unamuno writes of the shoemaker who aspired to become for his fellow townspeople the one and only shoemaker, indispensable and irreplaceable. Then, writes Unamuno, this man made the theoretical fact that each one of us is unique and irreplaceable, a practical truth.

Everything I do should speak of that belief, that adjustment. What I do is a visible sign of what I believe. My actions are the answer to the question, "What would I do if I knew what I should be doing?"

What you do earns its value from the way you do it. When running becomes for me, as my poet friend put it, "a totally entered experience," it becomes a religious experience. I give it my body. I give it my mind. I give it the yearnings of my heart, the further reaches of my soul. From the act of running—now an act of awareness, of love, of stretching myself—comes whatever wholeness, whatever certitude I possess then and for the rest of the day.

One can, of course, obtain wholeness and certitude ready-made.

There are any number of people trained and ready to tell me what is best. There is a truth already given. Why question or criticize it? Why not accept it and free myself for other activities? There is no need, and there is more than a little danger, in seeking it myself.

The answer, for me, is the suspicion that nothing that I need to know is known. There is no one who knows just how I should live and die. I must discover that for myself.

William James, who spent his life in the pursuit of truth, died with a note on his dresser stating there were no conclusions. "There is no advice to give," the note said, "no fortunes to be told. Farewell."

When I read James, however, what I see is very specific advice. There is no substitute for experience. There is no substitute for finding out for one's own self, for the personal revelation, for knowing firsthand.

When I run, that happens. The body and the spirit become one. Running becomes prayer and praise and applause for me and my Creator. When I run, I am filled with confidence and the faith that word contains. I can face unanswerable questions, certain that there are answers.

That is something my poet friend would understand. Poets see other worlds, other consciousnesses. They do not see boundaries. They can deal with contraries. They refuse limits. In the commonplace, they see the miraculous. But most of all, they disdain logic.

"Swiftly rose and spread about him," sang Whitman, "the peace and knowledge that pass all argument of the earth."

That is something even I understand. The peace and knowledge that pass all argument I do indeed know. I run and feel it rise up and spread around me. That ordinary act contains all that need be seen and heard and tasted and felt and spoken—as can anything we do each day.

The religious experience, you see, is too important to be confined to church. It must be available to me at every moment. When it is absent I am, in that sense, no longer living. I am existing. I am on life supports, outside of life, like a patient in a coma. I am unconscious, unaware of what being human means. One way to come out of that coma is to be a runner.

17

The Ends

"
There is no substitute,
therefore, for the orthodox virtues—discipline,
hard work, pleasure postponed, duty followed.
We must keep our eye on the goal,
keep looking at the hills.
"

"WE LIVE IN AN OPEN UNIVERSE," said William James, "in which uncertainty, choice, hypothesis, novelties and possibilities are natural."

But if the universe is unfinished, so are we. Each one of us is, in fact, an open universe. Each one of us is a microcosm of uncertainty, choice, hypothesis, novelties and possibilities. Each one of us is an unfinished person in this unfinished universe. And each one of us feels an infinite and mysterious obligation to complete ourselves and somehow contribute to the completion of the universe.

One manifestation of the preoccupation with human potential is what is happening in Marin County, California, the subject of a TV special called "I Want It All Right Now." Marin is a "more" county—more money, more schooling, more foreign cars, more expensive houses. Marin also has more drinking, more psychiatrists, more divorces and more suicides. It is filled with people who have made it and have found that making it is not enough.

Many people in Marin are discovering the truth in the old platitudes. More is never enough. Beauty and power and success do not bring peace. To go forward, you must go back into yourself.

And they have in Marin County. The search for happiness has become the search for self. Body awareness has become a major industry. You can find there almost every one of the self-realization and self-knowledge movements. You name it, and it has moved to Marin County.

What happens in this concentration on the self is not always for the best. Obsession with the self can create chaos in individual lives and leave behind the wreckage of other people. Families, friends and lovers are frequently the victims of this complete self-absorption. Everything and everyone is sacrificed in this remaking of a human being.

The self is, of course, initially selfish. Stripped of all those social devices that permit us to live together with a minimum of discord, the self stands there naked and completely selfish. That is what the critics see—the selfishness and self-absorption of many people who move toward their goals at the expense of other people, destroying human potential rather than increasing it. Such people, they say, are not going toward meaning but away from it, not learning how to love other people but how to get along without them, not finding satisfaction in the remaking of the world but in removing themselves from it.

As usual, everyone is right—the critics and those they criticize. The human potential movement is, in the beginning, and for a long time must be, selfish. Only by going deep into ourselves can we come back with a complete and natural acceptance of our need for others. Then, what was a duty becomes a delight, what was obligatory flows from the source.

It is apparent that for many people this final stage comes only after a long period of self-discovery. It may even take a lifetime. I, for one, know that I must go through a lot more isolation and study, search and solitude before I become a social being.

In a way, it is like being a ninety golfer and wanting to be better. We have to destroy our game and rebuild it, go back to the basics and start over. But it is not easy to begin at the beginning, to give up our little securities and satisfactions. We are reluctant to do away with our minor pleasures, to leave the comfort of the status quo. We do not want to risk what we have for the unknown.

But we must take that risk. Given all this leisure and freedom, we must live up to it. Given all this time and money, we cannot stand pat. We cannot bury these assets any more than we can bury our talents. We are accountable, and we know it.

I feel that accountability every day. I am filled with what Joan Didion called "that low dread" of having to go out and better myself. I move through days filled with failure of the body and the mind and the spirit —still trusting I am going on in the right direction, hoping that the real me is infinitely better than the acceptable me I am leaving behind.

We are always in the process of becoming. We have a commitment strongly spent or weakly kept, as Robert Frost said, to the work or career of person in progress. The original commitment may alter as we grow or be diverted by outside influences. But change or not, the commitment is there—and with it our word of honor to do what is necessary for its fulfillment.

There is no substitute, therefore, for the orthodox virtues—discipline, hard work, pleasure postponed, duty followed. We must keep our eye on the goal, keep looking at the hills.

That is the good life—coping and striving and eventually becoming the person you are, the self you were born to be. That self is the final product of a lifetime of dedication, of finding what you are good at and then doing it well.

The highest, happiest and most perfect moments of our lives are the reward for the good becoming. In our pure and dedicated drive toward the future, we are likely to be, as C. S. Lewis said, "surprised by joy." We suddenly do have it all right now. That is the paradox. Only by aiming at the future will we become lost in the present. Only be deferring gratification will we get it immediately. Happiness, we come to discover, is found in the pursuit of happiness.

I see this in everything I do. I am runner, doctor, writer—body, mind and spirit, you might say—and each I do with all my might. Let me tell you about the running.

When I am training for a marathon, I am not running for fun. I am working on my limits of pain and exhaustion, so I will do well in the race. It is a classic instance of deferred gratification.

But oddly, each workout becomes an end instead of a means. It is as Emerson said: "All that is not performance is preparation—or performance shall be." I am already part of the event I am preparing for.

Either what we do every day is important, or nothing is. In a sense, we can live our entire life every day. I see this most clearly the day of a race. Then, the full cycle is evident.

The planning, the anticipation, the anxiety, the tension, the worry that fills my life comes before every race. This is followed by the race itself, the soon-evident inadequacies, the continuing failure, the falling behind —all the while knowing pain and fatigue, suffering and despair—and finally the finish, and joy and the peace beyond understanding.

The half-marathon in Atlanta was no exception. With seconds to go, I still hadn't gotten my shoelaces quite right. Every time I adjusted them, they were too tight or too loose. And then there was the matter of what to wear. It had been cold the last two days. The temperature had hovered around freezing, and there had been a threat of snow. Now, it was warming up. There was a bright sun and no wind. I had changed my clothes three times before settling for a cotton turtleneck, a nylon shirt, gloves and a wool hat.

My world was full of uncertainties. I had forgotten to warm up, and it was now too late. I had taken a Coke for the first time before a race and was worried about that. My stomach was full of butterflies. My mouth was dry, and my heart was speeding up in my chest. And just before the fun came an announcement: Only those who ran one hour and thirty-two minutes or better would receive medals.

So there it was, true to life even to the Final Judgement. The good news was that there was a hereafter. The bad news was that we would be separated into sheep and goats. there would indeed be an elect, the rest consigned to outer darkness with neither medals nor trophies. I stood with those hundreds. My mind, like theirs, had turned from the race to the outcome—from the living of my life to the rewards.

Every athlete knows that moment. Just before the gun, before the whistle, before the first center jump, it is that moment when all thought is about the prize, the championship, the winning and the losing. I knew it those last few seconds at Atlanta.

It took a while to lose it. Within minutes, we were into the first of what proved to be continuous hills. I am no hill runner, and with almost every yard I was passed by another runner. So added to the fear of the 1:32 barrier was the envy of those who were obviously going to break it.

Fortunately, I was unaware of what lay ahead. The man next to me was from Chicago. He had flown in the day before and driven the course in a rented car.

"There are," he told me, "three long hills."

I didn't ask him for any details. What was in sight was bad enough.

Then, the sweating began. And with the sweat came release from the fear of the future. With the sweat came play. I was no longer threatened by the race or my fellow runners. I can best describe it, perhaps, as a feeling of control and a feeling of freedom. I suddenly felt confident in a setting of uncertainty.

The paradox of play, however, is how serious it can be. Now it was just me and those Atlanta hills fighting it out. Mostly, I fought their injustice; the distance was surely enough of a test. But I asked no mercy, enjoying the struggle, seeking to be stretched, hoping for the summit, yet never slackening the pace until the crest was passed.

By now, I had taken the nylon shirt off and stuffed it into my shorts. Gone were the hat and gloves. I had slipped the turtleneck back over my shoulders and was running bare-chested in the thirty-eight-degree weather. I felt as strong as I had ever felt in my life. I had the 1:32 barrier beaten, and I didn't really care. I had stopped counting the hills. Let them come; I was ready.

Those final miles were filled with feeling and knowing, but most of all with believing. I believed in myself, for one, and in things about me I might never be able to explain or prove; in love, the love that is born in common suffering and anguish and therefore is really pity, and in God and the hereafter.

Afterward there was a plane to catch, so I missed the awards ceremony and the Final Judgement. Not that it mattered. There's another one every day.

EPILOGUE

A FELLOW RUNNER who is in the publishing field told me a story about meeting the wife of a former associate.

"What is Ted doing these days?" he asked.

"Training at seven minutes a mile," she said, "and looking to go under three hours in the marathon."

He still doesn't know if Ted has a job.

In running circles, such replies are standard. When a stranger asks me what I do, my reflex is to tell him my time for the marathon. The marathon, you see, is my bench mark. It is the status symbol in my community, the running community. It is my credibility factor, not only for others but for myself as well. My marathon time is in fact my most valued possession. By it, I can establish my value as a runner, and each year I raise or lower that value according to what I do in the Boston Marathon.

I tell you this so you may understand the apprehension I felt during the 1979 Boston race. The fear began soon after I had run the gauntlet of cheering women at Wellesley. Pains hit my thighs. They were those same ominous, stabbing pains in the quadriceps that are usually felt only in the final miles. I knew then I was in for a long, painful marathon —and worse, a bad time. The next thirteen miles would be filled with suffering, and with the danger that I would be reduced to walking and perhaps not finishing at all.

Before the marathon, a reporter had asked me what I expected to learn from this race. He had read something I had written about each Boston Marathon being a learning experience. At the time, I was at a loss to answer. Who knows what he will learn until it happens? I didn't know that this was to be one of my most instructive Boston Marathons.

As I ran with that constant pain, I gradually came to the realization that it was not my fault I was running a bad race. "It's not your fault, George," I kept saying to myself. "You're doing the best you can." And I was. I was running the best race I could, and I began to be proud of it.

There were times, of course, when my mind leaped forward to the finish at the Prudential Center and the image of my impending disgrace. There were times when I was reduced to a grotesque shuffle and with it the thought that I might not see my family until night-fall.

Yet even then I continued to chant to myself, sometimes loud enough for the spectators to hear, "Do your best, do your best." And I did. I was running the one and only race possible for me this day. I forgot about the final time. I forgot about everything but the running.

I finished in 3:15—four minutes slower than the previous year, but it was the best 3:15 I had ever run—not a defeat, but a victory.

Once I stopped running, I found it almost impossible to walk. And after the cramps came the chills. Someone put a sheet of metallic foil around me, and I made my way through the crowd up the escalator to the Prudential Building.

The crowds clogged the walkways and impeded my painful progress, so I went through a side door and started across the plaza at the second level. It was empty except for a woman who was standing in my path. As I approached her, I had to go down a set of three steps no more than a few inches high. The only way I could do it was by turning around and taking them one at a time, backwards. I saw that the woman was watching me very intently.

She said, "Who are you?"

That weekend, I had been a man of many identities, many selves: I had been lecturer, doctor, writer and even celebrity. Now, I was a shivering, wobbling scarecrow wrapped in tinfoil.

"Who are you?" she asked again.

"Just a runner," I answered.

Then, she leaned over and kissed me.

ABOUT THE AUTHOR

Athlete, author and physician, DR. GEORGE SHEEHAN is a well-known and respected expert on fitness and running. Born in Brooklyn in 1918, Dr. Sheehan took up running in the mid-1960s and began writing a weekly newspaper column on the sport in 1968. Two years later he stepped into his current position as monthly columnist and Medical Editor for *Runner's World* magazine. He has since authored seven books, *Dr. Sheehan on Running, Dr. Sheehan's Medical Advice, Running and Being: The Total Experience, This Running Life, How to Feel Great 24 Hours a Day, Personal Best* and *George Sheehan on Running To Win.* Dr. Sheehan has completed 20 Boston Marathons and set several age-group records for various distances. He now lives with his wife, Mary Jane, in Ocean Grove, New Jersey.